JavaScript

Rheinwerk Computing

The Rheinwerk Computing series from Rheinwerk Publishing offers new and established professionals comprehensive guidance to enrich their skillsets and enhance their career prospects. Our publications are written by leading experts in the fields of programming, administration, security, analytics, and more. Each book is detailed and hands-on to help readers develop essential, practical skills that they can apply to their daily work. For further information, please visit our website: *www.rheinwerk-computing.com*.

Sebastian Springer
Node.js: The Comprehensive Guide
2022, approx. 835 pp., paperback and e-book
www.rheinwerk-computing.com/5556

Philip Ackermann
Full Stack Web Development: The Comprehensive Guide
2023, 740 pp., paperback and e-book
www.rheinwerk-computing.com/5704

Johannes Ernesti, Peter Kaiser
Python 3: The Comprehensive Guide
2022, approx. 1078 pp., paperback and e-book
www.rheinwerk-computing.com/5566

Bernd Öggl, Michael Kofler
Git: Project Management for Developers and DevOps Teams
2023, approx. 407 pp., paperback and e-book
www.rheinwerk-computing.com/5555

Sebastian Springer
React: The Comprehensive Guide
2024, 676 pp., paperback and e-book
www.rheinwerk-computing.com/5705

Philip Ackermann

JavaScript

The Comprehensive Guide

Editor Hareem Shafi
German Edition Editor Patricia Schiewald
German Edition Technical Reviewer Sebastian Springer
Translation Winema Language Services, Inc.
Copyeditor Melinda Rankin
Cover Design Graham Geary
Photo Credit AdobeStock: 137196969/© Studio Peace
Layout Design Vera Brauner
Production Hannah Lane
Typesetting SatzPro (Germany)
Printed and bound in Canada, on paper from sustainable sources

ISBN 978-1-4932-2286-5
© 2024 by Rheinwerk Publishing, Inc., Boston (MA)
1st edition 2022, 1st reprint 2024
3rd German edition published 2021 by Rheinwerk Verlag GmbH, Bonn, Germany

Library of Congress Cataloging-in-Publication Control Number: 2022023983

Contents at a Glance

Dear Reader,

For as long as I can remember, I have wanted to learn to drive.

Due to an assortment of life events, I didn't get the opportunity to get my license until a few years ago, at 28. I hopped into the instructor's car on the day of my first lesson, drove through an intersection, made four right turns, parked haphazardly, and hobbled out of the car and to my front door, stiff with fear. Everything had gone well. But at the first traffic light, watching cars race past, I'd had an epiphany: cars were accursed death traps. I canceled my remaining lessons.

A year passed before I signed up again. When I relayed my previous experience to my new instructor, he, a college student working part time at the driving school, nodded knowingly. His adult drivers were often more anxious learners than his teenage pupils. "You overthink it," he noted. "Also, your brains are too developed. More impulse control, less risky behavior." (Here he shook his head regrettably, as if to say that a fully developed brain was an unfortunate characteristic to possess.) "You need to get out of your own way. Let yourself be a little reckless."

Reader, I did get out of my own way. I successfully learned to drive that year and I'm pleased to say that I love it. And I often find myself returning to my instructor's advice. When I think about adopting new hobbies or learning new skills, I do my best to learn without restraint.

Whether you have picked up this book for passion or practicality, whether you are a beginner or an experienced programmer, I hope you find similar success learning about JavaScript. Your driving instructor is expert author Philip Ackermann, who has written a meticulous manual to guide you on your JavaScript journey, from language basics to client-side and server-side programming.

What did you think about *JavaScript: The Comprehensive Guide*? Your comments and suggestions are the most useful tools to help us make our books the best they can be. Please feel free to contact me and share any praise or criticism you may have.

Thank you for purchasing a book from Rheinwerk Publishing!

Hareem Shafi
Editor, Rheinwerk Publishing

hareems@rheinwerk-publishing.com
www.rheinwerk-computing.com
Rheinwerk Publishing · Boston, MA

Contents

4   Working with Reference Types

6   Processing and Triggering Events

7   Working with Forms

8   Controlling Browsers and Reading Browser Information

9 Dynamically Reloading Contents of a Web Page 513

10   Simplifying Tasks with jQuery 555

13   Object-Oriented Programming

14   Functional Programming

15   Correctly Structuring the Source Code

19   Desktop Applications with JavaScript   897

20   Controlling Microcontrollers with JavaScript   909

21 Establishing a Professional Development Process 931

Book Resources

The code listings presented in this book are available for you to download from the website for this book.

Go to *https://www.rheinwerk-computing.com/5554*. Scroll down to the **Product Supplements** section and click the **Supplements List** button. You will see the downloadable files, along with a brief description of the file content. Click the **Download** button to start the download. Depending on the size of the file (and your internet connection), it may take some time for the download to complete.

Preface

JavaScript, the lingua franca of the web, has become increasingly popular in recent years and is now used in many different areas. Be it web, mobile or server application development: JavaScript does a good job in all areas.

This book provides comprehensive insight into this important language that has become indispensable to web developers. Don't worry if you've never programmed before—you will also get an introduction to the basics of programming.

Although JavaScript appears to be quite simple at first glance and has long been considered a simple scripting language, this is not quite true. The specification behind JavaScript, called the ECMAScript standard, comprises more than a thousand pages. The specifications of the various application programming interfaces (APIs) that we discuss in this book are even more extensive in total. You can also write entire books on the JavaScript jQuery library and the Node.js platform. In a nutshell: it is not possible to discuss all these topics in detail in a single book, nor is this my goal.

The word *comprehensive* used in the title is not meant in the sense of all-encompassing, but in the sense of *detailed*, *extensive*, and *versatile*. I'll show you the basics of JavaScript; how to build web, server-side, and mobile applications using JavaScript; how to control microcontrollers using JavaScript; and a lot more. It is more important for me to demonstrate the most central and practical aspects, i.e. the aspects that you need in every-day JavaScript development, instead of discussing every last detail in an all-encompassing way.

Target Audience

This book is aimed at different audiences: on the one hand, readers who generally have no programming experience at all, neither in JavaScript nor in any other programming language. These readers can expect background knowledge of programming concepts and paradigms in this book, in addition to an introduction to JavaScript. Regardless of individual background knowledge, the book provides a comprehensive introduction to the language itself and to the most important APIs and application areas. On the other hand, the book is also aimed at readers who are already familiar with JavaScript and now want to deepen their experience or simply have a reliable, comprehensive reference book at hand.

In any case, to understand the JavaScript manual, it is an advantage if you have some knowledge of HTML and at least some knowledge of CSS. After all, there is a good reason why these two languages plus JavaScript constitute the core of modern web development.

Structure of the Book

The book can be roughly divided into four parts: In the first four chapters, you will learn the basics of programming and the language core of JavaScript—that is, the essential components of the language. Chapter 5 through Chapter 12 then focus on the application of JavaScript in web development: how to create dynamic content, how to retrieve content from the server using JavaScript, how to create graphics dynamically using JavaScript, and much more. Chapter 13 to Chapter 21 then deal with more advanced concepts, such as object-oriented and functional programming, the Node.js platform, mobile and desktop application development, and the use of JavaScript with the Internet of Things (IoT).

How Should I Read This Book?

The answer to this question depends on your level of knowledge, of both programming in general and the JavaScript language in particular. If you would describe yourself as a beginner, it is certainly best to work through the book from cover to cover, especially the first two parts—that is, Chapter 1 to Chapter 12. This will ensure that you do not omit any essential aspects that are necessary for understanding the following chapters.

Advanced readers can also skip individual chapters depending on their level of knowledge. In the code examples, we have deliberately taken care to keep them self-contained and not to stretch them over several chapters. This allows you to select individual topics without having to go through several chapters at once. In any case, you can also use the book as a reference: thanks to the comprehensive reference section, the (hopefully) meaningful headings, and the extensive index, the relevant information can be found quickly.

Acknowledgments

Writing a book always involves a lot of time, time that has to be freed up elsewhere. Most of all, therefore, I thank my wife and children for giving me the time I needed to do this.

For this English edition I would like to thank the linguists at Lemoine International GmbH for the translation, Melinda Rankin for copyediting, the team at Rheinwerk Publishing, especially Hareem Shafi, Kelly O'Callaghan, Graham Geary, and Hannah Lane, and the team at Rheinwerk Verlag who published the original German book: my editors Patricia Schiewald and Stephan Mattescheck for their constructive suggestions and support, as well as Sibylle Feldmann and the entire team at Rheinwerk Verlag. I would also like to thank Sebastian Springer for his many helpful comments and, as always, extraordinarily thorough expert opinion. Thank you all very much for your support!

I would also like to thank the publisher Hans Heise, with whose kind permission I was allowed to reuse excerpts from articles I wrote for *iX* and for *heise Developer* in this book. In this regard, I would especially like to thank Julia Schmidt.

I would also like to thank Max Bold from Ebner Media Group GmbH & Co. KG, with whose kind permission I was allowed to use excerpts from articles I wrote for the trade magazine *web & mobile DEVELOPER*.

Last but not least, of course, I thank you for purchasing this book and for the time you spend reading and working through it, and I hope you enjoy it. I appreciate receiving feedback on the book at *jsguide@philipackermann.de*. If you're active on Twitter, I'd love for you to follow my account @cleancoderocker (*https://twitter.com/cleancoderocker*).

Philip Ackermann
Rheinbach, Germany

Chapter 1
Basics and Introduction

Before we get into creating JavaScript programs, this chapter will give you an overview of what's meant by programming in the first place, what types of programming languages there are, and the historical background of the JavaScript language: How has this language evolved over the years? What is the relationship between JavaScript and ECMAScript? In addition, we'll introduce the various application areas of JavaScript and explain how these have also changed in recent years.

This book is designed to not only teach you the JavaScript language but also introduce you to basic programming concepts in case you aren't yet familiar with any programming language. In this introductory chapter, we'll therefore first explain a few basic terms and concepts that will be helpful throughout the book. If you already have some experience in programming, you can skip at least the first part of this chapter. On the other hand, we have deliberately kept this part short because we don't want to bore you with theoretical treatises on programming but get you quickly started with JavaScript. Therefore, you might also consider this part a quick review.

One more quick note about the book before we get right into it: Occasionally, when discussing certain topics, we'll touch on concepts that will be explained fully later. In general, this can't always be avoided in a book on programming languages. In a way, as an author, you are faced with the chicken-and-egg problem: one cannot be explained without the other and vice versa. In such cases, for the sake of clarity, we have included references to the chapters or sections in which the respective concepts are discussed more fully.

1.1 Programming Basics

Before you can get started with actual programming, you need some basic understanding of what programming is all about. Why do we write programs? How do programs work? What role does JavaScript play in this context? And how does this language differ from other programming languages?

1.1.1 Communicating with the Computer

Let's start with the question of why we want to write programs in the first place, or rather, what goal we pursue by doing it. Primarily, programming is about letting a computer take over certain tasks. These can be, for example, complex problems that we humans would struggle to figure out ourselves or things that help us work more effectively in everyday life. For example, think of word processors, email programs, or your browser. All these tools have been programmed by someone.

Simply put, the task of a developer is to give *instructions* to the computer so that it is able to perform the tasks assigned to it. In other words, as a developer, you formulate individual *steps* for solving a specific problem, such as sorting data in a table or validating form data entered on a web page. The steps are then evaluated one by one by the computer. This is roughly comparable to a cooking recipe. There, too, individual steps are defined that you need to follow in order to reach your goal. In programming, the developer is the one who provides the computer with a recipe to follow.

In summary, the steps for solving a problem (i.e., the recipe) in computer science and software development are generally referred to as *algorithms*. Therefore, a *program* (also called *software* or an *application*) is a sequence of algorithms and, as such, a sequence of instructions that can be executed by the computer.

> **Definition**
>
> In software development, the steps defined for solving a problem are collectively called an *algorithm*. This is comparable to cooking recipes, operating instructions, or manuals. In this sense, an algorithm is a set of instructions for the computer for how to solve a particular problem.

> **Definition**
>
> A *program* or piece of *software* is composed of numerous different algorithms.

At the beginning, programming novices often find it difficult to think like a computer and to define the steps within an algorithm accordingly. After all, computers follow the instructions you give them in a very precise way. While you as a human being can always use your mind when going through a cooking recipe and vary certain steps according to your experience, a computer assumes that the steps you formulated should be carried out exactly as set out. Conversely, this also means that you as a developer must formulate the instructions just as precisely and put yourself in the position of the computer.

Tip

When I started programming in 2000, I kept wondering how anyone could ever learn how to write programs and admired experienced developers for their knowledge. After all these years, I can tell you: you only learn it by doing it yourself. Therefore, you should not only read this book, but really *work through* it and create programs yourself again and again. However, don't put too much pressure on yourself, and don't stress yourself out if something doesn't work right away. After all, as a developer, you need one thing more than anything: perseverance, and the willingness to learn something new every day.

1.1.2   Programming Languages

Deep down, computers work with zeros and ones; that much is common knowledge. A more professional term for "zeros and ones" is *binary code* or *machine code* or *machine language*. The background for this binary code is the technical level that only knows two states: zero for "power off" and one for "power on".

Simply put, various combinations of zeros and ones ultimately make the computer's hardware do various things, such as display a pixel on your monitor in this or that color, respond to mouse movements or keyboard input, or send an email over the network.

But because it would be incredibly complicated (and disproportionately time-consuming) for developers like us to phrase the instructions for the computer in zeros and ones, clever people at some point invented *programming languages* that abstract and simplify this interaction with the computer.

Programming languages can be further classified into different categories depending on their degree of abstraction. JavaScript is one of the so-called high-level programming languages, so it abstracts relatively far from the zeros and ones. *Assembly languages*, on the other hand, are much less abstract. They don't require you to work with zeros and ones either, but the commands used are nevertheless relatively cryptic, and programming is comparatively complex (see Figure 1.1). The commands you use in JavaScript, on the other hand, are quite catchy, understandable, and easy to remember after you get used to them, as you'll soon see.

Note

JavaScript is a high-level programming language.

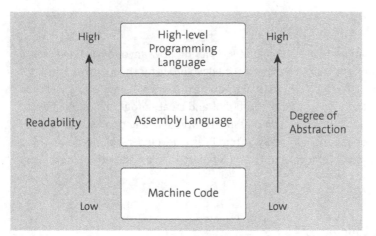

Figure 1.1 High-Level Programming Languages Abstract from Machine Code

As a developer, you store everything you program via a programming language in ordinary text files called *source files*. The content of such a file is called *source text* or *source code*.

Definition

The *source code* is what you as a developer write in a given programming language. *Machine code*, on the other hand, refers to the code that is read and executed by the computer.

For the computer to understand and implement the instructions written in the source code, the source code must be translated to a format that the computer can understand—that is, to the previously mentioned machine code made of zeros and ones (see Figure 1.2).

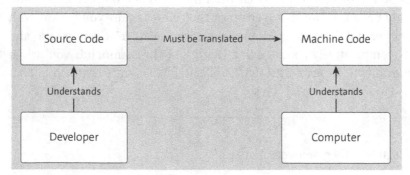

Figure 1.2 Source Code Understandable to Developers Must Be Converted into Machine Code That Is Understandable to Computers so That They Can Act on It

Basically, there are two different ways to achieve this: via *compilers* or via *interpreters*. (Explanations of both will follow shortly.) Depending on whether a programming language uses a compiler or an interpreter, it is a *compiled programming language*, an *interpreted programming language* or a so-called intermediate language.

Before we explain the exact differences among these three language types and clarify what a compiler or an interpreter is, let's note one point: JavaScript is an interpreted programming language. This has advantages, but also disadvantages, as we will see in a moment.

Compiled Programming Languages

In the case of compiled programming languages, a compiler converts the source code into machine code or into an *executable machine code file* (see Figure 1.3). This happens by translating the instructions written in the source code into a sequence of instructions for the computer. Programs generated by a compiler in this way can then be executed directly on the operating system for which they have been compiled, without the need for any other auxiliary components.

Figure 1.3 A Compiler Converts the Source Code into Executable Machine Code

Examples of compiled programming languages include C and C++. For example, in order to run a program written in C++, it must first be converted using an appropriate C++ compiler. But because the latter differs between operating systems, a separate version must be compiled for every operating system (see Figure 1.4).

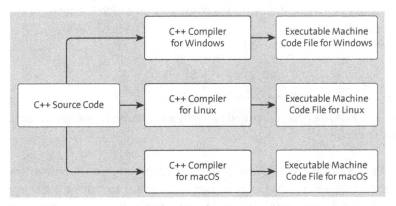

Figure 1.4 C++, for Example, Is a Compiled Programming Language

To this end, you need a separate compiler for every operating system. To run the program on Windows, it must first be compiled on Windows using an appropriate compiler. To run it on Linux, it must be compiled with a compiler on Linux, and the same applies to macOS if the program is to be run on a Mac. Although there are approaches to compile code on one operating system to run on another operating system (e.g., on Linux to run on Windows or vice versa; this technique is called *cross-compilation*), this does not change the fact that you have to spend quite a lot of effort to get a C++ program up and running on different operating systems. And we haven't even considered the processor architectures (32 bit and 64 bit), each of which requires a different compilation method.

Despite all the effort required, compiled programs still have a crucial advantage that we mentioned in passing: the machine code generated in each case can be executed on the respective operating system without auxiliary tools. Thus, no other programs need to be installed on the operating system to run a program compiled into machine code. This is a significant difference from interpreted programs, which we will discuss next.

> **Definition**
>
> Programs compiled for a specific operating system are also called *native programs* or *native applications*.

Interpreted Programming Languages

With interpreted programming languages, it isn't necessary to compile the source code. The source code is not translated by a compiler but evaluated by an interpreter (see Figure 1.5). Such an interpreter must be installed on the computer (or on the corresponding operating system) on which the program is to be executed (in contrast to the compiler, which only needs to be installed on the computer on which the corresponding source code is compiled).

Figure 1.5 An Interpreter Evaluates the Source Code Directly and Converts It Instruction by Instruction into Machine Code

JavaScript is therefore, as already revealed, an interpreted programming language (see Figure 1.6). This means that you can basically use any text editor to write a JavaScript program and execute the source code directly in a browser without any additional intermediate steps.

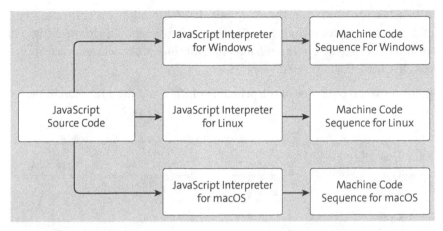

Figure 1.6 JavaScript Is an Interpreted Programming Language That Is Evaluated by a JavaScript Interpreter

---

Note

In the developer community, interpreted languages are usually very popular because they allow relatively fast development, precisely because the additional compilation step is omitted.

Interpreted programming languages thus require an interpreter to execute a program. Often this is a component of a so-called runtime environment (RTE). RTEs are used to enable application programs to run on a given operating system. In addition to an interpreter, RTEs also provide basic functions such as reading and writing files and access to peripheral devices (mouse, keyboard, printer, etc.).

In most cases and at the beginning, you will probably use one of the many browsers that already include a JavaScript RTE because they can natively interpret JavaScript. But there are also RTEs available that enable you to run JavaScript applications outside the browser.

Check Support for Individual Language Features

The individual RTEs differ to some extent with regard to the supported JavaScript language features. You can find a good overview on the website *www.caniuse.com*.

One RTE that has become very popular in recent years is Node.js. We've even dedicated an entire chapter to this topic (Chapter 17). Other JavaScript interpreters, which are very lightweight in terms of size (and therefore require little disk space), are also suitable for running JavaScript on microcontrollers. Chapter 20 deals with this topic.

In addition to RTEs for JavaScript, there are also RTEs for other programming languages. Well-known examples include *Java Runtime Environment (JRE)* for running Java programs or Microsoft's .NET *Common Language Runtime (CLR)*, which can run programs written in C#, Visual Basic, or C++.

Figure 1.7 again shows an overview of the principle of RTEs and their relation to native applications.

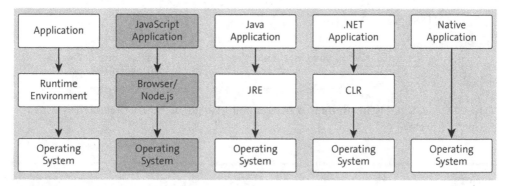

Figure 1.7 The Principle of Runtime Environments

Note

JavaScript is not a compiled language, but an interpreted language.

Both the compiler and the interpreter approach have advantages, but also disadvantages. Table 1.1 shows a brief summary.

Compiler	Interpreter
The program must be recompiled for execution every time.	The program can be executed directly.
Usually delivers very good performance because the source code doesn't have to be converted at runtime.	Tends to be less efficient than compiled programs as source code conversion occurs at program runtime. Nowadays, so-called just-in-time (JIT) compilers are often used in this context. They convert the source code or frequently executed source code into machine code that can then be executed relatively quickly.
Due to the additional compilation step, syntax errors are detected faster.	Because syntax errors are only detected at runtime, they can easily be overlooked.

Table 1.1 Advantages and Disadvantages of Compilers and Interpreters

Intermediate Languages

There are some programming languages that cannot be clearly assigned to one of the two categories mentioned (compiled and interpreted) as they use both compilers and interpreters. In Java, for example, the source code is compiled by a compiler into so-called bytecode, a kind of intermediate code, which in turn requires an interpreter in order to be executed (see Figure 1.8).

Figure 1.8 There Are Also Programming Languages That Use a Combination of Compiler and Interpreter

The advantage of this approach is that Java applications do not have to be compiled on the same operating system on which they will later be executed (in contrast to compiled languages) as the bytecode is independent of the operating system. The only thing that needs to be present on the respective target operating system is an interpreter for the bytecode—in other words, a runtime environment for Java (see Figure 1.9).

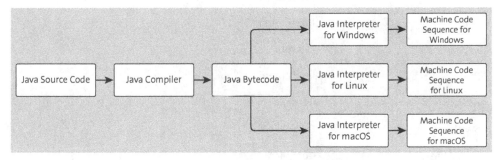

Figure 1.9 The Java Programming Language Is an Example of a Language That Uses Compilers and Interpreters

Overview of Different Programming Languages

You now know the difference between compiled and interpreted programming languages, and you also know that there are intermediate languages that use a combination of both approaches. You also learned about one example in each of these language categories: C or C++ as an example of compiled programming languages, Java as an example of an intermediate language, and finally JavaScript as an example of an interpreted language. But what about other well-known programming languages? You can find a selection of these in Table 1.2.

Programming Language	Type
Ada	Compiled
BASIC	Interpreted
C	Compiled
C++	Compiled
C#	Compiled
COBOL	Compiled
Fortran	Compiled
Go	Compiled
Java	Intermediate language
JavaScript	Interpreted
Lisp	Intermediate language
Objective-C	Compiled
Perl	Interpreted
PHP	Interpreted
Python	Interpreted
Ruby	Interpreted
Rust	Compiled
Swift	Compiled
Visual Basic	Compiled

Table 1.2 Categorization of Different Programming Languages

1.1.3   Tools for Program Design

As a developer, you're often itching to start with the *implementation* of an algorithm—but you should avoid being too hasty in the process. It's better to think about the structure of the algorithm first: Which individual steps are necessary to solve the given problem? What are the special cases to consider? What input data does the algorithm require? What is the result that should be returned?

It's best to initially follow these steps when implementing an algorithm:

1. **Set the goal of the algorithm**

   What do you want to achieve with the algorithm? What problem do you want the computer to solve for you? Is there something be calculated? Is there data to be sorted or user input to be checked?

2. **Define the steps**

Break down the problem into individual steps. In what order do these steps have to be performed? How are the steps related? Do individual steps need to be performed repeatedly? Or under certain conditions only? Soon, we'll introduce *flowchart notation* and the so-called pseudocode technique, which can help you plan the flow of an algorithm.

3. **Write the algorithm**

For the computer to understand your algorithm, you need to write it in a programming language. In this case, that's JavaScript. The following nearly 1,300 pages will help you with this.

Definition

In the context of programming and software development, *implementation* means the realization of an algorithm (or more generally, a program flow) in a specific programming language.

Note

The more complex the problem, the more important it is that you think about the individual steps before implementation.

Flowcharts

Flowcharts, also called *program flowcharts*, are graphical representations for describing algorithms that allow you to precisely define individual steps and the overall flow. The more experienced you are as a developer and the less complex a problem is, the more likely you are to avoid drawing flowcharts beforehand. In other cases, however, flowcharts can be enormously helpful in getting a clear idea of what an algorithm is supposed to do. Trust me: even if this seems redundant at first (after all, you still need to write the appropriate source code after drawing the flowchart), proper planning pays off later. The truth is that the more complex an algorithm or the preceding problem is, the more worthwhile is the preliminary work.

Flowcharts essentially consist of boxes in different shapes connected by lines. Figure 1.10 shows an example of a flowchart. It illustrates the flow of a program for the login process on a website. If a valid combination of username and password is entered, the user profile is to be loaded and redirected to the welcome page. If the input is incorrect, and if the maximum number of failed login attempts has not yet been exceeded, an error message is to be displayed and the user should be redirected back to the login page. If, on the other hand, the maximum number of failed login attempts *has* been exceeded, then the user should be blocked and a notification email should be sent to the responsible administrator.

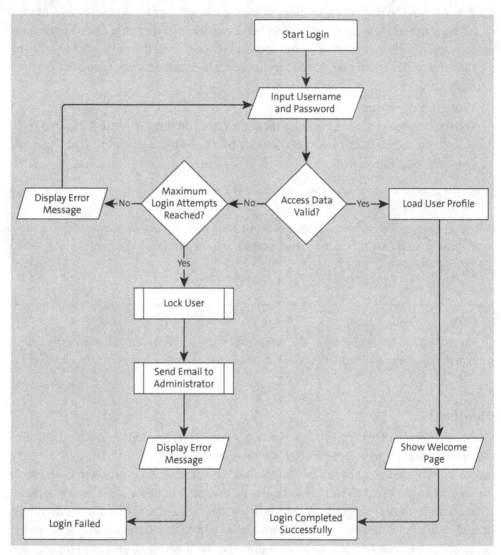

Figure 1.10 Flowchart Example

The elements in the flowchart are described ahead. Table 1.3 also gives an overview of these elements.

Start/stop control points are used to describe the beginning and the end of an algorithm. They are represented in flowcharts as rounded rectangles. They usually contain labels such as "Start," "Begin," "Stop," or "End" or more detailed wording that also includes the name of the algorithm, such as in the example "Start login," "Login failed," or "Login completed successfully."

Individual *statements* or *operations* of an algorithm are represented in a flowchart by normal rectangles. As a label, they contain a short, meaningful description of what is to be done in each step—for example, "Create user session."

The *input* and *output* of the program are represented by parallelograms. They are also labeled with a short description of what kind of input is expected by the program (e.g., "Input username and password") or what kind of output will be generated (e.g., "Show error message" or "Show welcome page").

If a decision has to be made at a certain point within an algorithm about which of the following instructions is to be executed, this is described in flowcharts using *decision points*, graphically represented as square diamonds with two paths leading away from each. As a rule, they are labeled with questions that can be answered with yes or no or with questions that can be answered with one of two possible answers. This is because a decision point is used to follow one path or the other in the flowchart, depending on the particular answer. The answers are written on the corresponding lines leading from the decision point. One of the decision points in the example is used to check whether the credentials entered are valid. If this is true (i.e., if the question "Access data valid?" is answered with "Yes"), the path shown on the right-hand side of the chart is the one to be followed. If not, the path shown on the left-hand side is to be followed.

Rectangles with two lines on the left and right sides are used to define calls to subroutines (or *subalgorithms*), which again consist of various steps. In the example flowchart, they describe the subroutines of locking the user and sending the notification email to the administrator.

Element	Label	Description
Start/Stop	Start/stop checkpoint	Used to describe the beginning and the end of an algorithm
Operation	Operation	Used to describe individual statements or operations of an algorithm
Input and Output	Input and output	Used to describe input or output
←No— Decision Point / Yes	Decision point	Used to describe branches in the algorithm

Table 1.3 The Most Important Elements of Flowcharts

Element	Label	Description
Subroutine	Execute a subroutine	Used to describe calls to subroutines
⟶	Connection	Used to connect individual elements in the flowchart and thus describe the flow of the algorithm

Table 1.3 The Most Important Elements of Flowcharts (Cont.)

Other Elements in Flowcharts

There are a few more elements that you can use in flowcharts, but they are not as commonly used and we don't need them for the remaining examples in the book. You can find an overview of these at *https://en.wikipedia.org/wiki/Flowchart*, for example.

Flowcharts Are Independent of the Programming Language

Another advantage of flowcharts is that they are independent of the programming language used. In our case, it doesn't really matter (after all, we want to program in JavaScript)—but in principle, this can be considered an advantage.

Pseudocode

As an alternative (or supplement) to flowcharts, you can also create so-called pseudocode for program design. This means that you write the individual steps of an algorithm in more or less natural language instead of in a concrete programming language. Listing 1.1 shows the algorithm from Figure 1.10, transferred to pseudocode.

```
program start login
  read username and password
  if user data valid then
    create user session
    show welcome page
  else
    if maximum number of login attempts reached then
      call subroutine to lock user
      call subroutine to send email to administrator
      display error message
      exit program
    else
      display error message
```

```
      redirect to input
      go to user data input
program end login
```

Listing 1.1 Pseudocode Example

Unlike flowcharts, where the elements used are predetermined, pseudocode has no restrictions in this regard. As a rule, you use words and sentence components such as "read", "if ... then ... else", "show", "output", "as long as ... execute", and the like. Approximate translations of elements from flowcharts to pseudocode are given in Table 1.4.

An essential feature of pseudocode (which also shows the similarity to real source code) are the indentations at the beginning of lines. As you can see in Listing 1.1, program lines that are executed depending on the respective preceding program line are indented further to the right (typically by two to four spaces).

Pseudocode	Element from Flowchart
program start program end	Start/stop checkpoint
Active sentences, starting with verbs like create, show, etc.	Operation
read, output	Input and output
if ... else	Decision point
as long as ... execute	Repetitions
subroutine call	Execute a subroutine

Table 1.4 Relationship between Sentence Components in Pseudocode and Elements in Flowcharts

The advantage of pseudocode, as with flowcharts, is that you can think about the flow of an algorithm in advance without having to start directly with the implementation in your chosen programming language. Although you already write text that is quite similar to the later source code, you do not have to deal with the syntactical peculiarities of the respective programming language. This allows you to focus entirely on the algorithm flow. In addition, especially for more complex algorithms, pseudocode is much more compact than flowcharts.

Flowcharts, Pseudocode, and Programming Languages

In the course of the book, you will notice that there are certain language constructs in programming languages (here, in JavaScript in particular) to which both flowcharts and pseudocode can be applied with relative ease.

1.2   Introduction to JavaScript

Now that we've looked at programming languages in general, this section will give a brief overview of JavaScript, but without going into the details of the language. Essentially, it will offer a brief historical overview of the language and introduce various application areas where JavaScript is used nowadays.

1.2.1   History

Histories of programming languages often are rather bland and rarely very interesting. For this reason, we'll keep this section as short as possible and give only the most important points without going into version details and the like.

Like software programs, programming languages are also updated from time to time. In that case, new features are added to the programming language to make the developer's work easier, while other features that caused problems in the past or were simply rarely used are dropped. So there were different versions of JavaScript in the past as well.

The history of JavaScript begins in 1995, when Brendan Eich designed the language for Netscape Navigator (a now outdated browser) in a record time of two weeks. In the beginning, JavaScript did not have its current name; it was initially called Mocha and LiveScript. Due to a cooperation between Netscape and Sun (the company behind the Java programming language) and for marketing reasons (the Java programming language was already quite popular at the time) the language was finally renamed to JavaScript. However, the similarity of the name to Java should not lead you to jump to conclusions: apart from the similar name, the two languages have little in common.

Shortly after the release of JavaScript, Microsoft followed up with a more or less compatible language (JScript) for Internet Explorer 3.0. To reconcile these two similar languages, Netscape then submitted JavaScript to the European Computer Manufacturers Association (ECMA), with the goal of creating a unified standard for the language. This standard has since been running under the name ECMAScript, which was adopted in version 6 in 2015 (ES6 or ES2015 for short). Since then, new features have been added to the standard every year, so it was agreed not to use a separate consecutive version number, but to simply list the respective calendar year in the version number (see Table 1.5).

Version Name	Year of Publication
ES1	1997
ES2	1998
ES3	1999

Table 1.5 JavaScript/ECMAScript Version History

Version Name	Year of Publication
ES4	Not released
ES5	2009
ES6/ES2015	2015
ES2016	2016
ES2017	2017
ES2018	2018
ES2019	2019
ES2020	2020
ES2021	2021

Table 1.5 JavaScript/ECMAScript Version History (Cont.)

Other Variants of ECMAScript

Thus, JavaScript is only one variant of this standard (examples of other variants are the ActionScript known from Flash and the ExtendScript used in numerous Adobe products).

1.2.2   Fields of Application

Nowadays, JavaScript not only plays a leading role in the development of web pages and web applications but also is a good choice for various other types of applications. The most important application areas are detailed ahead.

Definition of Terms

Since we use the terms *web page*, *website*, and *web application* repeatedly throughout the book, we will briefly explain them here. A *web page* is a single HTML document that can be accessed at a specific URL (e.g., *www.rheinwerk-computing.com/javascript_5554*). A *website* is a collection of various individual web pages (e.g., *www.rheinwerk-computing.com*).

A *web application*, however, is a web page that feels more like a desktop application than a web page. Examples include Google Documents and similar web-based software applications. Another term for such web applications is *rich internet applications*, which refers to web applications with rich content and features.

Frontend of Web Applications

When developing websites and web applications, a distinction is generally made between the part that takes place on the *client side* in the browser (the so-called frontend) and the part that takes place on the *server side* (the so-called backend). JavaScript has its roots in frontend development, and for a long time it was mainly used to "spruce up" the interface of a web page with dynamic effects.

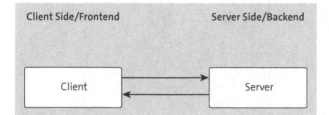

Figure 1.11 Relationship between Frontend and Backend (or Client Side and Server Side)

A related term coined back in the 1990s is *Dynamic HTML* (DHTML), which is the dynamic modification of HTML code using JavaScript. DHTML has been forgotten these days because, from today's point of view, it was based on rather ugly JavaScript code and was characterized more by bad practices than by best practices. Therefore, in Chapter 5 we will not deal with DHTML at all but with *DOM scripting*, which is another way of dynamically modifying the HTML of a web page.

Definition

DOM stands for *Document Object Model* and refers to the object model behind web pages. This topic will be discussed in detail in Chapter 5. There we will also explain what an object model is in the first place.

Definition

In the context of software development, *bad practices* refers to poor programming techniques, while *best practices* refers to particularly good programming techniques.

On various websites, you have probably seen functionality for sorting tables (see Figure 1.12) and filtering table entries according to certain criteria (see Figure 1.13). Both are typical use cases of dynamically modifying a web page and thus of using JavaScript.

An important milestone for JavaScript and the basis for more complex web applications was the introduction of the XMLHttpRequest object and the associated Ajax (Asynchronous JavaScript and XML), respectively, which allowed asynchronous requests to be sent from the browser to a server for the first time. Why this is so special, in which cases it can be useful, and what this `XMLHttpRequest` object is in the first place is explained in detail in Chapter 9. For now, note that it usually improves the usability of a web application, helps to avoid loading times, and makes a web application appear much more dynamic.

ID	First name	Last name	Age
5	James	Doe	35
4	Jane	Doe	32
1	John	Doe	44
2	Paul	Doe	44
3	Peter	Doe	40

Figure 1.12 Sorting Data Using JavaScript

Filter	Doe		
ID	First name	Last name	Age
1	John	Doe	44
2	Jane	Doe	44
5	James	Doe	40

Figure 1.13 Filtering Data with JavaScript

For a typical application example of dynamically reloading web page content, think of news tickers, which update themselves at certain intervals without the user having to retrieve the web page again. What is taken for granted today was not feasible in this form for a long time.

Another typical use case for using JavaScript within a web page is the *validation* of form input—for example, checking the validity of user input to determine whether a valid email address or a valid phone number has been entered (see Figure 1.14).

Although HTML—the *HyperText Markup Language*, for describing web documents—has made a big leap with the version change from HTML 4.01 to HTML5 and many form entries can now also be checked directly via HTML without using JavaScript, JavaScript is still a lot more flexible. In Chapter 7, we will show you, among other things, how to implement such validation using JavaScript.

If you know a bit about HTML (which we assume you do), you'll know that HTML comprises a number of basic components for defining the *user interface* (UI), including text fields, radio buttons, check boxes, tables, lists, and more.

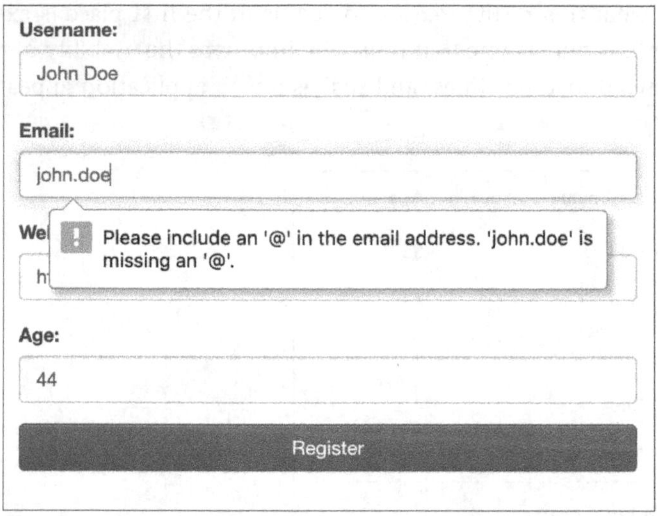

Figure 1.14 Validation of Form Input

However, HTML does not provide complex *interface elements* or *UI components*, including tabs, expandable and collapsible areas (*accordions*), customizable dialogs, and so on. Again, you have to resort to JavaScript instead.

Definition

The *user interface* is what allows a person to interact with a computer (or more generally, with a machine).

In Chapter 10, we'll introduce the popular JavaScript jQuery library and also show you how to use more complex UI components via this library or an extension of it (jQuery UI).

Definition

The term *library* or *software library* in the context of programming and software development refers to a collection of functionalities that can be accessed. For JavaScript, there is an extremely high number of libraries for a wide variety of uses.

Web Application Backend

Even if you don't notice it directly when interacting with a web application, a large part of the application logic takes place on the server side—that is, in the backend—especially in complex applications. Imagine a simple search function for a website: after you have entered the search criteria into the search form and the search form has been submitted, and before the search results are displayed, the essential part—namely, the search itself—takes place on the server (see Figure 1.15). This, too, needs to be programmed. Databases may need to be queried, the results put into a specific format, and more.

Until a few years ago, JavaScript could not be used for this purpose, or a considerable detour had to be taken. The server side was reserved for languages like Java or PHP. But the introduction of Node.js in particular, a runtime environment that can run JavaScript on the command line (and thus also on the server side), led to a continuing boom in server-side JavaScript applications. This will be detailed in Chapter 17.

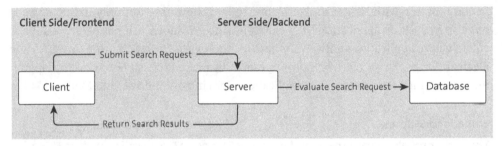

Figure 1.15 Many Requests That Are Started on the Client Side Involve the Server Side without the User Realizing This Directly

Mobile Applications

Mobile applications have become almost more important than web applications in recent years. Essentially, they can be divided into three categories:

- **Native applications**
  Native applications are those applications that have been developed for a specific (mobile) operating system, such as iOS, Android, or Windows Mobile. Native applications are compiled for a specific operating system: applications for iOS are programmed in Objective-C (or more recently in Swift), applications for Android in Java, and applications for Windows Mobile in C#, for example. Native applications tend to perform better than non-native applications. Native applications also offer more options to access certain features of a given mobile device.

- **HTML5 applications**
  HTML5 applications are developed using only standard HTML5, CSS3 (Cascading Style Sheets), and JavaScript technologies. The advantage is that because such applications do not need to be compiled, they do not depend on the operating system used (provided that a browser is installed). This means that one and the same HTML5 application can run on iOS and on Android and on Windows Mobile. But HTML5 applications usually do not offer the same performance as native applications. In addition, they cannot access the full functionality of a given mobile device.

- **Hybrid applications**
  Hybrid applications are a combination of native and HTML5 applications. They are developed entirely in HTML5, CSS3, and JavaScript, but run in a special native container, which also enables them to access mobile device functionality hidden from HTML5-only apps, just like native apps.

In Chapter 18, you'll learn how to build mobile apps with JavaScript using React Native (*https://reactnative.dev*).

Desktop Applications

In combination with HTML5 and CSS3, JavaScript is now used not only in the browser, but also in desktop applications. For example, since Windows 8, it has been possible to create native applications entirely in these technologies. The NW.js (*http://nwjs.io*) and Electron (*https://www.electronjs.org*) frameworks make it possible to develop operating system-independent desktop applications for Linux, Windows, and Mac.

Embedded Systems

You have probably heard the term *Internet of Things* (*IoT*; also called *Web of Things*). It refers to the networking of everyday objects (things) via the internet.

A classic example of this is the intelligent refrigerator that notices when there is no milk left and automatically updates the shopping list on your smartphone or, alternatively, purchases milk directly via a corresponding online store.

IoT also includes *wearables*—that is, portable microcomputers that are worn (invisibly) in articles of clothing or (visibly) directly on the body in the form of devices like, for example, smartwatches. Many of these devices are already programmable out of the box using JavaScript: for example, the Bangle.js smartwatch (*www.banglejs.com*) can be programmed via JavaScript, as can the Philips Hue smart LED lights (*www.philips-hue.com/en-us*).

Examples of programmable microcontrollers include Tessel (*https://tessel.io*) and Espruino (*www.espruino.com*). With the Johnny Five library (*https://github.com/rwaldron/johnny-five*), Arduino microcomputers can also be controlled remotely.

Naturally, the IoT domain also produces many different use cases for JavaScript. From reading temperature sensors to home surveillance systems that react to movements via cameras and start video recordings, many different things can now be realized with JavaScript (see Figure 1.16). You'll find a more detailed introduction to this topic in Chapter 20.

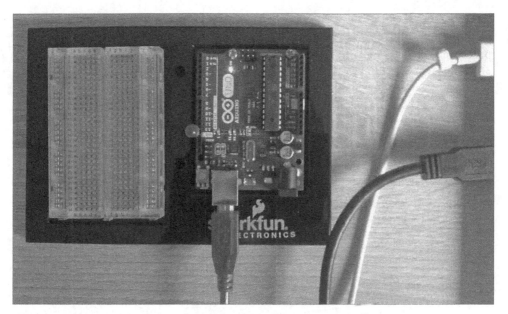

Figure 1.16 JavaScript Can Also Be Used for Controlling Microcontrollers

Games and 3D applications

Other use cases for JavaScript include browser games and 3D applications. However, both of these topics are so complex that we will not discuss them in this book.

JavaScript: Not the Best Choice for Everything

It may seem that you don't need any programming language except JavaScript because you can do everything with it anyway—but this of course is not true. In the last few years, a tremendous boom has developed around JavaScript, but this should also be questioned to some degree. A lot of things are not so easy to implement in JavaScript either, and for many other things it is more suitable to resort to other programming languages. Of course, you need experience to decide which programming language is the best choice for a given problem.

1.3 Summary

Hopefully, we haven't overwhelmed you with the terminology right at the beginning of the book (especially in the first section), and hopefully we've been able to illustrate what programming and programming languages are all about and how JavaScript fits into the overall picture. From now on, everything will be less theoretical, we promise.

But first, here is a brief summary of the key points of this chapter. Such summaries can be quite helpful to review what you have learned and to get an overview of the core points of a particular chapter. Therefore, you'll find a summary like the following at the end of each chapter in this book:

- *Flowcharts* are used to graphically illustrate the flow of algorithms or programs.
- *Pseudocode* is used to describe the flow of algorithms or programs in a text form.
- JavaScript is not a *compiled programming language*, but an *interpreted programming language*.
- JavaScript lets you program both the frontend and the backend of a web application.
- In addition, JavaScript enables you to develop mobile applications, desktop applications, embedded applications, and games and 3D applications.

Chapter 2
Getting Started

JavaScript is still mainly used for creating dynamic web pages—within a browser. Before we take a closer look at other application areas in later chapters, this chapter will show you the ways in which you can embed JavaScript in a web page and generate simple output. This chapter thus is the basis for the following chapters.

Before we go into further detail about the JavaScript language itself, you should first know how JavaScript relates to HTML and CSS within a web page, how to embed JavaScript in a web page, and how to generate output.

2.1 Introduction to JavaScript and Web Development

The most important three languages for creating web frontends are certainly HTML, CSS, and JavaScript. Each of these languages serves its own purpose.

2.1.1 The Relationship among HTML, CSS, and JavaScript

In HTML, you use *HTML elements* to specify the *structure* of a web page and the *meaning (semantics)* of individual components on a web page. For example, they describe which area on the web page is the main content and which area is used for navigation, and they define components such as forms, lists, buttons, input fields, or tables, as shown in Figure 2.1.

Artist	Album	Release Date	Genre
Monster Magnet	Powertrip	1998	Spacerock
Kyuss	Welcome to Sky Valley	1994	Stonerrock
Ben Harper	The Will to Live	1997	Singer/Songwriter
Tool	Lateralus	2001	Progrock
Beastie Boys	Ill Communication	1994	Hip Hop

Figure 2.1 HTML Is Used to Define the Structure of a Web Page

CSS, on the other hand, uses special *CSS rules* to determine how the individual components that you have previously defined in HTML should be displayed; this is used to define the *design* and *layout* of a web page. For example, you can define text color, text size, borders, background colors, color gradients, and so on. Figure 2.2 shows how CSS was used to adjust the font and font size of the table headings and table cells, add borders between table columns and table rows, and alternate the background color of the table rows. The whole thing looks a lot more appealing than the variant without CSS.

Artist	Album	Release Date	Genre
Monster Magnet	Powertrip	1998	Spacerock
Kyuss	Welcome to Sky Valley	1994	Stonerrock
Ben Harper	The Will to Live	1997	Singer/Songwriter
Tool	Lateralus	2001	Progrock
Beastie Boys	III Communication	1994	Hip Hop

Figure 2.2 With CSS, You Define the Layout and Appearance of Individual Elements of the Web Page

Last but not least, JavaScript is used to add *dynamic behavior* to the web page (or to the components on a web page) or to provide more interactivity on the web page. Examples of this are sorting and filtering the table data, as already mentioned in Chapter 1 (see Figure 2.3 and Figure 2.4). So while CSS takes care of the design of a web page, JavaScript can be used to improve the user experience and interactivity of a web page.

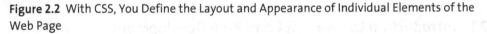

Q Search artist			
Artist ▾	Album	Release Date	Genre
Beastie Boys	III Communication	1994	Hip Hop
Ben Harper	The Will to Live	1997	Singer/Songwriter
Kyuss	Welcome to Sky Valley	1994	Stonerrock
Monster Magnet	Powertrip	1998	Spacerock
Tool	Lateralus	2001	Progrock

Figure 2.3 Sort Option to Make a Web Page More User-Friendly and Interactive with JavaScript

Q	Be			
Artist ▾	**Album**	**Release Date**	**Genre**	
Beastie Boys	III Communication	1994	Hip Hop	
Ben Harper	The Will to Live	1997	Singer/Songwriter	

Figure 2.4 Filter Option to Make a Web Page More User-Friendly and Interactive with JavaScript

Thus, in the vast majority of cases, a web page consists of a combination of HTML, CSS, and JavaScript code (see Figure 2.5). Note that though we just said that JavaScript takes care of the behavior of a web page, you can create functional web pages entirely without JavaScript. In principle, you can also create web pages without CSS; it is possible. In that case, only the HTML is evaluated by the browser. That means, however, that the web page is less fancy (without CSS) and less interactive and user-friendly (without JavaScript), as shown previously in Figure 2.1.

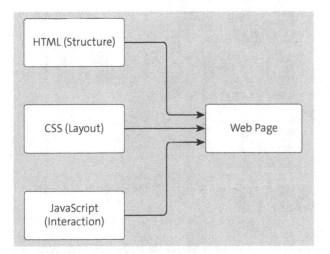

Figure 2.5 Usually, a Combination of HTML, CSS, and JavaScript Is Used within a Web Page

Note

HTML is used for the structure of a web page, CSS for layout and design, and JavaScript for behavior and interactivity.

Definition

Web and software developers also refer to three layers in this context: HTML provides the *content layer*, CSS the *presentation layer*, and JavaScript the *behavioral layer*.

Separating the Code for the Individual Layers

It is considered good development style not to mix the individual layers—that is, to keep HTML, CSS, and JavaScript code independent of each other and in separate files. This makes it easier to keep track of a web project and ultimately ensures that you can develop more effectively. In addition, this method enables you to include the same CSS and JavaScript files in various HTML files (see Figure 2.6) and thus to reuse the same CSS rules or JavaScript source code in several HTML files.

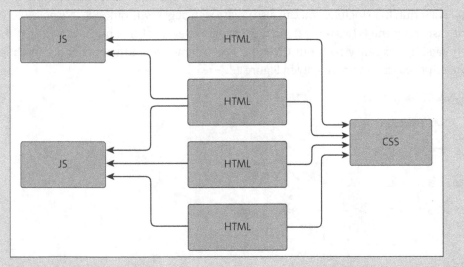

Figure 2.6 If You Write CSS and JavaScript Code into Separate Files rather than Directly into the HTML Code, It Is Easier to Reuse

A good approach to developing a website is to think about its structure first: What are the different areas of the web page? What are the headings? Is there any data presented in tabular form? What are the navigation options? Which information is included in the footer area and which in the header area of the page? Only HTML is used for this purpose. The website won't look nice or be very interactive, but that isn't the point of this first step, in which we do not want to be distracted from the essential element: the website content.

Building on this structural foundation, you then implement the design using CSS and the behavior of the web page using JavaScript. In principle, these two steps can also be carried out in parallel by different people. For example, a web designer may take care of the design with CSS, while a web developer programs the functionality in JavaScript (in practice, the web designer and web developer are often one and the same person, but especially in large projects with numerous websites, a distribution of responsibilities is not uncommon).

Phases of Website Development

When developing professional websites, there are several stages preceding the development step. Before development even begins, prototypes are designed in concept and design phases (either digitally or quite classically with pen and paper). The step-by-step approach just described (first HTML, then CSS, then JavaScript) thus only refers to development.

HTML Markup Language and CSS Style Language

By the way, HTML and CSS are not programming languages! HTML is a *markup language* and CSS is a *style language*; only JavaScript of the languages we're discussing here is a *programming language*. Strictly speaking, statements like "This can be programmed with HTML" are therefore not correct. You'd instead have to say something like "This can be realized with HTML."

Definition

The process of presenting a web page in the browser is called *rendering*. A common phrase among developers is "The browser renders a web page." This involves evaluating HTML, CSS, and JavaScript code, creating an appropriate model of the web page (which we'll talk about in Chapter 5), and "drawing" the web page into the browser window. In detail, this process is quite complex, and if you're interested in this topic, you might want to read the blog post at *www.html5rocks.com/en/tutorials/internals/ howbrowserswork*.

2.1.2 The Right Tool for Development

In principle, a simple text editor would be sufficient for creating JavaScript files (and for simple code examples this is perfectly fine), but sooner or later you should acquire a good editor that supports you when writing JavaScript and that is specifically designed for developing JavaScript programs (if you don't already have one installed on your computer anyway). Such an editor supports you, for example, by highlighting the source text in color, relieving you of writing recurring source text modules, recognizing errors in the source text, and much more.

Editors

There are a number of really good editors that can be used effectively. For example, Sublime Text (*www.sublimetext.com*; see Figure 2.7) and Atom (*https://atom.io*; see Figure 2.8), both available for Windows, macOS, and Linux, are popular editors in the developer community. While the former currently costs $99 (as of June 2021), the Atom editor is free of charge. In detail, both editors have their own features and strengths, but they are still quite similar. Try them out to see which one suits you more.

Figure 2.7 Sublime Text Editor

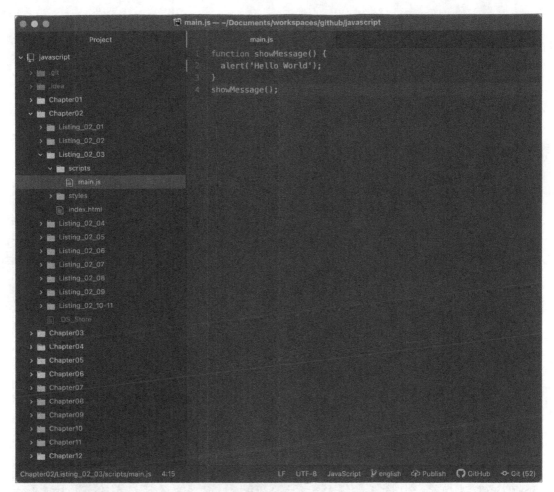

Figure 2.8 Atom Editor

Development Environments

Software developers switching from languages like Java or C++ to JavaScript are in most cases used to integrated development environments (IDEs), as known from their previous programming languages. In a way, you can think of a development environment as a very powerful editor that provides various additional features compared to a "normal" editor, such as synchronization with a source control system, running automatic builds, or integrating test frameworks. (If you're just shaking your head uncomprehendingly now and wondering what's behind all these terms, wait until Chapter 21, in which we'll go into more detail about these advanced topics of software development with JavaScript.)

WebStorm by IntelliJ (*www.jetbrains.com/webstorm/*; see Figure 2.9) is one example of a very popular and also very good development environment. A single license for WebStorm currently costs USD 129 (for personal use, there is another version that currently costs USD 59). However, if you want to test the program first, you can download a 30-day trial version from the WebStorm homepage. WebStorm is available for Windows and for macOS and Linux.

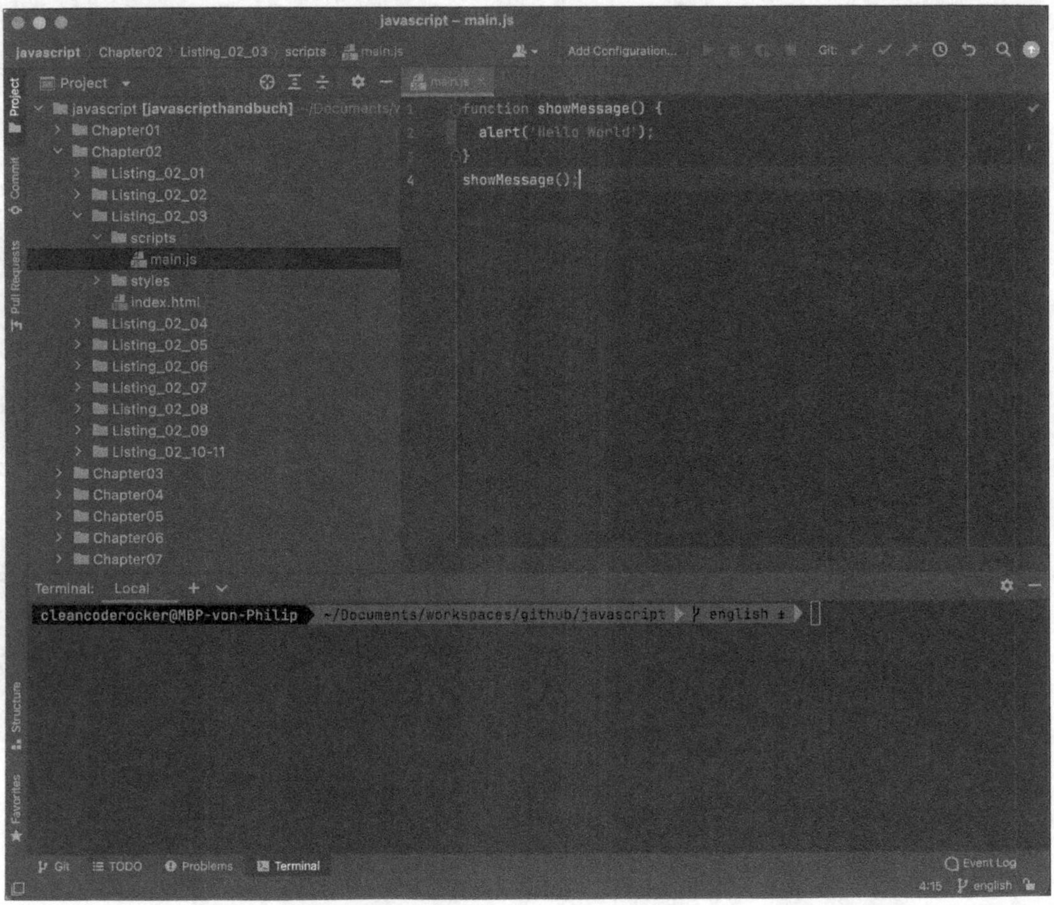

Figure 2.9 WebStorm IDE

Meanwhile a personal favorite among the development environments is Visual Studio Code by Microsoft (*https://code.visualstudio.com*; see Figure 2.10). It is available for download free of charge, can be flexibly extended via plug-ins, and its perceived performance is significantly better than that of WebStorm, for example.

A brief overview of the editors and development environments we've discussed is shown in Table 2.1.

Figure 2.10 Microsoft Visual Studio Code

Name	Price	macOS	Linux	Windows	Editor/Development Environment
Sublime Text	USD 99	Yes	Yes	Yes	Editor
Atom	Free of charge	Yes	Yes	Yes	Editor
Microsoft Visual Studio Code	Free of charge	Yes	Yes	Yes	Development environment
WebStorm	USD 129/ USD 59	Yes	Yes	Yes	Development environment

Table 2.1 Recommended Editors and Development Environments for JavaScript Development

Tip

For the beginning—for example, for trying out the code examples in this book—we recommend that you use one of the editors mentioned in this section and not a development environment (yet). The latter have the disadvantage that they are partly overloaded with menus and functionalities, so you have to deal not only with learning JavaScript but also with learning the development environment. Let's spare you that at least for the moment.

In addition, development environments only make sense when exceeding a certain project size. For smaller projects and the examples in this book, an editor is always enough (even though we will also cover complex topics). Plus, the editors are usually faster than the development environments in terms of execution speed.

2.2   Integrating JavaScript into a Web Page

Because we assume that you already know how to create an HTML file and how to embed a CSS file, and that you are "only" here to learn JavaScript, we don't want to waste any more time with details about HTML and CSS but will get started with JavaScript straight away. Don't worry: embedding and executing a JavaScript file is anything but difficult.

Learn HTML and CSS

If you have not worked with HTML or CSS a very good introductory book on this topic is *HTML and CSS: Design and Build Websites* by Jon Duckett (2011, John Wiley & Sons).

Per tradition (like almost every book on programming languages), we will start with a very simple *Hello World* example, which only produces the output Hello World. This is not very exciting yet, but right now the point is to show you how to embed a JavaScript file in an HTML file in the first place and how to execute the source code contained in the JavaScript file. We will take care of more complex things later.

2.2.1   Preparing a Suitable Folder Structure

For getting started and working through the following examples, we recommend that you use the directory structure shown in Figure 2.11 for every example. The HTML file is at the top level because this is the entry point for the browser and thus the file you will invoke in the browser right away.

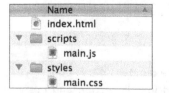

Figure 2.11 Example Folder Structure

However, it is a good idea to create different folders for the CSS and JavaScript files. The names *styles* (for CSS files) and *scripts* (for JavaScript files) are quite common. Especially if you are dealing with a lot of different JavaScript and CSS files during development, this separation (or an arrangement with subfolders in general) makes it easier to keep track of your project.

Starting Point of a JavaScript Application

Most of the examples in this book also follow the layout shown in Figure 2.11 as we will only run the JavaScript code in the browser at the beginning, using the *index.html* file as a kind of entry point to the program.

Later, in Chapter 17, you'll learn how you can also run JavaScript independent of a browser and thus independent of a corresponding HTML file. In this case, you don't need any HTML—and therefore no CSS files either.

Running JavaScript in the Browser

While you can execute JavaScript within a browser without creating an HTML file to embed the corresponding script (via special developer tools provided by browsers; Section 2.3.2), for now we don't want to use this feature.

2.2.2   Creating a JavaScript File

As mentioned earlier, it's better to save JavaScript code in a separate file (or in several separate files) that can then be embedded in the HTML code. So the first thing you need is a JavaScript file. Simply open the editor of your choice (or if you didn't take my advice, the development environment of your choice), create a new file, enter the lines of source code provided in Listing 2.1, and then save the file under the name *main.js*.

```
function showMessage() {
  alert('Hello World');
}
```

Listing 2.1 A Very Simple JavaScript Example That Defines a Function

---

Note

JavaScript files have the extension *.js*. Other file extensions are also possible, but the *.js* extension has the advantage that editors, development environments, and browsers directly know what the content is about. You should therefore always save all Java-Script files with the *.js* extension. (By the way, browsers recognize JavaScript files delivered by a web server via the *Content-Type header*, a piece of information that comes with the file from the server.)

Listing 2.1 defines a *function* with the name showMessage, which in turn calls another function (with the name alert) and passes it the message Hello World. The alert function is a JavaScript standard function, which we will briefly discuss later in this chapter. Functions in general, however, will be detailed in Chapter 3.

> **Supplemental Downloads for the Book**
>
> This code example and all those to come can also be found in the **Product Supplements** area for the book (see *https://www.rheinwerk-computing.com/5554*). There you can easily download the code and open it in your editor or directly in your browser (although we think that the most effective way to learn is to type the examples yourself, following them step by step).

2.2.3 Embedding a JavaScript File in an HTML File

To use the JavaScript source code within a web page, you need to link the JavaScript file to the web page or embed the JavaScript file in the HTML file. This is done via the HTML element named <script>.

This element can be used in two different ways: On the one hand, as we will demonstrate subsequently, external JavaScript files can be included in the HTML. On the other hand, JavaScript source code can be written directly between the opening <script> tag and the closing </script> tag.

An example of the latter method will be shown later, but this approach is only useful in exceptional cases because JavaScript code and HTML code are then mixed—that is, stored in one file (which is not a best practice for the reasons already mentioned). So let's first look at how to do it properly and include a separate file.

The <script> element has a total of six attributes, out of which the src attribute is certainly the most important one: it's used to specify the path to the JavaScript file that is to be included. (Table 2.2 shows an overview of what the other attributes do.)

Attribute	Meaning	Comment
async	Specifies whether the linked JavaScript file should be downloaded in an asynchronous way in order not to interrupt the download of other files (Section 2.2.5). This only makes sense in combination with the src attribute.	Optional

Table 2.2 The Attributes of the <script> Element

Attribute	Meaning	Comment
charset	Specifies the character set of the source code that is embedded via the src attribute. This only makes sense in combination with the src attribute, but is rarely used because most browsers do not respect this attribute. It is also considered better style to use UTF-8 everywhere within a website and define this in the \<meta\> element via the charset attribute.	Optional
defer	Specifies whether to wait to execute the linked JavaScript file until the web page content has been completely processed (Section 2.2.5). This only makes sense in combination with the src attribute, but is not always supported, especially not by older browsers.	Optional
language	Originally intended to indicate the version of JavaScript code used, but largely ignored by browsers.	Outdated
src	Specifies the path to the JavaScript file to be embedded.	Optional
type	Used to specify the MIME type (see box ahead) in order to identify the scripting language (in our case, JavaScript). However, you can also omit this attribute because text/javascript is used by default, which is supported by most browsers.	Optional

Table 2.2 The Attributes of the \<script\> Element (Cont.)

Now create an HTML file named *index.html* and insert the content shown in Listing 2.2.

```
<!DOCTYPE html>
<html>
<head lang="en">
  <meta charset="UTF-8">
  <title>Example</title>
  <link rel="stylesheet" href="styles/main.css" type="text/css">
</head>
<body>
<!--Here the JavaScript file will be included -->
<script src="scripts/main.js"></script>
</body>
</html>
```

Listing 2.2 Embedding JavaScript in HTML

If you now open this HTML file in the browser, nothing will happen yet because the function we defined in Listing 2.1 is not yet called at any point. Therefore, add the show-Message() call at the end of the JavaScript file, as shown in Listing 2.3, and reload the web page in the appropriate browser. Then a small hint dialog should open, containing the

67

message `Hello World` and with a slightly different appearance depending on the browser (see Figure 2.12).

```
function showMessage() {
  alert('Hello World');
}
showMessage();
```

Listing 2.3 Function Definition and Function Call

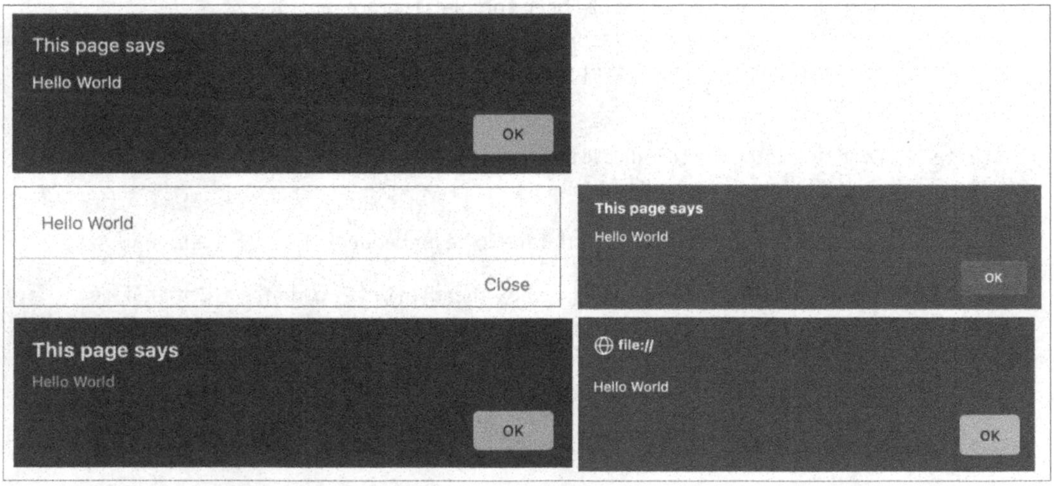

Figure 2.12 Hint Dialogs in Different Browsers

Definition

Multipurpose Internet Mail Extension (MIME) *types*, also called *internet media types* or *content types*, were originally intended to distinguish between content types within emails containing different content (such as images, PDF files, etc.). Now, however, MIME types are not only used in the context of email, but also whenever data is transmitted over the internet. If a server sends a file with a special MIME type, the client (e.g., the browser) knows directly what type of data is being transmitted.

For JavaScript, the MIME type wasn't standardized for a long time, so there were several MIME types—for example, `application/javascript`, `application/ecmascript`, `text/javascript` and `text/ecmascript`. Since 2006, however, there is an official standard (*www.rfc-editor.org/rfc/rfc4329.txt*) that defines the acceptable MIME types for JavaScript. According to this standard, `text/javascript` and `text/ecmascript` are both deprecated, and `application/javascript` and `application/ecmascript` should be used instead. Ironically, it's safest not to specify any MIME type for JavaScript at all (in the `<script>` element) as the `type` attribute is ignored by most browsers anyway.

> **Embedding Multiple JavaScript Files**
>
> Of course, you can embed several JavaScript files within one HTML file. Simply use a separate `<script>` element for each file you want to include.

2.2.4   Defining JavaScript Directly within the HTML

For the sake of completeness, we'll also show how you can define JavaScript directly within an HTML file. While this is usually not advisable because it means mixing HTML and JavaScript code in one file, it won't hurt to know that it still works.

Simply write the relevant JavaScript code inside the `<script>` element instead of linking it via the `src` attribute. Listing 2.4 shows the same example as in the previous section, but it doesn't use a separate JavaScript file for the JavaScript code. Instead, it embeds the code directly in the HTML. The `src` attribute is therefore omitted completely.

```
<!DOCTYPE html>
<html>
<head lang="en">
  <meta charset="UTF-8">
  <title>Example</title>
  <link rel="stylesheet" href="styles/main.css" type="text/css">
</head>
<body>
<script>
  function showMessage() {
    alert('Hello World');
  }
  showMessage();
</script>
</body>
</html>
```

Listing 2.4 Only Makes Sense in Exceptional Cases: Definition of JavaScript Directly in an HTML File

> **Note**
>
> Note that `<script>` elements that use the `src` attribute must not contain any source code between `<script>` and `</script>`. If there is any, this source code will be ignored.

Tip

Use separate JavaScript files for your source code instead of writing it directly into a <script> element. This creates a clean separation between the structure (HTML) and the behavior (JavaScript) of a web page.

The <noscript> Element

You can use the <noscript> element to define an HTML section that is displayed when JavaScript is not supported in the browser or has been disabled by the user (see Listing 2.5). However, if JavaScript is supported or enabled, the content of the <noscript> element will not be shown.

```
<noscript>
  JavaScript is not available or is disabled. <br />
  Please use a browser that supports JavaScript,
  or enable JavaScript in your browser.
</noscript>
```

Listing 2.5 Example of the Use of the <noscript> Element

2.2.5   Placement and Execution of the <script> Elements

If you had asked a web developer a few (many) years ago where to place a <script> element within a web page, they probably would have advised placing it in the <head> area of the web page. In the early days of web development, people thought that linked files such as CSS files and JavaScript files should be placed in a central location within the HTML code.

Since then, however, this idea has been abandoned. While CSS files are still placed in the <head> area, JavaScript files should be included before the closing </body> tag instead. The reason is this: when the browser loads a web page, it loads not only the HTML code but also embedded files such as images, CSS files, and JavaScript files. Depending on processor performance and memory usage, modern browsers are capable of downloading several such files in parallel. However, when the browser encounters a <script> element, it immediately starts processing the corresponding source code and evaluating it using the JavaScript interpreter. To be able to do this, the corresponding JavaScript source code must first be downloaded entirely. While this is happening, the browser pauses downloading all other files and *parsing* (i.e., processing) the HTML code, which in turn leads to the user impression that it takes longer to build the web page (see Figure 2.13).

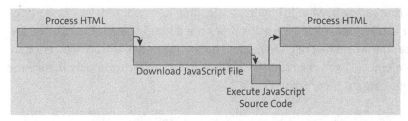

Figure 2.13 By Default, HTML Code Processing Stops when the Browser Encounters a <script> Element

In addition, you will often want to access HTML elements on a web page within the JavaScript source code. (You'll see how this works in Chapter 5.) If the JavaScript code is executed before these HTML elements have been processed, you'll encounter an access error (see Figure 2.14). If you place the <script> element before the closing </body> tag, though, you are on the safe side in this regard (see Figure 2.15), because in that case all elements included inside the <body> element are already loaded (with the exception of other <script> elements, of course).

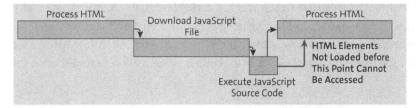

Figure 2.14 If JavaScript Accesses HTML Elements That Have Not Yet Been Loaded, an Error Occurs

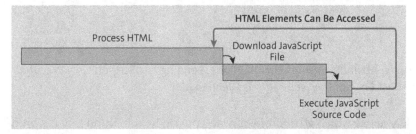

Figure 2.15 If the <script> Element Is Placed before the Closing </body> Tag, All Elements inside the <body> Element Are Loaded

> **Note**
>
> As a rule, you should position <script> elements at the end of the <body> element. This is because the browser first evaluates the JavaScript source code contained or embedded in each <script> element before continuing to load other HTML elements.

Two attributes that can be used to influence the loading behavior of JavaScript are the async and defer attributes, which we already mentioned briefly (see Table 2.2). The former ensures that the processing of HTML code is not paused when the browser encounters a <script> element. The JavaScript file is downloaded asynchronously (hence the name async). This concept is shown in Figure 2.16.

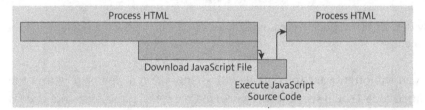

Figure 2.16 Due to the async Attribute, the HTML Code Continues To Be Processed until the Corresponding JavaScript Has Been Downloaded

As you can see, the JavaScript code is executed right away as soon as the corresponding JavaScript file has been completely downloaded.

The defer attribute takes this one step further. On the one hand, just like async, this attribute ensures that the HTML code processing is not paused. On the other hand, the JavaScript source code is executed only after the HTML code has been fully processed (see Figure 2.17). The execution of the JavaScript code is effectively deferred (hence the name defer).

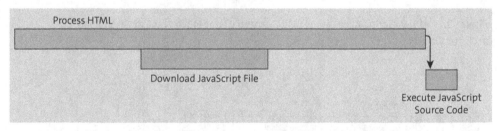

Figure 2.17 The defer Attribute Ensures That the Corresponding JavaScript Is Only Executed after the Entire HTML Code of the Web Page Has Been Loaded

So when should you use which attribute? For now, you can bear in mind that it's probably best not to use either attribute by default. The async attribute is only suitable for scripts that work completely independently and have nothing to do with the HTML on the web page. An example of this is the use of Google Analytics. The defer attribute, on the other hand, is currently not supported by all browsers, so you should also consider its use with caution.

Definition

Another way to ensure that all the content of the web page has been loaded before JavaScript code is executed is to use *event handlers* and *event listeners*. We'll introduce both of them in detail in Chapter 6. But for now, we'll show you roughly how both of them are used because they appear in the source code examples in the book before we get to the examples for Chapter 6.

In general, both event handlers and event listeners are used to respond to certain events that occur during the execution of a program and to execute certain code. (There is a small, subtle difference between event handlers and event listeners, but it's not important for now, and we'll explain it in Chapter 6.) Events can be mouse clicks, keystrokes, window resizing actions, and more. For web pages, too, there are various events that are triggered and can be answered by such event handlers and event listeners. For example, an event is triggered when the content of a web page is fully loaded.

To define an event handler for this event, you can use the onload attribute: The code you specify here as the value for such an attribute is invoked when the web page is fully loaded. As a value, you can specify a JavaScript *statement*, such as the call to a function, as shown in Listing 2.6.

```
<!DOCTYPE html>
<html>
<head lang="en">
  <meta charset="UTF-8">
  <title>Example</title>
  <link rel="stylesheet" href="styles/main.css" type="text/css">
</head>
<body onload="showMessage()">
<script src="scripts/main.js"></script>
</body>
</html>
```

Listing 2.6 Using an Event Handler

Event listeners, however, cannot be defined via HTML. Instead, you use the addEventListener() function of the document object (more on this later), to which you pass the name of the event and the function to be executed when the event is triggered (see Listing 2.7).

```
function showMessage() {
  alert('Hello World');
}
document.addEventListener('DOMContentLoaded', showMessage);
```

Listing 2.7 Using Event Listeners

The showMessage() call you just added to the end of the *main.js* file will need to be removed again in both cases. Otherwise, the function will be called twice (once by the script itself and once by the event handler/event listener), and as a consequence a message dialog will be displayed twice in succession.

2.2.6   Displaying the Source Code

All browsers usually provide a way to view the source code of a web page. This can be helpful in many cases—for example, if you want to check how a particular feature is implemented on a website you have discovered.

In Chrome, you can view the source code by following menu path **View • Developer • View Source** (see Figure 2.18); in Firefox, **Tools • Browser Tools • Page Source** (see Figure 2.19); in Safari, **Develop • Show Page Source** (see Figure 2.20); in Opera, **Developer • View Source** (see Figure 2.21); and in Microsoft Edge, **Tools • Developer • View Source** (see Figure 2.22).

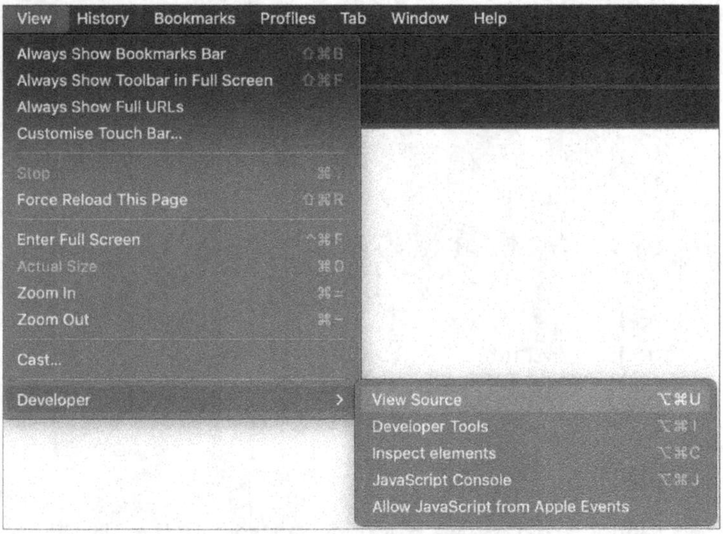

Figure 2.18 Show Source Code in Chrome

Source Code for More Complex Web Pages

If you look at the source code of more complex web pages, it's often very confusing. This is usually due to multiple reasons: on the one hand, content is often generated dynamically, and on the other, JavaScript is often deliberately compressed and obscured by web developers—the former to save space, the latter to protect the source code from prying eyes. This book does not deal with the compression and obfuscation of source code.

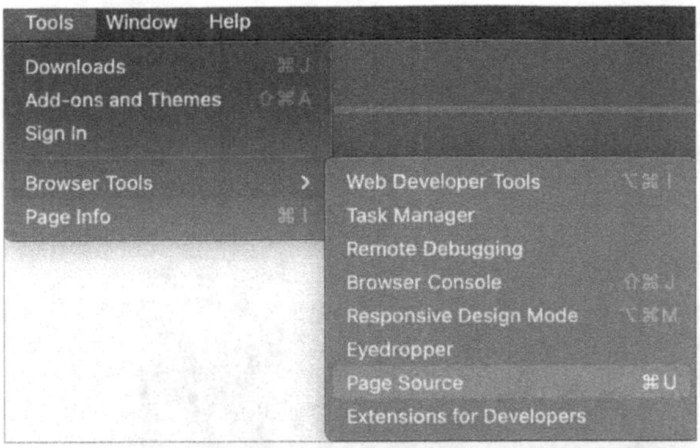

Figure 2.19 Show Source Code in Firefox

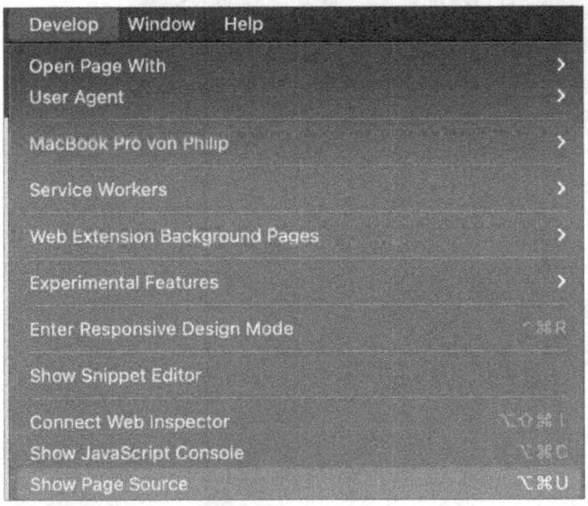

Figure 2.20 Show Source Code in Safari

Figure 2.21 Show Source Code in Opera

Figure 2.22 Show Source Code in Microsoft Edge

If you display the source code of a web page (no matter in which browser), you are first presented with the corresponding HTML code of the web page. Conveniently, however, embedded files such as CSS files or JavaScript files are linked in this source code view (see Figure 2.23) so that you can easily get to the source code of the linked file as well (see Figure 2.24).

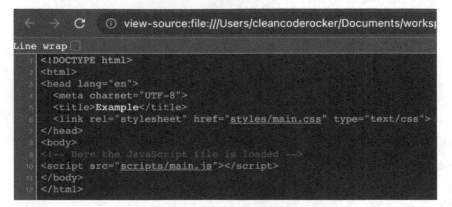

Figure 2.23 Source Code View for HTML in Chrome

Figure 2.24 Source Code View for JavaScript in Chrome

2.3 Creating Output

In the *Hello World* example, you have already seen how you can create simple output by calling the alert() function. However, there are several other options as well.

2.3.1 Showing the Standard Dialog Window

In addition to the already known hint dialog displayed by calling the alert() function (see Figure 2.25), the JavaScript language provides two more standard functions for displaying dialog boxes. The first one is the confirm() function. It's used to display *confirmation dialogs*—that is, yes/no decisions (see Figure 2.26). In contrast to the hint dialog, the confirmation dialog contains two buttons: one to confirm and one to cancel the corresponding message. The second one is the prompt() function. This function opens an *input dialog* where users can enter text (see Figure 2.27).

Figure 2.25 Simple Hint Dialog

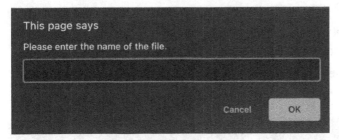

Figure 2.26 Simple Confirmation Dialog

Figure 2.27 Simple Input Dialog

In practice, however, these standard dialogs for hints, confirmation, and input are rarely used because they offer limited options for statements and—as already shown for the hint dialog—their design relies on the layout of the browser being used, which usually does not match the layout of the web page.

For this reason, web developers like to resort to one of the various JavaScript libraries that offer fancier and more functional dialogs (see Figure 2.28). One of these libraries is jQuery UI, which builds on the well-known jQuery library and extends it with various UI components. We will take a closer look at the main library, jQuery, as well as jQuery UI in Chapter 10.

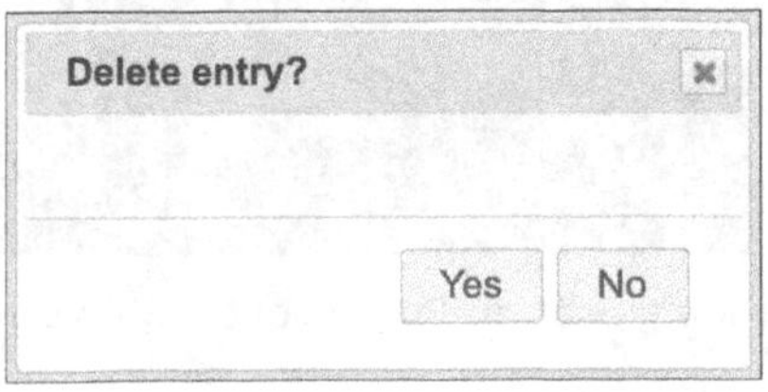

Figure 2.28 Custom Confirmation Dialog with JavaScript

2.3.2   Writing to the Console

When developing JavaScript applications, you'll often want to generate output for yourself for testing purposes only—for example, to return an intermediate result. For such test-only output, it obviously doesn't make sense to present it in dialogs that users would get to see as well. For this reason, all current browsers now offer a *console*, which is suitable for exactly such purposes and which you can access within a Java-Script program in order to output messages. By default, this console is hidden because users of a web page usually can do little with it.

Displaying the Console

To activate the console, proceed as follows, depending on your browser (we won't provide screenshots at this point as the menu items can be found in similar places as the menu items for displaying the source code, mentioned earlier in this chapter):

- In Chrome, select **View** · **Developer** · **JavaScript Console**, which opens the console within the Chrome DevTools.
- In Firefox, open the console via **Tools** · **Browser Tools** · **Browser Console**.
- In Safari, open the console via **Develop** · **Show JavaScript Console**.
- In Opera, you must first select **Developer** · **Developer Tools** and then the **Console** tab.
- In Microsoft Edge, open the console via **Tools** · **Developer** · **JavaScript Console**.

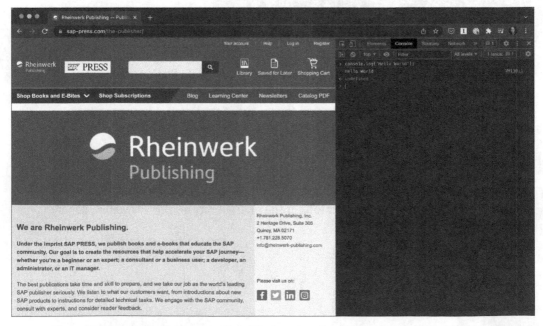

Figure 2.29 By Default, the Console Is Displayed on the Right or at the Bottom of the Browser Window (Google Chrome in This Case)

Figure 2.29 shows the console in the Chrome browser, for example. As you can see, it doesn't really look special, but it will be one of your main tools if you want to use JavaScript for web development. In addition to receiving output, you can also enter your input via the console (more about this in a few moments). In essence, the console is a kind of terminal (or command prompt, if you're a Windows user) that lets you issue JavaScript commands that are then executed in the context of the web page loaded.

Writing Output to the Console

For writing to the console, browsers provide the `console` object. This is a JavaScript object first introduced by the Firefox plug-in named Firebug (*https://getfirebug.com*), and it provides various ways to generate output to the console. Firebug itself has been discontinued, but the `console` object (although still not included in the ECMAScript standard) is available in almost every JavaScript runtime environment.

> **Standardized API for Working with the Console**
>
> The individual methods provided by the `console` object differ from runtime environment to runtime environment. To counteract this, there are efforts underway to create a standardized API.

A generally supported method is the `log()` method, which can be used to generate simple console output. To try using the console, simply replace the source code of the *main.js* file with the source code in Listing 2.8 and call the web page again.

```
// scripts/main.js
function showMessage() {
  console.log('Hello developer world');
}
```

Listing 2.8 Simple JavaScript Example

Depending on the browser, the result should be similar to that shown in Figure 2.30.

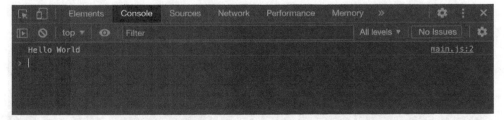

Figure 2.30 Output to the Console in Chrome

In addition to the log() method, console provides several other methods. An overview of the most important ones is provided in Table 2.3.

Method	Description
clear()	Clears the console.
debug()	Used to output a message intended for *debugging* (or *troubleshooting*). (You may first need to set the appropriate developer tools to return this type of output.)
error()	Used to output an error message. Some browsers display an error icon next to the output message within the console.
info()	This will display an info message in the console. Some browsers—Chrome, for example—also output an info icon.
log()	Probably the most commonly used method of console. Generates normal output to the console.
trace()	Outputs the *stack trace*—that is, the *method call stack* (see also Chapter 3) to the console.
warn()	Used to issue a warning to the console. Again, most browsers will display a corresponding icon next to the message.

Table 2.3 Most Important Methods of the console Object

Listing 2.9 shows the corresponding source code for using the console object. The output for the individual methods is highlighted with colors or icons, depending on the browser (see Figure 2.31).

```
console.log('Hello developer world');     // Output of a normal message
console.debug('Hello developer world');   // Output of a debug message
console.error('Hello developer world');   // Output of an error message
console.info('Hello developer world');    // Output of an info message
console.warn('Hello developer world');    // Output of a warning
```

Listing 2.9 Using the console Object

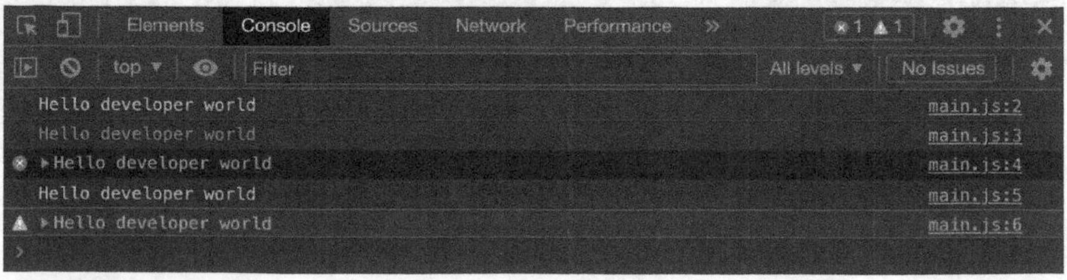

Figure 2.31 Different Message Types Are Highlighted with Colors or Icons

Writing Input to the Console

In the last few screenshots, you may have noticed the > sign below the output. Here, you can enter any JavaScript code and have it executed right away. This is a great way to quickly test simple scripts, and actually indispensable for web development. Try it: type the showMessage() command in the prompt and then press the Enter key to execute the command. The results are displayed in Figure 2.32.

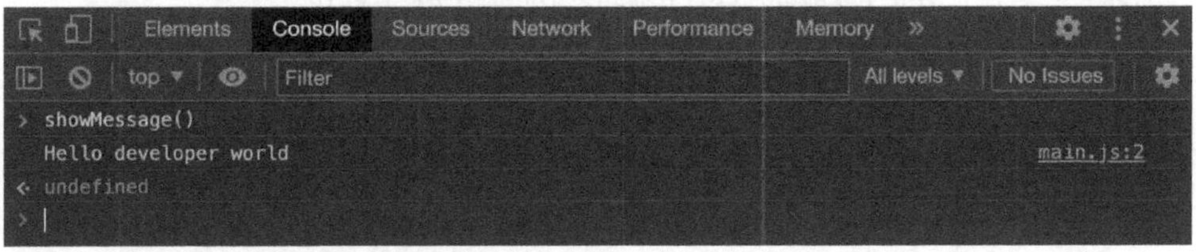

Figure 2.32 You Can Also Execute Source Code via the Console

Note

The console window and the console object are important tools for web developers. Make yourself familiar with both when you get a chance.

Logging Libraries

The console object works well for quick output during development. However, if a web page goes live or a JavaScript application is used in production, you don't really want to use console calls any longer (even though they are usually not displayed to the user). In practice, you often use special *logging libraries* that enable console output to be activated (for development) but also deactivated again (for productive use) via specific configuration settings. To start, and also for the examples in this book, however, the use of the console object should be sufficient.

2.3.3   Using Existing UI Components

Because the use of alert(), confirm(), and prompt() is rather outdated and only useful for quick testing, and the output via the console object is reserved for developers anyway, you obviously still need a way to create an appealing output for the user of a web page. To this end, you can write the output of a program into existing UI components such as text fields and the like.

Listing 2.10, Listing 2.11, and Figure 2.33 show an example. It consists of a simple form that can be used to determine the result of adding two numbers. The two numbers can be entered into two text fields, the addition is triggered by pressing the button, and the result is written into the third text field.

You don't need to understand the code for this example yet, and we won't into the details at this point. For now, just keep in mind that when developing for the web with JavaScript, it's relatively common to use HTML components for sending output from a program to the user.

```javascript
// scripts/main.js
function calculateSum() {
  const x = parseInt(document.getElementById('field1').value);
  const y = parseInt(document.getElementById('field2').value);
  const result = document.getElementById('result');
  console.log(x + y);
  result.value = x + y;
}
```

Listing 2.10 The JavaScript Code of the main.js File

```html
<!DOCTYPE html>
<html>
<head lang="en">
  <meta charset="UTF-8">
  <title>Example</title>
  <link rel="stylesheet" href="styles/main.css" type="text/css">
</head>
<body>
<div class="container">
  <div class="row">
    <label for="field1">X</label> <input id="field1" type="text" value="5">
  </div>
  <div class="row">
    <label for="field2">Y</label> <input id="field2" type="text" value="5">
  </div>
  <div class="row">
    <label for="result">Result: </label> <input id="result" type="text">
    <button onclick="calculateSum()">Calculate sum</button>
  </div>
</div>
<script src="scripts/main.js"></script>
</body>
</html>
```

Listing 2.11 The HTML Code for the Example Application

X	5
Y	5
Result:		Calculate sum

Figure 2.33 Example Application

> **DOM Manipulation**
>
> The most complex scenario is when you dynamically modify a web page to produce output—for example, dynamically modify a table to display tabular structured data. We will discuss this topic of DOM manipulation in more detail in Chapter 5.

2.4   Summary

In this chapter, you learned how to create JavaScript files and embed them in HTML. You now have the basic knowledge for executing the examples in the next chapters. The following key points were presented in this chapter:

- Three languages are important for frontend development: HTML as a *markup language* to define the structure of a web page, CSS as a *style language* to define design and layout, and JavaScript as a *programming language* to add additional behavior and interactivity to a web page.

- You can specify JavaScript directly using the <script> element or can embed a separate JavaScript file using the src attribute of the <script> element. We recommend the latter, as it ensures a clean separation between the structure (HTML) and behavior (JavaScript) of the web page.

- You should always place <script> elements before the closing </body> tag, as this ensures that the web page content is fully loaded.

- JavaScript inherently provides three functions for generating output: alert() for creating hint dialogs, confirm() for creating confirmation dialogs, and prompt() for creating input dialogs.

- In practice, however, instead of these (more or less obsolete) functions, people use fancier dialogs, such as those offered by the jQuery library.

- In addition, all current browsers provide the possibility to generate output via a console, which is primarily intended for you to use as a developer.

Chapter 3
Language Core

This chapter provides an introduction to the JavaScript language core. You will learn how to store individual values in variables and perform calculations, control the flow of a program using branches and repetitions, and structure the source code into reusable building blocks.

To learn a programming language, you need to learn the syntax and grammar, just like when you learn a "real" language like Italian, Chinese, or Latin. The *syntax* determines the words that can be used in the given language, and the *grammar* defines the rules according to which these words can be arranged. We have deliberately kept the source code examples in this chapter simple so that you can follow these examples easily and are well prepared for the later (more complex) examples in this book.

3.1 Storing Values in Variables

To solve a problem with an algorithm, it is in most cases necessary to store certain information temporarily. This is done via *variables*. These are nothing more than mutable (variable) *caches* where you store values to access them at a later time.

3.1.1 Defining Variables

To be able to use variables, you need to perform two steps. First, you need to create the variable. This process is generally referred to as *variable declaration*. To declare a variable in JavaScript, you can use the var keyword, followed by the variable name, as shown in Listing 3.1.

```
var firstName;
var lastName;
```

Listing 3.1 Declaration of Variables Using the var Keyword

As an alternative, it's possible since ES2015 to use the let keyword for defining variables, which is the recommended method, as shown in Listing 3.2.

```
let firstName;
let lastName;
```

Listing 3.2 Declaration of Variables Using the let Keyword

Both of these source code variants each define two variables: one named `firstName` and one named `lastName`. You don't need to understand the exact difference between `var` and `let` at this point. For now, just keep in mind that you should use the keyword `let` if the corresponding JavaScript runtime environment (or the browser) supports it.

Strict Mode

As you will see throughout this book, JavaScript has many quirks and features, some of which lead to errors that are hard to find within an application. To prevent this, *strict mode* was introduced with ES5. This mode ensures that these potentially error-prone features cannot be used within a script. So strict mode ultimately leads to the use of a somewhat "cleaned up" version of JavaScript (i.e., a subset of JavaScript).

You can activate strict mode either for the entire script or specifically for individual functions. In the first case, you include the statement `'use strict';` at the beginning of the script (as shown in Listing 3.3); in the second case, you include it in the first line of the corresponding function (more about this later).

```
'use strict';
let firstName;
let lastName;
```

Listing 3.3 Using Strict Mode

After declaring a variable, you can assign an actual value to it. This is also referred to as *value assignment* or *variable initialization*. It looks like the example in Listing 3.4.

```
firstName = 'John';
lastName = 'Doe';
```

Listing 3.4 Variable Initialization

By using the equals sign (=), you assign a concrete value to a variable. In JavaScript, the equals sign is the *assignment operator*. It doesn't represent two expressions that are equal in value as you would expect from the field of mathematics. In Listing 3.4, this operator is used to assign the value John to the `firstName` variable and the value Doe to the `lastName` variable.

Variables without Value

If a variable hasn't yet been assigned a value, it is not yet defined and accordingly has the value `undefined`.

The two steps of variable declaration and variable initialization can be conveniently combined into a single statement, as shown in Listing 3.5.

```
let firstName = 'John';
let lastName = 'Doe';
```

Listing 3.5 Variable Declaration and Variable Initialization

In addition, you have the possibility to declare and initialize several variables within a single statement:

```
let firstName='John', lastName='Doe';
```

Here, the two variables `firstName` and `lastName` are declared and initialized. In practice, however, the individual variables are often distributed over several lines for better readability:

```
let firstName = 'John',     // This creates one variable ...
    lastName = 'Doe';       // ... and this creates another one.
```

Declaration of Variables since ES2015

A best practice for declaring variables is as follows: use `let` for declaring variables for which the value can change at runtime (counter variables are a classic example). For all "variables" for which the value doesn't change, use `const` instead. In other words, define these "variables" as constants (see also Section 3.1.3). However, you should avoid using `var` to declare variables.

And that's exactly how we do it in this book:

- We use `var` only in examples where it is required by the version of the runtime environment used (like in code examples that are explicitly intended to work in older browsers).
- We use `let` for real variables—that is, variables for which the value changes within the code example shown (e.g., for the counter variables mentioned previously or for variables for which the value is "assembled" bit by bit).
- We use `const` for all other variables, which are actually constants.

Definition

Keywords represent an important part of the syntax of a programming language and, in the case of JavaScript, ensure that the interpreter knows what to do. In the case of `var`, `let`, and `const`, the interpreter knows that a variable is to be created and that the appropriate amount of space must be reserved for it.

> **Tip**
>
> Avoid declaring new variables without specifying `let` or `const`. Otherwise you may unintentionally overwrite already existing global variables with the same name. Strict mode will produce an error if you do try to do this, by the way.

As mentioned earlier, after variables have been assigned a value, they can be assigned a new value. Listing 3.6 demonstrates an example. In this case, the variable x is first assigned the value 4711, then the value 5.

```
let x = 4711;
console.log(x);   // Output: 4711
x = 5;
console.log(x);   // Output: 5
```

Listing 3.6 Variables Can Be Overwritten with New Values; They Are Variable, as the Name Suggests

3.1.2   Using Valid Variable Names

You are relatively free in the choice of names for variables, but there are a few restrictions that you must observe. If you don't, an error will occur when you run your program.

Keywords

First, there are some reserved keywords that are part of the language and serve as identifiers for the interpreter, such as the `var` and `let` keywords introduced earlier. If you were to use one of these keywords as a variable name, the interpreter would get confused and report an error accordingly.

In addition, there are other keywords in JavaScript that you can use to define certain things. Table 3.1 shows an overview of reserved keywords in JavaScript. Although not all of them are functional in the current version of JavaScript—but they are reserved for later versions of the language—you still must not use any of these keywords as variables. The keywords are described in the table, but most of them will be discussed in more detail in the sections or chapters listed in the right-hand column.

Keyword	Description	Chapter or Section with Further Discussion
async	Used to indicate asynchronous functions	Chapter 16
await	Used to wait for the result of asynchronous functions	Chapter 16

Table 3.1 Reserved Keywords in JavaScript

Keyword	Description	Chapter or Section with Further Discussion
break	Used to cancel multiway branches and loops	Chapter 3, Section 3.4.4 and Section 3.4.8
case	Used to define individual program branches in a multiway branch	Chapter 3, Section 3.4.4
class	Used to define classes	Chapter 13
catch	Used to intercept errors	Chapter 3, Section 3.6.5
const	Used to define constants	Chapter 3, Section 3.1.3
continue	Used to cancel loop iterations	Chapter 3, Section 3.4.8
debugger	Used to define breakpoints in the program	Section 3.7
default	Used to define a standard program branch for multiway branches	Chapter 3, Section 3.4.4
delete	Used to delete object properties	Chapter 4, Section 4.1.4
do	Used to define tail-controlled loops	Chapter 3, Section 3.4.7
else	Used to define an alternative program branch when branching	Chapter 3, Section 3.4.2
enum	Reserved keyword; no function assigned yet	N/A
export	Used in connection with modules	Chapter 16
extends	Used to define subclasses or superclasses	Chapter 13
finally	Used to define default behavior when handling errors	Chapter 3, Section 3.6.5
for	Used to define counting loops	Chapter 3, Section 3.4.5
function	Used to define functions	Chapter 3, Section 3.5.1
if	Used to define conditional statements and branches	Chapter 3, Section 3.4.1 and Section 3.4.2
implements	Reserved keyword	N/A
import	Used in connection with modules	Chapter 16
in	Checks whether an object contains a property or a method	Chapter 3, Section 3.3.9
interface	Reserved keyword	N/A

Table 3.1 Reserved Keywords in JavaScript (Cont.)

Keyword	Description	Chapter or Section with Further Discussion
instanceof	Checks whether an object is an instance of a prototype	Chapter 13
let	Used to define variables	Chapter 3, Section 3.1.1
new	Used to create object instances	Chapter 4
package	Reserved keyword; no function assigned yet	N/A
private	Reserved keyword; no function assigned yet	N/A
protected	Reserved keyword; no function assigned yet	N/A
public	Reserved keyword; no function assigned yet	N/A
return	Used to define a return value of a function	Chapter 3, Section 3.5.4
static	Used to define static properties and methods	Chapter 13
super	Used to access the superclass from a (sub)class	Chapter 13
switch	Used to define multiway branches	Chapter 3, Section 3.4.4
this	Used to access an object within the object itself	Chapter 4
throw	Used to throw an error	Chapter 3, Section 3.6.6
try	Used to define a code block in which errors can occur	Chapter 3, Section 3.6.5
typeof	Determines the type of a variable	Chapter 3, Section 3.3.9
var	Used to define variables	Chapter 3, Section 3.1.1
void	Reserved keyword; no function assigned yet	N/A
while	Used to define head-controlled loops	Chapter 3, Section 3.4.6
with	Reserved keyword; should not be used and is not allowed in strict mode, for example	N/A
yield	Used for generator functions	Chapter 16

Table 3.1 Reserved Keywords in JavaScript (Cont.)

Variable Names Already Assigned

While you cannot use keywords as variable names for syntactical reasons, there are also names that you *could* use but *should not*. We're referring to names that are already assigned to existing *global standard variables*.

The relevant standard variables essentially depend on the runtime environment: browsers define global standard variables that are different from those defined by a server-side runtime like Node.js. While browsers have predefined variables like alert, document, or window, Node.js has predefined variables such as process, module, and exports.

If you use one of these predefined words to define a new variable, this can have unintended consequences and lead to errors in the program. Listing 3.7 demonstrates this using the console object (which you already learned about in Chapter 2). In this case, a variable named console is defined and assigned the value 4711. The subsequent attempt to call the log() method on the console object fails.

```
const number = 22;      // Define variable
console.log(number);    // Output: 22
const console = 4711;   // Define variable
console.log(number);    // TypeError: console.log is not a function
```

Listing 3.7 The log() Function Is Not Found because the console Variable Has Been Redefined and Thus No Longer Addresses the Original Object

If you use one of these words as a variable name, you should at least be aware of the side effects this may have. In the previous example, it is obvious and the error is easy to find. But the visibility of variables also plays a role, as you will see in the course of the book. For now, remember this: if possible, you should avoid using predefined variable names for your own variables. A selection of predefined variable names in browser runtime environments is shown in Table 3.2. A detailed listing can be found on the internet—at *https://developer.mozilla.org/en-US/docs/Web/JavaScript/Reference/Global_Objects*, for example. See *https://nodejs.org/api/globals.html* for an overview of the global objects under Node.js.

Predefined Variable Names			
alert	closed	frames	open
blur	document	location	screen
close	focus	navigator	window

Table 3.2 Predefined Variable Names in Browsers

Allowed Characters

Regardless of keywords and predefined variable names, you may use only certain characters within variable names, including letters and numbers, and you can't start a variable name with a number.

For full details on the characters allowed, see the two blog posts at *https://mathiasbyn-ens.be/notes/javascript-identifiers* (for ECMAScript 5) and at *https://mathiasbynens.be/notes/javascript-identifiers-es6* (for ECMAScript 2015). But for starters, it's sufficient to follow these rules:

- A variable name may only start with a letter, the dollar sign ($), or an underscore (_).
- A variable name must not start with a number.
- A variable name may contain letters, numbers, dollar signs, and underscores, but no other characters, like periods or hyphens.

Listing 3.8 provides a few examples of valid and invalid variable names.

```
const 2ndName = 'James';    // invalid because it starts with a number
const first%Name = 'John'; // invalid because it contains special characters
const first-name = 'John'; // invalid because it contains a hyphen
const first_name = 'John'; // valid
const _firstName = 'John'; // valid
const $firstName = 'John'; // valid
```

Listing 3.8 Examples of Valid and Invalid Variable Names

Case Sensitivity

You should also note that variable names are case-sensitive. For example, name, Name, and nAme each represent different variables, as illustrated in Listing 3.9.

```
const name = 'John';    // This is a different variable ...
const Name = 'James';   // ... from this variable ...
const nAme = 'Peter';   // ... and this variable.
```

Listing 3.9 JavaScript Distinguishes between Uppercase and Lowercase Letters in Variable Names

In practice, however, you should avoid distinguishing variables only by their case. It is too likely that this will lead to confusion in your program.

CamelCase Spelling

You can use both uppercase and lowercase letters when assigning variable names. The only important thing is that you do it consistently. A generally accepted notation, for example, is the *lowerCamelCase* notation, where the variable name starts with a lowercase letter and then, if the name is composed of several words, each of the other words starts with an uppercase letter. The resulting variable name then resembles the form of camel humps. Listing 3.10 shows some examples.

```
const defaultValue  = 2345;
const firstName = 'John';
```

```
const lastName = 'Doe';
const isAdmin = true;
const userIsNotLoggedIn = true;
```

Listing 3.10 Examples of Variable Names in lowerCamelCase Notation

---

lowerCamelCase and UpperCamelCase Notation

The lowerCamelCase notation is commonly and frequently used for variable names by developers.

In addition to the lowerCamelCase notation, there is also the *UpperCamelCase* notation. The only difference is that the first letter is uppercase instead of lowercase. However, the UpperCamelCase notation is not used for variable names, but for class names (see Chapter 13).

Meaningful Names

Last but not least, we advise you to choose variables names that are as meaningful as possible so that you can tell the purpose of the variable from the name alone (i.e., without having to look at the surrounding code). For example, a name like uc is less meaningful than the name userConfiguration, and a name like x4 is less meaningful than the name xCoordinate4. Listing 3.11 shows some examples of meaningful and less meaningful variable names.

```
// not very meaningful variable names
const fn = 'John ';
const ln = 'Doe ';
// meaningful variable names
const firstName = 'John ';
const lastName = 'Doe ';
```

Listing 3.11 Examples of Meaningful and Less Meaningful Variable Names

---

Note

Use meaningful names when naming variables. This helps you and others who take a look at your source code to understand the code faster. Regarding the space it takes for these names, you don't have to pay attention to the length of variable names because it's possible to minify source code for productive use with special tools (called *minifiers*).

Book Recommendation

A very good book that deals with understandable source code in general is *Clean Code: A Handbook of Agile Software Craftsmanship* by Robert C. Martin (Pearson, 2008). In this book, the author details all sorts of aspects of clean code. Although the code examples are not written in JavaScript (but mostly in Java), they can be transferred to other programming languages relatively easily.

English Variable Names

In software development, it is common practice to name variables in English: on the one hand, English is often the common language in international teams, and on the other hand, it is the language with the fewest special characters.

3.1.3   Defining Constants

You have learned that you can change the value of variables any time; you can *overwrite* variables with a new value. Sometimes, however, you want to prevent this; that is, you actually need something like a variable, the value of which cannot be overwritten. These variables are called *constants* in programming because they are not variable but constant: once assigned, the value of a constant remains the same.

In JavaScript, there is a const keyword for defining constants. Accordingly, a constant is defined as shown in Listing 3.12.

```
const MAXIMUM = 5000;
```

Listing 3.12 Declaration of a Constant

Here, you can also see a common convention for naming constants: as a rule, these are written completely in uppercase. If the name consists of several words, separate them with an underscore (e.g., MAXIMUM_AGE).

If you try to overwrite a constant, as in Listing 3.13, it depends on the runtime environment whether the corresponding statement is silently ignored or an error is thrown.

```
const MAXIMUM = 5000;
MAXIMUM = 4711;        // potential runtime error
console.log(MAXIMUM);  // Output: 5000
```

Listing 3.13 Constants Cannot Be Overwritten

3.2   Using the Different Data Types

In total, JavaScript distinguishes among six different data types: on the one hand, there are the three *primitive data types* for representing numbers, strings, and Boolean values; on the other hand, there are the special data types null and undefined (also forms of primitive data types), plus the Object type, which serves as the basis for creating your own (complex) objects (see also Chapter 4).

In addition, we'll introduce so-called arrays in this section. Strictly speaking, these are not a separate data type in JavaScript, but they are so essential and important for programming that we'll briefly discuss them here (and then in detail together with objects in Chapter 4). In addition, some of the concepts that will follow in this chapter can be explained better or more practically using arrays. However, let's start with the three primitive data types first because they are the easiest to understand.

No Data Type in Variable Declarations

Unlike other programming languages, such as Java, JavaScript does not require you to specify a *data type* in the variable declaration because it is determined dynamically at runtime based on the value assigned to the variable.

Loose Typing and Strong Typing

Because the data type is not explicitly specified when declaring a variable in JavaScript, this is also referred to as *loose typing*. Other programming languages, such as Java, on the other hand, use what is known as *strong typing* or *strict typing*; that is, the data type must be explicitly defined in the variable declaration. If programmed carelessly, loose typing as in JavaScript can lead to unexpected problems, such as whenever you work with two or more variables of different data types. In addition, loose typing in JavaScript makes it possible to change the type of a variable during runtime—another potential source of errors.

3.2.1 Numbers

As you would expect, numbers (or more precisely, *numeric data*) are used in programming to perform calculations, describe quantities, define ranges of values, or simply to count—for example, to calculate the total of all items in a shopping cart, to count how often a user has accessed a web page, or to specify how fast an animation should play on a web page.

Defining Numbers

In JavaScript, numbers are represented by a numeric value. The value 9, for example, unsurprisingly stands for the number nine, the value 4711 for the number four thousand seven hundred and eleven. Decimals, or floating point numbers, are noted with a dot—for example, 0.5 or 0.3333. In addition, negative values can also be defined by simply prefixing the respective number with a minus sign—for example, -5 or -0.9. Since ES2021, it's also possible to use underscores as separators within numbers. Especially with longer numbers, these separators can noticeably increase readability. In fact, readability is also the main reason for this feature: the numbers are still represented internally as if they had been created without separators (as seen, for example, in the console output in the following listing).

Listing 3.14 shows some examples of defining variables containing numbers.

```
const number1 = 5;          // definition of an integer
const number2 = 0.5;        // definition of a decimal
const number3 = -22;        // definition of a negative integer
const number4 = -0.9;       // definition of a negative decimal
const number5 = 12_300;     // separator for decimal representation
const number6 = 1_000_000;  // separator for decimal representation

console.log(number1);       // 5
console.log(number2);       // 0.5
console.log(number3);       // -22
console.log(number4);       // -0.9
console.log(number5);       // 12300
console.log(number6);       // 1000000
```

Listing 3.14 Definition of Different Number Variables

Number Systems

Integers can be defined in JavaScript using different number systems. The spelling is different in each case. In addition to the decimal notation shown in Listing 3.14 (i.e., the base 10 number system), *binary notation* can be used for defining *binary numbers* (base 2 number system), the *octal notation* for defining *octal numbers* (base 8 number system), and the *hexadecimal notation* for defining *hexadecimal numbers* (base 16 number system). At the beginning, you probably won't use all three notations, or only very rarely. However, you should know that these notations exist and what they look like.

Binary numbers have the prefix 0b followed by a sequence of zeros and ones—for example, 0b01010101 for the decimal value of 85, as shown in Listing 3.15. Using other numbers will result in an error.

```
const number1 = 0b01010101; // definition of a binary number (decimal
                            // value of 85)
// const number2 = 0b01010102;         // invalid binary number
const number3 = 0b1010_0011_1010_0101; // separator for binary representation

console.log(number1);                  // 85
console.log(number3);                  // 41893
```

Listing 3.15 Examples of Valid and Invalid Binary Numbers

Octal numbers always start with a 0 followed by a sequence of numbers between 0 and 7—for example, 050 for the decimal value 40, as you can see in Listing 3.16. If one of the digits is outside the value range from 0 to 7, the leading 0 is ignored and the number is interpreted as a decimal number instead. (The exact calculation of octal numbers isn't important for our purposes at this point. If you're interested in this topic, you can find more information at *https://en.wikipedia.org/wiki/Octal*.)

```
const number1 = 050;      // definition of an octal number (decimal
                          // value of 40)
// const number2 = 078;  // invalid octal number (value of 78)
const number3 = 011147;  // definition of an octal
                          // number (decimal value of 4711)


console.log(number1);    // 40
console.log(number3);    // 4711
```

Listing 3.16 Examples of Valid and Invalid Octal Numbers

Hexadecimal numbers always start with the string 0x, followed by a sequence of hexadecimal values: the digits 0 to 9 and the letters A to F or a to f (details can be found at *https://en.wikipedia.org/wiki/Hexadecimal*). The hexadecimal value 0xF, for example, stands for the decimal value of 15. The use of a letter after F will result in a syntax error, as shown in Listing 3.17. In contrast to octal numbers, there is no automatic interpretation of the (wrong hexadecimal) value.

```
const number1 = 0xF;       // definition of a hexadecimal number (decimal
                           // value of 15)
const number2 = 0xb;       // definition of a hexadecimal number (decimal
                           // value of 11)
// const number3 = 0xG;    // invalid hexadecimal number (syntax error)
const number4 = 0xAF_BC_C0; // separator for hexadecimal representation


console.log(number1);      // 15
console.log(number2);      // 11
console.log(number4);      // 11517120
```

Listing 3.17 Examples of Valid and Invalid Hexadecimal Numbers

The Value Range of Numbers

The *value range* of numbers is limited in JavaScript; that is, you cannot define infinitely large or infinitely small numbers—and after all, your computer doesn't have infinite memory either. The smallest possible number—that is, the minimum value of numbers that can be used—is stored in the Number.MIN_VALUE variable (more precisely, in the MIN_VALUE *property* of the Number *object*). The largest possible number—that is, the maximum value of numbers—is stored in the `Number.MAX_VALUE` variable. In most runtime environments, the former has the value `5e-324`, the latter the value `1.7976931348623157e+308` (see Listing 3.18). Values outside of this value range cannot be displayed. Therefore, if a calculation has an (actual) result outside this value range, the value `-Infinity` (for a value below the value range) or `Infinity` (for a value above the value range) is used instead.

```
console.log(Number.MIN_VALUE);          // Output: 5e-324
console.log(Number.MAX_VALUE);          // Output: 1.7976931348623157e+308
console.log(Number.NEGATIVE_INFINITY);  // Output: -Infinity
console.log(Number.POSITIVE_INFINITY);  // Output: Infinity
```

Listing 3.18 Several Special Variables for Working with Numeric Values

To begin with, your applications will probably hardly ever touch these limits, but again, it doesn't hurt to know that the value range of numbers in JavaScript is limited and how you can determine those limits (and then, if you need to work with really big numbers, you should use the `BigInt` type anyway).

Invalid Numeric Values

Calculations that do not yield a valid numeric value return the special value `NaN` (an abbreviation for *not a number*).

3.2.2   Strings

In programming, *strings* are sequences of characters—for example, letters, digits, special characters, and control characters. You use strings whenever you are dealing with any form of text. For example, if a user enters his or her name on a store page, you would be dealing with a string of characters. The same is true if, say, you want to display a welcome message to the user; again, you would use a string as the data type.

Definition of Strings

The beginning and the end of a string are defined by quotation marks. You can use both single and double quotation marks. However, you must choose one of the two; a mixed form is not allowed. Listing 3.19 shows some examples for the definition of strings.

```
const firstName = 'John';        // single quotes
const lastName = "Doe";          // double quotes
const age = "22";                // not a number, but a string
const street = 'Sample Street";  // syntax error: mixed form
```

Listing 3.19 Examples of the Definition of Strings

> **Best Practice: Decide on a Style**
>
> Because in practice you will often want to use double quotes within a string, we recommend that you define strings using single quotes rather than double quotes. In this way, you avoid having to escape the double quotes.
>
> It's also best practice not to mix the types of quotes within a program—that is, not to define a string with single quotes in one place but another string with double quotes in another place. It's just good code style to decide on a type and stick to it consistently. For these reasons, we'll use single quotation marks in all examples from now on.
>
> There are even automatic tools that let you preset the code style you want to use and then automatically check that you've followed the appropriate preference throughout your program. Chapter 21 will address these automation tools, among other things.

Escaping of Characters within Strings

If you want to use quotation marks within a string, you have several options, depending on the type of quotation marks you want to use within the string and on the type of quotation marks you use to define the string.

Listing 3.20 shows four different cases: If you use single quotes to define the string (message1), you can easily use double quotes within the string. Similarly, you can use single quotes inside a string defined by double quotes (message2).

But in the remaining two cases—that is, when using single quotes in a string that was also defined using single quotes (message3) or when using double quotes in a string that was also defined using double quotes (message4)—you must tell the JavaScript interpreter not to interpret the second quote as the end of the string. You can achieve this via the backslash character (\). If you add this character directly before the quotation mark, the interpreter does not interpret the quote as the end of the string but displays it as the character itself.

```
const message1 = 'Your name is "John Doe"';
const message2 = "Your name is 'John Doe'";
const message3 = 'Your name is \'John Doe\'';
const message4 = "Your name is \"John Doe\"";
console.log(message1);   // Output: Your name is "John Doe"
console.log(message2);   // Output: Your name is 'John Doe'
console.log(message3);   // Output: Your name is 'John Doe'
console.log(message4);   // Output: Your name is "John Doe"
```

Listing 3.20 Use of Quotation Marks within Strings

The technical term for this prepending with the backslash character is *escaping* (the backslash character is also called an *escape character*). In other words, you *escape* the corresponding quotation mark for the interpreter so that it ignores it when determining the end of the string.

In addition to single and double quotes (regardless of what kind of quotes you use to define a string), you also need to escape other characters: the *control characters*, which are characters that cannot be represented as such—for example, line breaks, indentations, and so on.

Table 3.3 shows a selection of these characters. With \n, for example, you insert a line break; \t provides an indentation; and \f represents a form feed.

Characters	Meaning
\n	New line
\t	Tab character/indentation
\b	Backspace
\r	Carriage return
\f	Form feed

Table 3.3 Selection of Control Characters

Listing 3.21 shows a simple example of the use of control characters within a string: the \n character here ensures that a new line is started after the word Hello and after Mr., respectively, as shown in the output in Listing 3.22.

```
const message = 'Hello\nMr.\nDoe';
console.log(message);
```

Listing 3.21 Example of the Use of Control Characters within Strings

```
Hello
Mr.
Doe
```

Listing 3.22 Output of Listing 3.21

Outputting Strings within a Web Page

If you want to output a string not on the developer console as in the example, but directly within the content of a web page (we'll look at how to do this in detail in Chapter 5), you must use <br/> instead of \n for line breaks.

> **Using Backslash Characters in a String**
>
> To represent the backslash character itself within a string, it must also be escaped via a backslash character. This tells the interpreter that the escaped backslash character should not be interpreted as an escape character itself.

Using Template Strings

In everyday work with strings, you'll often want to insert calculated values or values stored in variables at certain positions within a string. As a rule, string concatenation is then used to assemble the individual parts into a string (see Listing 3.23).

```
const name = 'John Doe';
const age = 44;
const message = 'My name is ' + name + ', I am ' + age + ' years old.';
console.log(message); // "My name is John Doe, I am 44 years old."
```

Listing 3.23 Assembling a String

But this quickly becomes confusing when many variable parts are to be incorporated into a string. Moreover, this approach is not really advisable for performance reasons either. This is exactly the point where *template strings* come into play.

You can think of template strings as an extended form of normal strings. Instead of being defined by single or double quotes as in normal strings, they are defined by ` characters (called *backticks*), as shown in Listing 3.24.

```
const message = `Hello world.`;
console.log(message); // Hello world
```

Listing 3.24 Definition of a Template String

At first, this doesn't really look different from a normal string. However, you can do a lot more with template strings.

Defining Placeholders within Strings

Within template strings, you can define placeholders using the ${} notation, as shown in Listing 3.25. In this example, this populates the two placeholders ${name} and ${age} with the values of the corresponding variables and outputs the message "My name is John Doe, I am 44 years old."

```
const name = 'John Doe';
const age = 44;
const message = `My name is ${name}, I am ${age} years old.`;
console.log(message); // My name is John Doe, I am 44 years old.
```

Listing 3.25 Application of a Template String

Evaluating Expressions within Strings

Besides variable names, you can use any other expressions inside the curly braces. In Listing 3.26, for example, the first placeholder evaluates a function call, and the second placeholder evaluates an expression for adding two numbers.

```
const name = 'John Doe';
const age = 44;
function getName() {
  return name;
}
const message = `My name is ${getName()}, I am twice the age of ⊃
    ${age/2}.`;
console.log(message);
// "My name is John Doe, I am twice the age of 22."
```

Listing 3.26 Template Strings Can Contain Arbitrary Expressions

Defining Multiline Strings

Especially if you are dealing with long strings, in practice you will probably often split these strings into several parts and then distribute them over several lines connected by the + operator (see Listing 3.27). Line breaks that are to be included in the string output must be coded with \n as usual.

```
const message = 'Dear Mr. Doe, \n\nWe are happy to return ' +
                'the requested documents to you for review. \n\n' +
                'Yours sincerely, \nMrs. Smith, \nSample Company';
console.log(message);
// Output:
//
// Dear Mr. Doe,
//
// We are happy to return the requested documents to you for review.
//
// Yours sincerely,
// Mrs. Smith,
// Sample Company
```

Listing 3.27 Multiline String without Template Strings

Thanks to template strings, this misuse of the + operator is no longer necessary because line breaks are acceptable within template strings and are also considered as such when the string is output. So the example in Listing 3.27 could be rephrased using a template string as shown in Listing 3.28. In addition to the omission of + operators and the like, it's also noticeable that the line breaks defined in the template string are also transferred to the output. In other words, you can also dispense with \n as encoding for a line break. Also, blank lines and other white space characters are reproduced exactly as set (this is also, by the way, the reason that the code lines are all left-aligned and do not start with an indentation as in Listing 3.27).

```
const message = `Dear Mr. Doe,

we are happy to return the requested documents to you for review.

Yours sincerely,
Mrs. Smith,
Sample Company`;
console.log(message);
// Output:
//
// Dear Mr. Doe,
//
// We are happy to return the requested documents to you for review.
//
// Yours sincerely,
// Mrs. Smith,
// Sample Company
```

Listing 3.28 Multiline String with Template Strings

> **Note**
> We'll revisit template strings later in this chapter, when we deal with tagged templates in Section 3.5.8.

3.2.3   Boolean Values

Boolean values or *Booleans* are relatively easy to handle compared to numeric values and strings. This is because they can only take one of two values: true and false. Booleans are usually a good choice when a variable can take one of two values (see Listing 3.29).

```
const isLoggedIn = true;
const isAdmin = false;
```

Listing 3.29 Definition of Boolean Variables

Boolean values play a central role especially when it comes to defining branches within a program. We'll show you how to do this in Section 3.4.

3.2.4 Arrays

The variables you've gotten to know so far each only contain a single value: a single number or a single string or a single Boolean value. You should now also know which of these data types to use in which case.

As an example, let's consider the users of an online shopping website. For example, a user's age would be represented with a numeric value, the user's name with a string, and whether or not the user subscribed to the newsletter via a Boolean value.

But in order to represent the user's shopping cart, for example, which is in its simplest form a list of item names, you won't get far with the primitive data types alone because then you would need to define a separate variable for each entry in the shopping cart, as shown in Listing 3.30.

```
const shoppingCartItem1 = 'Record player';      // first item
const shoppingCartItem2 = 'Loudspeaker';        // second item
const shoppingCartItem3 = 'Preamplifier';       // third item
const shoppingCartItem4 = 'Loudspeaker cables'; // fourth item
```

Listing 3.30 In Some Cases, the Primitive Data Types Alone Will Not Work

This process would be more than unwieldy for several reasons: For one thing, you would have to provide for a certain number of variables from the outset, which in turn would mean that a user could not add more than the intended number of products to the shopping cart. Second, things like sorting products by name would also be disproportionately time-consuming, as you would have to manually compare each variable with every other variable. To cut a long story short, programming only with the primitive data types presented so far would be extremely impractical.

This is exactly where *arrays* come into play. Arrays are nothing but lists; that is, arrays can contain not only one but several values. For the shopping cart example, you would use an array to represent the shopping cart. The individual *entries* in this array would then be the names (and perhaps the identification numbers) of the products in the shopping cart.

The most common and easiest way to create an array in JavaScript is the *array literal notation*. Here, you simply use the two square brackets ([ ]) to define the beginning and the end of the array. The individual *entries* (or *values* or *elements*) to be included in the array are written between these two brackets, separated by commas.

An example is shown in Listing 3.31. In this case, a variable named shoppingCart is created and assigned such an array as its value. The array has four entries—namely, the Record player, Loudspeaker, Preamplifier, and Loudspeaker cables strings.

```
const shoppingCart = [    // start of array definition
  'Record player',        // first entry
  'Loudspeaker',          // second entry
  'Preamplifier',         // third entry
  'Loudspeaker cables'    // fourth entry
];                        // end of array definition
```

Listing 3.31 Creating an Array via Literal Notation

Note

Instead of dedicating a separate line to each entry in the array as in Listing 3.31, these can also be written to a single line, as shown in Listing 3.32. However, this adversely affects clarity, especially when there are many entries in the array. We would therefore rather advise against it.

```
const shoppingCart = [
  'Record player',
  'Loudspeaker',
  'Preamplifier',
  'Loudspeaker cables''
];
const highscores = [74334, 24344, 54533, 32553, 67556];
```

Listing 3.32 The Individual Entries Can Also Be Included on One Line When Defining an Array

---

In contrast to other programming, languages like Java, arrays can also contain entries of different types. In other words, one array can contain numbers as well as strings or Boolean values, objects (more on this later), and even other arrays (see Listing 3.33). This is possible in JavaScript due to loose typing. In addition, arrays grow dynamically, which means that when you create an array, you do not need to know or specify how many elements should be contained therein.

```
const values = [       // an array ...
  'John Doe',          // ... with a string ...
  22,                  // ... a number ...
  true                 // ... and a Boolean
];
```

Listing 3.33 Example of the Definition of an Array with Numeric Values

The Internal Structure of Arrays

You'll learn how to work with arrays and what you can do with them in Chapter 4. In that chapter, you'll learn how to insert elements into an existing array, delete elements from an array, search for specific elements within an array, sort the elements in an array by specific criteria, and much more. One thing we'll show you beforehand, though, is the internal structure of arrays. It isn't particularly complicated, but it's helpful for understanding the later examples in this chapter.

Arrays, in fact, have what is called an *index-based structure*, which means that every element in an array is stored at a particular index (you could also say at a particular position). The counting of these indexes starts at 0—as is quite common in computer science, by the way: the first element in the array is at index 0, the second element is at index 1, and so on until the last element is at index n-1, where *n* is the length of the array. For example, the array in Listing 3.31 has the structure shown in Figure 3.1.

0	'Record player'
1	'Loudspeaker'
2	'Preamplifier'
3	'Loudspeaker Cables'

Figure 3.1 The Positions of the Entries in the Array—the Indexes—Start at 0

The index-based structure is relevant for you during the development phase in that you can use the indexes to specifically access the individual elements of an array. To do this, simply write the index of the element you want to access in square brackets after the name of the respective array (see Listing 3.34).

```
const item1 = shoppingCart[0];   // first entry
const item2 = shoppingCart[1];   // second entry
const item3 = shoppingCart[2];   // third entry
const item4 = shoppingCart[3];   // fourth entry
console.log(item1);              // 'Record player'
console.log(item2);              // 'Loudspeaker'
console.log(item3);              // 'Preamplifier'
console.log(item4);              // 'Loudspeaker cables'
```

Listing 3.34 Access to the Elements of an Array

Multidimensional Arrays

You already learned that you can add numbers, strings, and Boolean values to an array. However, it's also possible to add other arrays to an array. This enables you to create *multidimensional arrays* (i.e., arrays of arrays). They can be useful whenever you want to store different records of the same data in an array, similar to an Excel spreadsheet (this is one example of a *two-dimensional array*).

> **Multidimensional Arrays**
>
> In principle, it's also possible to use three-dimensional arrays (i.e., arrays that contain arrays that in turn contain arrays) or arrays with any number of dimensions. Ahead, however, we'll only discuss two-dimensional arrays because they are ideal for illustrating the principle of multidimensional arrays.

For example, let's consider the shopping cart example, which is again shown in Listing 3.35. This is a one-dimensional array that contains only string entries representing product names.

```
const shoppingCart = [
  'Record player',
  'Loudspeaker',
  'Preamplifier',
  'Loudspeaker cables'
];
```

Listing 3.35 One-Dimensional Array

Suppose you now want to add additional properties to each entry in order to include not only the name but also the price and quantity of the product. This could be modeled, for example, using a multidimensional array, as shown in Listing 3.36. Each entry in the outer shoppingCart array is an array with three elements: the name of the product, the price, and the quantity.

```
const shoppingCart = [        // start of outer array
  [                           // first entry
    'Record player',          // first element in the first array
    200,                      // second element in the first array
    1                         // third element in the first array
  ],
  [                           // second entry
    'Loudspeaker',            // first element in the second array
    400,                      // second element in the second array
    2                         // third element in the second array
  ],
  [                           // third entry
    'Preamplifier',           // first element in the third array
    80,                       // second element in the third array
    1                         // third element in the third array
  ],
  [                           // fourth entry
    'Loudspeaker cables',     // first element in the fourth array
    20,                       // second element in the fourth array
```

```
    2                         // third element in the fourth array
  ]
];                            // end of outer array
```

Listing 3.36 Definition of a Multidimensional Array

Figure 3.2 illustrates the structure of this multidimensional array.

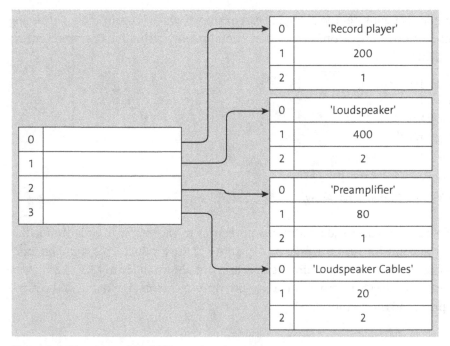

Figure 3.2 Structure of Multidimensional Arrays

Like with one-dimensional arrays, the individual values in a multidimensional array can be accessed via the index. However, depending on which array in which dimension you want to access, you will need to provide more details. For example, to access the first value of the first array (the Record player value), you need to write shopping-Cart[0][0]. The first [0] accesses the first array (in the first dimension); the second [0] accesses its first value (in the second dimension). Listing 3.37 shows how to output all values of all arrays in the shoppingCart array in this way.

```
console.log(shoppingCart[0][0]);  // Output: Record player
console.log(shoppingCart[0][1]);  // Output: 200
console.log(shoppingCart[0][2]);  // Output: 1
console.log(shoppingCart[1][0]);  // Output: Loudspeaker
console.log(shoppingCart[1][1]);  // Output: 400
console.log(shoppingCart[1][2]);  // Output: 2
console.log(shoppingCart[2][0]);  // Output: Preamplifier
console.log(shoppingCart[2][1]);  // Output: 80
```

```
console.log(shoppingCart[2][2]);  // Output: 1
console.log(shoppingCart[3][0]);  // Output: Loudspeaker cables
console.log(shoppingCart[3][1]);  // Output: 20
console.log(shoppingCart[3][2]);  // Output: 2
```

Listing 3.37 Access to the Values in a Multidimensional Array

3.2.5 Objects

Naturally, you can store all the data your program needs in numerous variables. At some point, you will have dozens, hundreds, or thousands of different variables and can't see the forest for the trees (not to mention the potential naming conflicts). It is better—and common practice in object-oriented programming—to combine related variables and functions in objects. This approach also creates clarity and increases the reusability of your source text.

In the context of objects, variables are called *properties* (*object properties*) or *attributes*, and functions are referred to as *methods* (*object methods*). Properties provide information about the object they are contained in, such as a person's name or age, the items in a shopping cart, or the number of links on a web page. Object methods represent certain tasks related to the object in which they are defined, such as adjusting a person's age or adding an item to a shopping cart.

Definition of Objects

The easiest way to create objects in JavaScript is to use *object literal notation*. You simply define the object using braces and list the object properties and object methods within these braces, separated by commas. For example, Listing 3.38 shows how to define an object that represents an item in a shopping cart.

```
const item = {
  name: 'JavaScript: The Comprehensive Guide',
  price: 55.95,
  author: 'Philip Ackermann',
  isbn: '978-1-4932-2286-5',
  printDescription: function() {
    console.log(`${this.author}: ${this.name}`);
  }
}
```

Listing 3.38 Creating an Object Using Object Literal Notation

The object in the example contains the four properties name, price, author, and isbn, as well as the printDescription() method. However, objects are actually key-value pairs, so you could also refer to name, price, author, isbn, and printDescription as *keys*. The key and value are separated from each other by a colon.

The structure of an object is illustrated in Figure 3.3.

item	
name	"JavaScript: The Comprehensive Guide"
price	55.59
author	"Philip Ackermann"
isbn	"978-3-8362-7272-8"
printDescription	[[Function]]

Figure 3.3 Properties and Methods Are Represented by Key-Value Pairs

The this Keyword

If you take a closer look at the above listing, you will notice the this keyword. This keyword is used to address the current object ("this" object). For example, this.author simply enables you to access the object's author property. The this keyword often causes confusion for JavaScript beginners, so we'll go into some specifics about it later in the book.

There are more ways to create objects in JavaScript, but we'll discuss those later in the book. They're listed here only for the sake of completeness:

- Via a constructor function
- Via the Object.create() method
- Via the instantiation of an ES2015 class

3.2.6   Special Data Types

In addition to the data types discussed so far, there are two more special data types in JavaScript that are often confused in practice and/or used for the same thing. Both data types have one thing in common: they each have only a single value, which is also reflected by the names of these data types: null and undefined.

If you declare a variable but do not initialize it yet (by assigning a value to it), it has the value undefined (see Listing 3.39).

```
let name;
console.log(name); // Output: undefined
```

```
name = 'John Doe';
console.log(name); // Output: John Doe
```

Listing 3.39 As Long as a Variable Has Not Yet Been Initialized, It Has the undefined Value

The `null` data type, however, represents an empty object. In Listing 3.40, for example, the `dog` and `person` objects are created first, and then the `dog` object is assigned to the `pet` property of the `person` object. Thus, if you access `person.pet`, the `dog` object is output, and the `person.pet` property points to the `dog` object. This relationship is shown in Figure 3.4. If you now set the `person.pet` property to `null`, the pointer to the `dog` object is disconnected (see Figure 3.5).

```
const dog = {
  name: 'Bello'
}
const person = {
  firstName: 'John',
  lastName: 'Doe',
  pet: dog
}
console.log(person.pet);  // Output: Object {name: "Bello"}
person.pet = null;
console.log(person.pet);  // Output: null
```

Listing 3.40 The null Value Is Used to Express that an Object Variable Is Not Populated

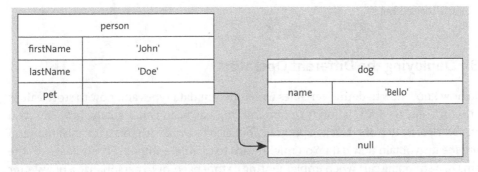

Figure 3.4 The pet Property Points to the dog Object

Figure 3.5 The pet Property Now Points to the Empty Object Represented by null

> **undefined versus null**
>
> The undefined value is not meant to be manually assigned to a variable, but the null value is. The undefined value indicates that a variable has not yet been initialized; the null value represents an empty object pointer.

3.2.7   Symbols

Symbols are another kind of primitive data type introduced with ES2015; they enable you to define unique and immutable values. Symbols can be created using the Symbol() function, optionally passing a symbol description as a parameter. Listing 3.41 shows a few examples.

```
const symbol1 = Symbol();
const symbol2 = Symbol('exampleDescription');
const symbol3 = Symbol();
const symbol4 = Symbol('exampleDescription');
console.log(symbol1);                // Output: Symbol()
console.log(symbol2);                // Output: Symbol(exampleDescription)
console.log(symbol3);                // Output: Symbol()
console.log(symbol4);                // Output: Symbol(exampleDescription)
console.log(symbol1 === symbol3);  // Output: false
console.log(symbol2 === symbol4);  // Output: false
```

Listing 3.41 Creating Symbols

You'll notice that regardless of whether you create a symbol with or without a description, and regardless of whether the descriptions of two symbols are the same, two symbols are always different from each other. Therefore, a comparison of two symbols will result in the value false, as shown in the listing.

We'll come back to symbols later—specifically, when we deal with objects and object properties in the next chapter. For now, you just need to remember that symbols are unique and immutable and in practice are not used nearly as often as the other data types presented here.

3.3   Deploying the Different Operators

You now know how to define variables with different data types and how to store values in them. Thus, the foundation for programming has been laid. Usually, however, you don't want only to store data in a program, but also to *work* with this data or *change* and *combine* it to obtain new data. You might want to calculate shipping costs based on the items in a shopping cart when implementing a store page, or to personalize a newsletter with the name of the recipient, adding a personal greeting such as "Your personal newsletter, John Doe." In JavaScript (and in programming in general), you use *operators* to achieve this.

From mathematics, you may remember the term *expression*. A mathematical formula, like 5 * 17, consists of *operands* and *operators*. In the example, 5 and 17 are the operands and * is the operator. Unlike statements, expressions always have a result that is returned by the expression. In the 5 * 17 example, the result is 85. This is relatively simple. In practice, expressions may well be more complex and contain multiple operands, different operators, function calls, and so on.

Note

The terms *statement* and *expression* are often confused, so here is a short description again. As described earlier, a program consists of various statements to be executed sequentially by the interpreter. In JavaScript, each statement is terminated with a semicolon. This semicolon indicates to the JavaScript interpreter that a statement is complete. In addition, braces can be used to group statements into *code blocks*. Expressions, however, are combinations of operators and operands that together yield a value and can be part of a statement (see Figure 3.6).

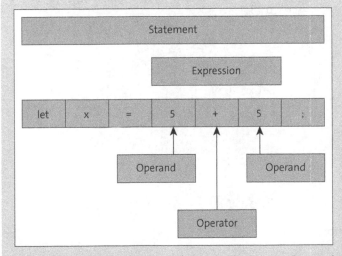

Figure 3.6 Relationship among the Terms Statement, Expression, Operand, and Operator

In JavaScript (and also in other programming languages), both variables and simple values (*literals*) can be used as operands. Operators link the individual operands within an expression. A distinction is made between the following types of operators, depending on the number of operands:

- An operator that refers to a single operand is called a *unary operator*. An example of this is the increment operator ++ that can be used, for example, to directly increment counter variables by one: counter++.

- An operator that refers to two operands is called a *binary operator*. An example of this is the addition operator +, which can be used to sum up two numbers—for example, x + y.

- JavaScript even provides an operator that refers to three operands. This is the *ternary operator* (Section 3.4.3).

3.3.1 Operators for Working with Numbers

JavaScript provides a set of *arithmetic operators*—that is, operators for working and calculating with numbers, including addition, subtraction, multiplication, division, and the remainder operator (*modulo*). In addition, there are the *increment* and *decrement* operators, which add 1 to a number (increment operator) or subtract 1 from a number (decrement operator), respectively. Since ES2016, the *exponential* operator is available, which can be used to calculate powers. Table 3.4 gives you an overview and examples of these operators.

Calculation Type	Operator	Example	Result of x
Addition	+	`let x = 20 + 20`	40
Subtraction	-	`let x = 20 - 5`	15
Multiplication	*	`let x = 20 * 5`	100
Division	/	`let x = 100 / 5`	20
Modulo	%	`let x = 20 % 6`	2
Increment	++	`let x = 5;` `x++;`	6
Decrement	--	`let x = 6;` `x--;`	5
Power calculation	**	`let x = 5**5;`	3125

Table 3.4 Arithmetic Operators

There isn't much more to say about arithmetic operators. The only thing you still need to know is the order in which the operators are evaluated, in case several arithmetic operators are used in an expression. You probably know about this issue from mathematics.

All you have to remember is that multiplication and division are evaluated before addition and subtraction. Therefore, the expression 4 + 4 * 5 results in 24, because 4 * 5 is evaluated first, and the first operand is added to this partial result (4 + 20) in a second step. However, if you want to evaluate the addition first and then the multiplication, you must enclose the operands of the addition in parentheses; for example, the result of (4 + 4) * 5 is 40.

3.3.2   Operators for Easier Assignment

It often happens that you want to use a variable that already contains a number as an operand, and at the same time assign the result of the operation to the variable as a new value. The statement result = result + 1 is such an example. The result variable is used on the one hand as an operand of the addition and on the other hand as a target variable for the addition result.

As an alternative to this long notation, you can also use a short notation for the addition, subtraction, multiplication, division, and remainder operators, which combines both steps: the operation and the assignment of the result to the corresponding variable. Listing 3.42 shows some examples, and Table 3.5 provides an overview of these operators.

```
let result = 5;
result += 11;  // the variable now has a value of 16 ...
result -= 1;   // ... now a value of 15 ...
result /= 3;   // ... now a value of 5 ...
result *= 4;   // ... now a value of 20 ...
result %= 5;   // ... and now a value of 0.
```

Listing 3.42 Various Short Forms in Practice

Operator	Description	Example	Long Form
+=	Adds the operand on the right to the value of the variable on the left and assigns the new value to the variable	result += 11	result = result + 11
-=	Subtracts the operand on the right from the value of the variable on the left and assigns the new value to the variable	result -= 11	result = result - 11
*=	Multiplies the value of the variable on the left by the operand on the right and assigns the new value to the variable	result *= 11	result = result * 11

Table 3.5 Various Short Forms to Combine Operation and Assignment

Operator	Description	Example	Long Form
/=	Divides the value of the variable on the left by the operand on the right and assigns the new value to the variable	result /= 11	result = result / 11
%=	Calculates the remainder of the division of the variable value on the left and the operand on the right and assigns the new value to the variable	result %= 11	result = result % 11
**=	Returns the result of raising the value on the left to the power of the operand on the right and assigns the new value to the variable	result **= 11	result = result ** 11

Table 3.5 Various Short Forms to Combine Operation and Assignment (Cont.)

3.3.3 Operators for Working with Strings

In practice, you will occasionally be faced with the task of combining two or more strings to form a new string, like in the example mentioned earlier of personalizing a newsletter. In this case, you would probably have two strings: the string Your personal newsletter and the string John Doe.

In JavaScript, the operator for joining two strings is the + operator. The joining itself is also called *concatenation*. Listing 3.43 shows an example. Here, the content of the salutation variable is concatenated with the content of the name variable, and the result of this operation is stored in the message variable, which then contains the value Your personal newsletter, John Doe (note the missing space after the comma). Hence, the first operand is the salutation variable, the second operand the name variable.

```
const salutation = 'Your personal newsletter,';  // string 1
const name = 'John Doe';                          // string 2
const message = salutation + name;                // concatenation
```

Listing 3.43 Concatenation of Two Strings

To insert a space after the comma, simply include it in the concatenation, as shown in Listing 3.44. Here, the + operator is used twice to join the variables salutation and name and a space (the string ' ') in between. As you can see, the + operator for string concatenation can also be used multiple times within an expression.

```
const salutation = 'Your personal newsletter,';  // string 1
const name = 'John Doe';                          // string 2
const message = salutation + ' ' + name;          // concatenation plus spaces
```

Listing 3.44 Concatenation of Three Strings

Besides the + operator, the only other operator you can use with strings is the assignment operator +=. As usual, this is used to add the value on the right side of the operator to the variable on the left side, which in the case of strings means that the two strings are concatenated.

Therefore, the example above could also be rephrased as shown in Listing 3.45. In the first step, the value "Your personal newsletter," is assigned to the message variable, then a space is appended (the variable now has the value "Your personal newsletter, "—i.e., the same message, but including the space), and in the last step, the content of the name variable is added (the variable now has the complete welcome message, "Your personal newsletter, John Doe").

```
let message = 'Your personal newsletter,';
message += ' ';
message += name;
```

Listing 3.45 Concatenation Using the Assignment Operator

Note

Operators that can be used with different data types, such as the + operator and the += operator, which work with both numbers and strings, are also referred to as *overloaded*. In the case of an *overloaded operator*, the operands' data type determines exactly which operation is to be performed. With respect to the two operators mentioned previously, that is whether a concatenation (of strings) or an addition (of numbers) is to be performed.

3.3.4   Operators for Working with Boolean Values

For working with Boolean values, there are various operators available in programming, which are referred to as *logical operators*. There are three operators in total: the && operator (*AND operator*), the || operator (*OR operator*), and the ! operator (*negation operator*), as shown in Table 3.6. The AND operator and OR operator are *binary operators*; that is, they expect two operands. The negation operator, on the other hand, is a *unary operator*; that is, it expects only a single operand.

Operator	Meaning
&&	Logical AND
||	Logical OR
!	Negation

Table 3.6 Logical Operators

The result of all Boolean operations is a Boolean value. The AND operator returns true if both operands are true. Otherwise, it returns false. The OR operator returns true whenever one of the two operands is true. It only returns false if both operands are false. The negation operator negates a Boolean value. In other words, if the operand is true, the operator returns false; if the operand is false, the operator returns true.

Listing 3.46 shows a simple code example for the various logical operators. The two initial variables isLoggedIn and isAdmin have the values true and false, respectively. Thus, the AND operation returns false (in the isLoggedInAndAdmin variable), the OR operation returns true (in the isLoggedInOrAdmin variable), and the negation of isLoggedIn returns false (in the isLoggedOut variable).

```
const isLoggedIn = true;
const isAdmin = false;
const isLoggedInAndAdmin = isLoggedIn && isAdmin; // AND operator
const isLoggedInOrAdmin = isLoggedIn || isAdmin;  // OR operator
const isLoggedOut = !isLoggedIn;                   // negation
console.log(isLoggedInAndAdmin);                   // false
console.log(isLoggedInOrAdmin);                    // true
console.log(isLoggedOut);                          // false
```

Listing 3.46 Use of the Various Logical Operators

Table 3.7 shows the results of the AND operator for the various combinations of operands, Table 3.8 shows the results of the OR operator, and Table 3.9 shows the results of negation.

Operand 1	Operand 2	Result
true	true	true
true	false	false
false	true	false
false	false	false

Table 3.7 Results for Logical AND Operations

Operand 1	Operand 2	Result
true	true	true
true	false	true
false	true	true
false	false	false

Table 3.8 Results for Logical OR Operations

Operand	Result
true	false
false	true

Table 3.9 Negation Results

Boolean Operators for Non-Boolean Operands

One thing that may seem a bit confusing at first is that Boolean operators can also be used with operands that are not Boolean values, such as numbers, strings, or objects. In such a case, the JavaScript interpreter works according to the special rules outlined ahead.

The following applies to the logical AND operation:

- If the first operand evaluates to false, the first operand is returned. A value that evaluates to false is also called a *falsy* value. Examples are the number 0 or an empty string.

- In all other cases, the second operand is returned.

Table 3.10 shows an overview, and Listing 3.47 demonstrates some examples.

Operand 1	Operand 2	Result
Object	x	x
true	x	x
false	x	false
x	null	null
null	x	null
x	NaN	NaN

Table 3.10 Results of the AND Operation of Non-Boolean Operands

Operand 1	Operand 2	Result
NaN	x	NaN
x	undefined	undefined
undefined	x	undefined

Table 3.10 Results of the AND Operation of Non-Boolean Operands (Cont.)

```
const john = {
  firstName: 'John',
  lastName: 'Doe'
};

const james = {
  firstName: 'James',
  lastName: 'Doe'
};

const isJohnAndJames = john && james;
console.log(isJohnAndJames);
// Output: Object {firstName: "James", lastName: "Doe"}

console.log(false && 'John');  // Output: false
console.log('John' && null);   // Output: null
console.log(null && 'John');   // Output: null
```

Listing 3.47 Use of the AND Operation for Non-Boolean Operands

The following applies to the logical OR operation:

- If the first operand evaluates to true, the first operand is returned.
- In all other cases, the second operand is returned.

Table 3.11 shows another overview, and Listing 3.48 presents some code examples.

Operand 1	Operand 2	Result
Object	x	Object
false	x	x
x	null	x
null	x	x

Table 3.11 Results of the OR Operation of Non-Boolean Operands

Operand 1	Operand 2	Result
null	null	null
x	NaN	x
NaN	x	x
NaN	NaN	NaN
x	undefined	x
undefined	x	x
undefined	undefined	undefined

Table 3.11 Results of the OR Operation of Non-Boolean Operands (Cont.)

```
const john = {
  firstName: 'John',
  lastName: 'Doe'
};

const james = {
  firstName: 'James',
  lastName: 'Doe'
};

const isJohnOrJames = john || james;
console.log(isJohnOrJames);
// Output: Object {firstName: "John", lastName: "Doe"}
console.log(false || 'John'); // Output: John
console.log('John' || null);  // Output: John
console.log(null || 'John');  // Output: John
```

Listing 3.48 Use of the OR Operation for Non-Boolean Operands

The following applies to negation:

- An empty string returns true; a nonempty string returns false.
- All numbers except 0 (including the special Infinity value) return false, but the number 0 returns true.
- Objects return false.
- The special values null, NaN, and undefined all return true.

Table 3.12 shows another overview, and Listing 3.49 presents some code examples.

Operand	Result
Empty string	true
Nonempty string	false
Number 0	true
Number not equal to 0 (including Infinity)	false
Object	false
null	true
NaN	true
undefined	true

Table 3.12 Results of the Negation of Non-Boolean Operands

```
const name = 'John Doe';
const emptyString = '';
console.log(!name);          // Output: false
console.log(!emptyString);   // Output: true
const amount = 0;
const age = 25;
console.log(!amount);        // Output: true
console.log(!age);           // Output: false
console.log(!john);          // Output: false
console.log(!null);          // Output: true
console.log(!NaN);           // Output: true
console.log(!undefined);     // Output: true
```

Listing 3.49 Use of Negation for a Non-Boolean Operand

Note

All of these special cases of using logical operators can be quite convenient in programming, as you will see in the course of the book.

You will use logical operators very often in programming. In Section 3.4.1, we'll revisit this topic of executing or not executing statements within a program depending on the results of Boolean operations.

The Nullish Coalescing Operator

Another logical operator introduced with ES2020 is the *nullish coalescing operator*, which consists of two consecutive question marks (see Listing 3.50). (For the sake of simplicity, we'll refer to it as the ?? operator ahead.) This logical operator works simi-larly to the logical OR operator (||), but there is a subtle difference: the ?? operator returns the value of the right operand only if the left operand is null or undefined. Remember that the logical OR operator returns the right operand even if the left oper-and is a falsy value—that is, a value that evaluates to false (e.g., 0, an empty string, or the like).

```
const someNullValue = null;
const someUndefinedValue = undefined;
const someNumber = 0;
const someText = '';
const someBoolean = false;

// Left operand is null --> return right operand
const a = someNullValue ?? 'Default value for null';
console.log(a);
// Output: Default value for null

// Left operand is undefined --> return right operand
const b = someUndefinedValue ?? 'Default value for undefined';
console.log(b);
// Output: Default value for undefined

// Left operand is 0 ("falsy") --> return left operand
const c = someNumber ?? 80;
console.log(c);
// Output: 0

// Left operand is an empty string ("falsy") --> return left operand
const d = someText ?? 'Default value for empty string';
console.log(d);
// Output: ''

// Left operand is false --> return left operand
const e = someBoolean ?? true;
console.log(e);
// Output: false

const x = 4711;

console.log({} ?? x);              // {}
console.log(false ?? x);           // false
console.log(x ?? null);            // 4711
console.log(null ?? x);            // 4711
```

```
console.log(null ?? null);            // null
console.log(x ?? NaN);                // 4711
console.log(NaN ?? x);                // NaN
console.log(x ?? undefined);          // 4711
console.log(undefined ?? x);          // 4711
console.log(undefined ?? undefined);  // undefined
```

Listing 3.50 The Nullish Coalescing Operator in Action

Similar to the tables for the && and || operators, Table 3.13 shows the result of the ?? operator for different operands.

Operand 1	Operand 2	Result
Object	x	Object
false	x	false
x	null	x
null	x	x
null	null	null
x	NaN	x
NaN	x	x
NaN	NaN	NaN
x	undefined	x
undefined	x	x
undefined	undefined	undefined

Table 3.13 Results of the ?? Operation for Non-Boolean Operands

3.3.5 Operators for Working with Bits

Bitwise operations enable you to work with single bits of values. You will probably do this only rather rarely in practice, but a list of these operators is shown in Table 3.14.

Operator	Meaning
&	Bitwise AND
|	Bitwise OR
^	Bitwise exclusive OR

Table 3.14 Bitwise Operators

Operator	Meaning
~	Bitwise NOT, where the result for a number x is -(x + 1). So for the number 65, for example, the result is -66.
<<	Bitwise left shift
>>	Bitwise right shift
>>>	Bitwise unsigned right shift

Table 3.14 Bitwise Operators (Cont.)

Listing 3.51 also shows the use of some operators and their corresponding results.

```
let BYTE_A = 0b00000001;       // Binary value 00000001, decimal value 1
// Bitwise left shift
BYTE_A = BYTE_A << 1;          // Binary value 00000010, decimal value 2
BYTE_A = BYTE_A << 1;          // Binary value 00000100, decimal value 4
BYTE_A = BYTE_A << 1;          // Binary value 00001000, decimal value 8
BYTE_A = BYTE_A << 1;          // Binary value 00010000, decimal value 16
// bitwise right shift
BYTE_A = BYTE_A >> 1;          // Binary value 00001000, decimal value 8
BYTE_A = BYTE_A >> 1;          // Binary value 00000100, decimal value 4
BYTE_A = BYTE_A >> 1;          // Binary value 00000010, decimal value 2
BYTE_A = BYTE_A >> 1;          // Binary value 00000001, decimal value 1

let BYTE_B = 0b01000001;       // Binary value 01000001, decimal value 65

// bitwise AND
let BYTE_C = BYTE_A & BYTE_B;  // Binary value 00000001, decimal value 1

// bitwise OR
let BYTE_D = BYTE_A | BYTE_B;  // Binary value 01000001, decimal value 65

 // bitwise exclusive OR
let BYTE_E = BYTE_A ^ BYTE_B;  // Binary value 01000000, decimal value 64
```

Listing 3.51 Use of Bitwise Operators

3.3.6 Operators for Comparing Values

Comparing two values is certainly one of the most frequently performed tasks in programming, be it comparing strings, numbers, or Boolean values. In this regard, JavaScript provides several operators, which are described in detail in Table 3.15.

Operator	Meaning	Description
==	Equal	Compares two values and checks if they are the same.
!=	Unequal to	Compares two values and checks if they are unequal.
===	Strictly equal to	Compares not only two values, but also the data types of the values. Only if the values and the data types are the same does this operator return true.
!==	Strictly unequal to	Compares not only two values, but also the data types of the values. If the values or the data types are not equal, this operator returns true.
<	Less than	Compares two values and checks if the left operand is smaller than the right operand.
>	Greater than	Compares two values and checks if the left operand is greater than the right operand.
<=	Less than or equal to	Compares two values and checks if the left operand is smaller than or equal to the right operand.
>=	Greater than or equal to	Compares two values and checks if the left operand is greater than or equal to the right operand.

Table 3.15 Relational Operators

The operators <, >, <=, and >= work for numeric values as expected in the way known from the field of mathematics: they are used to compare two values and check whether the left value is smaller (<) or greater (>) than the right value or smaller than or equal to (<=) or greater than or equal to (>=) the right value, respectively. Each of these operators returns a Boolean value.

So far, this is nothing really new. What's worth mentioning, however, is the behavior of the various equality or inequality operators. There are two operators for each: == and === for testing for equality and != and !== for testing for inequality. The difference is that == and != only compare the two values as such, while === and !== also compare the data types of the corresponding values.

Nonstrict Comparison versus Strict Comparison
The operators == and != perform a nonstrict comparison of two values, whereas the operators === and !== perform a strict comparison of two values.

Listing 3.52 and Listing 3.53 give a few concrete examples. (Go through the two listings in parallel line by line in order to better understand the difference between the operators.) For example, the == operator returns true for the comparison false == 0 because the interpreter tries to convert the second operand (0) into the data type of the first operand (i.e., a Boolean data type). Because 0 is converted to the Boolean value `false`, the result of the comparison is `true`. Conversely, 1 is converted to the Boolean value `true`, which is why the comparison in the second line returns `false`.

In the same way, for example, the numeric value 4711 is converted into a string if the first operand is also a string. Therefore, the comparison "4711" == 4711 also yields the value `true`.

```
console.log(false == 0);     // Output: true
console.log(false == 1);     // Output: false
console.log(true == 1);      // Output: true
console.log(true == 0);      // Output: false
console.log("4711" == 4711); // Output: true
console.log(false != 0);     // Output: false
console.log(false != 1);     // Output: true
console.log(true != 1);      // Output: false
console.log(true != 0);      // Output: true
console.log("4711" != 4711); // Output: false
```

Listing 3.52 Use of the Operators for Testing Equality and Inequality

---

Implicit Type Conversion

The automatic conversion of a value into another data type is also called *implicit type conversion*.

In contrast to the == and != operators, the two operators === and !== also check whether the data types of the two operands match. This is demonstrated in Listing 3.53, in which the comparison of the values `false` and 0 (which in Listing 3.52 resulted in `true`) now results in the value `false` because the first operand is a Boolean value and the second operand is a number.

```
console.log(false === 0);     // Output: false
console.log(false === 1);     // Output: false
console.log(true === 1);      // Output: false
console.log(true === 0);      // Output: false
console.log("4711" === 4711); // Output: false
console.log(false !== 0);     // Output: true
console.log(false !== 1);     // Output: true
console.log(true !== 1);      // Output: true
console.log(true !== 0);      // Output: true
console.log("4711" !== 4711); // Output: true
```

Listing 3.53 Use of the Operators for Testing Strict Equality and Strict Inequality

> **Tip**
>
> It's a best practice to always use the strict comparison operators for comparing two variables. This will prevent the automatic type conversion from taking effect, which can often lead to program errors that are hard to find.

> **Comparison Operators with Values that Are Not Numbers**
>
> The <, >, <=, and >= operators work reliably when used with numeric values. If you use the operators with a mixture of numeric values and other data types, the results are not always as expected due to automatic type conversion. However, we won't go into the details of these special cases.

3.3.7   The Optional Chaining Operator

The process of accessing nested properties or methods of an object was relatively cumbersome in JavaScript for a long time: on the path to the desired property, you had to gradually check for all properties whether they were present in the hierarchy. Suppose you wanted to access the nested property email in the object hierarchy john.contact. email, as shown in Listing 3.54. Up to and including ES2019, it was necessary to check whether each and every property existed in the hierarchy in order to prevent a runtime error caused by accessing a nonexistent property, as shown in the listing. The deeper the hierarchy, the more laborious the check, the more boilerplate code was required, and the more confusing the code.

```
const john = {
  firstName: 'John',
  lastName: 'Doe',
  contact: {
    email: 'john.doe@javascripthandbuch.com'
  }
};

const james = {
  firstName: 'James',
  lastName: 'Doe',
};

if (john.contact && john.contact.email) {
  console.log(john.contact.email);
}
// Output: "john.doe@javascripthandbuch.com"
```

```
// Runtime error!
// console.log(james.contact.email);

if (james.contact && james.contact.email) {
  console.log(james.contact.email);
}
// No output
```

Listing 3.54 Access to Nested Properties Up To and Including ES2019

With ES2020, the *optional chaining operator* was fortunately included in the standard. This operator is placed directly after a property when it is accessed, which ensures that the next hierarchy level is only accessed if the corresponding property exists. If it does not, the access attempt is aborted. So the previous example would look instead like Listing 3.55 when the optional chaining operator is used. The boilerplate code with the sequential Boolean expressions is omitted, and the code becomes much more readable.

```
const john = {
  firstName: 'John',
  lastName: 'Doe',
  contact: {
    email: 'john.doe@javascripthandbuch.com'
  }
};

const james = {
  firstName: 'James',
  lastName: 'Doe',
};

// Access to nested property via
// optional chaining operator:
console.log(john.contact?.email);
// Output: "john.doe@javascripthandbuch.com"

console.log(james.contact?.email);
// Output: undefined

// Alternative possibility: Using the
// operator on multiple hierarchy levels:
console.log(john?.contact?.email);
// Output: "john.doe@javascripthandbuch.com"
```

```
console.log(james?.contact?.email);
// Output: undefined
```

Listing 3.55 Access to Nested Properties Using the Optional Chaining Operator

> **Note**
>
> Conveniently, the optional chaining operator can be used not only for accessing properties, but also for accessing methods. In this case, the operator is simply placed after the method call, as shown in Listing 3.56.
>
> ```
> console.log(someObject.someFuntion()?.someValue);
> ```
>
> **Listing 3.56** Using the Optional Chaining Operator with Methods

3.3.8   The Logical Assignment Operators

Included in the standard with ES2021 are the *logical assignment operators*. This small group of operators combines logical operators and assignment expressions, making conditional value assignment easier for variables and object properties, among other things. There are a total of three logical assignment operators, each operating on two operands (see Listing 3.57).

The *logical OR assignment* operator ||= is a combination of the logical || operator and the assignment operator =; that is, it assigns the right operand to the left operand if the former has a falsy value and is thus a short form of the notation a || (a = b). The *logical AND assignment operator* &&= works similarly, but it combines the logical && operator and the assignment operator = and assigns the right operand to the left operand only if the former has a *truthy* value (i.e., a value that evaluates to true). This means it is a short form of the notation a && (a = b). The operator for the *logical nullish assignment* ??= in turn is a short form of the notation a ?? (a = b). It assigns the second operand to the first operand only if the former is null or undefined.

```
// logical OR assignment
let a1 = 5;
let a2 = null;
let a3 = false;
a1 ||= 7; // --> 5
a2 ||= 7; // --> 7
a3 ||= 7; // --> 7
console.log(`a1: ${a1}`); // "a1: 5"
console.log(`a2: ${a2}`); // "a2: 7"
console.log(`a3: ${a3}`); // "a3: 7"

// logical AND assignment
let b1 = 5;
```

3

```
let b2 = null;
let b3 = false;
b1 &&= 7; // --> 7
b2 &&= 7; // --> null
b3 &&= 7; // --> false
console.log(`b1: ${b1}`); // "b1: 7"
console.log(`b2: ${b2}`); // "b2: null"
console.log(`b3: ${b3}`); // "b3: false"

// logical nullish assignment
let c1 = 5;
let c2 = null;
let c3 = false;
c1 ??= 7; // --> 5
c2 ??= 7; // --> 7
c3 ??= 7; // --> false
console.log(`c1: ${c1}`); // "c1: 5"
console.log(`c2: ${c2}`); // "c2: 7"
console.log(`c3: ${c3}`); // "c3: false"
```

Listing 3.57 Comparison of Logical Assignment Operators

Real-Life Example: Initialization of Object Properties

The new logical assignment operators are especially useful for initializing object properties, as shown in Listing 3.58. For example, the statement james.lastName ||= 'Doe'; internally ensures that the lastName property of the object james is initialized with the value Doe if the property is not yet assigned. For comparison, the listing shows how the same task had to be handled before ES2021 (peter.lastName || (peter.lastName = 'Doe');).

```
const james = {
  firstName: 'James',
};
james.firstName ||= 'John';
james.lastName ||= 'Doe';
console.log(james);
// { firstName: 'James', lastName: 'Doe' }

// Prior to ES2021, the following was required:
const peter = {
  firstName: 'Peter'
};
peter.firstName || (peter.firstName = 'John');
peter.lastName || (peter.lastName = 'Doe');
```

```
console.log(peter);
// { firstName: 'Peter', lastName: 'Doe' }
```

Listing 3.58 The Logical Assignment Operators for Initializing Object Properties

3.3.9   Operators for Special Operations

In addition to the operators shown, there are a number of other operators in JavaScript, as listed in Table 3.16. We won't discuss these operators in detail now, but will do so at various points in the book.

Operation	Operator	Description
Conditional operator	`<condition> ? <value1> : <value2>`	Ternary operator that, depending on a condition (first operand), returns one of two values (defined by the second and third operands).
Deleting objects, object properties, or elements within an array	`delete`	Enables you to delete elements from arrays as well as object properties from objects.
Existence of a property in an object	`<property> in <object>`	Checks whether an object has a property.
Type verification	`<object> instanceof <type>`	Binary operator that checks whether an object is of a specific type.
Type determination	`typeof <Operand>`	Determines the data type of the operand. The operand can be an object, a string, a variable, or a keyword like `true` or `false`. Optionally, the operand can be specified in parentheses.

Table 3.16 Special Operators in JavaScript

3.4   Controlling the Flow of a Program

You now know how to store different values in variables and perform calculations with them. If you remember the flowcharts and pseudocode from Chapter 1, you will also remember that a program can go through different paths depending on certain conditions.

Suppose you want to display a specific message within a web page in case a user has already logged in, and not display this message if the user is not logged in. Or you want to dynamically generate a table on a web page from a list of data, but you don't know in advance how much data is contained in the list.

For cases like these, programming languages have *control structures* that allow you to determine whether a block of statements should be executed and how often a use case should be executed.

In programming, the former is handled via *conditional statements* or *branches*, the latter via *loops* or *repetitions*. Let's start with the first case, conditional statements.

3.4.1   Defining Conditional Statements

Relatively often, you will want to execute certain statements within a program only if a certain condition is met. In programming, such conditional statements can be implemented using an *if statement*.

The basic structure of such an `if` statement is shown in Listing 3.59. The keyword `if` initiates the `if` statement, the following parentheses contain the condition, and the braces enclose the statement(s) to be executed if the condition is true or fulfilled.

```
if(condition) {
  // Program code to be executed if condition is met
}
```

Listing 3.59 Basic Structure of a Conditional Statement

So, for example, to implement the use case described earlier in the introduction where a message is to be displayed depending on whether a user is logged in, you would use an `if` statement as in Listing 3.60. The content of the `if` statement (in braces) is executed only if the variable `userIsLoggedIn` contains the value `true`. The flowchart for this example is shown in Figure 3.7.

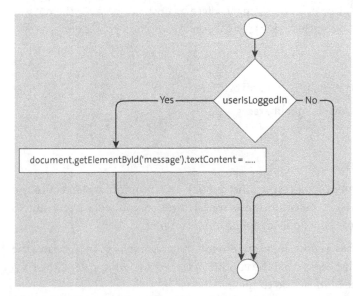

Figure 3.7 Flowchart for a Conditional Statement

```
const userIsLoggedIn = true;
if(userIsLoggedIn) {
  const message = 'Welcome, ' + userName;
  document.getElementById('message').textContent = message;
}
```

Listing 3.60 Example of a Conditional Statement

Note

You don't need to understand the concrete content in the if statement at this point, but it can be explained relatively quickly: The document variable is an object that represents the loaded web page. The getElementById() function provided by this object can be used to specifically access an HTML element on this web page by its ID. This function then returns a corresponding object that represents this HTML element and provides a textContent property that can subsequently be used to change the text content of this element. This will be discussed in more detail in Chapter 5.

Note

The userIsLoggedIn variable doesn't necessarily have to contain a Boolean value. If it contains another value, the if statement checks whether this value evaluates to true.

Omitting Braces

If the conditional statement contains only a single statement, the braces can also be omitted (see Listing 3.61). However, we strongly advise against this because the notation is not as clear as the one including braces, especially if you nest conditional statements.

```
if(condition)
  // Program code to be executed if condition is met
```

Listing 3.61 Use of if Statement without Braces

3.4.2   Defining Branches

With a conditional statement, you test against a Boolean condition and execute the corresponding statement(s) if the condition is met. However, you will often want to execute another statement if the Boolean condition is not met.

This case is not referred to as a conditional statement, but as *branching*. In this case, the code takes one of two paths: one path if the condition is met, the other path if the condition is not met. The code *branches*, so to speak.

To define a branch, use the `if` statement as for a conditional statement, but add another program branch to this construct, which is initiated by the `else` keyword. The basic structure is shown in Listing 3.62.

```
if(condition) {
  // Program code to be executed if condition is met
} else {
  // Program code to be executed if condition is not met
}
```

Listing 3.62 Basic Structure of a Branch

For example, the source code from the previous section could be extended as in Listing 3.63. There, a welcome message is still issued in case the user is logged in (i.e., the `user-IsLoggedIn` variable has a value of `true`). For the other case—namely, that the user is not logged in (and the `userIsLoggedIn` variable has a value of `false`)—the `displayLogin-Form()` function (not shown in detail here) is called.

```
const userIsLoggedIn = true;
if(userIsLoggedIn) {
  const message = 'Welcome, ' + userName;
  document.getElementById('message').textContent = message;
} else {
  displayLoginForm();
}
```

Listing 3.63 Example Basic Structure of a Branch

The corresponding flowchart for this example is shown in Figure 3.8. The only difference is that unlike the flowchart shown in Figure 3.7, a statement is now also executed in the No case.

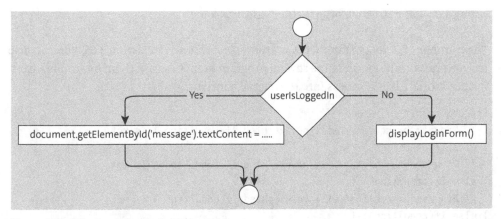

Figure 3.8 Flowchart for if-else Branching

135

Testing Multiple Conditions

There are other cases in which you will not want only to take one of two paths in the program. Sometimes you may want to test several conditions and execute a certain part of the program depending on which of the conditions is met. That is, you also need a way to be able to take one of *several* program branches.

Suppose you wrote an application in which a listing of appropriate film tips is generated for a specified age. For an age value of 8, different film tips should appear than for an age value of 16, and for a value of 11 there should be different ones than for a value of 35. In other words, depending on the selected age value, film tips for films with the corresponding film rating are to be listed.

You could also solve this kind of problem using several single consecutive conditional statements, but there is a better way: *if-else-if-else* branches. The basic structure of this construct is shown in Listing 3.64.

Begin as usual with the if statement and the condition to be checked first. However, you can add further conditions via else-if statements, which—if they are met—ensure that a different program branch is executed in each case. A final else statement also can be used to define the program branch that is to be executed if none of the preceding conditions is met (and thus none of the previous program branches has been taken).

```
if(condition1) {
  // Program branch that will be executed if condition 1 is met
} else if(condition2) {
  // Program branch that will be executed if condition 2 is met
} else {
  // Program branch that will be executed if none of the previous ...
  // ... conditions is met
}
```

Listing 3.64 Basic Structure of an if-else-if-else Branching

The number of else-if statements is arbitrary. As shown in Listing 3.65, you can also test several conditions or define several program branches with them by simply inserting additional else-if blocks into the overall construct.

```
if(condition1) {
  // Program branch that will be executed if condition 1 is met
} else if(condition2) {
  // Program branch that will be executed if condition 2 is met
} else if(condition3) {
  // Program branch that will be executed if condition 3 is met
} else if(condition4) {
  // Program branch that will be executed if condition 4 is met
```

```
} else {
  // Program branch that will be executed if none of the previous ...
  // ... conditions is met

}
```

Listing 3.65 The Number of else-if Statements Is Arbitrary

Furthermore, the closing `else` statement can also be omitted (see Listing 3.66).

```
if(condition1) {
  // Program branch 1
} else if(condition2) {
  // Program branch 2
}
```

Listing 3.66 The else Statement Is Optional and Can Also Be Omitted

With the help of the `if-else-if-else` statement, the program described above can also be implemented relatively easily, as shown in Listing 3.67. The `prompt()` method first asks for the age for which to display film tips. Then the first condition checks whether the entered age is greater than or equal to 18 (age >= 18). If this is the case, the message Show films with a rating of G, PG, PG-13, R, and NC-17. is output. (Naturally, there would be much more happening in the real application.) If, on the other hand, the age is less than 18, the testing continues: first, testing whether the age is greater than or equal to 17 (age >= 17), then whether it is greater than or equal to 13 (age >= 13), and finally whether it is greater than or equal to 6 (age >= 6). For example, when the number 17 is entered, the program provides the output Show films with a rating of G, PG, PG-13, and R..

```
const age = prompt('For what age are you looking for film tips?');
if(age >= 18) {
  console.log('Show films with a rating of G, PG, PG-13, R, and NC-17.');
} else if(age >= 17) {
  console.log('Show films with a rating of G, PG, PG-13, and R.');
} else if(age >= 13) {
  console.log('Show films with a rating of G, PG, and PG-13.');
} else if(age >= 6) {
  console.log('Show films with a rating of G and PG.');
}
```

Listing 3.67 Example of if-else-if-else Branching

For the sake of completeness and better understanding, Figure 3.9 again shows the corresponding flowchart for the code from Listing 3.67.

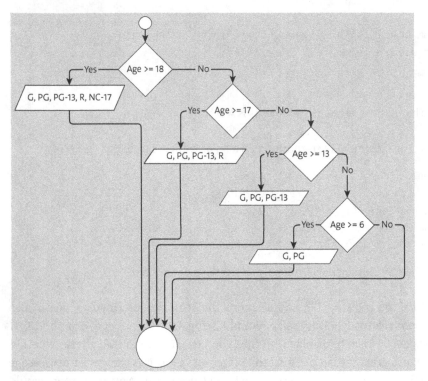

Figure 3.9 Flowchart for if-else-if-else Branching

This chart illustrates the program flow quite well so that it is easy to understand. In addition, this example also reveals that the order of the conditions is crucial. For example, if you change the order as in Listing 3.68, the program no longer behaves as originally intended. The output for the value 17 is now Show films with a rating of G and PG.. Why? After all, the conditions are only checked in reverse order. But that is precisely the cause of the problem. If, for example, an age value of 17 is entered, the first condition (age >= 6) is already met, and the output is Show films with a rating of G and PG.. The other conditions are no longer checked at all.

```
const age = prompt('For what age are you looking for film tips?');
if(age >= 6) {
  console.log('Show films with a rating of G and PG.');
} else if(age >= 13) {
  console.log('Show films with a rating of G, PG, and PG-13.');
} else if(age >= 17) {
  console.log('Show films with a rating of G, PG, PG-13, and R.');
} else if(age >= 18) {
  console.log('Show films with a rating of G, PG, PG-13, R, and NC-17.');
}
```

Listing 3.68 The Order of the Conditions Is Crucial for the Course of the Program

As a rule in this regard, it is recommended to always query the *more specific conditions* first and the *more general conditions* last. In our example, the condition age >= 18 is more specific than the condition age >= 17 (because it describes fewer possible values), which in turn is more specific than the condition age >= 13, which again is more specific than age >= 6.

Note

The conditions to be checked for if-else-if-else statements must be defined from *specific* to *general*: specific conditions must be tested first, more general conditions last. Basically, however, you should not use an exceedingly high number of different if-else branches; otherwise the code tends to be not quite as readable.

Using More Complex Conditions

In Section 3.3.4, you learned about the various Boolean operators: the AND operator, the OR operator, and the negation operator. In everyday programming, you will often use these operators with conditional statements or branches in order to be able to express more complex conditions. An example is shown in Listing 3.69. It uses the expression userIsLoggedIn && userIsAdmin as a condition for the if statement, which causes the corresponding program branch in braces to be executed only if the AND operation of the two variables userIsLoggedIn and userIsAdmin yields true.

```
const userIsLoggedIn = true;
const userIsAdmin = false;
if(userIsLoggedIn && userIsAdmin) {
  /* ... */
}
```

Listing 3.69 Using the Logical AND Operator to Ensure that Multiple Conditions Are Met

In practice, of course, much more complex conditions can be defined. There are no limits to your imagination. However, as is so often the case in programming, simply written code is also easier to understand for the developer.

Nesting Branches

The more complex a program becomes, the more you will need to test different conditions and provide for different program branches. Suppose you want to extend the preceding example, in which a user needs to enter an age, to include a check that ensures the value entered is actually a number. Only if this is the case is the entered value to be used for further processing. If, on the other hand, the value is not a number, a corresponding error is to be output. The implementation of this idea is shown in Listing 3.70.

```
const age = prompt('For what age are you looking for film tips?');
if(!isNaN(parseFloat(age)) && isFinite(age)) {
  if(age >= 18) {
    console.log('Show films with a rating of G, PG, PG-13, R, and NC-17.');
  } else if(age >= 17) {
    console.log('Show films with a rating of G, PG, PG-13, and R.');
  } else if(age >= 13) {
    console.log('Show films with a rating of G, PG, and PG-13.');
  } else if(age >= 6) {
    console.log('Show films with a rating of G and PG.');
  }
} else {
  console.error('Invalid age entered.');
}
```

Listing 3.70 Nesting Branches

In this example, a condition (!isNaN(parseFloat(age)) && isFinite(age)) is used to check whether the entered value is a number. (This condition is admittedly somewhat more complex, but not at all relevant for your understanding at this point.) Only if this condition is met is the part of the program that checks the concrete value of the age (the nested if-else-if-else statement) executed. If the condition is not met, the error message Invalid age entered. is output to the console.

3.4.3   Using the Selection Operator

In programming, you'll often want to assign one value or another to a variable depending on a condition. Suppose you want to find out if a user is at least 18 based on the age entered and then store the result of this check in the variable isAtLeast18. You could achieve this using an if-else statement, as shown in Listing 3.71. If the age is greater than or equal to 18, the variable is assigned the value true; otherwise, the value false.

```
const age = prompt('Please enter your age.');
let isAtLeast18;
if(age >= 18) {
  isAtLeast18 = true;
} else {
  isAtLeast18 = false;
}
console.log(isAtLeast18);
```

Listing 3.71 Variable Assignment Using a Branch

If you assign the variable an initial value right at the beginning, you can also omit the else part and only use a conditional statement (see Listing 3.72).

```
const age = prompt('Please enter your age.');
let isAtLeast18 = false;
if(age >= 18) {
  isAtLeast18 = true;
}
console.log(isAtLeast18);
```

Listing 3.72 Variable Assignment Using a Conditional Statement

This is already shorter than the code in Listing 3.71, but can be shortened further using the *selection operator*. The structure of this operator is shown in Listing 3.73.

```
const variable = condition ? value1 : value2;
```

Listing 3.73 Structure of the Selection Operator

So, for the time being, this is a very ordinary assignment: on the left side of the equals sign, you write the variable name, and on the right side you include the expression with the selection operator. This is a ternary operator as it has not one or two but three operands. The first operand is the condition to be checked, followed by a question mark. The second operand is the value to be assigned to the variable if the condition is met. And the third operand is the value to be assigned if the condition is not met. The two values are separated by a colon.

The previous example could be implemented using the selection operator as shown in Listing 3.74.

```
const age = prompt('Please enter your age.');
const isAtLeast18 = age >= 18 ? true : false;
console.log(isAtLeast18);
```

Listing 3.74 Variable Assignment Using the Selection Operator

The value you assign to the variable can be any value, such as a string, as shown in Listing 3.75.

```
const age = prompt('Please enter your age.');
const isAtLeast18 = age >= 18 ? true : false;
const message = isAtLeast18 ? 'Over 18' : 'Under 18';
console.log(message);
```

Listing 3.75 Assigning a String Using the Selection Operator

> **Note**
>
> Conditional statements and branches are used to take one of several paths in the program depending on one or more conditions and to execute the statements contained

therein. The selection operator, on the other hand, is used to assign one of two values to a variable depending on a single condition. Also note that you should neither nest the selection operator nor use code blocks, both of which result in very complex and unreadable expressions.

3.4.4   Defining Multiway Branches

You have already seen how to write conditional statements and branches that execute either one of two or one of several program branches. For the latter, there is an alternative to `if-else-if-else` statements, which is even the better choice in some use cases. We are talking about *multiway branching*, also called *switch branching* because of one of the keywords used. Basically, such `switch` statements are comparable to `if-else-if-else` branches, but their notation is somewhat clearer than a long sequence of `if-else-if-else` branches, especially when a variable to be checked can take several values. The basic structure of a `switch` statement is shown in Listing 3.76.

```
switch(expression) {
  case value1:
    // Statements
    break;
  case value2:
    // Statements
    break;
  case value3:
    // Statements
    break;
  case value4:
    // Statements
    break;
  default:
    // Statements
}
```

Listing 3.76 Basic Structure of a switch Statement

A `switch` statement is initiated by the keyword `switch`. This is followed by an expression in parentheses (in the listing: `expression`), the value of which will be used to control one of several program branches. The individual program branches are in turn defined by the keyword `case`. The value following such a `case` keyword (in Listing 3.76, the values `value1`, `value2`, `value3`, and `value4`) is compared with the expression. If the values match, the corresponding program branch is initiated; that is, those statements that follow the respective `case`, the value, and the colon are executed.

Within such a program branch, you can also use the keyword break to jump out of the entire switch statement and thus abort the respective program branch. Usually, you put a break at the end of every case program branch. But you can also omit it. We'll show you the effect later in this chapter.

To catch cases that are not caught by the case statements, you use the keyword default, which is roughly comparable to the terminating else of an if-else-if-else statement: if none of the previously defined case statements apply, the statements are executed in the default program branch.

Example

Let's explain the use of the switch statement and its advantage over if-else-if-else branches with a concrete example.

Suppose you wrote a web application that should output some kind of test results. Depending on the test result, different icons should be displayed. For example, failed tests should use an icon named *error.png*, passed tests should use an icon named *pass.png*, and so on (see Table 3.17). The test result is coded within the application using the values 0 to 3. All other values (like 4, 5 and -1) result in an icon named *unknown.png*.

Test Result	Meaning	Image Used
0	Test passed	*pass.png*
1	Info message	*info.png*
2	Warning	*warning.png*
3	Test failed	*error.png*
4	Unknown test result	*unknown.png*
5	Unknown test result	*unknown.png*
-1	Unknown test result	*unknown.png*

Table 3.17 Assigned Value for Different Variable Assignments

Now you could go ahead and test the test result inside an if-else-if-else branch according to the following principle: If the test result has a value of 0, load image *pass.png*; if the test result has a value of 1, load image *info.png*; and so on.

The corresponding code would then look like Listing 3.77.

```
const testResultElement = document.getElementById('testResult');
const testResult = 0;          // Test result, would normally be calculated
let icon = null;               // Variable to contain the image name
if(testResult === 0) {         // Check the test result. If it has the
                               // value 0, ...
```

```
  icon = 'pass.png';             // ... the image name "pass.tif" is used.
} else if(testResult === 1) {    // If the test result has the value 1, ...
  icon = 'info.png';             // ... the image name "info.tif" is used.
} else if(testResult === 2) {    // If the test result has the value 2, ...
  icon = 'warning.png';          // ... the image name "warning.tif" is used.
} else if(testResult === 3) {    // If the test result has the value 3, ...
  icon = 'error.png';            // ... the image name "error.tif" is used.
} else {                         // For all other values ...
  icon = 'unknown.png';          // ... the image name "unknown.tif" is used.
}
testResultElement.src = 'img/' + icon;  // Set the respective image
```

Listing 3.77 Use of if-else-if-else Branching

A program that does the same thing but uses a switch branch instead of an if-else-if-else branch is shown in Listing 3.78. The variable testResult (which contains the test result) is used here as input for the switch test; the case statements cover a total of four of the possible values (0 to 3) for this variable. In addition, there is the default statement, which is used if the variable has none of these values.

```
const testResultElement = document.getElementById('testResult');
const testResult = 0;          // Test result, would normally be calculated
let icon = null;               // Variable that will contain the image name
switch(testResult) {           // Check the test result.
  case 0:                      // If this has a value of 0, ...
    icon = 'pass.png';         // ... the image name "pass.tif" is used.
    break;                     // Abort the switch statement
  case 1:                      // If the test result has a value of 1, ...
    icon = 'info.png';         // ... the image name "info.tif" is used.
    break;                     // Abort the switch statement
  case 2:                      // If the test result has a value of 2, ...
    icon = 'warning.png';      // ... the image name "warning.tif" is used.
    break;                     // Abort the switch statement
  case 3:                      // If the test result has a value of 3, ...
    icon = 'error.png';        // ... the image name "error.tif" is used.
    break;                     // Abort the switch statement
  default:                     // For all other values ...
    icon = 'unknown.png';      // ... the image name "unknown.tif" is used.
}
testResultElement.src = 'img/' + icon;
```

Listing 3.78 Using the switch Application

Figure 3.10 illustrates this example once again using a flowchart.

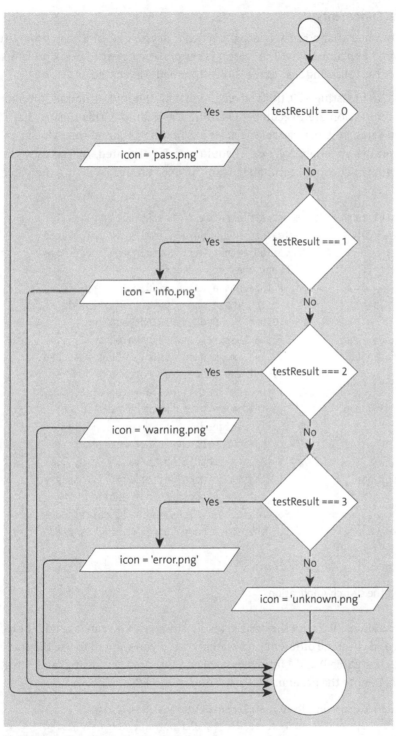

Figure 3.10 Flowchart for a switch Branch

Canceling switch Statements

We already mentioned that a break is usually written at the end of a case program branch, but haven't explained why. The reason is simple: the keyword break prevents the statements of the following case expressions from being executed.

If you omit break, as in Listing 3.79, this will ensure that all statements defined after an applicable case expression are executed. Regarding the example, this means that if testResult has a value of 2, the variable icon would first be assigned the value warning.png. However, the statement of case 3 would also be executed, followed by the default statement, which would ultimately result in icon always receiving the value unknown.png.

```
const testResultElement = document.getElementById('testResult');
const testResult = 0;          // Test result, would normally be calculated
let icon = null;               // Variable that will contain the image name
switch(testResult) {           // Check the test result.
  case 0:                      // If this has a value of 0, ...
    icon = 'pass.png';         // ... the image name "pass.tif" is assigned, ...
                               // ... but the process is not aborted.
  case 1:                      // If the test result has a value of 1, ...
    icon = 'info.png';         // ... the image name "info.tif" is assigned.
                               // ... but the process is not aborted.
  case 2:                      // If the test result has a value of 2, ...
    icon = 'warning.png';      // ... the image name "warning.tif" ...
                               // ... is assigned, ...
                               // ... but the process is not aborted.
  case 3:                      // If the test result has a value of 3, ...
    icon = 'error.png';        // ... the image name "error.tif" is assigned, ...
                               // ... but the process is not aborted.
default:                       // For all other values (and all cases above) ...
    icon = 'unknown.png';      // ... the image name "unknown.tif" is used.
}
testResultElement.src = 'img/' + icon;
```

Listing 3.79 Using the switch Application

In this specific example, this is not the desired result. However, you can take advantage of this behavior and combine different case statements. If you wanted to use the same icons for cases 0 (test passed) and 1 (info message) and for cases 2 (warning) and 3 (test failed), you could rewrite the program as shown in Listing 3.80.

```
const testResultElement = document.getElementById('testResult');
const testResult = 0;          // Test result, would normally be calculated
let icon = null;               // Variable that will contain the image name
switch(testResult) {           // Check the test result.
```

```
case 0:                      // If this has a value of 0 ...
case 1:                      // ... or a value of 1, ...
  icon = 'pass.png';         // ... the image name "pass.tif" is used.
  break;                     // Abort
case 2:                      // If the test result has a value of 2, ...
case 3:                      // ... or a value of 3, ...
  icon = 'error.png';        // ... the image name "error.tif" is used.
  break:                     // Abort
default:                     // For all other values ...
  icon = 'unknown.png';      // ... the image name "unknown.tif" is used.
}
testResultElement.src = 'img/' + icon;
```

Listing 3.80 Summarizing case Statements

Table 3.18 shows an overview.

Value of testResult	Assigned Value of Icon
0	pass.png
1	pass.png
2	error.png
3	error.png
4	unknown.png
5	unknown.png
-1	unknown.png

Table 3.18 Assigned Value for Different Variable Assignments

Note

If you want to take one out of several paths in the program depending on Boolean conditions, you should use conditional statements or branches. Multiway branches via the switch statement, however, are generally not suitable for testing Boolean conditions.

Remember the example of entering your age to output film tips? You could also implement this using a switch statement, as shown in Listing 3.81. Here, true is used as the base value for switch, and the respective condition is used for the individual test values within the individual case statements. Although this works, the switch statement is misused here. You should therefore rather use conditional statements or branches in such a case.

```
// No best practice: Boolean conditions within a switch statement
const age = prompt('For what age are you looking for film tips?');
switch(true) {
  case (age >= 18):
    console.log('Show films with a rating of G, PG, PG-13, R, and NC-17.');
    break;
  case (age >= 17):
    console.log('Show films with a rating of G, PG, PG-13, and R.');
    break;
  case (age >= 13):
    console.log('Show films with a rating of G, PG, and PG-13.');
    break;
  case (age >= 6):
    console.log('Show films with a rating of G and PG.');
    break;
}
```

Listing 3.81 Negative Example: switch Statements Should Usually Not Be Used with Boolean Conditions

3.4.5   Defining Counting Loops

You now know how to get your program to execute certain statements and not others depending on various conditions. Conditional statements, branches, and multiway branches are therefore one important construct that enables you to program more complex processes within an application. But there is also a second essential programming construct, one for executing statements *repeatedly*.

Do you remember the use case described in the introduction to this section, where a table was to be generated from a list of specific data? What would have to be done here from a purely procedural point of view? The entries in the list would have to be iterated one after the other, and for every entry, a new row would have to be created in the table. So every entry requires more or less the same steps to be performed, and thus the same (or at least quite similar) code would need to be executed every time.

Definition

In programming, *iteration* is the repeated execution of statements.

In programming, *loops* are the method of choice for such a repeated execution of program code. Overall, there are three different types of such loops, which are more or less suitable depending on the application. First there is the *counting loop,* which executes code repeatedly based on a *counter variable.* Then there are the *head-controlled loop* and the *tail-controlled loop*, both of which execute code for as long as a certain condition is met.

Ahead, we'll discuss these three types of loops in detail. This section starts with the counting loop.

Counting Loop Structure

Counting loops are always suitable when you know in advance how often certain statements are to be repeated—for example, to list all items in a shopping cart.

You can see the basic structure of a counting loop in Listing 3.82. The whole thing is initiated by the keyword for (that's why the counting loop is often called a *for loop*). Inside the following pair of parentheses, you define three things:

- **Initialization**
  Here you write the code that should be executed once *before executing the entire loop*. As a rule, this is where you initialize the counter variable (examples to follow shortly).

- **Condition**
  This is where you put the code that—*before executing a loop iteration*—first checks whether or not to continue executing the loop. Typically, here you check whether the counter variable has already reached a certain limit (e.g., the length of an array).

- **Increment expression**
  Here you write the code that should be executed *after each loop iteration*. Normally, the counter variable is incremented here.

Initialization, condition, and increment expressions are separated by semicolons. This is important so that the JavaScript interpreter can determine what code belongs where.

The actual code that is to be executed multiple times is written inside the braces into the *loop body* that immediately follows the closing parenthesis.

```
for (
  Initialization;        // is executed before the loop is executed
  Condition;             // is checked before executing an iteration
  Increment expression   // executed at the end of an iteration
) {
  Loop body              // is executed once in each iteration
}
```

Listing 3.82 The Basic Structure of a for Loop

Regarding the order, the following happens (see also Figure 3.11):

1. At the beginning of the loop, the initialization statement is executed once.

2. Then the condition is checked.

3. If it's true, the loop body is executed.

4. And then the increment expression is evaluated.

5. Then the process continues by checking the condition, executing the loop body, and executing the increment expression, until the condition is no longer fulfilled.

6. At this point—that is, when the condition returns false—the loop execution is terminated.

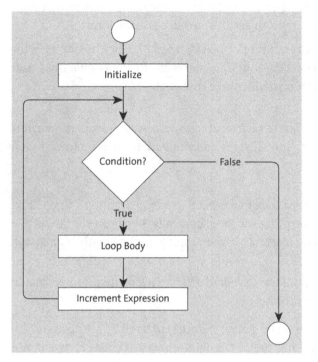

Figure 3.11 Flowchart for a Counting Loop

Example: Output of the Numbers 1 to 10

To add some practice to the theory, let's look at some real code examples. We'll start with a relatively simple example: the output of the numbers 1 to 10. The implementation of this example is shown in Listing 3.83.

```
for (
  let i = 1;      // Initialization: will be executed before the loop
                  // is executed
  i <= 10;        // Condition: is checked before executing an iteration
  i++             // Increment expression: is executed at the end of an ...
                  // ... iteration
) {               // Loop body: executed once in each iteration
  console.log(i);
}
```

```
// And here again in a notation suitable for everyday use:
for (let i = 1; i <= 10; i++) {
  console.log(i);
}
```

Listing 3.83 A Simple for Loop that Outputs Numbers from 1 to 10

At the beginning, the counter variable i is set to the initial value 1. Remember: this statement is executed only once before the entire loop is executed. Then i <= 10 is used to set the condition: the loop is to be executed as long as the counter variable i is less than or equal to 10. This condition is presently fulfilled (the counter variable has a value of 1). That is, the loop body is executed, the value of i is output, and then the variable i is incremented by one in the increment expression. The whole thing continues until the expression i <= 10 is no longer fulfilled; that is, the variable i has a value of 11. Table 3.19 shows the individual steps in detail.

Value of i before Checking the Condition	Condition	Execution of Loop Body	Output	Value of i after Increment Expression
1	1 <= 10	Yes	1	2
2	2 <= 10	Yes	2	3
3	3 <= 10	Yes	3	4
4	4 <= 10	Yes	4	5
5	5 <= 10	Yes	5	6
6	6 <= 10	Yes	6	7
7	7 <= 10	Yes	7	8
8	8 <= 10	Yes	8	9
9	9 <= 10	Yes	9	10
10	10 <= 10	Yes	10	11
11	11 <= 10	No, because the condition is not fulfilled		

Table 3.19 Detailed Listing of the Individual Steps in the Execution of the Loop

The i Variable

Of course, the name i by itself is not a meaningful variable name, but in the context of loops this name has become quite common for the counter variable. The letter i here is an abbreviation of *index*, which may be familiar in this form from mathematics—for example, from totals formulas.

Real-Life Example: Generating Values in a Pick List

In practice, you will probably rarely want to simply output the numbers from 1 to 10 to the console. So let's look at a more practical example of using counting loops. Suppose you needed to populate a pick list on a web page with values from an array using Java-Script. You could do this relatively easily with a counting loop, iterating over the values in the array and adding an entry for each value to the pick list.

Even though you don't know yet how to dynamically create elements within a web page (as mentioned, we won't cover that part until Chapter 5) and thus have to take some of the calls in the following listing at face value, the code in Listing 3.84 still shouldn't be that difficult to understand. The most important thing at the moment, the counting loop, is just as easy to understand in this example as in the earlier counting example.

```
const selectElement = document.getElementById('grade');  // the pick list
const options = [                                         // a list of values
  'A (90%-100%)',
  'B (80%-89%)',
  'C (70%-79%)',
  'D (60%-69%)',
  'F (0%-59%)',

];
for(let i=0; i<options.length; i++) {                     // For every value in ...
                                                          // ... the list ...
  const optionElement = document.createElement('option'); // ... create one ...
                                                          // ... selection element, ...
  const optionText = document.createTextNode(options[i]); // ... create the ...
                                                          // ... corresponding text, ...
  optionElement.appendChild(optionText);                  // ... append the Text to ...
                                                          // ... the element.
  selectElement.appendChild(optionElement);               // and append the element
                                                          // to the pick list.
}
```

Listing 3.84 Populating a Pick List Using a for Loop

What happens here in detail? First you access the pick list within the web page via document.getElementById('grade');. Then the options array is defined with the selection values that are to be inserted into this pick list. After that, the most important part for the moment begins: the counting loop.

As in the earlier counting example, the i variable serves as a counter variable. It is initialized to 0 this time because we need it right away to access the values of the array, and arrays are known to start at index 0.

The loop body is then executed once for each element in the array. This is taken care of by the expression i<options.length. Inside the loop body, there are many things happening in detail now, which we'll discuss in Chapter 5. The only important thing here is that the respective value in the array at index i is accessed via options[i]. The code around it then ensures that a corresponding entry is added to the pick list. The result of the code is shown in Figure 3.12.

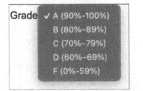

Figure 3.12 The Generated Pick List

Nested Counting Loops

There are no restrictions regarding the statements included in a loop body. For example, it's possible to execute other loops within a loop body. Due to the nesting, this construction is then also called *nested loops*.

For example, the code in Listing 3.85 outputs all combinations of numbers between 1 and 10. For each loop iteration of the *outer loop*, the complete *inner loop* is executed.

```
// outer loop
for (let i = 1; i < 11; i++) {
  // inner loop
  for (let j = 1; j < 11; j++) {
    console.log(`i has the value "${i}", j has the value "${j}"`);
  }
}
```

Listing 3.85 Nested Counting Loop that Outputs All Number Combinations of the Numbers from 1 to 10

Part of the output is shown in Listing 3.86. In the first iteration of the outer loop, i has a value of 1. In the course of this iteration, the inner loop is then executed completely; that is, the j variable sequentially takes on the values 1 through 10, while the value of i remains unchanged. After the inner loop is over, the next iteration of the outer loop begins; that is, the i variable is assigned the value 2, and the execution of the inner loop starts over. This is repeated until the condition for the outer loop is no longer fulfilled; that is, the variable i has the value 11.

```
i has the value "1", j has the value "1"
i has the value "1", j has the value "2"
i has the value "1", j has the value "3"
```

```
i has the value "1", j has the value "4"
i has the value "1", j has the value "5"
i has the value "1", j has the value "6"
i has the value "1", j has the value "7"
i has the value "1", j has the value "8"
i has the value "1", j has the value "9"
i has the value "1", j has the value "10"
i has the value "2", j has the value "1"
i has the value "2", j has the value "2"
i has the value "2", j has the value "3"
i has the value "2", j has the value "4"
i has the value "2", j has the value "5"
...
i has the value "10", j has the value "6"
i has the value "10", j has the value "7"
i has the value "10", j has the value "8"
i has the value "10", j has the value "9"
i has the value "10", j has the value "10"
```

Listing 3.86 Output of the Nested Counting Loop

Real-Life Example: Output of the Elements of Multidimensional Arrays

A quite common requirement in practice is to output the data of a multidimensional array. As an example, consider an array of coordinates as shown in Listing 3.87. Each coordinate is represented by an array of two values. The first value defines the latitude, the second value the longitude. The outer loop now iterates over the coordinates array. In each iteration of this loop, the coordinate variable is assigned the current element of this array (coordinates[i]), which, as mentioned, is also an array. The inner loop is now used to iterate over this array and output latitude and longitude information accordingly.

```
const coordinates = [
  [50.69, 8.94],
  [54.29, 11.97],
  [55.38, 12.88],
  [60.78, 9.94],
  [62.29, 7.69],
  [70.34, 8.24],
  [72.59, 11.29],
  [80.69, 8.56]
];
for(let i=0; i<coordinates.length; i++) {
  const coordinate = coordinates[i];
```

```
for(let j=0; j<coordinate.length; j++) {
    console.log(coordinate[j]);
  }
}
```

Listing 3.87 Iteration over a Multidimensional Array Using Nested Counting Loops

---

Counter Variables for Nested Loops

For nested loops, use a new counter variable for each loop. This will prevent the individual loops from getting in each other's way. It has become a convention to use the names i, j, k, l, and so on.

Maximum Depth of Nested Loops

Basically, you can nest loops as "deeply" as you like; that is, nested loops can again contain loops, and so on. In practice, however, It's quite unusual to use more than three nesting levels as the code required can quickly become very confusing or difficult to understand.

As mentioned earlier, there are two more types of loops in JavaScript besides the counting loop: the *head-controlled loop* and the *tail-controlled loop*. We'll present these loops ahead, which are very similar in principle.

3.4.6   Defining Head-Controlled Loops

Both head-controlled and tail-controlled loops basically function in the same way: the purpose of both loops is to execute one or more statements repeatedly so long as a given Boolean condition is fulfilled.

The difference between the two types of loops is the time at which the Boolean check takes place. The head-driven loop shown in Listing 3.88, also called a *while loop,* first checks whether the Boolean condition is met. If this is the case, the code in braces (the loop body) is executed. If, on the other hand, the condition is not or no longer fulfilled, the loop body is not (or no longer) executed, and the execution of the program continues after the loop (see also Figure 3.13).

```
while (expression) {
  // Statement(s)
}
```

Listing 3.88 The Basic Structure of a while Loop

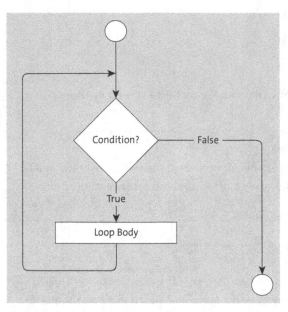

Figure 3.13 Flowchart of a Head-Controlled Loop

Unlike the for loop, which consists of an initialization expression, the condition, and the increment expression, the while loop only contains an expression that is used to set the condition. If you want to emulate a counting loop using a while loop and output the numbers 1 to 10, for example, you must write the initialization expression before the loop and place the increment expression inside the loop body, as shown in Listing 3.89.

```
let i = 1;          // Initialization
while (i < 11) {  // Condition
  console.log(i); // Statement
  i++;              // Increment
}
```

Listing 3.89 A Simple while Loop that Outputs the Numbers from 1 to 10

However, while loops are usually not used for such counter-oriented tasks. So let's look at a more practical example of using while loops next.

Real-Life Example: Moving HTML Elements within a Web Page

Suppose you have two lists on a web page and want to move all the list entries from one list (the source list) over to the other list (the target list) at the push of a button. The corresponding algorithm would look like the following: while there is still a list entry in the source list, this entry should be removed from the source list and moved to the target list. The word *while* already indicates that the while loop is the right choice for the language construct.

In this example, the HTML source code shown in Listing 3.90 will serve as a starting point. Here you can see the source list (with the ID source) and the target list (with the ID target). The source list contains four entries, the target list no entries (see also Figure 3.14).

```html
<ul id="source">
  <li>John Doe</li>
  <li>James Doe</li>
  <li>Peter Doe</li>
  <li>Jane Doe</li>
</ul>
<div>
  <button id="move"> &gt;&gt; </button>
</div>
<ul id="target">
</ul>
```

Listing 3.90 The Initial HTML with the Two Lists

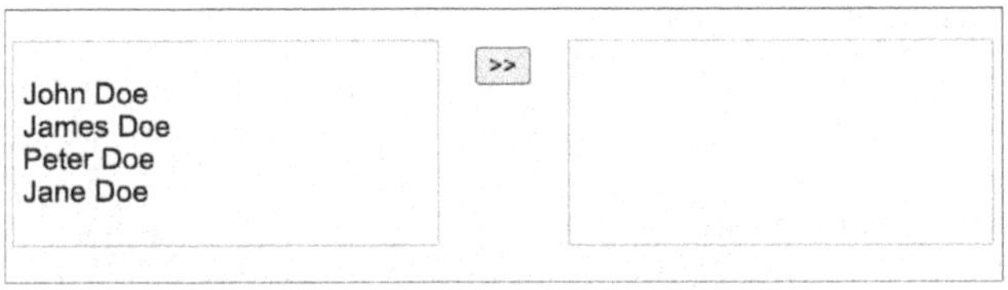

Figure 3.14 Before Moving, All Entries Are in the Source List

> **Note**
>
> Although most browsers tolerate or interpret the greater-than sign (>) without a preceding less-than sign (<) as a normal character, this still isn't valid HTML and should therefore be represented by the string > as in the example.

The corresponding JavaScript code is shown in Listing 3.91. As was true for the more complex counting loop example, at this point, you don't need to understand the details. What's important for now is only the highlighted source code—that is, the while loop (and don't worry: after Chapter 5, the code around it will seem easy to you).

The call of the hasChildNodes() function on the sourceList object is used here as the condition for the while loop: as long as the source list still contains entries, the first entry in each case is removed from the list and moved to the target list (see Figure 3.15). Once there are no more entries in the source list, sourceList.hasChildNodes() returns false and the loop is aborted.

```
const sourceList = document.getElementById('source');    // the source list
const targetList = document.getElementById('target');    // the target list
const copyButton = document.getElementById('move');      // the Move ...
                                                         // ... button
copyButton.addEventListener('click', function() {        // When clicking the ...
                                                         // ... button:
  while(sourceList.hasChildNodes()) {           // While there are items ...
                                                // ... in the source list, ...
    const item = sourceList.removeChild(        // ... the first item is ...
      sourceList.firstChild);                   // ... removed from this list ...
    targetList.appendChild(item);               // ... and added to the ...
                                                // ... target list.

  }
});
```

Listing 3.91 Real-Life Example of the Use of a while Loop

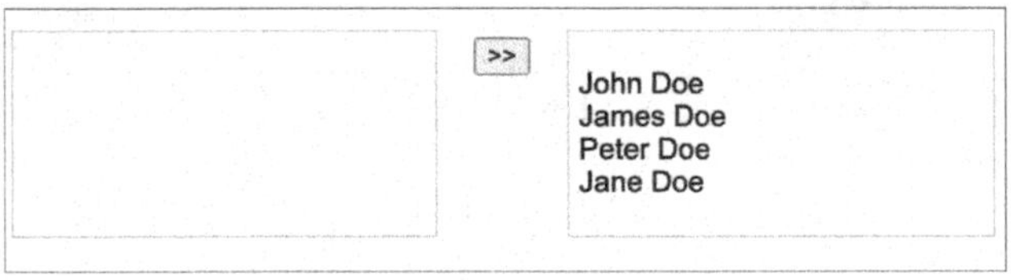

Figure 3.15 After Moving, All Entries Are in the Target List

3.4.7   Defining Tail-Controlled Loops

Basically, the tail-controlled loop works similarly to the head-controlled loop, but in exactly the opposite way. In other words: before the Boolean condition is checked, the loop body is already executed once. The basic structure is shown in Listing 3.92 and Figure 3.16. This loop is initiated by the keyword do, followed by a pair of braces enclosing the loop body. After the closing brace, there is at first the while keyword, followed by the Boolean condition.

```
do {
  // Statement(s)
} while (expression)
```

Listing 3.92 The Basic Structure of a do-while Loop

Note

The tail-controlled loop is also called a *do-while loop* because of the keywords used.

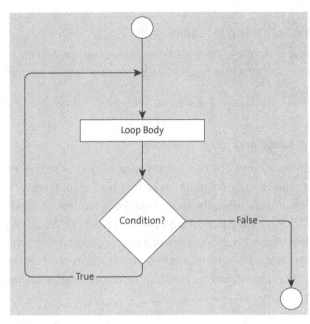

Figure 3.16 Flowchart for a Tail-Controlled Loop

Like the head-controlled loop (and unlike the counting loop), the tail-controlled loop does not contain an initialization expression or an increment expression. To use the do-while loop to output the numbers 1 to 10, both of these expressions must be added manually before the loop or in the loop body, similar to the head-driven loop, as shown in Listing 3.93.

```
let i = 1;           // Initialization
do {
  console.log(i);    // Statement
  i++;               // Increment
} while (i < 11)     // Condition
```

Listing 3.93 A Simple do-while Loop that Outputs the Numbers from 1 to 10

Head-Controlled versus Tail-Controlled Loops

A while loop is executed 0 to *n* times, and a do-while loop is executed 1 to *n* times. In practice, you will probably use the while loop more often than the do-while loop as it ensures that the loop body is executed only when the corresponding condition is met. The do-while loop, on the other hand, should normally be used when the loop body (regardless of the condition) is to be executed at least once.

> **Nesting of Head-Controlled and Tail-Controlled Loops**
>
> Like counting loops, head-controlled and tail-controlled loops can be nested. Indeed, you can use any of the loop types in all other loop types as well. However, we'll refrain from giving code examples at this point.

3.4.8   Prematurely Terminating Loops and Loop Iterations

You have seen that for counting loops and for head-controlled and tail-controlled loops, the loop definition specifies the condition that must be met for the loop body to be executed and that implicitly determines when the loop should be terminated. However, there are two other ways to influence the execution of loops (independent of the loop condition) from within the loop body: the break keyword enables you to abort the *complete loop* right away, and the continue keyword enables you to abort the *current loop iteration* and continue to the next loop iteration. How this works in detail is shown ahead.

Prematurely Terminating Loops

Sometimes you may want to terminate a loop prematurely. Let's look at a simple example: Suppose you want to output the individual numbers from a number array, but only until the first odd number is found, at which point the loop is to be aborted. We haven't yet covered how you can achieve this.

Of course, you could use branches within the loop body to distinguish odd and even numbers and use a variable to remember if an odd number has already been found, and then simply not output all subsequent numbers. However, this would not be ideal in terms of performance: Imagine an array with 100,000 numbers in which an odd number already appears at position 9. In such a case, the loop would also iterate over the remaining 99,991 numbers and execute the loop body, including numerous if tests.

This is where the break keyword comes into play. This keyword can be used to selectively terminate loops.

This is shown in Listing 3.94 using a counting loop. The numbers array contains even and odd numbers, where the number 65 is the first odd number. After initializing this array, the individual numbers are output via a counting loop. The modulo operator is used to check whether the respective number is an odd number (number % 2 === 1). If it is, the message Odd number found. is output and the loop is terminated.

```
const numbers = [2, 4, 56, 22, 65, 2, 54, 88, 29];
console.log('Before the loop.');
for (let i = 0; i < numbers.length; i++) {    // Iterate over ...
  const number = numbers[i];                  // ... the number array.
  if (number % 2 === 1) {                     // If a number is odd ...
```

```
    console.log('Odd number found.');      // ... output message ...
    break;                                 // ... and terminate the loop.
  }                                        // Otherwise ...
  console.log(number);                     // ... output the number.
}
console.log('After the loop.');
```

Listing 3.94 Loops Can Be Aborted via the break Keyword

The detailed output of the program is shown in Listing 3.95.

```
Before the loop.
2
4
56
22
Odd number found.
After the loop.
```

Listing 3.95 Output of the Example Program

The flowchart in Figure 3.17 illustrates this context once again. As you can see, break leads to the condition of the loop not being evaluated again. Instead, the complete execution of the loop is aborted.

In addition to counting loops, head-controlled and tail-controlled loops can also be aborted using break. Listing 3.96 shows the same example again, but this time rewritten using a head-controlled loop. For reasons of space, we won't give an example of the tail-controlled loop here, but it would be aborted in the same way as the head-controlled loop.

```
const numbers = [2, 4, 56, 22, 65, 2, 54, 88, 29];
console.log('Before the loop.');
let i = 0;                              // Initialize counter variable.
while(i < numbers.length) {             // Iterate over ...
  const number = numbers[i];            // ...  the number array.
  if (number % 2 === 1) {               // If a number is odd ...
    console.log('Odd number found.');   // ... output message ...
    break;                              // ... and terminate the loop.
  }                                     // Otherwise ...
  console.log(number);                  // ... output the number ...
  i++;                                  // ... and increment ...
                                        // ... the counter variable.

}
console.log('After the loop.');
```

Listing 3.96 Head-Controlled Loops Can Also Be Aborted via the break Keyword

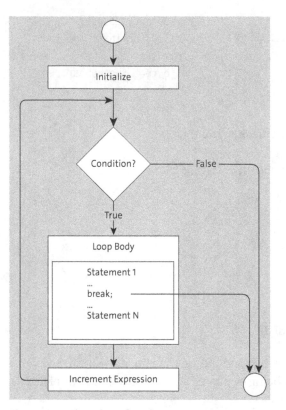

Figure 3.17 Flowchart for Aborting a Counting Loop

> **Note**
>
> In Chapter 4, when you learn how to work with arrays, among other things, you'll see yet another simpler way to search for specific values within an array. The examples shown so far are used only to illustrate the break keyword.

Prematurely Terminating Loop Iterations

If you want to abort only the current loop iteration rather than the entire loop, use the continue keyword. Suppose you want to modify the previous example so that after finding the first odd number the loop is not aborted, but only jumps to the next number in the array. In other words, the output of the odd number is to be skipped. Then, you can simply replace the keyword break with the keyword continue, as shown in Listing 3.97.

```
const numbers = [2, 4, 56, 22, 65, 2, 54, 88, 29];
console.log('Before the loop.');
for (let i = 0; i < numbers.length; i++) {    // Iterate over ...
  const number = numbers[i];                   // ...  the number array.
```

```
if (number % 2 === 1) {              // If a number is odd ...
  console.log('Odd number found.');  // ... output message ...
  continue;                          // ... and abort the
                                     // loop iteration.
}                                    // Otherwise ...
  console.log(number);               // ... output the number.
}
console.log('After the loop.');
```

Listing 3.97 Loop Iterations Can Be Aborted via the continue Keyword

What does this do? When the first odd number—that is, the number 65—is found, the message Odd number found. is output as before. But the subsequent continue keyword then ensures that the rest of the loop body for this iteration is no longer executed; that is, the last statement, the output of the number, is skipped. Instead, the loop continues to the next loop iteration: the increment expression is executed, the condition of the loop (i < numbers.length) is checked, and the loop body is executed again (see also Figure 3.18). In this way, only the even numbers of the array are output and the odd numbers are ignored.

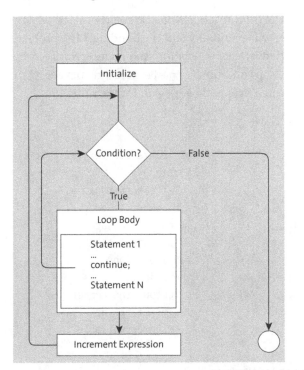

Figure 3.18 Flowchart for Terminating a Loop Iteration in a Counting Loop

Listing 3.98 again shows the detailed output of the program.

```
Before the loop.
2
4
56
22
Odd number found.
2
54
88
Odd number found.
After the loop.
```

Listing 3.98 Output of the Example Program

Infinite Loops

In the case of head-controlled and tail-controlled loops, you must be careful when using continue. If positioned incorrectly, the keyword can cause an *infinite loop* to occur—that is, a loop that is never aborted and thus sooner or later brings your application to its knees.

Listing 3.99 shows an example of such an infinite loop. (*Note:* Do not try this code! Otherwise, in the worst case, your browser will eventually stop responding!) The problem here is that the loop iteration is aborted by continue before the counter variable i is incremented. This in turn leads to the loop condition (i < numbers.length) never returning false so that the loop body is executed over and over again for the same i.

```javascript
const numbers = [2, 4, 56, 22, 65, 2, 54, 88, 29];
console.log('Before the loop.');
let i = 0;                          // Initialize counter variable.
while(i < numbers.length) {         // Iterate over ...
  const number = numbers[i];        // ... the number array.
  if (number % 2 === 1) {           // If a number is odd ...
    console.log('Odd number found.'); // ... output message ...
    continue;                       // ... and abort the
                                    // loop iteration.
  }                                 // Otherwise ...
  console.log(number);              // ... output the number and ...
  i++;                              // ... increment the ...
                                    // ... counter variable.
}
```

Listing 3.99 This Code Would Produce an Infinite Loop

In this case, you can solve this problem by simply increasing the counter variable before using continue, as shown in Listing 3.100, most simply right at the beginning of the loop body. But to ensure that the counter variable does not have a value of 1 when the array is accessed for the first time (which would cause the first number in the array to be skipped), you have to initialize it with the value -1.

```
const numbers = [2, 4, 56, 22, 65, 2, 54, 88, 29];
console.log('Before the loop.');
let i = 0;                              // Initialize counter variable.
while(i < numbers.length) {             // Iterate over number array.
  const number = numbers[i];            // Assign respective number.
  i++;                                  // Increment counter variable.
  if (number % 2 === 1) {               // If a number is odd ...
    console.log('Odd number found.');   // ... output message ...
    continue;                           // ... and terminate the loop
                                        // iteration.
  }                                     // Otherwise ...
  console.log(number);                  // ... output the number.
}
```

Listing 3.100 The Customized Code No Longer Produces an Infinite Loop

> **Note**
>
> To prevent infinite loops, you must always make sure that the termination condition of the respective loop will result in false at some point.

Defining Jump Labels

Thus, the continue keyword enables you to end the current loop iteration within a loop and continue to the next loop iteration. For nested loops, this always terminates the loop iteration of the loop in which continue is used. If the keyword appears in the outer loop, the loop iteration of the outer loop is terminated, but if it appears in the inner loop, the loop iteration of the inner loop is terminated.

It's also possible to terminate the loop iteration of the outer loop from an inner loop using *labels* or *jump labels*.

Suppose you need to search for duplicate numbers in the number array and move on to the next number once a duplicate number is found. To implement this, you have to compare each number in the array with all subsequent numbers, which just cries out for a nested counting loop. The implementation without jump labels is shown in Listing 3.101.

```
const numbers = [2, 4, 56, 22, 65, 2, 54, 88, 29];
for (let i = 0; i < numbers.length; i++) {
  const number = numbers[i];
  for (let j = i + 1; j < numbers.length; j++) {
```

```
    const number2 = numbers[j];
    console.log(`Compare ${number} with ${number2}`);
    if (number === number2) {
      console.log('Same numbers found');
      continue;
    }
  }
}
```

Listing 3.101 This Nested Loop Finds Duplicate Numbers in the Array

The only problem with this implementation is that it does not work as desired. It correctly outputs duplicate numbers, but it performs more comparisons than actually necessary. The reason is that continue aborts the loop iteration of the inner loop when a duplicate number is found, but still executes the inner loop to the end (see output in Listing 3.102).

```
Compare 2 with 4
Compare 2 with 56
Compare 2 with 22
Compare 2 with 65
Compare 2 with 2
Same numbers found
Compare 2 with 54
Compare 2 with 88
Compare 2 with 29
Compare 4 with 56
Compare 4 with 22
Compare 4 with 65
Compare 4 with 2
Compare 4 with 54
...
```

Listing 3.102 Output of the Previous Program

This is where jump labels come into play. You can use them to mark individual statements within a program with a name and then jump directly to this *named statement* via continue (and break). The adapted example is shown in Listing 3.103. In this example, both loops are each marked with a jump label: the outer loop with the name outer-Loop, the inner loop with the name innerLoop. The continue outerLoop statement then ensures that if a duplicate number is found, the process specifically jumps from the inner loop to the outer loop and continues with the next loop iteration of this outer loop. The corresponding output is shown in Listing 3.104.

```
const numbers = [2, 4, 56, 22, 65, 2, 54, 88, 29];
outerLoop:
```

```
for (let i = 0; i < numbers.length; i++) {
  const number = numbers[i];
  innerLoop:
    for (let j = i + 1; j < numbers.length; j++) {
      const number2 = numbers[j];
      console.log(`Compare ${number} with ${number2}`);
      if (number === number2) {
        console.log('Same numbers found');
        continue outerLoop;
      }
    }
}
```

Listing 3.103 Jump Labels Can Be Used to Specify the Target of a continue Statement

```
Compare 2 with 4
Compare 2 with 56
Compare 2 with 22
Compare 2 with 65
Compare 2 with 2
Same numbers found
Compare 4 with 56
Compare 4 with 22
Compare 4 with 65
Compare 4 with 2
Compare 4 with 54
...
```

Listing 3.104 Output of the Previous Program

Besides continue, jump labels can also be addressed using break. Listing 3.105 contains almost exactly the same code as Listing 3.103. The only difference is that instead of continue, the keyword break is used in the inner loop. The statement break outerLoop ensures that if a duplicate number is found, the process jumps from the inner loop to the outer loop, but then the *complete loop is aborted*! This can also be seen in the console output shown in Listing 3.106. Instead of continuing with the search for further number pairs after finding a number pair as before, the program exits right after the first number pair has been found.

```
const numbers = [2, 4, 56, 22, 65, 2, 54, 88, 29];
outerLoop:
  for (let i = 0; i < numbers.length; i++) {
    const number = numbers[i];
    innerLoop:
      for (let j = i + 1; j < numbers.length; j++) {
```

```
      const number2 = numbers[j];
      console.log(`Compare ${number} with ${number2}`);
      if (number === number2) {
        console.log('Same numbers found');
        break outerLoop;
      }
    }
  }
}
```

Listing 3.105 Jump Labels Also Work with a break Statement

```
Compare 2 with 4
Compare 2 with 56
Compare 2 with 22
Compare 2 with 65
Compare 2 with 2
Same numbers found
```

Listing 3.106 The Program Terminates When the First Pair of Numbers Has Been Found

Jump Labels in Practice

In practice, jump labels are used relatively rarely—even if they are quite useful for the example at hand. They often deteriorate the readability of the source text because you always need to check when and where and under what conditions the program jumps to which place exactly.

3.5   Creating Reusable Code Blocks

The more extensive your programs and the more complex the software you develop, the more source code you will have to manage. In addition, certain tasks become repetitive over time. Therefore, it makes sense to somehow group the source code into reusable code blocks. This has the advantage that on the one hand, you do not lose track of your program, and on the other hand, you can reuse these functions instead of continuously retyping individual statements every time. A function can be called at different places within a program.

3.5.1   Defining Functions

In JavaScript, you usually define a function using the function keyword. Since ECMA-Script 6, there is also a short notation that does not require the keyword, and we'll look at that in Section 3.5.7.

Defining Functions Using a Function Declaration

After the keyword `function`, you write the name of the function followed by a pair of parentheses (the meaning of which we explain in the next note box) and the statements to be executed in braces. For functions, the technical term for this is *function declaration* (analogous to the variable declaration).

Listing 3.107 shows a simple example of such a function declaration. When the function named `showMessage()` is called, it does nothing but output the phrase `Welcome` to the console. However, functions usually consist of several statements that perform much more complex tasks.

```
function showMessage() {
  console.log('Welcome');
}
```

Listing 3.107 Creating a Function Using a Function Declaration

---

Function Names

Function names are subject to the same restrictions as variable names (Section 3.1.2). To better distinguish function names from variable names within the text of this book, we have chosen the convention of always adding the pair of parentheses in the case of function names.

Defining Functions Using a Function Expression

In JavaScript, functions can be created not only via function declarations, but also via *function expressions*. Such function expressions can be used wherever it is permitted to use expressions—that is, wherever the interpreter expects an expression.

In that case, you usually do not specify a function name, which makes the function an anonymous function.

Definition

A function without a name is an *anonymous function*. A function with a name is a *named function*.

An example is shown in Listing 3.108. The function shown there is assigned to the variable `showMessage`. Afterward, the function can be called via this variable using `showMessage()`.

```
const showMessage = function() {
  console.log('Welcome');
}
showMessage();
```

Listing 3.108 Creating a Function Using a Function Expression

---

Note

The name showMessage in Listing 3.108 is not the name of the function, but the name of the variable. The function in the example has no name.

Function Declarations versus Function Expressions

Function declarations and function expressions differ from each other in the following ways:

- In the case of function declarations, the function must be given a name. For function expressions, the name is optional. If you omit it, the function is an anonymous function.

- In the case of function declarations, functions are called via the function name. In the case of function expressions, they are called via the variable to which the function has been assigned (see Listing 3.109).

```
const showMessage = function showMessageFunctionName() {
  console.log('Welcome');
}
showMessage();
// showMessageFunctionName();  // Function call not possible
```

Listing 3.109 With Function Expressions, the Function Cannot Be Called by Its Name

- Function expressions are processed by the interpreter only when it encounters the corresponding statement. This in turn means that such functions can only be used in the statements after that (see Listing 3.110). With function declarations, however, the interpreter ensures that the corresponding functions are also available before the declaration and can thus be called in statements before it (see Listing 3.111).

```
showMessage();  // Function call not possible, this statement produces an error.
const showMessage = function() {
  console.log('Welcome');
}
```

Listing 3.110 Functions Created Using Function Expressions Cannot Be Used before This Expression

```
showMessage();  // Function call possible
function showMessage() {
  console.log('Welcome');
}
```

Listing 3.111 Functions Created Using a Function Declaration Can Already Be Used before This Declaration

Creating Functions via a constructor Function

There is still the possibility to define functions via the *constructor function* named Function. However, this is relatively rarely done in practice, so we've presented this type of function generation with a simple code example in Listing 3.12 just for the sake of completeness.

```
const sum = new Function('x', 'y', 'return x + y');
console.log(sum(7, 8));
// Output: 15
```

Listing 3.112 Creating a Function via the Function Constructor Function

Strict Mode

As mentioned in Section 3.1.1, you can also use strict mode specifically for individual functions. To this end, you need to add the 'use strict'; statement as the first statement at the beginning of the function (see Listing 3.113).

```
function showMessage() {
  'use strict';
  const message = 'Welcome';
  console.log(message);
}
```

Listing 3.113 Using Strict Mode within a Function

3.5.2 Calling Functions

The showMessage() function we just declared can now be called at different places within a program. To do this, simply specify the function name followed by parentheses, as shown in Listing 3.114.

```
showMessage();  // Output: "Welcome"
showMessage();  // Output: "Welcome"
```

Listing 3.114 Calling a Function

The advantage, as shown in Listing 3.115, is that if you now decide to change the message from, say, Welcome to Hello world, you just need to customize this within the function.

```
function showMessage() {
  console.log('Hello world');
}
showMessage();  // Output: "Hello world"
showMessage();  // Output: "Hello world"
```

Listing 3.115 Functions Increase the Reusability of Source Code

3.5.3   Passing and Evaluating Function Parameters

Moving individual statements to a function and then being able to call this function in different places is already quite good in terms of reusability. However, it's often the case that a function requires certain information in order to be executed. Suppose you want to modify the showMessage() function so that it can be used to output an arbitrary message to the console. For this you need a way to pass this message to the function.

Defining Functions with a Parameter

This is where *function parameters* come into play. With their help, you can pass information to a function, and it is then available within the function. To define that a function expects parameters, simply write the names of the parameters in the parentheses after the function name. Regarding the choice of names for parameters—and for function names—the same rules apply as for variable names (Section 3.1.2). Listing 3.116 shows the modified showMessage() function that has been extended by the message parameter. Within the function, the parameters are then each available via their name. The example simply prints the message parameter to the console.

```
function showMessage(message) {
  console.log(message);
}
```

Listing 3.116 Function Declaration with Parameter

Calling Functions with a Parameter

To call a function with a concrete argument, write it inside the parentheses when calling the function, as shown in Listing 3.117 (see the box ahead for a description of the terms *parameter* and *argument*).

```
showMessage('James: Hello John');
showMessage('John: Hello James');
```

Listing 3.117 Calling a Function with an Argument

Parameters versus Arguments

In practice, the terms *parameter* and *argument* are often used synonymously, even though they actually have different meanings. Parameters are what are listed within the *signature* of a function or method. In JavaScript, the signature of a function or method is composed of the name and the number of parameters.

In Listing 3.118, for example, `createNewUser(username, email, password)` is the signature of the `createNewUser()` method. Thus, `username`, `email`, and `password` are the parameters of the function.

```
function createNewUser(username, email, password) {
  /* ... */
}
```

Listing 3.118 Parameters Can Be Found in the Signature of a Function or Method

The term *argument*, on the other hand, usually refers to what is specifically passed as a value to the respective function or method when it is called. In Listing 3.119, for example, in which the `createNewUser()` function is called, the values `John`, `john@example.com`, and `secret` are arguments of the function.

```
const john = createNewUser('John', 'john@example.com', 'secret');
```

Listing 3.119 Arguments Are Used when Calling a Function or Method

Defining Functions with Multiple Parameters

As explained in the preceding box, functions can also accept multiple parameters. In this case, you simply list the individual parameters separated by commas in the function declaration. Listing 3.120 shows an example. Here, the `printPersonInformation()` function is defined, which accepts the three parameters: `firstName`, `lastName`, and `age`. All three parameters are available within the function via their respective names.

```
function printPersonInformation(firstName, lastName, age) {
  console.log(`First name: ${firstName}`);
  console.log(`Last name: ${lastName}`);
  console.log(`Age: ${age}`);
}
```

Listing 3.120 Declaration of a Function with Multiple Parameters

Parameter Data Types

In strictly typed programming languages, you must also define the data types of the individual parameters when declaring the function. In JavaScript, however, this is not necessary.

Next, let's look at how to call such a function that expects multiple parameters.

Calling Functions with Multiple Parameters

To call a function that expects multiple parameters, simply write the corresponding arguments in a row and separate them with commas, as shown in Listing 3.121.

```
printPersonInformation('John', 'Doe', 44);
printPersonInformation('James', 'Doe', 55);
```

Listing 3.121 Calling a Function with Multiple Parameters

The output of the program is shown in Listing 3.122.

```
First name: John
Last name: Doe
Age: 44
First name: James
Last name: Doe
Age: 55
```

Listing 3.122 Output of the Above Program

Calling Functions with Fewer Arguments than Specified Parameters

One special feature of using functions, which distinguishes JavaScript from languages like Java, for example, is that a function can also be called with fewer arguments than parameters defined in the function declaration. The `printPersonInformation()` function discussed previously can be called not only with three arguments, but also with only two arguments, with a single argument, or with no argument at all (see Listing 3.123).

```
printPersonInformation('John', 'Doe');
```

Listing 3.123 Calling a Function with Fewer Arguments than Parameters

However, the parameters for which you do not pass any arguments when calling the function behave within the function like variables that have not been initialized. In other words, they have the value `undefined`. The output for the preceding function call is therefore as shown in Listing 3.124 as the `age` parameter is not defined within the `printPersonInformation()` function.

```
First name: John
Last name: Doe
Age: undefined
```

Listing 3.124 Parameters for Which No Arguments Have Been Passed Have the Value undefined

> **Note**
>
> In compiled programming languages that are strictly typed for this purpose, the compiler returns an error if you try to call a function with fewer or more arguments than existing parameters. This is not the case in JavaScript. Here, you must make your own arrangements as to what should happen when fewer or more arguments are used.

Within the function, you can now check whether an argument has been passed for the respective parameter by testing whether it contains the value undefined. Listing 3.125 shows the adapted printPersonInformation() function, in which each parameter is now checked to see whether a corresponding argument has been passed. Only if this is the case is the respective argument output.

```
function printPersonInformation(firstName, lastName, age) {
  if(firstName !== undefined) {
    console.log(`First name: ${firstName}`);
  }
  if(lastName !== undefined) {
    console.log(`Last name: ${lastName}`);
  }
  if(age !== undefined) {
    console.log(`Age: ${age}`);
  }
}
```

Listing 3.125 Within a Function, the Behavior Can Be Adjusted Depending on the Arguments Passed

Calling Functions with More Arguments than Specified Parameters (Using the arguments Variable)

Conversely, it's also possible to call a function with more arguments than specified parameters, as shown in Listing 3.126.

```
printPersonInformation('John', 'Doe', 44, 1.80);
```

Listing 3.126 Calling a Function with More Arguments than Parameters Defined

However, in this case the value passed is not directly available as a parameter (see Figure 3.19).

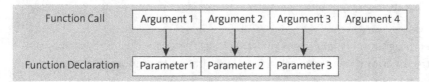

Figure 3.19 If a Function Is Called with More Arguments than Parameters, the Respective Arguments Are Not Directly Available as Parameters within the Function

Transferred to the example, this means that the fourth argument, 1.80, within the printPersonInformation() function is not assigned to any parameter as only the three firstName, lastName, and age parameters were explicitly specified in the function declaration:

```
function printPersonInformation(firstName, lastName, age) {
  ...
}
```

However, there is still a way to access *all* passed arguments within a function, thanks to the arguments variable that is implicitly available within a function. This is an object that contains all passed arguments and provides them via indexes (like an array): arguments[0] brings you to the first argument, arguments[1] to the second, and so on. The length property can also be used to determine how many arguments were passed in total. This, in turn, can be used to allow a variable number of arguments. Listing 3.127 shows the somewhat customized printPersonInformation() function from earlier.

```
function printPersonInformation(firstName, lastName, age) {
  console.log(`First name: ${firstName}`);
  console.log(`Last name: ${lastName}`);
  console.log(`Age: ${age}`);

  if(arguments.length > 3) {
    console.log(`Size: ${arguments[3]}`);
  }
  if(arguments.length > 4) {
    console.log(`Weight: ${arguments[4]}`);

  }
}
printPersonInformation('John', 'Doe', 44, 1.88, 88);
/* Output
First name: John
Last name: Doe
Age: 44
Size: 1.88
```

```
Weight: 88
*/
```

Listing 3.127 Via the arguments Object, All Arguments of a Function Call Are Available within a Function

> **Array-Like Objects**
>
> The arguments object is not an array, but an *array-like object*. Although access to the individual elements in the arguments object works like in an array via the corresponding index, and although a length property is also available for determining the number of elements, the arguments object does not have the methods that real arrays have (as we will discuss in Chapter 4).

The fact that the arguments object is not a true array and that it is therefore not possible to call an array method on it led to some cumbersome code in the past, in which the arguments object was first converted into an array, or array methods were "borrowed" using special techniques to be able to call them on the arguments object after all (details on this later in Chapter 4). However, this was never really satisfactory.

Calling Functions with More Arguments than Specified Parameters (Using Rest Parameters)

Since ES2015, there is therefore an alternative to, even a genuine replacement for the arguments object, which makes its use virtually superfluous. We are referring to rest parameters.

Rest parameters summarize all the arguments in a function call for which no parameter is provided in the function declaration. The principle behind this scenario is shown in Figure 3.20.

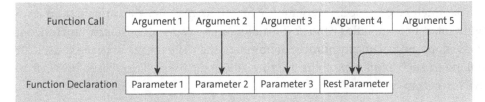

Figure 3.20 The Principle of Rest Parameters

The previous example can be rewritten with rest parameters. The rewritten code is shown in Listing 3.128.

```
function printPersonInformation(firstName, lastName, age, ...restArgs) {
  console.log('First name: ' + firstName);
  console.log('Last name: ' + lastName);
```

```
  console.log('Age: ' + age);
  if(restArgs.length > 0) {
    console.log(`Size: ${restArgs[0]}`);
  }
  if(restArgs.length > 1) {
    console.log(`Weight: ${restArgs[1]}`);
  }
}
printPersonInformation('John', 'Doe', 44, 1.88, 88);
/* Output
First name: John
Last name: Doe
Age: 44
Size: 1.88
Weight: 88
*/
```

Listing 3.128 Rest Parameters Provide All Arguments of a Function Call within a Function for which There Is No Corresponding Parameter in the Function Declaration

As you can see, rest parameters are defined by three consecutive points, immediately followed by an arbitrary parameter name. Rest parameters are also accessed via an index, and here too the length property represents the number of arguments. However, there are significant differences between rest parameters and the arguments object. On the one hand, a rest parameter is a real array; on the other hand, this array contains not all arguments of the function call, but only the arguments for which there is no matching parameter. In Listing 3.128, for example, these are the values 1.88 and 88 for the method call.

Functions with a Variable Number of Arguments

Rest parameters are especially useful for functions that allow a variable number of arguments. These are called *variadic functions*. As an example, consider a sum function that is supposed to sum any number of numbers and write the result to the console. To implement such a function, there are three different possibilities based on what we have learned so far:

- No parameter specified in the function declaration, but access to the arguments object. The function can then be called with any number of arguments.

- An array parameter specified in the function declaration, and access to this array. Strictly speaking, however, it is then no longer a variadic function because the function must always be called with a single argument—namely, the array.

- A rest parameter specified in the function declaration and access to the array implicitly provided. Again, the function can be called with any number of arguments.

While the former implementation is no longer recommended from today's point of view (because one usually wants to do without the arguments object), the latter two implementations will be briefly discussed here.

The implementation using an array is shown in Listing 3.129. In the function declaration, numbers stands for the array of numbers that can be passed. The sum of the numbers is then calculated using a counting loop. The only thing that is important at this point is that an array must always be passed when the function is called.

```javascript
function sum(numbers) {
  let result = 0;
  for (let i = 0; i < numbers.length; i++) {
    result += numbers[i];
  }
  console.log(result);
}
sum([2,3,4,5]);                    // Output: 14
sum([2,3,4,5,6,7,8,9]);            // Output: 44
sum([2,3,4,5,6,7,8,9,10,11]);     // Output: 65
```

Listing 3.129 Implementation of a Variadic Function via Array

The implementation of the function using rest parameters hardly differs from the implementation using an array. The only difference is in the function declaration, as you can see in Listing 3.130. The statements within the function remain the same as rest parameters are also arrays and can therefore be iterated in the same way as in Listing 3.129. What is different, however, is the call of the function: individual arguments are now passed instead of an array.

```javascript
function sum(...numbers) {
  let result = 0;
  for (let i = 0; i < numbers.length; i++) {
    result += numbers[i];
  }
  console.log(result);
}
sum(2,3,4,5);                    // Output: 14
sum(2,3,4,5,6,7,8,9);            // Output: 44
sum(2,3,4,5,6,7,8,9,10,11);     // Output: 65
```

Listing 3.130 Implementation of a True Variadic Function via Rest Parameters

Defining Functions within Functions

In contrast to other languages, such as the oft mentioned Java, JavaScript enables you to define functions within other functions. Such functions are then only visible or valid within the function in which they were defined (more on the topic of visibility or validity will be presented later in Section 3.5.9).

Listing 3.131 shows an example. First, the sum() function is defined here, which adds up two numbers. Inside the function, normalize() is defined, which simply returns the value 0 for negative arguments. However, this function can only be called within the sum() function. Outside of this function, normalize() is not visible, so trying to call it there will result in an error.

```
function sum(x, y) {
  const result =
    normalize(x) +
    normalize(y);

  function normalize(i) {
    if(i < 0) {
      return 0;
    }
    return i;
  }

  return result;
}
console.log(sum(-5, 5));     // Output: 5
console.log(normalize(-5));  // ReferenceError: normalize is not defined
```

Listing 3.131 Functions Can Be Defined within Other Functions

Note

Defining functions inside other functions has the disadvantage that the inner functions are recreated each time the outer function is called. For example, in the previous listing, each call of sum() generates the inner normalize() function.

3.5.4   Defining Return Values

Just as it's possible to *pass* specific information to a function via arguments or parameters, it's also possible to *return* information from within a function to the calling code. This information returned by a function is called a *return value*. You define a return value within a function using the return keyword followed by the value to be returned.

As an example, we'll again use a sum function similar to the one from the previous section, but we'll reduce the number of parameters to two. Listing 3.132 shows a corresponding function that adds up the two parameters x and y, stores the result in the intermediate result variable, and returns it.

```
function sum(x, y) {
  const result = x + y;  // Add the two passed parameters
  return result;         // Return result
}
```

Listing 3.132 A Function That Returns a Value

> **Note**
>
> Alternatively, the intermediate variable can be omitted in the present example, and the result of the expression x + y can be returned directly, as shown in Listing 3.133.
>
> ```
> function sum(x, y) {
>   return x + y;  // Addition und return
> }
> ```
>
> **Listing 3.133** Direct Return of the Result

The result of a function call can then be stored in a variable, for example, and reused in the calling code, as shown in Listing 3.134. Here, the result of the function call sum(5, 5) is stored in the variable resultOne, and the result of the sum(8, 8) function call in the variable resultTwo.

```
const resultOne = sum(5, 5);
const resultTwo = sum(8, 8);
console.log(resultOne); // 10
console.log(resultTwo); // 16
```

Listing 3.134 Values Returned by a Function Can Be Reused within the Calling Code

In principle, functions can return arbitrary return values: numeric values, as just shown, but also strings, Boolean values, objects, arrays, and even functions. In Listing 3.135, you can see an example of a function that returns an object.

```
function createUser(username, email, password) {
  const user = {
    username: username,
    email: email,
    password: password
  }
  return user;
}
const john = createUser('John Doe', 'john.doe@example.com', 'secret');
console.log(john.username);  // John Doe
```

```
console.log(john.email);    // john.doe@example.com
console.log(john.password); // secret
```

Listing 3.135 A Function That Returns an Object

Multiple Return Values

The keyword return can only be followed by a single value or variable; that is, a function can only have a single return value. It isn't possible for a function to return multiple values. But to return several results from a function, it's possible to use the common trick of combining these results in an array or an object and returning this array or object.

However, a function can of course have several different exit points and thus *different* return values—by using if branches, for example.

Note

We'll look at how to create functions that return functions and when this can be useful in Chapter 4.

3.5.5   Defining Default Values for Parameters

The fact that you can call functions in JavaScript with a variable number of arguments—regardless of how many parameters were specified in the function declaration—now leads to the question of how to handle cases within the function where fewer arguments were passed as parameters.

Of course, there is no general answer to this question. Instead, every function must be considered individually: for an addition function that expects two parameters but is passed only one argument, you would probably get a warning or even an error (Section 3.6.6 for information on how to return such errors).

However, it's often possible to continue working within the function by simply using *default values* for omitted arguments. Let's take the createUser() function discussed earlier as an example. It expects three arguments for the userName, email, and password parameters. However, if no password is passed, it's also possible to use a default password.

Since ES2015, there is a relatively simple notation for this using default parameters: As you can see in the password parameter in Listing 3.136, the default value of a parameter is simply written after the parameter, separated by an equal sign. If you now call the createUser() function in the example without passing an argument for the password parameter, the default value DeFaUlTPaSsWoRd is used.

```
function createUser(username, email, password = 'DeFaUlTPaSsWoRd') {
  const user = {
    username: username,
    email: email,
    password: password
  }
  return user;
}
const john = createUser('John Doe', 'john.doe@example.com', 'secret');
console.log(john.username);     // John Doe
console.log(john.email);        // john.doe@example.com
console.log(john.password);     // secret
const james = createUser('James Doe', 'james.doe@example.com');
console.log(james.username);    // James Doe
console.log(james.email);       // james.doe@example.com
console.log(james.password);    // DeFaUlTPaSsWoRd
```

Listing 3.136 Default Values in ES2015

However, providing default values was not always so convenient (and even at this point, not all JavaScript runtime environments support the default parameters introduced in ES2015). Therefore, Listing 3.137 briefly shows how default values were (and still can be) implemented using ES5 methods. The idea is to overwrite or reinitialize the corresponding parameter within the function depending on the value of the corresponding argument: If the parameter is set (in the example, password !== undefined), the corresponding argument continues to be used (in the example password). But if the parameter is not set, it is reinitialized with the default value (in the example, 'DeFaUlT-PaSsWoRd'). The selection operator is normally used for this purpose, which allows a relatively space-saving (although not very clear) notation.

```
function createUser(username, email, password) {
  password = password !== undefined ? password : 'DeFaUlTPaSsWoRd';
  const user = {
    username: username,
    email: email,
    password: password
  }
  return user;
}
const john = createUser('John Doe', 'john.doe@example.com', 'secret');
console.log(john.username);     // John Doe
console.log(john.email);        // john.doe@example.com
console.log(john.password);     // secret
const james = createUser('James Doe', 'james.doe@example.com');
```

```
console.log(james.username);    // James Doe
console.log(james.email);       // james.doe@example.com
console.log(james.password);    // DeFaUlTPaSsWoRd
```

Listing 3.137 Reproducing Default Values Using ES5 Methods

3.5.6 Using Elements from an Array as Parameters

Every now and then, you will want to use values in an array as individual arguments to a function. As an example, we'll use the createUser() function already shown in this chapter, which uses the username, email, and password parameters to create an object that represents the respective user. Let's assume this data, the user name, email address, and password, is available to you as an array, and you want to call the function with this data. There are three ways to achieve this:

- Access the individual values of the array by index and pass the respective value as an argument.
- Use the apply() method, which can be called on functions directly. (This is an advanced technique that we'll introduce in Chapter 4.)
- Use the *spread operator* available since ES2015.

So let's deal with the first and the last option at this point, and we'll look at the second possibility when appropriate. Option 1 is shown in Listing 3.138. The user data is available in the userData1 and userData2 arrays. To create the corresponding objects from these two arrays, you have to access the individual elements in the arrays via userData1[0], userData1[1], and userData1[2] (or userData2, respectively) and then use them as arguments.

```
function createUser(username, email, password) {
  const user = {
    username: username,
    email: email,
    password: password
  }
  return user;
}
const userData1 = ['John Doe', 'john.doe@example.com', 'secret'];
const userData2 = ['James Doe', 'james.doe@example.com', 'password'];
const john = createUser(
  userData1[0],
  userData1[1],
  userData1[2]
);
const james = createUser(
  userData2[0],
```

```
  userData2[1],
  userData2[2]
);
```

Listing 3.138 Using Array Values as Arguments of a Function

Because this procedure involves a relatively large amount of typing, ES2015 introduced the spread operator just mentioned. This operator allows the elements of an array to be spread over the parameters of a function (hence the name *spread*) so that the elements can be used directly as arguments (see Figure 3.21).

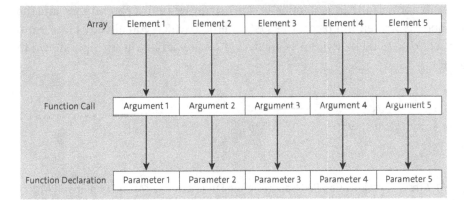

Figure 3.21 The Principle of the Spread Operator

To apply the spread operator to an array, simply prepend three dots to the name of the corresponding array. Listing 3.139 shows the use of the operator related to the preceding example. The effect is the same as in Listing 3.138, but you save yourself some typing as you don't have to manually access the individual indices of the array.

```
const userData1 = ['John Doe', 'john.doe@example.com', 'secret'];
const userData2 = ['James Doe', 'james.doe@example.com', 'password'];
const john = createUser(
  ...userData1
);
const james = createUser(
  ...userData2
);
```

Listing 3.139 Using Array Values as Arguments to a Function Using the Spread Operator

3.5.7 Defining Functions Using Short Notation

We mentioned earlier that since ES2015, there is a short notation for defining functions. More precisely, it's an alternative notation for function expressions. Due to the syntax used, these functions are also called *arrow functions* or *fat arrow functions*. The character string => is a central part of these arrow functions (see also Listing 3.140), which separates the function parameters (on the left side) from the function body (on the right side).

```
(parameters) => {function body}
```

Listing 3.140 Basic Structure of an Arrow Function

The syntax for the parameters and the function body varies for arrow functions depending on how many parameters the function expects and what you want to express. As in normal functions, parameters are usually written in parentheses, and the function body is written in braces. The sum() method, which you already know from previous sections, could be written as an arrow function, as in the example shown in Listing 3.141.

```
const sum = (x, y) => {return x + y;}
// ... is the same as ...
const sum = function(x, y) {
  return x + y;
}
```

Listing 3.141 Arrow Functions Can Be Used to Define Functions in a Much Simpler and More Space-Saving Way

Because this example uses only one statement within the function body, you can even omit the braces. Furthermore, the keyword return can be omitted because the result of the expression x + y is returned automatically. Therefore, the arrow function can be simplified as shown in Listing 3.142.

```
const sum = (x, y) => x + y;
```

Listing 3.142 Braces and the return Keyword Can Be Omitted if Only One Statement Occurs in the Function Body

For functions with one parameter, the parentheses around this parameter can also be omitted (see Listing 3.143).

```
const showMessage = message => console.log(message);
```

Listing 3.143 An Arrow Function with One Parameter

For functions without parameters, on the other hand, you would use an empty pair of parentheses (see Listing 3.144).

```
const printHelloWorld = () => console.log('Hello world');
```

Listing 3.144 An Arrow Function without Parameters

If you want to omit the braces from an arrow function but still return an object, the object must be written in parentheses in order to prevent the object's braces from being misinterpreted as the function body (see Listing 3.145).

```
const createUser = (username, email, password) =>
(
  {
    username: username,
    email: email,
    password: password
  }
);
// ... is the same as ...
function createUser(username, email, password) {
  const user = {
    username: username,
    email: email,
    password: password
  }
  return user;
}
```

Listing 3.145 An Arrow Function That Returns an Object

So, in summary, the notations shown in Table 3.20 are permitted.

Syntax	Meaning
() => { <function body> }	Function without parameters
x => { <function body> }	Function with one parameter
(x, y) => { <function body> }	Function with multiple parameters
<function parameter> => { return x*x }	Function body as a block
<function parameter> => x*x	Function body as a single statement

Table 3.20 The Different Notations for Arrow Functions

Arrow Functions in Practice

Since ES2015, arrow functions have been popular in practice, especially when it comes to using functions as arguments of other functions. We'll show you exactly how to do this in Chapter 4.

> **Other Features of Arrow Functions**
>
> In addition to the simplified syntax compared to functions defined using the `function` keyword, arrow functions offer several other features that simplify much of JavaScript development. However, to understand them, a deeper knowledge of JavaScript is required, so we'll revisit the following points later in this chapter or later in the book:
>
> - The value referenced by `this` arises from the context in which the function is *defined*, not from the context in which it is *executed* (Section 3.5.9 in this chapter).
> - Arrow functions cannot be called using `new`, so they cannot serve as constructor functions (see Chapter 4).
> - The `this` variable cannot be changed (Section 3.5.9 in this chapter).

3.5.8 Modifying Strings via Functions

When you learned about strings at the beginning of this chapter, we also briefly touched on the subject of template strings, which can be used to assemble strings very easily by using placeholders. A special possibility to influence the result of the string evaluation for template strings is offered by *tagged templates*. The template string is prefixed with the name of a function called *tag function* (see Listing 3.146). Internally, the JavaScript interpreter then ensures that the corresponding function (`tagFunction` in the example) is called with two parameters: the first parameter represents the fixed parts, the second parameter the variable parts—that is, the values for the placeholders of the corresponding template string.

```
const name = 'John Doe';
const age = 44;

function tagFunction(strings, ...replacements) {
  ...
}

const message = tagFunction`My name is ${name}, I am ${age} years old.';
console.log(message);
```

Listing 3.146 Tagged Template Example

Within the tag function, you then have the option to access these values and use them, for example, to influence the result value of the function and thus the result of the template string. In Listing 3.147, the tag function ensures that a different string is generated depending on the age passed. The parameter `replacements` contains the dynamic values of the underlying string: `John Doe` and `44` and `88`, respectively. The `strings` parameter contains the strings divided by the dynamic values: `'My name is '`, `', I am '`, and `' years old.'`.

```
function tagFunction(strings, ...replacements) {
  const name = replacements[0]; // "John Doe"
  const age = replacements[1];  // 44 or 88, respectively
  if (age > 80) {
    return `${strings[0]}${replacements[0]}.`;
    // --> "My name is John Doe."
  }
  return `${strings[0]}${name}${strings[1]}${age}${strings[2]}.`;
  // --> "My name is John Doe, I am 44 years old."
}

const name = 'John Doe';
let age = 44;

let message = tagFunction`My name is ${name}, I am ${age} years old`;
console.log(message);
// My name is John Doe, I am 44 years old.

age = 88;
message = tagFunction`My name is ${name}, I am ${age} years old`;
console.log(message);
// My name is John Doe
```

Listing 3.147 Implementation and Usage of a Tag Function

3.5.9 Functions in Detail

To be comfortable with using functions, it's necessary for a good JavaScript developer to also know what happens behind the scenes when functions are called. So in this section, we'll show you what the terms *call stack*, *execution context*, and *scope* are all about.

The Function Call Stack

Within a JavaScript application, all statements are executed by the interpreter sequentially, from top to bottom. If the interpreter now encounters a function call during execution, it jumps into this function and executes all the statements contained therein. At the end of the respective function, the interpreter jumps out of the function again and continues with the execution of the statement following the function call in the program. If the called function returns a value, this value can be used in the calling code (see Figure 3.22).

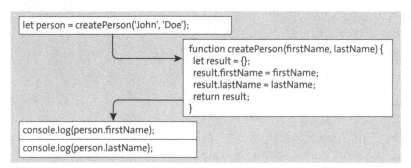

Figure 3.22 Sequence of Function Calls

Internally, as with other programming languages, a *function call stack* (or *method call stack*) is managed for this purpose. This is a stack of functions that can be used to trace which function called which other function.

Consider the (admittedly somewhat meaningless) example in Listing 3.148. It shows four functions that call each other in sequence: the doSomething() function calls the doSomethingB() function, which in turn calls the doSomethingC() function, which then calls the doSomethingD() function. What happens now in detail with the individual function calls is illustrated in Figure 3.23.

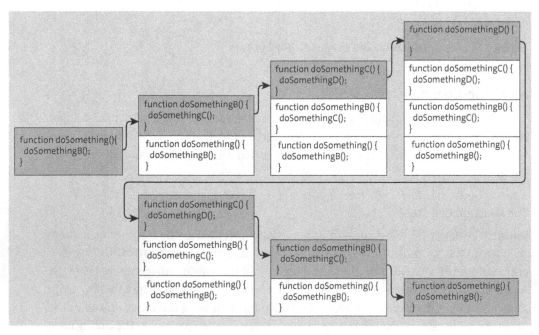

Figure 3.23 Function or Method Call Stack

Each time the interpreter jumps into a called function, information about that function is placed on the call stack. If the interpreter jumps out of the function again, the corresponding information is removed from the call stack again.

```
function doSomething() {
  doSomethingB();
}
function doSomethingB() {
  doSomethingC();
}
function doSomethingC() {
  doSomethingD();
}
function doSomethingD() {

}
```

Listing 3.148 Code Example to Illustrate the Call Stack

Execution Contexts

Whenever you jump into a new function, you also enter a new *execution context* (this contains the information we just mentioned). This execution context determines, among other things, which variables and functions are available. Overall, there are three different types of execution contexts, analogous to the different types of Java-Script code:

- **Execution context of the global code**
  Code that is not located within a function is also called *global code* (i.e., code that can be reached from anywhere). Consequently, the context in which this code is executed is also called the *global execution context*. Within a program, there can only be one global execution context.

- **Execution context of a function call**
  Code within a function is also called *function code*. This code is only accessible within the respective function. The execution context of functions determines which variables, which other functions (within the function), which parameters (according to the function signature), and which concrete arguments are available. Consequently, a separate, new execution context is created for each function call.

- **Execution context of an eval() function call**
  The eval() method is used to interpret and execute source text passed in the form of a string. When the function is called, a separate form of execution context is created for the code passed (as a string). But because the eval() method should be used with caution and the use of this method is considered a bad practice, we won't discuss it in detail in this book.

> **Note**
> There is only one global execution context, but there can be multiple execution contexts for functions because a new execution context is created for each function call.

An execution context essentially specifies the following three things (see also Figure 3.24).

- **Scope**
  The variables, functions, and, in the case of an execution context for function code, the parameters and arguments that are directly available in the respective execution context.

- **Scope chain**
  Defines where to search for variables and functions—for example, if identifiers are used in the code for which no corresponding variable or function with the same name was found in the respective (own) scope.

- **Context object**
  Within an execution context, the special this property is available, which references the context object.

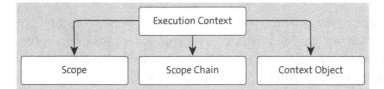

Figure 3.24 Execution Contexts Contain Important Information

Scopes

The scope or visibility is the area in a program in which a variable or function is valid or visible and can therefore be used. The execution context contains information about this scope. For programming languages, the scope can be set in two different ways, which are mutually exclusive:

- A *lexical* (or *static*) scope means that the scope is derived from the surrounding source text.

- A *dynamic* scope means that the scope is dynamically derived at runtime depending on the execution of the program.

Thus, as both types are mutually exclusive, only one of them can be used within a programming language. In the case of JavaScript, the scopes are determined lexically. Take a look at Figure 3.25. The rounded rectangles each represent scopes of variables and functions. The outermost rectangle represents the global scope: the variables defined here (number1 and number2) and the function someFunction() are visible throughout the program. The latter, in turn, defines its own scope: the variable result and the function sum() are only visible within the function someFunction(). They cannot be accessed from outside this function. This principle continues accordingly for nested functions: the variables and functions defined within the sum() function are only visible within the sum() function (and all functions nested below it).

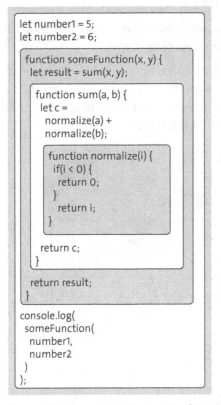

```
let number1 = 5;
let number2 = 6;

function someFunction(x, y) {
  let result = sum(x, y);

  function sum(a, b) {
    let c =
      normalize(a) +
      normalize(b);

    function normalize(i) {
      if(i < 0) {
        return 0;
      }
      return i;
    }

    return c;
  }

  return result;
}

console.log(
  someFunction(
    number1,
    number2
  )
);
```

Figure 3.25 Scopes Are Determined Statically in JavaScript

Note

Global variables and global functions are visible everywhere in a program. Variables and functions defined within a function are only visible within this function and in all other functions defined within this function.

Scope Chain

If an identifier (e.g., the name of a variable, a function, or a parameter) is used within the code but there is no variable, function, or parameter for this identifier in the respective execution context, the *scope chain* is used to search in the preceding or higher-level execution contexts.

Take a look at the code in Figure 3.26. Among other things, it shows the three variables x, y, and z, each defined in a different scope: x is defined in the global scope, y within the function someFunction(), and z within the nested function someFunctionB().

Within the latter function, the three variables are now accessed. The variable z is in the scope of the someFunctionB() function and is therefore output directly.

The variable y, on the other hand, is not directly in the scope of someFunctionB(), which is why the interpreter now moves upward in the scope chain and into the scope of the someFunction() function to search it for the variable (successfully).

For the variable x, the whole process works in the same way: x is not in the scope of someFunctionB(), which again means that the interpreter continues searching in the scope of someFunction(). This time, however, it doesn't find it there either, and continues to move up the chain to the global scope (and finds it there).

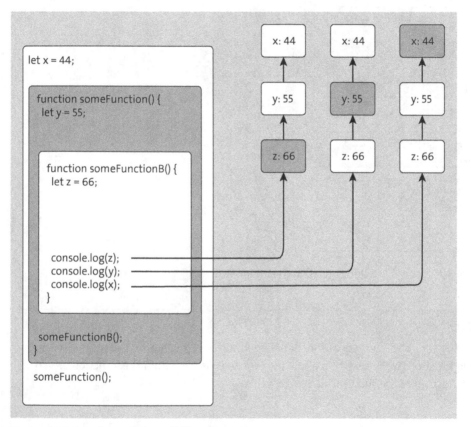

Figure 3.26 Principle of the Visibility Chain

Context Object

We've mentioned the this keyword before. This keyword is used within an object method (or a constructor) to address the respective object instance, the current object—that is, "this" object. More precisely, this object is called the *context object*.

You can think of this a bit like a property of a function that, when called, is assigned the value of the object on which it is called. (More precisely, this is even an implicit parameter, just like arguments, that is available within the function for every function call.)

So depending on whether a function is called as a global function or as a method of an object, this has a different value. Let's first consider the simple case of an object method in which a property of the object is read via this, as shown in Listing 3.149.

```
const person = {
  name: 'John',                // Object property
  getName: function() {
    return this.name;
  }
}

console.log(person.getName()); // Output: John
```

Listing 3.149 The this Keyword in the Context of an Object Refers to the Object

The output of the program is John, as expected, because this refers to the person object here.

Let's go one step further and also define a global function getNameGlobal() (see Listing 3.150).

```
function getNameGlobal() {
  return this.name;
}
console.log(getNameGlobal()); // undefined
```

Listing 3.150 A Simple Global Function in which this Is Used

When this function is called, it refers to the global context. There, the variable name is not defined, so you get undefined as the return value.

You can easily test that this in a global function refers to the global object by creating a global variable name (using var!) and calling the getNameGlobal() function again, as shown in Listing 3.151.

```
var name = "global name";
function getNameGlobal() {
    return this.name;
}
console.log(getNameGlobal()); // Output: global name
```

Listing 3.151 The this Keyword in the Global Context Refers to the Global Object

> **Note**
>
> Under the JavaScript Node.js runtime (see Chapter 17), the code shown in Listing 3.151 only returns undefined as output.

Now let's take two more objects, each defining the name property and reusing the global function getNameGlobal() as a method. This is achieved by referencing the global function from the object method as shown in Listing 3.152.

```
const person = {
  name : 'James',
  getName : getNameGlobal
}

const artist = {
  name : 'Kyuss',
  getName : getNameGlobal
}
console.log(person.getName()); // Output: James
console.log(artist.getName()); // Output: Kyuss
```

Listing 3.152 The this Keyword Refers to the Context of the Function

Now, at this point, it should be clear that this is set dynamically on the function call: getNameGlobal() as the object method in the context of person returns the value James and in the context of artist the value Kyuss.

Figure 3.27 shows a graphical illustration of this relationship.

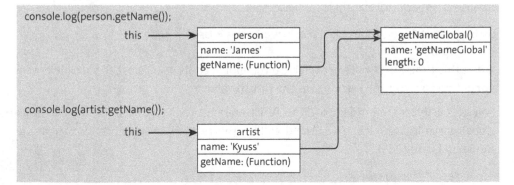

Figure 3.27 The this Keyword Is Determined Dynamically on Function Call

So the this variable has a different value depending on the context in which the function is called. In summary, the following rules apply:

- When calling a global function, this refers to the global object or is undefined in strict mode.
- If a function is called as an object method, this refers to the object.
- If a function is called as a constructor function (details to follow later in Chapter 4), this refers to the object created by the function call.

3.5.10 Calling Functions through User Interaction

In the previous sections, you learned a lot about functions. At this point, we'll give you a little preview of Chapter 5 by showing you how to call a function within a web page by pressing a button.

This process can be explained fairly quickly (we'll deal with the details in Chapter 5). The principle is known to you already from the previous chapter: the event listeners that enable you to call specific functions when an event occurs. (We'll come back to them in detail in Chapter 6.)

Now, to react to the click of a button and call a function, simply add an event listener for the click event of the corresponding button. The HTML code for this is shown in Listing 3.153, the JavaScript code in Listing 3.154. This is a simple web page where a small form can be used to calculate the sum of two numbers. The form contains three input fields (for the two input numbers and the result) as well as a button that is to trigger the calculation.

In the JavaScript code, the addEventListener() method we introduced in the previous chapter is used to register an event listener for the DOMContentLoaded event. The anonymous function passed here as an event listener isn't executed until all elements on the web page are loaded. This ensures that the input fields and button are present when accessed further down in the code.

Inside this event listener, another event listener is registered to be executed when the click event is triggered: the calculateSum() function. This, in turn, accesses the two input fields, reads their values, adds them up, and uses the showResult() function to display the result in the third input field.

```html
<!DOCTYPE html>
<html>
<head lang="en">
  <meta charset="UTF-8">
  <title>Example</title>
  <link rel="stylesheet" href="styles/main.css" type="text/css">
</head>
<body>
<div class="container">
  <div class="row">
    <label for="field1">X</label> <input id="field1" type="text" value="5">
  </div>
  <div class="row">
    <label for="field2">Y</label> <input id="field2" type="text" value="5">
  </div>
  <div class="row">
    <label for="result">Result: </label> <input id="result" type="text">
```

```
      <button id="button-calculate-sum">Calculate sum</button>
    </div>
  </div>
  <script src="scripts/main.js"></script>
</body>
</html>
```

Listing 3.153 HTML Code

```
document.addEventListener('DOMContentLoaded', function() {
  const button = document.getElementById('button-calculate-sum');
  button.addEventListener('click', calculateSum);
});

function calculateSum() {
  const x = parseInt(document.getElementById('field1').value);
  const y = parseInt(document.getElementById('field2').value);
  const result = x + y;
  showResult(result);
}

function showResult(result) {
  const resultField = document.getElementById('result');
  resultField.value = result;
}
```

Listing 3.154 A Simple Function

3.6   Responding to Errors and Handling Them Correctly

When running programs, errors can occur in various ways—for example, when a function is called with invalid arguments, when a user enters incorrect login information, or the like. As a developer, you need to know how to react to errors within a program on the one hand and how to trigger errors yourself on the other. Distinctions are made between different types of errors, as described ahead.

3.6.1   Syntax Errors

Syntax errors occur when the syntactic rules of JavaScript are disregarded—for example, if you omit the parentheses around the condition in an if statement or a while loop, or if you write funktion instead of function (i.e., with a *k* instead of a *c*) in the function declaration (see Listing 3.155).

```
funktion divide(x, y) {
  return normalize(x) / normalize(y);
}
function normalize(x) {
  return x <= 0 ? 1 : x;
}
```

Listing 3.155 Example of a Syntax Error

Syntax errors are not detected in JavaScript before runtime, because JavaScript is an interpreted programming language, not a compiled one (see Chapter 1). Depending on the editor or development environment you're using, however, it may also point out syntax errors during development.

> **Finding Syntax Errors**
>
> Syntax errors are usually easy to find because the interpreter points exactly to the erroneous code location (including the line number).

3.6.2 Runtime Errors

Runtime errors are errors that occur only at runtime—that is, when a program is executed. In JavaScript, the syntax errors just mentioned actually also fall into this category, because they don't occur before runtime either. What's really meant by runtime errors, though, are not syntax errors but errors that wouldn't occur before runtime even in compiled programs.

Another distinction is as follows: syntax errors always occur when the erroneous piece of code is *interpreted*, whereas runtime errors only occur when the erroneous piece of code is *executed* as well—for example, when you access variables within your program that have not been declared, or when you call a function that is not defined, as shown in Listing 3.156. Here, within the divide() function, an attempt is made (thanks to a typo) to call the normalized() method. When the entire code is loaded by the interpreter, there is still no error message (which would be shown in the case of syntax errors). The two calls of the normalize() function do not lead to an error yet either. Only when the divide() function in the last line of the sample code, and thus also the nonexistent normalized() function, is called does the program return an error message.

```
function divide(x, y) {
  return normalized(x) / normalized(y);
}
function normalize(x) {
  return x <= 0 ? 1 : x;
}
```

```
console.log(normalize(-2));   // Output: 1
console.log(normalize(5));    // Output: 5
console.log(divide(-2, 5));   // ReferenceError: normalized is not defined
```

Listing 3.156 Example of a Runtime Error

Finding Runtime Errors

Runtime errors are somewhat more difficult to find than syntax errors because the erroneous part of a program must also be executed. For smaller programs, this is quickly tested. However, the more extensive a program is—it isn't uncommon for a program to contain several hundred thousand lines of source code or more—the less simple it becomes. In Chapter 21, you'll see, among other things, how to use unit tests to test your source code automatically. For finding runtime errors, such unit tests can be of enormous help.

3.6.3   Logic Errors

Last, but not least, *logic errors* or *bugs* refer to those types of errors that are caused by incorrect logic of your program. As a rule, logic errors are caused by code that is supposed to solve a certain problem according to the requirements but has been implemented incorrectly by the developer. They can also arise when something in the program behaves differently than you suspect (e.g., due to the peculiarities of a library).

Let's take a look at the example in Listing 3.157. Here, a "small" logic error has been integrated compared to Listing 3.156: the normalize() method now returns 1 only for values less than 0, but no longer for values equal to 0. However, this bug is not noticeable every time the divide() function is called: the calls divide(5, -1) and divide(5, -2) work without problems because the second parameter is assigned the value 1 and the result of the divide() function remains valid. Only the call in the last line of the example produces an error (or returns the value Infinity and is therefore incorrect).

```
function divide(x, y) {
  return normalize(x) / normalize(y);
}
function normalize(x) {
  return x < 0 ? 1 : x;
}
console.log(divide(5, -1));   // Output: 5
console.log(divide(5, -2));   // Output: 5
console.log(divide(5, 0));    // Output: Infinity
```

Listing 3.157 Example of a Logic Error

Bugs

The term *bug* stems from the story that one of the first errors in a computer program was actually caused by a (real) bug.

Finding Logic Errors

Logic errors are the most difficult errors to find. Unlike runtime errors, they do not always occur when the faulty part of the program is executed, but only when certain conditions are met. Here too the unit tests mentioned earlier can help, and we'll present them in Chapter 21.

3.6.4 The Principle of Error Handling

Now, the inevitable question arises: How can the previously mentioned error types be found? In the case of syntax errors, the answer should be clear: as already indicated, these errors are relatively easy to find. It's usually sufficient to execute the respective program part once in the corresponding runtime environment. However, as mentioned earlier, editors and development environments often point out syntax errors already during development.

You can react to runtime errors with *error handling*, which will be the topic of this section. In Section 3.7, we'll then introduce a tool that can help you detect and eliminate logic errors.

If a runtime error occurs (you can also say that "an error is thrown"), JavaScript (at least within browsers) provides two options to *react* to the respective error (or "catch the error") and *handle* it. The individual steps are shown in Figure 3.28.

First, you have the possibility to catch errors via *try-catch code blocks* (more about this in a moment). If the error is not caught by such a try-catch code block, you have the additional option of reacting to the error via the window.onerror event handler (you'll find general information about event handlers and the underlying event-driven programming in Chapter 6). However, this can only be done within browsers because only they provide the window object. If the error isn't responded to here either, it eventually ends up with the user, which usually means that the error is output to the console.

Exceptions and Exception Handling

In software development, *exceptions* is often used as an alternative to the term *errors*, and *error handling* therefore also frequently is referred to as *exception handling*.

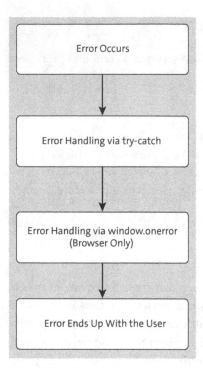

Figure 3.28 The Lifecycle of JavaScript Error Handling in the Browser

3.6.5   Catching and Handling Errors

First, let's look at how error handling works with try-catch code blocks. The name try-catch code blocks traces back to the keywords that are used here:

- The try keyword can be used to execute a block of code that potentially produces errors.

- Via catch, it's possible to catch or react to errors.

Figure 3.29 illustrates this principle, and Listing 3.158 shows the basic structure of a try-catch code block. The keyword try is used to initiate the code block (in braces) that could potentially throw errors. After the closing brace, you use the catch keyword to define the block of code (also in braces) that should be executed when an error occurs. After catch, you define the name of the error object in parentheses. This can be accessed afterward in the catch code block. You can think of this roughly as a kind of function parameter: the name can also be freely chosen.

In JavaScript, there are different types of errors, each represented by a different object type. Table 3.21 shows an overview of the error types that JavaScript provides by default. In addition, you have the possibility to create your own error types.

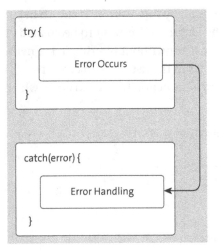

Figure 3.29 The Principle of Error Handling Using try-catch

```
try {
  // Execute code that potentially produces errors
} catch (error) {
  // Handle the error
}
```

Listing 3.158 The Basic Structure of a try-catch Block

Error Type	Description
Error	Base type from which other error types are derived.
EvalError	May occur if the eval() function is used incorrectly.
RangeError	Occurs when a number is outside a range of values—for example, when trying to create a negative length array: new Array(-5).
ReferenceError	Occurs when an object (a reference type) is expected at a specific position. Typically, this type of error occurs when trying to access a nonexistent variable.
SyntaxError	Occurs when an error is found in the syntax when parsing the source code with the eval() function.
TypeError	Occurs when a variable or parameter is called with an invalid type.
URIError	Occurs when an error has occurred in connection with a URI (Uniform Resource Identifier)—for example, when incorrect arguments are passed to the encodeURI() or decodeURI() function.

Table 3.21 The Different Types of Errors

An example program containing code that can potentially throw errors is shown in Listing 3.159. The createArray() function expects the length of the array to be created as parameter and passes this value to the array constructor without filtering it. If a negative or even invalid numeric value is now entered (as in the listing, using the prompt() call), the array constructor and thus the createArray() function throws an error, which is caught by the try-catch block.

```
const userInput = prompt('Please enter the length of the array');
const length = parseInt(userInput);
let array;
try {
  array = createArray(length);
} catch (error) {
  console.log(error.name);       // Output: RangeError
  console.log(error.message);    // Invalid array length
}

function createArray(length) {
  return new Array(length);
}
```

Listing 3.159 Example of the Use of a try-catch Block

The error object, which is available inside the catch block via the variable usually named error, provides two properties that can be used to get more detailed information about the reason for the error (see Table 3.22).

Property	Description
name	Error type
message	Description of the error

Table 3.22 The Properties of an Error Object

Other Properties of the Error Object

Depending on the runtime environment, the error object still has other properties, such as the fileName, lineNumber, and columnName properties in Firefox, which can be used to draw conclusions about the position in the source code where the corresponding error occurred. However, because these properties are not standardized, you shouldn't use them (or at least not in production systems).

3.6.6   Triggering Errors

For an error to be caught, it must naturally have been triggered and thrown somewhere. In the examples we've looked at so far, this happens through the standard JavaScript methods we called. However, you also have the option of throwing errors within a function yourself.

To this end, you use the throw keyword, as shown in the example in Listing 3.160. After the throw keyword, you include the error object that represents the respective error. In the example, an error is thrown within the checkAge() function if the argument passed is negative.

```
console.log(checkAge(22));    // true
console.log(checkAge(-22));   // Error: Age must not be negative
function checkAge(age) {
  if (age < 0) {
    throw new Error('Age must not be negative.');
  } else {
    return true;
  }
}
```

Listing 3.160 A Function That Throws an Error

If the interpreter hits throw, it will jump out of the respective function. The statements that follow in the function therefore are no longer executed.

So you could also adapt the example as shown in Listing 3.161 as the last statement (return true) wouldn't be executed anyway if the throw statement was executed before.

```
console.log(checkAge(22));    // true
console.log(checkAge(-22));   // Error: Age must not be negative
function checkAge(age) {
  if (age < 0) {
    throw new Error('Age must not be negative.');
  }
  return true;  // In case of error, this statement will no longer be executed.
}
```

Listing 3.161 The Code After throw Is No Longer Executed in Case of an Error

Within a function, of course, different errors can be thrown at different points, as shown in Listing 3.162. Here, the checkAge() function has been extended by a test that checks whether the passed argument is a numeric value at all. If this is not the case, a (different) error is thrown.

```
console.log(checkAge(22));          // true
console.log(checkAge("John Doe"));  // Error: Age must be a number
function checkAge(age) {
  if(isNaN(parseFloat(age))) {
    throw new Error('Age must be a number.');
  } else if (age < 0) {
    throw new Error('Age must not be negative.');
  }
  return true;  // In case of error, this statement will no longer be executed.
}
```

Listing 3.162 One Function Can Throw Multiple Errors

The error you throw should ideally allow you to draw conclusions about the nature of the error. The example could be adapted to throw a TypeError in case of a "not a number" value and a RangeError in case of a negative number value (see Listing 3.163).

```
console.log(checkAge(22));          // true
console.log(checkAge("John Doe"));  // TypeError: Age must be a number
function checkAge(age) {
  if(isNaN(parseFloat(age))) {
    throw new TypeError('Age must be a number.');
  } else if (age < 0) {
    throw new RangeError('Age must not be negative.');
  }
  return true;  // In case of error, this statement will no longer be executed.
}
```

Listing 3.163 Use Different Error Objects Depending on the Type of Error

One more thing to consider with regard to catching errors: For example, if you call the checkAge() function several times with invalid arguments, as seen in Listing 3.164, without surrounding the individual function calls with a try-catch block, only one error is issued for the first function call with an invalid argument, since the following statements (and thus the following function calls of—in this case—checkAge()) are no longer executed. In order to catch the individual errors, you need to surround the individual function calls with a try-catch block as seen in Listing 3.165.

```
console.log(checkAge(22));          // true
console.log(checkAge("John Doe"));  // TypeError: Age must be a number
console.log(checkAge(-22));         // will not be called
```

Listing 3.164 As Soon as the checkAge() Function Throws an Error, the Following Function Calls Are Ignored by the Interpreter

```
try {
  console.log(checkAge(22));           // true
} catch(error) {
  console.log(error);                  // will not be called
}
try {
  console.log(checkAge("John Doe")); // no output
} catch(error) {
  console.log(error);                  // TypeError: Age must be a number
}
try {
  console.log(checkAge(-22));          // no output
} catch(error) {
  console.log(error);                  // RangeError: Age must not be negative
}
```

Listing 3.165 To Be Able to React to Individual Errors, the Corresponding Function Calls Must Be Surrounded by a try-catch Block

Figure 3.30 once again illustrates the relationship between throwing an error and catching an error.

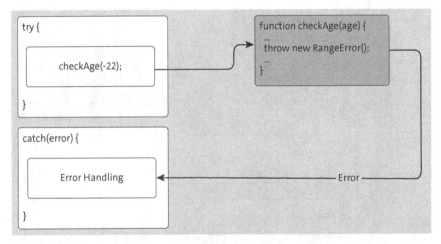

Figure 3.30 The throw Keyword Can Be Used to Throw Errors

Number of catch Blocks

In each try-catch block, you can use at most one catch entry. In other programming languages, like Java, this restriction doesn't apply: you can directly catch different types of errors via several catch statements in a try-catch block. However, because JavaScript doesn't apply the strict typing used in Java, it doesn't offer this possibility—at least, not according to the ECMAScript standard: the Firefox browser, or rather its underlying runtime environment, does support this via a special syntax (see *https://developer.mozilla.org/en-US/docs/Web/JavaScript/Reference/Statements/try...catch*). Still, you should generally refrain from using nonstandard features in production systems.

3.6.7   Errors and the Function Call Stack

The exact relationship between thrown errors and the function call stack is shown in Figure 3.31. If an error is thrown inside a function, the interpreter jumps out of that function, as you already know. If the error is not caught in the function to which the interpreter jumps (i.e., the function that called the error-throwing function), the interpreter jumps out of that function as well. If the error is still not caught in the next function (or more precisely, in the previous function in the function call stack), the interpreter jumps out here as well. This is done until the error is caught. If the error is not caught in any function and also not in the global code, the error ends up with the user—that is, on the console—and the application is terminated. (That isn't the case in the figure, though; here the error is caught by the doSomething() function.)

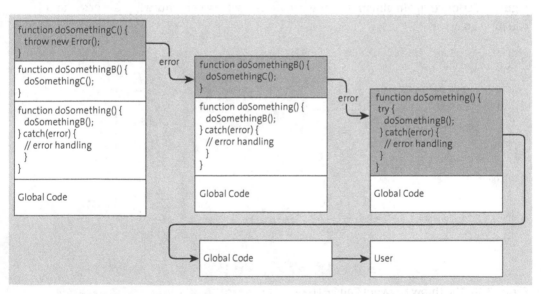

Figure 3.31 Errors That Are Caught and Handled Do Not End Up with the User

You now know how to throw errors and how to catch errors. Finally, there remains the question of how and at what point in the code it's best to handle errors. However, there is no general answer to this question as the way in which errors are handled heavily depends on the type of error. Basically, keep in mind that you should only forward errors to the user if the user can actually do something with the error information or, ideally, knows how to prevent the error in the future.

Let's take the checkAge() function from earlier as an example. If this is used, for example, in the context of a web application in which the user is to enter his or her age in a form field (see Listing 3.166), it would make sense to inform the user if the entries are incorrect. You can see the JavaScript code that does just that in Listing 3.167. In this code, the error message is written as the text of a specially designed HTML element (with the ID message).

```
<!DOCTYPE html>
<html>
<head lang="en">
  <meta charset="UTF-8">
  <title>Example</title>
  <link rel="stylesheet" href="styles/main.css" type="text/css">
</head>
<body>
<div class="container">
  <div class="row">
    <div id="message"></div>
  </div>
  <div class="row">
    <label for="age">Enter your age:</label>
    <input id="age" type="text" value="16">
  </div>
  <div class="row">
    <button onclick="enter()">Next</button>
  </div>
</div>
<script src="scripts/main.js"></script>
</body>
</html>
```

Listing 3.166 A Simple HTML Form That Allows Users to Enter Their Age

```
function enter() {
  const age = document.getElementById('age').value;
  try {
    checkAge(age);
  } catch (error) {
    document.getElementById('message').textContent = error.message;
    return;
  }
}
```

Listing 3.167 User-Friendly Output of an Error Message

Forward Error to the User or Not?

Errors that the user can respond to or work around should also be forwarded to the user. On the other hand, errors the user can't handle anyway should either be solved in other ways within the program or at least be written to the error console via `console.error()`.

3.6.8   Calling Certain Statements Regardless of Errors That Have Occurred

In some cases, whether an error occurs or not, you may want to execute special statements after executing the error-producing code. In this case, you can use the `finally` keyword to place yet another block of code with these statements at the end of a try-catch block. All statements in this `finally` block are executed in any case: whether an error occurs or not (see Figure 3.32).

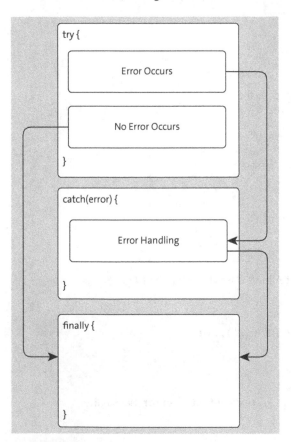

Figure 3.32 The Principle of try-catch-finally

The basic structure and the corresponding source code are shown in Listing 3.168.

```
try {
  // Execute code that potentially produces errors
} catch (error) {
  // Handle the error
} finally {
  // Everything that is written here will always be executed, regardless of
  // whether an error has occurred or not.
}
```

Listing 3.168 The Basic Structure of a try-catch-finally Block

The question arises in which cases the use of such a finally block can be useful. To answer this, we need to digress a bit and explain it with a practical example. So, imagine you want to access a database with JavaScript. Typically, such access consists of three steps:

1. Opening a database connection
2. The actual access, such as selecting specific data records (e.g., all users with the name John)
3. Closing the database connection

These three steps are shown (simplified, for didactic reasons) in an example program in Listing 3.169. Step 1 is represented by the openDatabaseConnection() function, step 2 by the getUsersByName() function, and step 3 by the closeDatabaseConnection() function. The accessDatabase() function in turn calls these three functions in exactly the order just described.

Let's assume that an error occurs in step 2—that is, in the getUsersByName() function—because a wrong argument is passed, as shown in the listing. In the accessDatabase() function, the call of getUsersByName() isn't surrounded by a try-catch block, and therefore the error is passed on (in the example, to the global code) so that the closeDatabaseConnection() function is no longer called and the database connection is no longer closed (see also Figure 3.33).

In practice, if many errors occur, this can quickly lead to many such unclosed connections, which can impact the performance of a system.

```
function openDatabaseConnection() {
  console.log('Database connection open');
}

function closeDatabaseConnection() {
  console.log('Database connection closed');
}
```

```
function getUsersByName(name) {
  if(typeof name !== 'string') {
    throw new TypeError('String expected');
  }
  /* ... */
}

function accessDatabase() {
  openDatabaseConnection();    // 'Database connection open'
  getUsersByName(22);          // TypeError: String expected
  closeDatabaseConnection();   // will not be executed
}
accessDatabase();
```

Listing 3.169 Already Known: If an Error Is Not Caught, Subsequent Statements in the Function Will Not Be Executed

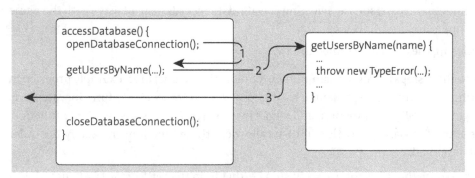

Figure 3.33 Without a try-catch Block, the Error Is Not Caught, and the Following Function Call Is No Longer Executed

You already know from the previous steps that you can easily work around this issue, as shown in Listing 3.170, by surrounding the call of getUsersByName() with a try-catch block.

Now the error can be handled within the accessDatabase() function, and the following statements (in this case, the closeDatabaseConnection() function) are executed as well (see also Figure 3.34).

```
function accessDatabase() {
  openDatabaseConnection();    // 'Database connection open'
  try {
    getUsersByName(22);
  } catch(error) {
    console.error(error);      // TypeError: String expected
```

```
  }
  closeDatabaseConnection();   // 'Database connection closed'
}
```

Listing 3.170 Also Known: If Errors Are Caught, Subsequent Statements Are Executed in the Current Function

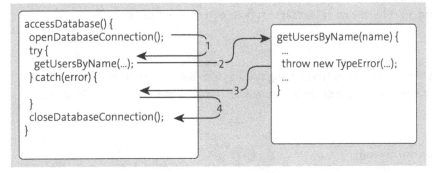

Figure 3.34 Using a try-catch Block, the Error Is Caught, and Subsequent Statements Are Executed

However, you may also want to handle the error within the `accessDatabase()` function, but still pass an error to the caller of the `accessDatabase()` function to inform them that something has gone wrong. This can be very useful. Imagine that the `accessDatabase()` function is called within a web application, and an error occurs. It then makes perfect sense that the function itself handles the error, but also that the calling code ensures that an appropriate error message is displayed to the user.

Listing 3.171 shows the corresponding adjusted example. The `accessDatabase()` function still calls the `getUsersByName()` function in a `try-catch` block and takes care of (database-related) error handling. To inform the caller of `accessDatabase()`—that is, the `showUsers()` function—about such errors, a database error is thrown via `throw new DBError()` (the `DBError` error object does not exist and is only used here to illustrate the concept). The `showUsers()` function then takes care of displaying an appropriate (user-friendly) message to the user. The only problem is that the `closeDatabaseConnection()` function is not called in the case of an error (see also Figure 3.35) because the process jumped out of the `accessDatabase()` function.

```
function accessDatabase() {
  openDatabaseConnection();     // 'Database connection open'
  try {
    getUsersByName(22);
  } catch(error) {
    console.log(error);         // TypeError: String expected
    throw new DBError('Error communicating with the database');
  }
```

```
    closeDatabaseConnection();    // will not be executed
}

function showUsers() {
  try {
    accessDatabase();
  } catch(error) {
    document.getElementById('message').textContent = error.message;
  }
}
```

Listing 3.171 If an Error Occurs That Is Caught via a catch Block and a New Error Is Thrown within This catch Block, Subsequent Statements in the Current Function Are No Longer Executed

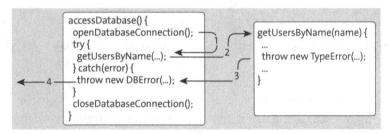

Figure 3.35 If You Throw a New Error within the catch Block, Subsequent Statements Are No Longer Executed

Of course, this can be counteracted by calling the closeDatabaseConnection() function in two places in the code, as in Listing 3.172: once after the whole try-catch block; and once inside the catch block, but before the new error is thrown. This has the disadvantage, though, that the function call is written in both places. For such simple cases as here in the example, where only a single function call occurs twice, this may still be tolerable. However, as soon as several statements are to be executed in both cases (i.e., in the case of an error and in the normal case), the code is accordingly difficult to maintain.

```
openDatabaseConnection();    // 'Database connection open'
try {
  getUsersByName(22);
} catch(error) {
  console.log(error);        // TypeError: String expected
  closeDatabaseConnection(); // 'Database connection closed'
  throw new DBError('Error communicating with the database');
}
closeDatabaseConnection();    // will not be executed
```

Listing 3.172 Not Good: The Code for Closing the Database Connection Is in Two Places in the Code

This is exactly where the `finally` block comes into play: it solves this problem in that the statements in such a `finally` block are executed in all cases, before any new errors are thrown within the corresponding `catch` block. The example could therefore also be adapted as in Listing 3.173. The progress of this program is shown in Figure 3.36.

```
openDatabaseConnection();     // 'Database connection open'
try {
  getUsersByName(22);
} catch(error) {
  console.log(error);         // TypeError: String expected
  throw new DBError('Error communicating with the database');
} finally {
  closeDatabaseConnection(); // 'Database connection closed'
}
```

Listing 3.173 Statements in the finally Block Are Executed in Any Case, Even if a New Error Is Thrown within the Corresponding catch Block

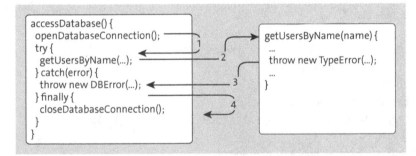

Figure 3.36 The Statements in the finally Block Are Always Executed, Even if a New Error Is Thrown inside the catch Block

Note

There are a total of three options for `try` statements:

- **Use of** `try` **in combination with** `catch`
  Error-producing code is called, and errors, if any, are caught.

- **Use of** `try` **in combination with** `finally`
  Error-producing code is executed, and errors, if any, are not caught, but the statements in the `finally` block are executed in any case.

- **Use of** `try` **in combination with** `catch` **and** `finally`
  Error-producing code is called, errors, if any, are caught, and the statements in the `finally` block are executed in any case.

3.7   Commenting the Source Code

Although purists claim that good source code is self-explanatory, you should especially comment more complex program sequences or source code that you know someone else will use as well. A comment is simply text that you can include in your code that human readers of your code (e.g., other developers in your team) can read to better understand the code, but that doesn't have any effect on the program itself. You have two options for this: single-line comments and multiline comments.

You always start a *single-line comment* with two consecutive slashes (//). As soon as the JavaScript interpreter finds this character combination in the source code, everything on the same line is considered a comment. You start a (potentially) *multiline comment* with the string /* and end it with the string */. Everything between these two strings (even across lines) is recognized as a comment by the JavaScript interpreter.

Listing 3.174 shows an example program that briefly demonstrates the use of both comment types.

```
/* This function adds two positive numbers
and returns the result. */
function add(x, y) {
  let result = 0;          // Variable for the result
  // If one of the two numbers is less than 0 ...
  if(x < 0 || y < 0) {
    // ... an error is returned ...
    throw new Error('Numbers must be greater than or equal to 0.');
  } else {
    // ... otherwise the two numbers are added ...
    result = x + y;
  }
  // ... and the result is returned.
  return result;
}
```

Listing 3.174 A Simple Program for Demonstrating Comments

3.8   Debugging the Code

When I started programming—at that time, with the Java programming language—one of the aha! moments that contributed significantly to my understanding of programming was the use of a *debugger*. With the help of such a debugger, it's possible to pause a program at a certain point, to go through the following statements step by step, to look at the variable assignments, and much more.

3.8.1 Introduction

Most programming books only present an introduction to *debugging* in later chapters—if any. However, this doesn't seem didactically clever because it means that one of the essential tools of everyday programming, and particularly one that contributes to the understanding of programming, remains unmentioned for a long time.

So we've included this topic fairly early in the book, hoping that it will be as helpful to you in learning JavaScript—and programming in general—as it was to me when I started.

The easiest way to get started is to use the Chrome DevTools, which we introduced briefly in Chapter 2. Other popular browsers have similar tools for debugging as well, which all work quite similarly in principle. Even various development environments like WebStorm have built-in debuggers.

The reason why we mention and explain debugging here is that debuggers are a great way to understand the flow of a program. This allows you to reinforce what you have learned so far in this chapter—conditional statements, branching, repetition, function calls, and error handling—and thus kill two birds with one stone, so to speak.

3.8.2 A Simple Code Example

Let's take the `findDuplicates()` function shown in Listing 3.175 as an example. This function is to output the duplicate entries for the numbers array. However, the function contains a small error that causes each entry to be recognized as duplicate.

```javascript
function findDuplicates() {
  const numbers = [2, 4, 5, 2, 5, 8, 5, 4711];
  for(let i=0; i<numbers.length; i++) {
    const numberAtI = numbers[i];
    for(let j=0; j<numbers.length; j++) {
      const numberAtJ = numbers[j];
      if(numberAtI === numberAtJ) {
        console.log(`Found duplicate: ${numberAtI}`);
      }
    }
  }
}

document.addEventListener('DOMContentLoaded', findDuplicates);
```

Listing 3.175 Example Function for Debugging

The HTML file that embeds the code in Listing 3.175 is shown in Listing 3.176. This is also the file you open next in the browser (in Chrome, in this case) to debug the JavaScript code there.

```
<!DOCTYPE html>
<html>
<head lang="en">
  <meta charset="UTF-8">
  <title>Debugging example</title>
  <link rel="stylesheet" href="styles/main.css" type="text/css">
</head>
<body>
<script src="scripts/main.js"></script>
</body>
</html>
```

Listing 3.176 HTML File That Embeds the Sample Code

3.8.3   Defining Breakpoints

To open the debugging section of CDT, select **View · Developer · JavaScript Console**, and then go to the **Sources** tab. On the left side, you'll see (among other things) the Java-Script source code file that is embedded in the called HTML file. Double-click this file (*main.js*) to select it and open it in the built-in editor (see Figure 3.37).

Figure 3.37 In the Sources View, Select the Corresponding Source Code File

This view can now be used to define *breakpoints* at which the execution of the program is to be stopped. Such breakpoints enable the developer to jump into a program at a certain point in time and execute the following statements step by step, starting at the breakpoint.

To define a breakpoint, simply click to the left of the corresponding line in the source code (where the line number is). The blue mark shows that a breakpoint is defined for the corresponding line (see Figure 3.38).

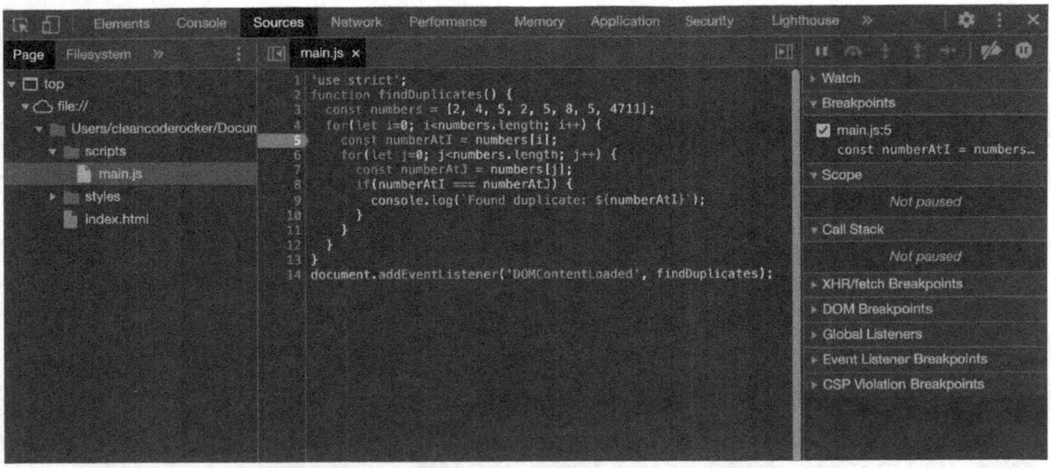

Figure 3.38 Define Breakpoints in the Program

When you subsequently reload the HTML file in the browser, the program stops exactly at the defined breakpoint (see Figure 3.39).

Figure 3.39 If You Now Run the Program, Execution Pauses at the Breakpoint Defined Earlier

Defining Breakpoints Using the debugger Keyword

As an alternative to defining breakpoints using CDT, you can also define breakpoints within the source code using the debugger keyword (see Figure 3.40).

The keyword is part of the language and thus independent of the debugging tool used (there are others besides CDT, but we won't discuss them here).

Figure 3.40 The debugger Keyword Causes the Debugging Tool to Stop the Program

3.8.4   Viewing Variable Assignments

Once the program has been stopped, you can view the variable assignments—that is, the current values of the visible variables. These can be found in the **Sources** view on the right side under the **Scope** tab (see Figure 3.41). In the example, you can see that the numberAtI variable still has the value undefined (after all, the line where the program is stopped hasn't been executed yet), and the i variable has a value of 0.

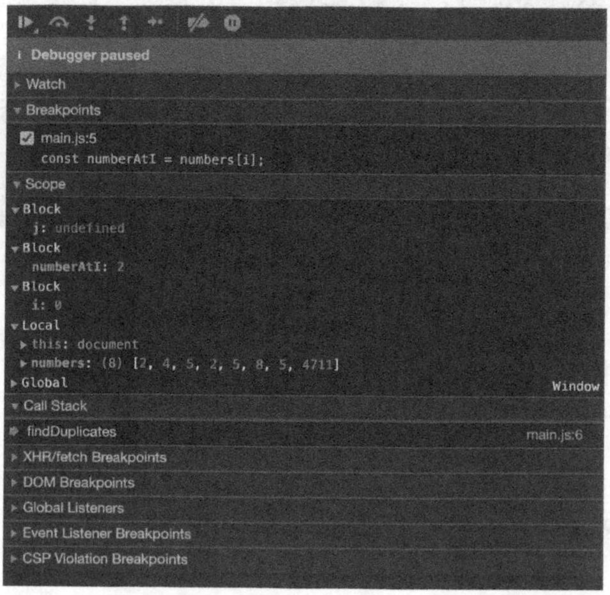

Figure 3.41 The Scope Tab Allows You to View the Variable Assignments

3.8.5 Running a Program Step by Step

Using the navigation (on the top-right side), you also have the option to execute the source code manually step by step or statement by statement. The exact meanings of the different buttons are summarized in Table 3.23.

Button	Meaning
	Continue the execution of the program (to the end or to the next breakpoint)
	Execute the next statement
	Jump into the next function call
	Jump out of the current function call
	Disable/enable breakpoints
	Pause in case of an error

Table 3.23 Meanings of the Different Buttons to Control the Debugger

If you now click the button to execute the next statement from the breakpoint defined in Figure 3.38, the `const numberAtI = numbers[i]` statement is executed, assigning the `numberAtI` variable a value of 2 (see Figure 3.42).

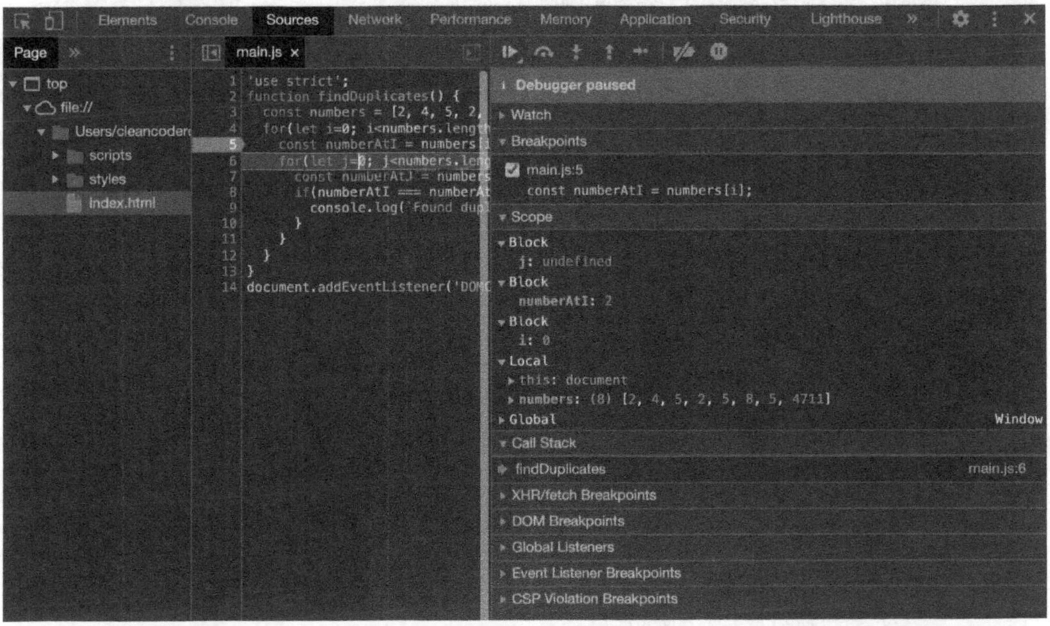

Figure 3.42 Using the Navigation on the Right Side, You Can Execute a Program Statement by Statement and Always Have an Overview of the Current Variable Assignment

If you now execute the statements up to line 7 (see Figure 3.43), you will be able to see straightaway where the error is in the program. The inner counting loop compares each element of the array (in the `numberAtJ` variable) with the current element of the outer loop (in the `numberAtI` variable), which means that each element—that is, each number—is also compared with itself.

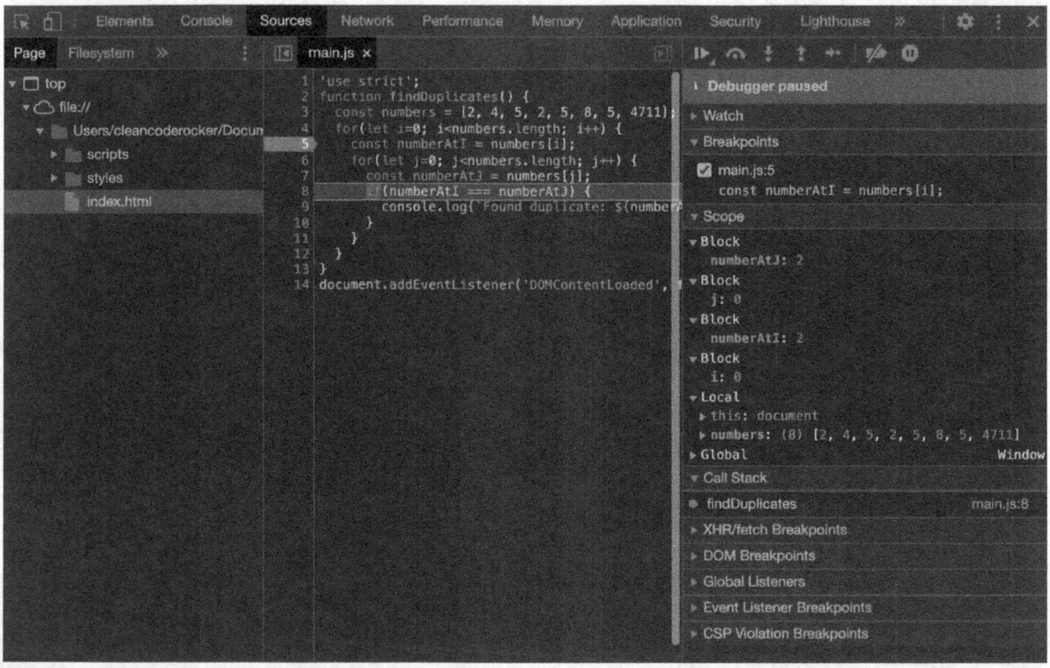

Figure 3.43 The Problem of the Program Has Been Recognized: The Inner Loop Counts from the Wrong Position

To solve this problem (and thus fix the bug), it's sufficient to let the inner counting loop count from position `i+1`. This compares the current element with all subsequent elements: the first element in the array (2) with the elements 4, 5, 2, 5, 8, 5, and 4711; the second element (4) with the elements 5, 2, 5, 8, 5, and 4711; and so on.

In this way, you not only prevent each element from being compared with itself, but also prevent two elements from being compared twice. The adapted source code is shown in Listing 3.177.

```
function findDuplicates() {
  const numbers = [2, 4, 5, 2, 5, 8, 5, 4711];
  for(let i=0; i<numbers.length; i++) {
    const numberAtI = numbers[i];
    for(let j=i+1; j<numbers.length; j++) {
      const numberAtJ = numbers[j];
      if(numberAtI === numberAtJ) {
        console.log(`Found duplicate: ${numberAtI}`);
```

```
      }
    }
  }
}
```

```
document.addEventListener('DOMContentLoaded', findDuplicates);
```

Listing 3.177 Example Function for Debugging, Correct Version

3.8.6 Defining Multiple Breakpoints

Of course, there is no reason that you shouldn't define several breakpoints within a program. You can then use the **Continue** button to "jump" to the next breakpoint occurring in the program flow (see Figure 3.44).

Figure 3.44 Alternatively, You Can Have the Debugger Pause at a Breakpoint Only When a Certain Condition Is Met

The breakpoints are not limited to a single source code file but can be used arbitrarily within a program, even if your program consists of several source code files.

3.8.7 Other Types of Breakpoints

Besides "normal" breakpoints, where a program stops whenever the corresponding line of code is reached, there are other types of breakpoints:

- *Conditional breakpoints* allow the execution to stop at the corresponding line of code only if the condition associated with the breakpoint is met (see Figure 3.45).

- *DOM breakpoints* allow the execution to stop when the content of a web page has been dynamically modified (we'll discuss the DOM topic in detail in Chapter 5).

- *Event listener breakpoints* allow the execution to stop when a specific event is triggered within a web page (we'll show you what events are in Chapter 6).

- *XHR breakpoints* allow the execution to stop when an Ajax call is executed (we'll show you exactly what Ajax means and what you can do with it in Chapter 9).

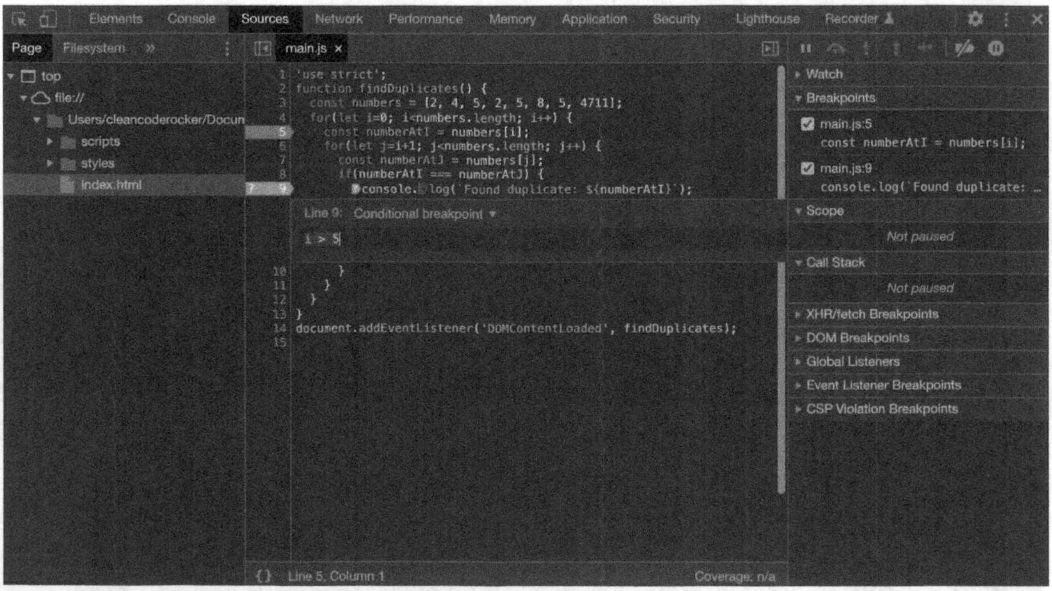

Figure 3.45 Example of a Conditional Breakpoint

3.8.8   Viewing the Function Call Stack

In addition to the variable assignment, you can also display the function call stack. The best way to illustrate this is to change the code example from earlier to call multiple functions.

In Listing 3.178, some of the logic from the findDuplicates() function has been moved to new functions: the contents of the outer loop are now in the checkNumber() function, which is called with the current number as the first argument and the entire array as the second argument.

In addition, the contents of the inner loop are in the compareNumbers() function. That is, the findDuplicates() function calls the checkNumber() function for each number in the array, which in turn calls the compareNumbers() function for each subsequent number.

```
function compareNumbers(numberAtI, numberAtJ) {
  if(numberAtI === numberAtJ) {
    console.log(`Found duplicate: ${numberAtI}`);
  }
```

```
}

function checkNumber(numberAtI, numbers, i) {
  for(let j=i+1; j<numbers.length; j++) {
    const numberAtJ = numbers[j];
    compareNumbers(numberAtI, numberAtJ);
  }
}

function findDuplicates() {
  const numbers = [2, 4, 5, 2, 5, 8, 5, 4711];
  for(let i=0; i<numbers.length; i++) {
    checkNumber(numbers[i], numbers, i);
  }
}

document.addEventListener('DOMContentLoaded', findDuplicates);
```

Listing 3.178 Adapted Example Function for Debugging

If you now set a breakpoint within the compareNumbers() function, as shown in Figure 3.46, you can nicely see the function call stack. To do this, simply select the **Call Stack** tab in the right pane. There, the function name on top represents the current function, the function below it the one from which the current function was called, and so on.

Figure 3.46 The Function Call Stack Can Be Viewed via the Call Stack Tab

225

3.9   Summary

In this chapter, you learned about the most important programming basics for Java-Script. Let's briefly summarize the most important points:

- *Variables* can be defined in JavaScript using the keywords var and (since ES2015) let. If you have a runtime environment that supports ES2015, you should get into the habit of always defining variables with let.

- You define *constants* in JavaScript using the const keyword.

- Even though JavaScript is not a strictly typed programming language, there are still different *data types*:

  - The *primitive standard data types* for numbers, strings and Boolean values, and the special data types undefined and null as well as symbols

  - The *reference data types*

  - *Template strings*, a powerful tool for working with strings that enables you, for example, to define placeholders in strings

- There are several types of *operators* in JavaScript:

  - Arithmetic operators for working with numbers

  - Operators for working with strings

  - Logical operators for working with Boolean values

  - Bitwise operators for working with bits

  - Operators for comparing values

  - Special operators—for type checking, for example

- You can handle the *control flow* in JavaScript using conditional statements, branches, multiway branches, counting loops, and head-controlled and tail-controlled loops:

  - *Conditional statements* and *branches* are suitable whenever you want to execute one of several program branches based on a Boolean condition. *Multiway branches*, on the other hand, are suitable if you want to execute one of several program branches depending on the value of a variable.

  - *Counting loops* are particularly suitable when the number of loop iterations is known in advance. *Head-controlled loops* and *tail-controlled loops* are suitable when code is to be executed repeatedly depending on a Boolean condition.

  - You can abort the execution of a loop using the break keyword.

  - You can use the continue keyword to abort the execution of a loop iteration and continue with the next loop iteration.

- To make code reusable, you can define your own *functions* in JavaScript. Functions can be called with *arguments* and return a *return value.*

- There are several types of *errors* in JavaScript:
  - *Syntax errors* occur when JavaScript syntactic rules are ignored.
  - *Runtime errors* are errors that occur only at runtime—that is, when a program is executed.
  - *Logic errors* or *bugs* refer to such types of errors that are caused by incorrect logic in your program.
- If an error occurs during the execution of a program, it's possible to handle such an error. The `try` keyword is used to mark the code part that could potentially throw errors, the `catch` keyword is used to mark the code part that should be executed in case of an error, and `finally` is used to mark the code part that should be called in any case.
- You can use *comments* to add notes to the source text. This can be helpful so that other developers (or yourself when you look at older source code again after some time) can understand the source code faster.
- To detect logic errors (also called *bugs*), such as for debugging purposes, a debugger is used, which enables you, among other things, to execute a program step by step and view the values of variables.

Chapter 4

Working with Reference Types

In addition to primitive data types and the special data types null and undefined, which you know from the previous chapters, JavaScript also provides so-called reference types.

Reference types like objects and arrays have already been mentioned in previous chapters. In this chapter, we'll introduce reference types in a little more detail.

4.1 Difference between Primitive Data Types and Reference Types

In Chapter 3, we discussed the various primitive data types in detail, and you learned about two reference types (or reference data types): objects and arrays. However, we haven't explained the exact difference between primitive data types and reference data types yet. Let's go over this now.

4.1.1 The Principle of Primitive Data Types

The difference between primitive data types and reference types is the way the respective values are stored. Each time a variable is declared, the computer provides memory for it and stores the variable, including its value, in a designated memory address. For primitive data types, each time a variable is assigned a value, the entire value is copied to that memory address. For example, if you create a variable x using let x = 4;, the computer stores this variable internally and assigns it the value 4 (see Figure 4.1).

Figure 4.1 For Primitive Variable x the Value Is Stored in a Corresponding Register

If you now execute the statement let y = x;, the variable y is assigned the value of x—that is, 4. Internally, the computer copies this value into the register provided for the variable (see Figure 4.2).

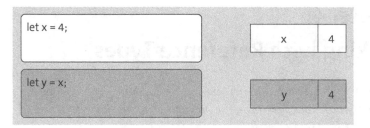

Figure 4.2 For Each Primitive Variable the Value Is Stored in a Corresponding Register

4.1.2   The Principle of Reference Types

This is different for reference types. Here, the computer does not store the value itself in the register provided for the respective variable, but only a reference to it (this is referred to as a *pointer*). Figure 4.3 illustrates this principle. The john variable is initialized with an object—that is, a reference type. However, this object (which itself is composed of various primitive data types) is not stored directly in the register but is only referenced via a pointer.

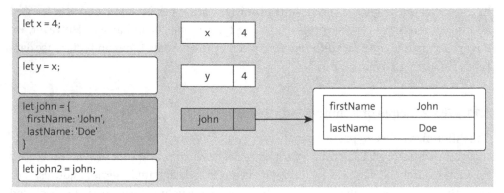

Figure 4.3 With Reference Types, a Reference to the Stored Object is Stored in the Register, Rather Than the Value Itself

If you now create a second variable (john2) and assign the content of the variable john to it (as shown in Figure 4.4), not the object stored therein is copied, but the pointer to the object. Both variables then point to the same object.

If, as in the example, two or more variables point to the same object, this also means that you always work with the same object, no matter which of the variables you access. So if you change a property of the referenced object using one of the variables, as shown in Listing 4.1, this also has an effect on the other variable (see Figure 4.5).

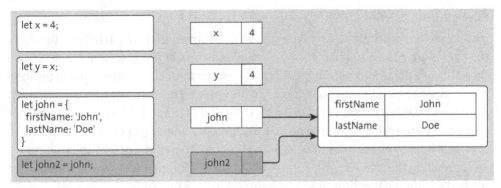

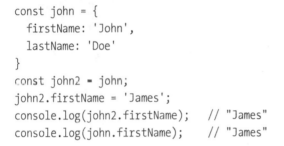

Figure 4.4 With Reference Types, Several Variables Can Point to the Same Object

```
const john = {
  firstName: 'John',
  lastName: 'Doe'
}
const john2 = john;
john2.firstName = 'James';
console.log(john2.firstName);   // "James"
console.log(john.firstName);    // "James"
```

Listing 4.1 Access to Object Properties and Object Methods via Dot Notation

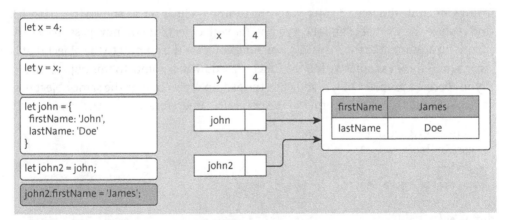

Figure 4.5 If You Change the Stored Object via a Variable, This Object Will Also Change for All Other Variables That Point to This Object

> **Note**
>
> For variables of a primitive data type, the computer copies the entire value into the memory address for the variable. For variables with a reference type, on the other hand, only the pointer or reference to the corresponding object is stored in the memory address.

4.1.3   Primitive Data Types and Reference Types as Function Arguments

If arguments of a primitive data type such as the number 4711 are passed to a function, the values are copied to the corresponding parameters of the function. If you change the value of a parameter within the function, this does not change the value of the variable that was passed to the function as an argument. This is illustrated in Listing 4.2. Here the variable y is first initialized with the value 4711 and then passed to the example() function. Within this function, in turn, the x parameter is set to the value 5. However, this doesn't change the value of y. The program therefore outputs the values 4711 (before calling the example() function), 4711 (at the beginning within the function), 5 (at the end within the function), and 4711 (after calling the function).

```
function example(x) {
  console.log(x);
  x = 5;
  console.log(x);
}
let y = 4711;
console.log(y);
example(y);
console.log(y);
```

Listing 4.2 For Function Calls with Primitive Data Types, the Value Is Passed

Things are quite different if you change the example a little bit, as shown in Listing 4.3, and replace the y variable and the x parameter with objects. If you now pass the y variable as an argument to the example() function, you pass the pointer to the object that is assigned to the y variable. Within the function, x now also points to this object; that is, if you change a property of x, as shown in the example, you change the same object that is also referred to by y. The output of the program is therefore 4711, 4711, 5, and 5.

```
function example(x) {
  console.log(x.value);
  x.value = 5;
  console.log(x.value);
}
let y = {
  value: 4711
};
console.log(y.value);
example(y);
console.log(y.value);
```

Listing 4.3 For Function Calls with Reference Types, the Pointer Is Passed

> **Note**
>
> If you pass an argument of a primitive data type to a function, the entire value is passed and copied into the function's parameter. However, if an argument with a reference type is passed to a function, only the reference to the corresponding object is passed.

4.1.4   Determining the Type of a Variable

Because you don't specify the type of a variable when you declare it, the question is how to recognize it. Suppose you want to check within a function whether a primitive data type (Boolean, number, string) or a reference type (object, array) has been passed. This can be effected using the typeof operator. This is a unary operator; that is, it expects only one operand—namely, the value or variable the type of which is to be determined. The operator returns a string, one of the values listed in Table 4.1.

Return Value of the typeof Operator	Is Returned For ...
boolean	Boolean values
number	Numeric values
string	Strings
symbol	Symbols, a new data type introduced in ES2015, which we'll talk about in Chapter 6, "Processing and Triggering Events"
function	Functions (which, by the way, are also objects in JavaScript, but more on that later)
object	All (other) types of objects as well as the value null
undefined	Undefined variables

Table 4.1 The Different Return Values of the Typeof Operator

Some examples of the use of the typeof operator are shown in Listing 4.4. You see that the operator returns the value boolean for Boolean values, the value number for numeric values (both for integers and floating point numbers), the value string for strings, the value function for functions, the value object for objects, the value undefined for undefined variables, and the value symbol for symbols.

```
console.log(typeof true);        // boolean
console.log(typeof false);       // boolean
console.log(typeof 4711);        // number
console.log(typeof 22.22);       // number
```

```
console.log(typeof 'John Doe');        // string
console.log(typeof function () {});     // function
console.log(typeof {});                 // object
console.log(typeof []);                 // object
console.log(typeof null);               // object
console.log(typeof undefined);          // undefined
console.log(typeof Symbol('B'));        // symbol
```

Listing 4.4 Application of the typeof Operator for Different Values

However, two things are worth mentioning at this point: first, the operator returns the value object for the value null; second, it returns the value object for arrays. Regarding the former, the committee responsible for the development of the ECMAScript standard has acknowledged that this is a bug in the specification, but one that cannot be easily fixed for reasons of backward compatibility with older versions. Regarding the latter, it can be stated that the typeof operator returns the value object for all objects (i.e., all reference types) except for functions. This includes arrays and other reference types, which you'll learn about later in this chapter.

> **Note**
>
> You can use the typeof operator to
>
> - distinguish primitive data types from reference types,
> - distinguish the individual primitive data types from each other, and
> - find out if a value is a function.
>
> You cannot use the operator to distinguish between different reference types—for example, to determine whether a variable is an array or a "normal" object.

Besides the typeof operator, there is another operator that deals with determining the type of variables, and that is the instanceof operator. In simple terms, this operator determines whether a variable is of a certain reference type (this is not quite correct, but the exact operation of instanceof is a bit more complicated, and the detailed explanation is only of little use at this point). The operator returns a Boolean value.

Some examples of using the instanceof operator are shown in Listing 4.5. You see that the john object is of the Object type, but not of the Array type. The numbers object, on the other hand, is of the Object type and of the Array type. This is because the Array type in JavaScript is a subtype of Object (don't worry, we'll come back to this topic later). The type of functions, Function, is also a subtype of Object, so the instanceof operator for the add() function returns true in both cases in the listing.

```
const john = {
  firstName: 'John',
  lastName: 'Doe'
```

```
}

const numbers = [2,3,4,5,6,7,8,9];

function add(x, y) {
  return x + y;
}
console.log(john instanceof Object);      // true
console.log(john instanceof Array);       // false
console.log(numbers instanceof Object);   // true
console.log(numbers instanceof Array);    // true
console.log(add instanceof Function);     // true
console.log(add instanceof Object);       // true
```

Listing 4.5 Application of the instanceof Operator for Different Values

> **Note**
>
> Object is the type from which all other reference types are derived. The instanceof operator therefore returns true for all variables of any reference type.

Unlike the typeof operator, the instanceof operator works only for values that contain a reference type. For values of primitive data types, however, the operator always returns false, as shown with the examples in Listing 4.6.

```
console.log(true instanceof Object);        // false
console.log(4711 instanceof Object);        // false
console.log('John Doe' instanceof Object);  // false
```

Listing 4.6 For Values of Primitive Data Types, the instanceof Operator Always Returns false

> **Note**
>
> To check whether a variable is an array, you can use the Array.isArray() method as an alternative to the instanceof operator, as shown in Listing 4.7.
>
> ```
> const john = {
> firstName: 'John',
> lastName: 'Doe'
> }
> const numbers = [2, 3, 4, 5, 6, 7, 8, 9];
> console.log(Array.isArray(john));    // false
> console.log(Array.isArray(numbers)); // true
> ```
>
> **Listing 4.7** Using the Array.isArray() Method for Different Values

4.1.5   Outlook

Now that you've learned about the difference between primitive data types and reference types and know how to perform type checking with the `typeof` and `instanceof` operators, the rest of the chapter will go more into detail about the various reference types available in JavaScript by default. These include the following:

- The `Object` reference type, which represents all types of objects (Section 4.2)
- The `Array` reference type, representing arrays, discussed in the previous chapter (Section 4.3)
- The `RegExp` reference type, which represents regular expressions that can be used to search for specific patterns within strings (Section 4.9)
- The `Date` reference type, which represents date and time information (Section 4.8.1)
- The `Math` reference type, which can be used to perform more complex calculations than those discussed in the previous chapter with the primitive data types (Section 4.8.2)

Furthermore, there are various *wrapper objects* that provide additional functionalities to the primitive data types. We'll also address this topic in Section 4.8.3. In addition, we'll go into a bit more detail about the functions introduced in the previous chapter (in Section 4.10) because these are also reference types in JavaScript.

4.2   Encapsulating State and Behavior in Objects

As mentioned earlier, JavaScript is a programming language that also supports the object-oriented programming paradigm. We'll look at the subject of object orientation in a little more detail in Chapter 13. At this point, we'll focus on the way you work with objects, but we'll also give you a short introduction to object-oriented programming.

4.2.1   Introduction to Object-Oriented Programming

Software systems can sometimes become quite complex and extensive. Object-oriented programming (or object orientation) aims to take some of the complexity out of software systems by trying to describe the system through different objects. In this context, objects from the real world are often also described as objects in the respective software system. For this purpose, imagine an online bookstore: in object-oriented programming, you would probably use objects that represent a user, a book, and a shopping cart.

Objects have a state and a behavior. The *state* of an object is described by its properties and connections to other objects. The *behavior* of an object is defined by its methods. Figure 4.6 shows the state and behavior of the just mentioned objects in the form of a *class diagram*.

The state of the ShoppingCart object, for example, essentially comprises the individual items that are in the respective shopping cart and represents them via the items property. The methods of ShoppingCart represent the behavior of the particular shopping cart: addItem() enables you to add new items, removeItem() to remove items, and clear() to clear the shopping cart.

As noted, we'll come back to the topic of object orientation later. For now, just remember that the focus in object-oriented programming is on the use of objects, as the name suggests. So next, let's look at the ways in which you can create objects in JavaScript.

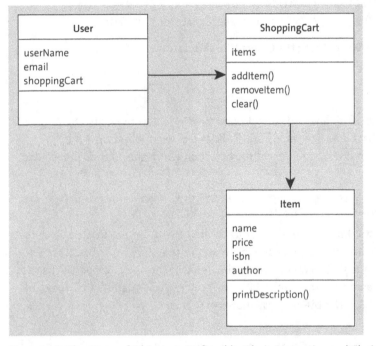

Figure 4.6 The State of Objects Is Defined by Their Properties and Their Connections to Other Objects, the Behavior of Objects by Their Methods

4.2.2   Creating Objects Using Literal Notation

In JavaScript, there are several ways to create objects. One of them, the *literal notation* (or *object literal notation*), was introduced in the previous chapter. As a reminder, Listing 4.8 briefly shows the corresponding code again. Here, the item object is created with four properties—name, price, author, and isbn—as well as the printDescription() method.

```
const item = {
  name: 'JavaScript: The Comprehensive Guide',
  price: 59.95,
  author: 'Philip Ackermann',
```

```
  isbn: '978-1-4932-2286-5',
  printDescription: function() {
    console.log(`${this.author}: ${this.name}`);
  }
}
console.log(item.name);      // "JavaScript: The Comprehensive Guide"
console.log(item.price);     // 59.95
console.log(item.author);    // "Philip Ackermann"
console.log(item.isbn);      // "978-1-4932-2286-5"
item.printDescription();     // "Philip Ackermann:
                             // JavaScript: The Comprehensive Guide"
```

Listing 4.8 Creating an Object Using the Object Literal Notation

The this Keyword

Remember that the this keyword—mentioned briefly in the previous chapter and which we'll come back to a few times in this book—is used in Listing 4.8 inside the printDescription() method to represent the object on which the method is executed.

Creating Objects via Object.entries()

Since ES2019, you still have the possibility to create objects based on arrays via the Object.entries() method. The individual elements in the array must be arrays with two elements each: the first element defines the name of the object property, the second element the value that this property is to receive. Code that creates the same object as in Listing 4.8 in this other way is shown in Listing 4.9.

```
const array = [
  [ 'name', 'JavaScript: The Comprehensive Guide' ],
  [ 'price', 59.95 ],
  [ 'author', 'Philip Ackermann' ],
  [ 'isbn', '978-1-4932-2286-5' ],
  [ 'printDescription', function() {
    console.log(`${this.author}: ${this.name}`);
  }]
];

const item = Object.fromEntries(array);
console.log(item.name);    // "JavaScript: The Comprehensive Guide"
console.log(item.price);   // 59.95
console.log(item.author);  // "Philip Ackermann"
console.log(item.isbn);    // "978-1-4932-2286-5"
```

```
item.printDescription();   // "Philip Ackermann:
                           // JavaScript: The Comprehensive Guide"
```

Listing 4.9 Creating an Object Using the Object.entries() Method

4.2.3   Creating Objects via Constructor Functions

The second way to create objects in JavaScript is via *constructor functions*. In terms of structure, these are initially nothing more than normal functions, as shown in Listing 4.10.

```
function Item(name, price, author, isbn) {
  this.name = name;
  this.price = price;
  this.author = author;
  this.isbn = isbn;
  this.printDescription = function() {
    console.log(`${this.author}: ${this.name}`);
  }
}
```

Listing 4.10 Example of a Function That Can Be Used as a Constructor Function

What makes a function a constructor function in the first place is the new keyword prepended when it's called (more about this in a few moments). The function then creates a new object and returns it. As you can see in Listing 4.10, it isn't necessary to use return within the function. Instead, the newly created object is implicitly returned—which can be accessed within the constructor function via the this keyword, by the way.

Notation for Constructor Functions

Following the convention, functions that can be called as constructor functions start with an uppercase letter—or to be more precise, they follow *UpperCamelCase notation*. This means that if a function name consists of several words, each word starts with an uppercase letter.

To call the function shown in Listing 4.10 as a constructor function, prefix it—as mentioned previously—with the new keyword (see Listing 4.11). You see that arguments can also be passed to a constructor function. Within the function (see Listing 4.10), these arguments are then available via the parameter variables, as is common in "normal" functions. So in the example, this method is used to create an object, the name property of which is given the value of the name parameter, the price property of which is given the value of the price parameter, and so on.

You also see that a constructor function can be used multiple times to create different object instances. This isn't the case with the literal notation, in which you always create individual objects.

```
const item = new Item(
  'JavaScript: The Comprehensive Guide',
  59.95,
  'Philip Ackermann',
  '978-1-4932-2286-5'
)
console.log(item.name);        // "JavaScript: The Comprehensive Guide"
console.log(item.price);       // 59.95
console.log(item.author);      // "Philip Ackermann"
console.log(item.isbn);        // "978-1-4932-2286-5"
item.printDescription();       // "Philip Ackermann:
                               // JavaScript: The Comprehensive Guide"
const item2 = new Item(
  'Node.js: The Comprehensive Guide',
  49.94,
  'Sebastian Springer',
  '978-1-4932-2292-6'
)
console.log(item2.name);       // "Node.js: The Comprehensive Guide"
console.log(item2.price);      // 49.94
console.log(item2.author);     // "Sebastian Springer"
console.log(item2.isbn);       // "978-1-4932-2292-6"
item2.printDescription();      // "Sebastian Springer:
                               // Node.js: The Comprehensive Guide"
```

Listing 4.11 Creating an Object via a Constructor Function

The context of calling a function as a constructor function is shown in Figure 4.7.

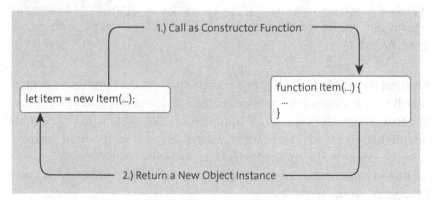

Figure 4.7 Calling a Function as a Constructor Function

Note

A function only becomes a constructor function when you call it using the new keyword. If you call a function as a constructor function, it isn't necessary to include a return statement within the function. Instead, a new object instance is automatically returned.

Calling Constructor Functions

In principle, it's also possible to call a function intended as a constructor function as a "normal" function—that is, without prepending new. Conversely, you can also prefix "normal" functions with new and thus call them as constructor functions. However, neither usually makes sense.

Constructor Functions of Standard Objects

Actually, you already used constructor functions in Chapter 3, although we didn't explicitly refer to them as such. For example, when you create a new array via new Array(), you use the Array() function as a constructor function. Likewise, when creating an error object via new Error(), you use a function (Error()) as a constructor function.

Prototypes

Each constructor function internally manages a *prototype*, an object that serves as the basis for the objects to be created via the constructor function. This prototype is stored in the prototype property of the function. If an object is now created using such a constructor function, the object is therefore based on the prototype stored there.

After the object is created, the prototype can be obtained either through the __proto__ property of the object or through the Object.getPrototypeOf() method. The constructor property can also be used to determine which constructor function was used to create an object instance. Listing 4.12 and Figure 4.8 demonstrate this using the already familiar Item constructor function and the item object instance just created.

```
console.log(Item.prototype);              // Item {}
console.log(item.__proto__);              // Item {}
console.log(Object.getPrototypeOf(item)); // Item {}
console.log(item.constructor);            // function Item(...)
```

Listing 4.12 Using Various Properties and Methods, Conclusions Can Be Drawn About the Prototype Used and the Constructor Function Used

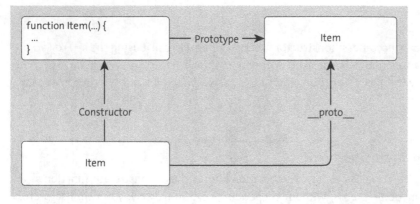

Figure 4.8 The Relationship among Object Instances, Constructor Functions, and Prototypes

When you create an object using a constructor function, the `typeof` operator for that object (as for all objects) returns the value `object`. The `instanceof` operator, on the other hand, can be used to check whether an object was created with a particular constructor function. If you write `item instanceof Item`, as shown in Listing 4.13, this expression returns `true` if the `item` object was created with the `Item()` constructor function.

```
console.log(typeof item);          // object
console.log(item instanceof Item);   // true
```

Listing 4.13 Applying the typeof and instanceof Operators to an Object Created via a Constructor Function

---

Prototype Chain

In detail, the issue is a bit more complicated when using a constructor function and applying the `instanceof` operator. Indeed, prototypes can in turn also have prototypes, which then leads to a whole chain of prototypes—the *prototype chain* (we'll discuss this topic in more detail in Chapter 13). The `instanceof` operator therefore checks, more precisely, whether the object in question is based on one of the prototypes in the prototype chain.

4.2.4   Creating Objects Using Classes

With the ECMAScript 6 version, so-called classes were introduced in ECMAScript and thus in JavaScript. In software development (more precisely, in object-oriented programming), classes are a kind of blueprint for objects. Within a class, you define the properties and methods for the objects to be created.

Class Diagrams

Do you remember the class diagram from Figure 4.6? These diagrams are called *class diagrams* because, strictly speaking, they illustrate the structure and relationships of individual classes.

Classes are defined in JavaScript using the `class` keyword. This keyword is followed by the name of the class (in UpperCamelCase notation) and the *class body* (the contents of the class) in braces.

Within the class body, you define the methods that should be available for object instances of the class. The method named `constructor()` takes a special role: it is called implicitly when you create a new object instance of the corresponding class (more on that in a moment).

Listing 4.14 shows an example of defining a budget profile. Looking closely, you will see that the content of the `constructor()` method is exactly the same as the content of the constructor function shown in Listing 4.10. The `constructor()` method doesn't require `return` either, but implicitly returns the corresponding object instance, as mentioned. Just as with constructor functions, the `this` keyword refers to the object instance created by calling the method.

```
class Item {
  constructor(name, price, author, isbn) {
    this.name = name;
    this.price = price;
    this.author = author;
    this.isbn = isbn;
  }
  printDescription() {
    console.log(`${this.author}: ${this.name}`);
  }
}
```

Listing 4.14 Example of a Class

As shown in Listing 4.15, the process of creating an object instance of a class is the same as for constructor functions—that is, using the `new` keyword. For example, `new Item()` creates a new object instance of the `Item` class. Implicitly, this calls the `constructor()` method of the class.

```
const item = new Item(
  'JavaScript: The Comprehensive Guide',
  59.95,
  'Philip Ackermann',
```

```
  '978-1-4932-2286-5'
)
console.log(item.name);      // "JavaScript: The Comprehensive Guide"
console.log(item.price);     // 59.95
console.log(item.author);    // "Philip Ackermann"
console.log(item.isbn);      // "978-1-4932-2286-5"
item.printDescription();     // "Philip Ackermann:
                             // JavaScript: The Comprehensive Guide"
const item2 = new Item(
  'Node.js: The Comprehensive Guide',
  49.94,
  'Sebastian Springer',
  '978-1-4932-2292-6'
)
console.log(item2.name);     // "Node.js: The Comprehensive Guide"
console.log(item2.price);    // 49.94
console.log(item2.author);   // "Sebastian Springer"
console.log(item2.isbn);     // "978-1-4932-2292-6"
item2.printDescription();    // "Sebastian Springer:
                             // Node.js: The Comprehensive Guide"
```

Listing 4.15 Creating an Object Using a Class

The principle of calling a class is illustrated in Figure 4.9.

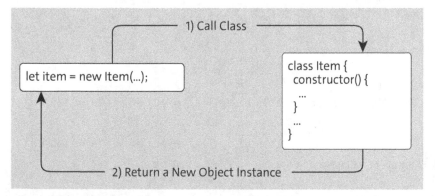

Figure 4.9 Calling a Class

The new ES2015 class syntax is ultimately just a syntactic alternative to the use of constructor functions. This is illustrated in Listing 4.16. Like constructor functions, classes also have a prototype property, which contains the base object, the prototype, based on which instances of the class are created. Instances of the class in turn (the item object in the example) also have the __proto__ and constructor properties (like instances created via constructor functions). The former references the prototype of the instance, the latter the class through which the instance was created (see Figure 4.10).

```javascript
class Item {
  constructor(name, price, author, isbn) {
    ...
  }
  ...
}
const item = new Item(
  'JavaScript: The Comprehensive Guide',
  59.95,
  'Philip Ackermann',
  '978-1-4932-2286-5'
)
console.log(Item.prototype);              // Item {}
console.log(item.__proto__);              // Item {}
console.log(Object.getPrototypeOf(item)); // Item {}
console.log(item.constructor);            // function class Item(...)
```

Listing 4.16 Using Various Properties and Methods, Conclusions Can Be Drawn About the Prototype Used and the Constructor Function Used

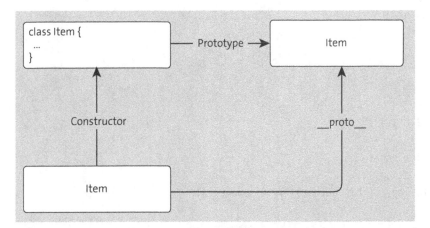

Figure 4.10 The Fact That Classes in JavaScript Are Only a Syntactic Simplification Can Also Be Seen in the Relationship between Prototypes and Object Instances

typeof versus instanceof

When you create an object using a class, the typeof operator returns the value object for that object. In turn, you can use the instanceof operator to check whether the object was created with the respective class (see Listing 4.17).

```
console.log(typeof item);          // object
console.log(item instanceof Item);   // true
```

Listing 4.17 Applying the typeof and instanceof Operators to an Object Created via a Constructor Function

4.2.5   Creating Objects via the Object.create() Function

Since ECMAScript 5, there is the possibility to create objects via the `Object.create()` helper method. As the first parameter, this method expects the prototype of the object to be created, and as the second parameter, a configuration object that can be used to configure the properties and methods of the object. The properties of this configuration object represent the names of the properties of the object to be created (in Listing 4.18, these are the properties `name`, `price`, `author`, and `isbn`). The value in each case is an object, which can be used to define the value (as shown in Listing 4.18) and the *property attributes*.

```
const item = Object.create(Object.prototype, {
  name: {
    value: 'JavaScript: The Comprehensive Guide'
  },
  price: {
    value: 59.95
  },
  author: {
    value: 'Philip Ackermann'
  },
  isbn: {
    value: '978-1-4932-2286-5'
  },
  printDescription: {
    value: function() {
      console.log(`${this.author}: ${this.name}`);
    }
  }
});
console.log(item.name);     // "JavaScript: The Comprehensive Guide"
console.log(item.price);    // 59.95
console.log(item.author);   // "Philip Ackermann"
console.log(item.isbn);     // "978-1-4932-2286-5"
item.printDescription();    // "Philip Ackermann:
                            // JavaScript: The Comprehensive Guide"
```

Listing 4.18 Creating an Object via the Object.create() Helper Function

Property Attributes

You can use these property attributes to configure individual object properties. In addition to the `value` property, which can be used to define the value of the property, there are other property attributes:

- `writable`
  This property attribute specifies via a Boolean value whether the respective property may be *overwritten*—that is, assigned a new value after initialization. By default, this attribute has a value of `false`.

- `enumerable`
  This property attribute specifies via a Boolean value whether the respective property is *enumerable*—that is, whether this property is included when iterating over the properties of the corresponding object (e.g., using a `for...in` loop). By default, this attribute has a value of `false`.

- `configurable`
  This property attribute specifies via a Boolean value whether the property attribute itself can be changed for the respective property—that is, whether the property can be *configured* via the attributes afterward. The default value for this attribute is also `false`.

- `set`
  This property attribute specifies which function is called when there is *write* access to the property (only usable for *access properties*; Section 4.2.6).

- `get`
  This property attribute specifies which function is called when there is *read* access to the property (can only be used for access properties; Section 4.2.6).

Some examples of this are shown in the source code in Listing 4.19. For all of the object properties defined there, the three property attributes `writable`, `configurable`, and `enumerable` are assigned different values. The properties for which `writable` is set to `false` cannot be assigned new values after the object is created. The `price` property is the exception here: it's the only property for which the value can be reset. The properties for which the `enumerable` attribute is set to `true` are output during the iteration over the object properties (which, by the way, is possible using the for-in loop). The exception in this respect is the `isbn` property: this property is the only one not output.

```
const item = Object.create(Object.prototype, {
  name: {
    value: 'JavaScript: The Comprehensive Guide',
    writable: false,
    configurable: true,
    enumerable: true
  },
  price: {
```

```
      value: 59.95,
      writable: true,
      configurable: true,
      enumerable: true
    },
    author: {
      value: 'Philip Ackermann',
      writable: false,
      configurable: true,
      enumerable: true
    },
    isbn: {
      value: '978-1-4932-2286-5',
      writable: false,
      configurable: true,
      enumerable: false     // During iteration, the "isbn" property is
                            // not output.


    },
    printDescription: {
      value: function() {
        console.log(`${this.author}: ${this.name}`);
      }
    }
  });
  for(let property in item) {
    console.log(property);    // Output: "name", "price", "author"
  }


  item.name = 'Cool new Java book';
  console.log(item.name);     // "JavaScript:
                              // The Comprehensive Guide", because the
                              // "name" property is not "writeable".


  item.price = 54.95;
  console.log(item.price);    // "54.95", because for the "price" property,
                              // the "writable" attribute has a value of "true".
```

Listing 4.19 Using Property Attributes

For accessing the property attributes of a property or method, the Object.getOwnProp-ertyDescriptor() method is available. This method expects the respective object as the first parameter and the name of the property/method for which the attributes are to be determined as the second parameter. The method returns an object with the known properties: value, writable, enumerable, configurable, and (for access properties) set and get (see Listing 4.20).

```
const item = {
  name: 'JavaScript: The Comprehensive Guide',
  price: 59.95,
  author: 'Philip Ackermann',
  isbn: '978-1-4932-2286-5',
  printDescription: function() {
    console.log(`${this.author}: ${this.name}`);
  }
}


const propertyDescriptor = Object.getOwnPropertyDescriptor(item, 'name');
console.log(propertyDescriptor.enumerable);     // true
console.log(propertyDescriptor.configurable);   // true
console.log(propertyDescriptor.writable);       // true
console.log(propertyDescriptor.value);          // "JavaScript:
                                                // The Comprehensive Guide"
```

Listing 4.20 Access to the Property Attributes

Conclusion About Creating Objects

Finally, the question arises as to which type of object creation you should use. Here's some advice:

- For simple objects that you want to create on the fly and of which you need only one instance, use the object literal notation.

- On the other hand, if you want to create multiple object instances of one object type, we recommend that you switch to the new class syntax rather than using constructor functions. The latter are only used in exceptional cases.

- You can use the Object.create() method if the class syntax isn't available to you (e.g., if you're working in a runtime environment that does not yet support ES2015 features) or if you want to use property attributes when creating an object.

4.2.6   Accessing Properties and Calling Methods

To access object properties or call object methods, JavaScript usually uses *dot notation*. Listing 4.21 shows two examples: the name property of the item object is accessed here, and the printDescription() method of the same object is called.

```
const itemName = item.name;
item.printDescription();
```

Listing 4.21 Access to Object Properties and Object Methods via Dot Notation

As an alternative to dot notation, you can also access properties and methods by writing the name of the property or method in square brackets after the name of the object, as shown in Listing 4.22. You see that to access the `printDescription()` object method via this notation, you only include the name of the method in brackets, not the pair of parentheses (through which the method is called).

```
const itemName = item['name'];
item['printDescription']();
```

Listing 4.22 Access to Object Properties and Object Methods via Bracket Notation

So in principle, you can use dot notation or bracket notation to access the properties and methods of an object. In some cases, however, you can only use the bracket notation: whenever the name of the respective property or method contains the minus sign (see Listing 4.23). If such names were used in combination with dot notation, the interpreter would report a syntax error because it would interpret the minus sign as a subtraction operator, which doesn't make sense in the present example at the corresponding position. Even if the name of the property or method is in a variable or isn't assembled until runtime, you must resort to the bracket notation (also see Listing 4.23).

```
const person = {
  'first-name': 'John',
  'last-name': 'Doe'
}
// console.log(person.first-name);  // Syntax error
// console.log(person.last-name);   // Syntax error
console.log(person['first-name']);  // "John"
console.log(person['last-name']);   // "Doe"

const firstName = 'first-name';
const lastName = 'last-name';
```

```
console.log(person[firstName]);  // "John"
console.log(person[lastName]);   // "Doe"

const name = 'name';
const prefixFirstName = 'first-';
const prefixLastName = 'last-';

console.log(person[prefixFirstName + name]);  // "John"
console.log(person[prefixLastName + name]);   // "Doe
```

Listing 4.23 In Various Cases, Properties (and Methods) Can Only Be Accessed Using the Bracket Notation

Setters and Getters

Instead of accessing properties directly, it's common in object-oriented programming to use special methods to reset properties or return the values of properties. Those types of methods that set a new value for a property are called *setter methods*, or *setters* for short, and those that return the value of a property are called *getter methods* or *getters*. The advantage of setter methods in particular is that they provide a good opportunity to validate values that are to be assigned to a property—that is, to check their validity.

In JavaScript, there are two special keywords to designate setter and getter methods: set for setter methods and get for getter methods. You can use these keywords in combination with object literal notation, with constructor functions, with classes, and with the Object.create() method.

Listing 4.24 shows how getters and setters are used in combination with literal notation. To avoid naming conflicts between properties and methods, it's common practice to prefix the former with an underscore.

```
const item = {
  _name: 'JavaScript: The Comprehensive Guide',
  _price: 59.95,
  _author: 'Philip Ackermann',
  _isbn: '978-1-4932-2286-5',
  set name(newName) {
    if(typeof newName === 'string') {
      console.log('Set new name');
      this._name = newName;
    } else {
      throw new TypeError('Name must be a string.')
    }
  },
```

```
  get name() {
    console.log('Return name');
    return this._name;
  }
  /* Same for the other properties. */
}
console.log(item.name);    // "Return name"
                           // "JavaScript: The Comprehensive Guide"
item.name = 'JavaScript: The Comprehensive Guide by Philip Ackermann';
                           // "Set new name"
```

Listing 4.24 Getters and Setters when Using Object Literal Notation

---

Data Encapsulation

In object-oriented programming, the technical term for allowing access to the properties of an object only via (setter and getter) methods is *data encapsulation* (*encapsulation* for short). The properties are thus protected from direct access from the outside.

In the code example in Listing 4.24, the properties in question (_name, _price, _author, and _isbn) are accessible even without using the setters and getters and thus are not protected from direct access. Strictly speaking, it's only recently become possible to define private properties in JavaScript. We'll show you how to do that in Chapter 13.

For comparison, Listing 4.25 shows the use of setter and getter methods in combination with constructor functions, Listing 4.26 in combination with classes, and Listing 4.27 in combination with the Object.create() method.

```
function Item(name, price, author, isbn) {
  this._name = name;
  this._price = price;
  this._author = author;
  this._isbn = isbn;
}

Item.prototype = {
  set name(newName) {
    if(typeof newName === 'string') {
      console.log('Set new name');
      this._name = newName;
    } else {
      throw new TypeError('Name must be a string.')
    }
  },
```

```
  get name() {
    console.log('Return name');
    return this._name;
  }
  /* Same for the other properties. */
};
const item = new Item(
  'JavaScript: The Comprehensive Guide',
  59.95,
  'Philip Ackermann',
  '978-1-4932-2286-5'
)


console.log(item.name);     // "Return name"
                            // "JavaScript: The Comprehensive Guide"
item.name = 'JavaScript: The Comprehensive Guide by Philip Ackermann';
                            // "Set new name"
```

Listing 4.25 Getters and Setters when Using Constructor Functions

```
class Item {
  constructor(name, price, author, isbn) {
    this._name = name;
    this._price = price;
    this._author = author;
    this._isbn = isbn;
  }
  set name(newName) {
    if(typeof newName === 'string') {
      console.log('Set new name');
      this._name = newName;
    } else {
      throw new TypeError('Name must be a string.')
    }
  }
  get name() {
    console.log('Return name');
    return this._name;
  }
  /* Same for the other properties. */
}
const item = new Item(
  'JavaScript: The Comprehensive Guide',
  59.95,
```

```
  'Philip Ackermann',
  '978-1-4932-2286-5'
)

console.log(item.name);      // "Return name"
                             // "JavaScript: The Comprehensive Guide"
item.name = 'JavaScript: The Comprehensive Guide by Philip Ackermann';
                             // "Set new name"
```

Listing 4.26 Getters and Setters when Using Classes

```
const item = Object.create(Object.prototype, {
  name: {
    set: function(newName) {
      if (typeof newName === 'string') {
        console.log('Set new name');
        this._name = newName;
      } else {
        throw new TypeError('Name must be a string.')
      }
    },
    get: function() {
        console.log('Return name');
        return this._name;
    }
    /* Same for the other properties. */
  }
});
// "Set new name"
item.name = 'JavaScript: The Comprehensive Guide by Philip Ackermann';
// "Return name"
console.log(item.name);
// Output:
// "JavaScript: The Comprehensive Guide by Philip Ackermann"
```

Listing 4.27 Getters and Setters when Using Object.create()

Note

You don't necessarily have to define a setter *and* getter method for a property. You can also specify only a setter method or only a getter method.

Data Properties and Access Properties

Now and then, you'll also find a distinction between data properties and access properties in literature. *Data properties* are those object properties that can be accessed without setters and getters, like some kinds of simple variables within an object that only contain data. *Access properties*, on the other hand, do not contain any data themselves but provide setter and getter methods that access or return the actual data.

In Listing 4.28, for example, the isbn property is a data property, while the name property (without a leading underscore) is an access property (even though the _name data property is accessed within the setter or getter method). Read and write access looks the same in both cases.

```javascript
const item = {
  isbn: '',
  _name: '',
  /* Here are the other properties. */
  set name(newName) {
    if(typeof newName === 'string') {
      console.log('Set new name');
      this._name = newName;
    } else {
      throw new TypeError('Name must be a string.')
    }
  },
  get name() {
    console.log('Return name');
    return this._name;
  }
  /* Same for the other properties. */
}
// Data property
item.isbn = '978-1-4932-2286-5';
console.log(item.isbn);
// Possible, but not desired, because access
// is to take place using set and get.
item._name = 'JavaScript: The Comprehensive Guide';
console.log(item._name);
// Access property
item.name = 'JavaScript: The Comprehensive Guide by Philip Ackermann';
console.log(item.name);
```

Listing 4.28 Data Properties and Access Properties

4.2.7   Adding or Overwriting Object Properties and Object Methods

As cannot be stressed enough, JavaScript is a dynamic programming language. This affects many areas, including the handling of objects. That is, you can add new properties and methods to objects in JavaScript any time. Many other languages do not provide this possibility—not even Java, which we so often use for comparison.

Creating Object Properties and Object Methods via Dot Notation

Adding a new property or a new method to an object works similarly to the initialization of variables regarding notation, except that on the left side of the assignment you state the name of the object, followed by the member operator and the name of the new property or method, as shown in Listing 4.29.

```
item.publisher = 'Rheinwerk Verlag';
item.order = function() {
  console.log('The book has been ordered successfully.');
}
```

Listing 4.29 Adding New Properties and Methods

Afterward, the new properties and methods are available as usual (see Listing 4.30).

```
console.log(item.publisher); // Output: Rheinwerk Verlag
item.order();                // Output: The book has been ordered successfully.
```

Listing 4.30 Access to Properties and Methods Defined Subsequently

In the same way, properties and methods of an object can also be overwritten or assigned new values, as shown in Listing 4.31.

```
item.publisher = 'Rheinwerk Verlag;
item.order = function() {
  console.log('The book has been ordered successfully.');
}
console.log(item.publisher); // Output: Rheinwerk Verlag
item.order();                // Output: The book has been ordered successfully.
// Overwrite the property
item.publisher = 'Rheinwerk Publishing';
// Overwrite the method
item.order = function() {
  console.log(`The book was ordered successfully from ${this.publisher}.`);
}
console.log(item.publisher); // Output: Rheinwerk Publishing
item.order();                // Output: The book was ordered ...
                             // successfully from Rheinwerk Publishing.
```

Listing 4.31 Overwriting Properties and Methods

In principle, it doesn't matter whether you specify all properties and methods directly when creating an object using literal notation or whether you add them individually afterward using dot notation. As you can see in Listing 4.32, the result is the same (although in direct comparison, literal notation better represents the coherence of the properties and methods as an object and is somewhat easier to read due to the indentation).

```javascript
const item = {
  name: 'JavaScript: The Comprehensive Guide',
  price: 59.95,
  author: 'Philip Ackermann',
  isbn: '978-1-4932-2286-5',
  printDescription: function() {
    console.log(`${this.author}: ${this.name}`);
  }
}
const item2 = {};
item2.name = 'JavaScript: The Comprehensive Guide';
item2.price = 59.95;
item2.author = 'Philip Ackermann';
item2.isbn = '978-1-4932-2286-5';
item2.printDescription = function() {
  console.log(`${this.author}: ${this.name}`);
}
```

Listing 4.32 Creating Objects and Defining Properties and Methods

Note, however, that when using literal notation, you must separate the name and value of the properties/methods with a colon and the individual properties/methods with commas. In dot notation, on the other hand, you use the equals sign and end with a semicolon because these are individual statements.

Preventing Properties and Methods from Being Overwritten

It isn't always desirable for the properties and methods of an object to be able to be overwritten. In some cases, you will explicitly want to prevent them from being overwritten later. In other cases, you'll want certain object properties and object methods to be available only from within, but not from outside of, an object. In JavaScript, much of this is relatively complex but still implementable via appropriate techniques.

Creating Object Properties and Object Methods via Bracket Notation

As for accessing object properties and object methods, bracket notation also can be used to create new properties and methods of an object. To do this, write the name of the respective property/method in square brackets after the object name on the left side of the respective assignment, and then write the value to be assigned on the right side, as shown in Listing 4.33.

```
const item = {};
item['name'] = 'JavaScript: The Comprehensive Guide';
item['price'] = 59.95;
item['author'] = 'Philip Ackermann';
item['isbn'] = '978-1-4932-2286-5';
item['printDescription'] = function() {
  console.log(`${this.author}: ${this.name}`);
}
```

Listing 4.33 Definition of Properties and Methods via Bracket Notation

Creating Object Properties and Object Methods via Helper Methods

Since ES5, JavaScript provides two helper methods for defining object properties and object methods: `Object.defineProperty()` lets you define a single new property (or method), and `Object.defineProperties()` enables you to define several in one go.

As shown in Listing 4.34, the object for which the new property/method is to be added is passed to the `Object.defineProperty()` method as the first argument, the name of the respective property/method is passed as the second argument, and finally a configuration object for defining the property attributes is passed as the third argument.

```
const item = {};
Object.defineProperty(item, 'name', {
    value: 'JavaScript: The Comprehensive Guide'
});
Object.defineProperty(item, 'price', {
    value: 59.95
});
Object.defineProperty(item, 'author', {
    value: 'Philip Ackermann'
});
Object.defineProperty(item, 'isbn', {
    value: '978-1-4932-2286-5'
});
Object.defineProperty(item, 'printDescription', {
    value: function() {
      console.log(`${this.author}: ${this.name}`);
    }
});
```

```
console.log(item.name);   // "JavaScript: The Comprehensive Guide"
console.log(item.price);  // 59.95
console.log(item.author); // "Philip Ackermann"
console.log(item.isbn);   // "978-1-4932-2286-5"
```

Listing 4.34 Adding New Properties and Methods via the Object.defineProperty() Method

The `Object.defineProperties()` method works much in the same way. As the first parameter, it's passed the object that is to be assigned the new properties/methods. As the second parameter, it's passed a configuration object, the structure of which corresponds to the configuration object that you already know from the `Object.create()` method: the property names of this configuration object each represent the names of the property/method to be created, and the respective configuration object defines the property attributes. An example of this is shown in Listing 4.35.

```
const item = {};
Object.defineProperties(item, {
  name: {
    value: 'JavaScript: The Comprehensive Guide'
  },
  price: {
    value: 59.95
  },
  author: {
    value: 'Philip Ackermann'
  },
  isbn: {
    value: '978-1-4932-2286-5'
  },
  printDescription: {
    value: function() {
      console.log(`${this.author}: ${this.name}`);
    }
  }
});
console.log(item.name);   // "JavaScript: The Comprehensive Guide"
console.log(item.price);  // 44.9
console.log(item.author); // "Philip Ackermann"
console.log(item.isbn);   // "978-1-4932-2286-5"
```

Listing 4.35 Adding New Properties and Methods via the Object.defineProperties() Method

4.2.8 Deleting Object Properties and Object Methods

In addition to dynamically adding object properties, it's also possible to dynamically remove object properties from an object again. To do this, use the delete operator, and pass it the object property to be removed as an operand.

An example is shown in Listing 4.36. First the item object is defined with four properties and one method. Then the in operator is used to check whether the item object includes the price property; this is done by the 'price' in item line.

The delete item.price statement ensures that the price property is deleted from the item object (see also Figure 4.11). Subsequently, the in operator returns false.

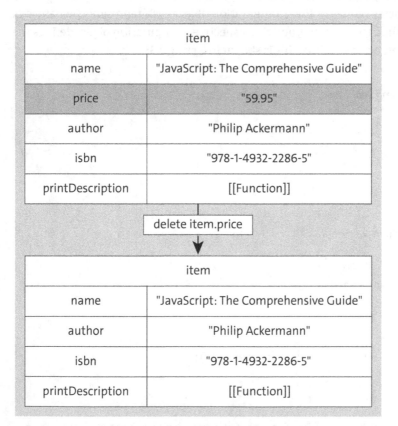

Figure 4.11 The delete Operator Is Used to Delete a Property from the Object

```
const item = {
  name: 'JavaScript: The Comprehensive Guide',
  price: 59.95,
  author: 'Philip Ackermann',
  isbn: '978-1-4932-2286-5',
  printDescription: function() {
```

```
    console.log(`${this.author}: ${this.name}`);
  }
}
console.log('price' in item);    // Output: true
console.log(item.price);         // Output: 44.9
delete item.price;               // Delete property
console.log('price' in item);    // Output: false
console.log(item.price);         // Output: undefined
```

Listing 4.36 Removing an Object Property

> **Note**
>
> The in operator returns true if the property passed as the first operand exists in the object passed as the second operand.

> **delete Operator versus null and undefined**
>
> By the way, using the delete operator is not the same as assigning the null value or the undefined value of an object property. The latter merely ensures that the property is given the value null or undefined, but not that the property is removed from the object, as demonstrated in Listing 4.37 and illustrated in Figure 4.12.
>
> ```
> const item = {
>   name: 'JavaScript: The Comprehensive Guide',
>   price: 59.95,
>   author: 'Philip Ackermann',
>   isbn: '978-1-4932-2286-5',
>   printDescription: function() {
>     console.log(`${this.author}: ${this.name}`);
>   }
> }
> console.log('price' in item);    // Output: true
> console.log(item.price);         // Output: 44.9
> item.price = null;               //
> console.log('price' in item);    // Output: true
> console.log(item.price);         // Output: null
> item.price = undefined;          //
> console.log('price' in item);    // Output: true
> console.log(item.price);         // Output: undefined
> ```
>
> **Listing 4.37** Assigning the Value null or undefined to an Object Property Does Not Delete the Property from the Object

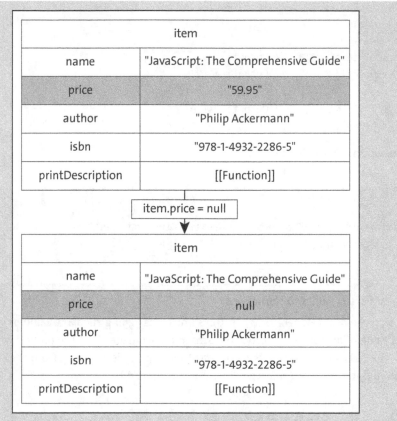

Figure 4.12 Setting an Object Property to null Does Not Delete the Property

4.2.9   Outputting Object Properties and Object Methods

To output all properties and methods of an object, there are two options: you can use the `for-in` loop, or you can use the `Object.keys()`, `Object.values()`, and `Object.entries()` methods. There are some notable differences between the techniques.

Outputting Object Properties and Object Methods via the for-in Loop

The `for-in` loop can be used to iterate over all enumerable properties (and methods) of an object—that is, those that have their property attribute `enumerable` set to `true`. An example of this is shown in Listing 4.38. In each iteration of the `for-in` loop, the `property` variable is assigned the corresponding name of the property or method of the `item` object. Using bracket notation, it's then possible to access the respective values of the properties via the variable. (This wouldn't be possible using dot notation, for example.)

```
const item = {
  name: 'JavaScript: The Comprehensive Guide',
  price: 59.95,
```

```
  author: 'Philip Ackermann',
  isbn: '978-1-4932-2286-5',
  printDescription: function() {
    console.log(`${this.author}: ${this.name}`);
  }
}
for(let property in item) {
  console.log(`Name: ${property}`);
  console.log(`Value: ${item[property]}`);
}
```

Listing 4.38 Listing All Object Properties and Object Methods via the for-in Loop

Outputting Object Properties and Object Methods via the Helper Methods

So the for-in loop provides an easy way to iterate over all the enumerable properties and methods of an object. Since ES5, the Object.keys() method provides an alternative that, for an object, returns the names of all (enumerable) properties and methods as an array. Using these methods instead of the for-in loop is suitable whenever you need the names of an object's properties and methods in list form—for example, to pass them to a function or to further process the array using array methods.

In the example shown in Listing 4.39, the result of calling Object.keys() is assigned to the properties array variable, which in turn is passed as an argument to the printArray() function. Within this function, a normal for loop is then used to iterate over the names in this array and output each name.

```
const properties = Object.keys(item);
for(let i=0; i<properties.length; i++) {
  const property = properties[i];
  console.log(`Name: ${property}`);
  console.log(`Value: ${item[property]}`);
}
printArray(properties);
function printArray(array) {
  for(let i=0; i<array.length; i++) {
    console.log(array[i]);
  }
}
```

Listing 4.39 Listing All Object Properties and Object Methods via the Object.keys() Method

In addition, since ES2017, there are the Object.values() and Object.entries() methods. The former returns the values of all (enumerable) properties and methods as an array; the latter returns name-value pairs of all (enumerable) properties and methods (see Listing 4.40).

```
const keys = Object.keys(item);
console.log(keys);
// [
//   'name',
//   'price',
//   'author',
//   'isbn',
//   'printDescription'
// ]
const values = Object.values(item);
console.log(values);
// [
//   'JavaScript: The Comprehensive Guide',
//   44.9,
//   'Philip Ackermann',
//   '978-1-4932-2286-5',
//   [Function: printDescription]
// ]
const entries = Object.entries(item);
console.log(entries);
// [
//   [ 'name', 'JavaScript: The Comprehensive Guide' ],
//   [ 'price', 44.9 ],
//   [ 'author', 'Philip Ackermann' ],
//   [ 'isbn', '978-1-4932-2286-5' ],
//   [ 'printDescription', [Function: printDescription] ]
// ]
```

Listing 4.40 Comparison of the Object.keys(), Object.values(), and Object.entries() Methods

> **Note**
>
> If you need the property names and method names of an object or their values as an array, use the Object.keys(), Object.values(), or Object.entries() method. However, if you need to iterate over the names only once, use the for-in loop.

One important difference between the for-in loop and the Object.keys() method worth mentioning is that the for-in loop also iterates over (enumerable) properties and methods of an object's prototypes, while the Object.keys() method only returns the names of (enumerable) properties and methods defined on the respective object instance itself.

In Listing 4.41, for example, two objects are created: the john object with the firstName property and the johnDoe object with the lastName property. Because the john object is specified as the prototype when creating the latter object, the johnDoe object also inherits the firstName property from this object.

Inheritance

We'll go into the topic of inheritance in detail in Chapter 13. For now, keep in mind that in JavaScript, properties and methods of objects are *inherited* by other objects, or objects can *inherit* properties and methods from other objects.

If you now apply the for-in loop to the johnDoe object, both the lastName property defined on the johnDoe object and the firstName property defined on the prototype of the object—that is, on the john object—are output. The Object.keys() method, on the other hand, only returns the name of the lastName property, but not the firstName property, because the properties and methods of the prototypes are not taken into account here.

```
const john = {
  firstName: 'John'
}
const johnDoe = Object.create(john, {
  lastName: {
    value: 'Doe',
    enumerable: true
  }
});
console.log(john.firstName);       // John
console.log(john.lastName);        // undefined
console.log(johnDoe.firstName);    // John
console.log(johnDoe.lastName);     // Doe
// Output: lastName, firstName
for(let i in johnDoe) {
  console.log(i);
}
const properties = Object.keys(johnDoe);
// Output: ["lastName"]
console.log(properties);
```

Listing 4.41 Difference between the for-in Loop and Object.keys()

4.2.10   Using Symbols to Define Unique Object Properties

Symbols can be used to define unique names for object properties. Object properties that are defined by symbols can subsequently only be read by specifying these symbols. As opposed to the definition of object properties by strings, collisions due to identical names are thus excluded.

Listing 4.42 shows the use of symbols to define unique object properties. The firstName and lastName symbols are used here as properties for the person object. Subsequently, the values of the properties can only be accessed using these symbols; both the access via the index and the access via the property names themselves fail.

```
const firstName = Symbol('firstName');
const lastName = Symbol('lastName');
const person = {};
person[firstName] = 'John';
person[lastName] = 'Doe';
console.log(person[firstName]);     // "John"
console.log(person[lastName]);      // "Doe"
console.log(person[0]);             // undefined
console.log(person[1]);             // undefined
console.log(person.firstName);      // undefined
console.log(person.lastName);       // undefined
console.log(person['firstName']);   // undefined
console.log(person['lastName']);    // undefined
```

Listing 4.42 Symbols Are Suitable as Unique Keys for Object Properties

For comparison, Listing 4.43 shows that this is different when using strings as property names: even though the index cannot be used, access is still possible via the name of the property.

```
const firstName = 'firstName';
const lastName = 'lastName';
const person = {};
person[firstName] = 'John';
person[lastName] = 'Doe';
console.log(person[firstName]);     // "John"
console.log(person[lastName]);      // "Doe"
console.log(person[0]);             // undefined
console.log(person[1]);             // undefined
console.log(person.firstName);      // "John"
console.log(person.lastName);       // "Doe"
console.log(person['firstName']);   // "John"
console.log(person['lastName']);    // "Doe"
```

Listing 4.43 Definition of Object Properties Based on Strings

Symbol.iterator

An example of using symbols to define object properties is the Symbol.iterator symbol, shown earlier in this chapter, which defines the method within iterable objects that returns the iterator for the object.

4.2.11   Preventing Changes to Objects

In some cases, it may be useful to protect objects from changes—that is, to prevent new properties or methods from being added to an object. JavaScript offers three different ways to do this:

- Preventing extensions to objects
- Sealing objects
- Freezing objects

We'll discuss these next.

Preventing Extensions to Objects

The first way to protect objects from changes is to use the `Object.preventExtensions()` method. As the name suggests, if you pass an object to this method, it will no longer be possible to extend the object. In other words: no new properties and methods can be added. If you try to do this anyway, an error occurs, as shown in Listing 4.44: the attempt to add the new `weight` property to the `john` object is not successful.

Values of existing properties and methods can be changed, though. In the example, after calling the `Object.preventExtensions()` method, a new value is assigned to the `firstName` property. This statement is allowed and therefore does not generate an error. It's also allowed to change property attributes, as shown in the example for the `enumerable` attribute of the `firstName` property.

```
const john = {
  firstName: 'John',
  lastName: 'Doe'
}
console.log(Object.isExtensible(john));    // true
john.age = 44;                             // define new property
console.log(john.age);                     // 44
Object.preventExtensions(john);            // prevent extensions
console.log(Object.isExtensible(john));    // false
john.firstName = 'James';                  // permitted: change existing
                                           // property
console.log(john.firstName);               // "James"
console.log(Object.getOwnPropertyDescriptor(john,
                             'firstName').enumerable);  // true
Object.defineProperty(john, 'firstName', { // permitted: change property
                             // attributes
    enumerable: false
});
console.log(Object.getOwnPropertyDescriptor(john,
                             'firstName').enumerable);  // false
```

```
john.weight = 88;                       // TypeError: Can't add property weight,
                                        // object is not extensible
```

Listing 4.44 Preventing Extensions to an Object

By the way, the `Object.isExtensible()` method enables you to check whether an object is extensible or not, as shown in the listing. As a parameter, this method expects the object for which the corresponding test is to be performed. As a result, the method returns a Boolean value.

Sealing Objects

The second way to prevent changes to an object is to use the `Object.seal()` method, which can be used to "seal" objects. Like objects for which `Object.preventExtensions()` has been called, sealed objects are not extensible, but in addition, their existing properties are not configurable either.

An example is shown in Listing 4.45. The `john` object is sealed here by calling the `Object.seal()` method. Subsequently, the `firstName` property of the `john` object can no longer be configured. Similar to the `isExtensible()` method, the `isSealed()` method can be used to determine whether an object is sealed.

```
const john = {
  firstName: 'John',
  lastName: 'Doe'
}
console.log(Object.isExtensible(john));    // true
console.log(Object.isSealed(john));        // false
john.age = 44;                             // define new property
console.log(john.age);                     // 44
Object.seal(john);                         // seal object
console.log(Object.isExtensible(john));    // false
console.log(Object.isSealed(john));        // true
john.firstName = 'James';                  // permitted: change existing
                                           // property
console.log(john.firstName);               // "James"
console.log(Object.getOwnPropertyDescriptor(john,
                          'firstName').enumerable);  // true
Object.defineProperty(john, 'firstName', { // Uncaught TypeError: Cannot
                                           // redefine
                                           // property: firstName
    enumerable: false
});
```

Listing 4.45 Sealing an Object

> **Sealed Objects Are Not Expandable**
>
> Because sealed objects are also nonextensible, the `Object.isExtensible()` method in Listing 4.45 returns `false` for the `john` object after sealing.

Freezing Objects

The `Object.freeze()` method goes one step further than the previously shown options. It freezes objects: like `Object.preventExtensions()`, it ensures that objects cannot be extended by new properties and methods, and like the `Object.seal()` method, it ensures that property attributes cannot be changed, but in addition, values of existing properties (and methods) cannot be changed. The `Object.isFrozen()` method can be used to determine whether an object is frozen or not.

An example of this is shown in Listing 4.46. The `john` object is frozen here by calling the `Object.freeze()` method, and subsequently, it's no longer possible to assign a new value to the `firstName` property. Calling `Object.isExtensible()` returns `false` for the frozen object, and calling `Object.isSealed()` returns `true`, because frozen objects are always also sealed and not extensible.

```
const john = {
  firstName: 'John',
  lastName: 'Doe'
}
console.log(Object.isExtensible(john));   // true
console.log(Object.isSealed(john));       // false
console.log(Object.isFrozen(john));       // false
john.age = 44;                            // new property
console.log(john.age);                    // 44
Object.freeze(john);                      // freeze object
console.log(Object.isExtensible(john));   // false
console.log(Object.isSealed(john));       // true
console.log(Object.isFrozen(john));       // true
john.firstName = 'James';                 // TypeError: Cannot assign to
                                          // read only
                                          // property 'firstName' of #<Object>
```

Listing 4.46 Freezing an Object

Comparison of the Techniques Shown

The relationship between the `Object.preventExtensions()`, `Object.seal()`, and `Object.freeze()` methods is shown in Figure 4.13: `Object.preventExtensions()` ensures that no new properties can be added to the respective object, `Object.seal()` further ensures that existing properties cannot be configured, and `Object.freeze()` additionally ensures that values of existing properties cannot be changed.

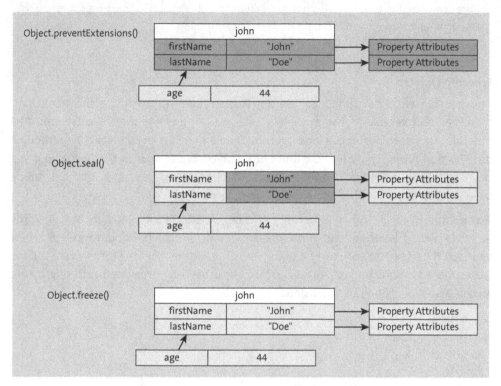

Figure 4.13 Comparison of the Different Methods for Preventing Object Changes

4.3   Working with Arrays

You got to know arrays briefly in Chapter 3. Nevertheless, at this point we'll first give you a brief recap of how to create and initialize arrays.

4.3.1   Creating and Initializing Arrays

In JavaScript, arrays can be created in two different ways: via a *constructor function* and via the short notation shown in the previous chapter, the *array literal notation*. Using the array constructor function, an array is created as shown in Listing 4.47.

```
const names = new Array();
```

Listing 4.47 Creating an Array

If you know a priori the number of values to be stored in the array, you can also pass this number to the constructor function as an argument as shown in Listing 4.48 (though you don't necessarily have to as arrays grow dynamically).

```
const names = new Array(20);
```

Listing 4.48 Creating an Array with a Specified Length

If you even know the values to be stored in the array, you can also pass them directly as arguments, as shown in Listing 4.49.

```
const names = new Array('John', 'James', 'Peter');
```

Listing 4.49 Creating an Array with Specified Values

Calling the Array() Constructor Function

Note that if you call the `Array()` constructor function with a single value and this value is a number, it is used to define the length of the array. If you call the constructor function with two numbers as arguments, the length of the array is implicitly 2, and the array contains the two number elements.

As you already know, the length of an array can be determined via the `length` property.

```
const names = new Array('John', 'James', 'Peter');
console.log(names.length); // Output: 3
```

Listing 4.50 Determining the Length of an Array

Creating Arrays without the new Keyword

In the case of arrays, you can also omit new when calling the constructor function. The source code in Listing 4.50 could therefore be rephrased as follows:

```
const names = Array('John', 'James', 'Peter');
```

Because developers often have to deal with arrays in practice or need to use arrays relatively often, JavaScript provides a convenient short notation (array literal notation) for creating arrays. The individual values are simply written in square brackets, as shown in Listing 4.51.

```
const names = ['John', 'James', 'Peter']; // Create an array with specific
                                           // values
const colors = [];                         // Create an empty array
```

Listing 4.51 Creating an Array Using Short Notation

Conveniently, array literal notation can be combined with object literal notation to, for example, create an array of objects, as in Listing 4.52.

```
const contacts = [
  {
    firstName: 'John',
    lastName: 'Doe',
    email: 'john.doe@javascripthandbuch.de'
  },
  {
    firstName: 'James',
    lastName: 'Doe',
    email: 'james.doe@javascripthandbuch.de'
  },
  {
    firstName: 'Peter',
    lastName: 'Doe',
    email: 'peter.doe@javascripthandbuch.de'
  }
];
```

Listing 4.52 Creating an Array of Objects Using Short Notation

---

Different Types in Arrays

Unlike other languages, JavaScript provides the possibility to store values of different types in a single array. This means, for example, that you can store both strings and numbers in the same array (see Listing 4.53).

```
const values = [];
values[0] = 'John';
values[1] = 4711;
values[2] = true;
```

Listing 4.53 Arrays Can Contain Values of Different Data Types

---

Now that you know how to create arrays, we'll show you next what you can do with arrays. The possibilities include the following:

- **Adding and removing elements**
  The push(), pop(), shift(), and unshift() methods can be used to add and remove elements.

- **Using arrays as stacks and queues**
  In other programming languages, there are data structures such as *stacks* and *queues* that are sometimes permanently built into the language. In JavaScript (up to ES6), there are only arrays. (As of ES6, there are *sets* and *maps*, which we'll show you later in Chapter 16). However, arrays can be used just like the stack and queue data structures thanks to the push(), pop(), shift(), and unshift() methods (Section 4.3.7 and Section 4.3.8).

- **Sorting arrays**

  The individual elements of an array can be sorted according to certain criteria using the reverse() and sort() methods (Section 4.3.6).

- **Finding elements in the array**

  There are several methods for finding elements in an array, including the indexOf(), lastIndexOf(), and find() methods, which we'll introduce in Section 4.3.9.

- **Functional aspects**

  Arrays have various methods that support *functional programming*. We'll discuss the corresponding every(), filter(), forEach(), map(), some(), and reduce() methods in connection with functional programming in Chapter 14.

An overview of the most important methods of arrays is presented in Table 4.2.

Method	Description
concat()	Appends elements or arrays to an existing array
filter()	Filters elements from the array based on a filter criterion passed in the form of a function
forEach()	Applies a passed function to each element in the array
join()	Converts an array into a string
map()	Maps the elements of an array to new elements based on a passed conversion function
pop()	Removes the last element of an array
push()	Inserts a new element at the end of the array
reduce()	Combines the elements of an array into one value based on a passed function
reverse()	Reverses the order of the elements in the array
shift()	Removes the first element of an array
slice()	Cuts individual elements from an array
splice()	Adds new elements at any position in the array
sort()	Sorts the array, optionally based on a passed comparison function

Table 4.2 The Most Important Methods of Arrays

4.3.2 Accessing Elements of an Array

Arrays, like objects, have different key-value pairs, where the keys are actually index numbers. As usual in computer science, counting starts at 0: that is, the first element is placed at index 0, the second element at index 1, and so on (see Figure 4.14).

0	"Clean bathroom"
1	"Go shopping"
2	"Tidy up"
3	"Mow lawn"

Figure 4.14 Array Structure

Individual elements in the array are accessed via this index, as shown in Listing 4.54. To do this, you use square brackets to specify the index you want to access. (Accessing a nonexistent index returns undefined as a return value.)

```
const todoList = [
  'Clean bathroom',       // element at index 0
  'Go shopping',          // element at index 1
  'Tidy up',              // element at index 2
  'Mow lawn'              // element at index 3
];
console.log(todoList[0]);    // "Clean bathroom"
console.log(todoList[1]);    // "Go shopping"
console.log(todoList[2]);    // "Tidy up"
console.log(todoList[3]);    // "Mow lawn"
console.log(todoList[4]);    // undefined
```

Listing 4.54 Accessing Individual Elements of an Array by Index

To iterate over the individual elements of an array, you can use a for loop, as shown in Listing 4.55.

```
for (let i = 0; i < todoList.length; i++) {
  console.log(todoList[i]);
}
```

Listing 4.55 Accessing Individual Elements of an Array via Loop and Index

4.3.3   Adding Elements to an Array

To add elements to an array, JavaScript provides several methods. They allow you to insert elements at the beginning or end of an array or at any position in the array. Ahead, we'll introduce the appropriate methods.

Adding an Element to the End of an Array

The most commonly used method when it comes to working with arrays is probably the push() method. It can be used to add elements to the end of an array. You can pass either one element or several elements as arguments. The method returns the new length of the array.

An example is shown in Listing 4.56. It uses push() to twice add one string to the todo-List Array and then to add two strings in one call. After each call, the length of the array is assigned to the length variable, which takes the values 1, 2, and 4 in succession. Figure 4.15 shows the state of the array before and after adding the respective elements.

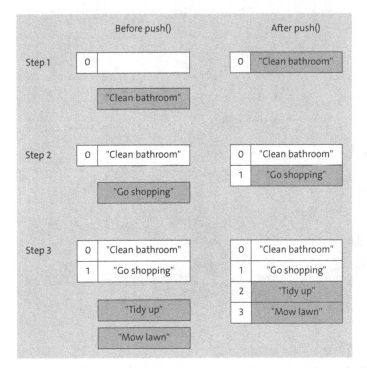

Figure 4.15 The push() Method Inserts New Elements at the End of an Array

```
const todoList = [];
let length;
length = todoList.push('Clean bathroom');
console.log(length);   // 1
length = todoList.push('Go shopping');
console.log(length);   // 2
length = todoList.push('Tidy up', 'Mow lawn');
console.log(length);   // 4
console.log(todoList); // ["Clean bathroom", "Go shopping",
                       // "Tidy up", "Mow lawn"]
```

Listing 4.56 Adding Elements to an Array via the push() Method

Adding an Element to the Beginning of an Array

If you want to insert new elements at the beginning of an array rather than at the end of it, you can use the unshift() method. Basically, this method works like the push() method, with the difference that it changes the index assignments of all the following elements. The push() method too can be passed a single element, or several elements separated by commas, which are then added to the beginning of the array in order. Again, the new length of the array is returned. Listing 4.57 shows how two new elements are added to the todoList array individually and then another two elements in one step. The corresponding intermediate results are illustrated in Figure 4.16.

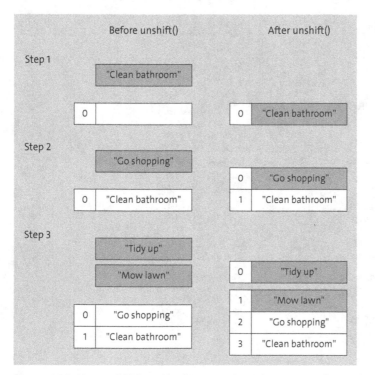

Figure 4.16 The unshift() Method Inserts New Elements at the Beginning of an Array

```
const todoList = [];
let length;
length = todoList.unshift('Clean bathroom');
console.log(length);   // 1
length = todoList.unshift('Go shopping');
console.log(length);   // 2
length = todoList.unshift('Tidy up', 'Mow lawn');
console.log(length);   // 4
console.log(todoList); // ["Tidy up", "Mow lawn",
                       // "Go shopping", "Clean bathroom"]
```

Listing 4.57 Adding Elements to an Array Using the unshift() Method

Inserting Elements at Any Position in the Array

Sometimes, you need the flexibility to add elements not only at the beginning or end of an array, but at arbitrary positions. You can achieve this using the splice() method.

> **Various Uses of the splice() Method**
>
> As you will see in the course of this chapter, the splice() method can be used not only for inserting elements, but also for deleting or replacing them. But first things first: let's first show you how to use splice() to add elements to arbitrary locations in the array.

To this end, you pass several arguments to the method: The first argument represents the position in the array from which the new elements should be added. The second argument represents the number of elements to be deleted from the array. For now, we always leave this argument at the value 0 as we only want to use splice() to add elements (not to replace or delete elements). All other arguments represent the elements to be added to the array.

Listing 4.58 again shows a source code example, Figure 4.17 the corresponding intermediate steps. In the first step, the Paint garage string is added to the todoList array at position 2. The subsequent elements (i.e., the Tidy up and Mow lawn strings) are moved back one position within the array. In the second step, the Lay sod and Lay out vegetable garden strings are added (again at position 2). Again, this moves the elements already present in the array from this position downward, but this time by two positions as two elements are newly added.

```javascript
const todoList = [
  'Clean bathroom',
  'Go shopping',
  'Tidy up',
  'Mow lawn'
];
todoList.splice(
  2,                    // Index from which to insert elements
  0,                    // Number of elements to be deleted
  'Paint garage'        // Element to be added
);
console.log(todoList);
// [
//   "Clean bathroom",
//   "Go shopping",
//   "Paint garage",
//   "Tidy up",
//   "Mow lawn"
```

```
// ]
todoList.splice(
  2,                              // Index from which to insert elements
  0,                              // Number of elements to be deleted
  'Lay sod',                      // Elements to be ...
  'Lay out vegetable garden'  // ... added
);
console.log(todoList);
// [
//   "Clean bathroom",
//   "Go shopping",
//   "Lay sod",
//   "Lay out vegetable garden",
//   "Paint garage",
//   "Tidy up",
//   "Mow lawn"
// ]
```

Listing 4.58 Adding Elements to an Array Using the splice() Method

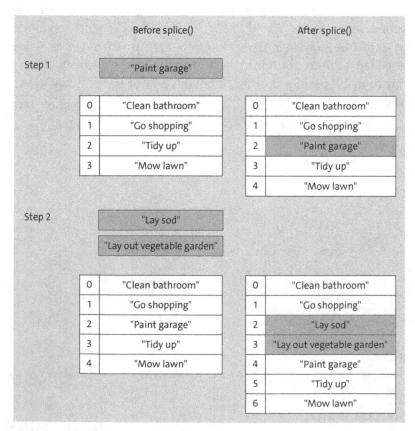

Figure 4.17 Using the splice() Method, Elements Can Be Inserted at Any Position in the Array

4.3.4 Removing Elements from an Array

Similar to adding elements to an array, there are also different ways to remove elements from an array again. Here too you have a choice: Do you want to remove an element from the end or from the beginning of an array? Do you even want to remove a whole part in the middle of the array? We'll show you how in the following sections.

Removing the Last Element from an Array

Just as the push() method is used for adding elements, the pop() method is used for removing elements from an array. That is, this method enables you to remove the last element of an array. As a return value, the method returns the removed element or—if there are no elements in the array—the value undefined. An example is shown in Listing 4.59. Figure 4.18 illustrates the first step shown in the listing, where the last element of the array (Mow lawn) is removed from the array.

```
const todoList = [
  'Clean bathroom',
  'Go shopping',
  'Tidy up',
  'Mow lawn'
];
const item1 = todoList.pop();
console.log(item1);              // Output: Mow lawn
const item2 = todoList.pop();
console.log(item2);              // Output: Tidy up
const item3 = todoList.pop();
console.log(item3);              // Output: Go shopping
const item4 = todoList.pop();
console.log(item4);              // Output: Clean bathroom
const item5 = todoList.pop();
console.log(item5);              // Output: undefined
```

Listing 4.59 The pop() Method Removes the Last Element from an Array

Figure 4.18 The pop() Method Removes the Last Element from an Array

Removing the First Element from an Array

If you want to remove not the last element from an array but the first one, use the shift() method instead of the pop() method. Essentially, it works opposite to the unshift() method; that is, it removes the first element from an array and returns it. If there are no elements in the array, the method—like pop()—returns the value unde-fined.

An example of this is shown in Listing 4.60. Here, the first elements are sequentially removed from the array and output. And Figure 4.19 shows the state of the array before and after the first removal.

```
const todoList = [
  'Clean bathroom',
  'Go shopping',
  'Tidy up',
  'Mow lawn'
];
const item1 = todoList.shift();
console.log(item1);              // Output: Clean bathroom
const item2 = todoList.shift();
console.log(item2);              // Output: Go shopping
const item3 = todoList.shift();
console.log(item3);              // Output: Tidy up
const item4 = todoList.shift();
console.log(item4);              // Output: Mow lawn
const item5 = todoList.shift();
console.log(item5);              // Output: undefined
```

Listing 4.60 The shift() Method Removes the First Element from an Array

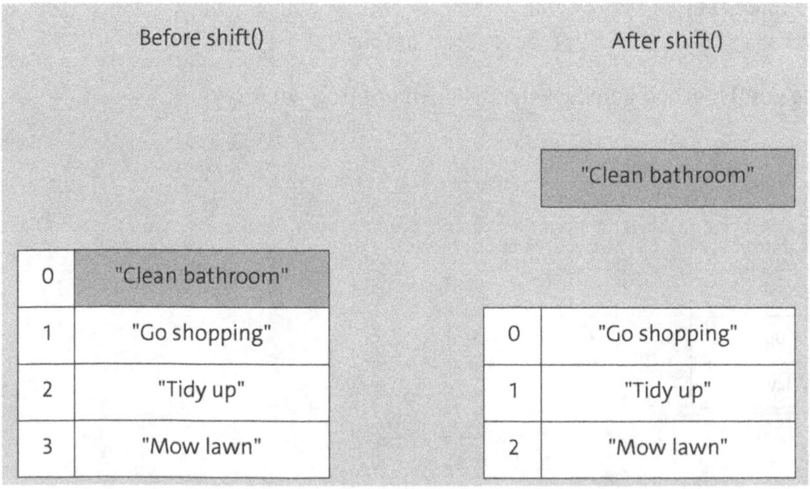

Figure 4.19 The shift() Method Removes the First Element from an Array

Removing Some of the Elements from an Array

When we introduced the `splice()` method in the context of adding elements to an array, we mentioned that elements can also be removed from an array via this method. Remember that if `splice()` is used for adding elements, the second argument is set to the value 0, and the elements to be added are then passed to it. If, on the other hand, you want to use `splice()` to remove elements, the parameters are set slightly differently, as shown in Listing 4.61.

The first argument represents the position in the array from which elements are to be removed, and the second argument represents the number of elements to be removed. Unlike when adding elements, no further arguments need to be passed (because no new elements are to be added).

In Listing 4.61, the two middle elements of the `todoList` array are removed in this way: `splice(1, 2)` removes two elements starting from position 1. As a return value, `splice()` returns an array containing the removed elements. Figure 4.20 illustrates the state of the `todoList` array before and after removing the elements.

```
const todoList = [
  'Clean bathroom',
  'Go shopping',
  'Tidy up',
  'Mow lawn'
];
const deletedTodos = todoList.splice(1, 2);
console.log(deletedTodos);              // ["Go shopping", "Tidy up"]
console.log(todoList);                  // ["Clean bathroom", "Mow lawn"]
```

Listing 4.61 The splice() Method Can Be Used to Delete Elements from an Array

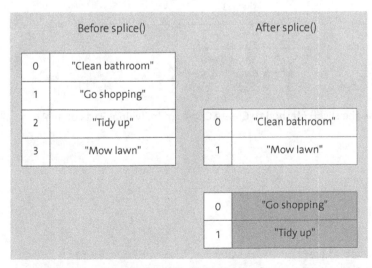

Figure 4.20 You Can Use the splice() Method to Remove Elements from an Array

4.3.5   Copying Some of the Elements from an Array

You've already seen how you can remove some of the elements from an array using the splice() method. On the other hand, the slice() method, which we'll present now, enables you to *copy* some of the elements of an array. The return value is an array with copies of the corresponding elements. The original elements remain in the array.

Two arguments can be passed to the method. The first argument denotes the position from which the extraction of the elements is to start, and the second (optional) argument denotes the position where the extraction of the elements should end. Listing 4.62 shows some examples. The individual steps are illustrated in Figure 4.21.

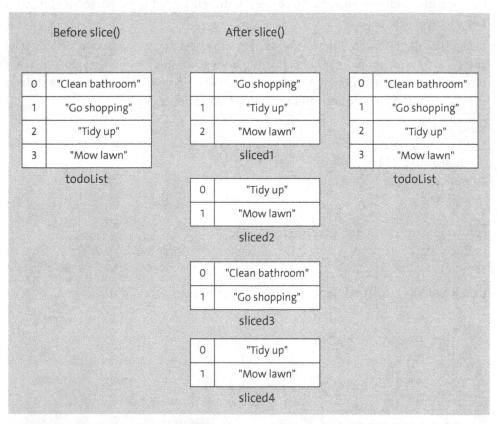

Figure 4.21 You Can Use the slice() Method to Create Copies of Individual Parts of an Array

```
const todoList = [
  'Clean bathroom',
  'Go shopping',
  'Tidy up',
  'Mow lawn'
];
const sliced1 = todoList.slice(1);      // starting from second element
```

```
console.log(sliced1);               // ["Go shopping", "Tidy up", "Mow lawn"]

const sliced2 = todoList.slice(2);  // starting from third element
console.log(sliced2);               // ["Tidy up", "Mow lawn"]

const sliced3 = todoList.slice(0, 2); // first and second element
console.log(sliced3);               // ["Clean bathroom", "Go shopping"]

const sliced4 = todoList.slice(2, 4); // third and fourth element
console.log(sliced4);               // ["Tidy up", "Mow lawn"]

// Original array remains unchanged:
console.log(todoList);              // ["Clean bathroom", "Go shopping",
                                    // "Tidy up", "Mow lawn"]
```

Listing 4.62 The slice() Method Can Be Used to Extract Parts of an Array

As shown, the slice() method can be called with positive numeric values as arguments, but also with negative numbers, which in turn affects which part of the array is extracted.

Table 4.3 shows the different possible combinations and their respective meanings. Some examples are shown in Listing 4.63.

First Parameter	Second Parameter	Meaning
Positive value	Positive value	Extracts the part of the array from the index defined by the first argument to the index defined by the second parameter.
Positive value	Not specified	Extracts the part of the array from the index defined by the first argument to the end of the array.
Negative value	Not specified	Extracts part of the array starting from the end of the array, where the number of extracted elements is determined by the negative value. For example, calling slice(-2) causes the last two elements of an array to be extracted.
Positive value	Negative value	Extracts the part of the array from the index defined by the first argument to the position defined by the second argument. For example, calling slice(1, -2) causes the elements from index 1 to the third-to-last index to be extracted.

Table 4.3 The Different Call Options of the slice() Method

```
const sliced5 = todoList.slice(-2);        // the last two elements
const sliced6 = todoList.slice(1,          // the second element from the
                                           // beginning to ...
                        -1);               // ... the second element from the end
const sliced7 = todoList.slice(1,          // the second element from
                                           // the beginning to ...
                        -2);               // ... the third element from the end
const sliced8 = todoList.slice(1,          // the second element from the
                                           // beginning to ...
                        -3);               // ... the fourth element from the end
console.log(sliced5);                      // ["Tidy up", "Mow lawn"]
console.log(sliced6);                      // ["Go shopping", "Tidy up"]
console.log(sliced7);                      // ["Go shopping"]
console.log(sliced8);                      // []
```

Listing 4.63 The Behavior of slice() Can Be Further Controlled by Specifying Negative Parameters

4.3.6   Sorting Arrays

Sorting data within an array is relatively simple. Two methods are available for this purpose: reverse() and sort(). The former simply reverses the order of the elements in the array; the latter allows sorting the elements according to specific individual criteria.

Reversing the Order of Elements in an Array

If you just want to reverse the order of elements in an array, the simplest way is to use the reverse() method. This method arranges the elements in reverse order (i.e., it changes the array) and additionally returns the reversed array as a return value.

An example is shown in Listing 4.64. The names array initially contains the strings John, James, and Peter in exactly this order. After calling the reverse() method, the strings are listed in the array in reverse order—that is, Peter, James, John. Obviously, you can't do much with this method.

```
const names = ['John', 'James', 'Peter'];
names.reverse();
console.log(names); // Output: Peter, James, John
```

Listing 4.64 Reversing the Order of Elements in an Array

Sorting the Elements in an Array According to Specific Criteria

The sort() method provides more flexibility because it enables you to optionally define your own sort criterion to influence the order. The sort criterion is specified in the form of a *comparison function*, which is passed as an argument to the sort() method. The comparison function, in turn, has two parameters and is internally invoked in pairs for the values of the array when sort() is called. The return value of the function determines which of two values is greater than the other:

- The return value -1 means that the first value is smaller than the second value.
- The return value 1 means that the first value is greater than the second value.
- The return value 0 means that both values are equal.

A comparison function that compares, for example, numeric values according to their size is shown in Listing 4.65.

```
function compare(value1, value2) {
  if (value1 < value2) {
    return -1; // The first value is smaller than the second value.
  } else if(value1 > value2) {
    return 1;  // The first value is greater than the second value.
  } else {
    return 0;  // Both values are of equal size.
  }
}
```

Listing 4.65 Basic Structure of a Comparison Function

This comparison function can now be passed to the sort() method, as shown in Listing 4.66. The initially unsorted values array is sorted after calling this method.

```
const values = [7, 6, 4, 8, 7, 2, 4];
values.sort(compare);
console.log(values); // 2, 4, 4, 6, 7, 7
```

Listing 4.66 Sorting with Your Own Comparison Function

Functions as Parameters of Other Functions

By the way, what's happening and shown in Listing 4.66 is that in JavaScript, you can use functions as arguments to other functions. This is a special feature of JavaScript that isn't provided by any other programming language. We'll come back to this topic later. For now, you only need to know that functions can be passed as arguments to another function. Note, however, that you must omit the parentheses here. If you wrote values.sort(compare()); in the preceding example, the compare() function would be called and the return value of the function would be passed as an argument, not the function itself.

Sorting Objects in Arrays

A slightly more complex example of using the sort() method is shown in Listing 4.67. Here you can see how to sort an array containing objects using the sort() method. For this purpose, there are three comparison functions, compareByFirstName(), compareBy-LastName(), and compareByEmail(), which compare individual elements with respect to various properties.

Within the comparison functions, we use the localeCompare() method, which is available for strings by default and takes into account country-specific settings for date and time formats and also for sorting strings. This method also returns one of three possible values: the value -1 for a case in which the string on which the method is called is "smaller" (in terms of alphabetical sorting) than the string passed as an argument; the value 1 for the case in which the string is "larger"; and the value 0 for the case in which both strings are of equal size—in other words, in which they are the same string.

```javascript
const contacts = [
  {
    firstName: 'John',
    lastName: 'Doe',
    email: 'john.doe@javascripthandbuch.de'
  },
  {
    firstName: 'James',
    lastName: 'Dean',
    email: 'superjames@javascripthandbuch.de'
  },
  {
    firstName: 'Peter',
    lastName: 'Dickens',
    email: 'dickens@javascripthandbuch.de'
  }
];
function compareByFirstName(contact1, contact2) {
  return contact1.firstName.localeCompare(contact2.firstName);
}
function compareByLastName(contact1, contact2) {
  return contact1.lastName.localeCompare(contact2.lastName);
}
function compareByEmail(contact1, contact2) {
  return contact1.email.localeCompare(contact2.email);
}
contacts.sort(compareByFirstName);  // sort by first name
console.log(contacts[0].firstName); // James
console.log(contacts[1].firstName); // John
console.log(contacts[2].firstName); // Peter
contacts.sort(compareByLastName);   // sort by last name
console.log(contacts[0].firstName); // James
console.log(contacts[1].firstName); // Peter
```

```
console.log(contacts[2].firstName); // John
contacts.sort(compareByEmail);      // sort by email address
console.log(contacts[0].firstName); // Peter
console.log(contacts[1].firstName); // John
console.log(contacts[2].firstName); // James
```

Listing 4.67 Sorting Objects within an Array

4.3.7   Using Arrays as a Stack

In programming (and in computer science in general), a *stack* refers to a data structure that operates according to the *last in, first out (LIFO) principle*, which means that the last element added to the stack is the first element to be removed. Usually, the method for adding elements is push() and the method for removing elements is pop() (see Figure 4.22).

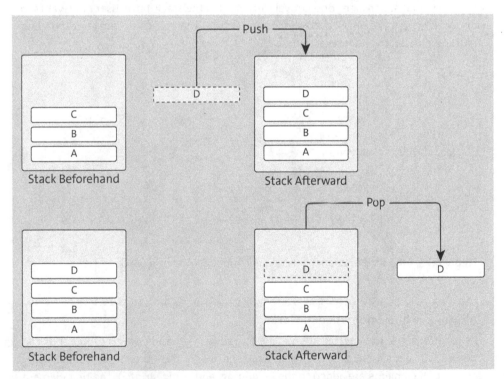

Figure 4.22 How Stacks Work

Although JavaScript does not provide any explicit stack data structure in the form of a special object or anything similar, it's possible to emulate the described behavior using arrays. To achieve this, you use the push() and pop() methods, which basically do what stacks do. A simple example is shown in Listing 4.68.

```
const stack = [];            // Declaration of a normal array
stack.push(1);               // Add one element ...
stack.push(2);               // ... and another one ...
stack.push(3);               // ... and another one ...
stack.push(4, 5, 6, 7, 8);   // ... and several in one go
console.log(stack.pop());    // Return the element that was
                             // added last: 8.
```

Listing 4.68 Simple Example of Using an Array as a Stack

Practical Example of Stacks

A practical example of using the stack data structure (in addition to the function call stack; see Chapter 3) is the implementation of an *undo functionality*—that is, the possibility within an application to undo the last user action (see Figure 4.23). To do this, the individual actions are consecutively arranged in the stack. If the user now wants to undo an action, the respective action is taken from the stack, and the corresponding part is executed to undo the action.

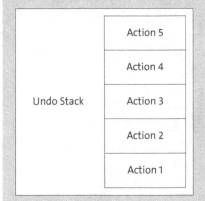

Figure 4.23 An Undo Functionality Is Usually Implemented by a Stack

Alternative Implementation of Stacks

As an alternative to using push() and pop(), the shift() and unshift() methods can be used to implement a stack. The stack then works the other way around: using unshift(), elements are added to the beginning, and using shift(), the first element is removed.

4.3.8   Using Arrays as a Queue

Like the stack, a *queue* is also a data structure, but it works in exactly the opposite way: a queue always returns the element that was added as the first of the elements contained in the queue, via the *first in, first out (FIFO) principle*. In other words, elements are added to the end of a queue, but removed from the beginning of the queue (see Figure 4.24). Usually, the corresponding methods are called enqueue() (for adding elements) and dequeue() (for removing elements).

Queues can also be emulated using arrays in JavaScript. As with stacks, the push() method ensures that elements are added to the end of the array. The rest is done by the shift() method, which returns and at the same time removes the first element of an array. Listing 4.69 shows a simple example.

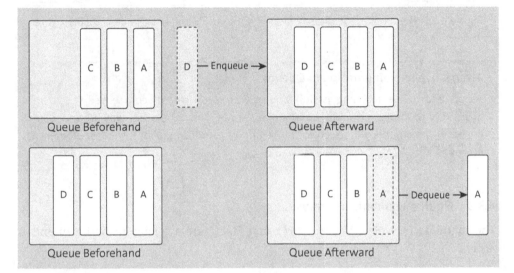

Figure 4.24 How Queues Work

```
const queue = [];                  // Declaration of a normal array
queue.push(1);                     // Add one element ...
queue.push(2);                     // ... and another one ...
queue.push(3);                     // ... and another one ...
queue.push(4, 5, 6, 7, 8);         // ... and several in one go
console.log(queue.shift());        // Return the element that was
                                   // added first: 1.
```

Listing 4.69 Simple Example of Using an Array as a Queue

Practical Example of Queues

For a practical example of using the queue data structure, consider message queues (see Figure 4.25). These type of queues decouple senders and receivers, so that they do not communicate directly with each other, but via the message queue. Messages are then stored in the message queue in the order they were sent and are processed accordingly.

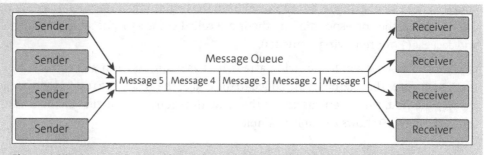

Figure 4.25 Message Queues Are a Classic Example of Using the Queue Data Structure

Alternative Implementation of Queues

As an alternative to using push() and shift(), you can of course use pop() and unshift() to implement a queue. The queue then works the other way around: using unshift(), elements are added to the beginning, and using pop(), the last element is removed.

4.3.9   Finding Elements in Arrays

The methods indexOf(), lastIndexOf(), and find() are available to find elements in arrays.

Searching from the Beginning of the Array

For the passed value, the indexOf() method determines the position (i.e., the index) where it occurs for the first time within the array. If it doesn't exist in the array, the method returns -1. An optional second parameter can be used to control from which index to start the search. Some examples are shown in Listing 4.70 and illustrated in Figure 4.26.

```
const transactions = [
  -20.0, 500.50, -40.0, -34.50, 200, 500.50, -20, 200
];
console.log(transactions.indexOf(-20.0));     // Output: 0
console.log(transactions.indexOf(500));       // Output: -1
console.log(transactions.indexOf(200));       // Output: 4
console.log(transactions.indexOf(200, 5));    // Output: 7
```

Listing 4.70 The indexOf() Method Enables You to Search for Elements within an Array

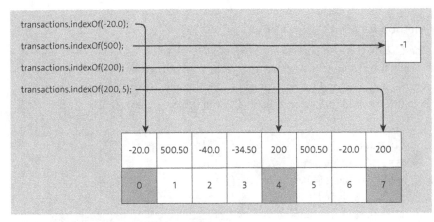

Figure 4.26 How the indexOf() Method Works

Searching from the End of an Array

The indexOf() method returns the first index where the passed value was found in the array. Any subsequent occurrences are not taken into account. Alternatively, you can use the lastIndexOf() method, which searches from the end of an array and accordingly finds the last occurrence of the passed value in the array. Optionally, as with indexOf(), a second parameter can be used to define from which index to start the search, and this method also returns -1 if the element searched for does not occur in the array (see Listing 4.71 and Figure 4.27).

```
console.log(transactions.lastIndexOf(-20.0));    // Output: 6
console.log(transactions.lastIndexOf(500));      // Output: -1
console.log(transactions.lastIndexOf(200));      // Output: 7
console.log(transactions.lastIndexOf(200, 5));   // Output: 4
```

Listing 4.71 The lastIndexOf() Method Enables You to Search for Elements within an Array Starting from the End

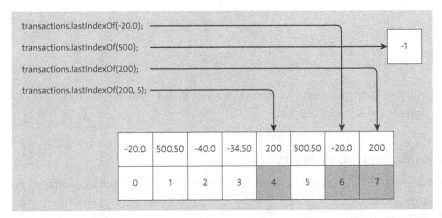

Figure 4.27 How the lastIndexOf() Method Works

Another Method for Arrays

With version ES2016 (i.e., the successor of ES6 or ES2015), the includes() method was introduced for arrays. It checks whether the passed value is contained in the array or not and returns a corresponding Boolean value. Optionally, the index from which the element is to be searched for can be specified as the second parameter.

```
[4, 5, 6].includes(4);                  // true
[2, 7, 8].includes(4);                  // false
['John', 'James'].includes('Peter');    // false
['John', 'James'].includes('James');    // true
[4, 5, 6, 4711, 50, 87].includes(6, 2); // true
[4, 5, 6, 4711, 50, 87].includes(6, 4); // false
```

Listing 4.72 Simple Check of whether an Array Contains a Certain Element

---

Finding Elements by Search Criterion

Besides the indexOf() and lastIndexOf() methods, there are also the findIndex() method and, since ES2016, the find() method. Both methods pass a function as an argument, which is called for each element in the array and determines by its (Boolean) return value whether the respective element fulfills the search criterion or not. The findIndex() method returns the index of the first occurrence as the result, whereas the find() method returns the element itself. An example is shown in Listing 4.73. The search criterion passed here is a function that returns true for odd numbers. Using the find() method with this function returns the value 3 as an argument because this is the first odd value in the array. The findIndex() method returns the value 1 accordingly because 3 occurs for the first time at index 1 in the array.

```
const result = [2,3,4,5,6,7,2,3,4,5]
  .find(element => element % 2 !== 0)
console.log(result);  // 3

const result2 = [2,3,4,5,6,7,2,3,4,5]
  findIndex(element => element % 2 !== 0);
console.log(result2); // 1
```

Listing 4.73 The find() and findIndex() Methods Use a Search Criterion to Find the First Occurrence That Matches the Search Criterion

4.3.10 Copying Elements within an Array

With version 6 of the ECMAScript standard, some new methods for working with arrays have been added. One of them is the copyWithin() method, which can be used to copy elements within an array.

As arguments, you pass it the index to which the elements are to be copied, the index from which the elements are to be copied, and optionally the index at which the copying of the elements should end. The elements currently in the place to which the elements are to be copied will be replaced by these elements.

Listing 4.74 and Figure 4.28 show an example. In the todoList array, the elements from index 2 and up to (not including) index 4 (i.e., the strings Tidy up and Mow lawn) are copied to index 0 in the array. The two elements at index 0 and index 1 (Clean bathroom and Go shopping) are replaced accordingly.

```
const todoList = [
  'Clean bathroom',
  'Go shopping',
  'Tidy up',
  'Mow lawn'
];
todoList.copyWithin(
  0,  // target start position to which the elements will be copied
  2,  // source start position from which the elements are copied
  4   // source end position up to which the elements are copied
);
console.log(todoList);
// ["Tidy up", "Mow lawn", "Tidy up", "Mow lawn"]
```

Listing 4.74 Using copyWithin(), Elements Can Be Copied within an Array

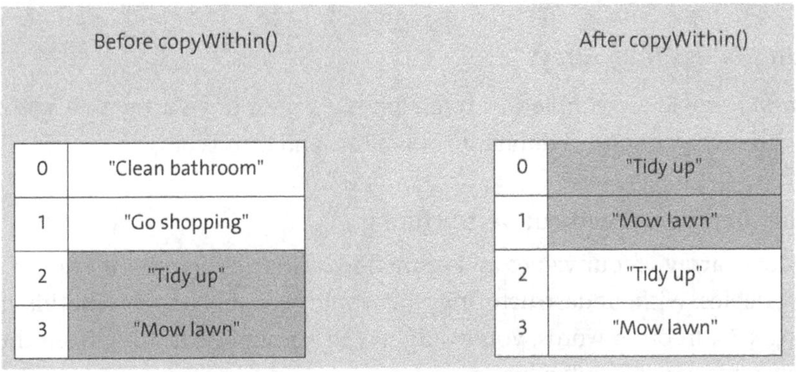

Figure 4.28 The copyWithin() Method Copies Elements within an Array

4.3.11 Converting Arrays to Strings

To convert arrays into a string (and output it to the console, for example), you have several options. On the one hand, you can use the toString(), toLocaleString(), and valueOf() methods. On the other hand, arrays offer the join() method, which can be used to join the individual elements of an array into a string. In this case, it's possible to specify a string as a parameter that is to be used as a separator. The usage of these methods is shown in Listing 4.75.

```
const names = ['John', 'James', 'Peter'];
const namesString = names.toString();
console.log(namesString);              // Output: John,James,Peter
const namesLocaleString = names.toLocaleString();
console.log(namesLocaleString);        // Output: John,James,Peter
const namesValue = names.valueOf();
console.log(namesValue);               // Output: ["John", "James", "Peter"]
const namesJoined = names.join('-');
console.log(namesJoined);              // Output: John-James-Peter
```

Listing 4.75 Converting an Array into a String

4.4   Extracting Values from Arrays and Objects

You're now familiar with objects and arrays, two of the most important reference data types. Before we introduce the other reference data types, let's briefly present the principle of destructuring or destructuring statements in a short intermezzo because it's directly related to arrays and objects. *Destructuring* enables you to relatively easily assign values stored in object properties or arrays to different variables (i.e., to "extract" them from the object or array). A distinction is made between array destructuring and object destructuring.

4.4.1   Extracting Values from Arrays

Array destructuring provides a simple way to assign the values of an array to a set of variables. This can save you some redundant statements and thus typing.

Extracting Values from Arrays without Destructuring

Suppose you had an array of four values and wanted to quickly assign those values to four different variables. Without destructuring, you would probably implement this as shown in Listing 4.76. In other words, you would have to assign each value from the array to the respective variable individually.

```
const bestOfStonerrock = [
  'Kyuss',
  'Spiritual Beggars',
  'Spice and the RJ Band',
  'Band of Spice'
];
```

```
const one = bestOfStonerrock[0];
const two = bestOfStonerrock[1];
const three = bestOfStonerrock[2];
const four = bestOfStonerrock[3];
```

Listing 4.76 Extracting Values from an Array without Destructuring

Extracting Values from Arrays with Destructuring

With the destructuring statement, however, the whole process is much easier and clearer, as shown in the corresponding example in Listing 4.77. The values that you want to assign to the values from the corresponding array are written, separated by commas, in square brackets after the let keyword (or the const keyword) in the order in which values are to be extracted from the array. That is, the first variable receives the value of index 0, the second variable receives the value of index 1, and so on.

```
const [
  one,
  two,
  three,
  four
] = bestOfStonerrock;
console.log(one);      // "Kyuss"
console.log(two);      // "Spiritual Beggars"
console.log(three);    // "Spice and the RJ Band"
console.log(four);     // "Band of Spice"
```

Listing 4.77 Extracting Values via Array Destructuring

This notation is easy to remember if you recall how arrays are created in JavaScript—namely, with reverse notation (see Listing 4.78).

```
const bestOfStonerrock = [
  one,
  two,
  three,
  four
];
```

Listing 4.78 Creating an Array Based on Variables

> **Note**
> Although we always refer to *extracting* and *extracted values*, note that the original values do remain in the source array.

295

Using Already Existing Variables for Destructuring

If the variables to which the values are to be assigned already exist and do not have to be declared first, you can also omit let (const cannot be used in this case!) and start the destructuring statement directly with the opening square bracket (see Listing 4.79).

```
let one;
let two;
let three;
let four;

[
  one,
  two,
  three,
  four
] = bestOfStonerrock;
```

Listing 4.79 For Already Existing Variables, let Can Also Be Omitted during Destructuring

Value Assignment with Fewer Elements in the Array

If the array contains fewer elements than variables are specified, the corresponding variable receives the value undefined, as shown in Listing 4.80.

```
const [
  one,
  two,
  three,
  four,
  five
] = bestOfStonerrock;
console.log(five); // undefined
```

Listing 4.80 Undefined Values in Array Destructuring Are Initialized with the Value undefined

Defining Default Values for Variables

Alternatively, with array destructuring, as with function parameters, you have the option of specifying default values for variables. Instead of undefined, the corresponding variable is then assigned the default value if no corresponding entry exists in the array (see Listing 4.81).

```
const bestOfStonerrock = [
  'Spiritual Beggars',
  'Spice and the RJ Band'
];
```

```
const [
  one = 'Kyuss',
  two = 'Kyuss',
  three = 'Kyuss',
  four = 'Kyuss'
] = bestOfStonerrock;
console.log(one);      // "Spiritual Beggars";
console.log(two);      // "Spice and the RJ Band";
console.log(three);    // "Kyuss";
console.log(four);     // "Kyuss";
```

Listing 4.81 Default Values in Array Destructuring

Extracting Only Specific Values

If you want to map only certain values from the array, you can do so by not providing a variable at the corresponding position. In Listing 4.82, for example, no further variable is specified between the variables one and three, but the corresponding position is left empty. The result: the value Kyuss from the array is assigned to the variable one, the value Spiritual Beggars to no variable and the values Spice and the RJ Band and Band of Spice to the variables three and four, as usual.

```
const bestOfStonerrock = [
  'Kyuss',
  'Spiritual Beggars',
  'Spice and the RJ Band',
  'Band of Spice'
];
const [
  one,
  ,                      // No variable is specified here.
  three,
  four
] = bestOfStonerrock;
console.log(one);      // "Kyuss"
// console.log(two);   // Error, not defined
console.log(three);    // "Spice and the RJ Band"
console.log(four);     // "Band of Spice"
```

Listing 4.82 Extracting Only Specific Values

Extracting Values from Multidimensional Arrays

However, destructuring works not only with one-dimensional arrays, but also with multidimensional ones. This is not as complicated as it might seem, if you just think of how a multidimensional array is created (see Listing 4.83).

```
const coordinates = [
  [2,3,4],
  [5,6,7],
  [8,9,10]
];
```

Listing 4.83 Creating a Multidimensional Array

Because then, even the notation for destructuring an array is no longer difficult, as shown in Listing 4.84.

```
const [
  [x1,y1,z1],
  [x2,y2,z2],
  [x3,y3,z3]
] = coordinates;
```

Listing 4.84 Array Destructuring of a Multidimensional Array

4.4.2   Extracting Values from Objects

Basically, the destructuring of objects works in the same way as the destructuring of arrays. Again, the notation is opposite to the construction—in this case, to the construction of objects. In Listing 4.85, for example, the values of the firstName and last-Name properties are extracted into the new firstNameExtracted and lastNameExtracted variables.

```
const person = {
  firstName : 'John',
  lastName : 'Doe'
};
const {
  firstName : firstNameExtracted,
  lastName : lastNameExtracted
} = person;
```

Listing 4.85 Creating an Object Compared to Destructuring an Object

If variables and object properties are the same, extracting is even easier. In Listing 4.86, the firstName and lastName variables are named just like the object properties of person. Implicitly, a corresponding assignment of property values to variables is then performed.

```
const {
  firstName,
```

```
      lastName
} = person;
```

Listing 4.86 Object Destructuring for Variables and Object Properties of the Same Name

Extracting Values from Nested Objects

Even nested objects are no problem for destructuring, as you can see in Listing 4.87. This example extracts the values of the postCode and street properties of the nested object stored with the address property and assigns them to the postCodeExtracted and streetExtracted variables.

```
const person = {
  firstName : 'John',
  lastName : 'Doe',
  address : {
    postCode : '23456',
    street : '22, Sample Street'
  }
}

const {
  firstName : firstNameExtracted,
  lastName : lastNameExtracted,
  address : {
    postCode : postCodeExtracted,
    street : streetExtracted
  }
} = person;
console.log(firstNameExtracted); // "John"
console.log(lastNameExtracted);  // "Doe"
console.log(postCodeExtracted);  // "23456"
console.log(streetExtracted);    // "22, Sample Street"
```

Listing 4.87 Object Destructuring of Nested Objects

Listing 4.88 alternatively shows the corresponding code if the object properties are to be extracted into variables of the same name.

```
const person = {
  firstName : 'John',
  lastName : 'Doe',
  address : {
    postCode : '23456',
    street : '22, Sample Street'
  }
```

```
}
const {
  firstName,
  lastName,
  address : {
    postCode,
    street
  }
} = person;
console.log(firstName); // "John"
console.log(lastName);  // "Doe"
console.log(postCode);  // "23456"
console.log(street);    // "22, Sample Street"
```

Listing 4.88 Object Destructuring of Nested Objects with Variables and Object Properties of the Same Name

If an object property doesn't exist, the variable is assigned the value `undefined`, analogous to the procedure for array destructuring. Unlike array destructuring, where you can also omit `let`, object destructuring will produce an error, even if the variables are already declared. The following notation is therefore not allowed:

```
{firstName} = person;
```

The reason: `{firstName}` is not interpreted as a destructuring statement, but as a *code block*. However, you can work around this conflict by enclosing either `{firstName}` or even the entire expression in parentheses:

```
({firstName}) = person;
({firstName} = person);
```

The parentheses ensure that the braces are no longer interpreted as a code block by the JavaScript interpreter.

Combining Object Destructuring with Array Destructuring

Conveniently, object destructuring and array destructuring also work in combination. You want to extract the email addresses from an array of person objects? No problem. You want to extract the second entry from an array that is stored as the property of an object? This is also possible. A similar example is shown in Listing 4.89. You see an object that contains an array of strings behind the `phoneNumbers` property, where (besides all other properties of the object) these strings are extracted into the `phoneNumber1Extracted` and `phoneNumber2Extracted` variables.

```
const person = {
  firstName : 'John',
  lastName : 'Doe',
  address : {
    postCode : '23456',
    street : '22, Sample Street'
  },
  phoneNumbers : [
    '02345/23456786',
    '02345/23456789'
  ]
}

const {
  firstName : firstNameExtracted,
  lastName : lastNameExtracted,
  address : {
    postCode : postCodeExtracted,
    street : streetExtracted
  },
  phoneNumbers : [
    phoneNumber1Extracted,
    phoneNumber2Extracted
  ]
} = person;
console.log(firstNameExtracted);      // "John"
console.log(lastNameExtracted);       // "Doe"
console.log(postCodeExtracted);       // "23456"
console.log(streetExtracted);         // "22, Sample Street"
console.log(phoneNumber1Extracted);   // "02345/23456786"
console.log(phoneNumber2Extracted);   // "02345/23456789"
```

Listing 4.89 Object Destructuring in Combination with Array Destructuring

Note
Array destructuring and object destructuring, and especially the combination of both, should not be excessively used in practice. Especially when you're dealing with complex hierarchies, you should consider whether the simple bracket notation for accessing array elements or the dot notation for accessing object properties is simpler or clearer in terms of code.

4.4.3   Extracting Values within a Loop

Another convenient feature of destructuring is that you can even use it inside a for-of loop. An example is shown in Listing 4.90: First the persons array is defined here, which contains objects that, in turn, contain information about persons and their contact data. Then the array is iterated using a for-of loop. Note the destructuring within the loop (before the of keyword). This causes a destructuring statement to be applied to the current object in each iteration; that is, the values from the object properties are extracted from the object.

Within the loop body, the variables defined by destructuring can then be accessed.

```
const persons = [
  {
    firstName: 'John',
    lastName: 'Doe',
    contact: {
      email: 'john.doe@javascripthandbuch.de',
      phone: '02345/23456789'
    }
  },
  {
    firstName: 'Jane',
    lastName: 'Smith',
    contact: {
      email: 'jane.smith@javascripthandbuch.de',
      phone: '02345/23456789'
    }
  }
];

for (let
  {
    firstName: firstName,
    lastName: lastName,
    contact: {
      email: email,
      phone: phone
    }
  } of persons) {
  console.log(`${firstName} ${lastName}`);
  console.log(`Email: ${email}`);
  console.log(`Phone: ${phone}`);
}
```

Listing 4.90 Destructuring within a for-of Loop

In Listing 4.90, the destructuring process is very detailed and spans several lines. Of course, it can also be done more compactly, such as by shortening the names of the variables, as shown in Listing 4.91.

```
for (let {firstName:f, lastName:l, contact:{email:e, phone:p}} of persons) {
  console.log(`${f} ${l}`);
  console.log(`Email: ${e}`);
  console.log(`Phone: ${p}`);
}
```

Listing 4.91 More Compact Notation for Destructuring in a for-of Loop

4.4.4 Extracting Arguments of a Function

Just as convenient as the use of destructuring in for-of loops (see previous section) is its use in combination with functions or their parameters. An example of this is shown in Listing 4.92, where the printPerson() method applies destructuring to an object passed to it as an argument. In the familiar way, the values are extracted as variables (or parameters) from the passed object and made available within the function.

```
function printPerson(
  {
    firstName: firstName,
    lastName: lastName,
    contact: {
      email: email,
      phone: phone
    }
  }
) {
  console.log(`${firstName} ${lastName}`);
  console.log(`Email: ${email}`);
  console.log(`Phone: ${phone}`);
}

const person = {
  firstName: 'John',
  lastName: 'Doe',
  contact: {
    email: 'john.doe@javascripthandbuch.de',
    phone: '02345/23456789'
  }
};
printPerson(person);
```

Listing 4.92 Extracting Function Arguments Using Destructuring

By the way: it's also possible to extract only some of the properties of an object, as shown in Listing 4.93. Here, only the email and phone properties are extracted; the other properties are disregarded.

```
function printContactInformation(
  {
    contact: {
      email: email,
      phone: phone
    }
  }
) {
  console.log(`Email: ${email}`);
  console.log(`Phone: ${phone}`);
}

const person = {
  firstName: 'John',
  lastName: 'Doe',
  contact: {
    email: 'john.doe@javascripthandbuch.de',
    phone: '02345/23456789'
  }
};

printContactInformation(person);
```

Listing 4.93 Extracting Some of the Object Properties Using Destructuring

4.4.5   Copying Object Properties to Another Object

In Chapter 3, you learned how any number of function parameters can be provided as an array via rest parameters. With version ES2018, *rest properties* were introduced, which enable a similar possibility for object properties. The definition of rest properties is also specified via three preceding points:

```
const {
  firstName,
  lastName,
  ...properties
} = person;
```

In Listing 4.94, this statement ensures that all properties of the person object that are defined as enumerable and are not assigned to another variable via the destructuring rule (firstName and lastName in the example) are copied to the properties object.

```
const person = {
  firstName: 'John',
  lastName: 'Doe',
  age: 33,
  hairColor: 'brown',
  height: 1.8
};

const {
  firstName,
  lastName,
  ...properties
} = person;

console.log(firstName);    // John
console.log(lastName);     // Doe
console.log(properties);   // {
                           //   age: 33,
                           //   hairColor: 'brown',
                           //   height: 1.8
                           // }
```

Listing 4.94 Extracting Object Properties via Rest Properties

4.4.6 Copying Object Properties from Another Object

Spread properties are in some ways the counterpart of rest properties and behave similarly to the spread operator (see Chapter 3). Remember: using this operator, it's possible to distribute values present in an array to several elements—like function parameters, for example. Spread properties work in a similar way for objects: The statement

```
const person = {
  firstName,
  lastName,
  ...properties
};
```

in Listing 4.95 causes all properties of the properties object (which are enumerable) to be copied to the person object.

```
const firstName = 'John';
const lastName = 'Doe';
const properties = {
  age: 33,
  hairColor: 'brown',
  height: 1.8
```

```
};

const person = {
  firstName,
  lastName,
  ...properties
};

console.log(person);
// {
//   firstName: 'John',
//   lastName: 'Doe',
//   age: 33,
//   hairColor: 'brown',
//   height: 1.8
// }
```

Listing 4.95 Inserting Object Properties via Spread Properties

This is where the (not so short) intermezzo on the topic of destructuring ends. In the next section, we'll turn to the other reference data types of JavaScript.

4.5   Working with Strings

In Chapter 3, you learned about strings as one of the primitive data types. In fact, you'll use strings so naturally in your everyday programming that you won't even think about them. Whether it's a user's form input you want to process or you want to generate HTML dynamically (we'll cover this in Chapter 5) or you want to write data to a file—in all of these cases, you're dealing with strings.

4.5.1   The Structure of a String

First of all, it's important to understand how strings are internally constructed or represented in JavaScript (and in other programming languages). Basically, strings are comparable to arrays, where each character within the string takes one element of this imaginary array. The first character is therefore at position (or index) 0, the second character at position (or index) 1, and so on. Figure 4.29 shows an example of the structure using the Max Mustermann character string.

M	a	x		M	u	s	t	e	r	m	a	n	n
0	1	2	3	4	5	6	7	8	9	10	11	12	13

Figure 4.29 Internal Structure of a String

4.5.2 Determining the Length of a String

Suppose you want to create a registration form for a website that allows users to register with a username, email address, and password, as is common with this type of form, and you want to ensure that the username entered is at least five characters long, but no longer than eight characters. To be able to enforce this, you must be able to determine the length of the string.

For this purpose, the string data type provides the length property, which contains exactly the number of characters in a string. Every string you define within a program has this property. For example, for the Max Mustermann string, which we'll use as an example throughout this section, this property has a value of 14 (see again Figure 4.29).

We haven't yet shown you how you can actually read values from form fields (you'll learn about this in Chapter 5 and in detail in Chapter 7), but we can implement this example independently of any forms.

Listing 4.96 shows how the check could be implemented. The checkUsername() function expects a string (the user name) as an argument and uses the length property to determine the number of characters in the passed string. If there are fewer than five characters, the error message Username must contain at least 5 characters. is displayed. If there are more than eight characters, the error message Username may contain a maximum of 8 characters. is displayed. In all other cases (i.e., the length is somewhere between five and eight characters), you receive the message Valid username.

```
function checkUsername(userName) {
  if(userName.length < 5) {
    console.error('Username must contain at least 5 characters.');
  } else if(userName.length > 8) {
    console.error('Username may contain a maximum of 8 characters.');
  } else {
    console.log('Valid username');
  }
}
checkUsername('Max');                // error, too short
checkUsername('Max Mustermann');     // error, too long
checkUsername('MaxMuste');           // valid
```

Listing 4.96 Using the length Property

To test the functionality of the function, it's called three times: once with the value Max, which leads to an error due to too few characters, once with the value Max Mustermann, which leads to an error due to too many characters, and finally with the valid value Max-Muste.

4.5.3   Searching within a String

Strings, like arrays, offer the `indexOf()` and `lastIndexOf()` methods. Unlike with arrays, where you use these methods to search for elements in the array, you can search for individual characters or (sub)strings within strings.

Searching for the First Occurrence

You determine the first occurrence of a character or a (sub)string within another string via the `indexOf()` method, which is essentially similar in use to the corresponding array method: the first argument is a character or string to search for and the second argument is optionally the position in the string from which to start the search. In Listing 4.97, for example, the character M is first searched for within the string Max Mustermann, and then the string son is searched for. Figure 4.30 and Figure 4.31 illustrate both processes.

```
const name = 'Max Mustermann';
console.log(name.indexOf('M'));      // Output: 0
console.log(name.indexOf('mann'));   // Output: 10
```

Listing 4.97 The indexOf() Method Can Be Used to Search for Characters and Strings within Another String

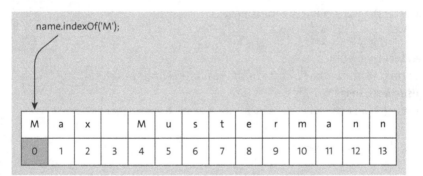

Figure 4.30 The indexOf() Method Can Be Used to Search for Single Characters within a String

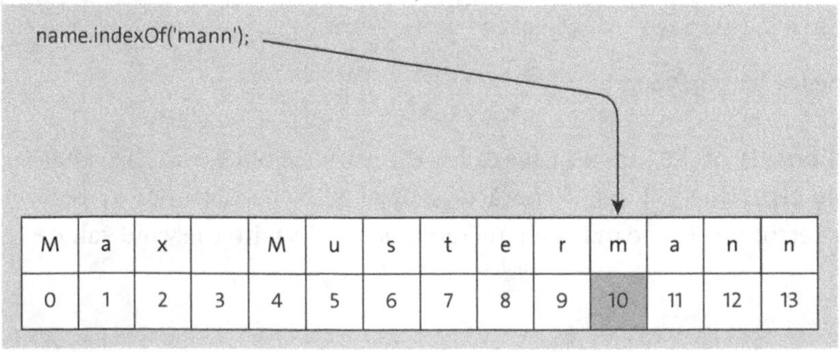

Figure 4.31 The indexOf() Method Also Can Be Used to Search for Whole Strings

As mentioned, the index from which to start the search can optionally be specified as the second argument. Listing 4.98 again searches for the character M, but this time starting from index 2. The first two characters in the string are therefore skipped during the search; the result of the method call is therefore 4 (see also Figure 4.32) because the M of Mustermann is now the one that is found first.

```
const name = 'Max Mustermann';
console.log(name.indexOf('M', 2));  // Output: 4
```

Listing 4.98 Optionally, the Second Argument of the indexOf() Method Can Be Used to Control from which Index in the String to Start the Search

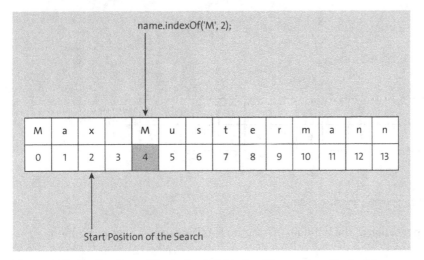

Figure 4.32 Application of the indexOf() Method from a Specific Position

Searching for the Last Occurrence

Analogous to indexOf(), the lastIndexOf() method searches from the end of a string. Here too the second parameter can be used to control from which index to start the search (where the index does not count from the end, but refers to the "normal" index). An example of this is shown in Listing 4.99, and the principle is again illustrated in Figure 4.33 and Figure 4.34.

```
const name = 'Max Mustermann';
console.log(name.lastIndexOf('M'));     // Output: 4
console.log(name.lastIndexOf('M', 2));  // Output: 0
```

Listing 4.99 The lastIndexOf() Method Searches for the First Occurrence Starting from the End of a String

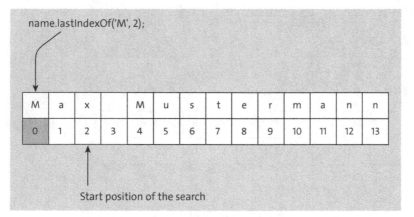

Figure 4.33 Application of the lastIndexOf() Method

Figure 4.34 Application of the lastIndexOf() Method Starting from a Specific Position

4.5.4 Extracting Parts of a String

Besides the indexOf() and lastIndexOf() methods, arrays and strings have another thing in common: the slice() method. Remember: for arrays, this method was used to copy parts of an array. In the case of strings, the method behaves similarly: it copies parts of a string. As an argument, the method is passed the start index from which to copy and optionally the end index up to which to copy. If the latter is omitted, the copy ranges from the start index to the end of the string. Some examples are shown in Listing 4.100. Figure 4.35, Figure 4.36, and Figure 4.37 show the corresponding results.

```
const name = 'Max Mustermann';
console.log(name.slice(0, 3));    // Output: "Max"
console.log(name.slice(4));       // Output: "Mustermann"
console.log(name.slice(4, 10));   // Output: "Muster"
```

Listing 4.100 Parts of a String Can Be Extracted via the slice() Method

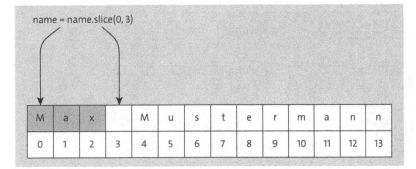

Figure 4.35 Copying the Beginning of a String

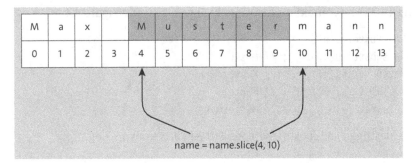

Figure 4.36 Copying the End of a String

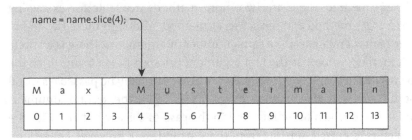

Figure 4.37 Copying a Middle Part of a String

As in the case of arrays, you can pass negative numeric values as arguments to the slice() method for strings (see Listing 4.101 and Figure 4.38).

```
const name = 'Max Mustermann';
console.log(name.slice(-10, -4)); // Output: "Muster"
```

Listing 4.101 The slice() Method Can Also Be Passed Negative Numeric Values

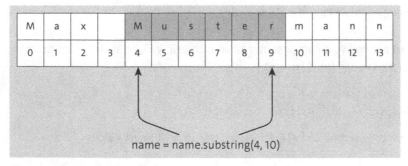

Figure 4.38 Using the slice() Method with Negative Numeric Values

Besides the slice() method, there are two more methods available for extracting strings: the substring() method and the substr() method. Although these two methods have similar names and expect the same number of arguments, there is a subtle difference. Both methods expect as the first argument the start index from which the substring is to be extracted, and both methods can also optionally be passed a second argument. The difference is that in the case of substring(), the second argument denotes the index up to which to extract, and in the case of substr(), it specifies the number of characters to extract starting from the start index. If, however, the second argument is omitted, both methods behave in the same way because then extraction simply starts from the start index and continues to the end of the string. Examples are shown in Listing 4.102. The context is illustrated in Figure 4.39 and Figure 4.40.

```
const name = 'Max Mustermann';
console.log(name.substring(4, 10)); // Muster
console.log(name.substring(4));     // Mustermann
console.log(name.substr(4, 6));     // Muster
console.log(name.substr(4));        // Mustermann
```

Listing 4.102 The substring() and substr() Methods Extract Parts from a String

Figure 4.39 Application of the substring() Method

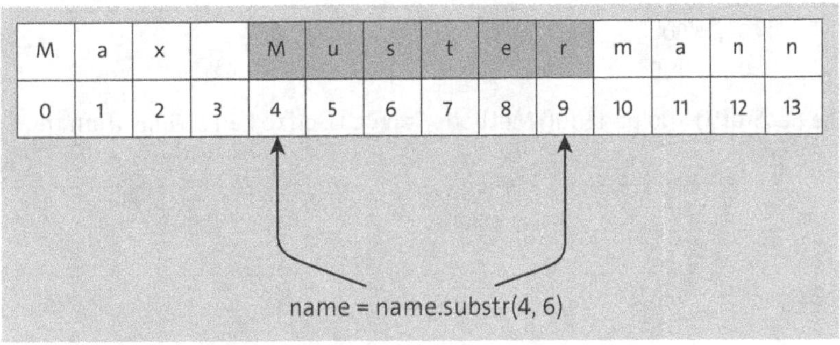

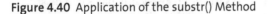

name = name.substr(4, 6)

Figure 4.40 Application of the substr() Method

More Methods for Strings

In addition to the methods presented in this section, there are a few more for strings. For example, toLowerCase() and toUpperCase() can be used to convert all characters in a string to lowercase or uppercase, respectively. The repeat() method, which is passed a number as an argument, uses a string to create a new string in which the original string occurs as often as specified. And the charAt() method allows you to target individual characters of a string at a specific index.

The padStart() and padEnd() methods, which were introduced with version ES2017, are particularly worth mentioning at this point. Both methods pad a given string from the beginning (padStart()) or the end (padEnd()), using another string until a certain length is reached. For example, the expression 'Hello'.padStart(9, 'H') causes the string Hello to be padded from the beginning up to a string length of 9 using the string H, resulting in the string HHHHHello. Conversely, 'Hello'.padEnd(9, 'o') causes the string (again, up to a length of 9) to be padded from the end using the string o, resulting in the string Hellooooo.

The two methods are particularly convenient when it comes to formatting numbers, as shown in Listing 4.103.

```
for (let i=1; i<15; i++) {
  console.log(`${i}`.padStart(3,'0'));
}
// Output consecutively:
// "001", "002", "003", "004", "005"
// "006", "007", "008", "009", "010"
// "011", "012", "013", "014"

for (let i=1; i<15; i++) {
  console.log(`${i}`.padEnd(3,'0'));
}
// Output consecutively:
// "100", "200", "300", "400", "500"
```

```
// "600", "700", "800", "900", "100"
// "110", "120", "130", "140"
```

Listing 4.103 The padStart() and padEnd() Methods Can Be Used to Pad Strings from the Beginning and the End

4.6 Using Maps

In programming, *maps* refers to data structures in which key-value pairs can be stored. Or in other words, within a map, individual values can be stored for keys and then be retrieved via the keys. The keys within a map must be unique, but values can occur more than once.

4.6.1 Creating Maps

Maps are represented in JavaScript by the Map type; consequently, instances can be created using the appropriate constructor function, as shown in Listing 4.104. As a parameter, you pass an array of arrays, where the latter contain the key as the first element (in the example, these are strings) and the value as the second element (in the example, these are numbers). The structure of the map created in this way is illustrated in Figure 4.41.

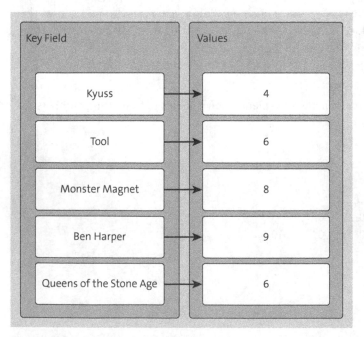

Figure 4.41 Exemplary Structure of a Map

```
const numbersOfAlbums = new Map(    // Create a map ...
  [                                 // ... based on an array
    ['Kyuss', 4],
    ['Tool', 6],
    ['Monster Magnet', 8],
    ['Ben Harper', 9],
    ['Queens of the Stone Age', 6]
  ]
);
console.log(numbersOfAlbums.size);  // Output: 5
```

Listing 4.104 Creating a Map Based on an Array

Iterable Objects

More precisely, the constructor function of Map does not necessarily expect an array, but an object that is iterable. We'll come back to this type of object in Chapter 16 when we turn to the topic of iterators. At this point, only note the following: an *iterable* object is one that defines its own iteration behavior so that it can be used directly as input in a loop, for example.

Some of the standard objects like string, array, map, and also set, presented in the next section, are already iterable by default. In Chapter 16, we'll also show you how to create your own iterable objects.

4.6.2   Basic Operations

Table 4.4 shows a listing of the methods of maps, and Listing 4.105 contains an example of how to use the various methods. For example, the set() method can be used to add a new key-value pair to a map. The get() method returns the stored value for a key, if such a value exists in the map. The number of all key-value pairs present in the map can be determined via the size property. The has() method can also be used to check whether a key has a value in the map. For deleting individual key-value pairs, you can use the delete() method, and for deleting all key-value pairs, you can use the clear() method.

```
const numbersOfAlbums = new Map();         // Create the map
numbersOfAlbums.set('Kyuss', 4);           // Add multiple entries
numbersOfAlbums.set('Tool', 6);
numbersOfAlbums.set('Monster Magnet', 8);
numbersOfAlbums.set('Ben Harper', 9);
numbersOfAlbums.set('Queens of the Stone Age', 6);
console.log(numbersOfAlbums.get('Kyuss'));  // Output: 4
console.log(numbersOfAlbums.size);          // Output: 5
console.log(numbersOfAlbums.has('Kyuss'));  // Output: true
```

```
numbersOfAlbums.delete('Kyuss');          // Delete an entry
console.log(numbersOfAlbums.has('Kyuss')); // Output: false
console.log(
  numbersOfAlbums.has('Justin Bieber')    // Output: false
);
numbersOfAlbums.clear();                   // Clear all entries
console.log(numbersOfAlbums.size);         // Output: 0
```

Listing 4.105 Using Maps

Method/Property	Description
clear()	Deletes all key-value pairs from the map.
delete()	Deletes the value of a given key from the map. If the deletion is successful, the method returns true, otherwise false.
get()	Returns the associated value for a key. If the key does not exist in the map, the method returns undefined.
has()	Checks for a key whether there is a value in the map. If yes, the method returns true, otherwise false.
set()	Sets the corresponding value for a key. If the key already exists in the map, the value associated with it will be overwritten.
size	Contains the number of key-value pairs in the map.
entries()	Returns an iterator that can be used to iterate over the key-value pairs of the map.
keys()	Analogous to entries(), this method returns an iterator for the keys of the map.
values()	Analogous to entries(), this method returns an iterator for the values of the map.

Table 4.4 Overview of the Methods and Properties of Maps

Conveniently, the method calls of set() can be chained, as shown in Listing 4.106, because the method returns the map as a return value and you can call set() again directly.

```
const numbersOfAlbums = new Map()    // Create a map ...
  .set('Kyuss', 4)                   // ... using method chaining
  .set('Tool', 6)
  .set('Monster Magnet', 8)
  .set('Ben Harper', 9)
```

```
  .set('Queens of the Stone Age', 6);
console.log(numbersOfAlbums.size);  // Output: 5
```

Listing 4.106 Creation of a Map Using Method Chaining

4.6.3 Iterating over Maps

As mentioned earlier, the `keys()`, `values()`, and `entries()` methods return *iterators*, which can be used to iterate over the individual entries of the map, as shown in the following listings.

Iterating over the Keys of a Map

Listing 4.107 iterates over the keys of the `numbersOfAlbums` map using the `keys()` method and the `for-of` loop also introduced in ES2015 (see the following box). Consequently, the program delivers the output Kyuss, Tool, Monster Magnet, Ben Harper and Queens of the Stone Age.

```
const numbersOfAlbums = new Map(    // Create a map ...
  [                                 // ... based on an array
    ['Kyuss', 4],
    ['Tool', 6],
    ['Monster Magnet', 8],
    ['Ben Harper', 9],
    ['Queens of the Stone Age', 6]
  ]
);
for (let artist of numbersOfAlbums.keys()) {
  console.log(artist);
}
```

Listing 4.107 Iteration over the Keys of a Map

The for-of Loop

With ES2015, an additional for loop was introduced, the *for-of* loop. It differs from the for-in loop, which has longer been a standard, in that it does not iterate over the names of the object properties, but over the values associated with these properties. An example is shown in Listing 4.108. The for-in loop outputs the indices (which are the properties for arrays) and the manually added name property, while the for-of loop outputs the values stored in the array.

```
const numbers = [ 18, 22, 26, 30, 34 ];
numbers.name = "number array"; // Arrays are objects and can be ...
                               // ... extended by properties.
```

```
// for-in loop
for (let i in numbers) {
    console.log(i); // 0, 1, 2, 3, 4, name
}
// for-of loop
for (let i of numbers) {
    console.log(i); // 18, 22, 26, 30, 34
}
```

Listing 4.108 Comparison of the Classic for-in Loop with the New for-of Loop

Iterating over the Values of a Map

In Listing 4.109, you can see how to iterate over the values contained in the map using the values() method. The output in this case is 4, 6, 8, 9, 6.

```
const numbersOfAlbums = /* ... */
for (let number of numbersOfAlbums.values()) {
  console.log(number);
}
```

Listing 4.109 Iteration over the Values of a Map

Iterating over the Key-Value Pairs of a Map

If you want to iterate over the keys and values—that is, the key-value pairs—you proceed as in Listing 4.110 and use the entries() method. The corresponding iterator returned by this method returns an array with two entries in each iteration: the key in the first place and the stored value in the second place.

```
const numbersOfAlbums = /* ... */
for (let entry of numbersOfAlbums.entries()) {
  console.log(entry[0]);      // Key
  console.log(entry[1]);      // Value
}

// Alternative access via array destructuring:
for (let [ bandName, numberOfAlbums ] of numbersOfAlbums.entries()) {
  console.log(bandName);
  console.log(numberOfAlbums);
}
```

Listing 4.110 Iteration over the Key-Value Pairs of a Map

Because the iterator returned by entries() is also the iterator that is by default stored in the (iterable) Map object, in this case you can also use the map directly as input to the for-of loop, as shown in Listing 4.111.

```
const numbersOfAlbums = /* ... */
for (let entry of numbersOfAlbums) {
  console.log(entry[0]);      // Key
  console.log(entry[1]);      // Value
}


// Alternative access via array destructuring:
for (let [ bandName, numberOfAlbums ] of numbersOfAlbums) {
  console.log(bandName);
  console.log(numberOfAlbums);
}
```

Listing 4.111 Alternative Iteration over the Key-Value Pairs of a Map

4.6.4 Using Weak Maps

In addition to the Map data type, the ECMAScript standard also provides the WeakMap data type. In principle, the weak maps represented by this type are similar to normal maps, but they differ fundamentally in one important respect: objects used as keys can be deleted as part of garbage collection, provided that these objects are no longer referenced (outside the weak map). The objects in a weak map are referenced "weakly", hence the name *weak* map.

> **Definition: Garbage Collection**
>
> In software development, the term *garbage collection* refers to a mechanism that ensures that memory areas that are no longer required are regularly released during the runtime of a program in order to minimize the program's memory requirements.

This property of weak maps has a direct impact on the API of weak maps compared to the API of normal maps: For one thing, only objects can be used as keys in weak maps and not primitive data types—as is possible with normal maps. This means that strings are also not allowed as keys in a weak map, for example.

On the other hand, the keys(), values(), and entries() methods are not available with weak maps. The reason is this: all of these methods would return iterators for which there would be no guarantee that the internal state would still be true after a garbage collection. Objects might have already been deleted via garbage collection but still appear in the internal count of the iterator.

For a similar reason, the `size` property is also not available in weak maps. However, the rest of the API doesn't differ from normal maps except for one more exception: the `clear()` method has since been removed from the standard for weak maps.

An example of using a weak map is shown in Listing 4.112, which modifies the familiar example from the section on normal maps to suit the requirements: objects instead of strings are now used as keys.

```
const artist1 = {
  name: 'Kyuss'
};
const artist2 = {
  name: 'Tool'
};
const artist3 = {
  name: 'Monster Magnet'
};
const artist4 = {
  name: 'Ben Harper'
};
const artist5 = {
  name: 'Queens of the Stone Age'
};
const artist6 = {
  name: 'Justin Bieber'
};
const numbersOfAlbums = new WeakMap();         // Create the map
numbersOfAlbums.set(artist1, 4);               // Add multiple entries
numbersOfAlbums.set(artist2, 6);
numbersOfAlbums.set(artist3, 8);
numbersOfAlbums.set(artist4, 9);
numbersOfAlbums.set(artist5, 6);
console.log(numbersOfAlbums.get(artist1));     // Output: 4
console.log(numbersOfAlbums.has(artist1));     // Output: true
numbersOfAlbums.delete(artist1);               // Delete an entry
console.log(numbersOfAlbums.has(artist1));     // Output: false
console.log(numbersOfAlbums.has(artist6));     // Output: false
console.log(numbersOfAlbums);
```

Listing 4.112 Using Weak Maps

> **Private Object Properties with Weak Maps**
>
> For an interesting use case for weak maps, see the blog post by Nicholas C. Zakas at *www.nczonline.net/blog/2014/01/21/private-instance-members-with-weakmaps-in-java-script/*. It describes how weak maps can be used to realize private object properties.

4.7 Using Sets

In programming, a *set* is a data structure similar to a list in which values may occur only once; that is, duplicate values are not allowed.

Sets are available since ES2015 and are represented by the new Set object. Whether two values are equal is checked according to the same rules as for the === operator—that is, strict equality, considering both value and type of a variable.

4.7.1 Creating Sets

To create a set, you simply use the Set constructor function. As with maps, the value passed can be an array (or an iterable object) that contains the initial values to be added to the set. In Listing 4.113, for example, a set is created that contains five strings as values. The duplicate string Kyuss is copied into the set only once, which results in a set size of 5 (the size can be determined via the size property).

```
const artists = new Set(      // Create a set ...
  [                           // ... based on an array
    'Kyuss',
    'Kyuss',
    'Tool',
    'Monster Magnet',
    'Ben Harper',
    'Queens of the Stone Age'
  ]
);
console.log(artists.size);   // Output: 5
```

Listing 4.113 When Creating an Array, the Elements Can Be Passed as an Array

4.7.2 Basic Operations of Sets

Sets provide a number of methods (see also Table 4.5), the usage of which is shown in some examples in Listing 4.114. For example, the add() method can be used to add new elements to the set. If you try to add the same element (in this case the same string)

multiple times, as in Listing 4.115, the set remains unchanged. In the example, after adding the total of six strings, the set therefore has a size of 5.

The `has()` method can be used to check whether an element is already contained in a set or not. As a return value, the method logically returns a corresponding Boolean value.

If you want to delete a single element from a set, you can use the `delete()` method. You pass it the respective element as an argument, and the method returns the result that the `has()` method would have returned for the element. In other words, if an element that is contained in the set is passed to the `delete()` method and the element is deleted, the method returns `true`; if an element that is not contained in the set is passed to it instead, the `delete()` method returns `false`. To delete not only a single element but all elements of a set, the `clear()` method is the right choice.

```javascript
const artists = new Set();            // Create the set
artists.add('Kyuss');                 // Add different values
artists.add('Kyuss');
artists.add('Tool');
artists.add('Monster Magnet');
artists.add('Ben Harper');
artists.add('Queens of the Stone Age'(
console.log(artists.size);            // Output: 5
console.log(artists.has('Kyuss'));    // Output: true
artists.delete('Kyuss');              // Delete a value
console.log(artists.has('Kyuss'));    // Output: false
console.log(
  artists.has('Justin Bieber')        // Output: false
);
artists.clear();                      // Clear all values
console.log(artists.size);            // Output: 0
```

Listing 4.114 Using Sets

Method/Property	Description
add()	Adds an element to the set.
clear()	Deletes all elements from the set.
delete()	Deletes the passed element from the set.
has()	Checks if the passed element is included in the set.

Table 4.5 Overview of the Methods and Properties of Sets

Method/Property	Description
entries()	Returns an iterator containing the value-value pairs of the set. The order of the pairs corresponds to the order in which they were added to the set. The fact that value-value pairs are returned is due to the fact that sets have the same API as the entries() method of Map (which, as stated above, returns key-value pairs).
keys()	Returns an iterator containing the values of the set. The order of the values corresponds to the order in which they were added to the set.
values()	Like keys(), returns an iterator containing the values of the set. Again, the order of the values corresponds to the order in which they were added to the set.
size	Property representing the number of elements in the set.

Table 4.5 Overview of the Methods and Properties of Sets (Cont.)

In the same way that you can chain calls of the set() method for maps, you can do the same with the add() method for sets (see Listing 4.115).

```
const artists = new Set()    // Create a set ...
  .add('Kyuss')              // ... using chaining
  .add('Tool')
  .add('Monster Magnet')
  .add('Ben Harper')
  .add('Queens of the Stone Age');
console.log(artists.size);   // Output: 5
```

Listing 4.115 Creation of a Set Using Method Chaining

4.7.3 Iterating over Sets

As with maps, the keys(), values(), and entries() methods are available to iterate over the entries in a set and return individual iterators. The difference from the equivalents with maps is that because sets don't contain keys, the keys() method returns an iterator for the values in the respective set just like the values() method does, and the entries() method returns an iterator that in each iteration returns an array with two entries, both of which represent the respective value. The usage of these methods is shown in Listing 4.116.

```
const artists = new Set(
  [
    'Kyuss',
    'Tool',
    'Monster Magnet',
```

```
    'Ben Harper',
    'Queens of the Stone Age'
  ]
);
// Output: "Kyuss", "Tool", "Monster Magnet", "Ben Harper", "Queens of the
// Stone Age"
for (let artist of artists.keys()) {
  console.log(artist);
}
// Output: "Kyuss", "Tool", "Monster Magnet", "Ben Harper", "Queens of the
// Stone Age"
for (let artist of artists.values()) {
  console.log(artist);
}
for (let artist of artists.entries()) {
  console.log(artist[0]);  // value, e.g. "Kyuss"
  console.log(artist[1]);  // value, e.g. "Kyuss"
}
// Output: "Kyuss", "Tool", "Monster Magnet", "Ben Harper", "Queens of the
// Stone Age"
for (let artist of artists) {
  console.log(artist);
}
```

Listing 4.116 The Individual Elements of a Set Can Be Iterated over Using a for-of Loop

4.7.4   Using Weak Sets

Analogous to weak maps for maps, there is the *weak sets* alternative for sets, represented by the type WeakSet. This means that the objects that are no longer referenced elsewhere are regularly deleted from the set during garbage collection. Weak sets, like weak maps, do not provide the keys(), values(), and entries() methods, and they do not have a size property or a clear() method. In addition, it's also true here that no primitive data types can be added as values of a weak set.

Listing 4.117 shows the usage of a weak set based on the familiar example.

```
const artist1 = {
  name: 'Kyuss'
};
const artist2 = {
  name: 'Tool'
};
const artist3 = {
  name: 'Monster Magnet'
```

```
};
const artist4 = {
  name: 'Ben Harper'
};
const artist5 = {
  name: 'Queens of the Stone Age'
};
const artist6 = {
  name: 'Justin Bieber'
};

const artists = new WeakSet(
  [
    artist1,
    artist2,
    artist3,
    artist4,
    artist5
  ]
);
console.log(artists.has(artist1));   // Output: true
artists.delete(artist1);             // Delete a value
console.log(artists.has(artist1));   // Output: false
console.log(artists.has(artist6));   // Output: false

console.log(artists);
```

Listing 4.117 Usage of Weak Sets

4.8   Other Global Objects

In addition to the global objects presented in the previous sections, there are others that are summarized (admittedly rather briefly) ahead.

4.8.1   Working with Date and Time Information

For working with date and time information, JavaScript provides the Date object. To access date and time information, you must first create an instance of Date, as shown in Listing 4.118. Arguments can be passed (details to follow), but they can also be omitted. In the latter case, an instance is created that represents the current date and time.

Then, for example, you can use getMonth() to get the month, getFullYear() to get the year, getDate() to get the current day in the month, getDay() to get the current day in the week, getHours() to get the current hour, and so on. Table 4.6 gives an overview of the most common methods.

```
const today = new Date();
console.log(today.getMonth());    // Returns the current month (0-11).
console.log(today.getFullYear()); // Returns the year in the format YYYY.
console.log(today.getDate());     // Returns the current day in the
                                  // month (1-31).
console.log(today.getDay());      // Returns the day of the week (starts
                                  // on Sunday with 0).
console.log(today.getHours());    // Returns the current hour of the day (0-23).
console.log(today.getTime());     // Returns the milliseconds since 1/1/1970.
```

Listing 4.118 Access to the Individual Components of a Date/Time Object

Method	Description
getDate()	Returns the day of the month (1–31) for the respective date.
getDay()	Returns the day of the week (0–6) for the respective date.
getFullYear()	Returns the year for the respective date.
getHours()	Returns the hour for the given date.
getMilliseconds()	Returns the milliseconds (0–999) for the respective date.
getMinutes()	Returns the minutes (0–59) for the respective date.
getMonth()	Returns the month (0–11) for the respective date.
getSeconds()	Returns the seconds (0–59) for the respective date.
getTime()	Returns the number of milliseconds that have elapsed since 01/01/1970, 00:00:00 UTC for the given date.
getYear()	Returns the year for the respective date. However, this method is outdated. Instead, you should use the Date.prototype.getFullYear() method.
setDate(dayValue)	Sets the day in the month for the respective date.

setFullYear(
  yearValue
  [, monthValue
  [, dayValue]]
)
	Sets the year for the respective date. Optionally, you can specify the month (0–11) and the day (1–31).

Table 4.6 The Main Methods of Date

Method	Description

`setHours(`
`  hoursValue`
`  [, minutesValue`
`  [, secondsValue`
`  [, msValue]]]`
`)`
	Sets the hours for the given date. Optionally, you can specify minutes (0–59), seconds (0–59), and milliseconds (0–999).

`setMilliseconds (milli-` `secondsValue)`	Sets the milliseconds (0–999) for the respective date.

`setMinutes(`
`  minutesValue`
`  [, secondsValue`
`  [, msValue]]`
`)`
	Sets the minutes (0–59) for the respective date. Optionally, you can specify seconds (0–59) and milliseconds (0–999).

`setMonth(`
`  monthValue`
`  [, dayValue]`
`)`
	Sets the month (0–11) for the respective date. Optionally, the day (1–31) can be specified.

`setSeconds(`
`  secondsValue`
`  [, msValue]`
`)`
	Sets the seconds (0–59) for the respective date. Optionally, you can specify milliseconds (0–999).

`setTime(`
`  timeValue`
`)`
	Sets the date and time based on a numeric value that indicates the milliseconds that have elapsed since 01/01/1970, 00:00:00 UTC.

`setYear()`	Outdated

Table 4.6 The Main Methods of Date (Cont.)

When you create an instance of Date, you have several options regarding the arguments (see also Listing 4.119):

- Without arguments, an object is created that represents the current date and time (as mentioned previously).

- If you pass a numeric value as an argument, this is evaluated as the number of milliseconds that have passed since 01/01/1970; that is, an object is created that represents the corresponding point in time.

- Alternatively, you can pass a string that is constructed according to the IETF standard RFC 2822 (*http://tools.ietf.org/html/rfc2822#page-14*) and contains a corresponding date specification (e.g., 02 14 2021 for 02/14/2021).

- In addition, the individual date and time specifications can also be passed individually as numeric values, in this order: year, month, day, hour, minute, second, millisecond.

```
const date1 = new Date();              // current date and time
                                       // here: Sat Aug 15 2021
                                       //       17:34:25 GMT+0200 (CEST)
const date2 = new Date(1438654000000); // date based on milliseconds
                                       // since 01/01/1970
                                       // here: Tue Aug 04 2015
                                       //       04:06:40 GMT+0200 (CEST)
const date3 = new Date("02 08 2021");  // date based on string
                                       // here: Sun Feb 08 2021
                                       //       00:00:00 GMT+0100 (CET)
const date4 = new Date(               // date based on ...
  2021,                                // ... year ...
  8,                                   // ... month ...
  15,                                  // ... day ...
  17,                                  // ... hours ...
  36,                                  // ... minutes ...
  30,                                  // ... seconds ...
  30                                   // ... and milliseconds
);                                     // here: Tue Sep 15 2021
                                       //       17:36:30 GMT+0200 (CEST)
```

Listing 4.119 The Different Ways to Create a Date Object

4.8.2   Performing Complex Calculations

In Chapter 3, you learned how to perform simple calculations with numbers. But if you want to perform more complex calculations, it's better to use the Math object instead. This object provides a whole set of different methods that can be used to perform all sorts of calculations. Some examples are shown in Listing 4.120.

```
console.log(Math.min(0, 4711, 30, 5, -8, -40)); // Output: -40
console.log(Math.max(0, 4711, 30, 5, -8, -40)); // Output: 4711
console.log(Math.random());                      // Output a random number
console.log(Math.round(4.7));                     // Output: 5
console.log(Math.round(4.4));                     // Output: 4
console.log(Math.ceil(4.4));                      // Output: 5
console.log(Math.floor(4.7));                     // Output: 4
```

Listing 4.120 Examples of Using the Math Object

4.8.3   Wrapper Objects for Primitive Data Types

There are also separate objects for the two primitive data types of numbers and Boolean values: `Number` represents numeric values and `Boolean` represents Boolean values. These objects are also called *wrapper objects* (as is `string`) because they can act like a "wrapper" around primitive values and extend them with, for example, methods. In Listing 4.121, the (primitive) numeric values 2 and 4711 are converted to corresponding objects, which then allows the `toExponential()` method to be called.

```
const number2 = new Number(2);
const number4711 = new Number(4711);
console.log(number2.toExponential());        // 2e+0
console.log(number4711.toExponential());     // 4.711e+3
```

Listing 4.121 Examples of Using Wrapper Objects

4.9   Working with Regular Expressions

Regular expressions are specific character patterns that are used to check whether a text (or a string) contains a specific combination of characters. For working with regular expressions, the `RegExp` type is available; strings also offer different methods to evaluate regular expressions. This means that you have a total of six different methods at your disposal:

- The `test()` method of the `RegExp` type checks whether a specific character pattern occurs in a string and returns a corresponding Boolean value.
- The `exec()` method of the `RegExp` type searches for occurrences of a respective character pattern and returns them as an array.
- The `match()` method of strings searches a string for occurrences matching a character pattern and returns them as an array.
- The `replace()` method of strings replaces occurrences within a string that match a corresponding character pattern.
- The `search()` method of strings searches for occurrences for a corresponding character pattern and returns the index of the first occurrence.
- The `split()` method of strings separates a string based on a corresponding character pattern and returns the individual parts of the string as an array.

We'll present these methods in detail ahead. But first, let's explain how regular expressions can be initialized.

4.9.1 Defining Regular Expressions

As for objects and arrays, there is also the possibility to create regular expressions via a constructor function or via the literal notation. Listing 4.122 shows the usage of the constructor function. The character pattern (the structure of which we'll discuss in detail in a moment) is passed as an argument.

```
const regExp = new RegExp('abcde');
```

Listing 4.122 Creating a Regular Expression via the Constructor Function

Listing 4.123, on the other hand, shows literal notation. In that case, the regular expression is surrounded by two slashes (/).

```
const regExp = /abcde/;
```

Listing 4.123 Creating a Regular Expression Using Literal Notation

> **Note**
>
> If you want to create a regular expression dynamically during the runtime of a program, perhaps based on user input, for example, use the constructor function to create the regular expression (because then you can specify the user input as a string).
>
> If, on the other hand, the regular expression is fixed and doesn't change at program runtime, it's better to use literal notation because it works faster than the constructor function in terms of execution speed.

4.9.2 Testing Characters against a Regular Expression

Before we show you what you can do with regular expressions and what the different symbols inside regular expressions mean, we need a way to test regular expressions against a string and verify that the string matches the regular expression. The method that allows you to do this is test(). As an argument, this method expects the string to be checked. The return value is a Boolean value that indicates whether the string matches the regular expression or not. A simple example is shown in Listing 4.124. The test() method returns true because the passed string contains the regular expression /abcde/.

```
const regExp = /abcde/;
console.log(regExp.test('abcdefghijklmnopqrstuvwxyz'));  // Output: true
```

Listing 4.124 The test() Method Can Be Used to Test whether a Character Pattern Occurs within a String

Admittedly, the regular expression /abcde/ isn't particularly complex: it merely checks whether the string abcde is contained in the string passed. Usually, you'll want to express more complex things—for example, extract all email addresses from a text. We'll therefore use a practical example to illustrate how you can formulate various things in regular expressions. The goal is to create a regular expression for international phone numbers. In doing so, we'll gradually introduce the different phrases in regular expressions and thus progressively improve the regular expression.

The following rules apply to valid international telephone numbers, although we deliberately relaxed or simplified them somewhat for didactic reasons (and so that the resulting regular expression doesn't become too complex):

- International phone numbers consist of a country code with two digits.
- This is followed by a space.
- After that is the area code, also with two digits.
- This is followed by another space.
- Finally, the actual phone number with five to seven digits follows.
- Optionally, international phone numbers can start with a + sign.

Now, let's implement these relaxed requirements one by one. If you aggregate the requirements, the result is that international telephone numbers must contain at least 11 characters and a maximum of 13 characters. First, let's look at how to phrase a regular expression that checks if a string contains at least 13 characters (yes, that may not fit the "maximum of 13 characters" part of the requirement at first glance, but we'll get back to that later on).

Besides the regular expression shown in the previous example (/abcde/), which specifies exactly the characters that the corresponding string must contain, there are special characters within regular expressions. For example, a dot means that any character matches the regular expression (see Table 4.7).

Expression	Meaning
.	Any character (except the line break)
a	The character *a*
ab	The string *ab*
a|b	The characters *a* or *b*

Table 4.7 Basic Formulations for Regular Expressions

So, to use a regular expression to ensure that a string contains at least 13 characters, just write 13 dots in a row, as shown in Listing 4.125. The method test() then returns the value true for the phone number 49 30 1234567 (which will be the simplified international phone number in our example), the value false for the shorter phone number 49 30 12345, and the value true for longer phone numbers.

```
const regExp = /............/;
console.log(regExp.test('49 30 1234567'));          // true
console.log(regExp.test('49 30 12345'));            // false
console.log(regExp.test('49 30 123456789'));        // true
```

Listing 4.125 First Version of the Regular Expression for Testing International Phone Numbers

However, the dot really means *any character*, and thus even strings that have at least 13 characters but contain only letters pass the test, as shown in Listing 4.126.

```
const regExp = /............/;
console.log(regExp.test('Hello World'));            // false
console.log(regExp.test('Max Mustermann'));         // true
console.log(regExp.test('Hello Max Mustermann'));   // true
```

Listing 4.126 All Strings That Contain at Least 13 Characters Fit the Regular Expression, Even Those That Do Not Contain Numbers

Figure 4.42 illustrates what happens when the regular expression is applied to the strings shown in the examples. For the regular expression shown, the test() method returns true for all strings that have at least 13 characters—incorrectly, including those that contain letters. So before we go on with the further implementation of the requirements, we must first implement the implicit requirement that only numbers should be allowed.

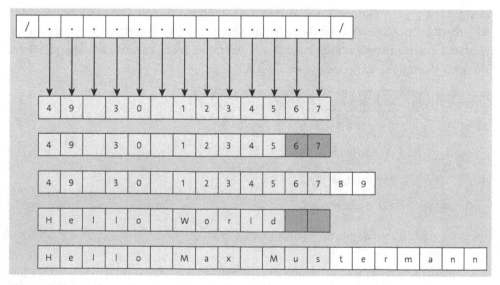

Figure 4.42 Regular Expressions Can Be Used to Search for Specific Occurrences within a String

4.9.3   Using Character Classes

To make sure that the regular expression for the international phone numbers fits only those strings that have the required numbers in the appropriate places, you can use *character classes* (see Table 4.8). You define a character class within a regular expression using square brackets: the opening square bracket starts the character class; the closing square bracket ends the character class. For example, to express that a string contains one of the letters *a*, *b*, *c*, *d*, or *e*, *in one place*, you can write the code in Listing 4.127.

```
const regExp = /[abcde]/;
console.log(regExp.test('a'));        // true
console.log(regExp.test('f'));        // false
console.log(regExp.test('afghj'));    // true
console.log(regExp.test('fghij'));    // false
```

Listing 4.127 Definition of a Character Class

> **Note**
>
> By the way, this is not to be confused with the expression /abcde/. A character class refers to a single character.

Name	Syntax	Meaning
Simple class	[xyz]	One of the characters *x*, *y*, or *z*
Negation	[^xyz]	None of the characters *x*, *y*, or *z*, but any other character
Range	[a-zA-Z]	A lowercase letter or an uppercase letter—that is, one of the characters between *a* and *z* or between *A* and *Z*

Table 4.8 The Different Character Classes in Regular Expressions

With this knowledge, we can now also adjust the phone number example or the corresponding regular expression. To ensure that there are numbers at the corresponding places in the phone number, we simply replace the dots there with the character class [0-9], which defines just that. Listing 4.128 shows the adapted source code and Figure 4.43 the corresponding diagram. You see that the test() method now no longer returns true for the string Hello Max Mustermann because the characters contained there are not defined in the character class.

```
const regExp = /[0-9][0-9].[0-9][0-9].[0-9][0-9][0-9][0-9][0-9][0-9][0-9]/;
console.log(regExp.test('49 30 1234567'));      // true
console.log(regExp.test('49 30 12345'));        // false
console.log(regExp.test('49 30 123456789'));    // true
```

```
console.log(regExp.test('Hello World'));            // false
console.log(regExp.test('Hello Max Mustermann')); // false
```

Listing 4.128 Character Classes Can Be Used to Restrict the Allowed Characters

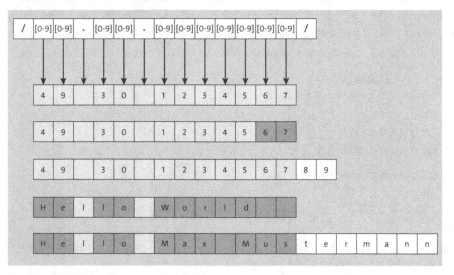

Figure 4.43 Using Character Classes

However, any character is still allowed in the two places in the phone number where spaces are supposed to be. Thus, the string 49X30X1234567 also fits the present regular expression (see Listing 4.129).

```
console.log(regExp.test('49X30X1234567'));        // true
```

Listing 4.129 The Regular Expression Still Returns true Even for Invalid Strings

However, this can be adjusted relatively easily by inserting a space instead of the dots in each case (see Listing 4.130).

```
const regExp = /[0-9][0-9] [0-9][0-9] [0-9][0-9][0-9][0-9][0-9][0-9][0-9]/;
console.log(regExp.test('49X30X1234567'));        // false
```

Listing 4.130 The Two Spaces Now Ensure That No Other Characters Are Allowed between the Digits

Predefined Character Classes

In addition to the possibility of defining your own character classes shown previously, you can also use *predefined character classes* (see Table 4.9). For example, instead of using [0-9] as a character class for a number between 0 to 9, it's enough to write \d, and instead of [^0-9], the predefined character class \D is sufficient.

Syntax	Meaning	Short Form For
.	Any sign	
\d	Integer between 0 and 9	[0-9]
\D	A character that is not a number	[^0-9]
\s	Everything that is a whitespace	[\t\n\x0B\f\r]
\S	Everything that is not a whitespace	[^\s]
\w	Everything that is a word character	[a-zA-Z_0-9]
\W	Everything that is not a word character	[^\w]

Table 4.9 The Different Predefined Character Classes in Regular Expressions

Continuation of the Phone Number Example

The regular expression for international phone numbers can be rephrased using predefined character classes as shown in Listing 4.131. The mechanism is the same (see Figure 4.44).

```
const regExp = /\d\d\s\d\d\s\d\d\d\d\d\d\d/;
console.log(regExp.test('49 30 1234567'));        // true
console.log(regExp.test('Hello World'));          // false
console.log(regExp.test('Hello Max Mustermann')); // false
console.log(regExp.test('49 30 12345678'));       // true
console.log(regExp.test('49X30X1234567'));        // false
```

Listing 4.131 Predefined Character Classes Are Available for Some Characters

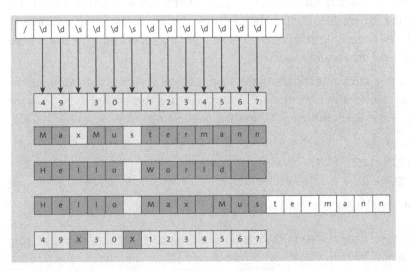

Figure 4.44 Usage of Predefined Character Classes

4.9.4   Limiting Beginning and End

The current version of the regular expression for phone numbers also returns true for strings in which a matching part is found at any position. Listing 4.132 shows two examples. For the two strings 12349 30 12345678 and 449 30 123456789, the test() method returns true because both strings contain a part that matches the regular expression (highlighted in bold in the listing; see also Figure 4.45).

```
const regExp = /\d\d\s\d\d\s\d\d\d\d\d\d\d\d/;
console.log(regExp.test('12349 30 12345678'));        // true
console.log(regExp.test('449 30 123456789'));         // true
```

Listing 4.132 The Beginning and End of the Phone Number Is Not Restricted

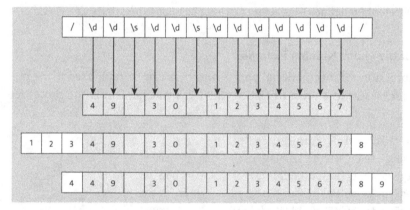

Figure 4.45 The Current Regular Expression Does Not Limit the Beginning or the End

If, however, you want to ensure that true is returned only for strings that not only contain a sequence of characters matching the regular expression at some point but also match the regular expression completely (i.e., do not contain any other characters), you must limit the beginning and the end of the regular expression. This is achieved using the two special characters ^ and $.

The ^ character (the circumflex) defines the beginning of a string. For example, the expression /^S/ matches the string Southampton, but not the string In Southampton because the S is not at the beginning of the string (see Listing 4.133).

```
const regExp = /^S/;
console.log(regExp.test('Southampton'));              // true
console.log(regExp.test('In Southampton'));           // false
```

Listing 4.133 Limiting the Beginning of a String

The $ character represents the end of a string: the expression /n$/ matches the string Southampton, but not the string Southampton Port because the n is not at the end (see Listing 4.134).

```
const regExp = /n$/;
console.log(regExp.test('Southampton'));          // true
console.log(regExp.test('Southampton Port'));     // false
```

Listing 4.134 Limiting the End of a String

Of course, both expressions can also be combined, as shown in Listing 4.135. Here, the regular expression fits only the string Southampton because in the other two strings, the value is not at the beginning and at the end at the same time.

```
const regExp = /^Southampton$/;
console.log(regExp.test('Southampton'));          // true
console.log(regExp.test('In Southampton'));       // false
console.log(regExp.test('Southampton Port'));     // false
```

Listing 4.135 Limiting the Beginning and End of a String

In addition to limiting the entire string, you can also use \b to test for the boundaries of individual words: For example, the expression /\bplay\b/ matches the string I play the electric guitar. because it contains the word play. However, it doesn't match the string I am a teamplayer. because the part play isn't a whole word here (see Listing 4.136).

```
const regExp = /\bplay\b/;
console.log(regExp.test('I play the electric guitar.'));  // true
console.log(regExp.test('I am a teamplayer.'));           // false
```

Listing 4.136 Limiting the Beginning and End of a Word

Conversely, \B can be used to describe that exactly no word boundary should be present. If you replace \b from Listing 4.136 with \B, as in Listing 4.137, the string I play the electric guitar. is no longer accepted, but the string I am a teamplayer. is.

```
const regExp = /\Bplay\B/;
console.log(regExp.test('I play the electric guitar.'));  // false
console.log(regExp.test('I am a teamplayer.'));           // true
```

Listing 4.137 Explicitly No Boundary at the Beginning and End of a Word

Table 4.10 summarizes the various expressions for describing word boundaries and the beginning and end of strings.

Expression	Meaning
^	beginning of a string
$	end of a string

Table 4.10 Characters for Describing Word Boundaries and the Beginning and End of Strings

Expression	Meaning
\b	beginning or end of a word
\B	no word boundary

Table 4.10 Characters for Describing Word Boundaries and the Beginning and End of Strings (Cont.)

Meaning of the Circumflex Character

Inside square brackets, the circumflex has another meaning, that of negation. For example, the expression /[^0-9]/ represents a character that is not a number.

Continuation of the Phone Number Example

You can now extend the regular expression for the phone numbers in this way, as shown in Listing 4.138, so that only strings that consist entirely of a phone number are accepted (see also Figure 4.46).

```
const regExp = /^\d\d\s\d\d\s\d\d\d\d\d\d\d$/;
console.log(regExp.test('49 30 1234567'));        // true
console.log(regExp.test('Hello World'));          // false
console.log(regExp.test('Hello Max Mustermann')); // false
console.log(regExp.test('49X30X1234567'));        // false
console.log(regExp.test('49 30 12345678'));       // false
console.log(regExp.test('449 30 1234567'));       // false
console.log(regExp.test('49 30 12345'));          // false
```

Listing 4.138 Limitation of Beginning and End

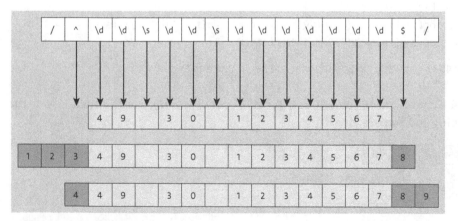

Figure 4.46 Limiting Beginning and End

4.9.5 Using Quantifiers

Quantifiers allow you to define how many occurrences of a character or character class must be present in the string for it to be accepted by the regular expression.

You can determine the following:

- A character or character class can optionally exist exactly once or not at all.
- A character or a character class can exist any number of times (even no times).
- A character or character class must exist at least once.
- A character or character class must exist exactly *n* times.
- A character or character class must exist at least *n* times.
- A character or character class must exist at least *n* times and at most *m* times.

Defining Optional Occurrences

To define that a character may occur optionally, simply place a question mark (?) after this character in the regular expression. For example, the regular expression in Listing 4.139 returns true for both the string abcde and the string abcdef because the f has been marked as optional. For the string abcdeff, however, the regular expression returns false because only one single f may occur.

```
const regExp = /^abcdef?$/;
console.log(regExp.test('abcde'));    // true
console.log(regExp.test('abcdef'));   // true
console.log(regExp.test('abcdeff'));  // false
```

Listing 4.139 Defining Optional Occurrences

Defining Any Number of Occurrences

To define that a character may occur any number of times, place an asterisk (*) after the character. The regular expression in Listing 4.140 returns true for all three strings shown there.

```
const regExp = /^abcdef*$/;
console.log(regExp.test('abcde'));    // true
console.log(regExp.test('abcdef'));   // true
console.log(regExp.test('abcdeff'));  // true
```

Listing 4.140 Defining Any Number of Occurrences

Defining at Least One Occurrence

To define that a character must occur at least once (but may occur any number of times), place a plus sign (+) after the character. Accordingly, the regular expression in Listing 4.141 returns true only if there is at least one f at the end of the string.

```
const regExp = /^abcdef+$/;
console.log(regExp.test('abcde'));     // false
console.log(regExp.test('abcdef'));    // true
console.log(regExp.test('abcdeff'));   // true
```

Listing 4.141 Defining at Least One Occurrence

Defining an Exact Number of Occurrences

You also have the possibility to define that a character should occur a specific number of times. To do this, include the number in braces after the corresponding character. Accordingly, the regular expression in Listing 4.142 returns true only if there are exactly two occurrences of f at the end of the string.

```
const regExp = /^abcdef{2}$/;
console.log(regExp.test('abcde'));      // false
console.log(regExp.test('abcdef'));     // false
console.log(regExp.test('abcdeff'));    // true
console.log(regExp.test('abcdefff'));   // false
console.log(regExp.test('abcdeffff'));  // false
```

Listing 4.142 Defining the Exact Number of Occurrences

Defining a Minimum Number of Occurrences

You can also define a minimum number of required occurrences via the brace notation. To do this, place a comma after the number (in braces). Accordingly, the regular expression in Listing 4.143 returns true only if the f appears at least twice at the end of the string.

```
const regExp = /^abcdef{2,}$/;
console.log(regExp.test('abcde'));      // false
console.log(regExp.test('abcdef'));     // false
console.log(regExp.test('abcdeff'));    // true
console.log(regExp.test('abcdefff'));   // true
console.log(regExp.test('abcdeffff'));  // true
```

Listing 4.143 Defining a Minimum Number of Occurrences

Defining a Minimum and a Maximum Number of Occurrences

To define both a minimum and a maximum number of occurrences, proceed similarly to defining the minimum number. The only difference is that you include the maximum number of occurrences after the comma. Accordingly, the regular expression in Listing 4.144 returns true only if f occurs exactly twice or three times at the end of the string.

```
const regExp = /^abcdef{2,3}$/;
console.log(regExp.test('abcde'));      // false
```

```
console.log(regExp.test('abcdef'));      // false
console.log(regExp.test('abcdeff'));     // true
console.log(regExp.test('abcdefff'));    // true
console.log(regExp.test('abcdeffff'));   // false
```

Listing 4.144 Defining a Minimum and a Maximum Number of Occurrences

Continuation of the Phone Number Example

The regular expression for the phone numbers can now be customized using quantifiers as shown in Listing 4.145. This also fulfills another of the requirements listed at the beginning: that the actual phone number may consist of a minimum of five and a maximum of seven digits (see also Figure 4.47).

```
const regExp = /^\d{2}\s\d{2}\s\d{5,7}$/;
console.log(regExp.test('49 30 1234567'));          // true
console.log(regExp.test('Hello World'));            // false
console.log(regExp.test('Hello Max Mustermann'));   // false
console.log(regExp.test('49X30X1234567'));          // false
console.log(regExp.test('49 30 12345678'));         // false
console.log(regExp.test('449 30 1234567'));         // false
console.log(regExp.test('49 30 12345'));            // true
console.log(regExp.test('+49 30 1234567'));         // false
```

Listing 4.145 The Phone Number Example Using Quantifiers

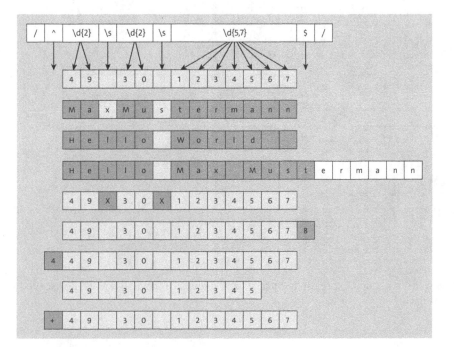

Figure 4.47 Using Quantifiers

Using the ? quantifier, the regular expression can also be extended to allow a phone number to optionally start with a + sign. However, as the + sign has a special meaning within regular expressions, it must be escaped with a backslash (\; see Listing 4.146 and Figure 4.48).

```
const regExp = /^\+?\d{2}\s\d{2}\s\d{5,7}$/;
console.log(regExp.test('+49 30 1234567'));        // true
console.log(regExp.test('49 30 1234567'));         // true
console.log(regExp.test('Hello World'));           // false
console.log(regExp.test('Hello Max Mustermann'));  // false
console.log(regExp.test('49X30X1234567'));         // false
console.log(regExp.test('49 30 12345678'));        // false
console.log(regExp.test('449 30 1234567'));        // false
console.log(regExp.test('49 30 12345'));           // true
console.log(regExp.test('+49 30 1234567'));        // true
```

Listing 4.146 The Customized Phone Number Example with Optional + Sign

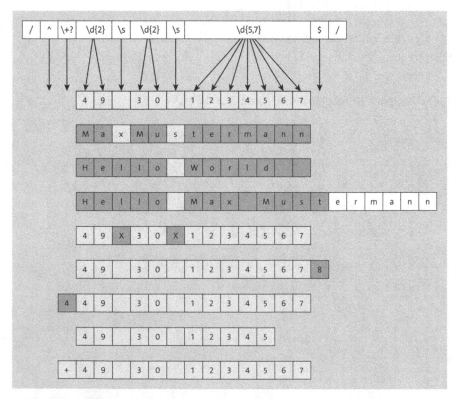

Figure 4.48 Within Regular Expressions, Special Characters Like the + Sign Must Be Escaped Using a Backslash

4.9.6 Searching for Occurrences

So far, we've only used the test() method to check if a string matches a regular expression, and we've gotten a Boolean value every time. As mentioned at the beginning, however, there are several other methods for working with regular expressions: one more that is called directly on a regular expression and four more that are called on strings. Let's look at these methods in turn.

To search a string for occurrences that match a regular expression, use the exec() method. Like the test() method, this method expects an argument in the form of a string to which the regular expression is to be applied. However, exec() does not return a Boolean value, but information about the occurrence.

More precisely, the return value is an array that contains in the first position the string that matches the regular expression (the purposes of the other positions in the array are detailed in Section 4.9.8). In addition to the normal array properties, the array has two more properties: the index property contains the index where the occurrence in the passed string was found, and the input property contains the passed string (see Table 4.11).

Property/Element	Description
index	The position where the occurrence was found
input	The string passed to the exec() method
[0]	The occurrence
[1], [2], ..., [n]	The substring of the occurrence (Section 4.9.8)

Table 4.11 Properties and Elements of the Return Value of exec()

An example is shown in Listing 4.147. Here the regular expression for the phone numbers is applied to the text The phone number is +49 30 1234567. using exec(). The result array, which is stored in the result variable, then contains at position 0 the telephone number found, and its index property contains the index of this occurrence in the passed string. As output, the program returns Number +49 30 1234567 found at index 25..

Note

By the way, for the example to work and the phone number to be found, the ^ and $ delimiters must be removed from the regular expression.

```
const text = 'The phone number is +49 30 1234567.';
const regExp = /\+?\d{2}\s\d{2}\s\d{5,7}/;
const result = regExp.exec(text)
console.log(
```

```
  'Number ' + result[0]
  + ' found at index ' + result.index
  + '.'
);
```

Listing 4.147 The exec() Method Returns More Detailed Information (the Index)

4.9.7   Searching All Occurrences within a String

If you want to search for multiple occurrences in a string, you need to modify this program a bit. For one thing, you must add g after the regular expression. This is a so-called flag or modifier that can be used to configure the way the regular expression works. The g stands for *global*, which means that not only the first occurrence but all occurrences should be found. Then you have to call the exec() method several times to find all occurrences one by one. The easiest way to do this is to use a loop, as shown in Listing 4.148.

```
const text = 'The private phone number is +49 30 1234567,' +
             ' the business phone number is +49 30 1234568.';
const regExp = /\+?\d{2}\s\d{2}\s\d{5,7}/g;
let result;
while ((result = regExp.exec(text)) !== null) {
  console.log(
    'Number ' + result[0]
    + ' found at index ' + result.index
    + '.'
  );
}
```

Listing 4.148 The g Flag Can Be Used to Search for All Occurrences within a String

The output of the program is shown in Listing 4.149.

```
Number +49 30 1234567 found at index 33
Number +49 30 1234568 found at index 88
```

Listing 4.149 Output of the Previous Program

The acceptable modifiers are listed in Table 4.12.

Flag/Modifier	Description
g	Stands for *global*: the regular expression is to be applied globally.
i	Stands for *ignore case*: the regular expression is not case-sensitive.

Table 4.12 The Different Modifiers for Regular Expressions

Flag/Modifier	Description
m	Stands for *multiline*: the regular expression is to be applied over several lines if the corresponding string spans several lines.

Table 4.12 The Different Modifiers for Regular Expressions (Cont.)

Note

Since ES2021, the replaceAll() method is available for strings. It replaces all found occurrences by default, without specifying flags. For many use cases, the usage of replaceAll() is therefore more intuitive.

4.9.8   Accessing Individual Parts of an Occurrence

Groups are a helpful feature of regular expressions. This feature enables you to access specific parts of a string that matches a regular expression. Groups are defined within a regular expression using parentheses. The opening parenthesis defines the beginning of the group, the closing parenthesis the end of the group. When using groups, the return value of exec() contains the characters that fall into each of the defined groups starting with index 1.

Another Advantage of Grouping Characters

Grouping characters has another advantage: using groups, quantifiers can be applied not only to individual characters, but to strings. For example, the regular expression (la)+ represents one or more occurrences of the string la.

The easiest way to understand groups is to use an example, as shown in Listing 4.150 and Figure 4.49. The regular expression shown defines different groups, each comprising the different components of a date: groups are defined for the year, the month, and the calendar day. Subsequently, it's possible to access these three parts via the indexes 1, 2, and 3 of the result of exec(). Any characters that don't fall into any of the groups (in the example, the two places defining spaces, \s) aren't included in the result.

```
const pattern = /^(\d{4})-(\d{2})-(\d{2})$/u;
const result = pattern.exec('2018-03-27');
console.log(result[0]);     // 2018-03-27
console.log(result[1]);     // 2018
console.log(result[2]);     // 03
console.log(result[3]);     // 27
```

```
console.log(result.index);   // 0
console.log(result.input);   // 2018-03-27
```

Listing 4.150 By Defining Groups, You Can Also Access Individual Parts of an Occurrence

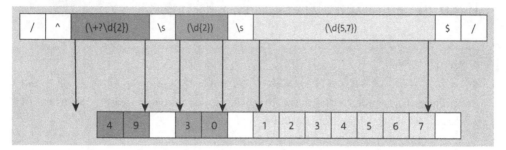

Figure 4.49 Groups Can Be Used to Access Individual Parts of an Occurrence

Since ES2018, it's also possible to specify named groups, where the name is defined by a preceding question mark within two angle brackets. The individual occurrences can then also be accessed via the name of the respective group (see Listing 4.151).

```
const pattern = /^(?<year>\d{4})-(?<month>\d{2})-(?<day>\d{2})$/u;
const result = pattern.exec('2018-03-27');
console.log(result.groups.year);  // '2018'
console.log(result.groups.month); // '03'
console.log(result.groups.day);   // '27'
```

Listing 4.151 Named Groups Allow Access via a Defined Name

4.9.9   Searching for Specific Strings

Basically, the match() method available for strings works similarly to the exec() method of regular expressions. The difference is that if you use the g flag, as shown in Listing 4.152, the match() method returns all found occurrences, but the exec() method still returns only the first occurrence found.

```
const regExp = /\+?\d{2}\s\d{2}\s\d{5,7}/g;
const string = 'A phone number: 49 30 1234567, and one more: 49 30 1234568';
const result = string.match(regExp);
console.log(result[0]);      // 49 30 1234567
console.log(result[1]);      // 49 30 1234568
const result2 = regExp.exec(string);
console.log(result2[0]);     // 49 30 1234567
console.log(result2[1]);     // undefined
```

Listing 4.152 The match() Method Is Called on Strings and Works Similarly to the exec() Method

4.9.10   Replacing Occurrences within a String

The replace() method can be used to replace individual occurrences of a pattern with a new string. The method can be passed both a regular expression and a string as its first argument. As the second argument, you pass the string with which the respective occurrence is to be replaced.

In Listing 4.153, for example, replace() replaces all found phone numbers with the string <number hidden>.

```
let text = 'The private phone number is +49 30 1234567,' +
           ' the business phone number is +49 30 1234568.';
const regExp = /(\+?\d{2})\s(\d{2})\s(\d{5,7})/g;
text = text.replace(regExp, '<number hidden>');
console.log(text);
// The private phone number is <number hidden>,
// the business phone number is <number hidden>.
```

Listing 4.153 The replace() Method Can Be Used to Replace Occurrences in a String

The replacement options are much more flexible if you pass a function instead of a string as the second argument. This function, in turn, is passed each found string as an argument. The return value of the function then is the value with which the found string is replaced. The example from Listing 4.153 can be slightly modified in this way, as shown in Listing 4.154, so that not the complete phone number but only the last five digits are replaced with the string XXXXX.

```
let text = 'The private phone number is +49 30 1234567,' +
           ' the business phone number is +49 30 1234568.';
const regExp = /(\+?\d{2})\s(\d{2})\s(\d{5,7})/g;
text = text.replace(regExp, function(number) {
  return number.substring(0, 9) + 'XXXXX';
});
console.log(text);
// The private phone number is +49 30 12XXXXX,
// the business phone number is +49 30 12XXXXX.
```

Listing 4.154 The New Value to Be Inserted Can Also Be Determined by a Function

4.9.11   Searching for Occurrences

You can use the search() method to search a string for the first occurrence that matches the corresponding regular expression.

An example is shown in Listing 4.155. The regular shown expression applies to phone numbers. The search() method consequently finds the first phone number within a string and returns the index within the string where the phone number was found. If no phone number was found, the method returns the value -1.

```
const text = 'This text contains a phone number: +49 30 1234567';
const text2 = 'This text does not contain any phone number.';
const regExp = /(\+?\d{2})\s(\d{2})\s(\d{5,7})/g;
console.log(text.search(regExp));    // Output: 40
console.log(text2.search(regExp));   // Output: -1
```

Listing 4.155 The search() Method Can Be Used to Search for Occurrences within a String

4.9.12   Splitting Strings

Using the split() method, you can split strings based on a regular expression or on another string. A simple yet quite practical example of this is shown in Listing 4.156.

The starting point is a string containing different values separated by commas. This string is split into the individual values at exactly these points using the split() method.

```
const text = 'John,Doe,4711,45,180,80';
const result = text.split(',');
const firstName = result[0];
const lastName = result[1];
const id = result[2];
const age = result[3];
const height = result[4];
const weight = result[5];
console.log(firstName);    // John
console.log(lastName);     // Doe
console.log(id);           // 4711
console.log(age);          // 45
console.log(height);       // 180
console.log(weight);       // 80
```

Listing 4.156 Most Often, split() Is Probably Used to Split a String at a Particular Delimiter

---

Note

Regular expressions are a powerful tool in a developer's toolbox. At this point, however, we won't go into this topic in more detail. It could fill several hundred pages, and there is simply not enough space here. After all, we still want to introduce you to many other exciting topics.

4.10   Functions as Reference Types

Functions are also objects in JavaScript. This isn't self-evident and not true for all programming languages (not for Java, for example). Functions can therefore be used like "normal" variables as arguments or as return values of other functions. Also, like other objects, functions have methods that can be called on corresponding function objects.

4.10.1   Using Functions as Arguments

Functions can be used as arguments to another function in JavaScript. A simple example of this is shown in Listing 4.157. It defines a function1() function that expects another function as its first parameter and calls it. If you want to pass another function to this function, you have several options. On the one hand, you can pass functions via the appropriate variable that references that function (in the example, the variable function2, which was implicitly created when creating the function2() function). On the other hand, you can also define the function right at the place where the argument is expected—that is, in the argument list of the function that is called. Typically, you would use anonymous functions in this case. The output of the program is shown in Listing 4.158.

```
// Definition of the function that expects another function as an argument
function function1(f) {
  console.log('Function 1 start'); // Calling the passed function
  f();
  console.log('Function 1 end');
}
function function2() {
  console.log('Function 2 start');
  console.log('Function 2 end');
}
// Call with a function using its name
function1(function2);
// function1(function2());      // This does not work.

// Call with an anonymous function as an argument
function1(function() {
  console.log('Anonymous function start');
  console.log('Anonymous function end');
});
```

Listing 4.157 Passing Functions as Arguments of Another Function

```
Function 1 start
Function 2 start
Function 2 end
Function 1 end
Function 1 start
Anonymous function start
Anonymous function end
Function 1 end
```

Listing 4.158 Output of the Preceding Program

Usage Example: Calling Functions for All Elements of an Array

A somewhat more useful and practical example is shown in Listing 4.159. Here, we first define a function called every(), which expects an array as the first argument and a function as the second argument. This latter function is then called for each element in the array.

Two more functions are defined: the print() function, which simply prints the argument passed to it on the console, and the (arrow) function printModulo(), which prints the modulo 2 calculation for the argument passed to it (provided this is a numeric value).

These two functions are then used as arguments for the every() function. The output shows that for each element in the numbers array, the print() function is called first, followed by the printModulo() function for each element.

```
const numbers = [2,3,4,5];

function every(array, f) {
  for(let i=0; i<array.length; i++) {
    f(array[i]);
  }
}

function print(item) {
  console.log(`Item: ${item}`);
}

const printModulo = (item) => {
  console.log(`${item} % 2 = ${item % 2}`);
}

every(numbers, print);
// Output:
// Item: 2
```

```
// Item: 3
// Item: 4
// Item: 5
```

```
every(numbers, printModulo);
// Output:
// 2 % 2 = 0
// 3 % 2 = 1
// 4 % 2 = 0
// 5 % 2 = 1
```

Listing 4.159 Passing a Function as a Parameter

The forEach() Method

The functionality we implemented ourselves in the every() function in the example is already provided natively by arrays in JavaScript, in the form of the forEach() array method. This method executes a function passed to it for each element in the array or calls it with the respective element as an argument. The example from Listing 4.159 could thus also be implemented as shown in Listing 4.160 (we'll talk about the forEach() method in Chapter 14).

```
const numbers = [2,3,4,5];
function print(item) {
  console.log('Item: ' + item);
}
function modulo(item) {
  console.log(item + ' % 2 = ' + item % 2);
}
numbers.forEach(print);
numbers.forEach(modulo);
```

Listing 4.160 The forEach() Method of Arrays Executes a Function Passed to It for Each Element in the Array

---

4.10.2   Using Functions as Return Values

A function in JavaScript can also be used as the return value of another function. How this works is shown in Listing 4.161, again using a simple example: the createAddFunction() function here returns an (anonymous) function which, in turn, calculates the result of two numbers.

The createAddFunction() function can then be called normally. As shown in the example, the result can be assigned to different variables (addFunction1 and addFunction2), which then represent different function objects and can be called as usual via their respective names.

```
function createAddFunction() {
  return function(x, y) {
    return x + y;
  }
}
const addFunction1 = createAddFunction();
const addFunction2 = createAddFunction();
console.log(addFunction1(22, 55));        // 77
console.log(addFunction2(33, 66));        // 99
```

Listing 4.161 Functions as Return Values

Chaining Function Calls

If a function returns another function as return value, you can also call the returned function directly without assigning it to a variable first. An example is shown in Listing 4.162. The sayHello() function prints the word Hello on the console and returns an anonymous function that prints the word World and also returns an anonymous function that outputs the message My name is John Doe. To the console.

If you now call the "outer" function via sayHello(), only the first message is output. By calling sayHello()() (i.e., with two pairs of parentheses), on the other hand, you ensure that not only the outer function is called, but also the function returned by it (the "middle" function), and thus the second message is output. Via sayHello()()() (i.e., with three pairs of parentheses), in turn, the "inner" function is called as well, and thus all three messages are output.

```
function sayHello() {
  console.log('Hello');
  return function() {
    console.log('World');
    return function() {
      console.log('My name is John Doe.');
    }
  }
}

sayHello();        // Calling the "outer" function
                   // Output:
                   // "Hello"
sayHello()();      // Calling the "outer" and "middle" functions
                   // Output:
                   // "Hello"
```

```
                    // "World"
sayHello()()();    // Calling all functions
                    // Output:
                    // "Hello"
                    // "World"
                    // "My name is John Doe."
```

Listing 4.162 Returned Functions Can Be Called Directly

4.10.3 Standard Methods of Each Function

Functions are objects, which means that they can contain methods. By default, every function already provides three methods: apply(), call(), and bind(). What these methods do, how they differ, and in which cases you can use them we'll show you next.

Binding Objects Using the bind() Method

You have already seen that this within a function refers to the context in which the function is called, not to the one in which it was defined. However, this behavior is not always what you want. Imagine you want to pass an object method that accesses this as an argument to a function—for example, as a *callback handler* (i.e., a function that is called by the function to which it is passed). This can lead to a runtime error, as shown in Listing 4.163.

```
const button = {
  handler : null,
  // Function that expects a callback handler
  onClick : function(handler) {
    this.handler = handler;
  },
  click : function() {
    this.handler();
  }
};

const handler = {
  log : function() {
    console.log("Button clicked.");
  },
  // Object method registered as a callback handler further below
  handle: function() {
    this.log();
  }
}
```

```
// Register callback handler
button.onClick(handler.handle);
// Implicit activation of the callback handler
button.click();
```

Listing 4.163 If an Object Method Is Used Outside an Object, this No Longer Refers to the Object

The program ends with an error: "TypeError: Object #<Object> has no method 'log'". The problem is passing handler.handle as a callback function to the onClick() method of button. As soon as this function is called within click() (this.handler()), this within the function refers not to the handler object, but to the button object. Because this object doesn't have a log() method, the runtime error noted occurs.

How can this problem be solved? Relatively easily, if you know how. The bind() function can be used to bind this to a specific object for a function. The bind() method is called on the corresponding function, passing as an argument the object that represents the execution context. If the function itself has parameters, these are simply appended at the end. As a result, bind() returns a new function object that is identical to the source function but has the execution context bound to the passed object (see Listing 4.164).

```
button.onClick(handler.handle.bind(handler));
```

Listing 4.164 The bind() Method Enables You to Define the Execution Context of a Function

For the sake of clarity, you could also write the following, as seen in Listing 4.165.

```
const boundFunction = handler.handle.bind(handler);
button.onClick(boundFunction);
```

Listing 4.165 Explicit Assignment of the Bound Function to a Variable

Note

One more note at this point: this problem also can be solved using an anonymous function that is passed as a callback and controls the call of the handler object (see Listing 4.166).

```
button.onClick(function() {
  handler.handle();
});
```

Listing 4.166 Anonymous Functions Are Often an Alternative to Functions That Are Passed Directly

This works because handle() is called on the handler object (not in the context of button, like before) and thus this refers to handler.

Calling Functions via the call() Method

Using the `call()` method, it's also possible to define the execution context of a function. However, `call()` doesn't create a new function object as in the case of `bind()` but calls the corresponding function directly. The execution context is passed as the first argument; optionally, further arguments can be defined for the function to be called.

A particularly common use case for using `call()` is to use the `forEach()` method to iterate over the `arguments` object (which you got to know in Chapter 3). This method is actually only available to real arrays; `arguments`—as you know—is not a real array and therefore does not provide this method. Thus, the source code shown in Listing 4.167 would result in an error.

```
function logNames() {
  console.log(arguments); // Output: { '0': 'John', '1': 'Doe' }
  /* Error: arguments is not an array
  arguments.forEach(function(argument) {
    console.log(argument);
  });
  */
}
logNames('John', 'James');
```

Listing 4.167 Because the arguments Object Is Not a Real Array, It Does Not Provide the forEach() Method

However, the functionality of the `forEach()` method can also be used for array-like objects like `arguments`. The technical term for this is *function borrowing* or *method borrowing*.

The simplest way to iterate over an array-like object is shown in Listing 4.168.

```
function logNames() {
  Array.prototype.forEach.call(arguments, function(argument) {
    console.log(argument);
  });
}
logNames('John', 'James');
```

Listing 4.168 Iteration over the Array-Like arguments Object by Borrowing the forEach() Method

What exactly is happening here? First of all, the global array object or its prototype is accessed via `Array.prototype`. This prototype contains all methods that are available to array instances in the context of prototypical inheritance (see also Chapter 13). The `forEach()` method is one of them. Via `Array.prototype.forEach`, you can access this method without calling it. The actual call takes place only by calling the `call()` method.

The first argument of call() defines the execution context, which must be the arguments object in the example. The second argument is the one passed to the forEach() method: a callback function that is called for each element in the array or, in this case, in the arguments object.

Calling Functions via the apply() Method

Basically, apply() works similarly to the call() method. The only difference is that the arguments of the called function are not passed as individual arguments but aggregated as an array. The previous example therefore could be realized using apply(), as shown in Listing 4.169.

```
function logNames() {
  Array.prototype.forEach.apply(arguments, [function(argument) {
    console.log(argument);
  }]);
}
logNames('John', 'James');
```

Listing 4.169 The apply() Method Works Similarly to call() but Expects an Array as a Second Argument Instead of Individual Values

4.11   Summary

In addition to primitive data types, there are also the so-called reference types you learned about in this chapter:

- The Object reference type represents the base type for all objects in JavaScript.
- The Array reference type represents arrays.
- The String reference type represents strings.
- The Map, WeakMap, Set, and WeakSet data structures are alternatives to normal arrays.
- Using *array destructuring* and *object destructuring*, it's relatively easy to assign values or properties from arrays and objects to several variables.
- Date and time are represented by the Date reference type.
- With the help of the Math reference type, it's possible to perform complex mathematical calculations.
- Regular expressions are represented by the RegExp reference type.
- Because functions are also objects in JavaScript, there is the corresponding Function reference type representing functions.

Chapter 5
Dynamically Changing Web Pages

*So far, we've used the browser as a means to an end: for running rela-
tively simple examples. But the language's potential within the browser
isn't fully utilized until you use it to create a dynamic web application.
An important basis for this is the Document Object Model, which manages the structure of a web page in the form of a tree structure and can
be changed dynamically using JavaScript.*

Some of the examples in previous chapters already dynamically generated content within an HTML page, but we need to take a closer look at this topic. In general, content can be generated dynamically both on the backend (i.e., on the side of the server that sends the content of a webpage to the client) and on the frontend. In this chapter we will focus on creating content dynamically on the frontend, which means generating content using JavaScript.

5.1 Structure of a Web Page

You already know that object-oriented programming tries to describe objects from the real world as objects in program modeling. Even a web page (for which you can argue whether it belongs to the real world) is represented internally in the browser as an object.

5.1.1 Document Object Model

Each time you access a web page, the browser creates a corresponding model of the web page in memory, called a *Document Object Model* (*DOM*). The DOM is primarily used to access web page content via JavaScript to modify existing content or add new content, for example. It represents the components of a web page hierarchically in a *tree representation*, also known as a *DOM tree*. A DOM tree, in turn, is composed of *nodes*. Their hierarchical arrangement reflects the structure of a web page (see Figure 5.1).

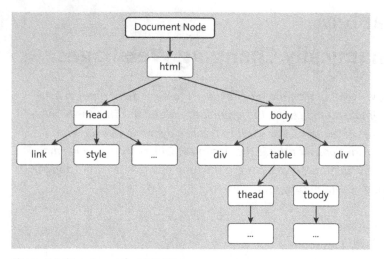

Figure 5.1 Structure of a DOM Tree

Background Information

The tree representation is a data structure frequently used in computer science and programming, especially when part-whole relationships are to be represented. In the case of the DOM, the initial element (the root) is at the top, and the tree "grows" downward.

5.1.2   The Different Types of Nodes

In total, there are four main types of nodes (there are a few more, twelve in total to be exact, but eight of them are less relevant at this stage). These are best explained using an example. Listing 5.1 shows an example HTML file in which you can see the HTML code of a simple table for displaying a contact list. The corresponding DOM is shown in Figure 5.2 (although the illustration is not complete for reasons of space and clarity).

```
<!DOCTYPE html>
<html>
  <head lang="en">
    <title>Contacts Example</title>
  </head>
  <body>
    <main id="main">
      <h1>Contacts</h1>
      <table id="contact-list-table" summary="Contacts">
        <thead>
          <tr>
```

```
            <th id="table-header-first-name">First name</th>
            <th id="table-header-last-name">Last name</th>
            <th id="table-header-email">E-mail address</th>
          </tr>
        </thead>
        <tbody>
          <tr class="row odd">
            <td>John</td>
            <td>Doe</td>
            <td>john.doe@javascripthandbuch.de</td>
          </tr>
          <tr class="row even">
            <td>James</td>
            <td>Doe</td>
            <td>james.doe@javascripthandbuch.de</td>
          </tr>
          <tr class="row odd">
            <td>Peter</td>
            <td>Doe</td>
            <td>peter.doe@javascripthandbuch.de</td>
          </tr>
          <tr class="row even">
            <td>Paul</td>
            <td>Doe</td>
            <td>paul.doe@javascripthandbuch.de</td>
          </tr>
        </tbody>
      </table>
    </main>
  </body>
</html>
```

Listing 5.1 Example HTML Page

When working with the DOM, you'll most often use the following four node types:

- The *document node* (outlined in bold in Figure 5.2) represents the entire web page and is the root of the DOM tree. It's represented by the document global object, which you might already have noticed in some listings. This object is also the entry object for any work with the DOM. The document node is also called the *root node*.

- *Element nodes* (shown in Figure 5.2 with a white background) represent individual HTML elements of a web page. In the example, these are the <main>, <h1>, <table>, <thead>, and <tbody> elements, for example.

- *Attribute nodes* (shown in Figure 5.2 surrounded by dashed lines and with a white background) stand for attributes of HTML elements—in the example, the attribute nodes for the lang, id, and summary attributes.

- The text within HTML elements is represented by its own type of node, called a *text node* (shown in Figure 5.2 surrounded by dashed lines and colored in gray). In the example, these are the nodes for the Contacts Example, Contacts, First name, Last name, and E-mail address texts. Text nodes can't have child nodes themselves and are thus inevitably leaves in the DOM tree (in the example, not all text nodes are shown due to space restrictions, as mentioned earlier).

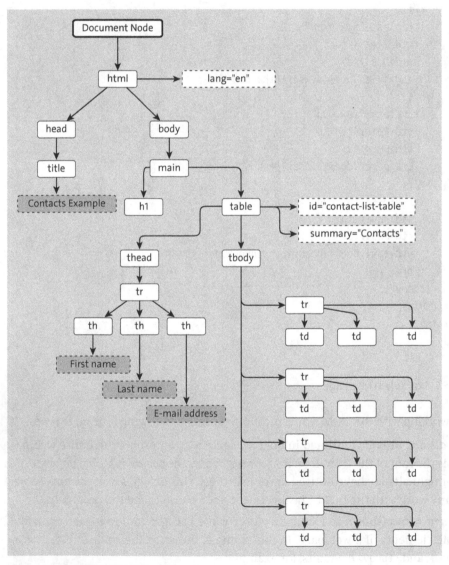

Figure 5.2 Example DOM Tree Structure

Note

The example from Listing 5.1 and Figure 5.2 forms the basis for the next sections. Using this example, we'll show you how to access and modify nodes on a web page.

Examining the DOM in the Browser

You can view the DOM of a web page in a special view with the respective JavaScript debugging tools of the different browsers. In Chrome DevTools, this view is located on the **Elements** tab (see Figure 5.3).

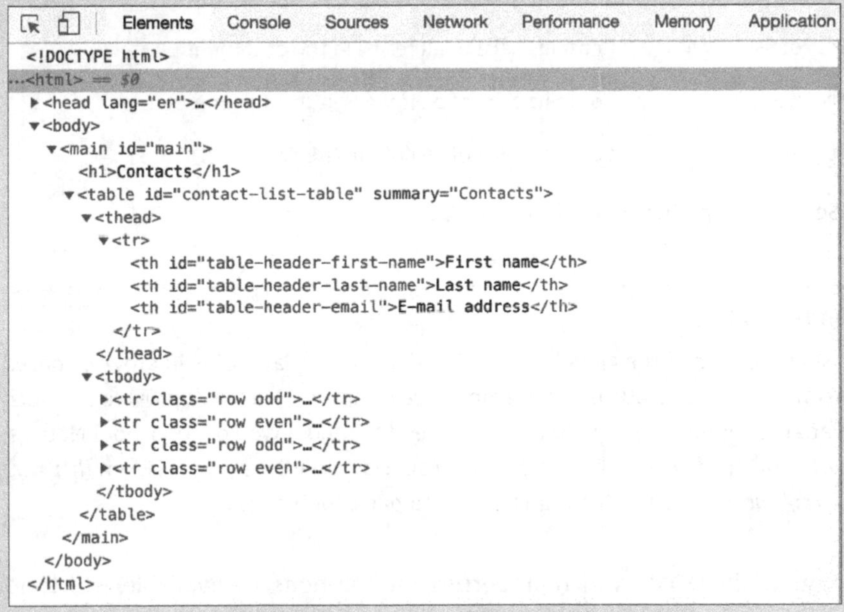

Figure 5.3 Representation of the DOM in Chrome DevTools

You can usually even change the DOM manually via this view. Test this by double-clicking one of the nodes within the DOM tree—for example, a text node. Then you can change the corresponding text of the node.

In practice, this can be quite helpful to quickly test a certain constellation of HTML. However, the changes you make in this view don't affect the underlying HTML file. If you reload the file in the browser, the changes are lost.

5.1.3 The Document Node

The document node, as mentioned earlier, is the entry point for the DOM and is represented by the document global object, which has various properties and methods.

Selected properties are listed in Table 5.1, while the various methods will be discussed in detail throughout this chapter.

Property	Description
document.title	Contains the title of the current document
document.lastModified	Contains the date when the document was last modified
document.URL	Contains a URL of the current document
document.domain	Contains the domain of the current document
document.cookie	Contains a list of all cookies for the document
document.forms	Contains a list of all forms in the document
document.images	Contains a list of all images in the document
document.links	Contains a list of all links in the document

Table 5.1 Selected Properties of the document Object

DOM under Node.js

The DOM in the form of the global document variable is only available in browser-based runtime environments. Node.js, for example (see Chapter 17), doesn't provide any such global variable because Node.js isn't typically used to render web pages. Under Node.js, a DOM of a web page can only be created via special modules such as jsdom (*https:// github.com/jsdom/jsdom*), which can be used to parse web pages.

The structure of the DOM—which properties and methods are available, which node types are provided, and so on—is defined in the DOM application programming interface (API), a specification of the World Wide Web Consortium (W3C). This API is independent of the programming language; that is, there are implementations not only for JavaScript, but also for other programming languages like Java or C++.

Interface, Implementation, and API

In object-oriented programming, *interfaces* are used to define the methods that must be present in *implementations* (i.e., concrete realizations of the respective interface). An *API* defines a set of interfaces provided by a software system.

Accordingly, the DOM API is a set of interfaces that browsers provide for working with web pages.

5.2   Selecting Elements

Whether you want to change existing information on a web page or add new information, you must first select an element on the web page that you want to change or to which you want to attach the new information. For this purpose, the DOM API offers various properties and methods, as shown in Table 5.2.

As you can see, there are some methods that return multiple elements and other methods that return single elements. We'll look at the details in the following sections.

Property/Method	Description	Return Code	Section
getElementById()	Selects an element based on an ID	Single element	Section 5.2.1
getElementsBy-ClassName()	Selects elements based on a class name	List of elements	Section 5.2.2
getElementsBy-TagName()	Selects all elements with the specified element name	List of elements	Section 5.2.3
getElementsBy-Name()	Selects elements by their name	List of elements	Section 5.2.4
querySelector()	Returns the first element that matches a given CSS selector	Single element	Section 5.2.5
querySelectorAll()	Returns all elements that match a given CSS selector	List of elements	Section 5.2.5
parentElement	Returns the parent element for a node	Single element	Section 5.2.6
parentNode	Returns the parent node for a node	Single node	Section 5.2.6
previousElement-Sibling	Returns the previous sibling element for a node	Single element	Section 5.2.8
previousSibling	Returns the previous sibling node for a node	Single node	Section 5.2.8
nextElementSibling	Returns the next sibling element for a node	Single element	Section 5.2.8

Table 5.2 The Different Methods and Properties for Selecting Elements

Property/Method	Description	Return Code	Section
nextSibling	Returns the next sibling node for a node	Single node	Section 5.2.8
firstElementChild	Returns the first child element for a node	Single element	Section 5.2.7
firstChild	Returns the first child node for a node	Single node	Section 5.2.7
lastElementChild	Returns the last child element for a node	Single element	Section 5.2.7
lastChild	Returns the last child node for a node	Single node	Section 5.2.7
childNodes	Returns all child nodes for a node	List of nodes	Section 5.2.7
children	Returns all child elements for a node	List of elements	Section 5.2.7

Table 5.2 The Different Methods and Properties for Selecting Elements (Cont.)

Selection Methods

Selection methods and properties are not only available for the document node, but also for other nodes (Section 5.2.9).

5.2.1   Selecting Elements by ID

Elements on a web page can be assigned an ID (which is unique on that web page) via the id attribute. This ID can be used in CSS rules, and you can select the corresponding element via JavaScript using the getElementById() method of the document object. You simply pass the ID of the element to be selected to the method in the form of a string.

In Listing 5.2, the element with the main ID is selected (see also Figure 5.4) and stored in the mainElement variable. Then, the className property is used to change the class attribute of the element to the value border, which in the example results in the element having a red border with rounded corners (see Figure 5.5; the complete example, including HTML and CSS code, can be found in the download area for the book).

```
const mainElement = document.getElementById('main');
mainElement.className = 'border';
```

Listing 5.2 Accessing an Element via the ID

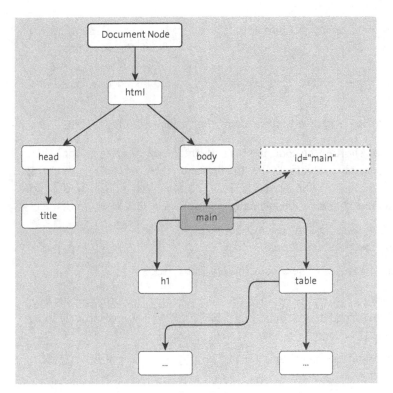

Figure 5.4 The getElementById() Method Selects One Element at Most

Contacts

First name	Last name	E-mail address
John	Doe	john.doe@javascripthandbuch.de
James	Doe	james.doe@javascripthandbuch.de
Peter	Doe	peter.doe@javascripthandbuch.de
Paul	Doe	paul.doe@javascripthandbuch.de

Figure 5.5 The Returned Element Is Assigned a New CSS Class, Giving the Element a Highlighted Border

Tip

In practice, it's not a bad idea to program a little more *defensively* and check that a variable to be accessed is not null or undefined. This also applies to working with the DOM, as the getElementById() method returns the value null if no element with the passed ID is found. If you then try to access a property or method on the assumed element, a runtime error occurs. To prevent this, you should use an if query to ensure that the return value of getElementById() is not null, as shown in Listing 5.3.

```
const mainElement = document.getElementById('main'); // Select element by ID.
if(mainElement !== null) {                            // If the element
                                                      // is not empty,
  mainElement.className = 'border';                   // assign new CSS class.
}
```

Listing 5.3 If There Is No Element with the main ID, the Variable Is Not Accessed

Alternatively, you can shorten the code and take advantage of the && operator, where the second operand is only evaluated if the first operand returns true. Thus, in Listing 5.4, the operand (mainElement.className = 'border') is evaluated (or executed) only if mainElement has a value that does not evaluate to false—in other words, is not null.

```
const mainElement = document.getElementById('main'); // Select element by ID.
mainElement && (mainElement.className = 'border');
```

Listing 5.4 You Can Use the && Operator to Shorten This Check

The check is even shorter using the *optional chaining operator* ?, which has only been available since ES2020. In Listing 5.5, the className property is accessed only when mainElement is not null or undefined.

```
const mainElement = document.getElementById('main'); // Select element by ID.
mainElement?.className = 'border';
```

Listing 5.5 You Can Use the ? Operator to Check whether a Property Is Defined

---

Performance of Selection Methods

Compared to other selection methods, selecting an element by ID is quite fast in terms of performanceas a web page isn't allowed to have multiple elements with the same ID, and thus the search can very quickly find the appropriate element for an ID. Other selection methods, like the getElementsByClassName() method presented in the next section, are much slower in comparison because they require checking every element on the web page. You usually won't notice the speed difference, but you should keep it in mind.

Tip

You shouldn't overuse DOM methods. If you need to use the result of a DOM method in multiple places within a program, store the result in a variable instead of calling the DOM method over and over again. Consider that every call of a DOM method that searches for elements in the DOM tree will cost computing time. This computing time can be minimized by using variables for caching results.

5.2.2 Selecting Elements by Class

Like IDs, *CSS classes* can be assigned to individual elements on a web page. These classes are managed via the `class` attribute. An element can have multiple classes, and unlike IDs, multiple elements can have the same class.

This, in turn, results in the corresponding `getElementsByClassName()` DOM method—which enables the selection by CSS class—returning not only a single element, but several elements, if necessary.

As an argument, the method is passed the class name as a string, as shown in Listing 5.6. In this example, all elements containing the `even` CSS class are selected—that is, the two even table rows (see Figure 5.6).

```
const tableRowsEven = document
    .getElementsByClassName('even');      // Select all even table rows.
```

Listing 5.6 Accessing an Element by Class Name

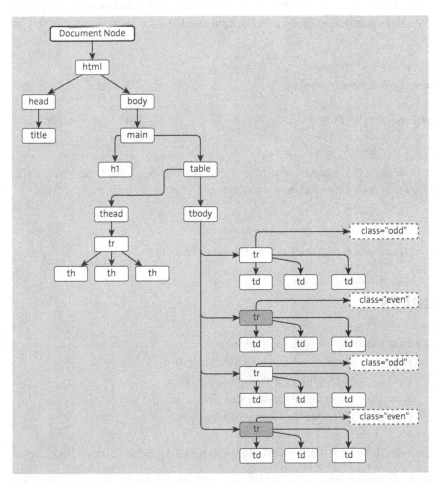

Figure 5.6 The getElementsByClassName() Method Can Return Multiple Elements

The return value of getElementsByClassName() is a *node list* (more precisely, an object of the NodeList type), which is used in a similar way as an array (but which is not an array; more about that in a moment). This node list contains the elements in the exact order in which they appear on the web page.

Although node lists look like arrays at first glance, they are not arrays. This is a fact that JavaScript beginners must always keep in mind as its nonobservance frequently leads to errors in the program.

A feature that node lists have in common with arrays is that you can access the individual elements in a node list via an index. That is, you can use tableRowsEven[0], for example, to access the first element, tableRowsEven[1] to access the second element, and so on. Another common feature is the length property, which can be used to determine the number of elements in the node list.

So, for example, to iterate over all elements of a node list, you can proceed as shown in Listing 5.7. This listing uses a for loop to iterate over all elements of the list. As with iteration over real arrays, you can use the length property and the access by index. Using these features, the example assigns a new background color to each element in the list (see Figure 5.7).

```
const tableRowsEven = document
  .getElementsByClassName('even');            // Select all even
                                              // table rows.

if(tableRowsEven.length > 0) {                // If at least one element
                                              // is found.

  for(let i=0; i<tableRowsEven.length; i++) { // Iterate all elements.
    const tableRow = tableRowsEven[i];        // Assign element to a variable.
    tableRow.style.backgroundColor = '#CCCCCC'; // Set new background color.
  }
}
```

Listing 5.7 Iteration over a List of Nodes Using the Array Syntax

Contacts

First name	Last name	E-mail address
John	Doe	john.doe@javascripthandbuch.de
James	Doe	james.doe@javascripthandbuch.de
Peter	Doe	peter.doe@javascripthandbuch.de
Paul	Doe	paul.doe@javascripthandbuch.de

Figure 5.7 The Even Table Cells Were Assigned a Different Background Color via JavaScript

Modifying the CSS of an Element

The style property of an element allows you to access or modify the CSS properties of an element. The object stored in this property contains all CSS properties as object properties (style.color, style.border, etc.). For CSS properties such as background-color that contain a hyphen, the corresponding object properties are defined in CamelCase notation (e.g., style.backgroundColor or style.fontFamily).

As an alternative to the array syntax with square brackets, individual nodes of a node list can be accessed using the item() method. In this case, the argument to be passed is the index of the element to be returned. The loop above could also be rephrased as shown in Listing 5.8.

```
const tableRowsEven = document
  .getElementsByClassName('even');              // Select all even
                                                // table rows.

if(tableRowsEven.length > 0) {                  // If at least one element
                                                // is found.

  for(let i=0; i<tableRowsEven.length; i++) {   // Iterate all elements.
    const tableRow = tableRowsEven.item(i);     // Assign element to a variable.
    tableRow.style.backgroundColor = '#CCCCCC'; // Set new background color.
  }
}
```

Listing 5.8 Iteration over a List of Nodes Using the item() Method

Method Borrowing

Because node lists aren't real arrays (they are objects of the NodeList type) but array-like objects (like the arguments object, remember?), in practice you'll often use the technique of *method borrowing* (see Chapter 4) to still be able to use Array methods (see Listing 5.9).

```
Array.prototype.forEach.call(tableRowsEven, (tableRow) => {
  tableRow.style.backgroundColor = '#CCCCCC';
});
```

Listing 5.9 Iteration over a Node List via Method Borrowing

Active Node Lists versus Static Node Lists

A distinction is made between *active* and *static node lists*. The former are node lists in which changes made to individual nodes in the list have a direct impact on the web page; that is, the changes are immediately reflected on the web page.

> With the latter, on the other hand, changes to nodes within the node list have no direct effect on the web page; they are not immediately reflected. The `getElementsByClassName()`, `getElementsByTagName()`, and `getElementsByName()` methods return active node lists, whereas the `querySelectorAll()` method returns a static node list.

5.2.3   Selecting Elements by Element Name

The `getElementsByTagName()` method can be used to select elements by their element name. The method expects the name of the element. For example, to select all table cells (see Figure 5.8), proceed as shown in Listing 5.10.

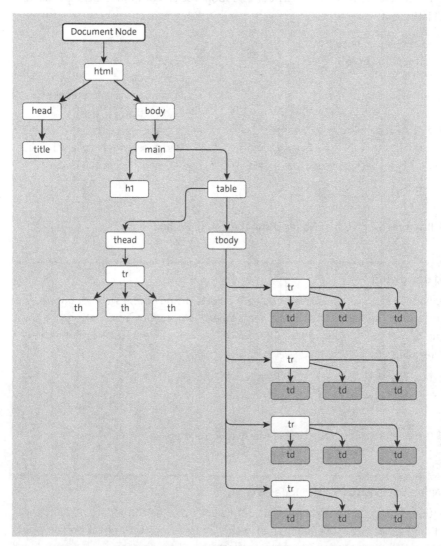

Figure 5.8 The getElementsByTagName() Method Selects Elements by Their Element Name

First, all table cells are selected via the getElementsByTagName() method, and then each element is assigned a new font and a new font size. The results are displayed in Figure 5.9.

```
const tableCells = document.getElementsByTagName('td');
if(tableCells.length > 0) {                    // If at lease one element is
                                               // found.
  for(let i=0; i<tableCells.length; i++) {     // Iterate all elements.
    const tableCell = tableCells[i];           // Assign element to a variable.
    tableCell.style.fontFamily = 'Verdana';    // Set new font.
    tableCell.style.fontSize = '9pt';          // Set new font size.
  }
}
```

Listing 5.10 Accessing an Element via Element Name

Contacts

First name	Last name	E-mail address
John	Doe	john.doe@javascripthandbuch.de
James	Doe	james.doe@javascripthandbuch.de
Peter	Doe	peter.doe@javascripthandbuch.de
Paul	Doe	paul.doe@javascripthandbuch.de

Figure 5.9 The Table Cells Are Assigned a New Font and Font Size

> **Note**
>
> Ensure that you only pass the name of the element to the getElementsByTagName() method, without additional angle brackets or the like. For example, the getElements-ByTagName('<td>') call wouldn't work.

5.2.4   Selecting Elements by Name

Some elements can be assigned a name attribute in HTML—for example <input> elements of the radio type—to indicate their association with a selection group. In Listing 5.11, for example, the three radio buttons are assigned to the genre group.

```
<form action="">
  <label for="artist">Artist</label>
  <input id="artist" type="text" name="artist">
  <br>
  <label for="album">Album</label>
```

```
<input id="album" type="text" name="album">
<br>
<p>Genre:</p>
<fieldset>
  <input type="radio" id="st" name="genre" value="Stonerrock">
  <label for="st">Stonerrock</label>
  <br>
  <input type="radio" id="sp" name="genre" value="Spacerock">
  <label for="sp">Spacerock</label>
  <br>
  <input type="radio" id="ha" name="genre" value="Hardrock">
  <label for="ha">Hardrock</label>
</fieldset>
</form>
```

Listing 5.11 A Simple HTML Form

Using the getElementsByName() method, elements can be selected based on this name attribute. In Listing 5.12, this method is used to select all elements with a name attribute of the value genre. (The other two form elements with the values artist and album are not selected, though; see Figure 5.10.)

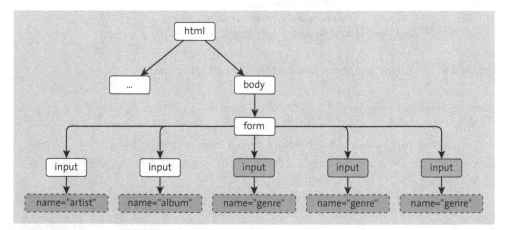

Figure 5.10 The getElementsByName() Method Selects Elements by Their name Attribute

In loop in Listing 5.12, the values of these elements (inputElement.value) are output: Stonerrock, Spacerock, and Hardrock.

```
const inputElementsForGenre = document
  .getElementsByName('genre');                    // Select all elements
                                                   // by name.

if(inputElementsForGenre.length > 0) {             // If at least one
                                                   // element is found.
```

372

```
for(let i=0; i<inputElementsForGenre.length; i++) {   // Iterate all elements.
  const inputElement = inputElementsForGenre[i];      // Assign element to a
                                                      // variable.

  console.log(inputElement.value);                    // Output: Stonerrock,
                                                      // Spacerock, Hardrock

}
}
```

Listing 5.12 Accessing Elements by Element Names

Browser Support of getElementsByName()

The getElementsByName() method doesn't work consistently in all browsers. For example, in some versions of the Internet Explorer and Opera browsers, the method returns not only those elements with a name attribute that matches the passed value, but also those with an id attribute that matches the passed value. In my opinion, the other selection methods (presented so far and to be presented in a moment) provide sufficient possibilities for selecting elements so that you can actually do without this method in practice.

5.2.5 Selecting Elements by Selector

The DOM methods for selecting elements presented so far already accomplish a lot but are quite restricted in the form of expression. The element you want to select might not have an ID or class at all; the getElementById() or getElementsByClassName() methods don't help in such cases. The getElementsByTagName() method, on the other hand, is very unspecific because it tends to select many elements. And getElementsByName() should be used with caution anyway, for the reasons mentioned earlier.

The querySelector() and querySelectorAll() methods are much more versatile and expressive for returning elements for a given CSS selector. The former method returns the *first element* that matches the corresponding CSS selector, while the latter method returns *all elements* that match the CSS selector.

Listing 5.13 shows an example of using querySelector(). This example passes the #main table td:nth-child(2) CSS selector, which describes the second table cells of each row (td:nth-child(2)) inside a table (table) within an element with the main ID (#main). But because the querySelector() method selects only the first element matching a selector, only the first <td> element is returned (see Figure 5.11 and Figure 5.12).

```
const tableCell = document.querySelector('#main table td:nth-child(2)');
tableCell.style.border = 'thick solid red';
```

Listing 5.13 Accessing an Element by CSS Selector

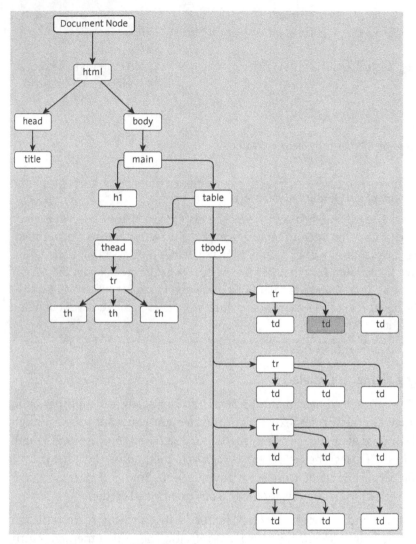

Figure 5.11 The querySelector() Method Returns at Most One Element

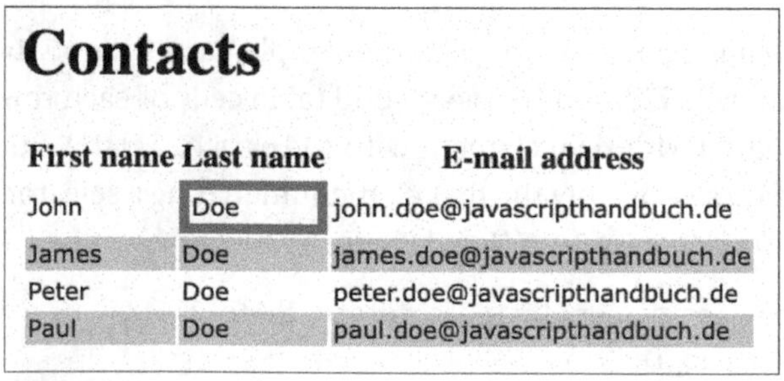

Contacts

First name	Last name	E-mail address
John	Doe	john.doe@javascripthandbuch.de
James	Doe	james.doe@javascripthandbuch.de
Peter	Doe	peter.doe@javascripthandbuch.de
Paul	Doe	paul.doe@javascripthandbuch.de

Figure 5.12 The querySelector() Method Returns the First Element That Matches the CSS Selector

Listing 5.14, on the other hand, shows the use of the querySelectorAll() method. This listing uses the same CSS selector as above. This time, however, you receive *all* elements that match this selector—that is, all second <td> elements (see Figure 5.13).

```
const tableCells = document.querySelectorAll('#main table td:nth-child(2)');
if(tableCells.length > 0) {
  for(let i=0; i<tableCells.length; i++) {
    const tableCell = tableCells[i];
    tableCell.style.border = 'thick solid red';
  }
}
```

Listing 5.14 Accessing Multiple Elements by CSS Selector

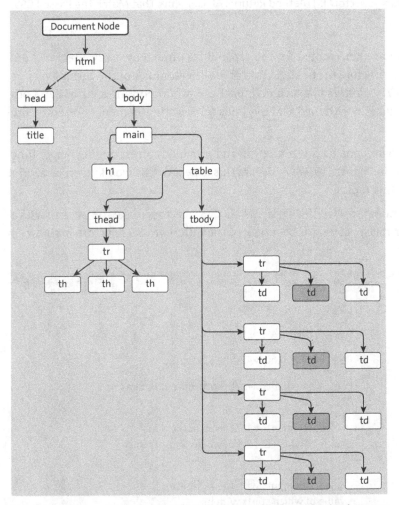

Figure 5.13 The querySelectorAll() Method Can Return Multiple Elements

Within the loop, these elements are then marked with a red frame in the same way as before (see Figure 5.14).

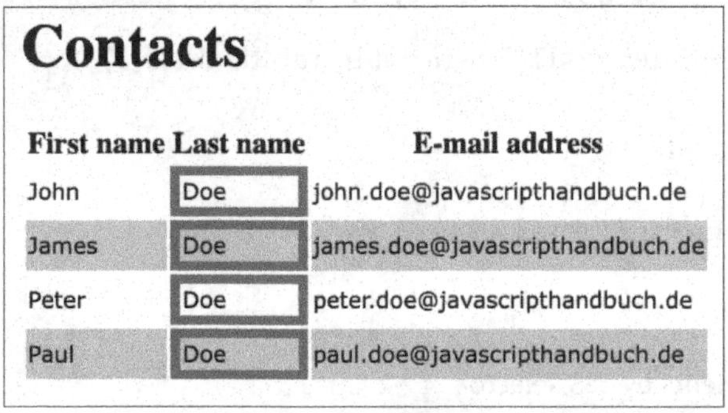

Figure 5.14 The querySelectorAll() Method Returns All Elements That Match the Passed CSS Selector

Web developers have long waited for the capabilities offered by querySelector() and querySelectorAll(). Before the introduction of the Selector API (for the current version, see *www.w3.org/TR/selectors4*), which defines these two important methods and others, you had to make do with the DOM methods for selecting elements presented previously.

The jQuery library recognized this limitation and provided corresponding helper functions quite early. In Chapter 10, we'll discuss this aspect of this well-known JavaScript library, among other topics.

Overall, the methods for selecting elements via CSS selectors make the work of a JavaScript developer much easier. An overview of the different CSS selectors is shown in Table 5.3.

Selector	Description	Since CSS version
*	Selects every element	2
E	Selects elements of type E	1
[a]	Selects elements with the attribute a	2
[a="b"]	Selects elements with the attribute a that has the value b	2
[a~="b"]	Selects elements with the attribute a the value of which is a list of values, one of which is equal to b	2
[a^="b"]	Selects elements with the attribute a the value of which starts with b	3

Table 5.3 The Different Selectors in CSS3

Selector	Description	Since CSS version
[a$="b"]	Selects elements with the attribute a the value of which ends with b	3
[a*="b"]	Selects elements with the attribute a the value of which contains b as a substring	3
[a|="b"]	Selects elements with the attribute a the values of which are a series of values separated by minus signs, where the first value is b	2
:root	Selects the root element of a document	3
:nth-child(n)	Selects the nth child element of an element	3
:nth-last-child(n)	Selects the nth child element of an element starting from the end	3
:nth-of-type(n)	Selects the nth sibling element of a specific type of an element	3
:nth-last-of-type(n)	Selects the nth sibling element of a specific type of an element starting from the end	3
:first-child	Selects the first child element of an element	2
:last-child	Selects the last child element of an element	3
:first-of-type	Selects the first sibling element of an element	3
:last-of-type	Selects the last sibling element of an element	3
:only-child	Selects elements that are the only child element of their parent element	3
:only-of-type	Selects elements that are the only element of their type among their sibling elements	3
:empty	Selects elements that have no child elements	3
:link	Selects links that have not yet been clicked	2
:visited	Selects links that have already been clicked	2
:active	Selects links that are being clicked at that moment	2
:hover	Selects links over which the mouse is currently located	2
:focus	Selects links that are currently focused	2

Table 5.3 The Different Selectors in CSS3 (Cont.)

Selector	Description	Since CSS version
:target	Selects jump labels that can be reached via links within a web page	3
:lang(en)	Selects elements the lang attribute of which has the value en	2
:enabled	Selects form elements into which values can be entered or which can be operated (and are not disabled)	3
:disabled	Selects form elements that cannot be operated or for which input has been disabled via the disabled attribute	3
:checked	Selects checkboxes and radio buttons that are enabled	3
.className	Selects elements the class attribute of which has the value className	1
#main	Selects elements the id attribute of which has the value main	1
:not(s)	Selects elements that do not match the selector s specified in parentheses	3
E F	Selects elements of type F that occur somewhere within an element of type E	1
E > F	Selects elements of type F that are child elements of an element of type E	2
E + F	Selects elements of type F that are sibling elements immediately following an element of type E	2
E ~ F	Selects elements of type F that are sibling elements of an element of type E	3

Table 5.3 The Different Selectors in CSS3 (Cont.)

5.2.6   Selecting the Parent Element of an Element

Element nodes have various properties that allow you to access related elements. Related elements are parent nodes or elements, child nodes or elements, and sibling nodes or elements.

For the selection of parent nodes/elements, the parentNode and parentElement properties are available; for the selection of child nodes/elements, there are the firstChild, firstElementChild, lastChild, lastElementChild, childNodes, and children properties;

and for the selection of sibling nodes/elements, the previousSibling, previousElementSibling, nextSibling, and nextElementSibling properties are provided.

These characteristics will be explained in a little more detail ahead. Let's start with the selection of parent nodes or elements.

To select the parent node of an element (or node), the parentNode property is available, while the parent element can be selected via the parentElement. In most cases, the parent node is always an element as well; that is, the parentNode and parentElement properties contain the same value (see Listing 5.15 and Figure 5.15).

```
const table = document.querySelector('table');
console.log(table.parentNode);    // <main>
console.log(table.parentElement); // <main>
```

Listing 5.15 Accessing a Parent Node or Parent Element

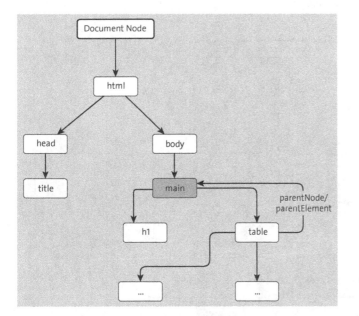

Figure 5.15 Selection of the Parent Element

Nodes and Elements

Not all nodes in the DOM tree are elements, but all elements are always nodes.

It's important to understand that some of the preceding properties return nodes, while other properties return elements. The parentNode, childNodes, firstChild, lastChild, previousSibling, and nextSibling properties return nodes, while the parentElement, children, firstElementChild, lastElementChild, previousElementSibling, and nextElementSibling properties return elements.

The following example illustrates what this means in practice. Look at the HTML code in Listing 5.16 and its DOM in Figure 5.16. They show a relatively simple web page with only two <span> elements inside the <body> element, each enclosed in text.

```
<!DOCTYPE html>
<html>
<body>
  Text
  <span></span>
  Text
  <span></span>
  Text
</body>
</html>
```

Listing 5.16 A Simple HTML Example

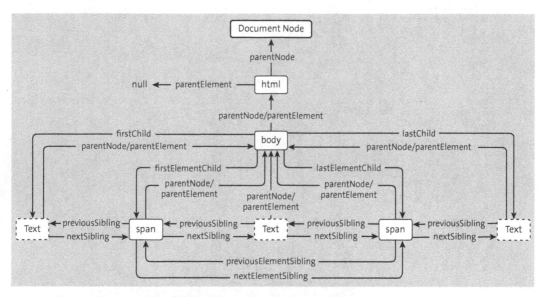

Figure 5.16 Overview of the Different Forms of Access

Accordingly, the corresponding DOM below the <body> element contains (in this order) a text node, an element node, a text node, an element node, and again a text node. For all these nodes, the <body> element represents both the parent node and the parent element at the same time. Thus, for all these nodes, the parentNode and parentElement properties return the same value: the <body> element.

Also, you can see in the DOM in Figure 5.16 that the parentNode and parentElement properties generally always reference the same element for all nodes. The only exception is the <html> element. This element does not have a parent element but "only" a parent node—the document node. In this case, the `parentElement` property returns the value `null`.

The other relationships between elements and nodes in the DOM will be discussed in the following sections.

5.2.7   Selecting the Child Elements of an Element

The child elements of an element can be determined via the `children` property, the child nodes via the `childNodes` property. Whether an element has child nodes can be determined using the `hasChildNodes()` method, which returns a Boolean value. You can determine whether an element has child elements using the `childElementCount` property: this contains the number of child elements.

Listing 5.17 shows some examples (again related to the HTML from Listing 5.1). You see that the `<tbody>` element has four child elements (the four `<tr>` elements; see Figure 5.17) and a total of nine child nodes (see Figure 5.18).

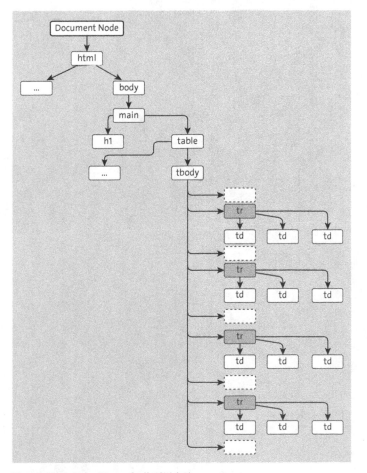

Figure 5.17 Selection of All Child Elements

```
const tbody = document.querySelector('tbody');
console.log(tbody.children.length);      // 4
console.log(tbody.childElementCount);    // 4
console.log(tbody.childNodes.length);    // 9
console.log(tbody.hasChildNodes());      // true
```

Listing 5.17 Accessing Child Nodes or Child Elements

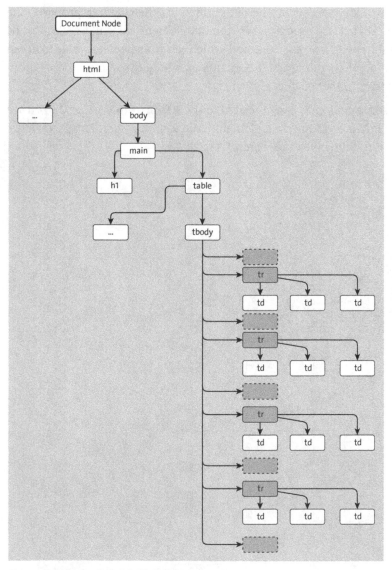

Figure 5.18 Selection of All Child Nodes

The reason for this is that although no text occurs between, before, and behind the four `<tr>` elements in HTML, so-called whitespace nodes are produced (see the following box). These whitespace nodes are created whenever line breaks are used between two elements in HTML, for example.

Whitespace Nodes

Whitespace within the HTML code, created by spaces, tabs, or line breaks, for example, always results in text nodes without text being created in the DOM. These are referred to as *whitespace nodes*.

In addition, various other properties are available that can be used to select individual child elements or child nodes:

- The `firstChild` property contains the first child node.
- The `lastChild` property contains the last child node.
- The `firstElementChild` property contains the first child element.
- The `lastElementChild` property contains the last child element.

Listing 5.18 shows some examples. The result of selecting the first and last child elements is shown in Figure 5.19, and the result of selecting the first and last child nodes is illustrated in Figure 5.20.

```
const tbody = document.querySelector('tbody');
console.log(tbody.firstChild);            // Text node
console.log(tbody.lastChild);             // Text node
console.log(tbody.firstElementChild);     // <tr>
console.log(tbody.lastElementChild);      // <tr>
```

Listing 5.18 Accessing Specific Child Nodes and Child Elements

---

Note

In most cases, you'll probably work with element nodes. In these cases, it's best to use properties that also return element nodes (such as `firstElementChild` and `lastElementChild`). There was a time when web developers only had properties available that returned all types of nodes (e.g., `firstChild` and `lastChild`) and they had to filter element nodes based on the node type itself. Fortunately, this has changed.

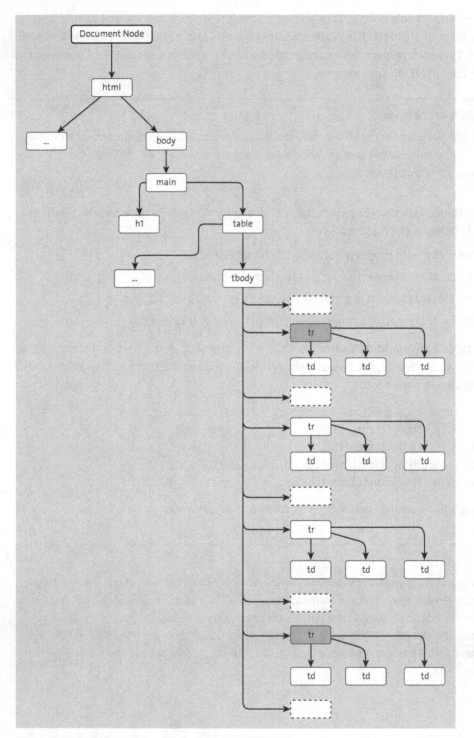

Figure 5.19 Selection of the First and the Last Child Element

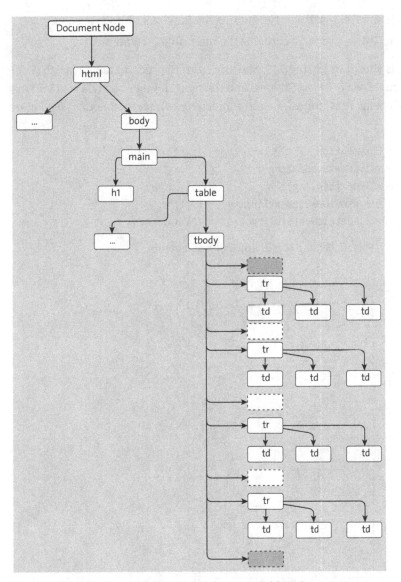

Figure 5.20 Selection of the First and the Last Child Node

5.2.8   Selecting the Sibling Elements of an Element

Now you know how to select nodes/elements in the DOM tree above (parent nodes/parent elements) and below (child nodes/child elements) a starting node/element using its properties. In addition, there is also the possibility to select the sibling nodes or sibling elements *within one level* of the DOM:

- The previousSibling property contains the previous sibling node.
- The nextSibling property contains the next sibling node.

- The previousElementSibling property contains the previous sibling element.
- The nextElementSibling property contains the next sibling element.

A code example is shown in Listing 5.19. Starting from the second table row, first the previous sibling node (via previousSibling) and the next sibling node (via nextSibling) are selected, both being text nodes—or more precisely, whitespace nodes (see Figure 5.21).

```
const tableCell = document.querySelector('tbody tr:nth-child(2)');
console.log(tableCell.previousSibling);        // Text node
console.log(tableCell.nextSibling);            // Text node
console.log(tableCell.previousElementSibling); // <tr>
console.log(tableCell.nextElementSibling);     // <tr>
```

Listing 5.19 Accessing Specific Sibling Nodes and Sibling Elements

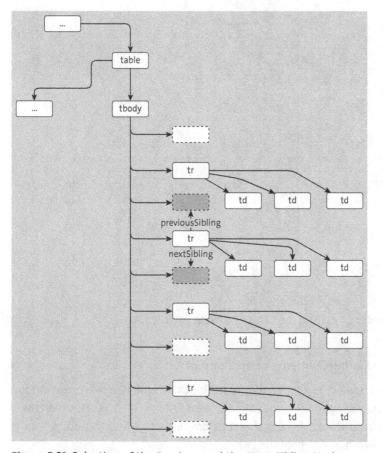

Figure 5.21 Selection of the Previous and the Next Sibling Node

Then `previousElementSibling` selects the previous sibling element, and `nextElementSibling` selects the next sibling element (see Figure 5.22).

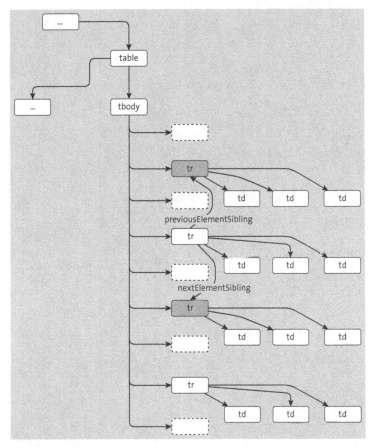

Figure 5.22 Selection of the Previous and the Next Sibling Element

5.2.9 Calling Selection Methods on Elements

Most of the presented DOM methods for selecting elements (`getElementsByClassName()`, `getElementsByTagName()`, `querySelector()`, and `querySelectorAll()`) can be called not only on the document node (i.e., on `document`), but also on all other element nodes of a web page (just `getElementById()` and `getElementsByName()` can be called only on the document node). In this case, the search for the elements includes only the subtree below the element on which the respective method was called.

Consider the HTML code in Listing 5.20, which contains nested lists. In the JavaScript code shown in Listing 5.21, the `getElementsByTagName()` method with the argument `li` is first called on the `document` node (which selects all list entries of the entire web page; see

Figure 5.23) and then on the nested list with the `list-2` ID (which, in turn, selects only those list entries that occur in this subtree of the DOM—i.e., below the nested list; see Figure 5.24).

```html
<!DOCTYPE html>
<html>
  <head lang="en">
    <title>Example of the selection of elements</title>
  </head>
  <body>
    <main id="main-content">
      <ul id="list-1">
        <li>List entry 1</li>
        <li>
          List entry 2
          <ul id="list-2">
            <li>List entry 2.1</li>
            <li>List entry 2.2</li>
            <li>List entry 2.3</li>
            <li>List entry 2.4</li>
          </ul>
        </li>
        <li>List entry 3</li>
        <li>List entry 4</li>
      </ul>
    </main>
  </body>
</html>
```

Listing 5.20 Example HTML Page

```javascript
const allListItemElements = document.getElementsByTagName('li');
console.log(allListItemElements.length); // Output: 8
const subList = document.getElementById('list-2');
const subListListItems = subList.getElementsByTagName('li');
console.log(subListListItems.length);    // Output: 4
```

Listing 5.21 Selection of Elements Starting from a Parent Element

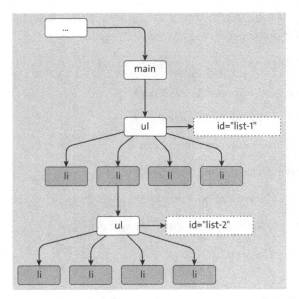

Figure 5.23 Calling the getElementsByTagName() Method on the Document Node

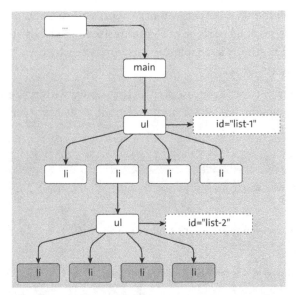

Figure 5.24 Calling the getElementsByTagName() Method on the <ul> Element with the list-2 ID

5.2.10   Selecting Elements by Type

In addition to the presented selection methods, the document object provides various properties for accessing specific elements of a web page directly, see Table 5.4. For example, the anchors property can be used to select all anchors (i.e., jump elements) on a web page, forms to select all forms, images to select all images, and links to select all links. In addition, the head property is available to access the <head> element directly, and the body property can be used for direct access to the <body> element.

Property	Description
document.anchors	Contains a list of all anchors of the web page
document.forms	Contains a list of all forms on the web page
document.images	Contains a list of all images on the web page
document.links	Contains a list of all links on the web page
document.head	Provides access to the <head> element of the web page
document.body	Provides access to the <body> element of the web page

Table 5.4 Various Properties for Selecting Elements by Type

5.3   Working with Text Nodes

Once you've selected one or more elements, you can modify them: you can add or remove text, add or remove attributes, and add or remove elements. Table 5.5 shows an overview of the main properties and methods available for this purpose, which we'll discuss in detail in the following sections.

As mentioned before, any text on a web page is represented as text nodes within the DOM tree. Now let's take a look at how you can access and also modify the text contents.

Property/Method	Description	Section
textContent	This property allows you to access the text content of a node.	Section 5.3.1
nodeValue	This property allows you to access the contents of a node.	Section 5.3.1
innerHTML	This property allows you to access the HTML content of a node.	Section 5.3.3
createTextNode()	This method allows you to create text nodes.	Section 5.3.4
createElement()	This method allows you to create elements.	Section 5.4.1
createAttribute()	This method allows you to create attribute nodes.	Section 5.5.3
appendChild()	This method allows you to add nodes to the DOM tree.	Section 5.4.1

Table 5.5 The Different Methods and Properties for Modifying Elements

Property/Method	Description	Section
removeChild()	This method allows you to remove nodes from the DOM tree.	Section 5.4.2

Table 5.5 The Different Methods and Properties for Modifying Elements (Cont.)

5.3.1   Accessing the Text Content of an Element

To access the plain text content of an element, it's best to use the textContent property. This property is convenient because any HTML markup within the respective element is ignored and excluded from the returned value. The next two listings illustrate this. First, Listing 5.22 shows a simple HTML list with one entry, where the contained text is marked up using <strong> and <em> elements.

```
<ul id="news">
  <li>
    <strong>Record news: </strong>New album by <em>Ben Harper</em> released.
  </li>
</ul>
```

Listing 5.22 HTML with Nested Elements

If you now access the textContent property as shown in Listing 5.23, you'll see that it contains only the plain text of the <li> element, but not the <strong> and <em> markup it contains.

```
const textContent = document.querySelector('#news li:nth-child(1)').textContent;
console.log(textContent);
// Output: Record news: New album by Ben Harper released.
```

Listing 5.23 The textContent Property Ignores Markup within the Corresponding Element

> **Note**
>
> The textContent property is very convenient because in practice, when accessing the text content of an element, it's often not relevant whether/what additional markup has been used.

5.3.2   Modifying the Text Content of an Element

If you want to reset the text content of an element, you also use the textContent property. As a value, you simply pass the new text, as shown in Listing 5.24. Here, a new text is assigned to the list element used previously.

```
const element = document.querySelector('#news li:nth-child(1)');
element.textContent = 'Record news: New album by Tool not yet ⊃
  released.';
```

Listing 5.24 The textContent Property Can Be Used to Reset the Text Content of an Element

Note, however, that textContent doesn't enable you to add HTML markup: although the string passed in the following listing contains markup, it is not interpreted but displayed as text (see Figure 5.25).

```
const element = document.querySelector('#news li:nth-child(1)');
element.textContent = '<strong>Record news:</strong> New album by ⊃
  <em>Tool</em> not yet released.';
```

Listing 5.25 The Markup within the Specified String Is Not Evaluated

- <strong>Record news:</strong> New album by <em>Tool</em> not yet released.

Figure 5.25 Markup Specified via textContent Is Not Evaluated

---

textContent versus innerText

In some browsers, you can also use the innerText property, which works in a similar way to textContent but is slightly different in detail. It is also not included in the DOM API and is thus not supported by Firefox, for example. We therefore advise that you avoid innerText and use textContent instead, as shown in the examples.

5.3.3 Modifying the HTML below an Element

If you want to insert not only text but also HTML into an element, you can use the innerHTML property. You'll learn about another possibility later, DOM manipulation, which in practice is often used to add HTML to the DOM. For starters, however, or for adding simple HTML components, innerHTML is sufficient. An example is shown in Listing 5.26: the same HTML block is added as in Listing 5.25, but this time it is also interpreted as HTML (see Figure 5.26).

```
const element = document.querySelector('#news li:nth-child(1)');
element.innerHTML = '<strong>Record news:</strong> New album by <em>Tool ⊃
  </em> not yet released.'
```

Listing 5.26 The innerHTML Property Is Used to Evaluate Markup Contained in the Passed String

- **Record news:** New album by *Tool* not yet released.

Figure 5.26 As Expected, the HTML Inserted via innerHTML Is Evaluated

Conversely, you can also use innerHTML to read the HTML content of an element. As with textContent, the result is a string that now contains not only the text content but also the HTML markup (see Listing 5.27).

```
const innerHTML = document.querySelector('#news li:nth-child(1)').innerHTML;
console.log(innerHTML);
// Output: <strong>Record news: </strong>New album by
// <em>Ben Harper</em> released.
```

Listing 5.27 The innerHTML Property Also Contains the HTML Markup

5.3.4 Creating and Adding Text Nodes

As an alternative to the options shown for accessing or modifying the text within a web page via the textContent and innerHTML properties, there is still the possibility to create text nodes and add them manually to the DOM tree. For this purpose, the DOM API provides the createTextNode() method. In Listing 5.28, a text node (with the text Example) is created via this method and then added to an existing element as a child node using the appendChild() method (more on this later). (This second step is necessary because the text node is not yet added to the DOM tree via the createTextNode() method.)

```
const element = document.getElementById('container');
const textNode = document.createTextNode('Example');
element.appendChild(textNode);
```

Listing 5.28 Creating and Adding a Text Node

Other Methods for Creating Nodes

In addition to the createTextNode() method, there are other methods for creating nodes, including createElement() for creating element nodes (Section 5.4.1) and createAttribute() for creating attribute nodes (Section 5.5.3).

Document Node Methods

The createTextNode() method and also the createElement() and createAttribute() methods described ahead are only available on the document node (i.e., the document object). These methods cannot be called on other nodes (and thus not on elements).

5.4 Working with Elements

Elements, too, can be created manually via methods and then added to the DOM tree (as opposed to using the innerHTML property, where you pass the HTML elements indirectly in the form of the text you assign to the property).

In this section, we'll show you how to create and add elements using these methods and how to work with elements in general.

5.4.1 Creating and Adding Elements

To create elements, use the createElement() method. This method expects the name of the element to be created as a parameter and returns the new element. By calling the method, the new element is not yet added to the DOM, though (same as with text nodes when using the createTextNode() method).

However, several other methods are available for adding generated elements to the DOM:

- Using insertBefore(), the element can be added as a child element before another element/node—that is, defined as a previous sibling element.
- Using appendChild(), the element can be added as the last child element of a parent element.
- Using replaceChild(), an existing child element (or an existing child node) can be replaced with a new child element. The method is called on the parent element and expects the new child node as the first parameter and the child node to be replaced as the second parameter.

Adding Text Nodes

By the way, these methods are also available for adding text nodes (Section 5.3.4).

A somewhat more complex—but practical—example is shown in Listing 5.29. Here an HTML table is generated based on a contact list (which is represented in the form of an array). The individual entries in the contact list contain the first name, the last name, and the email address of each contact.

```
const contacts = [
  {
    firstName: 'John',
    lastName: 'Doe',
    email: 'john.doe@javascripthandbuch.de'
  },
  {
    firstName: 'James',
```

```
      lastName: 'Doe',
      email: 'james.doe@javascripthandbuch.de'
   },
   {
      firstName: 'Peter',
      lastName: 'Doe',
      email: 'peter.doe@javascripthandbuch.de'
   }
];

function createTable() {
   const tableBody = document.querySelector('#contact-table tbody');
   for(let i=0; i<contacts.length; i++) {
      // For the current contact ...
      const contact = contacts[i];
      // ... a new line is created.
      // (1)
      const tableRow = document.createElement('tr');
      // Within the row, different cells are created ...
      // (2)
      const tableCellFirstName = document.createElement('td');
      // ... and filled with values.
      // (3)
      const firstName = document.createTextNode(contact.firstName);
      // (4)
      tableCellFirstName.appendChild(firstName);
      // (5)
      const tableCellLastName = document.createElement('td');
      // (6)
      const lastName = document.createTextNode(contact.lastName);
      // (7)
      tableCellLastName.appendChild(lastName);
      // (8)
      const tableCellEmail = document.createElement('td');
      // (9)
      const email = document.createTextNode(contact.email);
      // (10)
      tableCellEmail.appendChild(email);
      // (11)
      tableRow.appendChild(tableCellFirstName);
      // (12)
      tableRow.appendChild(tableCellLastName);
      // (13)
      tableRow.appendChild(tableCellEmail);
```

```
    // (14)
    tableBody.appendChild(tableRow);
  }
}
```

Listing 5.29 Creating a Table Based on the Contact List

Everything related to the creation of the corresponding elements takes place within the createTable() function. Here, the querySelector() method first selects the <tbody> element of the table that already exists in the HTML (see Listing 5.30) and then iterates the array containing the contact information. For each entry, the createElement() method is used to create a table row (<tr>) and to create a table cell (<td>) for each of the previously mentioned properties (firstName, lastName, and email). Using the createText-Node() method, text nodes are created for the values of the properties and added to the respective <td> element via appendChild() (alternatively, you could also use the text-Content property here).

At the end of each iteration, the created table cells are then added as child elements to the corresponding table row, and in the last row of the iteration, the table row is added as a child element of the table body—that is, the <tbody> element. The individual steps are explained using comments in the listing and can be traced with the help of Figure 5.27.

```
<!DOCTYPE html>
<html>
<head lang="en">
  <title>Contacts Example</title>
</head>
<body onload="createTable()">
<main id="main-content">
  <h1>Contacts</h1>
  <table id="contact-table" summary="Contacts">
    <thead>
    <tr>
      <th>First name</th>
      <th>Last name</th>
      <th>E-mail address</th>
    </tr>
    </thead>
    <tbody>
    </tbody>
  </table>
</main>
```

```
<script src="scripts/main.js"></script>
</body>
</html>
```

Listing 5.30 The HTML Template

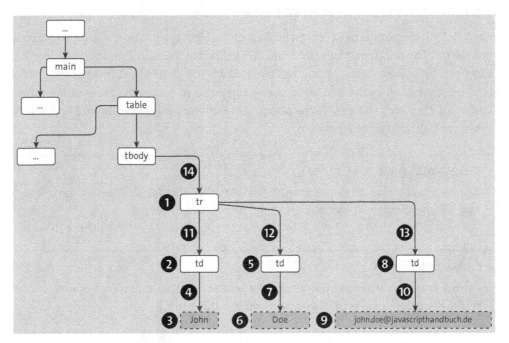

Figure 5.27 Sequence of Steps

5.4.2   Removing Elements and Nodes

To remove elements (or more generally nodes) from a parent element (or more generally a parent node), the removeChild() method is available. This method expects the element (or node) to be removed and also returns it as a return value. In Listing 5.31 (based on the listings from the previous section), you can see a method for filtering table data (sortByFirstName()) that takes advantage of the removeChild() method to remove all child nodes and child elements from the table body (i.e., all table rows).

```
function sortByFirstName() {
  const tableBody = document.querySelector('#contact-table tbody');
  while (tableBody.firstChild !== null) {
    tableBody.removeChild(tableBody.firstChild);
  }
  contacts.sort(function(contact1, contact2) {
    return contact1.firstName.localeCompare(contact2.firstName);
  })
```

```
    createTable();
}
```

Listing 5.31 Example of Using the removeChild() Method

5.4.3 The Different Types of HTML Elements

Every HTML element is represented by a specific object type within a DOM tree. These are set out in an extension to the DOM API called the DOM HTML specification. For example, links (<a> elements) are represented by the HTMLAnchorElement type, tables (<table> elements) by the HTMLTableElement type, and so on. An overview of the different HTML elements and their corresponding object types is given in Table 5.6. Obsolete types are italicized within the table.

The HTMLElement Supertype

All object types have the same supertype—that is, the HTMLElement type. Elements that have no specific type are assigned the HTMLElement type by default.

Obsolete Elements

For the sake of completeness, the elements and object types that have become obsolete in the meantime are still listed in the table in italics.

HTML Element	Type
<a>	HTMLAnchorElement
<abbr>	HTMLElement
<acronym>	HTMLElement
<address>	HTMLElement
<applet>	*HTMLAppletElement*
<area>	HTMLAreaElement
<audio>	HTMLAudioElement
<b>	HTMLElement
<base>	HTMLBaseElement
<basefont>	*HTMLBaseFontElement*
<bdo>	HTMLElement

Table 5.6 The Different HTML Elements and Their Respective Types in JavaScript

HTML Element	Type
<big>	HTMLElement
<blockquote>	HTMLQuoteElement
<body>	HTMLBodyElement
 	HTMLBRElement
<button>	HTMLButtonElement
<caption>	HTMLTableCaptionElement
<canvas>	HTMLCanvasElement
<center>	HTMLElement
<cite>	HTMLElement
<code>	HTMLElement
<col>, <colgroup>	HTMLTableColElement
<data>	HTMLDataElement
<datalist>	HTMLDataListElement
<dd>	HTMLElement
<del>	HTMLModElement
<dfn>	HTMLElement
<dir>	*HTMLDirectoryElement*
<div>	HTMLDivElement
<dl>	HTMLDListElement
<dt>	HTMLElement
<em>	HTMLElement
<embed>	HTMLEmbedElement
<fieldset>	HTMLFieldSetElement
<font>	*HTMLFontElement*
<form>	HTMLFormElement
<frame>	*HTMLFrameElement*
<frameset>	*HTMLFrameSetElement*

Table 5.6 The Different HTML Elements and Their Respective Types in JavaScript (Cont.)

HTML Element	Type
<h1>, <h2>, <h3>, <h4>, <h5>, <h6>	HTMLHeadingElement
<head>	HTMLHeadElement
<hr>	HTMLHRElement
<html>	HTMLHtmlElement
<i>	HTMLElement
<iframe>	HTMLIFrameElement
<img>	HTMLImageElement
<input>	HTMLInputElement
<ins>	HTMLModElement
<isindex>	*HTMLIsIndexElement*
<kbd>	HTMLElement
<keygen>	HTMLKeygenElement
<label>	HTMLLabelElement
<legend>	HTMLLegendElement
<li>	HTMLLIElement
<link>	HTMLLinkElement
<map>	HTMLMapElement
<media>	HTMLMediaElement
<menu>	*HTMLMenuElement*
<meta>	HTMLMetaElement
<meter>	HTMLMeterElement
<noframes>	HTMLElement
<noscript>	HTMLElement
<object>	HTMLObjectElement
<ol>	HTMLOListElement
<optgroup>	HTMLOptGroupElement
<option>	HTMLOptionElement

Table 5.6 The Different HTML Elements and Their Respective Types in JavaScript (Cont.)

HTML Element	Type
<output>	HTMLOutputElement
<p>	HTMLParagraphElement
<param>	HTMLParamElement
<pre>	HTMLPreElement
<progress>	HTMLProgressElement
<q>	HTMLQuoteElement
<s>	HTMLElement
<samp>	HTMLElement
<script>	HTMLScriptElement
<select>	HTMLSelectElement
<small>	HTMLElement
<source>	HTMLSourceElement
<span>	HTMLSpanElement
<strike>	HTMLElement
<strong>	HTMLElement
<style>	HTMLStyleElement
<sub>	HTMLElement
<sup>	HTMLElement
<table>	HTMLTableElement
<tbody>	HTMLTableSectionElement
<td>	HTMLTableCellElement
<textarea>	HTMLTextAreaElement
<tfoot>	HTMLTableSectionElement
<th>	HTMLTableHeaderCellElement
<thead>	HTMLTableSectionElement
<time>	HTMLTimeElement
<title>	HTMLTitleElement

Table 5.6 The Different HTML Elements and Their Respective Types in JavaScript (Cont.)

HTML Element	Type
`<tr>`	`HTMLTableRowElement`
`<tt>`	`HTMLElement`
`<u>`	`HTMLElement`
`<track>`	`HTMLTrackElement`
`<ul>`	`HTMLUListElement`
`<var>`	`HTMLElement`
	`HTMLUnknownElement`
`<video>`	`HTMLVideoElement`

Table 5.6 The Different HTML Elements and Their Respective Types in JavaScript (Cont.)

Listing 5.32 shows the principle of these object types using the example of tables represented by the `HTMLTableElement` type. This type—like all the other types shown in Table 5.6—has individual properties corresponding to the type, including the `caption` property, which contains the subtitle of a table (and is `null` in the example, because the table in Listing 5.1 has no `caption` attribute); the `tHead` property, which contains the header area—that is, the `<thead>` element—of a table; the `tBodies` property, which contains the various table bodies—that is, `<tbody>` elements—of a table; the `rows` property, which contains the table rows (including those in the header area); and the `tFoot` property, which contains the footer area—that is, the `<tfoot>` element.

```
const table = document.querySelector('table');
console.log(Object.getPrototypeOf(table));   // HTMLTableElement
console.log(table.caption);                  // null
console.log(table.tHead);                    // thead
console.log(table.tBodies);                  // [tbody]
console.log(table.rows);                      // [tr, tr, tr, tr, tr]
console.log(table.tFoot);                    // null
```

Listing 5.32 Each HTML Element Is Represented by Its Own Object Type

Besides individual properties, the different object types also have different methods: for example, the `HTMLTableElement` type, shown in Listing 5.33, contains the `insertRow()` method (among others), which can be used to directly create a new table row (without manually creating corresponding HTML elements via `document.createElement()`). This method returns an object of the type `HTMLTableRowElement`, which, in turn, comprises the `insertCell()` method (among others), via which a new table cell can be added directly to the corresponding row. In the example, a new table row with three cells is created in this way. This is much clearer than the example in Listing 5.29, don't you think?

```
const newRow    = table.insertRow(1);
const newCellFirstName = newRow.insertCell(0);
newCellFirstName.textContent = 'Bob';
const newCellLastName = newRow.insertCell(1);
newCellLastName.textContent = 'Doe';
const newCellEmail  = newRow.insertCell(2);
newCellEmail.textContent = 'bob.doe@javascripthandbuch.de';
```

Listing 5.33 The Different Object Types Also Have Individual Methods

Property Names versus Element Names

Note that object properties like tHead, tBodies, and tFoot are written in CamelCase notation, while the corresponding HTML elements are written in lowercase (<thead>, <tbody>, <tfoot>).

5.5   Working with Attributes

The DOM API provides several methods for working with attributes:

- You can use the getAttribute() method to access the attributes of an element (Section 5.5.1).
- You can use the setAttribute() method to change the value of an attribute or to add attributes to an element (Section 5.5.2).
- You can create attribute nodes via the createAttribute() method and add them using setAttributeNode() (Section 5.5.3).
- You can remove attributes using the removeAttribute() method (Section 5.5.4).

5.5.1   Reading the Value of an Attribute

To access the value of an attribute, use the getAttribute() method on the respective element. As a parameter, the method expects the name of the respective HTML attribute. It then returns the value of the corresponding attribute. Use the HTML code from Listing 5.34 as a starting point: it shows a link (an <a> element) with the id, class, and href attributes.

```
<a id="home" class="link" href="index.html">Home</a>
```

Listing 5.34 An HTML Link

To access these attributes, use the getAttribute() method, as shown in Listing 5.35.

```
const element = document.getElementById('home');
console.log(element.getAttribute('id'));    // home
console.log(element.getAttribute('class')); // link
console.log(element.getAttribute('href'));  // index.html
```

Listing 5.35 You Can Access Attributes of an HTML Element Using the getAttribute() Method

The attributes of an element are usually also available as properties with the same name—although the class attribute is an exception: this attribute can be accessed via the className property. Listing 5.36 shows a corresponding example: the id and href attributes can be read using the properties of the same name, the class attribute via the className property.

```
console.log(element.id);        // home
console.log(element.className); // link
console.log(element.href);      // index.html
```

Listing 5.36 The Attributes of an Element Are Also Available as Properties

However, you should note the following: for two attributes, the access via the getAttribute() method returns a different return value than the direct access via the property. For the style attribute, the getAttribute() method only returns the text contained as a value in the attribute. The access to the style property, on the other hand, returns an object of the CSSStyleDeclaration type, which can be used to access the corresponding CSS information in detail. In addition, all attributes that can be used to define event handlers (see also Chapter 6) return the JavaScript code to be executed as a function object via the corresponding property (e.g., onclick). If, on the other hand, the respective attribute is accessed via the getAttribute() method, the name of the function to be executed is returned as text.

Take a look at Listing 5.37 and Listing 5.38. The former shows an HTML button with various attributes, including a style attribute and an onclick attribute. In the latter, you can then see how both are accessed via the property of the same name and via the getAttribute() method, respectively.

```
<button id="create" class="link" style="background-color: green"
onclick="createContact()">Create contact</button>
```

Listing 5.37 An HTML Button

```
const button = document.getElementById('create');
console.log(button.onclick);                       // Output of the
                                                   // function object

console.log(typeof button.onclick);                // Output: function
console.log(button.getAttribute('onclick'));       // createContact()
console.log(typeof button.getAttribute('onclick')); // Output: string
```

```
console.log(button.style);                           // Output of
                                                     // CSSStyleDeclaration
console.log(typeof button.style);                    // Output: object
console.log(button.getAttribute('style'));           // background-color: green
console.log(typeof button.getAttribute('style'));    // Output: string
```

Listing 5.38 Accessing Event Handlers and the style Attribute Returns Different Return Values Depending on the Access Type

The reason that direct access to event handler attributes like onclick doesn't return a string but a function is that this property enables you to define event handlers for the respective element. That is, you can assign function objects to this property.

The reason that direct access to the style attribute doesn't return a string is that this attribute can be used to programmatically access the CSS information of the respective element, even with write access (as you've already seen in this chapter).

5.5.2   Changing the Value of an Attribute or Adding a New Attribute

To change the value of an attribute or add a new attribute, use the setAttribute() method on the element for which the attribute is to be changed. This method expects two parameters: the name of the attribute and the new value. If the corresponding element already has an attribute of the same name, the value of that attribute will be overwritten with the new value. If the attribute doesn't yet exist, a corresponding attribute is newly added to the element. An example is shown in Listing 5.39. This listing changes the class, href, and target properties for the previously selected link element.

```
const element = document.getElementById('home');
element.setAttribute('class', 'link active');
element.setAttribute('href', 'newlink.html');
element.setAttribute('target', '_blank');
console.log(element.getAttribute('class'));    // link active
console.log(element.getAttribute('href'));     // newlink.html
console.log(element.getAttribute('target'));   // _blank
```

Listing 5.39 You Can Change Existing Attributes of an HTML Element or Add New Attributes Using the setAttribute() Method

Alternatively, you can also change the values of attributes or add new attributes via the object properties of (usually) the same name (see Listing 5.40).

```
element.className = 'link active highlighted';
element.href = 'anotherLink.html';
element.target = '_self';
console.log(element.getAttribute('class'));    // link active highlighted
```

```
console.log(element.getAttribute('href'));     // anotherLink.html
console.log(element.getAttribute('target'));   // _self
```

Listing 5.40 Attributes Can Also Be Changed Directly via Corresponding Properties

> **Note**
> In the background, when the setAttribute() method is used, an attribute node is cre-
> ated and added to the DOM tree as a child node at the respective element node.

5.5.3   Creating and Adding Attribute Nodes

As with normal texts and when working with elements, you can also create attributes as attribute nodes using a special method, the createAttribute() method. As an argument, this method expects the name of the attribute to be created. It then returns the new attribute node. Like the text nodes and element nodes mentioned earlier, this node is not directly built into the DOM tree either. You have to do this manually using the setAttributeNode() method for the corresponding element (see Listing 5.41).

```
const element = document.getElementById('home');
const attribute = document.createAttribute('target');
attribute.value = '_blank';
element.setAttributeNode(attribute);
console.log(element.getAttribute('target'));  // _blank
```

Listing 5.41 Creating and Adding an Attribute Node

5.5.4   Removing Attributes

You can remove attributes from an element using the removeAttribute() method. In Listing 5.42, this is used to remove the two attributes class and href from the link element. Subsequently, the two attributes return the value null.

```
const element = document.getElementById('home');
element.removeAttribute('class');
element.removeAttribute('href');
console.log(element.getAttribute('class'));  // null
console.log(element.getAttribute('href'));   // null
```

Listing 5.42 You Can Remove Attributes from an HTML Element Using the removeAttribute() Method

5.5.5   Accessing CSS classes

Although you've already seen it (at least partially) in some examples throughout the chapter, we'll briefly explain how to read an element's CSS classes again.

First, there is the familiar `className` property, which is available in every element on a web page (i.e., every element node). This property simply contains the value of the `class` attribute of the corresponding element as a string. If the element has multiple CSS classes, these class names are separated by spaces within the string.

In the past, this has sometimes led to cumbersome code when, for example, you wanted to add new CSS classes to an element or—even worse—remove existing CSS classes. Why cumbersome? Because in each and every case, you had to parse the value of the attribute.

This was taken into account in version 4 of the DOM API. Since then, elements (in the DOM API, not in HTML) have the additional `classList` property, which contains the CSS classes as a list. Adding and removing individual CSS classes to or from an element has become much easier since then:

- The `add()` method can be used to add new CSS classes to the list.
- The `remove()` method enables you to remove CSS classes from the list.
- Via the `toggle()` method, CSS classes can be toggled. That is, if the CSS class exists in the list, it's deleted; if it doesn't exist, it's added. This method can even be linked to Boolean conditions.
- In addition, the `contains()` method can be used to check whether a CSS class is contained in the list.

Listing 5.43 shows some examples of these methods.

```javascript
const element = document.getElementById('home');
console.log(element.classList);                     // ["link"]
element.classList.add('active');                    // Add class
console.log(element.classList);                     // ["link", "active"]
element.classList.remove('active');                 // Remove class
console.log(element.classList);                     // ["link"]
element.classList.toggle('active');                 // Toggle class
console.log(element.classList);                     // ["link", "active"]
element.classList.toggle('active');                 // Toggle class
console.log(element.classList);                     // ["link"]
console.log(element.classList.contains('link'));    // true
console.log(element.classList.contains('active'));  // false
const i = 5;
const condition = i > 0;
element.classList.toggle('active', condition);      // Toggle class
console.log(element.classList);                     // ["link", "active"]
```

Listing 5.43 The classList Property of Elements Makes It Very Easy to Work with CSS Classes

5.6   Summary

In this chapter, you learned how to access and dynamically modify web page content using JavaScript. Let's summarize the main points:

- The *Document Object Model* represents the model for a web page, a hierarchical tree structure.

- The individual components in this tree structure are called *nodes*, and there are different types of nodes. The most important ones are *document nodes*, *element nodes*, *text nodes*, and *attribute nodes*. In addition, the element nodes are represented by different types, starting from the HTMLElement type.

- The *DOM API* defines properties and methods that enable you to access or modify the data on a web page.

- For example, you can add elements, delete elements, modify texts, and add or delete attributes using the DOM API.

- Elements on a web page can be selected in several ways: by ID, by CSS class, by element name, by name attribute, and by CSS selector.

- Starting from an element or node, the parent element/parent node, the child elements/child nodes, and the sibling elements/sibling nodes can be selected via various properties.

- The textContent property can be used to access or set the text content of a node, whereas the innerHTML property can be used to access the HTML content of an element.

- You can create text nodes via createTextNode(), element nodes via createElement(), and attribute nodes via createAttribute().

- After you create a node, you must first add it to the DOM tree using different methods: insertBefore(), appendChild(), and replaceChild().

Chapter 6
Processing and Triggering Events

An important concept in JavaScript programming is events and thus event-driven programming. In this chapter, we'll show you the principle behind events and how you can use event-driven programming to react to events triggered by users within a (web) application.

When you visit a web page and perform some actions, various *events* are triggered in the background. For example, when the page is fully loaded; when the user enters text into a text field, selects an option from a select box, or clicks on a button; or when elements enter or leave the visible area of the screen. Within your JavaScript code, you have the possibility to react to these events. For example, you could validate the text that the user has entered in a text field or send a form when the user clicks on a button. The principle of sending and responding to events is called *event-driven programming*.

6.1 The Concept of Event-Driven Programming

The concept of event-driven programming is not specific to JavaScript; it's also used in other programming languages. Basically, it works as follows (see also Figure 6.1): on one side, you have so-called triggers of events (also called *event emitters*). In the case of graphical user interfaces (UIs), for example, these can be buttons, text fields, or any other UI components. As soon as you click on a button or enter text in a text field, an *event* is triggered in the background by the respective component (the button or the text field).

After an event has been triggered, it's placed in an *event queue*, which ensures that events that were triggered first are also handled first. The *event loop* continuously checks whether there is a new event in the event queue, and if there is, the corresponding event is forwarded to *event handlers*.

In JavaScript, these event handlers are simple functions that allow you, the developer, to respond to the triggered event. So you can use event-driven programming to express things like "when this button is clicked, this or that function is to be called."

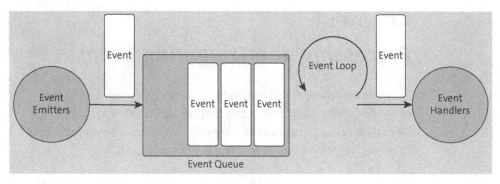

Figure 6.1 The Principle of Events and Event Handling

However, the principle of event-driven programming isn't limited to interactions with a user interface. In JavaScript development, there are also events that are triggered without the user interacting with the user interface—that is, events that are not triggered by the user but programmatically. In Chapter 17, for example, we'll introduce Node.js, a runtime environment for JavaScript that also uses events to control a lot of things in the background. In this chapter, however, we'll first use web pages (and thus primarily UIs) as an example to show you how to program using events.

6.2   Responding to Events

To trigger a function on user interactions within a web page, three steps are required:

1. Select the *element* on the web page that should respond to the user interaction. For example, if you want a function to be triggered when the user clicks on a column heading of a table, you must select the corresponding <th> element beforehand.

2. Specify the *event* that is to be caught. As you will see in a moment, there are many different types of events. For example, it's possible to capture mouse clicks, keystrokes, mouse movements, and much more. This step is also called *binding* an event to an element.

3. Specify the *function* to be called. Last but not least, you need to define the function to be called when the corresponding event occurs on the selected element. For example, will the data in the table be sorted on click? Will the text entered in a text field be validated?

Implicit Events

There are also events in web development that you can catch without having selected an element first. These include, for example, events that are triggered when a web page is fully loaded, plus many others.

In the previous chapter, you learned in detail how to select elements on a web page, so step 1 should be a piece of cake for you. So, let's take a look at how you can catch events or bind them to elements and how you define the code to be executed when an event is triggered. There are in fact three possibilities in this regard:

- **HTML event handlers**
  HTML event handlers provide one possibility to react to events, but they're no longer used nowadays. This option relies on special HTML attributes to define which function is to be called for which event. The reason for not using HTML event handlers anymore is that this option requires mixing HTML code and JavaScript code, which isn't considered a good choice in terms of maintainability and the like. Nevertheless, in Section 6.2.1, we'll show you the details of this type of event handler. You shouldn't use HTML event handlers yourself, but you may well come across them in older web applications, and then you should understand what's going on.

- **DOM event handlers**
  The second way to react to events is via so-called DOM event handlers. They got their name because they are part of the DOM specification and are defined via JavaScript. Compared to HTML event handlers, their advantage is that HTML code and JavaScript code are not mixed. In other words, the logic of the application (responding to events) is separate from the structure of the application (the HTML). Nevertheless, DOM event handlers also have a significant downside or limitation: they allow you to only specify a single function to be called for an event. We'll show you the details of all this in Section 6.2.2.

- **DOM event listeners**
  Last but not least, there is a third option to react to events: so-called DOM event listeners. These were introduced in 2000 as part of the second version of the DOM specification (*www.w3.org/TR/DOM-Level-2-Events/Overview.html*) and have ever since been the standard for event handling and the recommended way to respond to events. The reason: while in the case of event handlers it's only possible to register a single event handler for an event, event listeners allow you to register multiple event listeners for the same event. We'll show you how to define event listeners in Section 6.2.3.

The jQuery Helper Library

In addition, there are various JavaScript libraries that simplify or unify event handling. One of the more prominent examples is the jQuery library, which we'll present in more detail in Chapter 10. A part of Chapter 10 will also deal with event handling.

Definition of Terms

The terms *event handler* and *event listener* are often used synonymously in literature. However, in the case of JavaScript (as described earlier), a distinction is made between the two terms. That is, a function that has been defined as an HTML event handler or DOM event handler will be referred to as an event handler ahead, and a function that has been defined as an event listener will accordingly be referred to as an event listener.

The essential sequence when an event occurs is shown in Figure 6.2. First, there is a check for whether an event handler or an event listener is defined for the event.

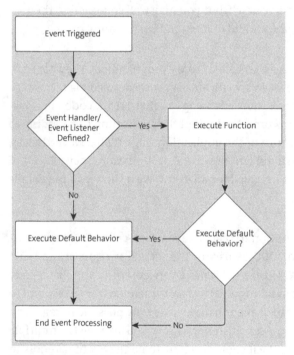

Figure 6.2 Event Handling Procedure

If this is the case, the corresponding code is executed. If, on the other hand, no event handlers/event listeners have been defined, the default actions of the browser that are associated with the respective event are triggered instead. Within an event handler/ event listener, you also have the possibility to disable these default browser actions for an event. We'll show you how to do this in Section 6.4.

6.2.1   Defining an Event Handler via HTML

Let's take a simple use case as an example of event handling: the validation of a form field that should only accept positive numbers. For starters, the only thing to check is that no negative value has been specified. Validation should be triggered every time the user quits the corresponding form field (i.e., when the user clicks outside of the form field).

Native Validation in HTML5

A few years ago, the validation of form fields was only possible using JavaScript. But HTML now includes certain options for checking form fields. However, it isn't yet as flexible as JavaScript, so it's still recommended for a web developer to know how to use JavaScript for checking the validity of data entered by a user on a web page.

Client-Side and Server-Side Validation

One more note: in a production application where users can fill out and submit forms, you should validate the entered data not only on the client side, but also on the server side. Essentially, the client-side validation is done for user-friendliness and to alert the user of any errors. The server-side validation, however, ensures that the transmitted data hasn't been (maliciously) manipulated by the user.

Now let's show you how this use case can be implemented using an HTML event handler. As mentioned earlier, HTML event handlers are defined within the HTML code using HTML attributes. HTML attributes always carry the name of the event preceded by on. For the example, the HTML attribute is onblur because the blur event is triggered when a form element is quit.

The value for the attribute is the function that is to be called when the event is triggered. All in all, this may result in the following HTML attribute if the function is called checkAgeNotNegative, as in the example:

```
onblur="checkAgeNotNegative()"
```

You can see the full HTML code in Listing 6.1. The input field with the age ID is used for entering the age and the <div> element with the output ID serves as a container for validation messages.

```
<!DOCTYPE html>
<html>
<head lang="en">
  <meta charset="UTF-8">
  <title>HTML event handler</title>
  <link rel="stylesheet" href="styles/main.css">
  <script src="scripts/main.js"></script>
</head>
<body>
  <div>
```

```
      <label for="age"></label>
      <input id="age" type="number" value="0" onblur="checkAgeNotNegative()"/>
    </div>
    <div id="output"></div>
  </body>
</html>
```

Listing 6.1 Definition of an HTML Event Handler That Is Called when an Input Field Is Exited

The called function (i.e., the event handler) is shown in Listing 6.2. Actually, there's nothing happening here that you don't already know about from the previous chapter: First, the input field and the container are determined by their ID and each assigned to a variable. The value of the input field is then read and checked. If the value is less than 0 (and thus invalid), a corresponding error message is written to the container. On the other hand, if the value is 0 or greater (and thus valid), the text content of the container is cleared (i.e., assigned an empty string). The latter is necessary to clear any error messages if a valid value is entered in the input field after an invalid value.

```
function checkAgeNotNegative() {
  const output = document.getElementById('output');    // Container for message
  const element = document.getElementById('age');      // Input field for age
  const age = element.value;                           // Current age value
  if(age < 0) {                                        // If value is negative ...
    output.textContent = 'Age cannot be negative.';    // ... output an error ...
                                                       // ... message...
  } else {                                             // ... else ...
    output.textContent = '';                           // ... delete message.
  }
}
```

Listing 6.2 The Function To Be Called as Event Handler

If you don't want to trigger the validation as soon as the input field is exited, but only at the push of a button, for example, the code can be adapted relatively easily, as shown in Listing 6.3. Here, the event handler for the blur event has been removed from the text field, and an additional button has been inserted for which the event handler for the click event has been defined (which is triggered when the corresponding button is clicked).

```
<input id="age" type="number" value="0"/>
<input type="submit" value="Check age" onclick="checkAgeNotNegative()"/>
```

Listing 6.3 Definition of an HTML Event Handler That Is Called when a Button Is Clicked

Although HTML event handlers seem relatively simple to use at first glance, they are now considered obsolete because they mix HTML code and JavaScript code, which can quickly become confusing in large web applications. Instead, you're better off using DOM event handlers, which we'll show you in the following section, or (even better) event listeners, which we'll present in Section 6.2.3.

6.2.2   Defining an Event Handler via JavaScript

DOM event handlers solve the problem of mixed HTML and JavaScript code. As shown in Listing 6.4, the HTML code remains free of JavaScript calls. Which element should result in which function being called for which event is defined in the JavaScript code.

```
<!DOCTYPE html>
<html>
<head lang="en">
  <meta charset="UTF-8">
  <title>HTML event handler</title>
  <link rel="stylesheet" href="styles/main.css">
  <script src="scripts/main.js"></script>
</head>
<body>
  <div>
    <label for="age"></label>
    <input id="age" type="number" value="0"/>
  </div>
  <div id="output"></div>
</body>
</html>
```

Listing 6.4 When Using DOM Event Handlers, the HTML Remains Free of JavaScript Code

How this works is shown in Listing 6.5. First, the input field for which the event handler is to be defined is again determined based on the ID. For the onblur property of this object, you define the name of the function to be called. Note that unlike with HTML event handlers, there is no function call, but really just the name of the function (i.e., without the pair of parentheses). If you were to write element.onblur = checkAgeNotNegative() instead of element.onblur = checkAgeNotNegative, the return value of the checkAgeNotNegative() function call would be defined as an event handler. In this case, this is not what we want.

```
function init() {
  const element = document.getElementById('age'); // (1) Get element
  element.onblur =                                 // (2) Define event
    checkAgeNotNegative;                           // (3) Define event handler
```

```
}

window.onload = init;
```

Listing 6.5 Definition of a DOM Event Handler

Event Listeners for Loading a Web Page

In Listing 6.5, you can also see that the onload property of the window object defines an event handler that's called when the web page is loaded. Without this event handler, the init() function would not be called, and thus no event handler would be registered on the form element.

DOM event handlers have a small disadvantage, as mentioned earlier: only one event handler can be defined per event on an element. For example, if you wanted to extend the previous validation to call not only a function that checks whether the entered value is non-negative but also another function that checks whether the entered value is a number at all (let's call it checkAgeIsNumber()), this wouldn't be possible, as shown in Listing 6.6. This listing first defines the checkAgeNotNegative function as an event handler for the onblur property and then the checkAgeIsNumber function. The latter, however, merely ensures that the onblur property is reset and the checkAgeNotNegative value is overwritten. The result is that only the checkAgeIsNumber function is called, but not the checkAgeIsNotNegative function.

```
function init() {
  const element = document.getElementById('age');
  element.onblur = checkAgeNotNegative;
  element.onblur = checkAgeIsNumber;  // Here, the event handler is overwritten.
}

window.onload = init;
```

Listing 6.6 Only One Event Handler Can Be Defined per Event

This can be remedied—at least with regard to the example—using anonymous functions. As shown in Listing 6.7, the checkAgeNotNegative and checkAgeIsNumber functions can simply be encapsulated within such an anonymous function, which is then defined as an event handler.

```
function init() {
  const element = document.getElementById('age');
  element.onblur = function() {         // anonymous function ...
    checkAgeNotNegative();              // ... in which both this function...
    checkAgeIsNumber();                 // ... and this function ...
                                        // ... are called
```

```
  };
}
```

```
window.onload = init;
```

Listing 6.7 Anonymous Functions Can Partially Circumvent the Described Problem but Are Relatively Inflexible

Although this approach works for the example at hand, you should define functions as event listeners rather than event handlers, if possible. We'll show you how in the following section.

6.2.3 Defining Event Listeners

The disadvantage of event handlers mentioned in the previous section doesn't apply to event listeners or to the related addEventListener() method (which is available to all elements on a web page via the DOM API). As parameters, it expects the name of the event to be responded to and the event listener—that is, the function to be called when the event occurs. Optionally, a third parameter can be specified to influence the *event flow* (details on this will follow in Section 6.4).

Listing 6.8 shows an example that does the same thing as the code from the previous sections: it calls the checkAgeNotNegative() function when quitting the corresponding form field for entering the age. The first parameter is the blur value (without on; don't use onblur); the second parameter is the name of the function, checkAgeNotNegative().

```
function init() {
  const element = document.getElementById('age');     // Get element
  element.addEventListener(                     // Register event listener
    'blur',                                     // Name of the event
    checkAgeNotNegative,                        // Name of the event listener
    false                                       // Event flow, details to follow later on
  );
}
document.addEventListener('DOMContentLoaded', init);
```

Listing 6.8 Definition of an Event Listener

Event Listener for Loading the Document Content

Although we already mentioned it earlier in this book (for example in Chapter 3), let's briefly touch on the DOMContentLoaded event again at this point. It's triggered whenever the entire DOM tree of a web page has been loaded, and it's perfect for executing initial code on a web page, such as registering event listeners (or event handlers). In the code examples within the book and especially in the download area for the book, we use this event in most cases to execute code inside a web page. A simple example is shown in Listing 6.9.

```
function init() {
  console.log('Document loaded');
}


document.addEventListener('DOMContentLoaded', init);
```

Listing 6.9 Definition of an Event Listener That Is Executed when the Web Page Is Loaded

If you want to define an event listener for the `load` event (analogous to `window.onload`), proceed as described in Listing 6.10. The difference between the `DOMContentLoaded` event and the `load` event is that the former is triggered when the full web document (meaning the DOM tree) has been loaded, while the latter is triggered when the full web document plus all external resources, such as JavaScript files, CSS files, and so on, have been loaded. By the way: there is no comparable property for the `window` object that can be used to define an event handler for the `DOMContentLoaded` event. This event can only be caught via event listeners.

```
function init() {
  console.log('Document and all resources loaded');
}


document.addEventListener('load', init);
```

Listing 6.10 Definition of an Event Listener That Is Executed when the Web Page Has Been Loaded, Including All Resources

---

The attachEvent() Method

The `addEventListener()` method isn't supported in older versions of Internet Explorer. Therefore, if you ever come across the `attachEvent()` method in someone else's code, don't be surprised: this is a proprietary method of Internet Explorer, but it isn't part of any standard and thus normally should not be used. Only to ensure backward compatibility with old versions of Internet Explorer do libraries like jQuery internally use this nonstandard method in some cases (see also Section 6.2.7).

6.2.4   Defining Multiple Event Listeners

Using the `addEventListener()` method, it's now also very easy to register several functions for one and the same event (which is possible with event handlers only via the detour of using a new, usually anonymous function).

Listing 6.11 shows an example where even three different functions are registered as event listeners for the blur event on the corresponding form field: the clearMessage() function ensures that the message is cleared, the checkAgeNotNegative() function checks that the age is not negative, and checkAgeIsNumber() ensures that the value entered is a number.

```
function checkAgeNotNegative() {
  const element = document.getElementById('age');     // Input field for age
  const age = element.value;                           // Current age value
  if(age < 0) {                                        // If value is negative ...
    showMessage('Age cannot be negative.');            // ... output warning.
  }
}

function checkAgeIsNumber() {
  const element = document.getElementById('age');     // Input field for age
  const age = element.value;                           // Current age value
  if(!(!isNaN(parseFloat(age)) && isFinite(age))) {   // If value is not
                                                       // a number ...
    showMessage('Age must be a number.');              // ... output message.
  }
}

function clearMessage() {
  showMessage('');
}

function showMessage(message) {
  const output = document.getElementById('output');
  output.textContent = message;
}

function init() {
  const element = document.getElementById('age'); // Get element
  element.addEventListener(                        // Register event listener
    'blur',                                        // Name of the event
    clearMessage                                   // Name of the event listener
  );
  element.addEventListener(                        // Register event listener
    'blur',                                        // Name of the event
    checkAgeNotNegative                            // Name of the event listener
  );
  element.addEventListener(                        // Register event listener
    'blur',                                        // Name of the event
```

```
    checkAgeIsNumber                                    // Name of the event listener
  );
}
```

```
document.addEventListener("DOMContentLoaded", init);
```

Listing 6.11 Definition of Multiple Event Listeners

> **Note**
>
> The use of event listeners or the addEventListener() method is much more flexible compared to event handlers because you can specify not only a single function, but any number of functions.

6.2.5   Passing Arguments to Event Listeners

Sometimes, you may want to pass arguments to the function you have registered as an event listener. However, this isn't possible out of the gate because you only pass the function itself to the addEventListener() method. Again the solution is using anonymous functions, as you can see in Listing 6.12.

The checkAgeNotNegative() and checkAgeIsNumber() functions now no longer access the form field with the age but expect a numeric value as a parameter to check. This makes both functions significantly more reusable because they no longer access the DOM tree directly and could in principle be used in a different context as well.

In addition, the code for accessing the DOM tree or the form field has been moved to the new getAgeValue() function. Within the event listeners (anonymous functions in both cases), the value returned by getAgeValue() is then passed to the two check methods.

```
function checkAgeNotNegative(age) {
  if(age < 0) {
    showMessage('Age cannot be negative.');
  }
}
```

```
function checkAgeIsNumber(age) {
  if(!(!isNaN(parseFloat(age)) && isFinite(age))) {
    showMessage('Age must be a number.');
  }
}
```

```
function clearMessage() {
  showMessage('');
```

```
}

function showMessage(message) {
  const output = document.getElementById('output');
  output.textContent = message;
}

function getAgeValue() {
  const element = document.getElementById('age');
  const age = element.value;
  return age;
}

function init() {
  const element = document.getElementById('age');
  element.addEventListener(
    'blur',
    clearMessage
  );
  element.addEventListener(
    'blur',
    function() {                  // anonymous function
      const age = getAgeValue();  // get value for age
      checkAgeNotNegative(age);   // call the actual function
    }
  );
  element.addEventListener(
    'blur',
    function() {                  // anonymous function
      const age = getAgeValue();  // get value for age
      checkAgeIsNumber(age);      // call the actual function
    }
  );
}
document.addEventListener("DOMContentLoaded", init);
```

Listing 6.12 Passing Parameters to Event Listeners

Event Listeners as Arrow Functions

There is also no reason why you shouldn't define event listeners as arrow functions. The preceding example can therefore be rephrased as shown in Listing 6.13.

```
element.addEventListener(
    'blur',
```

```
  () => {                            // anonymous arrow function
    const age = getAgeValue();       // get value for age
    checkAgeNotNegative(age);        // call the actual function
  }
);
element.addEventListener(
  'blur',
  () => {                            // anonymous arrow function
    const age = getAgeValue();       // get value for age
    checkAgeIsNumber(age);           // call the actual function
  }
);
document.addEventListener("DOMContentLoaded", init);
```

Listing 6.13 Event Listeners Can Also Be Defined as Arrow Functions

6.2.6   Removing Event Listeners

Event listeners that have been added to an element for an event can also be removed again using the removeEventListener() method. As parameters, you pass the name of the event and the event listener to be removed.

An example is shown in Listing 6.14. The age validation example from before has been extended here with a checkbox that can be used to deactivate or reactivate the validation. To this end, the checkbox is assigned an event listener for the change event (which triggers whenever the checkbox is enabled or disabled), and within this event listener, the checked property is used to check whether the checkbox is enabled or disabled. In the former case, the checkAgeNotNegative() and checkAgeIsNumber() event listeners are added, and in the latter case they are removed via the removeEventListener() method.

```
/* Here are the other functions. */
function init() {
  const element = document.getElementById('age');
  element.addEventListener('blur', clearMessage);
  element.addEventListener('blur', checkAgeNotNegative);
  element.addEventListener('blur', checkAgeIsNumber);
  const checkBox = document.getElementById('validation');
  checkBox.addEventListener('change', () => {
    if(checkBox.checked) {
      element.addEventListener('blur', checkAgeNotNegative);
      element.addEventListener('blur', checkAgeIsNumber);
    } else {
      clearMessage();
      element.removeEventListener('blur', checkAgeNotNegative);
```

```
    element.removeEventListener('blur', checkAgeIsNumber);
  }
});
}
document.addEventListener("DOMContentLoaded", init);
```

Listing 6.14 Removing Event Listeners

6.2.7   Defining Event Handlers and Event Listeners via a Helper Function

If you want to support as many browsers as possible but don't want to rely on a library like jQuery, you can use the addEvent() helper function shown in Listing 6.15. (Remember: Internet Explorer's proprietary method, mentioned above, is attachEvent().) The method expects three parameters: the element to which to add the event listener (or event handler), the event to respond to, and the function to register.

The function first checks if the addEventListener() method exists (this is usually checked on the window object). If it does, the function is registered as an event listener using this method. If, on the other hand, the method doesn't exist, the function checks in the same way whether the attachEvent() method exists; if so, the function is registered via that method. However, if the attachEvent() method doesn't exist either, the function is registered as an event handler.

```
function addEvent(element, eventType, eventListener) {
  if (window.addEventListener) {
    element.addEventListener(eventType, eventListener, false);
  }
  else if (window.attachEvent) {
    element.attachEvent('on' + eventType, eventListener);
  }
  else {
    element['on' + eventType] = eventListener;
  }
}
```

Listing 6.15 Helper Function for Defining Event Listeners or Event Handlers

The usage of the addEvent() helper function is shown in Listing 6.16.

```
function init() {
  const element = document.getElementById('age');
  addEvent(
    element,
    'blur',
    clearMessage
  );
```

```
addEvent(
  element,
  'blur',
  function() {
    const age = getAgeValue();
    checkAgeNotNegative(age);
  }
);
addEvent(
  element,
  'blur',
  function() {
    const age = getAgeValue();
    checkAgeIsNumber(age);
  }
);
}
```

Listing 6.16 Usage of the Helper Function

6.2.8 Accessing Information of an Event

Within a function that has been registered as an event handler or as an event listener, you can access certain information of the triggered event via a parameter that is passed when calling the corresponding function (but which we omitted in the previous listings for didactic reasons). Each event is represented by a specific object type—for example, mouse events by the MouseEvent object type and keyboard events by the KeyboardEvent object type. All of these object types have a common (super)type from which they derive: the Event type. The properties provided by this type are listed in Table 6.1. (The individual object types like MouseEvent and KeyboardEvent still provide other properties, some of which we'll discuss later in this chapter.)

Property	Description
bubbles	Contains an indication of whether or not an event moves upward in the DOM tree (Section 6.4).
cancelable	Contains an indication of whether an event can be canceled or not (Section 6.4.2).
currentTarget	Contains a reference to the current target of the event (Section 6.4).
defaultPrevented	Contains an indication of whether or not the preventDefault() method has been called on the event (Section 6.4.3).

Table 6.1 The Properties of Event

Property	Description
eventPhase	Contains a numeric value representing the phase the event is currently in (Section 6.4.1). Possible values: ■ 0 (or Event.NONE) ■ 1 (or Event.CAPTURING_PHASE) ■ 2 (or Event.AT_TARGET) ■ 3 (or Event.BUBBLING_PHASE)
target	Contains a reference to the original target of the event (Section 6.4).
timeStamp	Contains the time when the event was triggered.
type	Contains the name of the event.
isTrusted	Indicates whether the event was triggered by the browser (e.g., by clicking a button) or by JavaScript code (Section 6.5).

Table 6.1 The Properties of Event (Cont.)

A code example for accessing such an event object can be found in Listing 6.17. Here, you can see a function that is registered as an event listener for the click event of a button. When it's called, an object of the MouseEvent type is passed to it as a parameter (which is thus implicitly of the Event type as well). Within the function, the various properties of this object are then output (although we've omitted the properties defined by the MouseEvent type at this point).

```
function buttonClicked(event) {
  console.log(event.bubbles);            // true
  console.log(event.cancelable);         // true
  console.log(event.currentTarget);      // <input>
  console.log(event.defaultPrevented);   // false
  console.log(event.eventPhase);         // 2
  console.log(event.target);             // <input>
  console.log(event.timeStamp);          // e.g., 1453232649902
  console.log(event.type);               // "click"
  console.log(event.isTrusted);          // true
}

function init() {
  const element = document.getElementById('button'); // Get button
  element.addEventListener(              // Register event listener
    'click',                            // Name of the event
    buttonClicked,                      // Name of the event listener
    false                               // Event flow, details to follow later on
  );
```

```
}
```

```
document.addEventListener('DOMContentLoaded', init);
```

Listing 6.17 Access to the Event Object

The Event Object in Internet Explorer

As already mentioned, older versions of Internet Explorer do not always behave in a standards-compliant manner, which is also true with regard to the event object. In these browsers, this object isn't passed as an argument to the event handler (event listeners don't exist in these older browser versions) but is provided as an event property of the global window object (this property always contains only the currently triggered event).

Fortunately, the event object is still essentially structured as described in Table 6.1. However, the target element of the event (usually stored in the target property) must be accessed via the srcElement property.

You can access the event object and the target element in a browser-independent way as shown in Listing 6.18 (in the following examples in this book, however, we won't use this browser-independent solution for the sake of clarity).

```
function handler(ev) {
  var e = ev || window.event;              // Get event
  var target = e.target || e.srcElement;    // Target element
}
```

Listing 6.18 Browser-Independent Access to the Event Object and the Target Element

---

As mentioned earlier, the type of the event object differs depending on the type of the triggered event. The available types of events—and thus also the available object types—will be detailed in the following sections.

6.3   The Different Types of Events

Within a web application, there can be different types of events. Essentially, the following types can be distinguished:

- Events when interacting with the mouse (Section 6.3.1)
- Events when interacting with the keyboard or with text fields (Section 6.3.2)
- Events when working with forms (Section 6.3.3)
- Events when focusing elements (Section 6.3.4)
- Events related to the UI (Section 6.3.5)
- Events on mobile devices (Section 6.3.6)

Other Events

In addition to the events we'll present in this chapter, there are a number of others you'll encounter when developing with JavaScript. Some of these are discussed later in the book:

- In Chapter 9, we'll explain how to dynamically reload web page content from the server. This is another use case for events.
- In Chapter 10, we'll introduce the jQuery library, which simplifies and unifies many aspects of JavaScript development, including how events are handled.
- In Chapter 11, we'll address the topic of creating images using JavaScript, and that chapter also uses events.
- Also, the various web APIs outlined in Chapter 12 provide various events that you can respond to as a web developer.
- Node.js, the subject of Chapter 17, also uses the principle of event-driven programming.

In addition, you can find a good overview of the various events at *https://developer.mozilla.org/en-US/docs/Web/Events*.

6.3.1   Events when Interacting with the Mouse

The classic form of interaction with web pages is by using the mouse. Whenever a user moves the mouse or presses the mouse buttons, an event is triggered in the background. The related events are shown in Table 6.2. In addition to simple mouse clicks (click event), there is an event for double-clicking (dblclick) and for when the context menu has been opened (contextMenu).

The mousedown and mouseup events are triggered when the mouse button is pressed and released, respectively, and the mousemove event is triggered whenever the mouse is moved. In addition, there are various events that are triggered depending on whether the mouse pointer is moved over or away from an element on the web page.

Event	Description	Object Type
click	Triggered when the mouse button is pressed and released over an element	MouseEvent
dblclick	Triggered when the mouse button is pressed and released twice over an element	MouseEvent
contextmenu	Triggered when a context menu has been opened (usually via the right mouse button)	MouseEvent

Table 6.2 Overview of Events when Interacting with the Mouse

Event	Description	Object Type
mousedown	Triggered when the mouse button is pressed over an element	MouseEvent
mouseup	Triggered when the mouse button is released over an element	MouseEvent
mousemove	Triggered when the mouse has been moved	MouseEvent
mouseover	Triggered when the mouse is moved over an element (see also note box)	MouseEvent
mouseout	Triggered when the mouse is moved away from an element (see also note box)	MouseEvent
mouseenter	Triggered when the mouse is moved over an element (see also note box)	MouseEvent
mouseleave	Triggered when the mouse is moved away from an element (see also note box)	MouseEvent

Table 6.2 Overview of Events when Interacting with the Mouse (Cont.)

mouseenter/mouseleave versus mouseover/mouseout

The mouseenter and mouseover events and the mouseout and mouseleave events are quite similar at first glance. The former two are triggered when the mouse is moved over an element, the latter when the mouse is moved away from an element. The exact difference is illustrated in Figure 6.3: mouseenter and mouseleave are only triggered when the outer edge of the respective element is crossed, while mouseover and mouseout are additionally triggered when another element lies within the respective element and the mouse is moved over it (i.e., moved away from the outer element) or moved away from the inner element (and moved over the outer element).

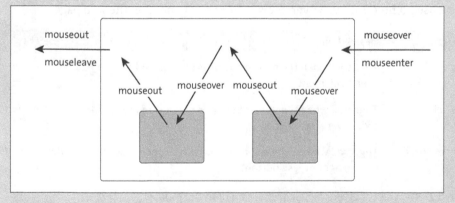

Figure 6.3 The mouseenter, mouseout, mouseover, and mouseleave Mouse Events in Comparison

428

Plus, you'll notice that all mouse events are of the MouseEvent object type. Besides the properties defined by the (super)type Event, this type provides the properties shown in Table 6.3.

Property	Description
altKey	Contains the Boolean indicating whether the ⌐Alt⌐ key was pressed when the event was triggered.
button	Contains the number of the mouse button that was pressed when the event was triggered.
buttons	Contains a number representing the mouse buttons pressed when the event was triggered. The number 1 represents the left mouse button, the number 2 the right mouse button, the number 4 the mouse wheel or the middle mouse button, the number 8 the fourth mouse button, and the number 16 the fifth mouse button. If several buttons were pressed when the event was triggered, buttons contains the sum of the respective numbers.
clientX	The x-coordinate (relative to the DOM content) where the mouse pointer is located when the event is triggered.
clientY	The y-coordinate (relative to the DOM content) where the mouse pointer is located when the event is triggered.
ctrlKey	Contains the Boolean indicating whether the ⌐Ctrl⌐ key was pressed when the event was triggered.
metaKey	Contains the Boolean indicating whether the *meta key* was pressed when the event was triggered (under macOS, the ⌐cmd⌐ key; under Windows, the ⌐Windows⌐ key).
movementX	The x-coordinate relative to the previous x-coordinate that occurred when the last mousemove event was triggered.
movementY	The y-coordinate relative to the previous y-coordinate that occurred when the last mousemove event was triggered.
region	Contains the ID of the region (or element) to which the event refers.
relatedTarget	Contains the related target element that is thematically connected to the current target element by the event. For example, when the mouse pointer is dragged away from one element and onto another, a mouseenter event is triggered for the latter. The relatedTarget property then refers to the element from which the mouse pointer was dragged away.
screenX	The x-coordinate (relative to the screen) where the mouse pointer is located when the event is triggered.

Table 6.3 Overview of the Properties of the MouseEvent Object Type

Property	Description
screenY	The y-coordinate (relative to the screen) where the mouse pointer is located when the event is triggered.
shiftKey	Contains the Boolean indicating whether the [Shift] key was pressed when the event was triggered.

Table 6.3 Overview of the Properties of the MouseEvent Object Type (Cont.)

Note

For reasons of space, we won't go into all properties in detail for the following object types of events, and we won't include the corresponding overview tables either. If you're specifically looking for the details of a particular object type or the various APIs in general, a good place to go is the web page mentioned earlier: *https://developer.mozilla.org/en-US/docs/Web/API/Event.*

An example of responding to mouse events, which is a bit ahead in terms of content but is quite illustrative and offers something to play around with, is shown in the following two listings. It illustrates how a part of the browser window can be used as a drawing area using the Canvas API (see also Chapter 11) and the mousemove event.

Listing 6.19 shows the necessary HTML code, which serves as a basis. The highlighted <canvas> element represents the drawing area (more on this in Chapter 11). Listing 6.20 shows the JavaScript code that ensures that when the mouse moves over the drawing area, corresponding lines are drawn along the mouse movements.

The handleMouseMove() function is registered at the drawing area as an event listener for the mousemove event. As soon as you move the mouse pointer over this drawing area, this event is triggered in the background, and the handleMouseMove() function is executed. Within this function, the clientX and clientY properties of the event object are then accessed, which are specific to the MouseEvent object type. These two properties contain the x and y coordinates of the mouse pointer at the time the event was triggered. Based on this position information, the following part of the function will then accordingly draw the path on the drawing area (you don't need to understand this code in detail now; it contains much that we won't discuss until Chapter 11).

```
<!DOCTYPE html>
<head lang="en">
  <meta charset="UTF-8">
  <title>Draw based on mouse position</title>
  <link rel="stylesheet" href="styles/main.css">
  <script src="scripts/main.js"></script>
</head>
```

```html
<body>
<div id="container">
  <canvas id="canvas" width="400" height="400">
  </canvas>
</div>
</body>
</html>
```

Listing 6.19 Source HTML with Drawing Area

```javascript
function init() {
  const canvas = document.getElementById('canvas');
  canvas.addEventListener('mousemove', handleMouseMove, false);
  const context = canvas.getContext('2d');  // Get drawing area.
  let started = false;                      // Notice start of path.
  function handleMouseMove(e) {
    let x, y;
    if (e.clientX              // If x position is specified ...
      || e.clientX == 0) {     // ... and not 0 ...
      x = e.clientX;           // ... remember x position ...
      y = e.clientY;           // ... remember y position.
    }
    if (!started) {            // If path not yet started ...
      context.beginPath();     // ... start path and ...
      context.moveTo(x, y);    // ... move to position.
      started = true;          // Notice that path has started.
    } else {                   // If path has started ...
      context.lineTo(x, y);    // ... move to position ...
      context.stroke();        // ... and draw connection.
    }
  }
}

document.addEventListener('DOMContentLoaded', init);
```

Listing 6.20 Drawing on the Canvas Using the Canvas API and the mousemove Event

6.3.2   Events when Interacting with the Keyboard and with Text Fields

Events are also triggered when the keyboard is used. Each time a user presses a key on the keyboard, three events are triggered: the keydown event when the respective key is pressed down, keyup when the key is released, and (in between) keypress, which virtually represents the typed character. The events that are triggered when interacting with the keyboard are of the KeyboardEvent type (see Table 6.4).

Event	Description	Object Type
keydown	Triggered when a key is pressed. If a key is pressed for a longer time, the event is triggered several times.	KeyboardEvent
keyup	Triggered when a key is released.	KeyboardEvent
keypress	Triggered when a character is inserted via the keyboard. The following principle applies here: if a key is pressed for a longer time, the event is triggered several times.	KeyboardEvent

Table 6.4 Overview of Events when Interacting with the Keyboard

For an example of using keyboard events, see the relatively extensive (but again, very practical) Listing 6.21, which shows how to move a web page element (in the example, a circular <div> element) using the arrow keys.

For this purpose, the keydown event is caught by means of an event listener. Within the event listener, the pressed key is determined, and depending on this information, one of four methods—moveUp(), moveDown(), moveRight(), or moveLeft()—is called. Each of these methods updates the position of the element stored in the position array and calls the move() method, which in turn updates the position of the element via CSS.

As you can also see in the example, the if-else statement checks whether the event object has the key property or the keyIdentifier property. The former is the property that is also specified in the current DOM standard. However, it isn't yet supported by all browsers, which is why the example still uses the older (but now obsolete) keyIdentifier property.

```
function init() {
  window.addEventListener('keydown', (event) => {
    if (event.key !== undefined) {
      // Included in current draft of DOM Events API.
      // Supported by Firefox and Internet Explorer, for example.
      console.log(event.key);
      switch (event.key) {
        case 'ArrowUp':
          moveUp();
          break;
        case 'ArrowLeft':
          moveLeft();
          break;
        case 'ArrowRight':
          moveRight();
          break;
        case 'ArrowDown':
```

```
        moveDown();
        break;
      default: return;
    }
  } else if (event.keyIdentifier !== undefined) {
    // Included in older draft of DOM Events API.
    // Supported by Chrome and Safari, for example.
    console.log(event.keyIdentifier);
    switch (event.keyIdentifier) {
      case 'Up':
        moveUp();
        break;
      case 'Left':
        moveLeft();
        break;
      case 'Right':
        moveRight();
        break;
      case 'Down':
        moveDown();
        break;
      default: return;
    }
  } else if (event.keyCode !== undefined) {
    // obsolete
  }
});

const circle = document.getElementById('circle');
const position = [0, 0];
function move() {
  circle.style.top = position[0] + 'px';
  circle.style.left = position[1] + 'px';
}
function moveUp() {
  position[0] -= 10;
  move();
}

function moveRight() {
  position[1] += 10;
  move();
}
```

```
function moveLeft() {
  position[1] -= 10;
  move();
}

function moveDown() {
  position[0] += 10;
  move();
  }
}

document.addEventListener('DOMContentLoaded', init);
```

Listing 6.21 Moving an Element Using the Arrow Keys and the keydown Event

6.3.3   Events when Working with Forms

There are also special events for working with forms. For example, corresponding events are triggered whenever the user modifies the text in an <input> or a <textarea> element; whenever the selected value in a dropdown list, a checkbox, or a group of radio buttons changes; or when a form is submitted or the values contained in a form are reset. All these events are represented by the Event object type, so they don't have their own specific object type like mouse events or keyboard events (see Table 6.5).

> **Note**
>
> We won't list any code examples here because we'll look at working with forms in more detail in Chapter 7, where you'll also see how to use form events.

Event	Description	Object Type
input	Triggered when the value of an <input> or a <textarea> element or an element with the contenteditable attribute has been changed	Event
change	Triggered when the selected value of a selection list, a checkbox, or a group of radio buttons has been changed	Event
submit	Triggered when a form has been submitted	Event
reset	Triggered when a form has been reset (via a reset button)	Event

Table 6.5 Overview of Events when Interacting with Text Fields and Forms

6.3.4   Events when Focusing Elements

In addition, an event is triggered every time an element on a web page goes into focus (e.g., by navigating to the element using the ⌨Tab key) or when it loses the focus. An overview is provided in Table 6.6. As you can see, the object types of the corresponding triggered events are each of the FocusEvent type.

Note

Remember that in the opening example in this chapter, you saw how the blur event can be used to validate text input in form fields.

Event	Description	Object Type
focus	Triggered when an element is focused.	FocusEvent
blur	Triggered when an element loses focus.	FocusEvent
focusin	Triggered when an element is focused. Unlike the focus event, this event bubbles (Section 6.4).	FocusEvent
focusout	Triggered when an element loses focus. Unlike the blur event, this event bubbles (Section 6.4).	FocusEvent

Table 6.6 Overview of Events when Focusing Elements

6.3.5   General Events of the User Interface

In addition to the events we've presented so far, there are a number of others that can be roughly categorized as UI events (where most, but not all, of these events are represented by the UIEvent type). An overview is presented in Table 6.7.

Event	Description	Object Type
load	Triggered when a web page is fully loaded	UIEvent
unload	Triggered when a web page is unloaded, usually when a new web page is requested in the corresponding browser window	UIEvent
abort	Triggered when the loading of a resource is canceled	UIEvent
Error	Triggered when there is a problem loading the web page, such as a JavaScript error	UIEvent
select	Triggered when text is selected on a web page	UIEvent

Table 6.7 Overview of the Events Related to the User Interface

Event	Description	Object Type
resize	Triggered when the size of the browser window has been changed	UIEvent
scroll	Triggered when scrolling up or down	UIEvent
beforeunload	Triggered just before a web page is unloaded, usually when a new web page is requested in the corresponding browser window	BeforeUnloadEvent
DOMContentLoaded	Triggered when the DOM tree is fully loaded	Event
cut	Triggered when content has been cut from a form field (e.g., using the keyboard shortcut ⌘cmd + X)	ClipboardEvent
copy	Triggered when content has been copied from a form field (e.g., using the keyboard shortcut ⌘cmd + C)	ClipboardEvent
paste	Triggered when content has been inserted into a form field (e.g., using the keyboard shortcut ⌘cmd + V)	ClipboardEvent
select	Triggered when text is selected in a form field	ClipboardEvent

Table 6.7 Overview of the Events Related to the User Interface (Cont.)

Usage of the load Event

You saw an example of using the load event earlier in this chapter, when we talked about executing initial JavaScript code (and registering further event handlers or event listeners) after the web page has loaded.

One use case for the scroll event, for example, is to display elements of a web page depending on the vertical scroll position. You've probably seen this effect before; nowadays, it's often used for so-called one-page web pages (i.e., web pages where the entire content is contained on a single, vertical, very long web page). If the user scrolls down on such a web page, further components of the web page gradually fade in, such as text or images (sometimes also moving into the screen from the left or right).

The next two listings show a very simple implementation (at least visually), which displays a text depending on the vertical scroll position. Listing 6.22 only contains the HTML code and is only intended to show you the structure of the web page (the complete example including CSS can be found, as always, in the download area for the book).

The `<span>` element with the name ID that contains the text John Doe is initially hidden when the web page loads. Listing 6.23 also registers an event listener (handleScroll-Event()) for the scroll event on the window object when the web page is loaded. Within this event listener, window.scrollY is used to determine the vertical scroll position (see also Chapter 8). When this scroll position exceeds a certain threshold (the value 10 in the example), the hide CSS class is removed from the hidden `<span>` element and replaced with the show CSS class. The CSS rule defined for this CSS class (not shown here) then ensures that the element is slowly faded in.

```
<!DOCTYPE html>
<html>
<head lang="en">
  <meta charset="UTF-8">
  <title>Fade in an element when scrolling</title>
  <link rel="stylesheet" href="styles/main.css">
  <script src="scripts/main.js"></script>
</head>
<body>
  <div id="content">
    Hello
    <span id="name" class="hide">John Doe</span>
  </div>
</body>
</html>
```

Listing 6.22 Source HTML for Fading in an Element Depending on the Scroll Position

```
function init() {
  let scrollPosition = window.scrollY;
  const nameElement = document.getElementById('name');

  function handleScrollEvent(e) {
    scrollPosition = window.scrollY;
    if(scrollPosition > 10) {
      nameElement.classList.remove('hide');
      nameElement.classList.add('show');
    }
    else {
      nameElement.classList.remove('show');
      nameElement.classList.add('hide');
    }
  }
```

```
  window.addEventListener('scroll', handleScrollEvent);
}
```

```
document.addEventListener('DOMContentLoaded', init);
```

Listing 6.23 Display an Element Depending on the Scroll Position Using an Event Listener for the Scroll Event

6.3.6   Events on Mobile Devices

When using mobile devices (smartphones, tablets, etc.), a number of other events are triggered. The background to this is primarily the fact that such end devices can be operated in quite a different way than conventional laptops or desktop computers: Instead of using a mouse and keyboard, you usually use your fingers or special input pens to interact with the corresponding website.

Based on these forms of interaction—which are very much designed for touching the display—there are corresponding events to be able to detect and respond to touches on the display of the end device.

In addition, there are other things that play a role with mobile devices, such as the device's tilt or orientation: Is it tilted sideways or tilted forward or backward? Events can also be used to respond to the movement of a mobile device. An overview of the most important events in this regard can be found in Table 6.8.

Event	Description	Object Type
orientationchange	Triggered when the orientation of the input device changes	Event
deviceorientation	Triggered when new data is available regarding the orientation of the end device	DeviceOrientationEvent
devicemotion	Is triggered at regular intervals and then indicates the acceleration force acting on the end device	DeviceMotionEvent
touchstart	Triggered when the input device (usually a finger) touches the display	TouchEvent
touchend	Triggered when the input device stops touching—in other words, when the finger is removed from the display	TouchEvent

Table 6.8 A Selection of Mobile Device Events

Event	Description	Object Type
touchmove	Triggered when the input device has been moved over the display	TouchEvent
touchcancel	Triggered when the tracking of the touch has been interrupted	TouchEvent

Table 6.8 A Selection of Mobile Device Events (Cont.)

> **Note**
>
> In order not to exceed the scope of this chapter, we won't include code examples here but will provide them in Chapter 12. In that chapter, we'll show you how to recognize and respond to the orientation and movements of a mobile device.

6.4   Understanding and Influencing the Flow of Events

Whenever an event is triggered, it goes through several event phases. As a JavaScript developer, it's important for you to understand what these phases are and how they're related to event triggering.

6.4.1   The Event Phases

Basically, the following three phases are distinguished with regard to the event flow:

1. **Capturing phase**
   In this phase, the event "descends" from the top node in the DOM tree (the document node) down to the element for which the event was triggered, the target element (see Figure 6.4).

2. **Target phase**
   In this phase, the event is triggered at the target element.

3. **Bubbling phase**
   In this phase, the event "rises" from the target element in the DOM tree back up to the document node (see Figure 6.5).

During the capturing phase and the bubbling phase, the event triggers the event handlers or event listeners that have been registered for this event at the respective element at which the event is currently located.

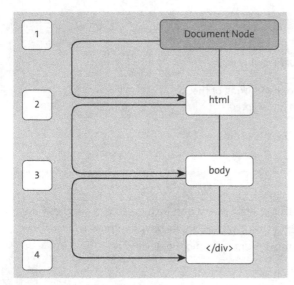

Figure 6.4 In Event Capturing, the Event Descends to the Bottom

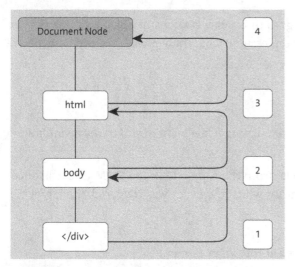

Figure 6.5 In Event Bubbling, the Event Rises to the Top

The capturing phase and the bubbling phase trace back to different opinions of the different browser manufacturers a long time ago. Browser manufacturer Netscape at the time was of the opinion that an event should always first call the event handler/event listener on the element that is further up in the DOM tree, and therefore proceeded according to so-called event capturing, which consisted only of the capturing phase (and the target phase). But Microsoft held a different opinion: in Internet Explorer, an event first triggered the event handlers/event listeners defined on the target element. That is, Microsoft followed the *event bubbling* principle, which in turn consisted only of the bubbling phase (and the target phase).

However, the event flow has been standardized by the W3C for some time now (see *www.w3.org/TR/DOM-Level-3-Events/#event-flow*), with care taken to combine both phases into one event flow model, as shown in Figure 6.6. In other words, when an event is triggered, it first goes through the capturing phase, executing all event handlers/event listeners registered for that phase (more on that later), then goes through the target phase, executing the event handlers/event listeners registered on the target element, and then goes through the bubbling phase, now executing all event handlers/event listeners registered for that phase.

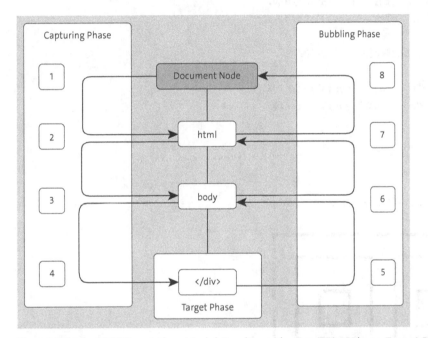

Figure 6.6 The W3C Event Flow Model Combines the Capturing Phase, Target Phase, and Bubbling Phase

The easiest way to understand this principle of event bubbling and event capturing is to use an example.

Event Bubbling Example

Let's start with an example of event bubbling. First look at the HTML code in Listing 6.24. It shows an outer `<div>` element (with the ID `outer`) that contains two `<div>` elements (with the IDs `first` and `second`), which, in turn, contain two `<div>` elements each. The structure is shown in Figure 6.7.

```
<!DOCTYPE html>
<html>
<head lang="en">
  <meta charset="UTF-8">
```

```
<title>Event capturing and event bubbling</title>
<link rel="stylesheet" href="styles/main.css">
<script src="scripts/main.js"></script>
</head>
<body>
<div id="outer" class="level1">
  <div id="first" class="level2">
    1
    <div id="A" class="level3">A</div>
    <div id="B" class="level3">B</div>
  </div>
  <div id="second" class="level2">
    2
    <div id="C" class="level3">C</div>
    <div id="D" class="level3">D</div>
  </div>
</div>
</body>
</html>
```

Listing 6.24 The HTML for the Event Example

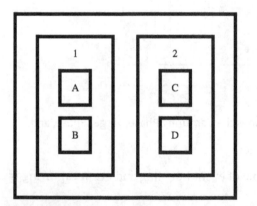

Figure 6.7 The Starting Point for the Event Example

In the JavaScript code in Listing 6.25, the same function is now added to each of these `<div>` elements as an event listener. This function does nothing but toggle the `selected` CSS class via `classList.toggle()` and thus switch between a white and gray background.

```
function handler(ev) {
  const e = ev || window.event;                    // Get event
  const target = e.target || e.srcElement;         // Target element
```

```
    this.classList.toggle('selected');              // CSS class
    console.log(                                     // Output clicked ...
      `Clicked on node with ID "${target.id}"`       // ... element
    );
    console.log(                                     // Output current ...
      `Event at node with ID "${this.id}"`           // ... element
    );
}
function init() {
  const elements = document.querySelectorAll(        // All elements ...
    '.level1, ' +                                    // ... of the first, ...
    '.level2, ' +                                    // ... the second, ...
    '.level3'                                        // ... and the third ...
  );                                                 // ... level...
  for(let i=0; i<elements.length; i++) {             // ... get a ...
    elements[i].addEventListener(                    // ... listener for the ...
      'click',                                       // ... click event.
      handler,
      false
    );
  }
}
document.addEventListener('DOMContentLoaded', init);
```

Listing 6.25 The Code for the Event Bubbling Example

If you now click on the <div> element that contains the C (i.e., on an element of the third <div> layer, so to speak), this element is colored gray. After that, the event is passed to the parent element (with the 2), which also colors this element gray. Then the event is forwarded again (to the outermost <div> element), the event listener is executed there as well, and accordingly the background color of this element is also set to gray. You can see the result in Figure 6.8, and the output of the program in Listing 6.26.

```
Clicked on node with ID "C"
Event at node with ID "C"
Clicked on node with ID "C"
Event at node with ID "second"
Clicked on node with ID "C"
Event at node with ID "outer"
```

Listing 6.26 Output for the Previous Program when Clicking on the <div> Element Labeled C

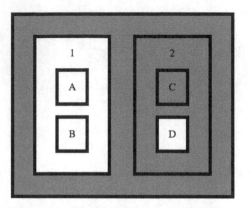

Figure 6.8 If You Click on the <div> Element Labeled C, All Preceding Elements Are Colored Gray during Event Bubbling, Starting from the Target Element

If, on the other hand, you click on the <div> element with the 2 (i.e., an element of the second <div> layer), its event listener is executed first, and the background color is set to gray. Then the event listener for the parent element—that is, the outermost <div> element—is executed, and its background color is also set to gray. You can see the result in Figure 6.9, and the output of the program in Listing 6.27.

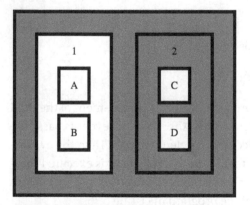

Figure 6.9 If You Click on the <div> Element Labeled 2, All Preceding Elements Are Colored Gray during Event Bubbling, Starting from the Target Element

```
Clicked on node with ID "second"
Event at node with ID "second"
Clicked on node with ID "second"
Event at node with ID "outer"
```

Listing 6.27 Output for the Preceding Program when Clicking on the <div> Element Labeled 2

You can see that event listeners that you register via the addEventListener() method are registered for the bubbling phase by default. Next, let's look at how you can register event listeners for the capturing phase.

> **Event Handlers in the Bubbling Phase**
>
> If you register an event handler (whether via HTML or via JavaScript), it's always executed in the bubbling phase. In contrast to event listeners, event handlers don't offer a way to influence the phase in which they are to be executed.

Event Capturing Example

Using the addEventListener() method, it's possible to register a function as an event listener for the capturing phase. This can be controlled via the third parameter of this method: you can specify a Boolean value that determines whether the respective function should be registered as an event listener for the bubbling phase or for the capturing phase.

By default, as already mentioned, the registration takes place for the bubbling phase, but if you want the event listener to be registered for the capturing phase, you need to pass the value true. An example of this is shown in Listing 6.28. It's essentially based on the previous examples in which we demonstrated event bubbling. The only difference is that the event listeners for the click event are now registered for the capturing phase rather than the bubbling phase.

```
function init() {
  const elements = document.querySelectorAll('.level1, .level2, .level3');
  for(let i=0; i<elements.length; i++) {
    elements[i].addEventListener('click', handler, true);
    // elements[i].onclick = handler;                 // always bubbling phase
    // elements[i].attachEvent('click', handler);  // IE<9 always bubbling phase
  }
}
```

Listing 6.28 Event Capturing

If you now click on the element with the value C again, the event won't trigger the event listeners in the bubbling phase starting from the target element, but in the capturing phase starting from the document node (of course, the bubbling phase is still run through in order to be able to execute other event handlers and such event listeners that were registered for the bubbling phase).

The first element that has an event listener registered for that event is the outermost <div> element, which means that the first thing to execute is the event listener for that element. Then the event moves down the DOM tree (we're in the capturing phase) and triggers the event listener for the element with the 2. Finally, the event listener is triggered for the element that was clicked (the target element with the C).

The output of the program, shown in Listing 6.29, illustrates this sequence.

```
Clicked on node with ID "C"
Event at node with ID "outer"
Clicked on node with ID "C"
Event at node with ID "second"
Clicked on node with ID "C"
Event at node with ID "C"
```

Listing 6.29 Output of the Preceding Program

The graphical result, in turn, resembles the result from the event bubbling example when the <div> element with the C was also clicked (see Figure 6.10; compare with Figure 6.8).

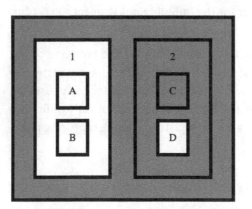

Figure 6.10 If You Click on the C <div> Element, All Preceding Elements Are Colored Gray during Event Capturing, Starting from the Outermost <div> Element

Even if you click on the <div> element with the 2, the graphical result looks the same as in the event bubbling example (see Figure 6.11; compare with Figure 6.9); only the order in which the event listeners are executed is different.

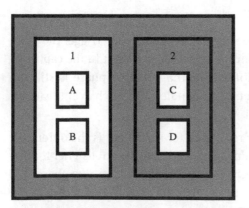

Figure 6.11 If You Click on the 2 <div> Element, All Preceding Elements Are Colored Gray during Event Capturing, Starting from the Outermost <div> Element

6.4.2   Interrupting the Event Flow

When an event is triggered, actions that normally occur as a result of the event can be prevented:

- The stopPropagation() method can be used to prevent the corresponding event from being propagated to the next element in the DOM tree, thereby triggering actions (or corresponding event handlers and event listeners) on other elements.

- The preventDefault() method, on the other hand, can be used to prevent the browser's default actions from being executed when an event occurs. For example, you can prevent the browser from opening a link when you click on it or from submitting a form when you click on a submit button.

In Listing 6.30, you can see how the program has been expanded a little bit: an additional if statement is used to check whether the current element (this) contains the CSS class level2—in other words, whether the current element is an element of the second level, one of the two <div> elements with the 1 or the 2 (the outermost <div> element has the CSS class level1, while the four innermost <div> elements have the CSS class level3; see also Listing 6.24). If this is the case, the stopPropagation() method is executed on the event object.

So if you now click on a third-level <div> element—for example, again on the <div> element containing the C—then by default (with an event listener registered for the bubbling phase) only that element and the element containing the 2 are colored gray, but not the outermost element (see Figure 6.12 and the output of the program in Listing 6.31). Because forwarding is prevented via the stopPropagation() method, the outermost <div> element is not reached (see Figure 6.13).

```
function handler(ev) {
  const e = ev || window.event;
  const target = e.target || e.srcElement;
  this.classList.toggle('selected');
  console.log(
    `Clicked on node with ID "${target.id}"`
  );
  console.log(
    `Event at node with ID "${this.id}"`
  );
  if(this.classList.contains('level2')) {   // Once level 2 has been reached ...
    e.stopPropagation();                     // ... the event will not ...
  }                                          // ... be forwarded.
}
```

Listing 6.30 Termination of the Event Flow

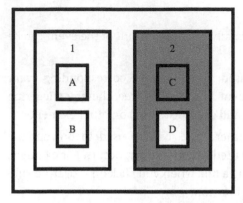

Figure 6.12 When Interrupting the Event Flow in the Bubbling Phase, Only the Target Element up to the 2 <div> Element Is Grayed

```
Clicked on node with ID "C"
main.js:8 Event at node with ID "C"
main.js:5 Clicked on node with ID "C"
main.js:8 Event at node with ID "second"
```

Listing 6.31 Output for the Preceeding Program when Clicking on the C <div> Element

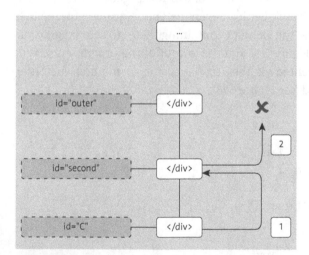

Figure 6.13 Calling stopPropagation() Prevents the Event from Rising in the DOM Tree during the Bubbling Phase

Event Listeners in the Capturing Phase

The example assumes that the event listeners have all been registered for the bubbling phase. If, on the other hand, the event listeners are registered for the *capturing* phase, the result looks different (see Figure 6.14) because the event listeners are evaluated at the respective elements starting from the document node (see Figure 6.15).

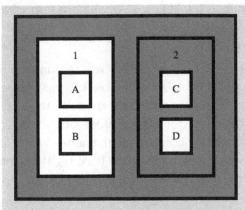

Figure 6.14 When Interrupting the Event Flow in the Capturing Phase, Only the Document Node up to the 2 <div> Element Is Grayed

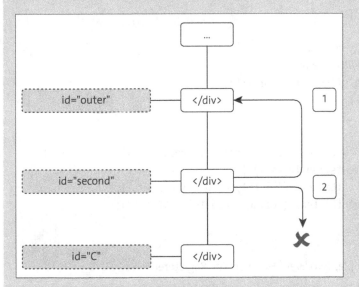

Figure 6.15 Calling stopPropagation() Prevents the Event from Descending in the DOM Tree during the Capturing Phase

Interrupting the Event Flow Immediately

As you know, you can register more than one event listener per element for an event. If you then call the stopPropagation() method in one of these event listeners, all other event listeners for this element are still executed.

This is illustrated in Listing 6.32. Here, the handleClickEvent1() and handleClickEvent2() functions are registered as event listeners for the click event on all <div> elements. As known from the previous examples, the handleClickEvent1() method toggles the selected CSS class and thus colors the background color of the respective element gray at first execution.

The handleClickEvent2() method works similarly but has the effect that the respective element gets a dashed frame. Both methods also prevent the event from being forwarded by calling the stopPropagation() method.

If you now click on the <div> element with the C, the handleClickEvent1() function is executed first, then the event object is propagated (despite the call of stopPropagation()), and the handleClickEvent2() function is executed. In other words, the stopPropagation() method doesn't prevent the event from being propagated between event listeners registered for the corresponding event on one and the same element. It only prevents the propagation to those event listeners that have been registered on other elements for the event. The result of the program is shown in Figure 6.16.

```
function handleClickEvent1(ev) {
  const e = ev || window.event;
  this.classList.toggle('selected');
  e.stopPropagation();
}
function handleClickEvent2(ev) {
  const e = ev || window.event;
  this.classList.toggle('selected-border');
  e.stopPropagation();
}
function init() {
  const elements = document.querySelectorAll('.level1, .level2, .level3');
  for(let i=0; i<elements.length; i++) {
    elements[i].addEventListener('click', handleClickEvent1);
    elements[i].addEventListener('click', handleClickEvent2);
  }
}
```

Listing 6.32 In the Example, Two Event Handlers Are Registered First

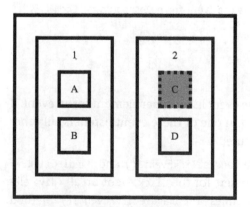

Figure 6.16 Both Registered Event Listeners Are Called when stopPropagation() Is Called

However, if you want to prevent the propagation of an event even for the event listeners registered on a single element, you have to resort to the `stopImmediatePropagation()` method. Listing 6.33 shows an example: the `handleClickEvent1()` function now calls exactly this method, which in turn ensures that the second registered event listener will no longer call the `handleClickEvent2()` function (see Figure 6.17).

```
function handleClickEvent1(ev) {
  const e = ev || window.event;
  this.classList.toggle('selected');
  e.stopImmediatePropagation();
}
function handleClickEvent2(ev) {
  const e = ev || window.event;
  this.classList.toggle('selected-border');
  e.stopPropagation();
}
```

Listing 6.33 Immediately Canceling the Propagation Also Prevents Other Event Handlers Registered on the Respective Element from Being Executed

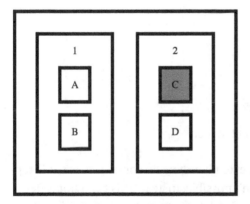

Figure 6.17 By Calling stopImmediatePropagation(), Further Event Listeners on the Same Element Will Not Be Executed

Note

The `stopPropagation()` method prevents events from being propagated to event listeners that are defined for the respective event on other elements, whereas the `stopImmediatePropagation()` method prevents events from being propagated even to those event listeners that were registered for the event on the same element.

6.4.3 Preventing Default Actions of Events

While you can use the stopPropagation() and stopImmediatePropagation() methods to prevent event propagation, it's possible to use the preventDefault() method to prevent the browser's default actions.

An example of this is shown in Listing 6.34. The handleLinkClicked() function is registered as an event listener for the click event of a link (i.e., an <a> element). However, if the link is clicked, the corresponding linked URL is not opened (which, as we know, would be the browser's default action for handling links); calling the preventDefault() method prevents the link from opening.

```
function handleLinkClicked(e) {
  console.log('Link clicked');
  e.preventDefault();
}

function init() {
  const element = document.getElementById('link');
  element.addEventListener(
    'click',
    handleLinkClicked,
    false
  );
}

document.addEventListener('DOMContentLoaded', init);
```

Listing 6.34 Preventing Default Actions for Event Listeners

A peculiarity worth pointing out is that with event handlers (in contrast to event listeners), calling the preventDefault() method isn't possible. Instead, this behavior is determined by the return value of the function defined as an event handler: if this value is false, the default actions are prevented, but if it's true or no return value is specified, the default functions are executed. A corresponding example is shown in Listing 6.35. The handleLinkClicked() function, defined as an event handler, returns false here, which prevents the browser from opening the URL of the clicked link.

```
function handleLinkClicked(e) {
  console.log('Link clicked');
  return false;
}

function init() {
  const element = document.getElementById('link');
```

```
  element.onclick = handleLinkClicked;
}

document.addEventListener('DOMContentLoaded', init);
```

Listing 6.35 Preventing Default Actions for Event Handlers

Generic Helper Function

A generic helper function that causes both event listeners and event handlers to prevent default browser actions is shown in Listing 6.36. This function first checks whether the preventDefault() method exists on the event object. If so, the method is called. Otherwise, the return value of the (now assumed) event handler is set to false via the returnValue property. The use of this helper function is shown in Listing 6.37.

```
function stopDefault(e) {
  if (e && e.preventDefault) {
    e.preventDefault();
  } else if (window.event && window.event.returnValue) {
    window.event.returnValue = false;
  }
}
```

Listing 6.36 Helper Function for Preventing Default Actions

```
function handleLinkClicked(e) {
  console.log('Link clicked');
  stopDefault(e);
}

function init() {
  const element = document.getElementById('link');
  element.onclick = handleLinkClicked;
  const element2 = document.getElementById('link2');
  element2.addEventListener(
    'click',
    handleLinkClicked,
    false
  );
}

document.addEventListener('DOMContentLoaded', init);
```

Listing 6.37 Usage of the Helper Function

> **Return Value of Event Handlers**
>
> The return value `false` in a function defined as an event handler prevents not only the default actions of the browser that are normally executed for the respective event, but also the propagation of the event. The return value `false` is virtually equivalent to calling `preventDefault()` and `stopPropagation()` for event listeners.

6.5   Programmatically Triggering Events

Events in JavaScript (and in event-driven programming in general) can be triggered not only by immediate user actions, but also programmatically—that is, by JavaScript code.

6.5.1   Triggering Simple Events

To programmatically trigger an event, simply create an object instance of `Event` and use it as an argument to the `dispatchEvent()` method available to any element in the DOM tree.

The first argument passed to the `Event` constructor is a string that defines the type of the event. Optionally, a configuration object passed as the second argument can be used to determine whether the event should go through the bubbling phase or not (via the `bubbles` property) and whether it is allowed to prevent the browser's default actions (via the `cancelable` property).

The object instance created via the constructor can then be passed to the `dispatch-Event()` method, which internally ensures that this event is triggered on the element on which you call the method. An example of this is shown in Listing 6.38.

```javascript
function init() {
  const element = document.getElementById('example')
  const event = new Event(
  'example',              // Type of the event
  {
    bubbles: true,        // Allow bubbling
    cancelable: false     // Default actions cannot ...
                          // ... be prevented.
  });
  element.addEventListener(
    'example',                          // Type of event
    (event) => {
      console.log('Event triggered');
      console.log(event.type);          // "example"
    },
    false
```

```
  );
  element.dispatchEvent(event);
}

document.addEventListener('DOMContentLoaded', init);
```

Listing 6.38 Example for Triggering an Event

6.5.2   Triggering Events with Passed Arguments

If you want to assign the triggered event or the corresponding event object-specific information that can then be accessed within the defined event handlers and registered event listeners, use the CustomEvent object type instead of the Event object type.

The constructor of CustomEvent can be passed corresponding data within the configuration object (which can also be passed as a second argument) via the detail property. An example of this is shown in Listing 6.39. Here an object (with the properties firstName, lastName, and id) is passed as an argument to the event object and read within the event listener.

```
function init() {
  const element = document.getElementById('example')
  const event = new CustomEvent('example', {
    detail: {
      firstName: 'John',
      lastName: 'Doe',
      id: 4711
    }
  });
  element.addEventListener(
    'example',
    (event) => {
      console.log('Event triggered');
      console.log(event.type);              // "example"
      console.log(event.detail.firstName); // "John"
      console.log(event.detail.lastName);  // "Doe"
      console.log(event.detail.id);        // 4711
    },
    false
  );
  element.dispatchEvent(event);
}

document.addEventListener('DOMContentLoaded', init);
```

Listing 6.39 Example of Specifying Parameters when Triggering an Event

6.5.3   Triggering Default Events

In addition, you also have the option to programmatically trigger other events (e.g., mouse events or keyboard events) and to virtually simulate user interactions in this way. To do this, simply create an object instance of the respective event object type, as shown in Listing 6.40 using a mouse event, and pass it to the dispatchEvent() method.

```
function init() {
  const element = document.getElementById('example')
  const event = new MouseEvent('click', {
    'view': window,
    'bubbles': true,
    'cancelable': true
  });
  element.addEventListener(
    'click',
    (event) => {
      console.log('Element clicked');
    },
    false
  );
  element.dispatchEvent(event);
}

document.addEventListener('DOMContentLoaded', init);
```

Listing 6.40 Example of Triggering an Event for Mouse Clicks

Browser Support

One final note to conclude this chapter: support of the events presented in this chapter (and other events not presented here) can vary between browsers. As always, when it comes to browser support of any features, the Can I Use website at *http://caniuse.com* provides a good overview.

6.6   Summary

In this chapter, you learned about the basic operation of event-driven programming in JavaScript. Among other things, you now know how to respond to user actions, whether mouse or keyboard interactions, form inputs, or other events that are triggered. The following are the most important points to remember from this chapter:

- In *event-driven programming*, events are triggered that can be acted upon within the code.

- In general, the code that responds to events is called an *event handler* or an *event listener.*

- In JavaScript, you can define event handlers using HTML (*HTML event handlers*) or JavaScript (*JavaScript event handlers*), but event listeners can only be defined via JavaScript.

- The advantage of event listeners over event handlers (in JavaScript) is that you can register several for one event.

- In this chapter, we have mainly shown how you can register event handlers/event listeners on elements in the DOM tree. In general, however, the concept of registering event handlers/event listeners goes further: they can also be registered to objects such as the `window` object.

- There are several types of events in JavaScript web development, including mouse events, keyboard events, form interaction events, and many more.

- When an event is triggered on an element in the DOM tree, it goes through different phases: In the *capturing phase*, starting at the document node, the event is passed downwards element by element to the target element, executing each of the event listeners registered for the capturing phase. In the *target phase*, the event handlers/event listeners registered on the target element are then executed. In the third phase, the *bubbling phase*, the event rises back up to the document node starting from the target element, executing all event handlers/event listeners registered for this phase.

- Last but not least, you have learned how you can trigger events programmatically, whether via the `Event` object type to trigger general events, via the `CustomEvent` object type to trigger events using arguments, or via the various other object types such as `MouseEvent`.

Chapter 7
Working with Forms

Forms or the associated form fields, such as input fields, selection lists, and so on, are an essential part of interactive web applications. Basically, forms also work without JavaScript, but JavaScript can significantly increase the interactivity and user-friendliness of forms. This chapter shows you how to use this benefit.

While the previous chapters, with the exception of the two introductory chapters, were relatively extensive, this chapter on form processing will give you a little breather—on the one hand because it isn't as extensive, and on the other hand because we'll revisit many concepts from the two previous chapters on the DOM and on event handling. This chapter specifically details the following topics:

- How can you select forms within a web page and access data within a form (Section 7.1)? Most of this will be relatively easy for you because of the previous two chapters. However, there are a few particularities to note here and there.

- How can you submit forms via JavaScript (Section 7.2)? You learned in Chapter 6 that you can programmatically trigger, for example, mouse events or keyboard events. Form submission can also be executed programmatically via JavaScript (although not in the same way as event triggering).

- How can you validate entered form data—that is, check its validity (Section 7.3)? We used this topic as a means to an end in Chapter 6 in order to explain event handling. In this chapter, however, we'll discuss the Constraint Validation API, which is specifically designed for validating forms.

7.1   Accessing Forms and Form Fields

In Chapter 5, you learned how you can use JavaScript to access individual elements within a web page. The access to forms works quite similarly.

7.1.1   Accessing Forms

You have several options to access forms on a web page:

- Via the methods for selecting elements presented in Chapter 5: getElementById(), getElementsByClassName(), getElementsByTagName(), getElementsByName(), querySelector(), and querySelectorAll()
- Via the forms property of the document object
- Via a property of the document object that corresponds to the name of the corresponding form

Let's demonstrate these three types of access. To do this, first look at the form shown in Listing 7.1. This is a simple login form with an input field for the username, a password field for entering a password, a checkbox for saving the entered login data, and a button for submitting the form (see also Figure 7.1).

```
<!DOCTYPE html>
<html>
<head lang="en">
  <meta charset="UTF-8">
  <title>Form example</title>
  <link rel="stylesheet" href="styles/main.css">
  <link
    href="https://maxcdn.bootstrapcdn.com/bootstrap/3.3.6/css/
      bootstrap.min.css"
    rel="stylesheet"
    crossorigin="anonymous"
  >
  <link
    rel="stylesheet"
    href="https://maxcdn.bootstrapcdn.com/bootstrap/3.3.6/css/
      bootstrap-theme.min.css"
    crossorigin="anonymous"
  >
</head>
<body>
<form
  id="login"
  name="login"
  method="post"
  action="login.html"
  class="form col-xs-4 center-block"
>
  <div class="form-group">
    <label for="username">Username:</label>
    <input
      type="text"
```

```
          id="username"
          name="username"
          class="form-control"
          value=""
          placeholder="Username"
        >
    </div>
    <div class="form-group">
      <label for="password">Password:</label>
      <input
        type="password"
        id="password"
        name="password"
        class="form-control"
        value=""
        placeholder="Password"
      >
    </div>
    <div class="checkbox">
      <label for="remember">
        <input
          type="checkbox"
          id="remember"
          name="remember"
          value="on"
        >
        Remember login on this computer
      </label>
    </div>
    <button
      type="submit"
      id="submit"
      name="submit"
      class="btn btn-primary btn-block"
    >
      Login
    </button>
</form>
<script src="scripts/main.js"></script>
</body>
</html>
```

Listing 7.1 HTML Code for a Simple Login Form

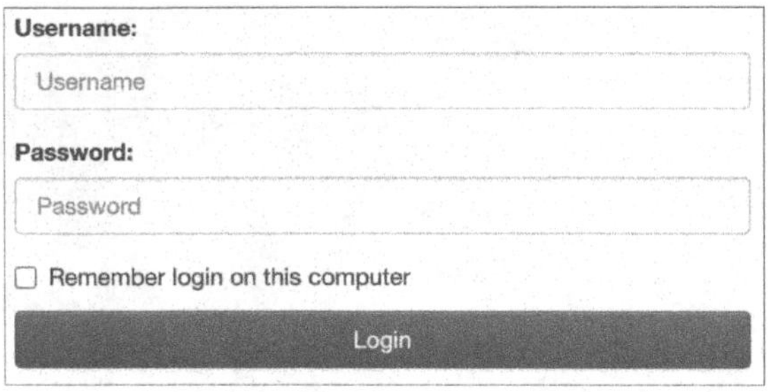

Figure 7.1 A Simple Login Form

The Bootstrap Framework

To make it look a bit prettier, the Bootstrap CSS framework (*http://getbootstrap.com*) was used for the layout.

In Listing 7.2, you can see the three previously mentioned ways to access this form. You already know about access via DOM selection methods. The other two access types are also interesting at this point.

For example, the forms property of the document object contains a list of all forms that are on the web page. The individual forms in this list can be accessed via the index. Within the list, the forms are sorted in the same order as they appear on the web page: the first form appears at position 0, the second at position 1, and so on. The example only contains one form, which is why it uses index 0.

In addition, for each form that has a name (i.e., has a name attribute), a property of the same name is implicitly provided on the document object and can be used to access that form. In the example, the form has the name login; consequently, the form can be accessed via document.login.

```javascript
// 1.) Access via DOM selection methods
const formById = document.getElementById('login');
const formByName = document.getElementsByName('login')[0];
const formBySelector = document.querySelector('form');
// 2.) Access via forms property
const formByFormsField = document.forms[0];
// 3.) Access via the name of the form
 const formByNameField = document.login;
console.log(formById.id);             // "login"
console.log(formByName.id);           // "login"
console.log(formBySelector.id);       // "login"
console.log(formByFormsField.id);     // "login"
console.log(formByNameField.id);      // "login"
```

Listing 7.2 Access to a Form

What way of selecting forms should you choose now? We would advise you to always use one of the DOM selection methods, and preferably the getElementById() or query-Selector() method.

The reason: although the forms property allows quick access to all forms on a web page, it has a disadvantage when you take a closer look. If there are several forms on a web page, it's necessary to know exactly where the desired form is located on the web page. In addition, if the order of the forms changes or if a (preceding) form is removed from the web page or a new (preceding) form is added, the index must also be adjusted for access.

The access via the name of the form using the document object's property of the same name is not ideal either because you have to be careful not to choose a name that's already taken by an existing property or method (of the document object).

The getElementById() and querySelector() methods, on the other hand, can be used to select elements unambiguously so that no problems arise in the cases mentioned earlier, and no adjustments to the corresponding JavaScript code are necessary.

Forms provide various properties, such as the elements property, which allows you to access the individual form elements contained in the form (details on this in the next section); the name property, which contains the name of the form; and the action and method properties, which contain information about what action should be triggered with the form (or to what URL the form data should be sent) and what HTTP method should be used for this purpose (POST or GET). Listing 7.3 shows some examples of the form in Listing 7.1.

```
const form = document.getElementById('login');
console.log(form.elements);        // Form elements, details to follow
console.log(form.length);          // Number of form elements
console.log(form.name);            // Name of the form, "login" in this case
console.log(form.action);          // Content of the "action" attribute
console.log(form.method);          // HTTP method, "post" in this case
```

Listing 7.3 Access to Selected Properties of a Form

7.1.2   Accessing Form Elements

To access individual form elements within a form, you have the following options:

- Using the methods for selecting elements, like getElementById(), getElementsByClassName(), getElementsByTagName(), getElementsByName(), querySelector(), and querySelectorAll()
- Using the elements property of the respective form object

Listing 7.4 shows some corresponding examples. Selection via the DOM selection methods is nothing new, so we'll move directly to the elements property provided by each form object. It stores a list of the form elements that are contained within the respective form. Individual elements in thisl list are accessed via the index, which (as with the forms property, discussed in Section 7.1.1) also reflects the position of the respective element within the form.

```
// 1.) Access via DOM selection methods
const fieldUserNameById = document.getElementById('username');
const fieldPasswordById = document.getElementById('password');
const fieldRememberById = document.getElementById('remember');
const buttonSubmitById = document.getElementById('submit');
console.log(fieldUserNameById.id);    // "username"
console.log(fieldPasswordById.id);    // "password"
console.log(fieldRememberById.id);    // "remember"
console.log(buttonSubmitById.id);     // "submit"

// 2.) Access via the elements property
const form = document.getElementById('login');
const formElements = form.elements;
console.log(formElements.length);      // 4
const fieldUserName = formElements[0];
const fieldPassword = formElements[1];
const fieldRemember = formElements[2];
const buttonSubmit = formElements[3];
console.log(fieldUserName.id);         // "username"
console.log(fieldPassword.id);         // "password"
console.log(fieldRemember.id);         // "remember"
console.log(buttonSubmit.id);          // "submit"
```

Listing 7.4 Access to Form Elements

Therefore, the same advice we just gave you about accessing forms also applies to accessing form elements: access via the DOM selection methods is the option that's the most resilient against changes to the HTML code, while access via the elements property is the least resilient option. If the order of the form elements (i.e., the elements within a form) changes, you have to adapt the JavaScript code again and again.

Each form element is represented by a special object type, as shown in Table 7.1. As you can see, text fields, password fields, radio buttons, and checkboxes are all represented by the HTMLInputElement object type, text areas by the HTMLTextAreaElement object type, selection lists by the HTMLSelectElement object type, and individual options within selection lists by the HTMLOptionElement object type.

Object Type	Form Element
Password field	HTMLInputElement
Text field	HTMLInputElement
Radio button	HTMLInputElement
Checkbox	HTMLInputElement
Text area	HTMLTextAreaElement
Selection list	HTMLSelectElement
Option in selection list	HTMLOptionElement

Table 7.1 The Most Important Form Elements and Their Corresponding Object Types

---

JavaScript Objects for HTML Components

As noted in Chapter 5, the different HTML components are also represented by different JavaScript objects, each of which has specific properties and methods. In the previous sections, this was demonstrated using forms (e.g., using the HTMLFormElement, HTMLInputElement, or HTMLOptionElement type).

Let's now show you how to access the individual form elements in the following sections.

7.1.3   Reading the Value of Text Fields and Password Fields

To access the value of a text field, you can use the value property of the corresponding element. An example of this is shown in Listing 7.5. Here, the two input fields of the opening example are accessed (the text field and the password field), and an event listener is registered for the change event, which is triggered whenever the value of an input field changes.

Within the event listener, the this keyword enables access to the respective element at which the event listener was triggered. In other words, the element for which an event listener has been registered represents its execution context. Plus, you'll notice that the text stored in the value property is stored in plain text, even for the password field; that is, it isn't encrypted in any way (both text fields and password fields are of the HTMLInputElement type).

```
const inputUsername = document.getElementById('username');
const inputPassword = document.getElementById('password');
inputUsername.addEventListener('change', function(e) {
```

```
  console.log(this.value);             // entered value
});
inputPassword.addEventListener('change', function(e) {
  console.log(this.value);             // entered value
});
```

Listing 7.5 Access to the Values of Text and Password Fields

However, there is one thing you must keep in mind when using this within an event listener: if the event listener was expressed as an arrow function, then this refers not to the element on which the event listener was defined, but to the context in which the arrow function was defined (see also Chapter 3).

Therefore, to access a form element within an event listener defined as an arrow function, there are two other ways: on the one hand, you can cache the corresponding form element in a variable and access it (an example is shown in Listing 7.6).

```
const inputUsername = document.getElementById('username');
const inputPassword = document.getElementById('password');
inputUsername.addEventListener('change', (e) => {
  console.log(inputUsername.value);    // entered value
  console.log(this.value);             // undefined
});
inputPassword.addEventListener('change', (e) => {
  console.log(inputPassword.value);    // entered value
  console.log(this.value);             // undefined
});
```

Listing 7.6 Within Event Listeners Defined via an Arrow Function, this Does Not Refer to the Respective Element

On the other hand, you can use the event object to access the respective form element. You already know how to do this from the previous chapter, but for the sake of completeness, it's illustrated once again in Listing 7.7.

```
inputUsername.addEventListener('change', (e) => {
  console.log(e.target.value);         // entered value
});
inputPassword.addEventListener('change', (e) => {
  console.log(e.target.value);         // entered value
});
```

Listing 7.7 Access via the Event Object

7.1.4 Reading the Value of Checkboxes

Checkboxes are read in a similar way as text fields and password fields. Here too the value of the checkbox can be accessed via the value property (by default, this property has the value on). To check whether the checkbox has been selected (i.e., been checked or not), however, you use the checked property, which returns a corresponding Boolean value. An example is shown in Listing 7.8.

```
const checkbox = document.getElementById('remember');
checkbox.addEventListener('change', (e) => {
  console.log(checkbox.value);    // by default, the "on" value
  console.log(checkbox.checked);  // true or false
});
```

Listing 7.8 Access to a Checkbox

7.1.5 Reading the Value of Radio Buttons

Typically, radio buttons always appear as a group within a web page. You probably know already that within a group of radio buttons, only one radio button can be selected at a time. The group to which a radio button belongs is determined by the value of the name attribute. The radio buttons shown in Listing 7.9, for example, all belong to the order group (see also Figure 7.2).

```
...
<body>
  <form id="orderform" name="orderform" class="form col-xs-12 center-block">
    <div class="form-group">
      <input type="radio" id="P001" name="order" value="P001">
        <label for="P001">Pizza Salami</label>
      </input>
    </div>
    <div class="form-group">
      <input type="radio" id="P002" name="order" value="P002">
        <label for="P002">Pizza Margherita</label>
      </input>
    </div>
    <div class="form-group">
      <input type="radio" id="P003" name="order" value="P003">
        <label for="P003">Pizza Tonno</label>
      </input>
    </div>
    <div class="form-group">
      <input type="radio" id="P004" name="order" value="P004">
        <label for="P004">Pizza Mozzarella</label>
      </input>
```

```
    </div>
    <div class="form-group">
      <input type="radio" id="P005" name="order" value="P005">
        <label for="P005">Pizza Hawaii</label>
      </input>
    </div>
  </form>
  <div class="form col-xs-12 center-block">
    Selection:
    <div id="selection">
    </div>
  </div>
</body>
...
```

Listing 7.9 HTML Code for Using Radio Buttons

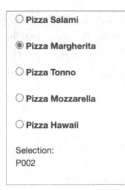

Figure 7.2 A Group of Radio Buttons

Listing 7.10 shows how to access the individual radio buttons within a group. The easi-est way to do this is to access the form's property that has the same name as the radio button group (in this case, the order property). In this property, all radio buttons of the group are stored as a list. In the example, we iterate over this list and register an event listener for each radio button. The latter ensures that when a radio button is selected (which triggers a change event), the value of the selected radio button (value property) is written to the <div> element with the ID selection (see also Figure 7.2).

```
const messageContainer = document
  .getElementById('selection');                    // Container for messages
const orderForm = document
  .getElementById('orderform');                    // Form
const radioButtons = orderForm.order;
for(let i=0; i<radioButtons.length; i++) {
  radioButtons[i].addEventListener('change', (e) => {
```

```
      console.log(e.target.value);                // e.g. "P002"
      messageContainer.innerText = e.target.value;  // Display message
  });
}
```

Listing 7.10 Access to the Radio Buttons of a Group

7.1.6 Reading the Value of Selection Lists

Next, let me show you how to access the values of a selection list. The selection list shown in Listing 7.11 serves as a basis.

```
...
<body>
  <form id="orderform" name="orderform" class="form col-xs-4 center-block">
    <select id="order" name="order" class="form-control">
      <option selected value="P001">Pizza Salami</option>
      <option value="P002">Pizza Margherita</option>
      <option value="P003">Pizza Tonno</option>
      <option value="P004">Pizza Mozzarella</option>
      <option value="P005">Pizza Hawaii</option>
    </select>
  </form>
  <div class="form col-xs-12 center-block">
    Selection:
    <div id="selection">
    </div>
  </div>
</body>
...
```

Listing 7.11 The HTML Code for the Selection List

It's also possible for selection lists to react to changes via the change event. This event is triggered whenever a value is selected in the selection list. Again, the value property is used to access the selected value. An example is shown in Listing 7.12. The updateOrder() function is registered as an event listener for the change event (this time not an arrow function, which is why the selection list can be accessed using this).

Among other things, selection lists have the selectedIndex property, which contains the index of the selected option. The item() method can be used to access the corresponding selection element (of type HTMLOptionElement) using this index. Each selection element has two properties that can be used to read the value of the underlying <option> element (value) and its text (text). (The latter is also contained in the value property of the selection list.)

```
function init() {
  const messageContainer = document
    .getElementById('selection');              // Container for messages
  const order = document.getElementById('order');   // <select> element
  order.addEventListener('change', updateOrder);    // Register listener

  function updateOrder(event) {                // this is of the ...
                                               // ... HTMLSelectElement type
    const value = this.value;                  // The currently selected value
    const index = this.selectedIndex;          // Index of the selected option
    const option = this.item(index);           // Selected <option> element
    const text = this.item(index).text;        // Text of the <option> element
    const message = text + ' (' + value + ')'; // Generate message
    messageContainer.innerText = message;      // Display message
  }
}
```

Listing 7.12 Access to the Selected Value of a Selection List

You can see the result of the example in Figure 7.3.

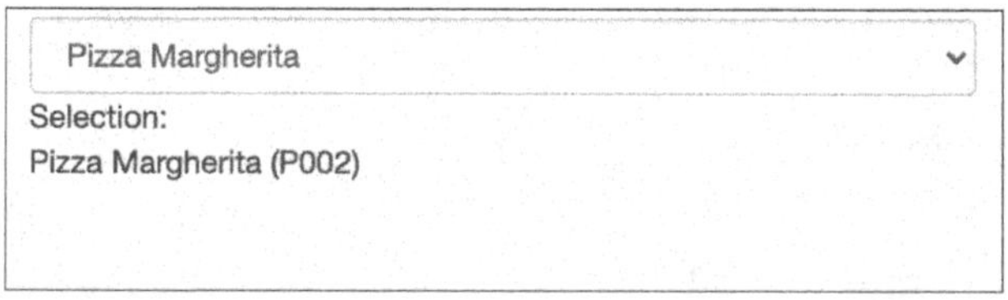

Figure 7.3 The Selected Value Is Displayed below the Selection List via JavaScript

7.1.7 Reading the Values of Multiple Selection Lists

As you know, the multiple attribute can be used in HTML to define selection lists in which several values can be selected—that is, *multiple selection lists* (see Listing 7.13).

```
...
<select id="order" name="order" size="4" multiple>
  <option selected value="P001">Pizza Salami</option>
  <option value="P002">Pizza Margherita</option>
  <option value="P003">Pizza Tonno</option>
  <option value="P004">Pizza Mozzarella</option>
  <option value="P005">Pizza Hawaii</option>
</select>
...
```

Listing 7.13 The HTML Code for the Selection List with Multiple Selection

In this case, however, the `selectedIndex` property used previously doesn't get you very far. Instead, you have to resort to the `selectedOptions` property, which contains a list of selected values (more precisely, an object of the `HTMLCollection` type, which, in turn, contains objects of the `HTMLOptionElement` type).

Listing 7.14 shows how to read all selected values using this property. You can see the result of the program in Figure 7.4.

```
...
function updateOrder(event) {
  while (messageContainer.firstChild) {         // delete all messages
    messageContainer.removeChild(
      messageContainer.firstChild
    );
  }
  const options = this.selectedOptions;         // selected options
  for (let i = 0; i < options.length; i++) {    // for each option ...
    const message = options[i].text             // ... generate ...
      + ' (' + options[i].value + ')';          // ... message ...
    const div = document.createElement('div');  // ... and add it ...
    const optionText = document                 //
      .createTextNode(message);                 //
    div.appendChild(optionText);                //
    messageContainer.appendChild(div);          // ... to container
  }
}
...
```

Listing 7.14 Access to All Selected Values of a Selection List

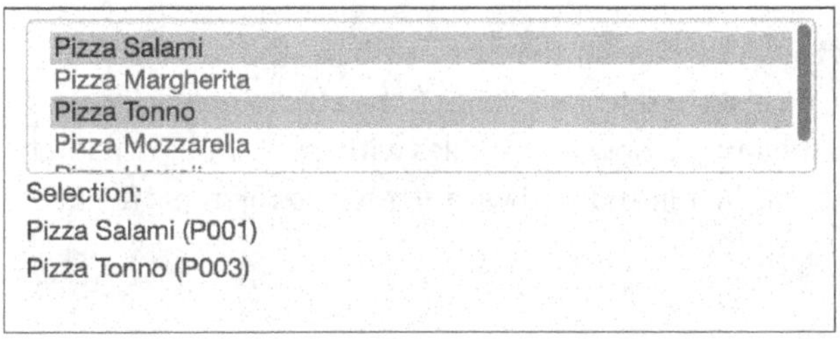
Pizza Salami
Pizza Margherita
Pizza Tonno
Pizza Mozzarella
Selection:
Pizza Salami (P001)
Pizza Tonno (P003)

Figure 7.4 All Selected Values Are Displayed below the Selection List via JavaScript

7.1.8 Populating Selection Lists with Values Using JavaScript

It can be helpful in some cases to generate the options within a dropdown list dynamically via JavaScript. To do this, you have the option of simply creating new object instances of the `Option` type and adding them to the corresponding selection list via the add() method. An example of this is shown in Listing 7.15. Based on the options array, which contains various objects, a counting loop is used to generate an entry for each of these objects and add it to the list.

```javascript
const messageContainer = document.getElementById('selection');
const order = document.getElementById('order');
const options = [
  {name: 'Pizza Salami', id: 'P001'},
  {name: 'Pizza Margherita', id: 'P002'},
  {name: 'Pizza Tonno', id: 'P003'},
  {name: 'Pizza Mozzarella', id: 'P004'},
  {name: 'Pizza Hawaii', id: 'P005'}
];
for(let i=0; i<options.length; i++) {
  order.add(
    new Option(         // constructor for <option> elements
      options[i].name,  // text to be displayed
      options[i].id,    // optional value associated with the selection
      false,            // optional specification that sets
                        // the "selected" attribute
      false             // optional specification of whether the value should
                        // be preselected
    )
  );
}
```

Listing 7.15 Adding Options to a Selection List via JavaScript

Selecting Files

If you assign <input> elements the value file for the type attribute, the corresponding form displays a button that can be used to select files (e.g., to be able to upload images or similar items via a form). We'll show you how to read files with JavaScript in Chapter 12. The process uses an API that was first introduced with HTML5, so the topic fits better in that chapter.

7.2   Programmatically Submitting and Resetting Forms

JavaScript offers the possibility to submit forms programmatically. For this purpose, the submit() method is available for form objects. In addition, the reset() method can be used to reset the values entered into a form.

To demonstrate the use of these methods, the default submit button from the preceding example has been replaced with two <span> elements in Listing 7.16 (see also Figure 7.5).

Listing 7.17 shows how to submit the form by calling the submit() method, and Listing 7.18 illustrates how the values of the form elements can be reset to the default values.

```
...
<body>
<form id="login" name="login" method="post" action="login.html"
  class="form col-xs-4 center-block">
  <div class="form-group">
    <label for="username">Username:</label>
    <input
      type="text"
      id="username"
      name="username"
      class="form-control"
      value=""
      placeholder="Username"
    >
  </div>
  <div class="form-group">
    <label for="password">Password:</label>
    <input
      type="password"
      id="password"
      name="password"
      class="form-control"
       value=""
      placeholder="Password"
    >
  </div>
  <div class="checkbox">
    <label for="remember">
      <input
        type="checkbox"
        id="remember"
        name="remember"
        value="on"
      >
      Remember login on this computer
    </label>
  </div>
  <span
    type="submit"
    id="submit"
    name="submit"
```

```
      class="btn btn-primary btn-block"
    >
      Login
    </span>
    <span
      type="reset"
      id="reset"
      name="reset"
      class="btn btn-default btn-block"
      >
      Reset
    </span>
</form>
</body>
...
```

Listing 7.16 The Adapted Login Form

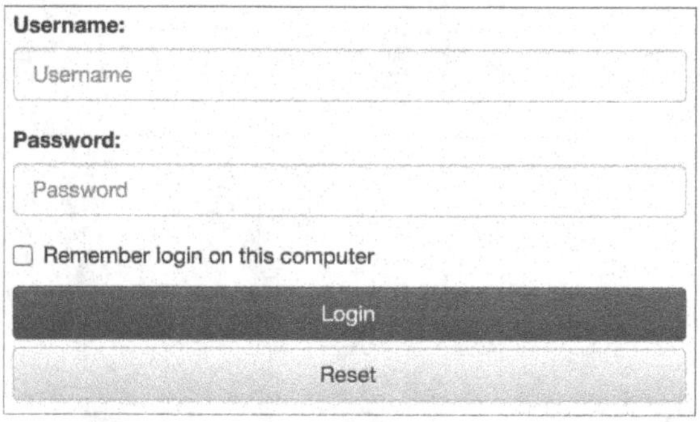

Figure 7.5 The Extended Login Form

```
const loginForm = document.getElementById('login');
const loginButton = document.getElementById('submit');
loginButton.addEventListener('click', (e) => {
  loginForm.submit();
});
```

Listing 7.17 Submitting a Form Programmatically

```
const loginForm = document.getElementById('login');
const resetButton = document.getElementById('reset');
resetButton.addEventListener('click', (e) => {
  loginForm.reset();
});
```

Listing 7.18 Resetting a Form Programmatically

Be Careful When Choosing Names for Form Elements

Note that submitting a form using the submit() method will not work if there is an element named submit in the form. To understand this, remember that within a form, the individual form elements can also be accessed by their names (Section 7.1.1). If you now use the submit value for a form element, the submit() method of the form is overwritten. (The same applies to the reset() method and other methods of forms not discussed here.)

Naturally, it immediately follows that you should only use the name submit for form elements if you definitely do not want to make use of the submit() method.

7.3   Validating Form Inputs

We showed you a simple example of validating forms or values entered in form fields in Chapter 6. But as mentioned in that chapter, validating input fields with HTML5 is a lot easier because it already offers some native validation options.

Definition

The term *native* in the context of programming languages or in the context of HTML means something like *built into the language* or *included in the language scope*. So, native validation in HTML5 means that it's already included in the language and doesn't need to be implemented by JavaScript.

Listing 7.19 shows an example of a simple registration form that uses appropriate attributes to trigger the native validation: the fields for entering the user name and email address, for example, are marked as required by the required attribute, and the latter is also marked by the type attribute (with the value email) as a field that only accepts email addresses. The field for entering the website uses the value of the type attribute to only allow (valid) URLs to be entered, and the field for entering the age only accepts numeric values (via the value number of the type attribute) within a specific range of values (defined by the min and max attributes).

```
...
<form id="register" name="register" method="post" action="register.html">
  <div class="form-group">
    <label for="username">Username:</label>
    <input
      type="text"
      id="username"
      name="username"
      required
      class="form-control"
```

```
      >
    </div>
    <div class="form-group">
    <label for="email">E-mail:</label>
    <input
      type="email"
      id="email"
      name="email"
      required
      class="form-control"
    >
    </div>
        <div class="form-group">
    <label for="url">Website:</label>
    <input
      type="url"
      id="website"
      name="website"
      class="form-control"
    >
    </div>
    <div class="form-group">
      <label for="age">Age:</label>
      <input
      type="number"
      id="age"
      name="age"
      min="18"
      max="99"
      value="18"
      class="form-control"
    >
    </div>
    <button
      type="submit"
      id="submit"
      name="submit"
      class="btn btn-primary btn-block"
    >
      Login
    </button>
</form>
...
```

Listing 7.19 Example of Native HTML5 Validation

Without a single line of JavaScript, you already have a working validation for such standard cases. If, for example, you leave the field for entering the email address empty and try to submit the form, the browser generates a corresponding (but very general) error message and applies the CSS rules defined for the CSS pseudoclass :invalid (see Figure 7.6 and Figure 7.7).

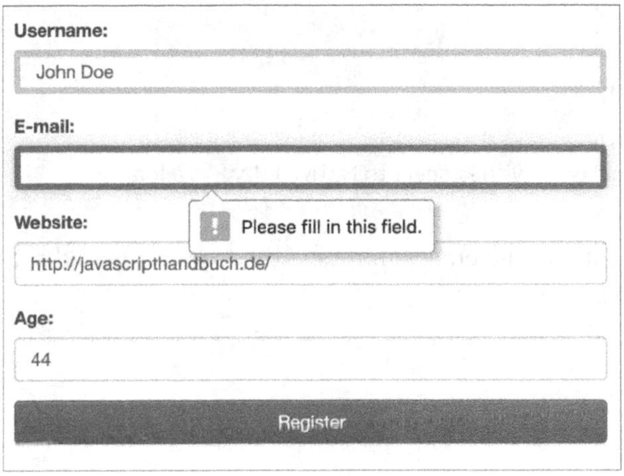

Figure 7.6 Native Validation in HTML5

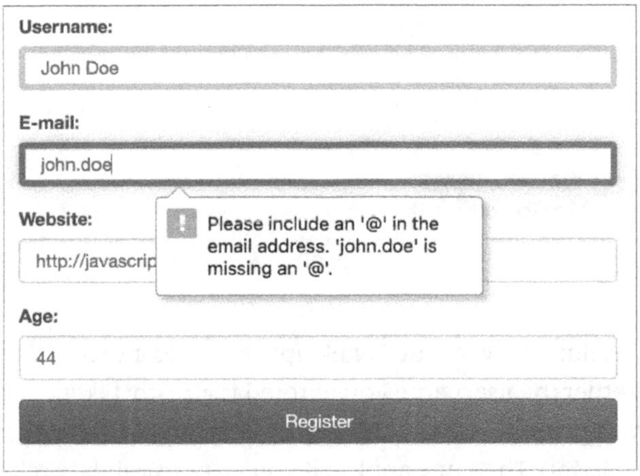

Figure 7.7 Depending on the Cause of the Error, There Are Different Messages for a Form Field

For form elements with valid values, the CSS rules for the :valid CSS pseudoclass are applied accordingly (in the example, this is the field for entering the username).

CSS Pseudoclasses for Forms

The :required, :invalid, and :valid CSS pseudoclasses can be used to define CSS rules that influence the appearance of the form elements, as shown in Listing 7.20. The :required pseudoclass denotes those form elements that have been marked as required fields, the `:invalid` pseudoclass denotes those form elements that contain invalid values, and the `:valid` pseudoclass denotes those form elements that contain valid values.

```
input:required:invalid, input:focus:invalid {
    border: thick solid red;
 }
input:required:valid {
    border: thick solid lightgreen;
}
```

Listing 7.20 Usage of CSS Pseudoclasses with Respect to Native HTML5 Validation

Figure 7.8 shows the same form with a valid email address. If the form is now submitted, it will work without problems.

Figure 7.8 The Form with Valid Values

However, as mentioned earlier, validation without JavaScript is not as flexible. For example, if you want to check whether the username you entered is already taken, you can't do this with HTML alone (you probably need a database query to do this, which you can only formulate using JavaScript). The same applies if you want to validate relationships between individual form elements—for example, whether two input fields contain the same value. Regarding the error messages and their appearance, you are also highly restricted with pure HTML.

Thanks to the Constraint Validation API (*https://html.spec.whatwg.org/multipage/forms.html#the-constraint-validation-api*), however, the native validation of HTML5 can also be controlled via JavaScript, and thus validation information can be accessed and validated much more flexibly. For this purpose, the Constraint Validation API defines various properties and methods that are available for forms and form elements (see Table 7.2).

Property	Description
willValidate	Returns an indication of whether validation is enabled or not for a form element. Set to true by default. If a form element is disabled via the disabled attribute, this property contains the value false. For other elements, such as <div> elements, the property returns the value undefined.
validity	Contains an object of type ValidityState, which, in turn, contains detailed information about the validity of the data entered into the corresponding form element. This information is listed in Table 7.3.
validationMessage	Contains the validation message displayed by the browser in case the entered data is invalid. This message differs depending on the browser. For the example just given, Chrome and Opera, for example, return the value Fill in this field., Firefox returns the value Please fill in this field. (a bit friendlier), and Safari simply returns the value Value missing (less friendly).

Table 7.2 Properties Related to Native Validation

The willValidate property provides information about whether validation is activated for a form element or not, the validationMessage property contains a corresponding error message in case of a validation error, and the validity property can be used to draw conclusions about the cause of the error. This property contains an object with various properties, each of which contains Boolean values (see Table 7.3)—for example, valueMissing for missing inputs, tooShort or tooLong for values below or above minimum or maximum length, or rangeUnderflow and rangeOverflow for values outside a defined value range.

Property	Description
Valid	Returns an indication of whether an input field contains an error or not
valueMissing	Returns an indication of whether an input field is a required field that does not contain any value
typeMismatch	Returns an indication of whether the required type of an input field (e.g., an email address) is not met by the entered value
patternMismatch	Returns an indication of whether the entered value matches the defined pattern or not
tooLong	Returns an indication of whether the entered value is too long
tooShort	Returns an indication of whether the entered value is too short

Table 7.3 Overview of the Properties Related to the Validation of Forms

Property	Description
rangeUnderflow	Returns an indication of whether the entered value is below the defined range of values
rangeOverflow	Returns an indication of whether the entered value is above the defined range of values
stepMismatch	Returns an indication of whether the entered value matches the definition of the step attribute
badInput	Returns an indication of whether the entered value is invalid
customError	Returns an indication of whether the entered value triggers a user-defined error

Table 7.3 Overview of the Properties Related to the Validation of Forms (Cont.)

Listing 7.21 provides an example of using native validation in JavaScript. There, an event listener for the change event has been registered on the text field for entering the email address. Within the event listener, some of the properties discussed previously are output.

```
function init() {
  const emailElement = document.getElementById('email');
  emailElement.addEventListener('change', validateEmail);
}

function validateEmail(e) {
  const event = (e ? e : window.event);                // Event
  const emailElement = (event.target                   // Target element
    ? event.target
    : event.srcElement);
  console.log(emailElement.willValidate);              // true
  console.log(emailElement.validity);                  // ValidityState: ...
  console.log(emailElement.validity.valueMissing);     // ... Value present?
  console.log(emailElement.validity.valid);            // ... Value valid?
  console.log(emailElement.validationMessage);         // Validation message
}

document.addEventListener('DOMContentLoaded', init);
```

Listing 7.21 Output of the Validation Data

The example can be made a little more practical—for example, to display the corresponding error message below the input field in case of an error (see Figure 7.9).

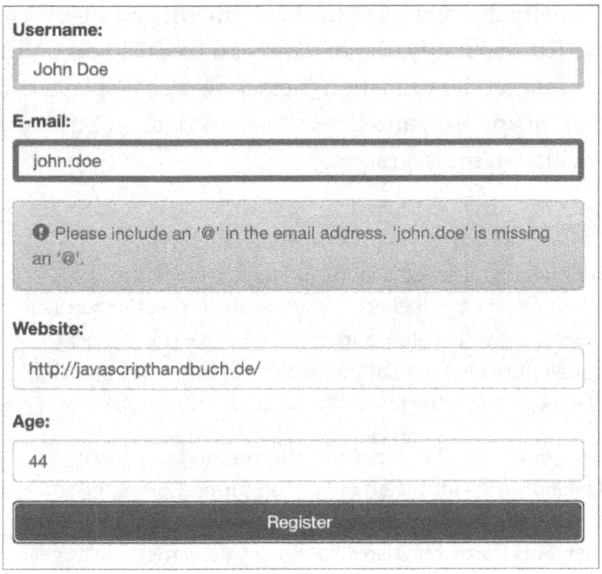

Figure 7.9 This Is Displayed Below the Input Field Instead of the Default Output for the Validation Message

Listing 7.22 shows the corresponding JavaScript code (as usual, the HTML code can be found in the download area for the book).

Depending on whether the input field contains a valid value (recognizable by the `emailElement.validity.valid` property), the validation message is displayed in the corresponding container element, if applicable.

```
function validateEmail(e) {
  ...

  const errorContainer = document.getElementById('email-error');
  const messageContainer = errorContainer.querySelector('.error-message');
  if(!emailElement.validity.valid) {
    messageContainer.textContent = emailElement.validationMessage;
    errorContainer.style.display = 'block';
  } else {
    messageContainer.textContent = '';
    errorContainer.style.display = 'none';
  }
}
```

Listing 7.22 Displaying the Validation Message below the Input Field

In addition to the mentioned properties, forms and form elements also have some methods related to validation thanks to the Constraint Validation API (see Table 7.4).

For example, the checkValidity() method can be used to check whether a single form element or an entire form is valid (consequently, the method can be called on both), the reportValidity() method ensures that the validation message is also displayed (in its default appearance) in the event of an error, and the setCustomValidity() method enables you to define your own validation messages.

Method	Description
checkValidity()	This method can be called on individual form elements or on forms. In the first case, it checks whether the respective form element contains a valid value, and in the second case, it checks whether all form elements of the respective form contain valid values. In both cases, the result is a Boolean value.
reportValidity()	Like the checkValidity() method, this method can also be called on individual form elements or on forms. Compared to checkValidity(), however, it not only checks the validity of the form elements/form, but also displays any validation messages (in their default appearance) in the browser.
setCustomValidity()	This method enables you to write a customized validation message.

Table 7.4 Methods Related to Native Validation

Listing 7.23 shows a real-world example of using setCustomValidity(). The form has been extended by a second text field that prompts a user to enter their email address a second time in order to counteract the input of a valid but incorrect email address. The validateEmail() function is registered at both input fields as an event listener for the change event and checks if the content of both input fields is the same. If this is not the case, a corresponding error message is set via setCustomValidity() (on the other hand, calling this method with an empty string means that the validation was successful). You can see the results of the program in Figure 7.10 (validation failed) and Figure 7.11 (validation successful).

```
function init() {
  const emailElement = document.getElementById('email');
  const emailElement2 = document.getElementById('email2');
  emailElement.addEventListener('change', validateEmail);
  emailElement2.addEventListener('change', validateEmail);
}

function validateEmail(e) {
  const emailElement = document.getElementById('email');
  const emailElement2 = document.getElementById('email2');
```

```
  if (emailElement.value !== emailElement2.value) {
    emailElement.setCustomValidity('E-mails must match.');
    emailElement2.setCustomValidity('E-mails must match.');
  } else {
    emailElement.setCustomValidity('');
    emailElement2.setCustomValidity('');
  }

  const errorContainer = document.getElementById('email-error');
  const messageContainer = errorContainer.querySelector('.error-message');
  if(!emailElement.validity.valid) {
    messageContainer.textContent = emailElement.validationMessage;
    errorContainer.style.display = 'block';
  } else {
    messageContainer.textContent = '';
    errorContainer.style.display = 'none';
  }
}

document.addEventListener('DOMContentLoaded', init);
```

Listing 7.23 Checking if Two Input Fields Contain the Same Value

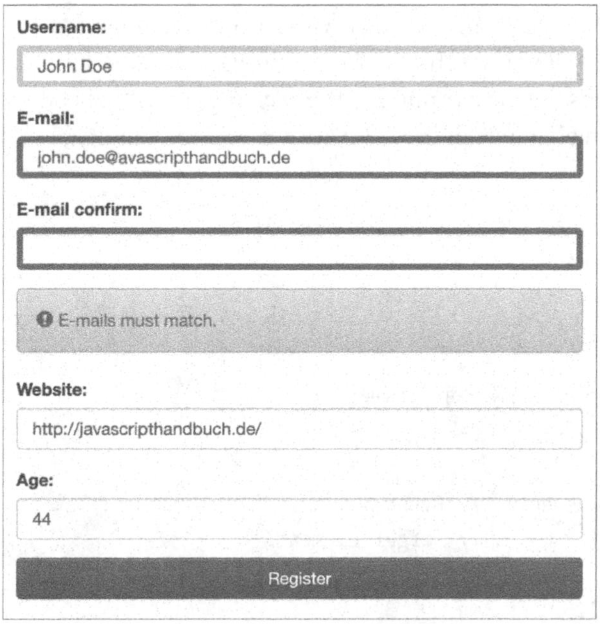

Figure 7.10 Example of a Validation That Cannot Be Implemented Using Only HTML

Figure 7.11 Only if Both Email Fields Contain the Same Value Is the Validation Successful

If, on the other hand, you want to trigger the native validation with JavaScript only after a form has been submitted or the corresponding submit button has been pressed, you have to set the noValidate property to true, as shown in Listing 7.24. By default, the native validation is performed *before* the submit event is triggered. This means that the browser's default outputs (including the standard validation messages) are displayed first, before you have the option to perform your own validations and generate customized outputs via JavaScript. But if you set the noValidate property to true, as in the example, you disable the browser's default output. (By the way, the rest of the code in the example ensures that all form elements of the form are checked for validity.)

```
function init() {
  const registerForm = document.getElementById('register');
  registerForm.noValidate = true;
  registerForm.addEventListener('submit', validateForm);
}

document.addEventListener('DOMContentLoaded', init);

function validateForm(e) {
  const event = (e ? e : window.event); // Event
  const form = (event.target           // Target element
          ? event.target
          : event.srcElement);
  let formIsValid = true;               // Validity of the form
  const formElements =                  // Form elements ...
```

```
    form.querySelectorAll(              // ... that support ...
      'input, textarea, select');       // ... native validation
  for (let i = 0; i < formElements.length; i++) {
    const formElement = formElements[i];
    if (formElement.willValidate !== 'undefined') {
      formElement.checkValidity();
    } else {
                                        // Browser does not support
                                        // native HTML5 validation.
    }
    if (!formElement.validity.valid) {  // If the value is not valid ...
      formIsValid = false;              // ... the form data is not valid.
    }
  }
  if (!formIsValid) {                   // If the form data is not valid ...
    if (event.preventDefault) {         // ...
      event.preventDefault();           // ... prevent default actions.
    }
  }
  return formIsValid;
}
```

Listing 7.24 Validating All Form Fields within a Form

7.4   Summary

In this chapter, you learned how to work with forms. You learned how to read values from the different type of form elements, how to validate form data, and how to submit forms. The following are the most important points to remember from this chapter:

- Forms within a web page can be selected in several ways: via the familiar DOM selection methods, via the forms property of the document object, and via properties of the document object that correspond to the name of the respective form.

- To avoid having to modify your JavaScript code when making changes regarding the order of forms on a web page, you should usually use DOM selection methods such as getElementById() or querySelector() to select forms.

- Individual form elements within a form can also be selected in different ways: via the DOM selection methods and via the elements property of the respective form.

- Accessing the values of individual form elements is generally quite similar. The values of text fields, password fields, checkboxes, and radio buttons can be accessed via the value property. In the case of the latter two, the checked property also can be used to check whether the respective element is selected or not.

- The `submit()` method can be used to submit forms via JavaScript, while the `reset()` method resets them to their default values.

- The Constraint Validation API is available for validating form inputs. Using this API, you can use the native HTML5 validations and perform your own validations.

Chapter 8
Controlling Browsers and Reading Browser Information

In addition to the Document Object Model, which you learned about in Chapter 5, browsers provide a second special object model that you can use to access browser-relevant information via JavaScript. In this chapter, we'll use this model to show you how to access window information, how to influence the navigation panel and browsing history, and how to identify the browser.

In browser runtime environments, the Browser Object Model (BOM or BOM API) is available in addition to the DOM. Through this object model, it's possible to control certain aspects of the browser (such as going back and forth in the browsing history) and to read certain information from the browser (such as information about the size and position of the current browser window).

8.1 The Browser Object Model

The entry point for the Browser Object Model is the global window object, as shown in Figure 8.1. This object represents a single browser window (or more precisely, a single browser tab as each browser tab contains its own object instance).

This global object is also the entry point to the Document Object Model (see Chapter 5), which, as you know, is represented by the document object. Strictly speaking, the latter is actually a property of the window object, but it's also implicitly provided as a global object by browsers (so you can write both document and window.document).

The standard JavaScript objects, like Object, Array, and Function, which we discussed in Chapter 4, are properties of the window object as well, but they're also available as global variables.

In addition, the window object also provides the entry point to various HTML5 Web APIs—for example, the Geolocation API, the Storage API, and many more, which we'll discuss in Chapter 12.

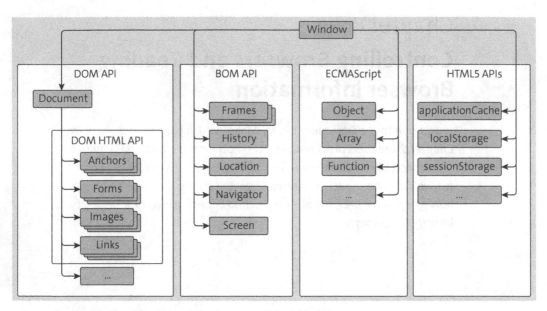

Figure 8.1 Classification of the Browser Object Model

In this chapter, however, we'll only deal with the BOM API for the time being. Specifically, we'll introduce the following five topics that result directly from the properties of the window object:

- First, there are some properties that contain concrete information regarding the browser window and methods that can be used to open various dialog boxes. We'll discuss these properties and methods in Section 8.2.

- Secondly, the location property contains information about the current URL of the browser window (Section 8.3). This property allows you to access the various components of the current URL.

- The history property contains a reference to an object of the History type. This allows you to access and modify the browsing history (Section 8.4).

- The navigator property contains a reference to an object of the navigator type. This object provides general information of the browser, like its name, manufacturer details, and so on (Section 8.5).

- The screen property contains a reference to an object of the Screen type, which you can use to retrieve information about the screen, like its height and width, color depth, pixel depth, and so on (Section 8.6).

Background Information

Strictly speaking, the window object represents the global object defined in ECMAScript and thus also has all the properties (undefined, NaN, etc.) and methods (parseFloat(), parseInt(), etc.) that are defined in the standard for this object and that you already

---

learned about in Chapter 3. The fact that the window object represents the global object is, in turn, the reason that all properties and methods of the window object are also available globally (and you don't always have to prepend window when accessing it).

8.2   Accessing Window Information

Let's start by introducing the general properties of the window object for accessing window information, as well as the methods provided by the window object.

8.2.1   Determining the Size and Position of a Browser Window

To determine the size and position of a browser window, there is a whole set of properties that provide every conceivable dimension (see Figure 8.2). The outerHeight and outerWidth properties represent the height and width of the browser window, including all displayed browser bars. The innerHeight and innerWidth properties, on the other hand, represent the height and width without the browser bars, but including scrollbars.

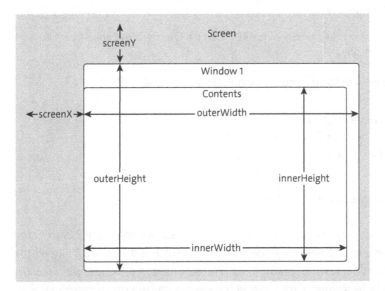

Figure 8.2 Size and Position Information of a Browser Window (or Browser Tab)

You can use the screenX and screenY properties to find out where the browser window is located horizontally and vertically on the screen. You can use the scrollX and scrollY properties to determine how far the content of the browser window has been scrolled horizontally and vertically (alternatively, simply use pageXOffset and pageYOffset). An overview of these properties can be found in Table 8.1, and some examples are shown in Listing 8.1.

Property	Description
innerHeight	Contains the height of the window content, including (if shown) the horizontal scrollbar but excluding other browser bars
innerWidth	Contains the width of the window content, including (if shown) the vertical scrollbar but excluding other browser bars
outerHeight	Contains the height of the browser window, including all browser bars
outerWidth	Contains the width of the browser window, including all browser bars
pageXOffset	An alias for window.scrollX
pageYOffset	An alias for window.scrollY
screenX	Contains the position of the browser window on the x-axis—in other words, the distance of the browser window from the left edge of the screen
screenY	Contains the position of the browser window on the y-axis—in other words, the distance of the browser window from the top of the screen
scrollX	Contains the number of pixels the web page has already been scrolled horizontally
scrollY	Contains the number of pixels the web page has already been scrolled vertically

Table 8.1 Properties Relevant to Size and Position of the window Object

```
console.log(window.innerHeight);   // e.g. 600
console.log(window.innerWidth);    // e.g. 1134
console.log(window.screenX);       // e.g. 100
console.log(window.screenY);       // e.g. 22
```

Listing 8.1 Determining the Size and Position of a Browser Window

You can also use the scrollX and scrollY properties (not shown in Figure 8.2) to determine how far the content of a web page has scrolled horizontally and vertically within the browser window. You saw an example of this in Chapter 6, where we used the scrollY property to fade elements into the web page depending on the vertical scroll position.

8.2.2   Changing the Size and Position of a Browser Window

Of course, you can not only determine the size and position of a browser window, but also resize a browser window and change its position on the screen. For this purpose, the window object offers various methods (see also Listing 8.2): The moveBy() method can be used to move a browser window horizontally and vertically by a specified number of pixels, and the moveTo() method can be used to move the window to a specific position. Via the resizeBy() method, you can scale a browser window by a certain factor, and via the resizeTo() method you can scale to a certain size. The scrollTo() method scrolls the window contents to a specified position, and the scrollBy() method scrolls the window contents by a specified horizontal and vertical number of pixels. An overview of all these methods can be found in Table 8.2.

```
// Move browser window by 200 pixels both horizontally and vertically
window.moveBy(200, 200);
// Move browser window to position (200, 200)
window.moveTo(200, 200);
// Enlarge browser window by 200 pixels in width and height
window.resizeBy(200, 200);
// Shrink browser window by 200 pixels in width and height
window.resizeBy(-200, -200);
// Move browser content by 200 pixels both horizontally and vertically
window.scrollBy(200, 200);
// Move browser content to position (200, 200)
window.scrollTo(200, 200);
```

Listing 8.2 Changing the Size and Position of a Browser Window

Method	Description
moveBy()	Moves the current browser window horizontally and vertically by a specified number of pixels. The first parameter determines the horizontal, the second parameter the vertical movement in pixels.
moveTo()	Moves the current browser window horizontally and vertically to a specified position. The first parameter determines the horizontal, the second parameter the vertical position in pixels.
resizeBy()	Scales the current browser window horizontally and vertically by a specified number of pixels. The first parameter determines the horizontal scaling value, the second parameter the vertical scaling value.
resizeTo()	Scales the current browser window horizontally and vertically to a specified size. The first parameter determines the width, the second parameter the height.
scroll()	Scrolls the window contents to a specified position. The first parameter indicates the horizontal position, the second parameter the vertical position.

Table 8.2 The Methods of the window Object to Define the Size and Position of the Browser Window and the Window Content

Method	Description
scrollBy()	Scrolls the window content by a specified factor. The first parameter specifies the horizontal scroll factor, the second parameter specifies the vertical scroll factor.
scrollTo()	Scrolls the window contents to a specified position. The first parameter indicates the horizontal position, the second parameter the vertical position.

Table 8.2 The Methods of the window Object to Define the Size and Position of the Browser Window and the Window Content (Cont.)

8.2.3   Accessing Display Information of the Browser Bars

A browser window typically consists of various components (see Figure 8.3). In addition to the content area that displays the web page, there is an address bar in which you can enter a URL (or in most modern browsers, also a search term, which then starts the pre-configured search engine); a status bar that indicates, among other things, whether a web page has been loaded or is in the process of being loaded; a menu bar; a toolbar; a "personal" bar (containing bookmarks, for example); and, last but not least, scrollbars, which display the horizontal and vertical position of the respective web page.

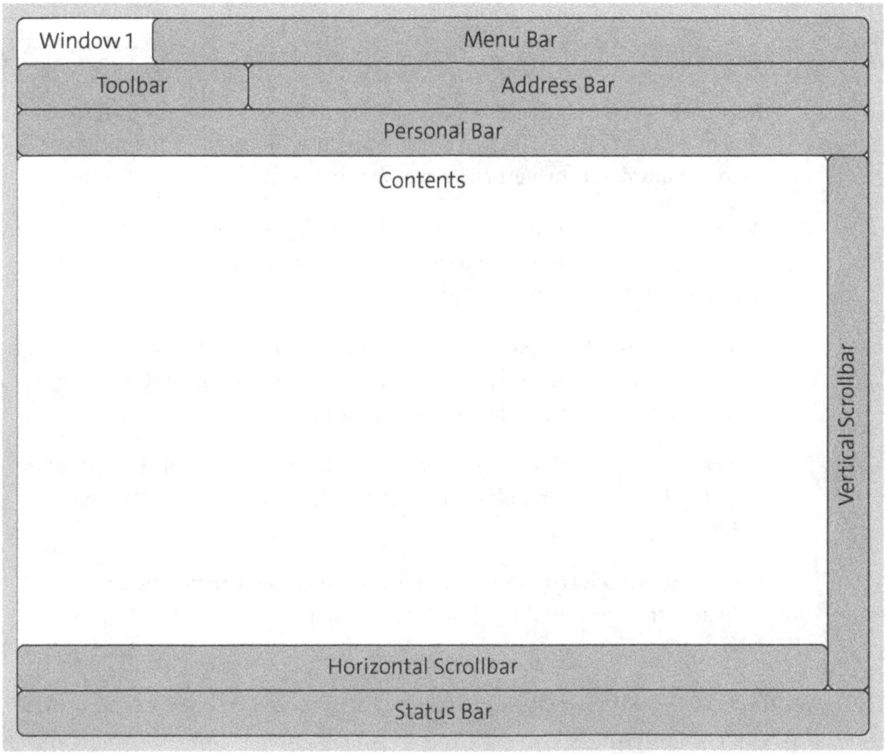

Figure 8.3 Structure of a Browser Window (or Browser Tab)

You can find out whether these browser bars are displayed or not using the properties listed in Table 8.3.

Property	Description
`locationbar`	Contains a reference to an object that provides information about whether the address bar is displayed or not
`menubar`	Contains a reference to an object that provides information about whether the menu bar is displayed or not
`personalbar`	Contains a reference to an object that provides information about whether the personal bar (e.g., the bookmark bar) is displayed or not
`scrollbars`	Contains a reference to an object that provides information about whether the scrollbars are displayed or not
`statusbar`	Contains a reference to an object that provides information about whether the status bar is displayed or not
`toolbar`	Contains a reference to an object that provides information about whether the toolbar is displayed or not

Table 8.3 Properties of the window Object with Respect to the Various Browser Bars

8.2.4 Determining General Properties

In addition to the properties presented in the previous sections, there are a few more properties that we'll briefly mention here (see Table 8.4). The name property, for example, contains the name of the browser window. This does not refer to the title of the loaded web page (which can be determined via document.title), but to a name that identifies the browser window as such (see also Section 8.2.5).

The opener property contains a reference to the browser window (object) from which the current browser window has been opened (again, Section 8.2.5). The self property, however, contains a reference to the window object itself. If you want to access the current window object within event listeners, this is particularly interesting to avoid conflicts with the this keyword.

Property	Description
`name`	Contains the name of the window.
`opener`	If you open a browser window from another browser window via JavaScript (Section 8.2.5), this property contains a reference to the original window.
`self`	Contains a reference to an object representing the current browser window.

Table 8.4 General Properties of the window Object

8.2.5   Opening New Browser Windows

The open() method is available for opening a new browser window. An example of this is shown in Listing 8.3. The first argument you pass to the method is the URL of the web page that you want to open in the new window. As a second argument, you can optionally specify the name of the new window (not to be confused with the name of the web page). In addition, the third argument gives you the possibility to influence the appearance and behavior of the window. You can pass a string consisting of the properties shown in Table 8.5. The value of the respective property is directly appended to the property using an equal sign; several property-value pairs are separated by commas.

In Listing 8.3, for example, a browser window is created with a width of 500 pixels (width property) and a height of 500 pixels (height property), which is resizable (resizable property) and has scrollbars and a status bar (scrollbars and status properties). For the latter properties, and generally for those properties that can take only one of two states, the allowed values are yes and no (in the resizable example) and 1 and 0 (in the scrollbars example). Alternatively, the value can be omitted, in which case the presence of the property name is evaluated as yes or 1 (in the status example).

```
const linkOpen = document.getElementById('link-open');
linkOpen.addEventListener('click', (e) => {
  const url = document.getElementById('url').value;
  window.open(
    url,                    // URL to open
    'Window title',         // Name of the window
    'width=500,' +          // Width of the window
    'height=500,' +         // Height of the window
    'resizable=yes,' +      // Resizing possible
    'scrollbars=1,' +       // Scrollbar enabled
    'status'                // Status bar enabled
  );
});
```

Listing 8.3 Opening a Browser Window

Parameter	Meaning
height	The height of the new browser window in pixels
innerHeight	The height of the display area of the new browser window in pixels
innerWidth	The width of the display area of the new browser window in pixels
left	Distance of the upper left corner of the new browser window to the left edge of the screen in pixels

Table 8.5 Selected Parameters for Opening Browser Windows

Parameter	Meaning
location	Indication of whether the new browser window should have an address bar or not
menubar	Indication of whether the new browser window should have a menu bar or not
resizable	Indication of whether the new browser window is resizable or not
screenX	Distance of the upper left corner of the new browser window to the left edge of the screen in pixels
screenY	Distance of the upper left corner of the new browser window to the top of the screen in pixels
scrollbars	Indication of whether the new browser window should have a scrollbar or not
status	Indication of whether the new browser window should have a status bar or not
toolbar	Indication of whether the new browser window should have a toolbar or not
top	Distance of the upper left corner of the new browser window to the top of the screen in pixels
width	The width of the new browser window in pixels

Table 8.5 Selected Parameters for Opening Browser Windows (Cont.)

8.2.6 Closing the Browser Window

Analogous to the open() method, you can also use the close() method to close a browser window again. Listing 8.4 shows an example that extends the previous example with a button (linkClose). In the event listener for the linkOpen button, the open browser window is saved (you can see that the open() method returns an object representing the open browser window). Inside the event listener for the linkClose button, the close() method is called on this object, closing the previously opened browser window again.

```
const windowReference;
const linkOpen = document.getElementById('link-open');
const linkClose = document.getElementById('link-close');
linkOpen.addEventListener('click', (e) => {
  const url = document.getElementById('url').value;
  windowReference = window.open(
    url,
    'Window title',
```

```
      'width=500,height=500,resizable,scrollbars=yes,status=1'
   );
});
linkClose.addEventListener('click', (e) => {
   windowReference.close();
});
```

Listing 8.4 Closing a Browser Window

> **Opening the Browser Window via JavaScript**
>
> Although we just showed you how it works, we advise against opening browser windows via JavaScript. Such windows always have the negative connotation of annoying advertising windows. They are ignored by most browsers by default and not opened until users have given their consent.

8.2.7   Opening Dialogs

In addition to the methods presented so far for opening and closing browser windows, the window object offers further methods (for a small selection, see Table 8.6). You already know about three of them from the previous chapters: you can use the alert() method to open alert dialogs, the confirm() method to open confirmation dialogs, and the prompt() method to open dialogs in which you can enter text.

In addition, the find() method can be used to search for text within a web page, and the print() method can be used to print the contents of the current web page (see Figure 8.4).

Method	Description
alert()	Opens a dialog with a message
close()	Closes the browser window (Section 8.2.6)
confirm()	Opens a dialog with a message
find()	Searches for a string in the browser window
open()	Creates a new browser window (Section 8.2.5)
print()	Opens a dialog for printing the window contents
prompt()	Opens a dialog that allows users to enter text

Table 8.6 Methods of the window Object for Opening Dialogs

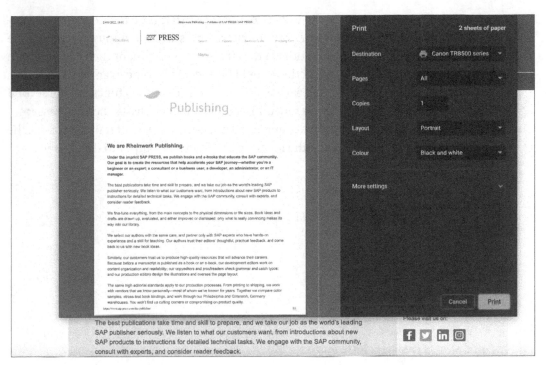

Figure 8.4 The print() Method Opens the Dialog for Printing the Current Web Page

8.2.8   Executing Functions in a Time-Controlled Manner

If you want to execute certain functions within a web page with a delay (once) or at certain intervals (repeatedly), the window object provides several helper methods for this purpose (see also Table 8.7).

Method	Description
setInterval()	Executes a function at specified time intervals. Returns an ID that can be passed as a parameter to the clearInterval() method to abort the execution of the function.
clearInterval()	Cancels the execution of the function triggered by setInterval().
setTimeout()	Executes a function after a specified period of time. Returns an ID that can be passed as a parameter to the clearTimeout() method to prevent the function from executing.
clearTimeout()	Cancels the execution of the function triggered by setTimeout().

Table 8.7 Methods of the window Object for the Time-Controlled Execution of Functions

The setTimeout() method can be used to define after what time period a certain function should be executed. As the first argument, you pass an anonymous function or the name of the corresponding function, and as the second argument the time period in milliseconds after which the function should be executed. Some examples are shown in Listing 8.5. The first call of setTimeout() passes an anonymous function, the second call passes an (anonymous) arrow function, and the third call passes the printMessage() function. All three calls ensure that after 5,000 milliseconds (i.e., after five seconds), the passed function is executed and the message Hello World is output to the console.

```
window.setTimeout(function() {
  console.log('Hello World');
}, 5000);

window.setTimeout(() => {
  console.log('Hello World');
}, 5000);
function printMessage() {
  console.log('Hello World');
}
window.setTimeout(printMessage, 5000);
```

Listing 8.5 Executing a Function after Five Seconds

Analogous to the setTimout() method, the window object provides the setInterval() method, which can be used to execute a function at specific time intervals. As the first argument, you pass either an anonymous function or the name of the function to be executed, and as the second argument the interval in milliseconds at which the function is to be executed. Listing 8.6 shows some examples. All three calls to setInterval() cause the passed function to be executed every 5,000 milliseconds.

```
window.setInterval(function() {
  console.log('Hello World');
}, 5000);

window.setInterval(() => {
  console.log('Hello World');
}, 5000);
function printMessage() {
  console.log('Hello World');
}
window.setInterval(printMessage, 5000);
```

Listing 8.6 Executing a Function Every Five Seconds

8.3 Accessing Navigation Information of a Currently Open Web Page

Using the object stored in the `location` property (which is of the `Location` type), you can access information regarding the URL of the web page currently loaded in the browser window or tab.

8.3.1 Accessing the Individual Components of the URL

A URL consists of different components, as shown in Figure 8.5. Among other things, a URL consists of a protocol, the host name, a port specification, a path specification, and query parameters. The properties to access the individual components of a URL are listed in Table 8.8.

https://	www.javascripthandbuch.de	/chapter08/	example.html	?firstName=John&lastName=Doe
Log	Host Name	Path	File Name	Query String

Figure 8.5 The Components of a URL

Property	Description
href	Contains the entire URL.
protocol	Contains the protocol of the URL including the colon, e.g. `https:`.
host	Contains the hostname of a URL—for example, `javascripthandbuch.de`. If a port specification is available, it will also be listed—for example, `philipackermann.de:8080`.
hostname	Contains the domain of a URL—for example, `javascripthandbuch.de`. Unlike the host property, hostname does not include a port specification.
port	Contains the port of a URL—for example, 8080.
pathname	Contains the path of a URL, starting with a `/`.
search	Contains the parameters of a URL—that is, the *query string* (also *search string*)—including a preceding question mark—for example, `?firstName=John`. Multiple parameter-value pairs are separated by an ampersand symbol—for example, `?firstName=John&lastName=Doe`.
hash	Contains the *fragment identifier*, including a preceding #. In the case of the URL `http://www.javascripthandbuch.de#services`, this would be `#services`. If you call a URL with a fragment identifier and there is an element with the corresponding ID on the respective web page, the display area is scrolled to this element.

Table 8.8 The Properties of Location

Property	Description
username	Contains the username specified in the URL. For the URL https:// john:secret@javascripthandbuch.de, this would be the value john. Not supported by all browsers.
password	Contains the password specified in the URL. For the URL https:// max:secret@javascripthandbuch.de, this would be the value secret. Not supported by all browsers.
origin	Contains the canonical form of the URL, consisting of the protocol, followed by ://, the domain, and—if the URL contains a port specification—a colon and the port specification.

Table 8.8 The Properties of Location (Cont.)

8.3.2   Accessing Query String Parameters

Unfortunately, there is no method available for accessing the individual parameters in the query string of a URL. Instead, you have to parse the query string itself or use a helper function, as shown in Listing 8.7. This function expects the name of the parameter for which the value is to be determined, creates a regular expression using this parameter, and extracts the value for the parameter (if available) from the query string of the URL (location.search).

```
function getParameterByName(name) {
  name = name.replace(/[\[]/, '\\[').replace(/[\]]/, '\\]');
  const regex = new RegExp('[\\?&]' + name + '=([^&#]*)'),
    results = regex.exec(location.search);
  return results === null ? '' : decodeURIComponent(results[1].replace(/\+/
g, ' '));
}
console.log(getParameterByName('tests'));
```

Listing 8.7 Helper Function for Extracting Individual Query String Parameters

8.3.3   Loading a New Web Page

To load a new web page in the current browser window, you have several options.

The assign() method expects a URL as argument and opens the corresponding web page. This also creates a new entry in the browsing history. You can see an example of this in Listing 8.8.

```
const linkLoad = document.getElementById('link-load');
linkLoad.addEventListener('click', (e) => {
  const url = document.getElementById('url').value;
  window.location.assign(url);
});
```

Listing 8.8 Loading a Web Page via the assign() Method

Basically, the replace() method works in the same way as the assign() method: the URL of the web page to be loaded is passed as an argument (see Listing 8.9). Unlike assign(), however, calling replace() doesn't result in a new entry being created in the browsing history. So in this case, you can no longer navigate back to the previously visited website.

```
const linkLoad = document.getElementById('link-load');
linkLoad.addEventListener('click', (e) => {
  const url = document.getElementById('url').value;
  window.location.replace(url);
});
```

Listing 8.9 Loading a Web Page Using the replace() Method

In addition, the href property of the location object can also be used to load a new web page, as shown in Listing 8.10.

```
const linkLoad = document.getElementById('link-load');
linkLoad.addEventListener('click', (e) => {
  const url = document.getElementById('url').value;
  window.location.href = url;
});
```

Listing 8.10 Loading a Web Page Using the href Property

If you want to reload the current web page, you can do this using the reload() method. Optionally, a Boolean value can be passed to the method to determine whether the web page should be reloaded from the server (in this case, pass the value true) or whether the browser can also reload the web page from its internal cache (in this case, pass the value false). An example of this is shown in Listing 8.11.

```
const linkReload = document.getElementById('link-reload');
linkReload.addEventListener('click', (e) => {
  window.location.reload(true);
});
```

Listing 8.11 Reloading a Web Page via the reload() Method

8.4   Viewing and Modifying the Browsing History

The history property of the window object takes you to an object that represents the browsing history. This object (of the History type) can be used to take a look at the history, but it can also enable you to change the history.

8.4.1   Navigating in the Browsing History

Each time the browser loads a new web page, or even jumps to a jump label (an *anchor*) within a web page, the browser creates a new entry in the browsing history by default (the exception here is the replace() method, as shown in Section 8.3.3).

A few years ago, it wasn't so easy to influence the browsing history. The only things you could do (and still can do) were use the length property to see the number of entries in the browsing history, the back() method to go back one entry, the forward() method to go forward one entry, and the go() method to go to a specific entry in the browsing history (see Table 8.9). Some examples are shown in Listing 8.12.

```
window.history.length;      // number of entries
window.history.back();      // back in history
window.history.forward();   // forward in history
window.history.go(-2);      // two entries back
window.history.go(2);       // two entries forward
window.history.go(0);       // reload current web page
```

Listing 8.12 Access to the Browsing History

Property/Method	Description
length	Contains the number of entries in the history, including the currently loaded web page.
back()	Goes to the previous web page in the history. Identical to the user pressing the browser's Back button.
forward()	Goes to the following web page in the history. Identical to the user pressing the browser's Next button.
go()	Goes to a specific web page in the history. The method is passed the increment starting from the current web page. For example, the value -1 causes the previous web page to be opened, and the value 1 causes the following web page to be opened. If a value is passed for which there is no corresponding web page in the history, this method does nothing. If, on the other hand, the method is called without a value or with the value 0, the current web page is reloaded.

Table 8.9 The Old Properties and Methods of History That Are Still Valid

8.4.2 Browsing History for Single-Page Applications

However, with the success of single-page applications, where only parts of a web page/ application are reloaded, a new or additional functionality was needed to describe individual entries in the browsing history. The reason: if only parts of a web page are reloaded, the URL doesn't change by default, so there is no new entry in the browsing history. Bookmarking then isn't possible either because different web pages (or more precisely, different states of a web page) don't have their own URLs.

Therefore, the fragment identifier of the URL was used for a long time (see hash property in Table 8.8). If parts of a web page were reloaded, you simply changed this fragment identifier and thus ensured that a new entry was created in the browsing history.

Here's a quick example: Suppose you were visiting a web page with the URL *www.javascripthandbuch.de* that has five different navigation entries: **Home**, **Services**, **Skills**, **About Us**, and **Contact**. The individual URLs would then be *www.javascripthandbuch.de# home*, *www.javascripthandbuch.de#services*, *www.javascripthandbuch.de#skills*, *www. javascripthandbuch.de#aboutus*, and *www.javascripthandbuch.de#contact*. Such URLs are also called *hashbang URLs* because of the # character they contain (see Listing 8.13).

```
...
<body>
  <nav>
    <ul>
      <li><a href="#home">Home</a></li>
      <li><a href="#services">Services</a></li>
      <li><a href="#skills">Skills</a></li>
      <li><a href="#aboutus">About Us</a></li>
      <li><a href="#contact">Contact</a></li>
    </ul>
  </nav>
  <main id="content"></main>
</body>
...
```

Listing 8.13 Hashbang URLs

But this technique isn't ideal; it has some limitations. For example, the fragment identifier is only available on the client side and is not sent to the server.

8.4.3 Adding Entries to the Browsing History

For some time now, several adjustments have therefore been available (within the framework of the History API) that make it easier to work with the browsing history in the previously mentioned cases as well. The API defines a new property and two new methods for this purpose: the state property contains the current entry in the browsing history, the pushState() method can be used to place a new entry in the history, and the replaceState() method can be used to replace the current entry (see Table 8.10).

Property/Method	Description
state	Contains the current entry in the browsing history.
pushState()	Adds an entry to the history. Any JavaScript object (the so-called state object), the title, and optionally a URL are passed.
replaceState()	Replaces the current entry in the history with a new entry. A state object, the title, and optionally a URL are passed.

Table 8.10 The Newer Properties and Methods of History

Let me demonstrate the use of these methods by adapting the previous example. First, hashbang URLs aren't used. Instead, normal URLs are used, as shown in the HTML code in Listing 8.14. The goal is not to load a new web page when one of the links is clicked, but to update the content in the <main> element while still creating a new entry in the browsing history.

```
...
<body>
  <nav>
    <ul>
      <li><a href="/home">Home</a></li>
      <li><a href="/services">Services</a></li>
      <li><a href="/skills">Skills</a></li>
      <li><a href="/aboutus">About Us</a></li>
      <li><a href="/contact">Contact</a></li>
    </ul>
  </nav>
  <main id="content"></main>
</body>
...
```

Listing 8.14 No Hashbang URLs Are Required when Using the New History API

Listing 8.15 shows the corresponding JavaScript code. For each link on the web page, an event listener is registered that calls the pushState() method, adding a new entry to the browsing history. The first argument passed here is the content to be displayed, which for simplicity is contained in the contents object (in practice, the content would be dynamically loaded from the server instead; see also Chapter 9).

The second parameter passed is the title to be displayed in the browser title bar when the corresponding link is clicked. For this purpose, the text content of the respective link element is used (event.target.textContent). Finally, the third parameter is the URL to be displayed in the address bar. Here, the content of the href attribute of the corresponding link element is used (event.target.href).

Calling preventDefault() on the event object also prevents the default action from being executed when the links are clicked. If you omitted this call, the browser would simply reload the URL of the link.

```javascript
function init() {
  // Container element for the content
  const contentElement = document.getElementById('content');
  // Sample content, normally loaded via Ajax
  const contents = {
    home: {
      content: 'Home'
    },
    services: {
      content: 'Services'
    },
    skills: {
      content: 'Skills'
    },
    aboutus: {
      content: 'About Us'
    },
    contact: {
      content: 'Contact'
    }
  };
  // Event listener for the links
  function handleClick(event) {
    const pageName = event.target.getAttribute('href').split('/').pop();
    const content = contents[pageName];
    updateContent(content.content);
    history.pushState(
      content,                    // State object
      event.target.textContent,   // Title
      event.target.href           // URL
    );
    return event.preventDefault();
  }
  // Register the event listeners
  const linkElements = document.getElementsByTagName('a');
  for (let i = 0; i < linkElements.length; i++) {
    linkElements[i].addEventListener('click', handleClick, true);
```

```
  }
  function updateContent(content) {
    contentElement.textContent = content;
  }
}

document.addEventListener('DOMContentLoaded', init);
```

Listing 8.15 Adding Entries to the Browsing History

Web Servers

The code in Listing 8.15 only works when the HTML is run through a web server, not when it's opened as a local file.

8.4.4   Responding to Changes in the Browsing History

Every time the current entry in the browsing history changes (e.g., when you press the **Back** button in the browser), the popstate event is triggered. At the moment (i.e., only with the source code from Listing 8.15), however, the content of the web page is not yet updated because the updateContent() method is only called when one of the links is clicked, not when the **Back** button is used (and also not when the **Next** button is clicked).

To achieve this and update the content of the <main> element even when using the browser buttons, you simply need to call the updateContent() method inside an event listener for the popstate event (see Listing 8.16).

The event listener is passed an event object of the PopStateEvent type, the state property of which gives you access to the entry removed from the browsing history. In the example, its content property is read and added to the container element for the content.

```
window.addEventListener('popstate', (event) => {
  updateContent(event.state.content);
});
```

Listing 8.16 Responding to Remote Entries in the Browsing History

8.4.5   Replacing the Current Entry in the Browsing History

To replace the current entry in the browsing history with another entry, you can use the replaceState() method. Like the pushState() method, this method is passed the state object, the name, and optionally a URL (see Listing 8.17).

```
history.replaceState(
  {
    content: contentElement.textContent
  },
  document.title,
  document.location.href
);
```

Listing 8.17 Replacing an Entry in the Browsing History

You can see the connection between browsing history and the pushState() and replaceState() methods in Figure 8.6 (where, for the sake of clarity, the respective entries are only represented by the URL instead of showing the complete information, including the state object).

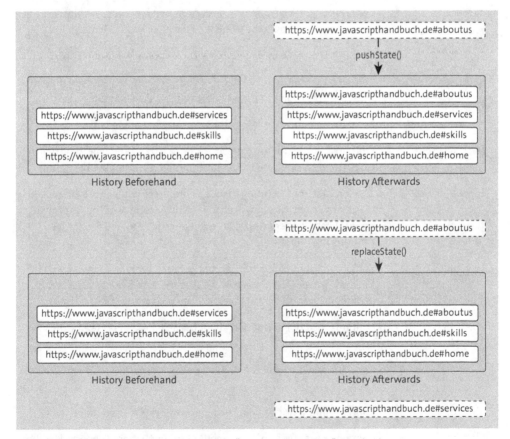

Figure 8.6 Difference between pushState() and replaceState() Methods

8.5 Recognizing Browsers and Determining Browser Features

So far, you've seen how you can access and partially change information tied to the browser window, the current URL, and the browsing history. But if you want to access general browser information (browser name, browser manufacturer, etc.), use the `navigator` property of the `window` object.

The object of the `Navigator` type stored in this property provides all sorts of such information (see Table 8.11), but some of it should be treated with caution or is marked as obsolete and should no longer be used.

Property	Description
appCodeName	Contains the internal codename of the current browser (not reliable, because every browser returns the value `Mozilla`).
appName	Contains the official name of the current browser (not reliable, because every browser outputs the value `Netscape`).
appVersion	Contains the version number of the current browser (not reliable).
battery	Contains a reference to an object of the `BatteryManager` type that provides the entry point to the Battery Status API (see Chapter 12).
cookieEnabled	Contains an indication of whether cookies are enabled or not.
geolocation	Contains a reference to an object of the `Geolocation` type, which provides the entry point to the Geolocation API (see Chapter 12).
language	Contains a string indicating the user's preferred language. Typically, this is the language that's also used within the interface of the respective browser. If no preferred language could be determined, this property contains the value `null`.
languages	Contains a list of strings indicating the user's preferred languages, with the most preferred language in the first position (which corresponds to the language contained in the `language` property).
mimeTypes	Contains a list of information about MIME types supported by the browser.
onLine	Boolean indicating whether the browser is connected to the internet or not.
platform	Contains information about the operating system used (not reliable).
plugins	Contains a list of information about plug-ins that are supported by the browser.

Table 8.11 Properties of the navigator Object

Property	Description
product	Contains the product name of the current browser. However, for backward compatibility, this returns the value Gecko in each browser.
productSub	Contains the sublabel of the current browser (either 20030107 or 20100101).
serviceWorker	Contains a reference to an object of the ServiceWorkerContainer type, which provides the entry point to the Service Worker API.
userAgent	Contains a string that identifies the browser used. However, it should be used with caution (see next note box).
vendor	Contains information about the browser manufacturer (one of the values Apple Computer, Inc., Google Inc., or an empty string).
vendorSub	Actually intended for further information about the browser manufacturer, but always contains an empty string.

Table 8.11 Properties of the navigator Object (Cont.)

For example, some time ago the navigator object was often used to draw conclusions about the browser used via the userAgent property in order to determine which features are supported by the browser and to execute the corresponding JavaScript code depending on this information. This technique is called *browser detection* or *browser sniffing*.

But today, browsers no longer use unique values for this property, so it's no longer possible to draw conclusions about the browser used. For example, the property in Chrome returns the value Mozilla/5.0 (Macintosh; Intel Mac OS X 10_8_5) AppleWebKit/ 537.36 (KHTML, like Gecko) Chrome/47.0.2526.111 Safari/537.36, which is anything but unique because it already contains different browser names.

This is also why browser detection technique is no longer used to draw conclusions about supported features. Instead, so-called feature detection directly searches for a feature. In other words, the specific browser used is usually not relevant for you as a web developer; more important is what features are supported by this browser.

For example, you can assume that a browser supports the new History API if the history object has a pushState() method (see Listing 8.18). So in feature detection, you directly test whether certain JavaScript objects have certain properties or methods that are indicative of the corresponding feature.

```
if(window.history.pushState) {
  // History API supported
} else {
  // History API not supported
}
```

Listing 8.18 Feature Detection Example

Note

To check whether a browser supports a particular feature, you shouldn't use the user-Agent property of the navigator object; it's considered very unreliable. Instead, you should use the feature detection technique.

8.6   Accessing Screen Information

The object stored in the screen property (of the Screen type) contains information related to the screen. These include the height (height) and width (width) of the screen, the color depth (colorDepth), and some information about how much space is available horizontally and vertically on the screen minus the fixed screen components (such as taskbars). Figure 8.7 illustrates these properties, and you can find an overview in Table 8.12.

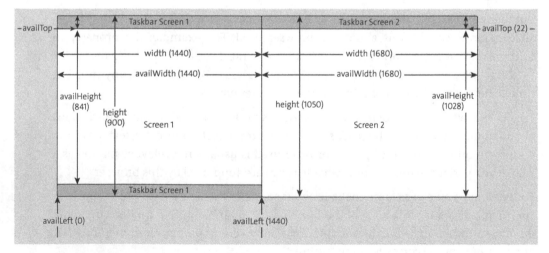

Figure 8.7 Properties of the Screen Window

Property	Description
availTop	Contains a pixel value that indicates how much space is taken up from the top by fixed screen components such as taskbars and the like.
availLeft	Contains a pixel value that indicates how much space is taken up from the left by fixed screen components such as taskbars and the like.
availHeight	Contains the maximum available screen height in pixels minus the height of components like, for example, taskbars that are always displayed
availWidth	Contains the maximum available screen width in pixels minus the width of components like, for example, taskbars that are always displayed
colorDepth	Contains the color depth of the screen
height	Contains the height of the screen in pixels
orientation	Contains a reference to an object of the ScreenOrientation type, which provides information about the orientation of the screen and is a part of the Screen Orientation API (*http://www.w3.org/TR/screen-orientation*)
pixelDepth	Contains the pixel depth of the screen
width	Contains the width of the screen in pixels

Table 8.12 Properties of the screen Object

8.7   Summary

In this chapter, you learned about the *Browser Object Model*, the object model through which you can access various components of the browser:

- The global window object represents the entry point into the BOM.
- The location object can be used to access components of the current URL and to reload web pages.
- Using the history object, you can navigate the browsing history and create new entries in the browsing history.
- The navigator object gives you detailed information about the browser, but not all of it is always reliable.
- Via the screen object, you get information regarding the screen, like height and width, as well as color depth, pixel depth, and so on.

Chapter 9

Dynamically Reloading Contents of a Web Page

For user interaction and in terms of user-friendliness, the concept of Ajax has become indispensable in the development of modern web applications. This technique enables you to dynamically update individual parts of a web page with content from the server instead of completely reloading the page.

In this chapter, we'll show you how to dynamically reload or replace parts of a web page without reloading the entire web page. The technology behind this is called Ajax (Asynchronous JavaScript and XML).

9.1 The Principle of Ajax

The name Ajax was first coined in 2005 by Jesse James Garrett in his essay "A New Approach to Web Applications." The idea is to use JavaScript for exchanging data with the server in the background without completely reloading the web page itself.

9.1.1 Synchronous Communication

Let's first look at how the classic communication between client and server works via Hypertext Transfer Protocol (HTTP). The client (usually the browser) sends a request (*HTTP request*) to the server, which then evaluates it and returns a corresponding response (*HTTP response*) to the client.

In terms of web page loading, this means that every time the user clicks on a link or fills out a form, for example, a corresponding HTTP request is sent to the server, which then generates the content of the new web page and returns it to the client (see Figure 9.1).

The less than ideal aspect of this process is that the client or browser has to wait while the server evaluates the request and prepares the response. As a user, you'll notice this because you'll no longer be able to interact with the website during this time; that is, no further requests can be made during the waiting time. For this reason, this type of communication, the orderly interplay between starting a request and waiting for the response, is also called *synchronous communication*.

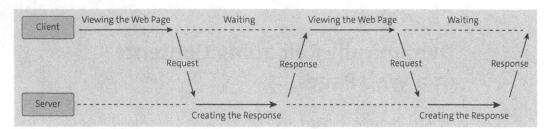

Figure 9.1 The Principle of Synchronous Communication

To use a more illustrative example, let's look at the implementation of a classic search function within a web page. A search form is used to enter the criteria for the search, and then the form is submitted. The server evaluates the search request, usually performs one or more database queries, and creates the web page containing the search results (see Figure 9.2). While the server is doing this, the user can do nothing but wait for the results. Only when all search results have been determined and the response has been loaded from the server can the user continue the interaction—for example, browse through the search results in the overview or view each result in detail.

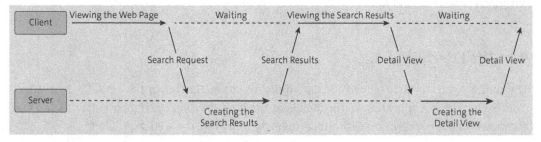

Figure 9.2 Sequence of a Synchronously Implemented Search

9.1.2   Asynchronous Communication

When using Ajax, the communication takes place asynchronously, not synchronously, which is why this is referred to as *asynchronous communication*. Like with synchronous communication, first a complete web page is loaded from the server, or the client makes a request to the server, which processes it and delivers an appropriate response. Unlike synchronous communication, however, asynchronous communication also enables you to send new requests to the server while you are still waiting for the response to requests that have already been sent (see Figure 9.3). This makes it possible, for example, to independently update individual parts of a web page with data from the server.

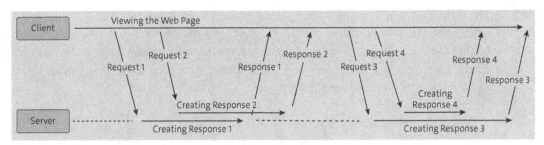

Figure 9.3 The Principle of Asynchronous Communication

If we apply this to the search example, then after submitting the search form, the form would be hidden, a progress bar would be displayed, and—after the search was completed—the search results would be displayed (see Figure 9.4). The other (fixed) components of the web page, such as the header, navigation, and footer areas, are not reloaded.

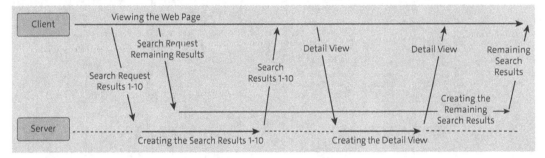

Figure 9.4 Workflow of an Asynchronous Search Implementation

This has some advantages: First, the data for the fixed components are not retransmitted from the server, which has an overall positive effect on the transmission time. Second, users have the possibility to continue interacting with other components on the website. For example, search results could be retrieved from the server piece by piece instead of all at once. A user could already view part of the search results, call detailed views of the results, and so on, while more search results were gradually retrieved from the server.

Note

Overall, asynchronous communication can significantly improve the user-friendliness and usability of a web page (or web application).

Technically, of course, HTTP requests are still sent during asynchronous communication as well. The only difference is that these are not triggered directly by the browser but are controlled via JavaScript calls (although synchronous calls are also possible using JavaScript, but more on that later).

The difference is illustrated once again in Figure 9.5. Without Ajax (left side in the diagram), the HTTP requests are executed directly by the browser, but when using Ajax (right side in the diagram), this is done by the corresponding JavaScript code. The JavaScript code also handles processing the response from the server—for example, to update the user interface accordingly.

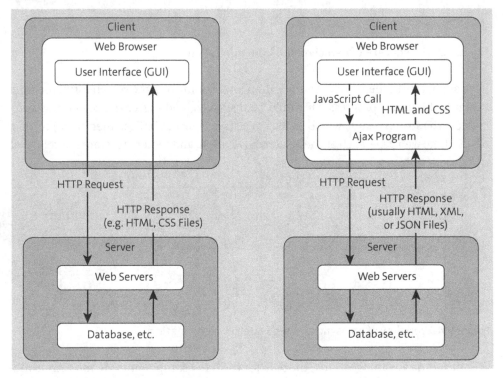

Figure 9.5 Difference between Classic and AJAX-Based Web Applications

9.1.3   Typical Use Cases for Ajax

In addition to the example described in the previous section of the search process running in the background, there are a number of other examples of using Ajax, which we'll briefly present ahead.

Automatic Completion of Input Fields

A classic example is the completion of input fields. The idea is to display input suggestions to the user in the form of a selection list while the user enters text in the corresponding input field (see Figure 9.6), thus preselecting possible selection values. Technically, you register an event listener for the change event of the respective input field, use Ajax to send a request containing the current input to the server, and display the matching values returned by the server in the dropdown list.

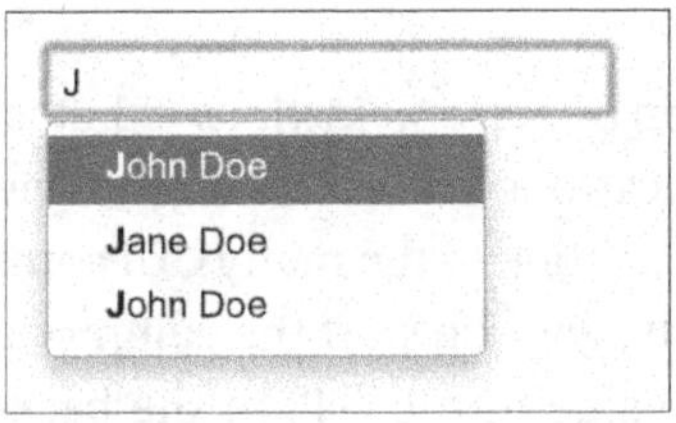

Figure 9.6 Automatic Completion of Input Fields

Pagination of Large Records

Another example is the pagination of records (i.e., splitting them into individual pages). Indeed, if there are many different records (e.g., a table of users), it makes sense not to display all records in one long table, but only a part of the data at a time, with the option to switch back and forth between individual parts. As a rule, a navigation option is provided above or below the corresponding table, as shown in Figure 9.7.

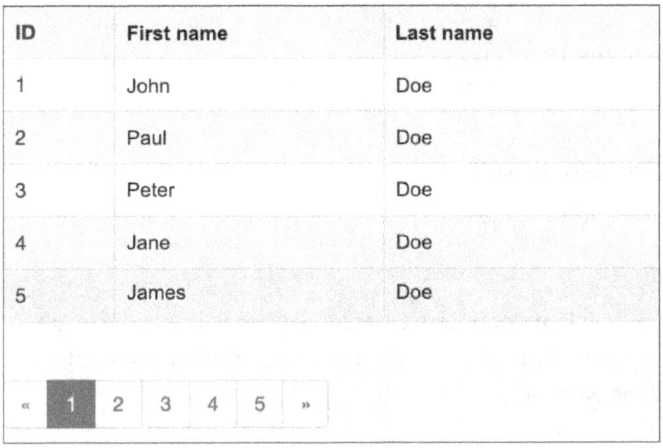

ID	First name	Last name
1	John	Doe
2	Paul	Doe
3	Peter	Doe
4	Jane	Doe
5	James	Doe

« 1 2 3 4 5 »

Figure 9.7 Ajax Is Often Used for Pagination

The example can be implemented by first loading only a part of the records from the server via Ajax (the "first page," so to speak, similar to the search results described earlier). If the user now clicks on the link to another page, the records for this selected page are loaded from the server accordingly.

News Tickers

News tickers, which you may see on news or sports pages, use Ajax to make regular requests to the server and display new messages, if available. To do this, you use the setInterval() method on the client side (see Chapter 8) to send requests to the server at specific intervals via Ajax. If the requests return new messages, these are incorporated into the news ticker accordingly.

Editable UI Components

The concept of Ajax has greatly propelled the proliferation of *web applications*—that is, web pages that look and feel like classic desktop applications while running in the browser. Tables that allow you to edit individual records are one of the many GUI components used in such applications (see Figure 9.8). Usually, you can start the edit mode by double-clicking on a table cell and then adjust the value in the cell. In the background, the corresponding record is then synchronized with the database on the server via Ajax.

ID	First name	Last name
1	John	Doe
2	Paul	Doe
3	Peter	Doe
4	Jane	Doe
5	James	Doe

Figure 9.8 Simple Editing of Table Records via Ajax

Note

Beyond these use cases, there are plenty of others where Ajax comes in handy. In general, Ajax is useful whenever you want to dynamically load data from or send data to the server without reloading the web page.

9.1.4   Data Formats Used

Now the question arises, what data is transferred between client and server, and in what format? In principle, you can use any format, but the following three are used most frequently:

- **HTML**
  This format is useful if you want to load ready-made GUI components (also called *widgets*; e.g., calendar components or the like) directly from the server and integrate them into the web page. We'll show you how to use HTML as a data format in Section 9.4.2.

- **Extensible Markup Language (XML)**
  This format is suitable if you load structured data from the server (e.g., individual records for a table) and want to generate content on the web page based on this data.

We'll show you how to use XML as a data format in Section 9.4.3. But first, we'll give you an introduction to this format in Section 9.2.

- **JavaScript Object Notation (JSON)**
  Like XML, this format is suitable whenever you want to load data from the server to generate content on the web page based on that data, but it's much leaner than XML and comparatively easy to process in JavaScript applications. We'll show you how to use JSON as a data format in Section 9.4.4. The structure of this format is explained in Section 9.3.

Various Exchange Formats

Obviously, the term *Asynchronous JavaScript and XML* is actually misleading because not only XML can be used as an exchange format.

9.2   The XML Format

XML is a markup language that can be used to structure data hierarchically.

9.2.1   The Structure of XML

In terms of syntax, XML looks similar to HTML (although there are some differences in detail, which we won't discuss at this point); that is, there are XML elements and XML attributes.

In principle, you're free to decide which elements you use within an XML document and which attributes you use within an element. As a rule, however, both are defined in an XML schema (or alternatively in a document type definition [DTD]). Both the XML schema and DTD contain rules, including which elements may be used in an XML document, which attributes these elements may have, and which child elements are allowed. As this book is primarily about JavaScript and not about XML, we'll stick to this general information regarding XML schema and DTD.

As an example, take a look at Listing 9.1, which shows a typical XML document. The first line contains information about the XML version used and the encoding; the rest of the document represents the actual content. The <artists> element represents the root node in this example. As with HTML, there can only be one of these within a document.

Below <artists>, there are two child elements of the type <artist>, each of which has a name attribute and also a child element of the type <albums>. The latter, in turn, has several child elements of the type <album>, each of which contains two child elements, <title> and <year>.

```xml
<?xml version="1.0" encoding="UTF-8"?>
<artists>
  <artist name="Kyuss">
    <albums>
      <album>
        <title>Wretch</title>
        <year>1991</year>
      </album>
      <album>
        <title>Blues for the Red Sun</title>
        <year>1992</year>
      </album>
      <album>
        <title>Welcome to Sky Valley</title>
        <year>1994</year>
      </album>
      <album>
        <title>...And the Circus Leaves Town</title>
        <year>1995</year>
      </album>
    </albums>
  </artist>
  <artist name="Ben Harper">
    <albums>
      <album>
        <title>The Will to Live</title>
        <year>1997</year>
      </album>
      <album>
        <title>Burn to Shine</title>
        <year>1999</year>
      </album>
      <album>
        <title>Live from Mars</title>
        <year>2001</year>
      </album>
      <album>
        <title>Diamonds on the Inside</title>
        <year>2003</year>
      </album>
    </albums>
  </artist>
</artists>
```

Listing 9.1 Example of an XML File

> **Note**
>
> XML files typically have the *.xml* file extension.

9.2.2 XML and the DOM API

Because of their hierarchical structure, it makes sense to represent XML documents as a tree. For example, Figure 9.9 shows the XML tree for the example in Listing 9.1.

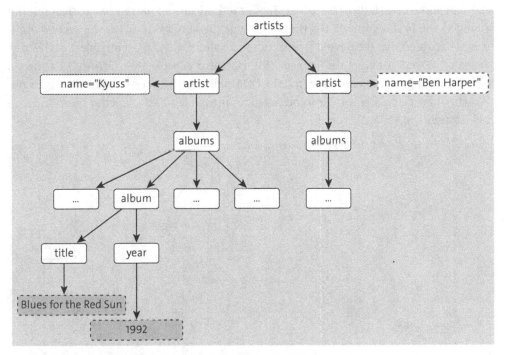

Figure 9.9 Hierarchical Tree Representation of an XML Document

Of course, you will have noticed immediately that the XML tree bears a strong resemblance to the DOM tree (see Chapter 5). This is no coincidence: the DOM API is also used for XML documents, so the contents of XML documents can be accessed in the same way as we discussed for HTML documents in Chapter 5. We'll show you examples later in this chapter in Section 9.2 and Section 9.4.3).

> **Note**
>
> More precisely, XML data within a JavaScript program is represented by the type Document in the same way as for web pages (i.e., the object stored in the document variable).

9.2.3   Converting Strings to XML Objects

When you send XML data to a server via Ajax or, conversely, retrieve XML data from a server via Ajax, the data is converted in the background. When XML objects (of the Document type) are converted into strings, this is called data *serialization*. The process of converting strings into XML objects, on the other hand, is called *parsing*. In principle, you don't need to know how both work, but having a bit of background knowledge in this regard certainly doesn't hurt.

To create XML objects based on a string that contains data in XML format, you can use the DOMParser object. Its parseFormString() method can be passed the corresponding string as the first argument and the MIME type (usually text/xml) as the second argument. Provided that the passed string contains valid XML, you get an object of the Document type that contains the parsed XML (see also Figure 9.10). Listing 9.2 shows a corresponding example. You see that the DOM selection methods you're already familiar with, like querySelector(), can be called on the parsed XML object to select individual elements in the XML tree.

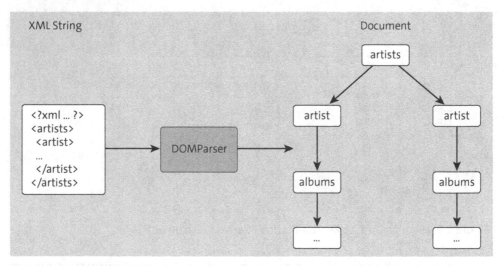

Figure 9.10 The DOMParser Object Can Be Used to Convert Strings into XML Objects

```
const xmlString = `<?xml version="1.0" encoding="ISO-8859-1"?>
              <artists>
                <artist name="Kyuss">
                  <albums>
                    <album>
                      <title>Wretch</title>
                      <year>1991</year>
                    </album>
                  </albums>
                </artist>
```

```
            </artists>`;
const domParser = new DOMParser();
const xmlDOM = domParser.parseFromString(xmlString, 'text/xml');
const firstArtist = xmlDOM.querySelector('artist');
console.log(firstArtist.getAttribute('name'));              // "Kyuss"
console.log(firstArtist.querySelector('title').textContent);  // "Wretch"
console.log(firstArtist.querySelector('year').textContent);   // 1991
```

Listing 9.2 Parsing a String to an XML Document

9.2.4   Converting XML Objects to Strings

Besides converting strings into XML objects of the Document type there's also the option of converting XML objects into strings. The helper object used in this context is the XMLSerializer object. This object provides the serializeToString() method, to which the XML object has been passed as an argument, as shown in Listing 9.3. The return value is the serialized XML object in the form of a string (see also Figure 9.11).

```
const xmlString = `<?xml version="1.0" encoding="ISO-8859-1"?>
               <artists>
                 <artist name="Kyuss">
                   <albums>
                     <album>
                       <title>Wretch</title>
                       <year>1991</year>
                     </album>
                   </albums>
                 </artist>
               </artists>`;
const domParser = new DOMParser();
const xmlDOM = domParser.parseFromString(xmlString, 'text/xml');
const xmlSerializer = new XMLSerializer();
const xmlStringSerialized = xmlSerializer.serializeToString(xmlDOM);
console.log(xmlStringSerialized);
```

Listing 9.3 Serializing an XML Document into a String

For a long time, XML was considered the exchange format par excellence when it came to exchanging data between applications (or between client and server). Now, however, a second format has become established, one that's particularly appealing due to its simple structure and its easy integration with JavaScript applications (anyone who has ever had to deal with XML for a long period of time knows that the format involves a relatively large amount of overhead, a lot of "trappings" in addition to the actual content—like closing tags of elements, to name just one of many examples). So let's briefly introduce this competitor.

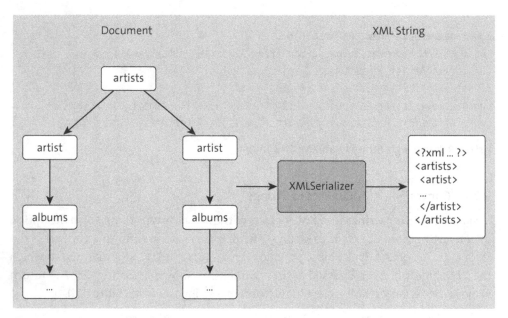

Figure 9.11 The XMLSerializer Object Can Be Used to Convert XML Objects into Strings

9.3 The JSON Format

JSON (pronounced like the name "Jason") is the format that has overtaken XML in many respects.

9.3.1 The Structure of JSON

At first glance, the JSON format looks like the object literal notation (see Chapter 3). However, there are some important differences in detail, which we'll show you in this section.

The essential characteristic of the JSON format is its braces, which are used to define individual objects. Properties of objects are enclosed in quotation marks and separated from the respective value by a colon. The values can be strings, numeric values, Boolean values, arrays, the value null, or other objects. Listing 9.4 shows an example of a JSON document that contains the same data as the XML document defined in Section 9.2.1 (see Listing 9.1 for comparison).

```
{
  "artists": [
    {
      "name": "Kyuss",
      "albums": [
        {
```

```
        "title": "Wretch",
        "year": 1991
      },
      {
        "title": "Blues for the Red Sun",
        "year": 1992
      },
      {
        "title": "Welcome to Sky Valley",
        "year": 1994
      },
      {
        "title": "...And the Circus Leaves Town",
        "year": 1995
      }
    ]
  },
  {
    "name": "Ben Harper",
    "albums": [
      {
        "title": "The Will to Live",
        "year": 1997
      },
      {
        "title": "Burn to Shine",
        "year": 1999
      },
      {
        "title": "Live from Mars",
        "year": 2001
      },
      {
        "title": "Diamonds on the Inside",
        "year": 2003
      }
    ]
  }
]
}
```

Listing 9.4 Example of a JSON File

> **Note**
>
> JSON files usually have the *.json* file extension.

The good thing about JSON is that it's very easy to use within a JavaScript application. More specifically, an object built in JSON can be used directly within JavaScript code, as shown in Listing 9.5. Here, the object discussed earlier (somewhat shortened for reasons of space) is defined directly in the JavaScript code and assigned to the `object` variable. You can access the properties of the JavaScript object created in this way using the dot notation, as you already know.

> **JSON Is a Subset of Object Literal Notation**
>
> Even more precisely, the JSON format is a subset of object literal notation and thus a subset of JavaScript. This, in turn, is the real reason that JSON can be used directly within JavaScript.

```
const object = {
  "artists": [
    {
      "name": "Kyuss",
      "albums": []
    },
    {
      "name": "Ben Harper",
      "albums": []
    }
  ]
}
console.log(object.artists);          // [Object, Object]
console.log(object.artists.length);   // 2
console.log(object.artists[0].name);  // "Kyuss"
console.log(object.artists[1].name);  // "Ben Harper"
```

Listing 9.5 JavaScript Directly Supports the JSON Format

9.3.2   Difference between JSON and JavaScript Objects

As mentioned, there are some fundamental differences between the JSON format and the object literal notation. For example, in JSON, properties must be enclosed in double quotation marks, whereas this isn't necessary in object literal notation. Single or double quotation marks can be used here, or they can even be omitted altogether if the name of the property allows it (if there are no hyphens in the name, for example).

Furthermore, as already mentioned, only strings, numbers, Boolean values, other (JSON) objects or arrays, and the value null can be used in JSON. In object literal notation, however, this restriction doesn't apply. For example, it also accepts functions, regular expressions, and any other object instances as values.

Validating JSON

If you aren't quite sure whether the JSON you have created is valid, one of the many online tools to check JSON for validity is the JSONLint validator tool at *http://jsonlint.com*—just in case your development environment or editor doesn't offer such functionality.

For working with JSON data, the global object JSON is available both in browsers and under Node.js. This object essentially provides two methods: one for converting JavaScript objects to a string in JSON format, and a second for converting strings in JSON format to JavaScript objects. Next, let's briefly show you how to use these two methods.

9.3.3 Converting Objects to JSON Format

Using the stringify() method of the JSON object, you can convert JavaScript objects into a string in JSON format. The method expects a JavaScript object as the first argument and returns the corresponding string containing the object in JSON format as the result.

As a second argument, you can optionally pass a function to control certain aspects of the conversion: this function is called for each property of the JavaScript object during the conversion. Its return value then determines the *target value*, the value to be transferred to the converted JSON for the respective property. If you don't want to convert the values but want to accept them as they are, you can simply pass the value null instead of a function.

The third argument can also be used to influence the indentation of the braces. Listing 9.6 shows an example of this, and Figure 9.12 accordingly illustrates the principle of the conversion.

```
const string = JSON.stringify(
  object,                      // JavaScript object
  (key, value) => {            // Replacement function
    return value;              // Return value determines target value
  },
  2                            // Indentation
);
console.log(string);
```

Listing 9.6 Converting a JavaScript Object to JSON Format

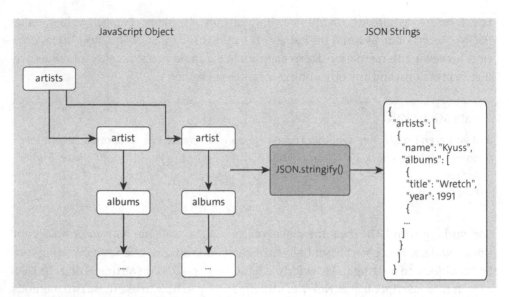

Figure 9.12 The JSON.stringify() Method Can Be Used to Convert JavaScript Objects to JSON Format

9.3.4 Converting Objects from JSON Format

While stringify() is provided for converting JavaScript objects to JSON format, the parse() method is designed for the reverse direction—that is, for converting a string in JSON format to a JavaScript object. As the first argument, the method expects the corresponding string. The function optionally passed as a second argument (similar to the use of stringify() just now) can be used to control which value should be used for the target object during the conversion. This function is called for each property. An example of using the parse() method is shown in Listing 9.7. Figure 9.13 illustrates the principle again in a graphic.

```
const objectParsed = JSON.parse(
  string,                              // JSON
  (key, value) => {                    // Replacement function
    return value;                      // Return value determines target value
  }
);
console.log(objectParsed.artists);            // [Object, Object]
console.log(objectParsed.artists.length);     // 2
console.log(objectParsed.artists[0].name);    // "Kyuss"
console.log(objectParsed.artists[1].name);    // "Ben Harper"
```

Listing 9.7 Converting a String in JSON Format to a JavaScript Object

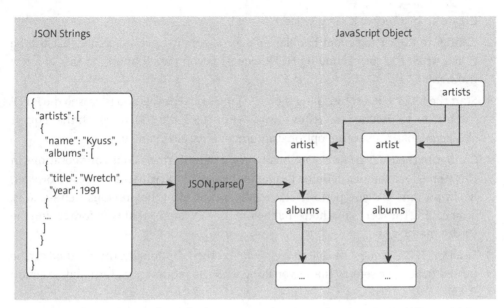

Figure 9.13 The JSON.parse() Method Can Be Used to Convert Strings in JSON Format into JavaScript Objects

9.4   Making Requests via Ajax

That's enough of the theory and the introduction to the exchange formats. Now let's show you how to specifically create queries using Ajax.

9.4.1   The XMLHttpRequest Object

The basis for all types of Ajax requests is the XMLHttpRequest object, originally developed by Microsoft and adopted over time by other browser manufacturers. Even the W3C is working on a standardization of this object (see *www.w3.org/TR/XMLHttpRequest/*).

> **Note**
>
> The Fetch API (Section 9.4.8) provides another way of making asynchronous HTTP requests (i.e., Ajax requests)—and it's much simpler. Nevertheless, we'll discuss the original variant first—not least for didactic reasons. After that, we'll present the Fetch API.

Flow of a Request via Ajax

The process of formulating an Ajax request is always similar when using the XMLHttpRequest object (see also Listing 9.8), and consists of the following steps:

1. Create an instance of XMLHttpRequest.

2. Configure the onload event handler or a corresponding event listener that will be called when the corresponding HTTP request is completed (more on this in a few moments).

3. Start the HTTP request by calling the open() method. The method is passed the HTTP method to be used for the request (e.g., GET or POST), the URL to which the request should be made, and other optional arguments (see also Table 9.1).

4. Configure the HTTP request. Optionally, you can perform various configurations in this step—for example, defining headers to be sent along with the request. However, it's important that you perform this configuration after the previous step—that is, after calling the open() method—but before the next step—that is, before calling the send() method.

5. Send the HTTP request by calling the send() method. Optionally, this method can be passed data to be sent to the server along with the request (e.g., form data; Section 9.4.5).

```
'use strict';
const request = new XMLHttpRequest();  // 1.) Create the XMLHttpRequest object
request.onload = (event) => {          // 2.) Definition of the event handler
  console.log('Response loaded');
}
request.open(                          // 3.) Start the request ...
  'GET',                               // ... specifying the HTTP method...
  'content/data.xml'                   // ... and URL
);
request.setRequestHeader('Accept', 'text/html'); // 4.) Configure the request
request.send();                                  // 5.) Send the request
```

Listing 9.8 Typical Process of Creating an Ajax Request

Setting Up a Web Server

To make Ajax requests to a web server, you first need such a web server. The easiest way is to run the server locally on your development computer while developing your application. Some development environments, such as WebStorm, start a local web server in the background when you open an HTML document in the browser preview. The examples from the download directory should work right away in this case. If you use an editor or another development environment that doesn't have such a feature, you'll have to start a local web server yourself and install it beforehand, if necessary.

Three better-known web servers are Apache (*https://httpd.apache.org*), nginx (*http://nginx.org*), and Lighttpd (*www.lighttpd.net*). For installation and configuration, see the servers' websites. However, it's easier in our case here to use the http-server Node.js

---

package (*https://github.com/indexzero/http-server*). You only need to install Node.js (which you'll be doing in the course of the book anyway; see Chapter 17) and then use its package manager, npm, to install this package (`npm install -g http-server`). After that, the `http-server` command is available to start a local web server that uses the current directory as its root directory. For the following examples, we recommend executing the command in the corresponding directory of the respective listing or alternatively in the directory for this chapter.

Methods of XMLHttpRequest

In addition, the `XMLHttpRequest` object provides several other methods. You can see an overview of this in Table 9.1.

Method	Description
`abort()`	Cancels a request.
`getAllResponseHeaders()`	Returns all headers of the HTTP response as a string.

`getResponseHeader(`
  `header`
`)`
	Returns the corresponding value for the name of a header.

`open(`
  `method,`
  `url,`
  `async,`
  `user,`
  `password`
`)`
	Starts a request. You need to pass the HTTP method to be used (e.g., `GET` or `POST`), the URL to which the request should be sent, a Boolean value specifying whether the request should be synchronous (`false`) or asynchronous (`true`), and possibly a username and password for access-protected URLs.

`overrideMimeType(`
  `mime`
`)`
	Overwrites the MIME type returned by the server.

`send()`	Sends a request.

`send(`
  `data`
`)`
	Sends a request and sends the passed data—for example, form data (Section 9.4.5).

`setRequestHeader(`
  `header,`
  `value`
`)`
	Sets the value for the specified header.

Table 9.1 The Methods of XMLHttpRequest

XMLHttpRequest Properties

In addition to the methods mentioned previously, the XMLHttpRequest object provides a number of properties (see Table 9.2). Some of them are used to configure the object or the corresponding request (e.g., the various event handlers) and some other properties are used to read the results of a request (e.g., as you'll see later, the response, responseText, and responseXML properties).

Property	Description
onabort	Event handler that is called when a request was aborted via the abort() method.
onerror	Event handler that is called when an error has occurred.
onload	Event handler that is called when the request is successfully executed and the response is available.
onloadend	Event handler that is called after the request is successfully executed.
onloadstart	Event handler that is called after the request is started.
onprogress	Event handler that is called when the request progresses.
onreadystatechange	Event handler that is called when the state of the request changes.
ontimeout	Event handler that is called if the request is aborted due to a timeout.
readyState	Contains the current state of the request encoded as a numeric value.
response	Contains the "body" of the response, which is either of type ArrayBuffer, Blob, or Document, or a JSON object, or a string, or null, in case the request has not yet completed or was not successful.
responseText	Contains the response as a string or the value null if the request has not yet completed or was not successful.
responseType	This property can be used to determine which data type the response should have. Can have one of the following values (the type of the response is included in parentheses): ■ Empty string (String) ■ arraybuffer (ArrayBuffer) ■ blob (Blob) ■ document (Document) ■ json (JavaScript object parsed from the response) ■ text (String)

Table 9.2 The Properties of XMLHttpRequest

Property	Description
responseXML	Contains the response as an object of the Document type.
status	Contains the HTTP status code of the request (e.g., 200).
statusText	In addition to the HTTP status code, this also contains the status message (e.g., 200 OK).
timeout	This property can be used to define the number of milliseconds a request may last before it's aborted by a time-out.
upload	Event handler that can be used to track the status when uploading data.
withCredentials	This property can be used to define whether requests should be made using credentials such as cookies or authorization headers.

Table 9.2 The Properties of XMLHttpRequest (Cont.)

Registering Event Listeners to XMLHttpRequest

In addition to the methods listed in Table 9.1, the XMLHttpRequest object also provides the addEventListener() method, which you can use to register event listeners for the various events, as you already know from the elements within the DOM tree (see Chapter 6). Analogous to the event handlers listed in Table 9.2, these are abort, error, load, loadend, loadstart, progress, readystatechange, and timeout (see Listing 9.9).

```
request.addEventListener('loadstart', (event) => {
  console.log('Request started');
});
request.addEventListener('progress', (event) => {
  console.log('Progress');
});
request.addEventListener('abort', (event) => {
  console.log('Request aborted');
});
request.addEventListener('error', (event) => {
  console.log('Error during request');
});
request.addEventListener('load', (event) => {
  console.log('Response loaded');
});
request.addEventListener('timeout', (event) => {
  console.log('Request aborted due to timeout');
});
```

```
request.addEventListener('loadend', (event) => {
  console.log('Request finished');
});
```

Listing 9.9 The Different Events Regarding Ajax Requests

Difference between the load and readystatechange Events

Older browser versions use the onreadystatechange event handler instead of the onload event handler (see Listing 9.10). The corresponding readystatechange event is triggered whenever the state of an Ajax-based request changes (all states available are shown in Table 9.3).

To get the final result of a request, you have to check whether the Loaded state has been reached—that is, whether the readyState property of the request object contains the value 4. You should also make sure that the request was successful—that is, that the status property of the request object contains the HTTP status code 200 (see Table 9.4).

```
// Script for older browsers, hence the var keyword
var request = new XMLHttpRequest();
request.onreadystatechange = function() {...
  if (request.readyState === 4 && request.status === 200) {
    var data = request.responseXML;
    var entries = data.getElementsByTagName('entry');
    for (var i = 0; i < entries.length; i++) {
      /* Insert XML*/
    }
  }
};
request.open('GET', 'content/data.xml', true);
request.send(null);
```

Listing 9.10 Using the onreadystatechange Event Handler

Value	Name	Meaning
0	Uninitialized	An instance of XMLHttpRequest (or an equivalent type) has been created, but the open() method has not yet been called.
1	Open	The open() method was called.
2	Sent	The send() method was called.

Table 9.3 The Different Values of the readyState Property

Value	Name	Meaning
3	Receiving	The server's response is downloaded.
4	Loaded	The server's response was downloaded completely.

Table 9.3 The Different Values of the readyState Property (Cont.)

Value	Name	Meaning
200	OK	The request was successful.
401	Unauthorized	The request was not successful because there was no authentication.
403	Forbidden	The request was not successful because access to the corresponding URL is not allowed.
404	Not Found	The request was not successful because the URL was not found.
500	Internal Server Error	The request was not successful due to an internal server error.

Table 9.4 A Selection of Different HTTP Status Codes

9.4.2 Loading HTML Data via Ajax

As mentioned, there are several options for the data format used for communication between the client and the server, or transferred from the server to the client, respectively. First, let's show you how to load HTML from the server using Ajax. You already know how to create a simple request using Ajax. After a successful request (and successful response), the only thing left to do is to read the responseText property of the request object for the load event within the corresponding event handler or event listener (see Listing 9.11). This property contains the "body" of the response returned by the server as a string (i.e., the transmitted data without header data, for example). You should also set the Accept header to text/html so that only responses that contain HTML are accepted by the server.

```
'use strict';
const request = new XMLHttpRequest();          // Create the XMLHttpRequest
                                               // object
request.onload = (e) => {                       // When result is loaded ...
  if(request.status === 200) {
    const html = request.responseText;         // HTML response as a string.
  }
};
```

```
request.open(
  'GET',                                          // Load the ...
  'content/snippet.html',                         // ... HTML file
);
request.responseType = '';                        // Response as a string ...
request.setRequestHeader('Accept', 'text/html');  // ... only of type HTML
request.send();                                   // Send request
```

Listing 9.11 Loading HTML Data via Ajax

Alternatively, you can use the responseType property to specify that the response should be parsed directly into an object of the Document type, which you access in the event handler/event listener via the responseXML property of the request object, as shown in Listing 9.12. You can then use the techniques we covered in Chapter 5 to access the contents of the parsed document, such as the body property, as shown in the listing.

```
const request = new XMLHttpRequest();             // Create the
                                                  // XMLHttpRequest
                                                  // object

request.onload = () => {                           // When result
                                                  // is loaded ...

  if(request.status === 200) {
    const html = request.responseXML.body.innerHTML; // HTML response as parsed
                                                  // object.

  }
};
request.open(
  'GET',                                          // Load the ...
  'content/snippet.html'                          // ... HTML file
);
request.responseType = 'document';                // Response as
                                                  // parsed object ...

request.setRequestHeader('Accept', 'text/html');  // ... only of type HTML
request.send();                                   // Send request
```

Listing 9.12 Loading HTML Data via Ajax

Usage Example: Loading HTML Content Dynamically from the Server

To dynamically reload individual contents of a web page, you can load them as HTML snippets via Ajax. These HTML snippets can either be loaded ready-made on the server or dynamically generated by the server at runtime (see Figure 9.14). The following listings show an example. In Listing 9.13, you first see the basic HTML framework, which

contains a navigation bar with two entries (Login and Register), and a <main> element
that serves as a container for the content loaded dynamically.

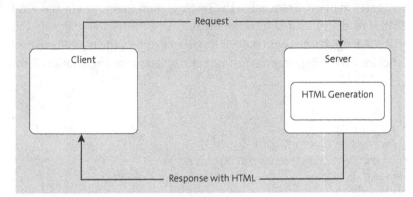

Figure 9.14 HTML Generation on the Server Side

```
<!DOCTYPE html>
<html>
<head lang="en">
    ...
</head>
<body>
  <div class="container">
    <nav>
      <ul class="nav nav-pills">
        <li role="presentation">
          <a id="login" href="#">Login</a>
        </li>
        <li role="presentation">
          <a id="register" href="#">Register</a>
        </li>
      </ul>
    </nav>
    <main id="main-content" class="container col-xs-offset-2 col-xs-8"></main>
  </div>
</body>
</html>
```

Listing 9.13 The HTML Framework

The JavaScript code in Listing 9.14 isn't particularly complicated. Within the init()
method, two event listeners are registered for the click event on the Login and Register navigation elements. When triggered, each event listener calls the loadContent()

method, specifying as argument the name of the HTML file to be loaded from the server (but without the file suffix *.html*).

Within the loadContent() method, a request to the server is then executed via Ajax, and the returned HTML is read and loaded into the content area of the web page via the innerHTML property. Clicking on the **Login** navigation item displays the login form (see Figure 9.15), and clicking on the **Register** navigation item displays the registration form (see Figure 9.16).

```
'use strict';
function init() {
  const login = document.getElementById('login');
  const register = document.getElementById('register');
  login.addEventListener('click', (e) => {
    e.preventDefault();
    loadContent('login');
  });
  register.addEventListener('click', (e) => {
    e.preventDefault();
    loadContent('register');
  });
}

function loadContent(name) {
  const request = new XMLHttpRequest();
  request.onload = (e) => {
    if(request.status === 200) {
      const htmlSnippet = request.responseText;
      document.getElementById('main-content').innerHTML = htmlSnippet;
    }
  };
  request.open(
    'GET',
    name + '.html'
  );
  request.responseType = '';
  request.setRequestHeader('Accept', 'text/html');
  request.send();
}
window.addEventListener('DOMContentLoaded', init);
```

Listing 9.14 Loading HTML Data via Ajax

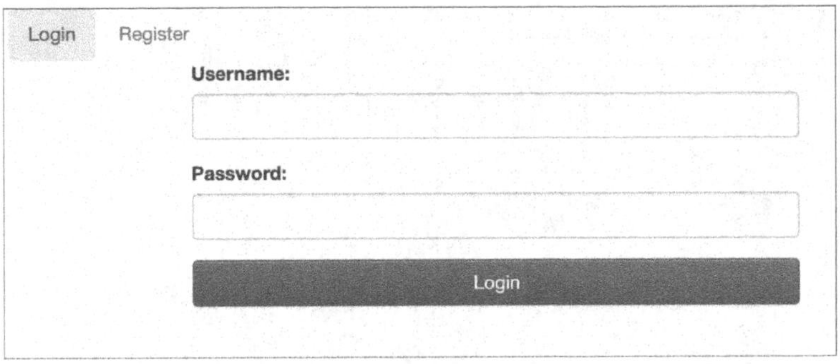

Figure 9.15 When You Click Login, the Login Form Is Loaded via Ajax

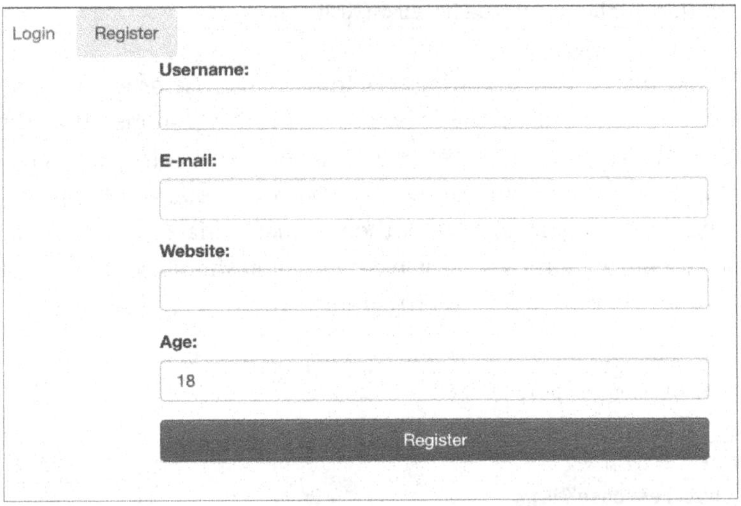

Figure 9.16 When You Click Register, the Corresponding Form for Registration Is Loaded via Ajax

9.4.3   Loading XML Data via Ajax

It often makes more sense not to load data in HTML format from the server, but to take care of generating the HTML code on the client side. For example, if you want to read different records from a database and display them in an HTML table, it makes little sense to generate the HTML table on the server side first and then send it back to the client. It's better to fetch only the individual records from the server—in the form of an XML document, for example—and generate the HTML table on the client side (see Figure 9.17). This ensures a clean separation between the data and the HTML code.

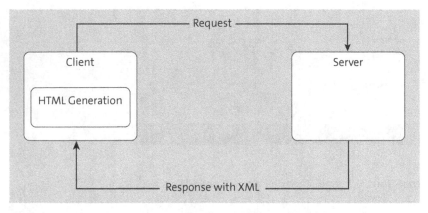

Figure 9.17 HTML Generation on the Client Side Based on XML Data

To load XML data via Ajax, proceed as in Listing 9.15. In principle, the browser recognizes from the MIME type returned by the server in the HTTP response that the returned content is data in XML format. However, you can help this automatic detection a bit by assigning the document value to the responseType property. Within the event handler/event listener, the parsed XML is then available via the responseXML property in the form of an object of the Document type. Also, you should set the Accept header to the value text/xml or application/xml to accept only data in XML format.

```
'use strict';
const request = new XMLHttpRequest();
request.onload = (e) => {
  if(request.status === 200) {
    const xml = request.responseXML;
    // here further processing of the XML data
    console.log(xml);
  }
};
request.open(
  'GET',
  'content/data.xml'
);
request.responseType = 'document';
request.setRequestHeader('Accept', 'text/xml');
request.send(null);
```

Listing 9.15 Loading XML Data via Ajax

Usage Example: Generating HTML Table Based on XML Data

Let me amplify the example a little. The goal is to load the data shown as an XML document in Section 9.2 from the server via Ajax and generate an HTML table from it. To do this, you can proceed as shown in Listing 9.16. Here, the *artists.xml* file is loaded via Ajax and processed within the onload event handler. Because the response is an object of the Document type, the DOM methods you learned about in Chapter 5 can be executed on this object.

In the example, all <artist> elements are selected in this way by calling the getElementsByTagName() method. Subsequently, the list of these selected elements is iterated, and (again by calling getElementsByTagName()) all <album> elements within the respective <artist> element are selected. Within the loop over these elements, a new row is then created in the table for each entry (with the code for this outsourced in the createRow() method). The results are displayed in Figure 9.18.

```javascript
'use strict';
function init() {
  const request = new XMLHttpRequest();
  request.onload = () => {
    if(request.status === 200) {
      const xmlDoc = request.responseXML;
      const table = initTable();
      // 1.) Select all <artist> elements
      const artists = xmlDoc.getElementsByTagName('artist');
      for (let i = 0; i < artists.length; i++) {
        const artist = artists[i];
        // 2.) Select the <album> elements
        const albums = artist.getElementsByTagName('album');
        for (let j = 0; j < albums.length; j++) {
          const album = albums[j];
          // 3.) Create a new table row
          const row = createRow(
            artist.getAttribute('name'),
            album.getElementsByTagName('title')[0].childNodes[0].nodeValue,
            album.getElementsByTagName('year')[0].childNodes[0].nodeValue
          );
          table.tBodies[0].appendChild(row);
        }
      }
      document.getElementById('artists-container').appendChild(table);
    }
  };
```

```
  request.open('GET', 'artists.xml', true);
  request.responseType = 'document';
  request.setRequestHeader('Accept', 'text/xml');
  request.send();
}

function initTable() {
  const table = document.createElement('table');
  const tableHeader = document.createElement('thead');
  const headerRow = document.createElement('tr');
  const headerColumnArtistName = document.createElement('th');
  const headerColumnAlbumTitle = document.createElement('th');
  const headerColumnAlbumYear = document.createElement('th');
  const tableBody = document.createElement('tbody');
  headerColumnArtistName.appendChild(document.createTextNode('Name'));
  headerColumnAlbumTitle.appendChild(document.createTextNode('Title'));
  headerColumnAlbumYear.appendChild(document.createTextNode('Year'));
  headerRow.appendChild(headerColumnArtistName);
  headerRow.appendChild(headerColumnAlbumTitle);
  headerRow.appendChild(headerColumnAlbumYear);
  tableHeader.appendChild(headerRow);
  table.appendChild(tableHeader);
  table.appendChild(tableBody);
  table.className = 'table table-striped';
  return table;
}

function createRow(artistName, albumTitle, albumYear) {
  const row = document.createElement('tr');
  const columnName = document.createElement('td');
  const columnTitle = document.createElement('td');
  const columnYear = document.createElement('td');
  columnName.appendChild(document.createTextNode(artistName));
  columnTitle.appendChild(document.createTextNode(albumTitle));
  columnYear.appendChild(document.createTextNode(albumYear));
  row.appendChild(columnName);
  row.appendChild(columnTitle);
  row.appendChild(columnYear);
  return row;
}
window.addEventListener('DOMContentLoaded', init);
```

Listing 9.16 Loading XML Data via Ajax and Generating HTML on the Client Side

Name	Title	Year
Kyuss	Wretch	1991
Kyuss	Blues for the Red Sun	1992
Kyuss	Welcome to Sky Valley	1994
Kyuss	...And the Circus Leaves Town	1995
Ben Harper	The Will to Live	1997
Ben Harper	Burn to Shine	1999
Ben Harper	Live from Mars	2001
Ben Harper	Diamonds on the Inside	2003

Figure 9.18 The HTML Table Generated from the XML Data

9.4.4   Loading JSON Data via Ajax

As mentioned, the JSON format is very well suited for direct use in JavaScript applications. To load JSON data via Ajax, proceed as in Listing 9.17. You can use the value json as the value for the responseType property. Browsers that support this value ensure that the response is parsed as JSON by the server and can be read directly as a JavaScript object via the response property.

When processing the response from the server within the onload event handler, in order to receive a JSON object, you should then read the responseType property. If this contains the value json, the response or the JSON object can be accessed directly via the response property of the request object. On the other hand, if the value of the property is not json (i.e., the browser does not support this value), you have to take a small detour and manually convert the contents of the responseText property into a JSON object using the parse() method.

You should use application/json as the value for the Accept header when querying JSON data in order to only accept data from the server that is actually of the JSON type.

```
'use strict';
let request = new XMLHttpRequest();
const.onload = () => {
  if(request.status === 200) {
    let json;
    if (request.responseType === 'json') {
      json = request.response;
    } else {
      json = JSON.parse(request.responseText);
    }
    // here further processing of the JSON data
    console.log(json);
```

```
  }
};
request.open('GET', 'data/content.json', true);
request.responseType = 'json';
request.setRequestHeader('Accept', 'application/json');
request.send();
```

Listing 9.17 Loading JSON Data via Ajax

Usage Example: Generating a HTML Table Based on JSON Data

Let's show how you would solve the example from Section 9.4.3 using the JSON format—that is, by generating an HTML table based on JSON data (see Figure 9.19).

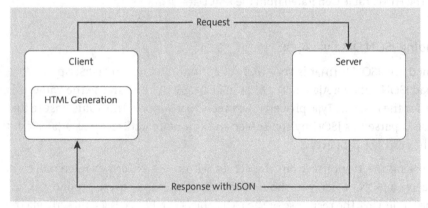

Figure 9.19 HTML Generation on the Client Side Based on JSON Data

The JSON document from Section 9.3 will be used as the basis. The code for initializing the table (initTable()) and for creating a table row (createRow()) remains unchanged compared to the XML example from Listing 9.16; therefore, these methods are not listed again in Listing 9.18. The example can actually be explained quite quickly because much is similar to the XML example explained earlier. Only the access to the data model—that is, to the parsed JavaScript object—is somewhat easier: instead of using DOM methods, the access can simply occur via dot notation.

The outer loop iterates over all artists (result.artists) and the inner loop iterates over their albums (artist.albums), generating a new row in the table each time by calling createRow(). The generated HTML doesn't differ in any way from the HTML generated in the XML example.

```
'use strict';
const request = new XMLHttpRequest();
request.onload = () => {
  if(request.status === 200) {
    let result;
```

```
    if (request.responseType === 'json') {
      result = request.response;
    } else {
      result = JSON.parse(request.responseText);
    }
    const table = initTable();
    const artists = result.artists;
    for (let i = 0; i < artists.length; i++) {
      const artist = artists[i];
      const albums = artist.albums;
      for (let j = 0; j < albums.length; j++) {
        const album = albums[j];
        const row = createRow(
          artist.name,
          album.title,
          album.year
        );
        table.tBodies[0].appendChild(row);
      }
    }
    document.getElementById('artists-container').appendChild(table);
  }
};
request.open('GET', 'artists.json', true);
request.responseType = 'json';
request.setRequestHeader('Accept', 'application/json');
request.send();
```

Listing 9.18 Loading JSON Data via Ajax

The jQuery Library

In Chapter 10, we'll show you, among other things, how you can also use the jQuery library to express Ajax requests in a slightly simpler and, most importantly, a browser-independent way.

9.4.5 Sending Data to the Server via Ajax

Naturally, it's not only possible to retrieve data from a server; you can also send data to the server. In this case, instead of using GET, you simply use POST as the HTTP method and pass the appropriate data to the send() method. Here too you can freely choose the format, but usually the JSON format is used because, as mentioned, it can be generated very easily with JavaScript.

An example is shown in Listing 9.19. First, the newArtist JavaScript object is created in the familiar way. When formulating the Ajax request, the value artist/create is specified as the URL under the assumption that a corresponding script is hidden behind this URL on the server side, which receives and processes the data sent to the server. In order not to let the server guess the format of the data sent, it's also advisable to set the Content-Type header accordingly. In this example for the JSON data, it's set to the value application/json.

```
'use strict';
const newArtist = {
  "name": "Deltron 3030",
  "albums": [
    {
      "title": "Deltron 3030",
      "year": 2000
    },
    {
      "title": "Event 2",
      "year": 2013
    }
  ]
}
const request = new XMLHttpRequest();
request.onload = () => {
  if(request.status === 200) {
    console.log('Data successfully sent.');
  }
};
request.open('POST', 'artists/create');
request.setRequestHeader('Content-Type', 'application/json');
request.send(newArtist);
```

Listing 9.19 Sending JSON Data to a Server via Ajax

9.4.6   Submitting Dorms via Ajax

With the FormData object, JavaScript provides a simple way to send form data to a server via Ajax. After creating an object instance of FormData, you can add individual properties and their values via the append() method as in Listing 9.20. Then you pass the object instance as an argument to the send() method. As the value for the HTTP method, you pass the POST value here as well.

```
'use strict';
function init() {
  const formData = new FormData();
```

```
  formData.append('username', 'john.doe');
  formData.append('email', 'john.doe@javascripthandbuch.de');
  formData.append('url', 'javascripthandbuch.de');
  formData.append('age', 44);
  const request = new XMLHttpRequest();
  request.open('POST', 'register', true);
  request.send(formData);
}
document.addEventListener('DOMContentLoaded', init);
```

Listing 9.20 Sending a Form via Ajax

Sending form data is made even easier by the fact that the FormData object can be bound directly to a form. To do this, simply pass the appropriate form to the constructor call of FormData, as shown in Listing 9.21. This way you bypass the manual calls to append() because all properties (or form input fields) of the corresponding form are implicitly added to the FormData object.

```
'use strict';
function init() {
  const form = document.getElementById('register');
  form.addEventListener('submit', (e) => {
    e.preventDefault();
    const formData = new FormData(form);
    const request = new XMLHttpRequest();
    request.open('POST', 'register', true);
    request.send(formData);
  });
}
document.addEventListener('DOMContentLoaded', init);
```

Listing 9.21 Binding a FormData Object to a Form

> **Note**
>
> Before the FormData object existed, you had to manually read the values from the corresponding form, use them to create your own JavaScript object, and pass this object to the Ajax call.

9.4.7 Loading Data from Other Domains

For security reasons, it isn't possible to load data via Ajax from a domain other than the one from which the JavaScript code was loaded; that is, cross-origin requests are not allowed (see Figure 9.20). The reason for this is mainly to prevent malicious code from being loaded from other domains. However, there are three different techniques that still allow you to load data from other domains, and we'll briefly discuss them in this section.

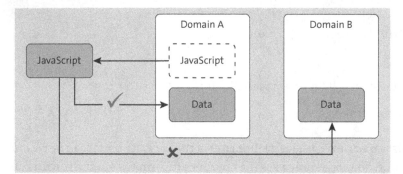

Figure 9.20 Cross-Origin Requests Are Not Allowed by Default

> **Note**
>
> We won't list any concrete implementations because in some cases, it would be necessary to create corresponding programs on the server side as well, which would exceed the scope of this section. Here, the point is primarily to explain the theoretical background to the various techniques.

Loading Data from Other Servers via Proxy

One way to load JavaScript code from another domain is to use a proxy (see Figure 9.21). This is a component on a server within the (own) domain from which the JavaScript code was loaded and which connects to the (foreign) domain from which the other data is to be loaded.

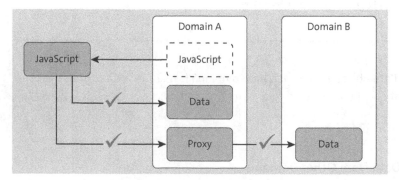

Figure 9.21 A Server-Side Proxy Is Used to Bypass Cross-Origin Requests

Now, instead of loading the data directly from the other domain via Ajax, you send the requests to the proxy. Based on the request, the proxy makes its own request to the other domain (on the server side, there are usually no restrictions regarding access to other domains). The proxy then processes the response of this request and forwards it to the client as a response to the original request from the client.

Loading Data from Other Servers via CORS

The second option to load JavaScript from a foreign server is to use the cross-origin resource sharing (CORS) principle (see Figure 9.22).

First, the client sends a preflight request to the foreign domain. The browser implicitly sends an additional (unchangeable) `Origin` header that specifies the domain from which the JavaScript code making the request was loaded. In addition, the `Access-Control-Request-Method` header is set to the value `OPTION`.

The server in the foreign domain then indicates in a preflight response whether the data may be loaded from there. Specifically, the server sends the `Access-Control-Allow-Origin` header. Only if the domain from which the request is to be made via JavaScript appears as a value in this header will the actual request subsequently be made and the actual response be sent.

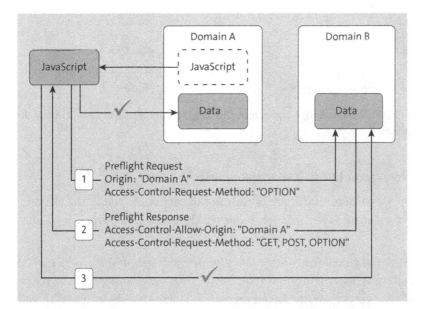

Figure 9.22 Cross-Origin Resource Sharing Allows Data to be Downloaded from Previously Defined Servers

---

Browser Support and Specification of CORS

CORS is only supported by more recent browsers. Older browsers do not support this technique. The specification can be found at *fetch.spec.whatwg.org/#http-cors-protocol*.

Loading Data from Other Servers via JSONP

The third way to load data from other servers is called JSON with Padding (JSONP). This takes advantage of the fact that JavaScript code can be loaded from *any* other domain via the <script> element. Essentially, you load two JavaScript files via the <script> element, as shown in Figure 9.23. The file that is loaded from your own domain defines a function that expects specific data. In turn, the file loaded from the foreign domain calls this function with the corresponding data. Within the function, you then have the usual access to the data.

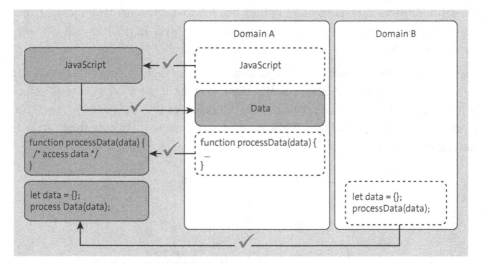

Figure 9.23 With JSONP, the JavaScript Code from the Foreign Domain Calls JavaScript Code from the Own Domain

9.4.8   The Newer Alternative to XMLHttpRequest: The Fetch API

It should be mentioned here that there is now an alternative to using the XMLHttp-Request object for creating asynchronous requests: the *Fetch API* (*https://fetch.spec.whatwg.org*).

The starting point is the global function fetch() (or one defined on the window object), which abstracts all kinds of asynchronous requests (GET, POST, etc.) and returns a Promise object. The then() and catch() methods can then be called on this object to define callbacks for result handling and error handling (see Listing 9.22) for cases where the response was successfully loaded from the server (then()) or where an error occurred (catch()).

Calling response.json() within the callback for the then() method creates a stream in the example, via which the body of the HTTP response can be read as JSON. In addition to JSON streams, there are other streams available for array buffers (via the array-Buffer() method), binary large objects (BLOBs; via the blob() method), form data (via the formData() method), and plain text (via the text() method).

```
'use strict';
function init() {
  // 1.) Query the artists.json file
  fetch('artists.json')
    .then((response) => {
      // The response object contains the following properties:
      console.log(response.status);      // 200
      console.log(response.statusText); // "OK"
      console.log(response.type);        // "basic"
      console.log(response.bodyUsed);    // false
      console.log(response.headers);     // []
      console.log(response.ok);          // true
      console.log(response.redirected); // false
      console.log(response.url);         // http://localhost:8080/artists.json
                        // (depending on the root directory of the web server)

      // 2.) Convert the response into a JavaScript object
      return response.json();
    })
    .then((result) => {
      // 3.) Evaluate the converted JavaScript object
      const table = initTable();
      const artists = result.artists;
      for (let i = 0; i < artists.length; i++) {
        const artist = artists[i];
        const albums = artist.albums;
        for (let j = 0; j < albums.length; j++) {
          const album = albums[j];
          const row = createRow(
            artist.name,
            album.title,
            album.year
          );
          table.tBodies[0].appendChild(row);
        }
      }
      document.getElementById('artists-container').appendChild(table);
    })
    .catch((error) => {
      console.error(error);
    });
}
```

Listing 9.22 Using the Fetch API for a GET Request

Because the Fetch API is based on promises, or a call to fetch() returns a Promise object, you can also use the API in combination with await. This makes the source text a bit more readable, as shown in Listing 9.23.

```javascript
'use strict';
async function init() {
  try {
    // 1.) Query the artists.json file
    const response = await fetch('artists.json');
    // The response object contains the following properties:
    console.log(response.status);     // 200
    console.log(response.statusText); // "OK"
    console.log(response.type);       // "basic"
    console.log(response.bodyUsed);   // false
    console.log(response.headers);    // []
    console.log(response.ok);         // true
    console.log(response.redirected); // false
    console.log(response.url);        // "http://localhost:8080/artists.json"
                        // (depending on the root directory of the web server)
    // 2.) Convert the response into a JavaScript object
    const result = await response.json();
    // 3.) Evaluate the converted JavaScript object
    const table = initTable();
    const artists = result.artists;
    for (let i = 0; i < artists.length; i++) {
      const artist = artists[i];
      const albums = artist.albums;
      for (let j = 0; j < albums.length; j++) {
        const album = albums[j];
        const row = createRow(
          artist.name,
          album.title,
          album.year
        );
        table.tBodies[0].appendChild(row);
      }
    }
    document.getElementById('artists-container').appendChild(table);
  } catch(error) {
  console.error(error);
  }
}
```

```
function initTable() {
  const table = document.createElement('table');
  // ... like above
  return table;
}
```

Listing 9.23 Using the Fetch API in Combination with await

For simple GET requests, it's sufficient to pass only the URL as a parameter to the fetch() method. For HTTP requests that are based on a different HTTP method or that require additional configurations, you can pass these configurations in the form of a second parameter. For example, Listing 9.24 shows you how to execute a POST request in this way. You can also see here that the configuration object can be used to configure not only the HTTP method, but also the HTTP headers and the body—that is, the data to be transferred with the request.

```
'use strict';
async function init() {
  try {
    const body = {
      firstName: 'John',
      lastName: 'Doe',
    }
    const response = await fetch('register',
      {
        method: 'post',
        headers: {
          'Accept': 'application/json',
          'Content-Type': 'application/json'
        },
        body: JSON.stringify(body)
      }
    );
    console.log(response);
  } catch (error) {
    console.error(error);
  };
}

document.addEventListener('DOMContentLoaded', init);
```

Listing 9.24 Using the Fetch API for a POST Request

9.5   Summary

In this chapter, you learned about an important tool for enhancing the user experience of web applications: asynchronous communication using Ajax. In summary, as always at the end of each chapter, here are the key points to remember:

- Using *Ajax*, it's possible to send asynchronous HTTP requests to a server using Java-Script. For example, this allows parts of a web page to be updated without having to completely reload a web page.

- *XML* is used mainly as an exchange format between applications or between client and server.

- *JSON* is a relatively new format—compared to XML—that's also used for exchanging data between applications or between client and server. It's very popular in this regard mainly because it's very lightweight compared to XML, doesn't have as much overhead, and is natively supported in JavaScript.

- The central object through which Ajax requests are made is the `XMLHttpRequest` object.

- With the help of the `FormData` object, form data can also be sent via Ajax relatively easily.

- In principle, it isn't possible to load data from servers via Ajax except from the server from which the corresponding JavaScript code was loaded. However, there are three techniques that allow you to load data from other servers:
  - Using a *proxy* on your own server
  - Using *CORS*
  - Using *JSONP*

- The Fetch API simplifies sending asynchronous requests compared to using the `XMLHttpRequest` object.

Chapter 10
Simplifying Tasks with jQuery

Many tasks that can now be performed relatively easily with JavaScript were for a long time only possible with a relatively large amount of source code due to browser differences. For this reason, various libraries have emerged to simplify different tasks such as working with the DOM. One of the most famous of these libraries is jQuery, which even today is part of every web developer's toolbox.

Probably one of the best-known JavaScript libraries is the jQuery library (*https://jquery.com*), which, in part, considerably simplifies working with JavaScript. Although many things are now also possible with standard methods of the DOM API, jQuery is still a library to be taken seriously. This chapter provides an overview of using jQuery, including how to simplify accessing and manipulating the DOM, working with events, and formulating Ajax requests.

> **Note**
>
> The jQuery library is so extensive that we can't cover all its aspects in one chapter. Instead, we'll offer a selection of topics that are representative and give a good introduction to the library. Also, we won't discuss the selected topics in great detail but will describe the code examples relatively concisely (we're assuming that you've already acquired the necessary basic knowledge, such as DOM processing, events, Ajax, and so on, throughout the preceding chapters).

10.1 Introduction

As you've seen in the previous chapters, there are differences between different browsers with regard to DOM manipulation, event processing, and Ajax. The jQuery library abstracts such browser-specific details and provides a unified interface, and not only for the aforementioned topics. So essentially, jQuery has the following advantages:

- **Simplified working with the DOM**
  jQuery simplifies access to elements of the DOM tree by providing various helper methods. In Section 10.2, we discuss this topic in more detail. By the way: standard methods of the current DOM API, like `querySelector()` and `querySelectorAll()` (which are not available in older browsers), are based on ideas from jQuery.

- **Simplified working with events**
  jQuery simplifies working with events and provides helper methods for this purpose, which we'll introduce in Section 10.3.

- **Simplified phrasing of Ajax requests**
  jQuery simplifies the phrasing of Ajax requests—again, by hiding browser-specific details. We'll present the corresponding helper methods in Section 10.4.

---

jQuery Isn't Always Necessary

Although jQuery is a really powerful library, you shouldn't make the mistake of equating jQuery with JavaScript and first learning jQuery and then the JavaScript language. jQuery can certainly be of support in many cases, but often the use of the library isn't even necessary because you can already solve the corresponding tasks with pure JavaScript code or even other, leaner libraries. Websites like You Might Not Need jQuery (*http://youmightnotneedjquery.com*) demonstrate this with various examples.

Tip

In principle, it's not bad for a JavaScript developer to both be able to use libraries like jQuery and have a firm grasp of the basic language concepts as well.

10.1.1   Embedding jQuery

The jQuery library can be embedded in several ways. At *https://jquery.com/download/*, you can download the current version of the library. Besides the "normal" version, a minified (i.e., compressed) version is available for download, which is as small as possible in terms of file size. After you've downloaded the file, you can include it as usual via the <script> element (see Listing 10.1).

```
<!DOCTYPE html>
<html>
<head lang="en">
  <title>jQuery example</title>
  <link rel="stylesheet" href="styles/main.css" type="text/css">
</head>
<body>
  <script src="scripts/jquery-3.6.0.min.js"></script>
  <script src="scripts/main.js"></script>
</body>
</html>
```

Listing 10.1 Embedding a Downloaded Version of jQuery

Minified Versions versus Nonminified Versions

Most libraries offer both a normal (nonminified) version and a minified version for download. In the latter, spaces and often comments within the code are removed, for example, and much more is optimized to reduce the file size and thus reduce download time. Consequently, minified versions of libraries are suitable for use in a production system. The nonminified version is actually only suitable if you also want to take a look at the corresponding library during development—during debugging, for example.

10.1.2   Embedding jQuery via a Content Delivery Network

If you download jQuery as described and embed it as a local dependency in your web page and then load your website onto a server, you must also load jQuery onto the appropriate server. Alternatively, you have the option of integrating jQuery via a *content delivery network* (*CDN*; see note box). For jQuery, the corresponding URL (for the current version of the library) is *https://code.jquery.com/jquery-3.6.0.min.js* (see Listing 10.2).

```
<!DOCTYPE html>
<html>
<head lang="en">
  <title>jQuery example</title>
  <link rel="stylesheet" href="styles/main.css" type="text/css">
</head>
<body>
  <script src="https://code.jquery.com/jquery-3.6.0.min.js"></script>
  <script src="scripts/main.js"></script>
</body>
</html>
```

Listing 10.2 Embedding jQuery via a Content Delivery Network

Content Delivery Network

A *content delivery network* (also known as a *content distribution network*) is a network of servers connected via the internet that distribute requests so that they can be answered as quickly as possible. Typically, the geographical location of a request plays a major role: for example, if a user from Germany accesses your web page and you have embedded jQuery there via a CDN URL (*https://code.jquery.com*), the corresponding code is sent to the user from a server in Germany. A user accessing your web page from the US, on the other hand, is served by a server located there.

10.1.3   Using jQuery

The core of jQuery is the `jQuery()` function or the equivalent shortcut function `$()` (called the *jQuery method* ahead). This function can be called with various arguments (see *http://api.jquery.com/jQuery* for details), three forms of which are used particularly frequently:

- **Call with CSS selector**
  In this case, you pass a selector to the jQuery method (similar to the CSS selectors, but more about that in a moment) and receive an object as the return value that contains the elements of the web page that match the selector. Examples of this are shown in Listing 10.3 and Listing 10.4. The object returned by the method represents a so-called wrapper object (called the *jQuery object* ahead) for the corresponding elements and provides various methods for these elements (more on this later).

  ```
  const selectedElements = jQuery('body > div > span');
  ```

  Listing 10.3 The jQuery() Function

  ```
  const selectedElements = $('body > div > span');
  ```

  Listing 10.4 The More Common Shortcut Function, $()

- **Call with nodes from the DOM tree**
  As an alternative to calling the jQuery method with a selector, it can also be called with a node of the DOM tree or with the corresponding JavaScript object representing the respective node. Here as well, the jQuery object represents a wrapper object around the passed node and provides additional methods. For example, to define an event listener that is called when the `document` object is fully loaded, proceed as in Listing 10.5. The `ready()` method doesn't exist for the `document` object but is provided indirectly by the jQuery object (see also Section 10.3.2).

  ```
  $(document).ready(() => {
    console.log('Web page loaded');
  });
  ```

  Listing 10.5 Calling the jQuery Method with a Node from the DOM Tree

- **Call with HTML string**
  You can also use the jQuery method to create new elements. To do this, simply pass the appropriate HTML code for the element you want to create to the method as a string, as shown in Listing 10.6.

  ```
  const newElement = $('<div>New element</div>');
  ```

  Listing 10.6 Calling the jQuery Method with an HTML String

> **Note**
>
> In all cases shown, the return value of the jQuery method is an object that adds additional functionality, the jQuery object, to the corresponding elements. This object contains references to one or more nodes of the DOM tree, hereafter referred to as *selected nodes* or *selected elements*.

10.1.4 Simplifying Tasks with jQuery

The fact that jQuery simplifies working with the DOM is best demonstrated using an example. Suppose you have an HTML list in which each list entry contains a URL (as text, not as a link), and you'd like to use JavaScript to create real links from the URLs at runtime. In other words: The text content of the list entries is to be converted into <a> elements.

Using pure JavaScript, you would probably proceed as shown in Listing 10.7. First, the appropriate <li> elements must be selected (here, for simplicity, all <li> elements of the entire web page). Then, in each case, the text content must be extracted and removed, and a new <a> element must be created, its href attribute and text content must be set, and the element must be added to the <li> element as a child element.

```javascript
'use strict';
function init() {
  const listItems = document.getElementsByTagName('li');
  for(let i=0; i<listItems.length; i++) {
    const listItem = listItems[i];
    const url = listItem.textContent;
    listItem.textContent = '';
    const link = document.createElement('a');
    link.setAttribute('href', url);
    const linkText = document.createTextNode(url);
    link.appendChild(linkText);
    listItem.appendChild(link);
  }
}
document.addEventListener('DOMContentLoaded', init);
```

Listing 10.7 Creating Links Using Pure JavaScript

Not exactly little code for actually a trivial task. And it doesn't get any better if you use the innerHTML property instead of the createElement(), setAttribute(), and createText-Node() DOM methods, as shown in Listing 10.8. This code also looks relatively cluttered and cobbled together.

```
'use strict';
function init() {
  const listItems = document.getElementsByTagName('li');
  for(let i=0; i<listItems.length; i++) {
    listItems[i].innerHTML = '<a href="'
    + listItems[i].textContent + '">'
    + listItems[i].textContent + '</a>';
  }
}
document.addEventListener('DOMContentLoaded', init);
```

Listing 10.8 Creating Links Using innerHTML

With jQuery, things get a little more elegant, to say the least. The corresponding code is shown in Listing 10.9. Here the wrapInner() method comes into play, which is made available to the selected elements by the jQuery object. This method wraps the contents of the selected elements with the HTML code returned by the passed function in the example. Much simpler than the previous code!

```
'use strict';
function init() {
  $('li').wrapInner(
    function() {
      return '<a href="' + this.textContent + '"></a>'
    }
  );
}
$(document).ready(init)
```

Listing 10.9 Creating Links Using jQuery

> **jQuery Plug-ins**
>
> By the way, if you don't find a functionality within jQuery, there are thousands of plug-ins available on the internet. A very good overview is given by the official jQuery registry at *https://plugins.jquery.com/*.

10.2   Working with the DOM

Working with the DOM wasn't always as comfortable as it is now thanks to methods like querySelector() and querySelectorAll(). For a long time, jQuery was the first choice when it came to processing the DOM in a relatively simple way—to select, modify, or add elements, for example. Even today, jQuery supports you in the following tasks, among others:

- Selection of elements (Section 10.2.1)
- Accessing and modifying content (Section 10.2.2)
- Filtering selected elements (Section 10.2.3)
- Accessing attributes (Section 10.2.4)
- Accessing CSS properties (Section 10.2.5)
- Navigating between elements (Section 10.2.6)
- Using effects (Section 10.2.7)

10.2.1 Selecting Elements

Using jQuery, elements can be selected using CSS-like selectors. These selectors can be divided into the following groups:

- **Basic selectors**
  Essential selectors that you already know from CSS (see Table 10.1)
- **Hierarchy selectors**
  Selectors involving the hierarchy of elements (see Table 10.2), also already known from CSS
- **Basic filter selectors**
  Selectors that allow you to more specifically filter individual elements, not all of which exist in CSS (see Table 10.3)
- **Content filter selectors**
  Selectors that include the content of elements (see Table 10.4)
- **Visibility filter selectors**
  Selectors involving the visibility of elements (see Table 10.5)
- **Attribute filter selectors**
  Selectors that include the attributes of elements (see Table 10.6)
- **Form filter selectors**
  Selectors that are specifically useful for selecting form elements (see Table 10.7)
- **Child filter selectors**
  Selectors for selecting child elements (see Table 10.8)

Selector	Description
`*`	Elements with any element name
`elementName`	Elements of type `elementName`

Table 10.1 Basic Selectors in jQuery

Selector	Description
#id	Element with the ID id
.class	Elements of the class class
selektor1, selector2	Elements that match either the selector1 selector or the selector2 selector

Table 10.1 Basic Selectors in jQuery (Cont.)

Selector	Description
element1 element2	All elements of type element2 that are inside an element of type element1
element1 > element2	All elements of type element2 that are direct child elements of an element of type element1
element1 + element2	All elements of type element2 that directly follow an element of type element1
element1 ~ element2	All elements of type element2 that follow an element of type element1

Table 10.2 Hierarchy Selectors in jQuery

Selector	Description
:animated	Selects elements that are currently used within an animation.
:header	Selects all heading elements—that is, <h1>, <h2>, <h3>, <h4>, <h5>, and <h6>.
:lang()	Selects all elements for the passed language.
:not()	Selects all elements that do not match the passed selector.
:root	Selects the root element (not the document node)—that is, the <html> element.
:target	Selects the element identified by the fragment ID of the corresponding URL. For example, if the URL is *http://www. javascripthandbuch.de#jquery*, then $(':target') will select the element with the ID jquery.

Table 10.3 Basic Filter Selectors in jQuery

Selector	Description
:contains()	Selects all elements that contain the passed text
:empty	Selects all elements that have no child elements or child nodes
:has()	Selects all elements that contain at least one element that matches the passed selector
:parent	Selects all elements that have at least one child node

Table 10.4 Content Filter Selectors in jQuery

Selector	Description
:hidden	Selects all elements that are not visible
:visible	Selects all visible elements

Table 10.5 Visibility Filter Selectors in jQuery

Selector	Description
[name|= "value"]	Selects elements with the attribute name for which the values are a series of values separated by minus signs and where the first value is value
[name*= "value"]	Selects elements with the attribute name, the value of which contains value as a substring
[name~= "value"]	Selects elements with the attribute name, the value of which is a list of values, one of which is equal to value
[name$= "value"]	Selects elements with the attribute name, the value of which ends with value
[name= "value"]	Selects elements with the attribute name that has the value value
[name!= "value"]	Selects elements with the attribute name that do not have the value value
[name^= "value"]	Selects elements with the attribute name, the value of which begins with value
[name]	Selects elements with the attribute name
[name= "value"] [name2= "value2"]	Selects elements with the attribute name having the value value and with the attribute name2 having the value value2

Table 10.6 Attribute Filter Selectors in jQuery

Selector	Description
:button	Selects all buttons
:checkbox	Selects all checkboxes
:checked	Selects all selected or activated elements
:disabled	Selects all disabled elements
:enabled	Selects all activated elements
:focus	Selects all elements that have the focus
:file	Selects all file input fields
:image	Selects all elements with the attribute type having the value image
:input	Selects all input fields
:password	Selects all password fields
:radio	Selects all radio buttons
:reset	Selects all elements with the attribute type having the value reset
:selected	Selects all selected elements
:submit	Selects all elements with the attribute type having the value submit
:text	Selects all text input fields

Table 10.7 Form Filter Selectors in jQuery

Selector	Description
:first-child	Selects the first child element
:first-of-type	Selects the first element of a given type
:last-child	Selects the last child element
:last-of-type	Selects the last element of a given type
:nth-child()	Selects the nth child element
:nth-last-child()	Selects the nth child element, counting from the end

Table 10.8 Child Filter Selectors in jQuery

Selector	Description
:nth-of-type()	Selects the nth element of a given type
:nth-last-of-type()	Selects the nth element of a given type, counting from the end
:only-child	Selects elements that are the only child element of their parent element
:only-of-type()	Selects elements that are the only child element of their parent element of a given type

Table 10.8 Child Filter Selectors in jQuery (Cont.)

You can find some examples of using these selectors in Listing 10.10, and complete lists of all corresponding selectors can be found in the tables ahead.

```
$(document).ready((() => {
  const inputElements = $('input');            // all <input> elements
  const john = $('#john');                     // element with the ID "john"
  const oddElements = $('.odd');               // elements of the class "odd"
  const elements = $('td, th');                // all <td>- und <th> elements
  const inputJohn = $('input[name="john"]');   // <input> elements the
                                               // name attribute of which
                                               // has the value "john"

  const oddRows = $('tr').odd());              // all "odd" <tr> elements
  const evenRows = $('tr').even();             // all "even" <tr> elements
  const listItemsAtIndex = $('li:eq(2)');      // all <li> elements at index 2
  const allOthers = $(':not(li)');             // all elements other than <li>
  const notExample = $(':not(.example)');      // all elements without the CSS
                                               // class "example"
});
```

Listing 10.10 A Few Examples of Using Selectors

> **Note**
>
> Some selectors such as :odd (for selecting all "odd" elements), :even (for selecting all "even" elements), :first (for selecting the first elements), and :last (for selecting the last elements) are deprecated since jQuery 3.4. Instead, you should first select the elements using the appropriate selector and apply the odd(), even(), first(), and last() methods on the result set (see Listing 10.10 for the use of odd() and even()).

> **Combination of Selectors**
>
> The individual selectors naturally can be combined with each other, as you know from CSS.

10.2.2   Accessing and Modifying Content

After you've selected elements via the jQuery method using the selectors presented in the previous section, the jQuery object provides various methods for the selected elements to access and modify the content. These include but are not limited to the following:

- Accessing and modifying HTML and text content (see Table 10.9)
- Adding content within an element (see Table 10.10 and Figure 10.1)
- Adding content outside an element (see Table 10.11 and Figure 10.1)
- Adding content around an element (see Table 10.12)
- Replacing content (see Table 10.13)
- Removing content (see Table 10.14)

Method	Description
html()	Without an argument, this method returns the HTML content of an element. With an argument, this method sets the HTML content of an element.
text()	Without an argument, this method returns the text content of an element. With an argument, this method sets the text content of an element.

Table 10.9 Methods for Retrieving and Defining Content

Method	Description
append()	Adds content to the end of the selected elements: $(a).append(b) adds content b to the end of element a (see Figure 10.1).
appendTo()	Opposite of append(); that is, $(a).appendTo(b) adds element a as content to the end of element b.
prepend()	Inserts content at the beginning of the selected elements: $(a).prepend(b) adds content b to the beginning of element a (see Figure 10.1).
prependTo()	Opposite of prepend(); that is, $(a).prependTo(b) adds element a as content to the beginning of element b.

Table 10.10 Methods for Adding Content within an Element

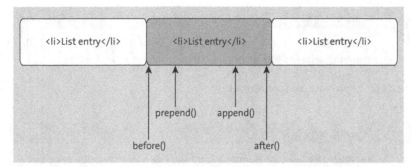

Figure 10.1 The Different Methods for Adding Content inside and outside Elements

Method	Description
after()	Adds content after each of the selected elements: $(a).after(b) inserts content b after element a (see Figure 10.1).
before()	Adds content before each of the selected elements: $(a).before(b) inserts content b before element a (see Figure 10.1).
insertAfter()	Opposite of after(); that is, $(a).insertAfter(b) inserts element a after element b.
insertBefore()	Opposite of before(); that is, $(a).insertBefore(b) inserts element a before element b.

Table 10.11 Methods for Adding Content outside an Element

Method	Description
clone()	Creates a copy of the selected elements. More precisely, a so-called deep copy is created, which also copies child elements of the selected elements.
wrap()	Adds new content around each of the selected elements.
wrapAll()	Adds new content around all selected elements.
wrapInner()	Adds new content around the content of each of the selected elements.

Table 10.12 Methods for Adding Content around an Element

Method	Description
replaceWith()	Replaces the selected elements with new content: $(a).replaceWith(b) replaces element a with content b.

Table 10.13 Methods for Replacing Content

Method	Description
replaceAll()	Opposite of replaceWith(); that is, $(a).replaceAll(b) replaces all elements selected by selector b with the content in a.

Table 10.13 Methods for Replacing Content (Cont.)

Method	Description
detach()	Removes the selected elements from the DOM tree but retains references to the removed elements so that they can be reincorporated into the DOM tree at a later time
empty()	Removes all child nodes from the selected elements
remove()	Removes the selected elements from the DOM tree
unwrap()	Removes the parent element from each of the selected elements

Table 10.14 Methods for Removing Content

Some examples of these methods are shown in Listing 10.11. For example, you can use the html() method to access the HTML content, the text() method to access the text content (both read and write access), append() to append new content to the existing content of the selected elements, prepend() to insert content before the existing content, after() to append new content to the selected elements, and before() to insert content before the selected elements.

```
// Add new HTML content
$('#main').html('<div>New content</div>');
// Access the HTML content
const htmlContent = $('#main').html();

// Add new text content
$('#main').text('New text content');
// Access the text content
const textContent = $('#main').text();

// Add new content after the
// existing content of each <div> element
// with the CSS class "example"
$('div.example').append('<p>Example</p>');

// Add new content before the
// existing content of each <div> element
// with the CSS class "example"
$('div.example').prepend('<p>Example</p>');
```

```
// Add new content after each
// <div> element with the CSS class "example"
$('div.example').after('<p>Example</p>');
```

```
// Add new content before each
// <div> element with the CSS class "example"
$('div.example').before('<p>Example</p>');
```

Listing 10.11 Some Examples of Changing and Adding Content

10.2.3 Filtering Selected Elements

The jQuery object also provides various methods for the selected elements, which you can use to further narrow down the currently selected elements (see Table 10.15). Some examples are shown in Listing 10.12: for example, the eq() method limits the selection to the element at index 2 (i.e., the third <li> element in the example); the first() and last() methods let you select the first and last of the currently selected elements, respectively; the filter() method limits the selection to the specified selector; and the not() method limits the selection to the elements that do not match the specified selector. You can also use the has() method to select the elements that have at least one child element that matches the given selector. Figure 10.2 illustrates the filter methods shown in Listing 10.12.

```
// Selection of the third <li> element
$('li').eq(2);
// Selection of the first <li> element
$('li').first();
// Selection of <li> elements that have the CSS class ".selected"
$('li').filter('.selected');
// Selection of all <li> elements that contain a <ul> element
$('li').has('ul');
// Selection of all elements that have the CSS class ".selected"
$('li').has('.selected');
// Selection of the last <li> element
$('li').last();
// Selection of all class attributes of the <li> elements
$('li').map(() => { this.className });
// Selection of all <li> elements that do not have the CSS class ".selected"
$('li').not('.selected');
// Selection of the first two <li> elements
$('li').slice(0, 2);
```

Listing 10.12 Usage of Different Filter Methods

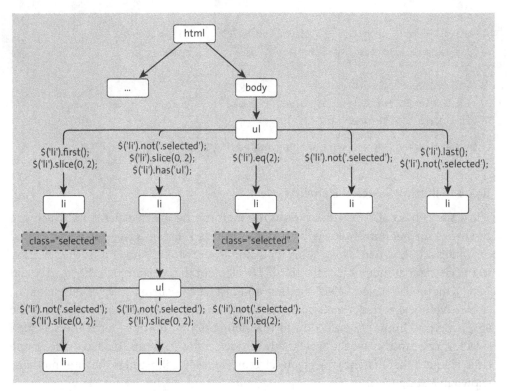

Figure 10.2 Narrowing Down Elements via jQuery Filter Methods

Method	Description
add()	Adds new elements to a selection of elements
addBack()	Adds a previous selection to the current selection of elements
eq()	Reduces the selected elements to one element at a given index
filter()	Reduces the selected elements to those elements (1) that match the passed selector or (2) for which the passed filter function returns true
find()	Selects the child elements of the selected elements that (1) match the passed selector, (2) are contained in the passed jQuery object, or (3) are equal to the passed element
first()	Reduces the selected elements to the first element
has()	Reduces the selected elements to those elements that have a child element that (1) matches the passed selector or (2) is equal to the passed element

Table 10.15 Methods for Filtering

Method	Description
is()	Checks if at least one of the selected elements (1) matches the passed selector, (2) returns true for the passed filter function, (3) is contained in the passed jQuery object, or (4) is one of the elements passed as parameter
last()	Reduces the selected elements to the last element
not()	Reduces the selected elements to those that (1) do not match the passed selector, (2) do not match the passed filter function, or (3) are not contained in the passed jQuery object
slice()	Reduces the selected elements to a subset defined by start and end index

Table 10.15 Methods for Filtering (Cont.)

10.2.4 Accessing Attributes

The jQuery object also provides some methods to access HTML attributes (see Table 10.16). The attr() method can be used to determine or reset values of attributes, as shown in Listing 10.13: if you pass the name of an attribute to the method, the method returns the corresponding value of the attribute; if, on the other hand, you pass another string as the second argument to the method, this string is used as the new value for the attribute.

Alternatively, you can pass an object to the method in order to add several attributes in one go. In this case, the object's property names are used as names for the attributes, and the object property values are used as values for the attributes.

To delete attributes, however, use the removeAttr() method. For adding and removing CSS classes, the methods addClass() and removeClass() are available. However, these two methods are actually redundant—at least for newer browsers that support the classList property, which provide equivalent functionality via the add() and remove() methods.

```
const element = $('a#main');
// Read access to the "href" attribute of the element
const href = element.attr('href');
// Write access to the "href" attribute of the element
element.attr('href', 'index.html');
// Alternative write access via configuration object
element.attr({
  href: 'index.html',
  target: '_blank'
});
// Remove the "href" attribute from the element
element.removeAttr('href');
```

```
// Add a CSS class
element.addClass('highlighted');
// Remove a CSS class
element.removeClass('highlighted');
```

Listing 10.13 Access to Attributes and CSS Classes

Method	Description
attr()	With one argument, this method returns the value for an attribute (e.g., $('a#main').attr('href')). With two arguments, this method sets the value of an attribute (e.g., $('a#main').attr('href', 'index.html')).
removeAttr()	Removes an attribute from an element, e.g., $('a#main').removeAttr ('href')).
addClass()	Adds a new CSS class to the values in the class attribute. In newer browsers, this is possible without jQuery thanks to the standardized classList property and its add() method.
removeClass()	Removes a CSS class from the values in the class attribute. This too is possible in newer browsers without jQuery thanks to the classList property and its remove() method. However, the removeClass() method can alternatively be passed a function that returns a comma-separated list of CSS classes. This functionality isn't possible via the remove() method of the classList property.
toggleClass()	Toggles a CSS class: if the element has the passed class, the class will be removed, and if the element doesn't have the passed class, the class will be added.

Table 10.16 Methods for Accessing Attributes and CSS Classes

10.2.5   Accessing CSS Properties

To access CSS properties, jQuery provides the css() method. Like other methods, such as html(), text(), and attr(), this method can be used to both read and set values. For the former, pass the method the name of the CSS property of which the value is to be read; for the latter, specify the value to be set as the second parameter.

Alternatively, as with the attr() method, an object can be passed as an argument, and the respective properties are then used as CSS properties. In addition, you can also pass an array of strings as an argument to read the values of several CSS properties in one step. Some examples are shown in Listing 10.14.

```
// Read the background color of the <body> element
const backgroundColor = $('body').css('background-color');
// Read the foreground color and the background color of the <body> element
```

```
const properties = $('body').css(['color', 'background-color']);
// Set the background color of the <body> element
$('body').css('background-color', 'blue');
// Set the foreground color and the background color of the <body> element
$('body').css({
  'color': 'white',
  'background-color': 'blue'
});
```

Listing 10.14 Accessing CSS Properties

10.2.6   Navigating between Elements

Starting from a selection of elements stored in a jQuery object, you can use the methods presented ahead to find elements that have a specific relationship to these elements, such as parent elements, sibling elements, and child elements. Some examples are shown in Listing 10.15. The corresponding descriptions of the methods can be found in Table 10.17.

```
// Child elements
// Selection of all child elements of <ul>
const listItems = $('ul').children();
// Selection of the next link within <ul>
const closestLink = $('ul').closest('a');


// Sibling elements
// Selection of the next sibling element
const nextSibling = $('ul').next();
// Selection of the next link element
const nextSiblingLink = $('ul').next('a');
// Selection of all next sibling elements
const nextSiblings = $('ul').nextAll();
// Selection of all next link elements
const nextSiblingLinks = $('div').nextAll('a');
// Selection of all next sibling elements up to the specified element
const nextSiblingsUntil = $('div').nextUntil('a');
// Selection of the previous sibling element
const previousSibling = $('ul').prev();
// Selection of all previous sibling elements
const previousSiblings = $('ul').prevAll();
// Selection of all previous sibling elements up to the specified element
const previousSiblingsUntil = $('div').prevUntil('a');
// Selection of all sibling elements
const siblings = $('div').siblings();
```

```
// Parent elements
// Selection of the parent element
const parent = $('ul').parent();
// Selection of all parent elements
const parents = $('ul').parents();
// Selection of all parent elements up to the specified element
const parentsUntil = $('ul').parentsUntil('div');
```

Listing 10.15 Various Examples of Navigating between Elements

Method	Description
children()	Selects the child elements of the selected elements. Optionally, a selector can be passed--in that case only those child elements are selected to which this selector applies..
closest()	Selects the first element of the selected elements that matches the selector passed as a parameter or for which one of the parent elements matches the selector.
next()	Selects the next sibling element of the selected elements. If a selector is passed, the next sibling element that matches this selector is selected.
nextAll()	Selects all next sibling elements of the selected elements. If a selector is passed, the next sibling elements that match this selector are selected.
nextUntil()	Selects all next sibling elements of the selected elements. If a selector is passed, the next sibling elements are selected up to the sibling element that matches this selector.
parent()	Selects the parent element of the selected elements.
parents()	Selects all parent elements preceding in the hierarchy of the selected elements.
parentsUntil()	Selects all parent elements preceding in the hierarchy of the selected elements up to an element that (1) matches the passed selector, (2) matches the passed element, or (3) is contained in the passed jQuery object.
prev()	Selects the previous sibling element of the selected elements. If a selector is passed, the previous sibling element that matches this selector is selected.
prevAll()	Selects all previous sibling elements of the selected elements. If a selector is passed, the previous sibling elements that match this selector are selected.

Table 10.17 Methods for Navigating the DOM Tree

Method	Description
prevUntil()	Selects all previous sibling elements of the selected elements. If a selector is passed, the previous sibling elements are selected up to the sibling element that matches this selector.
siblings()	Selects all sibling elements of the selected elements. If a selector is passed, the sibling elements that match this selector are selected.

Table 10.17 Methods for Navigating the DOM Tree (Cont.)

10.2.7   Using Effects and Animations

Effects such as fading in or out elements of a web page were not always as easy to implement as they are now with the help of CSS3 animations. It's little wonder then that jQuery offers several methods for this as well, the most important of which are shown in Table 10.18. For example, with fadeIn(), fadeOut(), and fadeToggle(), it's possible to fade the selected elements in and out, and slideDown(), slideUp(), and slideToggle() enable you to slide the selected elements in and out.

The most flexible option is provided by animate(). This method can be passed—in the form of a configuration object—various CSS properties to be animated, the speed or duration of the animation (either as a string, such as one of the values fast or slow, or as a numeric value specifying the duration in milliseconds), an *easing function* (which describes how the speed of the animation behaves in relation to the time within the animation), and a callback function that's called when the animation has been fully executed (see Listing 10.16).

Method	Description
animate()	Enables the animation of CSS properties.
clearQueue()	Removes all animations from the queue that have not yet been executed.
delay()	Delays an animation by a specified number of milliseconds.
dequeue()	Executes the next animation in the queue.
fadeIn()	Fades the selected elements in.
fadeOut()	Fades the selected elements out.
fadeTo()	Adjusts the opacity of the selected elements.
fadeToggle()	Fades the selected elements in or out, depending on their state: if an element is visible, it's faded out, but if it isn't visible, it's faded in.

Table 10.18 Methods for Displaying and Hiding Elements

Method	Description
finish()	Stops the current animation, removes all animations from the queue, and sets the CSS properties of the selected elements to the target value.
hide()	Hides the selected elements.
queue()	Accesses the animations in the queue.
show()	Shows the selected elements.
slideDown()	Slides the selected elements down, from top to bottom.
slideToggle()	Slides the selected elements in or out, depending on their state: if an element is visible, it slides out from bottom to the, but if it isn't visible, it slides in from top to bottom.
slideUp()	Slides the selected elements up, from bottom to top.
stop()	Stops the current animation.
toggle()	Hides or displays the selected elements: if an element is visible, it's hidden, but if it isn't visible, it's displayed.

Table 10.18 Methods for Displaying and Hiding Elements (Cont.)

```
'use strict';
$(document).ready(() => {
  $('main').animate(
    { opacity: 0.75 }, // Properties
    'fast',            // Speed
    'swing',           // Easing
    () => {
      // Animation completed
    }
  );
});
```

Listing 10.16 Accessing CSS Properties

10.3   Responding to Events

As you recall from Chapter 6, there are several options for catching events. Event handlers are usually available for the corresponding event, and there's also the possibility to register several event listeners for one event via the addEventListener() method. Older versions of Internet Explorer also use the attachEvent() method, which fulfills a similar task.

We also showed a corresponding browser-independent helper function in Chapter 6. The jQuery library offers a browser-independent solution as well.

10.3.1 Registering Event Listeners

jQuery provides several methods to respond to events or register event listeners. So, on the one hand, you can use the on() method, which is called on the jQuery object, as shown in Listing 10.17: you pass the name of the event to be responded to as the first parameter and the event listener in the form of a function as the second parameter.

```
$('#button').on('click', (event) => {
  console.log('Button pressed');
});
```

Listing 10.17 Registering an Event Listener

> **Note**
>
> If the jQuery object contains references to multiple elements, calling an event method for each element in the selection invokes the corresponding event listener.

As an alternative to the general on() method, jQuery offers various methods named specifically after the event to be caught, such as the click() method found in Listing 10.18. Logically, these event methods don't need to be passed the name of the respective event as a parameter, but only the event listener.

```
$('#button').click((event) => {
  console.log('Button pressed');
});
```

Listing 10.18 Registering an Event Listener via the Shorthand Method

Overall, the event methods can be classified as follows:

- General event methods (see Table 10.19)
- Event methods for handling general events (Section 10.3.2)
- Event methods for handling mouse events (Section 10.3.3)
- Event methods for handling keyboard events (Section 10.3.4)
- Event methods for handling form events (Section 10.3.5)

10

Method	Description
bind()	Adds an event listener for an event. Since jQuery 1.7, however, the on() method should be used according to the official documentation.
delegate()	For older jQuery versions, this is the preferred method to add an event listener for an event. However, since jQuery 1.7, the on() method should be used.
off()	Removes an event listener for an event.
on()	Adds an event listener for an event.
one()	Adds an event listener that is triggered at most once per event for each selected element.
trigger()	Runs all event listeners registered for an event.
triggerHandler()	Like the trigger() method, but doesn't perform the default behavior for an event (such as submitting a form).
unbind()	Removes an event listener for an event. Since jQuery 1.7, however, the off() method should be used according to the official documentation.
undelegate()	For older jQuery versions, this is the preferred method to remove an event listener for an event. However, since jQuery 1.7, the off() method should be used.

Table 10.19 Methods for Managing Event Handlers

10.3.2 Responding to General Events

Table 10.20 contains some methods for registering event listeners for general events: error() enables you to register event listeners that are triggered when an error event is raised on the selected elements, event listeners registered via ready() are called as soon as the corresponding elements have been loaded (see Listing 10.19), event listeners registered via resize() are called whenever a resize event occurs for the elements, and event listeners registered via scroll() are called whenever a scroll event occurs for the elements.

Method	Description
error()	Register event listeners that are executed when an error event occurs.
ready()	Register event listeners that are executed when the DOM or the element passed to the method is fully loaded.

Table 10.20 Different Methods for Registering Event Listeners

Method	Description
resize()	Register event listeners that are executed when a resize event occurs.
scroll()	Register event listeners that are executed when an element is scrolled.

Table 10.20 Different Methods for Registering Event Listeners (Cont.)

```
$(document).ready(() => {
  console.log('Web page loaded');
});
```

Listing 10.19 Registering an Event Listener for Loading the Document

10.3.3   Responding to Mouse Events

Table 10.21 shows the methods jQuery uses to register event listeners for mouse events. They basically correspond to the events you already know from Chapter 6: click() and dblclick() for mouse clicks; focusin() and focusout() for focusing elements; and mousedown(), mouseenter(), mouseleave(), mousemove(), mouseout(), mouseover(), and mouseup() for mouse movements over elements.

Method	Description
click()	Register event listeners that are executed when the mouse is clicked
dblclick()	Register event listeners that are executed when the mouse is double-clicked
focusin()	Register event listeners that are executed when an element receives focus
focusout()	Register event listeners that are executed when an element loses focus
hover()	Register event listeners that are executed when the mouse pointer hovers over an element
mousedown()	Register event listeners that are executed when the mouse pointer is over an element and the mouse button is pressed
mouseenter()	Register event listeners that are executed when the mouse pointer enters an element
mouseleave()	Register event listeners that are executed when the mouse pointer leaves an element
mousemove()	Register event listeners that are triggered when the mouse moves over an element

Table 10.21 Methods for Handling Mouse Events

Method	Description
mouseout()	Register event listeners that are executed when the mouse pointer leaves an element
mouseover()	Register event listeners that are executed when the mouse pointer enters an element
mouseup()	Register event listeners that are executed when the mouse pointer is over an element and the mouse button is released

Table 10.21 Methods for Handling Mouse Events (Cont.)

An example is shown in Listing 10.20.

```
$('button#target').click((event) => {
  console.log('Button was pressed');
});
```

Listing 10.20 Registering an Event Listener for a Mouse Event

By the way, it's also possible to use the event methods not for registering event listeners, but for triggering events. To do this, simply call the corresponding method without any arguments. In Listing 10.21, for example, within the second event listener (registered on the <button> element with the ID target2), the click event is triggered for the <button> element with the ID target.

```
$('button#target').click((event) => {
  console.log('Button was pressed');
});
$('button#target2').click((event) => {
  $('button#target').click();
});
```

Listing 10.21 Triggering an Event

Note

Most methods in jQuery can be called with a different number of arguments, and each has different functions. For example, as shown earlier in this chapter, you can use the attr() method to both read and write HTML attributes or, as just shown, you can use the event methods to both register event listeners and trigger events.

10.3.4 Responding to Keyboard Events

For registering event listeners for keyboard events, the methods listed in Table 10.22 are available: keydown(), keyup(), and keypress() for registering event listeners that are triggered when a key is pressed or released. Again, all of this should be familiar from Chapter 6.

Method	Description
keydown()	Register event listeners that are executed when a key on the keyboard is pressed. If a key is pressed for a longer time, the event listener is executed several times.
keypress()	Register event listeners that are executed when a key on the keyboard is pressed.
keyup()	Register event listeners that are executed when a key on the keyboard is released.

Table 10.22 Methods for Handling Keyboard Events

An example of using these methods is shown in Listing 10.22. This nicely illustrates how the individual event methods (or all jQuery methods in general) can be used one after the other.

```
$('input#username')
  .keypress((event) => {
    console.log('Key for entering username pressed.');
  })
  .keydown((event) => {
    console.log('Key is pressed.');
  })
  .keyup((event) => {
    console.log('Key for entering username released.');
  });
```

Listing 10.22 Registering Different Event Listeners for Keyboard Events

Fluent API

When an API allows you to call a method directly on the return value of a method, as in Listing 10.22, it is also called a fluent API.

10.3.5 Responding to Form Events

The methods listed in Table 10.23 for registering event listeners related to form events should also be essentially familiar from Chapter 6: blur() and focus() for registering

event listeners that are triggered when a form field loses or receives focus, change()
when the value of a form field changes, select() when a specific value is selected for a
form field, and submit() when a form is submitted.

Method	Description
blur()	Register event listeners that are executed when a form field loses focus
change()	Register event listeners that are executed when the selected value of a selection list, a checkbox, or a group of radio buttons has been changed
focus()	Register event listeners that are executed when a form field receives focus
select()	Register event listeners that are executed when the text of an input field (`<input>` element of the text type) or a text input area (`<textarea>` element) is selected
submit()	Register event listeners that are executed when a form is submitted

Table 10.23 Methods for Handling Form Events

Some examples are shown in Listing 10.23.

```
$('input#username')
  .focus((event) => {
    console.log('Input field focused.');
  })
  .blur((event) => {
    console.log('Input field no longer focused.');
  })
  .change((event) => {
    console.log('Text changed.');
  })
  .select((event) => {
    console.log('Text selected.');
  });
```

Listing 10.23 Registering Different Event Listeners for Form Events

10.3.6   Accessing Information from Events

The *event object*, which is available as a parameter within each event listener, contains
different information and provides different methods, as shown in Table 10.24. Basically, this is the information also contained in the standard event object, as discussed
in Chapter 6, supplemented by a few more details. But again, jQuery hides the browser-
specific details, allowing for browser-independent use.

Property/Method	Description
currentTarget	Contains the current element during the bubbling phase
data	Contains an optional data object passed to the event method
delegateTarget	Contains the element on which the event listener was registered
isDefaultPrevented()	Indicates whether preventDefault() was called on the event object
isImmediatePropagationStopped()	Indicates whether stopImmediatePropagation() was called on the event object
isPropagationStopped()	Indicates whether stopPropagation() was called on the event object
metaKey	Contains an indication of whether the so-called meta key (for Mac keyboards, the `cmd` key; for Windows keyboards, the `Windows` key) was pressed while the event was triggered.
namespace	Contains the namespace of the event
pageX	Contains the mouse position relative to the left edge of the document
pageY	Contains the mouse position relative to the top of the document
preventDefault()	Prevents the default action for an event from being executed
relatedTarget	For an element for which an event was triggered, contains the element directly related to the event (e.g., in the case of a mouseout event, the element on which the mouseover event was triggered by the same user action)
result	Contains the result of an event listener previously triggered for an event
stopImmediatePropagation()	Immediately prevents the event from rising further during the bubbling phase
stopPropagation()	Prevents the event from rising further during the bubbling phase

Table 10.24 Properties and Methods of the Event Object

Property/Method	Description
target	Contains the element that triggered the event
timeStamp	Contains a timestamp indicating the time when the event was triggered
type	Contains the type of the event
which	In the case of mouse or keyboard events, contains the mouse button or key on the keyboard that was pressed

Table 10.24 Properties and Methods of the Event Object (Cont.)

Listing 10.24 shows an example of how you can access this information. Most importantly, you can also see here that it's possible to pass an event a data object that you can then access within the event listener.

```
$('input').on(
  'change,
  {
    value : 4711                      // Data object
  },
  (event) => {
    console.log(event.currentTarget); // current element
    console.log(event.data);          // data object
    console.log(event.data.value);    // property of the data object
    console.log(event.pageX);         // x position of mouse
    console.log(event.pageY);         // y position of mouse
  }
);
```

Listing 10.24 Accessing the jQuery Event Object

10.4 Creating Ajax Requests

Generating Ajax requests is also considerably simplified by jQuery. In this section, we'll show you how to perform the examples in Chapter 9 for Ajax-based loading of HTML, XML, and JSON data via the appropriate jQuery methods.

10.4.1 Creating Ajax Requests

For creating Ajax requests, jQuery provides several methods, listed in Table 10.25. These are methods that—with the exception of the load() method—are called not on a selection of elements, as has been the case so far in this chapter, but directly on the $ object. Therefore, we call these methods *global jQuery methods* ahead.

Method	Description
$.ajax()	Performs an asynchronous HTTP request
$.get()	Performs an HTTP request using the HTTP GET method
$.getJSON()	Performs an HTTP GET request to load JSON data from a server
$.getScript()	Performs an HTTP GET request to load JavaScript data from a server and execute it directly
load()	Performs an HTTP GET request to load HTML data from a server and embed it directly into the selected elements
$.post()	Performs an HTTP request using the HTTP POST method

Table 10.25 Main Methods for Working with Ajax

The jQuery global method ajax() (or $.ajax()) allows you to create arbitrary Ajax requests. The configuration object expected by this method gives you the most leeway regarding the configuration of a request.

The get() and post() methods are used to create GET or POST requests, meaning that you don't have to worry about specific configurations for these request types, such as specifying the HTTP method.

In addition, special methods are available for loading HTML data (load()), loading JSON data (getJSON()), and loading JavaScript files (getScript()).

Listing 10.25 shows an example of using the ajax() method, which you already know about in principle from Chapter 9: the goal is to load JSON data from the server and dynamically create a table for this data.

The URL for the request is configured via the url property of the configuration object, the type expected as a response via the dataType property (possibilities include, for example, json, xml, or html), and the type of the request via the type property. Callback functions for the successful execution of a request or also for errors can be defined via the success and error properties. Within the success callback function, the response of the server is accessed via the data parameter in the example. Because this is JSON data, it can be processed directly to create the table, as already mentioned.

```
'use strict';
$(document).ready(() => {
  $.ajax({
    url: 'artists.json',
    dataType: 'json',
    type: 'GET',
```

585

```
  success: (data) => {
    const table = initTable();
    const artists = data.artists;
    for (let i = 0; i < artists.length; i++) {
      const artist = artists[i];
      const albums = artist.albums;
      for (let j = 0; j < albums.length; j++) {
        const album = albums[j];
        const row = createRow(
          artist.name,
          album.title,
          album.year
        );
        $(table).find('tbody').append(row);
      }
    }
    $('#artists-container').append(table);
  },
  error: (jqXHR, errorMessage, error) => {
  }
});
});
```

Listing 10.25 Generating an Ajax Request

As an alternative to specifying the callback functions via the success and error properties, you also have the option of defining them via the done() and fail() methods,
which (thanks to jQuery's Fluent API) can be combined directly with calling the ajax()
method (see Listing 10.26).

```
'use strict';
$(document).ready(() => {
  $.ajax({
    url: 'artists.json',
    dataType: 'json',
    type: 'GET'
  })
  .done((data) => {
    const table = initTable();
    const artists = data.artists;
    for (let i = 0; i < artists.length; i++) {
      const artist = artists[i];
      const albums = artist.albums;
      for (let j = 0; j < albums.length; j++) {
        const album = albums[j];
```

```
      const row = createRow(
        artist.name,
        album.title,
        album.year
      );
      $(table).find('tbody').append(row);
    }
  }
  $('#artists-container').append(table);
})
.fail((jqXHR, errorMessage, error) => {
});
});
```

Listing 10.26 Generating an Ajax Request via the Fluent API

10.4.2   Responding to Events

For responding to events related to working with Ajax requests, jQuery provides the methods shown in Table 10.26.

Method	Description
ajaxComplete()	Specify an event listener that is called when an Ajax request completes
ajaxError()	Specify an event listener for errors
ajaxSend()	Specify an event listener that is called when an Ajax request is sent
ajaxStart()	Specify an event listener that is called when the first Ajax request is started
ajaxStop()	Specify an event listener that is called when all Ajax requests have completed
ajaxSuccess()	Specify an event listener that is called whenever an Ajax request completes successfully

Table 10.26 Methods for Handling Ajax Events

An example is shown in Listing 10.27. There are two things to keep in mind here: first, the methods are each called on a selection of elements (or the corresponding jQuery object); second, the event listeners each have a different number of parameters. The event listeners for ajaxStart() and ajaxStop() have no parameters at all, the event listeners for ajaxSend() and ajaxComplete() each get the event object, plus an object representing the Ajax request and an object with configurations related to the request. The event listeners for the ajaxSuccess() and ajaxError() methods also receive the response data and the error object, respectively.

```
$(document)
  .ajaxStart(() => {
    console.log('Request started.');
  })
  .ajaxSend((event, request, settings) => {
    console.log('Request sent.');
  })
  .ajaxSuccess((event, request, settings, data) => {
    console.log('Request completed successfully');
  })
  .ajaxError((event, request, settings, error) => {
    console.log('Error on request: ' + error);
  })
  .ajaxComplete((event, request, settings) => {
    console.log('Request completed.');
  })
  .ajaxStop(() => {
    console.log('All requests completed.');
  });
```

Listing 10.27 Registering Different Event Listeners for Ajax Events

10.4.3 Loading HTML Data via Ajax

To load HTML data via Ajax, you can proceed as in Listing 10.28 and use the global jQuery get() method. The important thing here is that you pass the value html to the dataType property. You can then use html() in the corresponding callback function to assign the response data directly to an element as HTML content.

```
'use strict';
$(document).ready(() => {
  const login = $('#login');
  const register = $('#register');
  login.click((e) => {
    e.preventDefault();
    loadContent('login');
  });
  register.click((e) => {
    e.preventDefault();
    loadContent('register');
  });
});

function loadContent(name) {
  $.get({
```

```
    url: name + '.html',
    dataType: 'html'
  }).done((data) => {
    $('#main-content').html(data);
  });
}
```

Listing 10.28 Loading HTML Data via Ajax

But this process is even easier with the load() method, as shown in Listing 10.29. You can call this method directly on a jQuery object (or the selection of elements it represents). As arguments, you pass the URL from which the HTML data should be loaded and optionally a callback function that will be called when the data has been successfully loaded.

```
function loadContent(name) {
  $('#main-content').load(
    name + '.html',
    (
      responseText,
      textStatus,
      jqXHRObject
    ) => {
      console.log('HTML loaded');
    }
  );
}
```

Listing 10.29 Alternative Loading of HTML Data via Ajax

Sending Additional Data with the Request

You can optionally insert another argument between the URL and the callback function—namely to define the data to be sent to the server with the request (in the form of a string). This is useful, for example, if the server is to generate either this or that response based on the data.

10.4.4 Loading XML Data via Ajax

To load XML data, use the get() method as shown in Listing 10.30, passing the xml value for the dataType property. Within the callback function, the response data is then directly available as XML or as a DOM tree. The best thing about this is that the jQuery $() method can also use it—for example, to select all <artist> elements using the find() method as shown in the listing, to iterate over these elements using each()

(another helper method of jQuery, by the way), or to access the text content of the
<title> and <year> elements using text().

```javascript
'use strict';
$(document).ready(() => {
  $.get({
    url: 'artists.xml',
    dataType: 'xml'
  }).done((data) => {
    const table = initTable();
    const artists = $(data).find('artist');
    artists.each((index, artist) => {
      const albums = $(artist).find('album');
      albums.each((index, album) => {
        const row = createRow(
          artist.getAttribute('name'),
          $(album).find('title').text(),
          $(album).find('year').text()
        );
        $(table).find('tbody').append(row);
      });
    });
    $('#artists-container').append(table);
  });
});
```

Listing 10.30 Loading XML Data via Ajax

10.4.5   Loading JSON Data via Ajax

We showed you how to load JSON data using jQuery at the beginning of Section 10.4.1
using the ajax() method. Listing 10.31 shows the equivalent example using the get()
method. You specify json as the value for the dataType property and can then access the
JSON data sent by the server in the callback function as usual.

```javascript
'use strict';
$(document).ready(() => {
  $.get({
    url: 'artists.json',
    dataType: 'json'
  }).done((data) => {
    const table = initTable();
    const artists = data.artists;
    for (let i = 0; i < artists.length; i++) {
      const artist = artists[i];
```

```
      const albums = artist.albums;
      for (let j = 0; j < albums.length; j++) {
        const album = albums[j];
        const row = createRow(
          artist.name,
          album.title,
          album.year
        );
        $(table).find('tbody').append(row);
      }
    }
    $('#artists-container').append(table);
  });
});
```

Listing 10.31 Loading JSON Data via Ajax

Alternatively, jQuery provides the getJSON() method, which further simplifies request-ing JSON data (see Listing 10.32). As arguments, you pass this method the URL to be requested and a callback function to access the JSON data sent by the server.

```
'use strict';
$(document).ready(() => {
  $.getJSON(
    'artists.json',
    (
      data,
      textStatus,
      jqXHRObject
    ) => {
      // here is the already known content
    }
  );
});
```

Listing 10.32 Alternative Loading of JSON Data via Ajax

Sending Additional Data with the Request

As you saw with the load() method, you can optionally specify one more argument between the URL and the callback function to define those data that should be sent to the server with the request.

10.5   Summary

In this chapter, you learned about the popular jQuery JavaScript library, which simplifies many things, especially with regard to DOM manipulation, event handling, and creating Ajax requests. The following list summarizes the most important aspects:

- jQuery is a library that mainly hides browser-specific details and provides helper methods for recurring tasks that can be used across browsers.

- The linchpin for working with jQuery is the jQuery() or $() method.

- Among other things, you can pass a selector, an existing element, or an HTML string as an argument to this method.

- As a return value, the method provides a wrapper object (*jQuery object*) that extends the corresponding elements by additional methods (*jQuery methods*).

- Thus, a jQuery object provides various methods for working with the DOM, including the following:
  - Methods to access the content of elements
  - Methods to filter selected elements
  - Methods to access attributes
  - Methods to access CSS properties
  - Methods to navigate between elements
  - Methods to animate elements or their CSS properties

- For working with events, jQuery provides several methods to register event listeners, including the following:
  - Methods to register event listeners for general events
  - Methods to register event listeners for mouse events
  - Methods to register event listeners for keyboard events
  - Methods to register event listeners for form events

- Creating Ajax requests is also made easier by a number of helper methods, including the following:
  - A method to create arbitrary Ajax requests
  - A method to create GET requests
  - A method to create POST requests
  - A method to load HTML content directly into an element via Ajax
  - A method to load JavaScript files
  - A method to load JSON files

- Most helper methods can be used for various purposes; for example, HTML attributes can be both read and written via the attr() method, CSS properties can be read and written via the css() method, and event listeners can be registered or removed again via the event methods.

Finally, Table 10.27 compares how different problems can be handled with jQuery and with pure JavaScript. For more examples, we recommend looking at the *http://you-mightnotneedjquery.com* website mentioned earlier. There you can see very nicely how the code of both variants is about equally compact, especially in the DOM manipulation area. When working with events and with Ajax, the code is still a bit more compact with jQuery. In all cases, however, it's true that jQuery is largely browser-independent, while this doesn't always apply to the pure JavaScript variants.

Working with the DOM	
Add CSS class	jQuery: ```$(element).addClass(\n newClassName\n);```
	Pure JavaScript: ```if (element.classList) {\n element.classList.add(newClassName);\n} else {\n element.className += ' ' + newClassName;\n}```
Access child elements	jQuery: ```$(element).children();```
	Pure JavaScript: ```element.children```
Iterate over elements	jQuery: ```$(selector).each(\n (index, element) => {\n }\n);```
	Pure JavaScript: ```const elements = document.querySelectorAll(\n selector\n);\nArray.prototype.forEach.call(\n elements, (element, index) => {\n }\n);```

Table 10.27 Comparison between jQuery and Pure JavaScript

Working with the DOM	

Search elements below an element	jQuery:
	`$(element).find(`
	`  selector`
	`);`

	Pure JavaScript:
	`element.querySelectorAll(`
	`  selector`
	`);`

Search elements	jQuery: `$(selector);`
	Pure JavaScript: `document.querySelectorAll(selector);`
Access attributes	jQuery: `$(element).attr(name);`
	Pure JavaScript: `element.getAttribute(name);`
Read HTML content	jQuery: `$(element).html();`
	Pure JavaScript: `element.innerHTML;`
Write HTML content	jQuery: `$(element).html(content);`
	Pure JavaScript: `element.innerHTML = content;`
Read text content	jQuery: `$(element).text();`
	Pure JavaScript: `element.textContent;`

Table 10.27 Comparison between jQuery and Pure JavaScript (Cont.)

Working with the DOM	
Write text content	jQuery: `$(element).text(content);`
	Pure JavaScript: `element.textContent = content;`
Next element	jQuery: `$(element).next();`
	Pure JavaScript: `element.nextElementSibling;`
Previous element	jQuery: `$(element).prev();`
	Pure JavaScript: `element.previousElementSibling;`
Working with events	

Add event listener	jQuery:
	`$(element).on(`
	`  eventName,`
	`  eventHandler`
	`);`

	Pure JavaScript:
	`element.addEventListener(`
	`  eventName,`
	`  eventHandler`
	`);`

Remove event listener	jQuery:
	`$(element).off(`
	`  eventName,`
	`  eventHandler`
	`);`

	Pure JavaScript:
	`element.removeEventListener(`
	`  eventName,`
	`  eventHandler`
	`);`

Table 10.27 Comparison between jQuery and Pure JavaScript (Cont.)

Working with the DOM	
Execute function when loading the document	jQuery: ```js\n$(document).ready(() => {\n});\n```
	Pure JavaScript: ```js\nfunction ready(callback) {\n if (document.readyState != 'loading'){\n callback();\n } else {\n document.addEventListener(\n 'DOMContentLoaded',\n callback\n);\n }\n}\n```
Working with Ajax requests	
Send GET request	jQuery: ```js\n$.ajax({\n type: 'GET',\n url: url,\n success: response => {},\n error: () => {}\n});\n```
	Pure JavaScript: ```js\nfetch(url)\n .then(response => {})\n .catch(error => {});\n```
Send POST request	jQuery: ```js\n$.ajax({\n type: 'POST',\n url: url,\n data: data\n});\n```
	Pure JavaScript: ```js\nfetch('url', {\n method: 'POST',\n body: data,\n})\n.then(response => {})\n.catch(error => {});\n```

Table 10.27 Comparison between jQuery and Pure JavaScript (Cont.)

Working with the DOM	

Load JSON via Ajax	jQuery:
	
	``
	$.getJSON(
	  'data.json',
	  (data) => {}
	);
	``

	Pure JavaScript:
	
	``
	fetch('data.json')
	  .then(response => response.json())
	  .then(data => {})
	  .catch(error => {});
	``

Table 10.27 Comparison between jQuery and Pure JavaScript (Cont.)

Chapter 11
Dynamically Creating Images and Graphics

In this chapter, you'll learn about two different technologies for creating images and graphics dynamically using JavaScript.

For the creation of images or the drawing of graphics, two different technologies are available in JavaScript (or in the browser): first, the so-called Canvas API, through which it's possible to "draw" via JavaScript on a previously defined drawing surface, and second, the Scalable Vector Graphics (SVG) format, which enables the declarative definition of vector graphics that can be interpreted and displayed by all modern browsers. Because this format is an XML format, you can also create SVG graphics dynamically via JavaScript as usual using the DOM API.

11.1 Drawing Images

The Canvas API (*www.w3.org/TR/2dcontext*) allows you to perform program-based drawings within a browser window using JavaScript.

11.1.1 The Drawing Area

The basis for drawing graphics is the <canvas> element. This element represents the drawing area, as it were, which can be accessed within the JavaScript code and drawn on using the Canvas API.

The width and height attributes can be used to define the width and height the drawing area should occupy on the screen. If you omit these attributes, the area has a width of 300 pixels and a height of 150 pixels by default.

In addition, it's useful to give the <canvas> element an ID via the id attribute, as shown in Listing 11.1, to be able to select the element easily from JavaScript via getElement-ById().

```
<canvas id="canvas" width="500" height="300">
</canvas>
```

Listing 11.1 The Basis for Drawing with the Canvas API

Basically, the <canvas> element can be styled in any way via CSS, just like other HTML elements. For the following examples, we'll only provide the element with a frame (see Listing 11.2), in order to distinguish the drawing area from the surrounding area in this way.

```
canvas {
  border: 1px solid black;
}
```

Listing 11.2 The <canvas> Element Can Be Styled in Any Way via CSS

Listing 11.3 shows the entire HTML file that serves as the basis for the following examples.

```
<!DOCTYPE html>
<html>
<head lang="en">
  <title>Canvas example</title>
  <link rel="stylesheet" href="styles/main.css" type="text/css">
</head>
<body>
<main>
  <canvas id="canvas" width="500" height="300"></canvas>
</main>
<script src="scripts/main.js"></script>
</body>
</html>
```

Listing 11.3 The Entire HTML File, Including the Drawing Area

11.1.2   The Rendering Context

The <canvas> element provides one or multiple rendering contexts that can be used to manipulate the drawing area or its contents. The getContext() method of the <canvas> element can be used to access the corresponding context. As parameters, this method expects the context identifier (2d for a 2D rendering context, webgl for a 3D rendering context in browsers supporting WebGL version 1, and webgl2 for a 3D context in browsers supporting WebGL version 2; see Table 11.1) and optional context-specific configuration parameters.

> **2D and 3D Context**
>
> In this book, we'll focus on the 2D context. The topic of 3D programming in general and WebGL in particular is difficult to explain in a few pages.

Identifiers	Description
2d	Context for rendering 2D graphics. If you pass this identifier, the getContext() method returns an object of the type CanvasRenderingContext2D.
webgl	Context for rendering 3D graphics in browsers that implement WebGL version 1. If you pass this identifier, the getContext() method returns an object of the type WebGLRenderingContext.
webgl2	Context for rendering 3D graphics in browsers that implement WebGL version 2. If you pass this identifier, the getContext() method returns an object of the type WebGL2RenderingContext.

Table 11.1 The Identifiers for the Different Rendering Contexts That Can Be Used as Arguments for getContext()

Listing 11.4 shows the code that's required to access the 2D context of the drawing area. The object returned by the getContext() method is of the type CanvasRenderingContext2D and is the entry point to the Canvas API. All methods described ahead are called on this object.

```
const canvas = document.getElementById('canvas');
const context = canvas.getContext('2d');
```

Listing 11.4 Accessing the Rendering Context via JavaScript

The 2D context is based on a two-dimensional coordinate system (see Figure 11.1), on which you can draw with pixel precision using x and y coordinates (and using various helper functions that we'll introduce ahead).

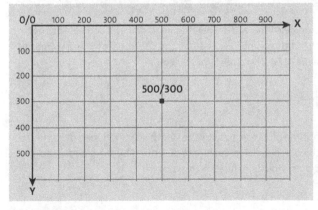

Figure 11.1 The Coordinate System

It's no surprise that the origin of this coordinate system is the coordinate (0,0) in the top-left-hand corner of the drawing area. Graphic elements such as rectangles, circles, curves, and so on are drawn in the drawing area in relation to this origin coordinate.

Checking Support for the Canvas API

In general, it's good style to perform certain checks within the JavaScript code before using an API that may not be supported by all browsers (or not by older browsers). *Feature detection* is the well-known technical term here. In the case of the Canvas API, it's therefore appropriate to proceed as shown in Listing 11.5.

```
const canvas = document.getElementById('canvas');
if (canvas.getContext){
  const context = canvas.getContext('2d');
  // continue here
}
```

Listing 11.5 Feature Detection for the Canvas API

Here we first check whether the object representing the <canvas> element (the return value of getElementById()) has the getContext() method at all. Only if this is the case can we assume that the Canvas API is supported by the browser.

11.1.3   Drawing Rectangles

To fill the still empty drawing area with some life, we'll first show how you can draw simple rectangles. The CanvasRenderingContext2D type provides three different methods for this purpose: the fillRect() method creates a rectangle filled with a previously defined background color, strokeRect() draws the outline of a rectangle (also with a previously defined border color), and clearRect() removes everything from the drawing area inside the defined rectangle (see Table 11.2).

Method	Description
fillRect(x, y, width, height)	Draws a rectangle of the width specified in width and the height specified in height at the point described by the coordinates x and y and fills it with a previously defined background color
strokeRect(x, y, width, height)	Draws the outline of a rectangle of the width specified in width and the height specified in height at the point described by the x and y coordinates, using a previously defined frame color

Table 11.2 Different Methods for Drawing Rectangles

Method	Description
clearRect(x, y, width, height)	Deletes everything from the drawing area that is inside the defined rectangle

Table 11.2 Different Methods for Drawing Rectangles (Cont.)

All three methods have the same four parameters: x and y coordinates to define the upper-left-hand point of the respective rectangle, as well as information about the width and height of the respective rectangle (see Figure 11.2).

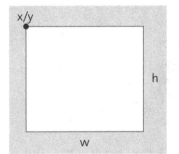

Figure 11.2 Structure of a Rectangle

Listing 11.6 shows some examples of drawing rectangles. You see that before the fill-Rect() and strokeRect() methods are called, the background color and frame color are first defined via the fillStyle and strokeStyle properties in the rendering context. Figure 11.3 shows the result of this source code: on the left you can see the two filled rectangles, on the right the two rectangles with frames, and on the far right the robot head.

> **Note**
>
> Once set, the settings you define affect not only the immediately following fillRect() or strokeRect() call, but all subsequent calls.

```
function draw() {
  const canvas = document.getElementById('canvas');
  if (canvas.getContext){
    const context = canvas.getContext('2d');
    context.fillStyle = 'rgb(200,0,0)';           // Set background color
    context.fillRect (10, 10, 80, 80);            // Draw 1st rectangle
    context.fillStyle = 'rgba(0, 0, 200, 0.5)';   // Set background color
```

```
    context.fillRect (100, 10, 80, 80);                 // Draw 2nd rectangle
    context.strokeStyle = 'rgb(200,0,0)';               // Set frame color
    context.strokeRect (190, 10, 80, 80);               // Draw 3rd rectangle
    context.strokeStyle = 'rgba(0, 0, 200, 0.5)';       // Set frame color
    context.strokeRect (280, 10, 80, 80);               // Draw 4th rectangle
    context.fillStyle = 'rgb(200,0,0)';                 // Set background color
    context.fillRect (370, 10, 80, 80);                 // Draw "head"
    context.clearRect (380, 20, 60, 20);                // Draw "eye area"
    context.fillRect (390, 25, 10, 10);                 // Draw left "eye"
    context.fillRect (420, 25, 10, 10);                 // Draw right "eye"
    context.clearRect (385, 60, 50, 10);                // Draw "mouth"
  }
}
```

Listing 11.6 Examples of Drawing Rectangles

Figure 11.3 Various Drawn Rectangles

Rectangles are the only basic geometric shape for which the Canvas API defines special methods; all other geometric shapes—circles, triangles, and so on—have to be drawn via so-called paths. In the following section, we'll describe the different types of paths that are available.

11.1.4   Using Paths

In the context of the Canvas API, a *path* is a string of coordinates connected by lines. A line between two points can be straight or curved.

Drawing Straight Lines

Basically, creating paths using the Canvas API always involves four steps: starting the path, drawing the path, closing the path (optional), and coloring the background or frame (optional).

Listing 11.7 shows a simple example of drawing a path that starts at point (50, 200) and goes straight to point (400, 50). The beginPath() method, called on the context object, starts creating the path. The imaginary drawing pen is then moved to the point defined by the passed x and y coordinates via moveTo(). With lineTo(), in turn, a straight line is drawn from this point to a second point, whose coordinates are passed to this method using the appropriate arguments. Finally, the stroke() method ensures that the drawn path also receives a color (black in this case because the strokeStyle property wasn't explicitly set up front and black is the default color). You can see the result of the source text in Figure 11.4.

```
const context = canvas.getContext('2d');
context.beginPath();         // Start of path
context.moveTo(50, 200);     // Define starting point
context.lineTo(400, 50);     // Straight line to specified point
context.stroke();            // Color frame
```

Listing 11.7 Example of Drawing a Path

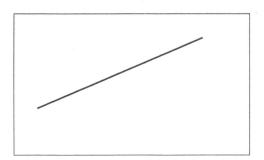

Figure 11.4 A Line Drawn by Means of a Path

If you don't want to use only a straight line, you can add more coordinates to the path by calling other methods (before calling stroke()), as shown in Listing 11.8 and Figure 11.5.

```
const context = canvas.getContext('2d');
context.beginPath();         // Start of path
context.moveTo(50, 200);     // Define starting point
context.lineTo(400, 50);     // Straight line to specified point
context.lineTo(400, 200);    // straight line to specified point
context.stroke();            // Color frame
```

Listing 11.8 Example of Drawing a Path with Multiple Path Components

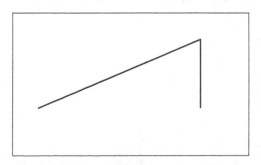

Figure 11.5 A Path Consisting of Several Path Components

Closing Paths

If you want to *close* a path—that is, automatically draw a line from the current point to the starting point—you can use the closePath() method for simplicity instead of manually drawing a line to the starting point of the path. Listing 11.9 shows an example of this, and you can see the result in Figure 11.6.

```
const context = canvas.getContext('2d');
context.beginPath();          // Start of path
context.moveTo(50, 200);      // Define starting point
context.lineTo(400, 50);      // Straight line to specified point
context.lineTo(400, 200);     // straight line to specified point
context.closePath();          // Close path
context.stroke();             // Color frame
```

Listing 11.9 Example of Closing a Path

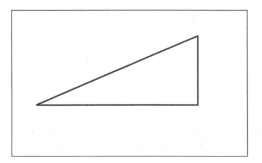

Figure 11.6 Example of Closing a Path

The Path2D Object

As you saw in the previous listings, you call the methods for drawing paths on the context object. Because this can become quite confusing when dealing with many paths, the Path2D object is available as an alternative. This object provides methods that are similar to those of the context object with regard to path creation, and it's particularly suitable for working with many paths in order to always keep track of the various paths. Listing 11.10 shows the corresponding source code, which leads to the same result as the source code in Listing 11.9.

```
const context = canvas.getContext('2d');
const path = new Path2D();
path.moveTo(50, 200);      // Draw path
path.lineTo(400, 50);      // Draw path
path.lineTo(400, 200);     // Draw path
path.closePath();          // Close path
context.stroke(path);      // Color frame
```

Listing 11.10 Example of Working with the Path2D Object

Drawing Square Curves

You can't really do much with straight lines alone when it comes to drawing. For this reason, there are several methods in the Canvas API to draw curves.

One of these methods is `quadraticCurveTo()`, which is used to draw so-called square curves (see Figure 11.7).

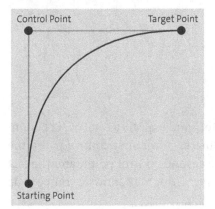

Figure 11.7 A Square Curve

For this purpose, four parameters are expected: The first two parameters form the x and y coordinate of the *control point*, which essentially influences the extent of the curve. Parameters three and four, on the other hand, represent the x and y coordinates of the point to which the curve is to be drawn (the *target point*).

Listing 11.11 shows an example of using `quadraticCurve()`.

```
const context = canvas.getContext('2d');
const path = new Path2D();
path.moveTo(25,100);      // Starting point
path.quadraticCurveTo(
    25,                   // control point x coordinate
    25,                   // control point y coordinate
    100,                  // target point x coordinate
    25                    // target point y coordinate
);
context.stroke(path);
```

Listing 11.11 Example of Drawing a Square Curve

Drawing Bezier Curves

In addition to drawing square curves, the Canvas API provides a method for drawing so-called Bezier curves. These are more flexible in terms of appearance or parameterization than square curves as they have not only one but two control points (see Figure 11.8).

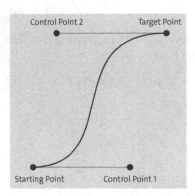

Figure 11.8 A Bezier Curve

The corresponding method is called bezierCurveTo() and expects a total of six parameters. The first two parameters define the coordinates of the first control point, the following two parameters the coordinates of the second control point, and the last two parameters the coordinates of the target point. Listing 11.12 shows a source code example.

```
const context = canvas.getContext('2d');
const path = new Path2D();
path.moveTo(25,100);  // Starting point
path.bezierCurveTo(
  100,              // control point x1 coordinate
  100,              // control point y1 coordinate
  25,               // control point x2 coordinate
  25,               // control point y2 coordinate
  100,              // target point x coordinate
  25                // target point y coordinate
);
context.stroke(path);
```

Listing 11.12 Example of Drawing a Bezier Curve

Drawing Arcs and Circles

To draw arcs or circles you can use two methods: the arcTo() method and the arc() method. Listing 11.13 contains an example of using arcTo(). The method expects five parameters: x and y coordinates of the first control point, x and y coordinates of the second control point, and the radius of the arc to be drawn (see also Figure 11.9).

```
const context = canvas.getContext('2d');
const path = new Path2D();
path.moveTo(25,200);  // Starting point
path.arcTo(
  25,               // x coordinate first control point
```

```
    25,                   // y coordinate first control point
    200,                  // x coordinate second control point
    25,                   // y coordinate second control point
    90                    // Radius of arc
);
path.lineTo(200, 25); // Target point
context.stroke(path);
```

Listing 11.13 Example of Drawing with the arcTo() Method

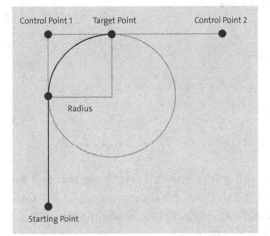

Figure 11.9 Example Using the arcTo() Method

Listing 11.14 shows how you can use the arc() method. The method expects six parameters: x and y coordinates of the arc center, the radius of the arc, start and end angles, and a Boolean specifying whether the arc should be drawn clockwise or counterclockwise (see also Figure 11.10).

```
const context = canvas.getContext('2d');
const path = new Path2D();
path.moveTo(25,200);    // Starting point
path.arc(
    100,                  // x coordinate of arc center
    100,                  // y coordinate of arc center
    50,                   // Radius of arc
    25,                   // Start angle
    25,                   // End angle
    false                 // draw clockwise
);
path.lineTo(200, 25);   // Target point
context.stroke(path);
```

Listing 11.14 Example of Drawing with the arc() Method

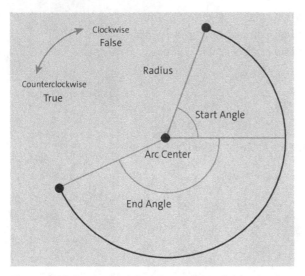

Figure 11.10 Example Using the arc() Method

11.1.5   Drawing Texts

Two methods are available to you for drawing text: the fillText() method and the strokeText() method. You'll probably guess their uses from their names: the former draws text filled with a (previously defined) background color, while the latter draws text outlined with a (previously defined) frame color.

Both methods expect at least three parameters and optionally a fourth one: the text itself, x position and y position, and (optionally) the maximum width the text may occupy in the drawing area.

Listing 11.15 contains an example of how you can use the method. In addition, various properties of the context object can be used to manipulate the appearance of the text, such as font size, font color, alignment, or text direction (see Table 11.3).

```
const context = canvas.getContext('2d');
context.font = '48px serif';              // Font properties
context.fillText('Hello World', 10, 50);     // Draw text
context.strokeText('Hello World', 10, 100); // Draw text
```

Listing 11.15 Example of Drawing Text

Property	Description
font	Contains information as a character string about the appearance of the text, such as font size, font color, and so on. The syntax is exactly the same for the font property from CSS.

Table 11.3 Various Properties for Configuring Text

Property	Description
textAlign	Contains information about the horizontal alignment of the text. Possible values are start, end, left, right, and center.
textBaseline	Contains information about the vertical position of the text. Possible values are top, hanging, middle, alphabetic, ideographic, and bottom.
Direction	Contains information about the text direction. Possible values are ltr (left to right), rtl (right to left), and inherit.

Table 11.3 Various Properties for Configuring Text (Cont.)

11.1.6 Drawing Gradients

Instead of using a single color, areas and frames can also be filled with a color gradient. You can choose between linear color gradients and radial color gradients—as you may already know from graphics programs.

Drawing Linear Gradients

You can draw linear gradients using the createLinearGradient() method. This method is passed the x and y coordinates of the starting point (the first two parameters) and the x and y coordinates of the end point (the last two parameters) in the form of four parameters.

The method returns an object of the CanvasGradient type, which can be used to determine the individual colors of the gradient via the addColorStop() method. The first parameter passed to the method is the relative position (as a value between 0.0 and 1.0) and the corresponding color value.

In Listing 11.16, a color gradient is created from point (0, 0) to point (0, 150), which has the value #FF0000 (red) at the beginning (at position 0.0), then #00FF00 (green) in the middle (at position 0.5), and #0000FF (blue) at the end (at position 1.0). The result is shown in Figure 11.11.

```
const context = canvas.getContext('2d');
const gradient = context.createLinearGradient(    // Create gradient
  0,                                              // x coordinate starting point
  0,                                              // y coordinate starting point
  0,                                              // x coordinate end point
  150                                             // y coordinate end point
);
gradient.addColorStop(0, '#FF0000');              // first color value
gradient.addColorStop(0.5, '#00FF00');            // second color value
```

```
gradient.addColorStop(1, '#0000FF');           // third color value
context.fillStyle = gradient;                   // Assign style
context.fillRect(20, 20, 460, 240);             // Draw rectangle
```

Listing 11.16 Creating a Linear Gradient

Figure 11.11 Structure of a Linear Gradient

Drawing Radial Gradients

In contrast to linear color gradients in which the colors run in one direction (i.e., *linearly*), radial color gradients run *radially*—that is, starting from one point in all directions. A radial gradient is defined by two circles, as shown in Figure 11.12: one circle defines the center of the gradient; the other defines the perimeter of the gradient.

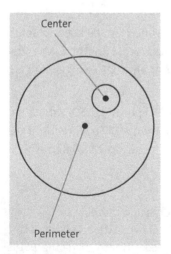

Figure 11.12 Structure of a Radial Gradient

The corresponding method in the Canvas API is named createRadialGradient() and expects—as shown in Listing 11.17—six parameters, where the first three parameters represent the x and y coordinates and the radius of the circle defining the center, and the last three parameters do the same for the circle defining the circumference. You can see the result of the source text in Figure 11.13.

```
const context = canvas.getContext('2d');
const gradient = context.createRadialGradient(    // Create gradient
  50,                                             // x coordinate circle 1 center
  100,                                            // y coordinate circle 1 center
  20,                                             // Radius circle 1
  100,                                            // x coordinate circle 2 center
  100,                                            // y coordinate circle 2 center
  80                                              // Radius circle 2
);
gradient.addColorStop(0, '#FF0000');              // first color value
gradient.addColorStop(0.5, '#00FF00');            // second color value
gradient.addColorStop(1, 'rgba(0,0,255,0)');      // third color value
context.fillStyle = gradient;                     // Assign style
context.fillRect(10,10,200,200);                  // Draw rectangle
```

Listing 11.17 Creating a Radial Gradient

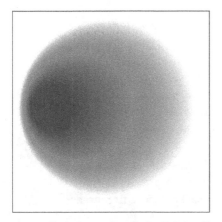

Figure 11.13 Example of a Radial Gradient

11.1.7 Saving and Restoring the Canvas State

You've seen that when you use methods like fillRect() or fillText(), you may need to make settings for the filling color, font, and so on in the context object up front. To save these settings, the context object provides the save() method. Each time you call this method, the current settings are placed on a stack and saved. The restore() method can then be used to restore the settings at a later time. This is especially useful if you want to reuse certain settings multiple times, but at different points in time.

Listing 11.18 shows an example of this, where the code generates the graphic shown in Figure 11.14. The procedure is as follows: First, a square of 150 pixels height and 150 pixels width is created using the default settings (filling color is black by default). By calling to save(), you can then save these defaults to the stack just mentioned. Then the filling color is set to the value #00FF00, green, and a slightly smaller (horizontally and vertically offset) square is created. Calling save() again will also save these settings to the stack. The background color is set to #FF0000, red, and again a smaller square is drawn.

The restore() call then loads the settings that were last saved on the stack, which are those where the filling color was set to green (so the subsequently created square has this color). In the same way, a second call of restore() will then load the default settings, again resulting in a black square.

```
'use strict';
function draw() {
  const ctx = document.getElementById('canvas').getContext('2d');

  ctx.fillRect(0, 0, 150, 150);     // Draw square with default settings
                                    // Background color black
  ctx.save();                       // Save current state (state 1)

  ctx.fillStyle = '#00FF00';        // Change settings
  ctx.fillRect(15, 15, 120, 120);   // Draw square with new settings
                                    // Background color green

  ctx.save();                       // Save current state (state 2)
  ctx.fillStyle = '#FF0000';        // Change settings
  ctx.fillRect(30, 30, 90, 90);     // Draw square with new settings
                                    // Background color red

  ctx.restore();                    // Load previous state (state 2)
  ctx.fillRect(45, 45, 60, 60);     // Draw square with previous
                                    // settings, background color green

  ctx.restore();                    // Load previous state (state 1)
  ctx.fillRect(60, 60, 30, 30);     // Draw square with default settings
                                    // Background color black
}
document.addEventListener('DOMContentLoaded', draw);
```

Listing 11.18 Saving and Loading States

Figure 11.14 States of the Settings Can Be Reused via save() and restore()

The states stored on the stack also contain information about the current transformation matrix. For this reason, using save() and restore() also plays an important role in the context of transformations, as you'll see in the examples in the following sections.

11.1.8 Using Transformations

For the purpose of transforming graphic elements within the drawing area, you can use the three operations shown in Figure 11.15:

- **Scaling**
  Here you change the width and/or the height.

- **Rotation**
  Here you change the angle.

- **Translation**
  Here you change the x and/or y position.

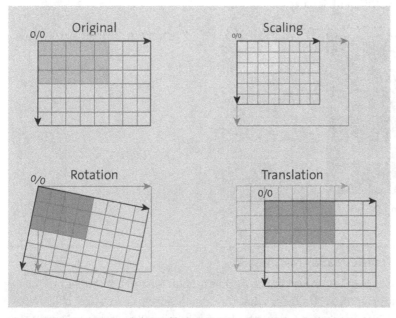

Figure 11.15 Overview of the Different Types of Transformations

Scaling

To scale a graphic element, you can use the scale() method. This method expects the horizontal scaling factor as the first parameter and the vertical scaling factor as the second parameter. Listing 11.19 contains an example of this. Here, three squares are created one after the other (see also Figure 11.16), whereby the same values are passed as arguments for width and height in each case. The difference in size is caused only by the respective preceding call of scale(). The red square is thus scaled by a factor of 7, the green one by a factor of 6, and the blue one by a factor of 5.

```
const context = document.getElementById('canvas').getContext('2d');
context.save();                    // Save initial state
context.fillStyle = '#FF0000';     // Filling color red
context.scale(7,7);                // Scaling
context.fillRect(0,0,40,40);       // Draw red square
context.restore();                 // Reset to initial state
context.save();                    // Save initial state
context.fillStyle = '#00FF00';     // Filling color green
context.scale(6,6);                // Scaling
context.fillRect(0,0,40,40);       // Draw green square
context.restore();                 // Reset to initial state
context.save();                    // Save initial state
context.fillStyle = '#0000FF';     // Filling color blue
context.scale(5,5);                // Scaling
context.fillRect(0,0,40,40);       // Draw blue square
```

Listing 11.19 Scaling Different Squares

Figure 11.16 Scaling Result

Changing the Transformation Matrix

To be precise, calling scale() doesn't scale a single graphic element; it changes the current transformation matrix. This means that the scaling settings first affect all graphic elements drawn into the drawing area after the method is called. If you only want to scale individual graphic elements, you must always reset the transformation matrix via the restore() and save() calls before drawing the relevant next element, as shown in the example.

Rotation

To rotate graphic elements, you can use the rotate() method. As a parameter, this method expects the angle by which you want to rotate. As is the case with scale(), using rotate() also affects the transformation matrix on which the drawing area is based, so it may be necessary to reset it again, as was the case with scale(), by calling restore() and save().

Listing 11.20 contains an example of using rotate(). Figure 11.17 shows the corresponding result.

```
const context = document.getElementById('canvas').getContext('2d');
context.save();                             // Save initial state
context.fillStyle = '#FF0000';              // Filling color red
context.rotate(7);                          // Rotation (rotation anglein radians)
context.fillRect(200,0,140,140);            // Draw red square
context.restore();                          // Reset to initial state
context.save();                             // Save initial state
context.fillStyle = '#00FF00';              // Filling color green
context.rotate(7);                          // Rotation (rotation anglein radians)
context.fillRect(200,-180,140,140);         // Draw green square
context.restore();                          // Reset to initial state
context.save();                             // Save initial state
context.fillStyle = '#0000FF';              // Filling color blue
context.rotate(7);                          // Rotation (rotation anglein radians)
context.fillRect(380,-180,140,140);         // Draw blue square
```

Listing 11.20 Rotation of Different Squares

Figure 11.17 Rotation Result

Translation

For the purpose of translation, you can use the translate() method, which expects values for the horizontal and vertical displacements as parameters. Listing 11.21 contains an example of this, while Figure 11.18 shows the result.

```
const context = document.getElementById('canvas').getContext('2d');
context.save();                             // Save initial state
context.fillStyle = '#FF0000';              // Filling color red
context.translate(40, 40);                  // Translation
context.fillRect(0,0,40,40);                // Draw red square
context.restore();                          // Reset to initial state
context.save();                             // Save initial state
context.fillStyle = '#00FF00';              // Filling color green
```

```
context.translate(100, 40);        // Translation
context.fillRect(0,0,40,40);       // Draw green square
context.restore();                 // Reset to initial state
context.save();                    // Save initial state
context.fillStyle = '#0000FF';     // Filling color blue
context.translate(160, 40);        // Translation
context.fillRect(0,0,40,40);       // Draw blue square
```

Listing 11.21 Translation of Different Squares

Figure 11.18 Translation Result

11.1.9 Creating Animations

Up to this point, you've only seen how you can make drawings using the Canvas API in the examples, but animations are also possible. But to create an animation, you need to draw every single frame of it yourself. In principle, this works as follows—and the last three steps can be carried out several times:

- Emptying the drawing area
- Optional saving of the state
- Drawing
- Optional loading of the state

These four steps are usually encapsulated within a function, which is then called at regular intervals (for each frame in the animation). Although this time-controlled repeated calling can be achieved using the setInterval() function, you should use the requestAnimationFrame() method instead. This method is specifically intended for working with animations within a web page and is the most efficient way to call a corresponding function repeatedly and at consistent time intervals.

Listing 11.22 shows an example of an animation in which three colored rectangles are rotated around a certain point. The redraw() function contains the code responsible for drawing the rectangles. This function is called once it's been passed as an argument to the requestAnimationFrame() method. The call of requestAnimationFrame() is necessary at two points: first, at the start within the draw() function, and second, at the end of the redraw() function. The first call causes redraw() to be called initially and to draw the first frame in the animation (effectively starting the animation), while the second call causes redraw() to continuously call itself to draw a new frame in the animation each time (continuing the animation indefinitely, as it were).

```
function draw() {
  const canvas = document.getElementById('canvas');
  if (canvas.getContext){
    window.requestAnimationFrame(redraw);
  }
}


function redraw() {
  const context = document.getElementById('canvas').getContext('2d');
  context.clearRect(0,0,500,300);     // (1) Clear drawing area
  const time = new Date();
  const angle = ((2*Math.PI)/6)*time.getSeconds()
             + ((2*Math.PI)/6000)*time.getMilliseconds();
                                       // red rectangle:
  context.fillStyle = '#FF0000';       //
  context.save();                      // (2) Save state
  context.translate(150,150);          // (3) Draw
  context.rotate(angle);               //
  context.translate(0,25);             //
  context.fillRect(5,5,20,20);         //
  context.restore();                   // (4) Load state
                                       // green rectangle:
  context.fillStyle = '#00FF00';       //
  context.save();                      // (2) Save state
  context.translate(150,150);          // (3) Draw
  context.rotate(angle);               //
  context.translate(0,50);             //
  context.fillRect(5,5,20,20);         //
  context.restore();                   // (4) Load state
                                       // blue rectangle:
  context.fillStyle = '#0000FF';       //
  context.save();                      // (2) Save state
  context.translate(150,150);          // (3) Draw
  context.rotate(angle);               //
  context.translate(0,75);             //
  context.fillRect(5,5,20,20);         //
  context.restore();                   // (4) Load state
  window.requestAnimationFrame(redraw);
}
window.addEventListener('DOMContentLoaded', draw);
```

Listing 11.22 Creating an Animation

11.2   Integrating Vector Graphics

In addition to being able to draw pixel-based graphics via JavaScript using the Canvas API, you can also use JavaScript to create vector graphics. One of the better-known formats, which has celebrated a comeback thanks to HTML5 in particular, is the SVG format.

11.2.1   The SVG Format

SVG is an XML-based markup language for describing two-dimensional vector graphics. For this purpose, the corresponding specification (*www.w3.org/TR/SVG2/*) provides various elements such as <circle>, <ellipse>, <line>, <polygon>, <polyline>, and <rect> to define geometric shapes (see Table 11.4).

You can create SVG graphics manually, but this is often quite tedious, especially when it comes to creating more complicated graphics. It's easier to create appropriate graphics in one of the numerous vector programs available, export them to SVG format (programs like Adobe Illustrator, Inkscape, and similar others usually offer such an option), and then use them in the appropriate web page. You can see a simple example of an SVG document in Listing 11.23: a white circle on a black background.

Element	Meaning	Attributes (Selection)
<rect>	Rectangle	<ul><li>x: x coordinate</li><li>y: y coordinate</li><li>width: rectangle width</li><li>height: rectangle height</li><li>rx: horizontal radius for rounded corners</li><li>ry: vertical radius for rounded corners</li></ul>
<circle>	Circle	<ul><li>cx: x coordinate of the circle center</li><li>cy: y coordinate of the circle center</li><li>r: radius</li></ul>
<ellipse>	Ellipse	<ul><li>cx: x coordinate of the center</li><li>cy: y coordinate of the center</li><li>rx: radius of the semiaxis in x-direction</li><li>ry: radius of the semiaxis in y-direction</li></ul>
<line>	Line with two points	<ul><li>x1: x coordinate of the first point</li><li>y1: y coordinate of the first point</li><li>x2: x coordinate of the second point</li><li>y2: y coordinate of the second point</li></ul>

Table 11.4 Overview of the Most Important Elements in SVG

Element	Meaning	Attributes (Selection)
`<polyline>`	Line with several intermediate points	■ `points`: list of x and y coordinates of the individual points to be connected by the lines, with the x-y pairs separated by commas or spaces
`<polygon>`	Polygon	■ `points`: list of x and y coordinates of the individual points to be connected by the lines, with the x-y pairs separated by commas or spaces
`<path>`	Path	
`<g>`	Group of graphic elements	
`<text>`	Text contents	■ `x`: x coordinate of the baseline ■ `y`: y coordinate of the baseline
`<a>`	Hyperlinks	
`<image>`	External images	■ `x`: x coordinate ■ `y`: y coordinate ■ `width`: image width ■ `height`: image height
`<linearGradient>`	Linear gradient	
`<radialGradient>`	Radial gradient	

Table 11.4 Overview of the Most Important Elements in SVG (Cont.)

```
<svg xmlns="http://www.w3.org/2000/svg">
  <rect width="100%" height="100%" fill="#000000" />
  <circle id="circle" cx="100" cy="100" r="80" fill="#ffffff" />
</svg>
```

Listing 11.23 Example of a Simple SVG Document

11.2.2 Integrating SVG in HTML

To integrate SVG in HTML, you have several options, the most important ones of which are briefly described in the following sections.

Integrating via the `<img>` Element

Here, the corresponding SVG file is simply linked via the src attribute of the `<img>` element (see Listing 11.24). Browsers that can handle SVG will then display the linked SVG document at the appropriate place in the HTML.

However, links defined within the SVG content are not supported by this type of integration. The same applies to JavaScript code that appears within the SVG document. This code won't get interpreted or executed.

```
<!DOCTYPE html>
<html>
<head lang="en">
  ...
</head>
<body>
  <img src="example.svg" alt="SVG-Grafik" width="500" height="500" >
</body>
</html>
```

Listing 11.24 Integrating via the <img> Element

Integrating via the <iframe> Element

SVG files can also be defined as the source for the content of <iframe> elements (see Listing 11.25). The SVG file is then displayed within the iFrame. Unlike integrating via the <img> element, this type of integration interprets links within the SVG content and also executes any JavaScript that may exist.

```
<!DOCTYPE html>
<html>
<head lang="en">
  ...
</head>
<body>
  <iframe src="example.svg" width="500" height="500" scrolling="no" >
    <!-- For older browsers that don't support SVG -->
    <img src="example.tif" width="500" height="500" alt="Alternative PNG image">
  </iframe>
</body>
</html>
```

Listing 11.25 Integrating via the <iframe> Element

Integrating via the <object> Element

You can also integrate SVG files as multimedia objects using the <object> element (see Listing 11.26). For older browsers that can't display SVG, you can also specify alternative content, such as an alternative image, between the opening and closing <object> tags.

Similar to integrating via the <iframe> element, this type of integration interprets links within the SVG content, and JavaScript is also supported.

```
<!DOCTYPE html>
<html>
<head lang="en">
  ...
</head>
<body>
  <object data="example.svg" width="500" height="500" >
    <!-- For older browsers that don't support SVG -->
    <img src="example.tif" width="500" height="500" alt="Alternative PNG image">
  </object>
</body>
</html>
```

Listing 11.26 Integrating via the `<object>` Element

Integrating as Background Image via CSS

SVG files can also be used (surrounded by `url()`) as a value for the `background` CSS property (see Listing 11.27). In this case, the content of the SVG file is used as the background image for the corresponding element (or elements) selected by the respective CSS rule. However, links within the SVG content and JavaScript code won't be interpreted.

```
<!DOCTYPE html>
<html>
<head lang="en">
  ...
</head>
<body>
  <div style="background: url(example.svg); width: 500px; height: 500px" ></div>
</body>
</html>
```

Listing 11.27 Integrating as Background Image via CSS

Inline Definition in HTML

A particularly convenient feature is the fact that SVG can also be defined directly "inline" within the HTML code (see Listing 11.28). The browser then interprets the SVG in place, so links and JavaScript are interpreted as well.

```
<!DOCTYPE html>
<html>
<head lang="en">
  ...
</head>
<body>
  <svg id="svg" version="1.1"
```

```
      baseProfile="full"
      width="500" height="500"
      xmlns="http://www.w3.org/2000/svg">
  <rect width="100%" height="100%" />
  <circle id="circle" cx="100" cy="100" r="80" />
  </svg>
</body>
</html>
```

Listing 11.28 Inline Definition within the HTML Code

11.2.3   Changing the Appearance of SVG Elements with CSS

The individual elements within an SVG document can be styled using CSS, although the properties are not the same as those you use when styling HTML elements. For a selection of permitted elements, see Table 11.5. You also can find a complete listing in the SVG specification at *www.w3.org/TR/SVG2/styling.html*.

Property	Description
cursor	Mouse pointer
fill	Filling color
fill-opacity	Filling color, opacity
font-family	Font
font-size	Font size
font-style	Font style
stroke	Frame color
stroke-opacity	Frame color, opacity
stroke-width	Frame width

Table 11.5 Selection of Various CSS Properties for SVG

Listing 11.29 contains an example in which the SVG from Listing 11.28 is styled using CSS.

```
rect {
  stroke-width: 4;
  fill: #FFFFFF;
  stroke: #3080D0;
}
```

```css
#circle:hover {
  cursor: pointer;
}

#circle {
  fill-opacity: 0.5;
  stroke-width: 4;
  fill: #3080D0;
  stroke: #3080D0;
}
#circle.active {
  fill: #000000;
}

text {
  fill: #FFFFFF;
  font-family: sans-serif;
}
```

Listing 11.29 The Appearance of SVG Elements Can Be Changed via Special Properties Using CSS

11.2.4 Manipulating the Behavior of SVG Elements via JavaScript

Not only can you style the elements in an SVG document using CSS, you can also access individual elements using JavaScript, modify them, add new elements, and basically perform all the other DOM operations you already know about from Chapter 5.

As an example of this, we'll describe two use cases: first, how to add event listeners to individual SVG elements using JavaScript, and second, how to dynamically change the position of a graphic element using JavaScript.

Registering an Event Listener for SVG Elements

Listing 11.30 contains an example of registering event listeners to SVG elements. Here the embedded <svg> element is first accessed via the getElementById() method and then the <circle> element is determined via a renewed call of this method (this time on the <svg> element found). After that, three different event listeners are registered via the addEventListener() method: the event listener for the click event is called when the <circle> element is clicked, and the event listeners for the mouseover and mouseout events are called whenever the mouse pointer is moved over or away from that element. In both cases, the active CSS class is switched back and forth, and thus the filling color is changed (see also the CSS in Listing 11.29).

```
'use strict';
function init() {
  const svgDocument = document.getElementById('svg');
  const circle = svg.getElementById('circle');
  circle.addEventListener('click', (e) => {
    console.log('Hello World');
  });
  circle.addEventListener('mouseover', (e) => {
    circle.classList.toggle('active');
  });
  circle.addEventListener('mouseout', (e) => {
    circle.classList.toggle('active');
  });
}

window.addEventListener('DOMContentLoaded', init);
```

Listing 11.30 Registering Event Listeners to SVG Elements

Dynamically Changing SVG Elements

SVG elements can of course also be changed dynamically via JavaScript—for example, the position of the <circle> element. For this purpose, the HTML/SVG is first extended by two sliders, as shown in Listing 11.31. Then, an event listener for the change event is added to each slider (see Listing 11.32), within which the moveCircle() function is called. This function expects the following parameters: first, a position specification, and second, a specification about the direction (horizontal or vertical or x or y). Based on this, either the cx attribute (x coordinate of the circle center) or the cy attribute (y coordinate of the circle center) is updated accordingly. The circle then is immediately moved to the corresponding position on the drawing area.

```
<!DOCTYPE html>
<html>
<head lang="en">
    <meta charset="UTF-8">
    <title>SVG example</title>
    <link rel="stylesheet" href="styles/styles.css"></head>
<body>
  <script src="scripts/main.js"></script>
  <svg id="svg" version="1.1"
      baseProfile="full"
      width="500" height="500"
      xmlns="http://www.w3.org/2000/svg">
    <rect width="100%" height="100%" />
```

```
      <circle id="circle" cx="100" cy="100" r="80" />
   </svg>
   <div>X: <input id="sliderX" type="range" min="1" max="500" value="100" />
</div>
   <div>Y: <input id="sliderY" type="range" min="1" max="500" value="100" />
</div>
</body>
</html>
```

Listing 11.31 The HTML Is Extended by Two Sliders

```
'use strict';
function init() {
  const sliderX = document.getElementById('sliderX');
  const sliderY = document.getElementById('sliderY');
  sliderX.addEventListener('change', (e) => {
    moveCircle(e.target.value, 'x');
  });
  sliderY.addEventListener('change', (e) => {
    moveCircle(e.target.value, 'y');
  });
}

function moveCircle(value, direction) {
  const svgDocument = document.getElementById('svg');
  const circle = svgDocument.getElementById('circle');
  circle.setAttribute('c' + direction, value);
}

window.addEventListener('DOMContentLoaded', init);
```

Listing 11.32 Changing the Position of a Graphic Element

11.3 Summary

This chapter has shown how to use JavaScript to create graphics within the browser window. The main points here are as follows:

- Using the *Canvas API*, you can create graphics within a defined drawing area in the browser window.

- The <canvas> element provides one or multiple rendering contexts through which the drawing area or its contents can be manipulated.

- For drawing rectangles, the Canvas API offers three methods:
  - `fillRect()` creates a rectangle filled with a previously defined background color.
  - `strokeRect()` draws the outline of a rectangle (also with a previously defined frame color).
  - `clearRect()` removes everything from the drawing area that is inside the defined rectangle.
- All other geometric shapes must be drawn using *paths*.
- Texts, on the other hand, can be generated using the `fillText()` and `strokeText()` methods.
- To draw linear gradients, you can use the `createLinearGradient()` method, while the `createRadialGradient()` method enables you to draw radial gradients.
- In addition, the following three operations are available for transforming graphic elements:
  - *Scaling* changes the width and/or the height.
  - *Rotation* changes the angle.
  - *Translation* changes the x and/or y position.
- The *SVG* format is used for the declarative definition of vector graphics.
- SVG can be integrated via the `<img>`, `<iframe>`, or `<object>` element, or via CSS as a background image, or it can be defined directly inline in HTML.
- SVG can be styled using CSS, although some of the properties are different from those used in CSS for styling HTML.
- JavaScript can be used to access the contents of SVG documents—for example, to register event listeners for individual graphic elements or to dynamically add new graphic elements.

Chapter 12
Using Modern Web APIs

HTML5 provides web developers with a number of new JavaScript APIs, among other things, that can be used to do all sorts of useful things. In this chapter, we'll cover a selection of these APIs and show you, for example, alternatives available for communicating with the server, how to store data so that it's available offline, how to play audio and video files, and how to determine the geographic location of users. All these techniques (and more) allow you to make your web applications even more dynamic and versatile.

You could easily fill whole books with info about web APIs, so in this chapter—although it's quite a long one—we'll only introduce a comparatively small selection of the best-known APIs. Specifically, we'll address the APIs listed in Table 12.1.

Web API	Description	Section
Web Socket API	Enables bidirectional communication between client and server	Section 12.1.2
Server-Sent Events	Enables actively sending messages to the client from the server	Section 12.1.3
Web Storage API	Enables access to browser storage	Section 12.3
Indexed Database API	Enables access to a browser database	Section 12.4
File API	Enables access to the file system	Section 12.5
Drag and Drop API	Enables components to be moved within a web page	Section 12.6
Web Worker API	Enables JavaScript programs to run in parallel	Section 12.7
Geolocation API	Enables accessing location information for the user	Section 12.8
Battery Status API	Enables reading the battery level of an end device	Section 12.9

Table 12.1 The Web APIs Discussed in This Chapter

Web API	Description	Section
Web Speech API	Enables speech to be recognized and speech to be output	Section 12.10
Web Animation API	Enables creating animations	Section 12.11
Command Line API	Enables working with the command line	Section 12.12
Internationalization API	Allows for creating multilingual applications	Section 12.13

Table 12.1 The Web APIs Discussed in This Chapter (Cont.)

In addition—because it's appropriate in the run-up to Web Storage API and Indexed Database API—we'll briefly discuss the principle of cookies and show you how to create and read them with JavaScript.

More Web APIs: Monthly Article Series

I regularly present various web APIs in the German *web & mobile DEVELOPER* magazine. In this context, I look at APIs other than those mentioned here, as well as those that are still at a very early stage. I would be very happy to welcome you as a reader there as well.

More Web APIs in This Book

We've already covered some APIs throughout the course of this book, including the Canvas API for drawing via JavaScript (see Chapter 11) and the Constraint Validation API, which can be used to validate form input via JavaScript (see Chapter 7).

W3C versus WHATWG

In the context of web APIs, it's also important to understand the difference between the World Wide Web Consortium (W3C) and the Web Hypertext Application Technology Working Group (WHATWG). The former is a standardization body for the technologies of the World Wide Web, including HTML, CSS, and the various web APIs. The WHATWG, on the other hand, is a working group whose creation in 2004 was primarily due to the fact that the development of various web standards at the W3C at that time was progressing rather sluggishly. This is because the W3C aims to always adopt final versions of web standards, which accordingly can take a while now and then. The WHATWG, on the other hand, is pursuing a different strategy: Here, so-called living standards are maintained—specifications that are continuously developed further in close cooperation with the various browser manufacturers (who, by the way, are also part of the working group). In terms of web APIs, this means that you're often dealing with two variants: a "final" variant that has been approved by the W3C and one that is being further developed by the WHATWG.

12.1   Communicating via JavaScript

This first section is about how to communicate with the server using JavaScript and appropriate web APIs. Specifically, we'll cover the Web Socket API and server-sent events. The former enables bidirectional communication between client and server, and the latter enables messages to be actively sent to the client from the server.

12.1.1   Unidirectional Communication with the Server

Before we turn our attention to the Web Socket API and thus to bidirectional communication between client and server, we'll first give you an introductory overview of "normal" communication between client and server—that is, *unidirectional communication*—and show which approaches have emerged in recent years to circumvent the limitations of this type of communication.

When communicating via HTTP, the communication happens from the client, regardless of whether it is a classic website or a modern web application based on Ajax. In all cases, it's the client that formulates the (HTTP) requests to the server, to which the server then responds with (HTTP) responses. The server can't send data to a client by itself via HTTP.

The communication between client and server is unidirectional—that is, in one direction from the client to the server. Although the server responds with replies and thus you are already communicating in two directions, that doesn't change the fact that *active* communication is only in one direction.

Suppose you developed an application where messages are to be stored on a server at irregular intervals and displayed in a web application in a relatively timely manner. It would be nice if the server would notify the client about new messages. Various techniques have emerged in the past to make such requirements feasible through hacks. One of them is so-called polling, in which the client requests new data from the server in the background (through Ajax requests), which the server then responds to accordingly (see Figure 12.1).

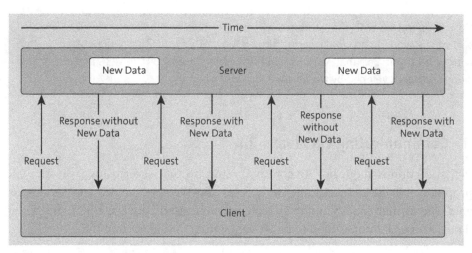

Figure 12.1 The Principle of Polling

A variant of the polling technique is so-called long polling, where the client also sends requests to the server in the background (see Figure 12.2). If new data is available on the server, the server immediately provides a response. If, on the other hand, no new data is available, the server keeps the HTTP connection open until either new data is available on the server or a previously specified time-out has been exceeded. In both cases, as soon as the client receives the appropriate response from the server, it sends another request, and the server keeps the connection open again, and so on.

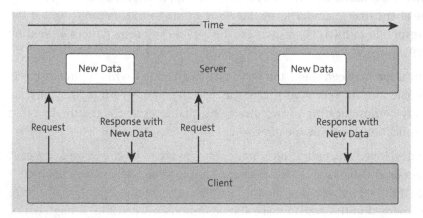

Figure 12.2 The Principle of Long Polling

However, there are also technologies where the server really sends data to the client, so you can do without the techniques we just described. One of these technologies is the so-called Web Socket API.

12.1.2   Bidirectional Communication with a Server

Socket connections between client and server can be established via the Web Socket API (*www.w3.org/TR/websockets/* or *https://html.spec.whatwg.org/multipage/comms. html#network*), through which it's possible both for the client to send data to the server and for the server to send data to the client. In other words, there is a permanent connection between client and server, and both can send data to the other at any time (see Figure 12.3).

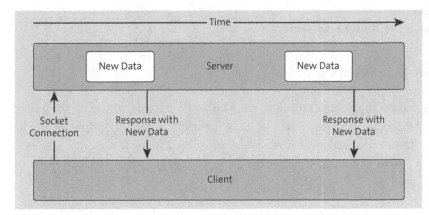

Figure 12.3 The Principle of Web Sockets

The specification includes only one type (or interface)—namely, WebSocket. To establish a web socket connection, you use the appropriate constructor function, as shown in Listing 12.1.

```
const connection = new WebSocket('ws://example.com/test');
```

Listing 12.1 Create a Web Socket Connection

Regarding the connection establishment, WebSocket provides three event handlers: the event handler onopen is called when the web socket connection has been opened, the event handler onerror when an error has occurred while establishing the connection, and finally the event handler onclose when the connection has been closed again (see Listing 12.2).

```
connection.onopen = (event) => {
  console.log('Connection opened');
};
connection.onerror = (error) => {
  console.log(`WebSocket Error: ${error}`);
};
```

```
connection.onclose = (event) => {
  console.log('Connection closed');
};
```

Listing 12.2 The Different Event Handlers for Establishment of a Connection

To send data to the server, use the send() method, which understandably makes sense only inside the onopen event handler (see Listing 12.3).

```
connection.onopen = (event) => {
  connection.send('Message to server').
};
```

Listing 12.3 Sending a Message to the Server

Here, strings, binary large objects (BLOBs), array buffers, and typed arrays can be passed to the send() method. So to send data in JSON format, the corresponding JavaScript objects must first be converted via JSON.stringify() as in Listing 12.4.

```
const message = {
  hello: 'world'
};
connection.send(JSON.stringify(message));
```

Listing 12.4 Sending a JSON Message to the Server

On the other hand, to be able to react to data sent by the server, WebSocket provides another event handler, onmessage (see Listing 12.5).

```
connection.onmessage = (event) {
  console.log(event.data.byteLength);
};
```

Listing 12.5 Receiving a Message from the Server

If you receive JSON data from the server, you have to transform it using JSON.parse(), as shown in Listing 12.6.

```
connection.onmessage = (event) => {
  try {
    const data = JSON.parse(event.data);
    console.log(data);
  } catch (error) {
    console.error('Error parsing');
  }
};
```

Listing 12.6 Receiving a JSON Message from the Server

Furthermore, as with sending messages to the server, BLOBs and array buffers can also be received from the server. This is done by setting the `binaryType` property to the value `blob` or `arraybuffer`, which has the former value by default (see Listing 12.7).

```
connection.binaryType = 'arraybuffer';
```

Listing 12.7 Determining the Binary Data Type

To close a connection, use the `close()` method.

```
connection.close();
```

Listing 12.8 Closing a Web Socket Connection

12.1.3   Outgoing Communication from the Server

Using *server-sent events* (*www.w3.org/TR/eventsource/* or in the living standard at *https://html.spec.whatwg.org/multipage/comms.html#server-sent-events*), it's possible for servers to send messages to a client on their own (see Figure 12.4).

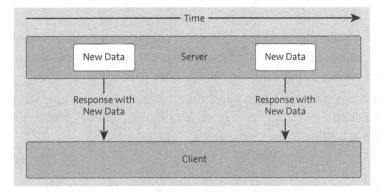

Figure 12.4 In Server-Sent Events, the Server Sends Messages to the Client.

Implementing the Client Side

The API defines the `EventSource` interface, which represents a server-side source that generates events or sends messages. To define such an event source, you pass the URL to the corresponding constructor function as shown in Listing 12.9 and define an event handler to be able to respond to the messages from the server.

```
const source = new EventSource('/events');
source.onmessage = (event) => {
  console.log(event.data);         // sent message
  console.log(event.origin);       // source
  console.log(event.lastEventId);  // ID of the last event sent
};
```

Listing 12.9 Specifying a Data Source for Server-Side Events

In addition to the onmessage event handler, the onopen and onerror event handlers are also available. The former is called when the connection to the server has been opened, the latter when an error has occurred.

As an alternative to the onmessage event handler, you can also register an event listener using the addEventListener() method (see Listing 12.10).

```
const source = new EventSource('/events');
source.addEventListener('message', (event) => {
  document.body.innerHTML += `${event.data}<br>`;
});
```

Listing 12.10 Registering an Event Listener

Implementing the Server Side

What's missing is the server-based code that sends the messages. And what could be more appropriate in our case than to write them in JavaScript as well, using Node.js? We're getting a little ahead of things here because we won't discuss Node.js in detail until Chapter 17—but it's still better than showing no server-based script at all or one implemented in PHP or Java.

So if you want to try the following example yourself on your computer, you need to install Node.js first; you can briefly refer to Chapter 17 for that. If you'd rather wait until we've fully discussed Node.js, you can come back to this chapter at a later time.

Listing 12.11 shows the server-based code for an application that generates a sample task for adding the numbers between 1 and 20 every five seconds (e.g., "5 + 9 = ") and sends the corresponding task as a string to the client (see Figure 12.5).

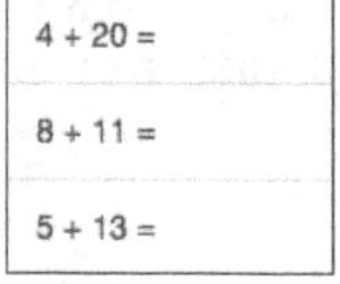

6 + 16 =
11 + 17 =
3 + 2 =
3 + 20 =
1 + 7 =
4 + 20 =
8 + 11 =
5 + 13 =

Figure 12.5 The Individual Tasks Are Sent from the Server to the Client

But everything in turn: first, the first two lines (or lines two and three if you disregard the 'use strict';) import two standard Node.js modules—the fs module (short for *file system*), which provides various functions related to working with the file system, and the http module, which can be used to start a web server.

```
const fs = require('fs');
const http = require('http');
const MIN = 1;
const MAX = 20;

const server = http.createServer((request, response) => {
  if (request.headers.accept && request.headers.accept === 'text/event-
stream') {
    // URL for the event source
    if (request.url === '/events') {
      sendEvent(request, response);
    } else {
      response.writeHead(404);
      response.end();
    }
  } else {
    // URL for the HTML file
    response.writeHead(200, {'Content-Type': 'text/html'});
    response.write(fs.readFileSync(__dirname + '/index.html'));
    response.end();
  }
})
server.listen(8000);

function sendEvent(request, response) {
  response.writeHead(200, {
    'Content-Type': 'text/event-stream',
    'Cache-Control': 'no-cache',
    'Connection': 'keep-alive'
  });

  const id = (new Date()).toLocaleTimeString();

  setInterval(() => {
    createServerSendEvent(response, id);
  }, 5000);

  createServerSendEvent(response, id);
}

function createServerSendEvent(response, id) {
  const exercise = createRandomExercise();
  response.write('id: ' + id + '\n');
```

```
    response.write('data: ' + exercise + '\n\n');
}

function createRandomExercise() {
  const number1 = Math.floor(Math.random() * MAX) + MIN;
  const number2 = Math.floor(Math.random() * MAX) + MIN;
  const exercise = number1 + ' + ' + number2 + ' = ';
  return exercise;
}
```

Listing 12.11 Implementation of a Web Server for Server-Sent Events

For this purpose, the http module provides the createServer() method, to which you pass a callback function that is then called for each HTTP request to the web server (more on this in a moment). With the listen() method, you start the web server. Here you can specify the port under which the server is to be reached (in the example, port 8000). Inside the callback function of createServer(), you have access to the HTTP request (request parameter) and the HTTP response (response parameter).

Two cases are dealt with in this example: the first part of the branch (the if part) checks if the request is one that wants to use the server as an event source, and the second part of the branch (the else part) causes the **index.html** file to be returned for all other requests (i.e., the content from Listing 12.12).

Sending individual events can be seen in the sendEvent() method: Here, a server-side event is generated every five seconds using the createServerSendEvent() function. The code for creating the random addition task is located in the createRandomExercise() function.

> **Starting the Server**
>
> To start the script—assuming that Node.js is installed—enter the node <filename> command, where you use the name of the JavaScript file for <filename>.

```
<!DOCTYPE html>
<html>
<head lang="en">
  <meta charset="utf-8" />
  <link rel="stylesheet" href="https://maxcdn.bootstrapcdn.com/bootstrap/3.3.6/
css/bootstrap.min.css" crossorigin="anonymous">
</head>
<body>
  <script>
    document.addEventListener('DOMContentLoaded', () => {
      const source = new EventSource('/events');
      const list = document.getElementById('exercises')
```

```
  source.addEventListener('message', (e) => {
    const listItem = document.createElement('li');
    listItem.classList.add('list-group-item');
    listItem.textContent += e.data;
    list.appendChild(listItem);
  });
});
</script>
<ul id="exercises" class="list-group">
</ul>
</body>
</html>
```

Listing 12.12 The HTML Code for Receiving the Server-Side Events

12.2   Recognizing Users

There are some use cases that require that you can also store data on the client side and retrieve it at a later time. In the following sections, you'll learn various techniques necessary for this. Let's start with cookies, which are not a pure HTML5 technology, but rather have a few years under their belt. However, the didactic structure may forgive explaining the principle and use of cookie technology at this point.

12.2.1   Using Cookies

The HTTP protocol is a *stateless protocol*, which means that any HTTP request from a client to a server is handled by the server independently of other requests, including those that the same client may have made previously. In other words, initially the server doesn't recognize when a client makes a request for the second time (see Figure 12.6).

However, you often have use cases where you want to know exactly which client is accessing a web page. As an example, imagine a web store where users can add items to a shopping cart (as is common in a web store). To remember which items the user has placed in the shopping cart and to list them correctly after reloading the web page, you need an option to recognize the user.

This is where cookies come into play. Cookies allow you to store small amounts of information on the client computer and—when the user visits your website again—to read this information on the server side (or through JavaScript). In principle, cookies are nothing more than smaller text files that the browser stores on the user's computer (if the user allows it and has not taken appropriate precautions in the browser settings) and which are then transmitted together with the HTTP request each time the associated website is called (see Figure 12.7).

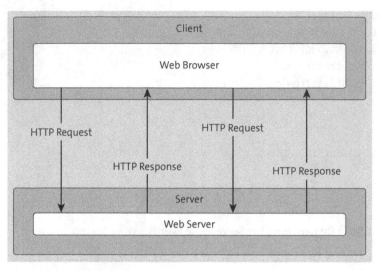

Figure 12.6 HTTP Is a Stateless Protocol

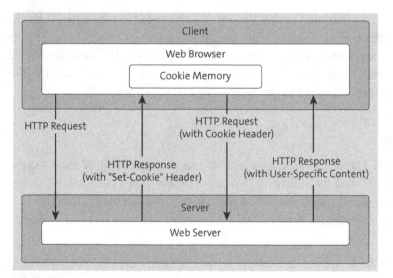

Figure 12.7 The Principle of Cookies

Such cookie files essentially contain the following information:

- The *name* and *value* of the cookie. The name is not case-sensitive, which means that, for example, *name* and *Name* refer to the same cookie. Only strings are allowed as values (and not, say, numbers). Name and value are the only mandatory pieces of information. Specifying the remaining information is optional (if it isn't specified, default values are used).

- The *domain* of the server and the *path* on the server to which the cookie should be sent. For example, a cookie with the domain *www.javascriptmanual.com* is also only sent with requests to this domain. A cookie with the domain *www.javascripthandbuch.de* and the path */samplechapter* is only sent with requests to *www.javascripthandbuch.de/samplechapter*, but not to *www.javascripthandbuch.de*.

- An *expiration date* until which the cookie is valid. After the expiration of the date specified here, the cookie expires, is deleted, and is no longer sent to the server. If no expiration date is specified when a cookie is created, it's deleted by default when the browser session is terminated.

- A *security flag* that can be used to optionally specify whether a cookie should only be sent on connections that use Secure Sockets Layer (SSL)—for example, to allow sending to *https://www.javascripthandbuch.de* but prevent sending to *http://www.javascripthandbuch.de*.

Content of Cookies

Cookies contain plain text—that is, no source code or executable code.

Alternative Options to Recognize Users

In addition to cookies, there are other options for recognizing users—for example, *URL rewriting*, which involves rewriting links within a web page and adding a parameter that identifies the user. If the user then clicks on a link, the URL parameter on the server side can be used to identify which user it is.

12.2.2 Creating Cookies

Cookies can be created in two ways: on the one hand, they can be sent from the server to the client in the header of an HTTP response; on the other hand, they can be generated on the client side—for example, by JavaScript. We'll look at the second case ahead.

The starting point for managing cookies is the cookie property of the document object. Cookies can be both read and created via this property. However, this is anything but comfortable, as you'll see. For example, to add cookies, you write the code shown in Listing 12.13.

```
document.cookie = 'username=John Doe';
document.cookie = 'shoppingCartItemIDs=22345,23445,65464,74747,46646,; expires=
Sa, 31 Dec 2021 23:59:59 UTC; path=/';
```

Listing 12.13 Creating Cookies in JavaScript

> **Cookies for Local HTML Files**
>
> When you open a local HTML file in the browser, your browser may not set cookies by default. In Chrome, for example, you must start with the `--enable-file-cookies` option to interpret cookies for local HTML files. Safari and Firefox, in contrast, also accept cookies for local HTML files by default.

Here, it's first somewhat confusing that the assignments after the creation of `document.cookie = newCookie` do not overwrite the `cookie` property, but instead add a new cookie. Referring to the preceding example, this means that after executing the two lines of code, two cookies will be created for the website: one cookie with the name `username` and the value `John Doe` and one cookie with the name `shoppingCartItemIDs` and the value `22345,23445,65464,74747,46646`. You can also define the expiration date and the path of the cookie by specifying `expires` and `path`.

> **Note**
>
> In the background, a setter method is called when the `cookie` property is assigned (this is an access property; also refer to Chapter 4). This setter method doesn't overwrite any existing values, but simply appends the new value.

12.2.3   Reading Cookies

Where defining cookies is already confusing, reading them is also unnecessarily complicated, as you can see in Listing 12.14. In fact, accessing `document.cookie` simply gives you a string of all the name-value pairs of the cookies for the current web page.

```
console.log(document.cookie);
// Output: username=John Doe;
// shoppingCartItemIDs=22345,23445,65464,74747,46646
```

Listing 12.14 Reading Cookies in JavaScript

This, in turn, means two things: on the one hand, you have no option to read other information, such as expiration date, for a cookie via `document.cookie`; on the other hand, it's very time-consuming to split the string in order to be able to access individual cookies and their values. Fortunately, there are some libraries available for this, such as the one at *https://github.com/ScottHamper/Cookies* or the jQuery plug-in available at *https://github.com/carhartl/jquery-cookie*.

But if you don't want to use an extra library, use the helper functions shown in Listing 12.15 (based on the blog post at *www.quirksmode.org/js/cookies.html*). The `create-Cookie()` function is used to create new cookies, the `readCookie()` function is used to read cookies, and the `deleteCookie()` function is used to remove cookies.

```
// File: cookie-utils.js
function createCookie(name, value, days) {
  let expires = '';
  if (days) {
    const date = new Date();
    date.setTime(date.getTime() + (days * 24 * 60 * 60 * 1000));
    expires = '; expires=' + date.toGMTString();
  }
  document.cookie = name + '=' + value + expires + '; path=/';
}

function readCookie(name) {
  const nameEQ = name + '=';
  const ca = document.cookie.split(';');
  for (let i = 0; i < ca.length; i++) {
    let c = ca[i];
    while (c.charAt(0) == ' ') {
      c = c.substring(1, c.length);
    }
    if (c.indexOf(nameEQ) == 0) {
      return c.substring(nameEQ.length, c.length);
    }
  }
  return null;
}

function deleteCookie(name) {
  createCookie(name, '', -1);
}
```

Listing 12.15 Helper Functions for Writing, Reading, and Deleting Cookies

The createCookie() function expects three parameters: the name and value of the cookie, and optionally the number of days the cookie is supposed to be valid. The read-Cookie() function expects the name of the cookie and returns the corresponding value of the cookie. There is no direct way to delete cookies in JavaScript. For the implementation of the deleteCookie() function, you now make use of the fact that cookies whose expiration dates are in the past expire immediately and are deleted by the browser.

Based on these helper functions, we'll show you next how cookies can be used to store user data and influence output depending on it, using a simple shopping cart example.

> **Application Cases for Cookies**
>
> Cookies are mainly used for two things: first, to recognize users (in which case you store corresponding user IDs in the cookies), and second, to store (small amounts of) data on the client side.

12.2.4   Example: Shopping Cart Based on Cookies

The example consists of three components / files: The **catalog.js** file (see Listing 12.16) contains dummy data for the shopping cart. In real life, you certainly would store this information not entirely on the client side in JavaScript, but on the server side, and then make it accessible via a web service. For the example and for clarifying cookies, however, this architecture should suffice.

```javascript
// File: catalog.js
const catalog = {
  id22345: {
    name: 'Jar of pickles (500 ml)',
    price: '2.50'
  },
  id23445: {
    name: 'Pears (2 kg)',
    price: '4.50'
  },
  id46647: {
    name: 'Cherries',
    price: '2.50'
  },
  id65464: {
    name: 'Apples (2 kg)',
    price: '4.50'
  },
  id46648: {
    name: 'Salad',
    price: '2.50'
  },
  id74747: {
    name: 'Jar of cherries (1000 ml)',
    price: '2.50'
  },
```

```
  id46646: {
    name: 'Bananas',
    price: '4.50'
  }
}
```

Listing 12.16 All Items in the Catalog, on Client Side for the Sake of Simplicity

Listing 12.17 shows the basic HTML structure in which the shopping cart output is to be generated. The JavaScript files for the cookie helper functions (cookie-utils.js), the offer catalog (catalog.js), and the shopping cart implementation (shopping-cart.js), which we'll talk about in a moment, are included as external JavaScript files as usual.

```
<!DOCTYPE html>
<html>
<head lang="en">
  <meta charset="UTF-8">
  <title>Shopping Cart with Cookies</title>
</head>
<body>
<div>Hello, <span id="username"></span></div>
<br>

<div id="shopping-cart">
  You have <span id="shopping-cart-item-count">0</span> items in your cart.
  <ul id="shopping-cart-items"></ul>
<div>
<script src="cookie-utils.js"></script>
<script src="catalog.js"></script>
<script src="shopping-cart.js"></script>
</body>
</html>
```

Listing 12.17 The Basic HTML Structure for the Shopping Cart

The implementation of the shopping cart is shown in Listing 12.18. You can see two functions here: showUsername() to show the user name and showShoppingCart() to show the shopping cart. Both functions access the previously defined readCookie() helper function to read the corresponding data from the respective cookies. For simplicity, the user name and the IDs of the products in the shopping cart are initialized using create-Cookie() at the beginning of the script. Normally, you would store the user name after the user logs in and the shopping cart after each addition or removal of a product. The results are displayed in Figure 12.8.

```
// File: shopping-cart.js
createCookie('username', 'John Doe', 7);
createCookie('shoppingCartItemIDs',
            'id22345,id23445,id65464,id74747,id46646',
            7);

showUsername();
showShoppingCart();

function showUsername() {
  const username = readCookie('username');
  document.getElementById('username').textContent = username;
}

function showShoppingCart() {
  const ids = readCookie('shoppingCartItemIDs').split(',');
  const itemsElement = document.getElementById('shopping-cart-items');
  ids.forEach(function (id) {
    const item = catalog[id];
    const itemElement = document.createElement('li');
    itemElement.appendChild(document.createTextNode(item.name));
    itemsElement.appendChild(itemElement);
  });
  document.getElementById('shopping-cart-item-count').textContent = ids.length;
}
```

Listing 12.18 Reading the Cookies and Displaying the Shopping Cart

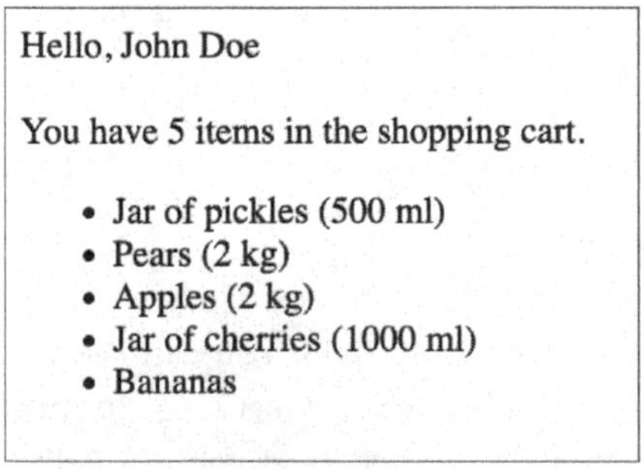

Hello, John Doe

You have 5 items in the shopping cart.

- Jar of pickles (500 ml)
- Pears (2 kg)
- Apples (2 kg)
- Jar of cherries (1000 ml)
- Bananas

Figure 12.8 Shopping Carts Are a Typical Example of Using Cookies

Showing Content of Cookies

The developer tools of the various browser manufacturers allow you to view the contents of cookies. In Chrome DevTools, you can find this feature under **Resources • Cookies** (see Figure 12.9).

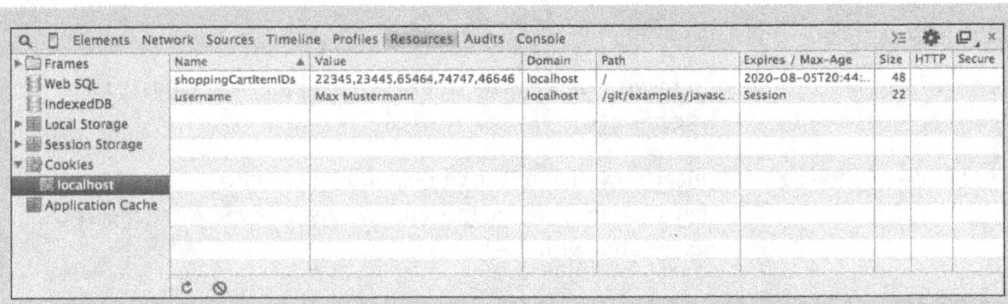

Figure 12.9 The Individual Browsers Provide Helper Tools with which You Can View the Cookies—Here, Chrome DevTools

12.2.5   Disadvantages of Cookies

All cookies for a corresponding domain and the relevant path are sent with each request, which affects the data volume. In addition, cookies that are sent via the HTTP protocol (and not via the secure HTTPS protocol) are transmitted unencrypted, which poses a security risk depending on the type of information transmitted. Another limitation of cookies is the allowed memory size of 4 KB.

12.3   Using the Browser Storage

The Web Storage API (*https://html.spec.whatwg.org/multipage/webstorage.html*) defines an interface for accessing an internal browser storage. In principle, there are two different types of browser storage: *local browser storage*, which is accessible across different browser windows and tabs, and *session storage*, which is only accessible within a browser tab (details on this later in the chapter in Section 12.3.6).

The former—that is, local storage—can be accessed via the localStorage global object (or window.localStorage), the latter, session storage, via the sessionStorage global object (or window.sessionStorage). In terms of API, the two browser storage options are identical (see Table 12.2); that is, both have the same methods and properties (the corresponding objects representing the browser storage options are both of type Storage).

Property/Method	Description
length	Contains the number of elements in the storage
clear()	Removes all key-value pairs from the storage
getItem(key)	Returns the corresponding value from the storage for a key
key(index)	Returns the name of the key at position index from the storage

Table 12.2 Properties and Methods of Storage

Property/Method	Description
removeItem(key)	Removes—if present—the key-value pair for the passed key from the storage
setItem(key, value)	Inserts a value for the corresponding key into the storage or—if a key with the same name already exists—overwrites the value associated with the key

Table 12.2 Properties and Methods of Storage (Cont.)

12.3.1   Storing Values in the Browser Storage

Storing values to browser storage is done using the setItem() method. To this method, you transfer a key under which the corresponding value is to be stored as the first parameter and the value to be stored as the second parameter. As mentioned previously, this works for the local browser storage (see Listing 12.19) and the session browser storage (see Listing 12.20).

```
localStorage.setItem('firstname', 'John');
localStorage.setItem('lastname', 'Doe');
```

Listing 12.19 Storing Values to the Local Browser Storage

```
sessionStorage.setItem('firstname', 'John');
sessionStorage.setItem('lastname', 'Doe');
```

Listing 12.20 Storing Values to the Session Browser Storage

The value to be stored must be a string only, which means you should first convert objects using JSON.stringify() into a string, as shown in Listing 12.21.

If you don't do that, the value returned by the toString() method of the respective object is used, which is the [object Object] string by default. That's not really what you want.

```
const user = {
  firstname: 'John',
  lastname: 'Doe'
}
localStorage.setItem(
  'user',
  user                    // Incorrect: The string [object Object] is stored.
);
localStorage.setItem(
```

```
  'user',
  JSON.stringify(user)  // Correct: The object is stored in JSON format.
);
```

Listing 12.21 Objects Must Be Converted to Strings before Storing

12.3.2   Reading Values from the Browser Storage

Analogous to the setItem() method for storing values in the object store, the getItem() method is available to read values from the object store based on their key (see Listing 12.22).

```
const firstname = localStorage.getItem('firstname');  // Reading the value
                                                       // of the "firstname"
                                                       // property
const lastname = localStorage.getItem('lastname'); // Reading the value
                                                   // of the "lastname" property
console.log(firstname);                            // John
console.log(lastname);                             // Doe
```

Listing 12.22 Reading Values from Local Storage

When reading objects that have previously been stored (and converted via JSON.stringify()), you must of course remember to convert the corresponding value back into an object via JSON.parse(). After all, this value is a string. For example, to read the user object previously stored in Listing 12.21 from the object store again accordingly, proceed as shown in Listing 12.23.

```
let user = localStorage.getItem('user');
user = JSON.parse(user);
console.log(user.firstname);                       // John
console.log(user.lastname);                        // Doe
```

Listing 12.23 Reading Objects from the Local Storage

12.3.3   Updating Values in the Browser Storage

There is no separate method for updating values in one of the browser storage options. This task is performed by the setItem() method. It ensures that the value for a key is overwritten if it already exists in the object store. You can see an example of this in Listing 12.24.

```
localStorage.setItem('firstname', 'John');
localStorage.setItem('lastname', 'Doe');
let firstname = localStorage.getItem('firstname');
```

```
let lastname = localStorage.getItem('lastname');
console.log(firstname);                              // John
console.log(lastname);                               // Doe
localStorage.setItem('firstname', 'James');
localStorage.setItem('lastname', 'Peterson');
firstname = localStorage.getItem('firstname');
lastname = localStorage.getItem('lastname');
console.log(firstname);                              // James
console.log(lastname);                               // Peterson
```

Listing 12.24 Updating Values in the Browser Storage

12.3.4   Deleting Values from the Browser Storage

The removeItem() method can be used to selectively delete individual items from the browser storage, passing the key of the corresponding item as a parameter (see Listing 12.25). If you want to delete not only one entry but all entries of a browser storage, you use the clear() method.

```
localStorage.setItem('firstname', 'John');
localStorage.setItem('lastname', 'Doe');
const firstname = localStorage.getItem('firstname');
const lastname = localStorage.getItem('lastname');
console.log(firstname);       // John
console.log(lastname);        // Doe
localStorage.removeItem('firstname');
localStorage.removeItem('lastname');
```

Listing 12.25 Deleting Values from the Browser Storage

12.3.5   Responding to Changes in the Browser Storage

To respond to changes in the browser storage, you can register an event listener for the storage event using the addEventListener() method of the window object. This event is triggered whenever the browser storage (either in localStorage or in sessionStorage) changes.

The corresponding event object passed as an argument to the event listener is of type StorageEvent and contains properties in addition to those available by default for event objects, which you can see in Listing 12.26 and Table 12.3. The key property contains the key for which the entry has changed, oldValue contains the old value, newValue contains the new value, the url property contains the URL of the document in which the entry has changed, and storageArea contains the storage object affected by the change.

```
window.addEventListener('storage', (e) => {
  console.log(e.key);          // Key of the updated entry
  console.log(e.oldValue);     // old value
  console.log(e.newValue);     // new value
  console.log(e.url)           // the URL of the document for which an entry ...
                               // ... was changed
  console.log(e.storageArea);  // the storage object that was changed
});
```

Listing 12.26 Registering an Event Listener

Property	Description
key	Contains the key of the updated entry
oldValue	Contains the old value that was stored behind the key
newValue	Contains the new value that is now stored behind the key
url	Contains the URL of the document for which an entry was changed
storageArea	Contains a reference to the storage object that was changed

Table 12.3 Properties of StorageEvent

12.3.6   The Different Types of Browser Storage

As you learned in the previous sections, there are two different types of browser storage: local storage (accessible via window.localStorage) and session storage (accessible via window.sessionStorage). We haven't yet explained the exact difference between the two. Let's make up for that now.

In principle, the two types of storage differ in where they are visible or from where they can be accessed. The local storage, as shown in Figure 12.10, is accessible from all windows and tabs within the respective browser (the local storage of another browser cannot be accessed, of course).

The session storage, on the other hand, is different for each window or tab, as shown in Figure 12.11. It therefore isn't possible to access the session storage of a window or tab from another window or tab.

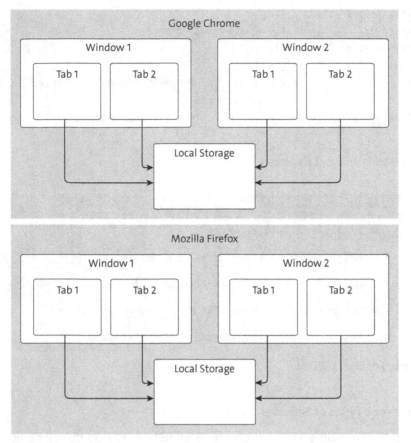

Figure 12.10 The Principle of the Local Storage

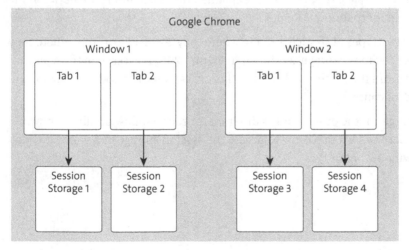

Figure 12.11 The Principle of the Session Storage

12.3.7   Example: Shopping Cart Based on the Browser Storage

The shopping cart example from Section 12.2.4, which was implemented there based on cookies, can be customized using the browser storage, as shown in Listing 12.27. The changes are printed in bold in the listing and affect only four lines: exactly the ones where the username and the IDs of the products in the shopping cart are stored and read again. The rest of the code and also the **catalog.js** (see Listing 12.16) and **index.html** (see) files remain unchanged.

```
// File: shopping-cart.js
localStorage.setItem('username', 'John Doe');
localStorage.setItem('shoppingCartItemIDs', JSON.stringify(
  ['id22345','id23445','id65464','id74747','id46646'])
);

showUsername();
showShoppingCart();

function showUsername() {
  const username = localStorage.getItem('username');
  document.getElementById('username').textContent = username;
}

function showShoppingCart() {
  const ids = JSON.parse(localStorage.getItem('shoppingCartItemIDs'));
  const itemsElement = document.getElementById('shopping-cart-items');
  ids.forEach(function (id) {
    const item = catalog[id];
    const itemElement = document.createElement('li');
    itemElement.appendChild(document.createTextNode(item.name));
    itemsElement.appendChild(itemElement);
  });
  document.getElementById('shopping-cart-item-count').textContent = ids.length;
}
```

Listing 12.27 Reading the Values from the Browser Storage and Displaying the Shopping Cart

Viewing the Contents of the Browser Storage

You can usually view the various browser storage areas via various browser tools. Figure 12.12 shows Chrome DevTools, for example. There you'll find the local browser storage under **Resources • Local Storage** and the session storage under **Resources • Session Storage**.

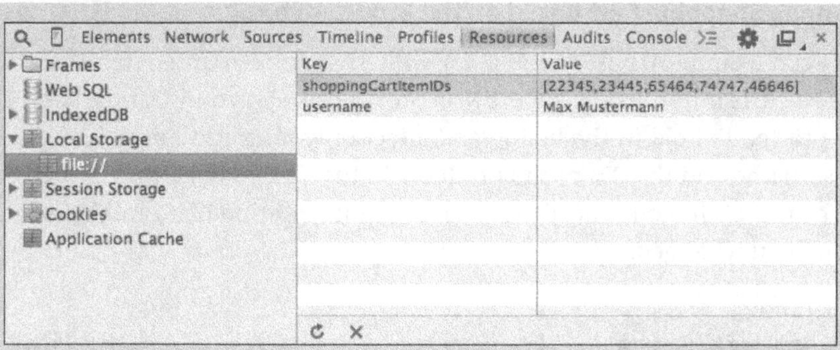

Figure 12.12 The Local Storage Can Be Inspected Using Various Browser Tools, as Shown Here for Chrome DevTools

12.4 Using the Browser Database

The Indexed Database API or IndexedDB API (*www.w3.org/TR/IndexedDB/*) is a database that resides in the browser or is implemented and made available by the browser. Before we show you specifically how to work with the IndexedDB API, we'll explain a few basic concepts about databases in general and the concepts used with IndexedDB in particular.

In principle, this (client-side) database works just like a server-side database; that is, you can create records in it, read records, update them, or delete them again.

CRUD Operations

Four key operations are often discussed in concert: create, read, update, and delete (*CRUD*).

IndexedDB is a *nonrelational database*, also referred to as a NoSQL database. On the other hand, there are *relational databases*, where the data is stored in the form of records in different tables. MySQL and PostgreSQL are examples of relational databases. In NoSQL databases, you store objects. A further distinction is made here between key-value stores, column families, graph databases, document databases, and others. Examples of nonrelational databases include MongoDB, CouchDB, Redis, or IndexedDB on the client side.

The basic idea behind IndexedDB is to store (JavaScript) objects under specific keys; that is, IndexedDB is a *key-value store*. In principle, this is comparable to the map data structure; that is, the individual objects in such a database are stored as values under certain keys.

The core of an IndexedDB database is formed by the object stores. These are roughly comparable to tables in relational databases and contain the various key-value pairs.

12.4.1 Opening a Database

You can access IndexedDB via the window object. Its indexedDB property comprises an object of type IDBFactory, which can be used to open databases, among other things. For this purpose, this object provides the open() method. As shown in Listing 12.28, you pass the name of the database to it and optionally a version number as a second parameter (the latter internally determines the database schema used for storing objects).

The return value of the open() method is an object of the IDBOpenDBRequest type; that is, at this point you don't have the database itself (or an object representing it) in your hands but have only made a request to open the corresponding database.

To be able to access the database itself or, in the event of an error, the corresponding error, various event handlers can be defined on this request object. For example, the onerror property can be used to formulate an event handler in case of an error, such as when the user doesn't have permissions in the browser to access the database. The onsuccess property can be used to define an event handler that is to be called when the database has been opened successfully.

```
const idbFactory = window.indexcdDB;      // Access to the helper object
const request = idbFactory.open(          // Open the database...
  'TestDatabase',                         // ... based on the name...
  1                                       // ... and optionally the version
);
request.onerror = (event) => {            // Event handler in case of error
  const error = event.target.error;       // Access to the error
  console.error(error.message);           // Output of the error
};
request.onsuccess = (event) => {.         // Event handler for the normal case
  const database = event.target.result;   // Access to the database
  console.log(database.name);             // Output: "TestDatabase"
  console.log(database.version);          // Output: 1
};
```

Listing 12.28 Opening a Database

Within these event handlers, you then have corresponding access to an error object (in case of an error) or a database object (in the normal case). For example, event.target.result within the onsuccess handler takes you to an object of type IDBDatabase, which in turn gives you access to further information such as the name, the version, or even the contained object stores, and it allows you to create and delete object stores, which will be important shortly.

Browser Prefixes

It's often the case that new features are already implemented by the various browsers before the corresponding specification has been given final approval. Usually, browsers use *browser prefixes* to indicate this. For example, in some older browser versions, IndexedDB is hidden not behind the indexedDB property but under the corresponding browser-prefixed property—for example, mozIndexedDB for Firefox and webkitIndexedDB for Chrome and Safari. If you want to include such browsers as well, it's recommended to use the initial code snippets shown in Listing 12.29.

```
window.indexedDB = window.indexedDB          // for the normal case
                || window.mozIndexedDB       // older Firefox versions
                || window.webkitIndexedDB    // older Chrome versions
                || window.msIndexedDB        // older IE versions
```

Listing 12.29 Fallback to Browser-Specific IndexedDB for Older Browsers

This simply resets the window.indexedDB property: if this property exists, its value is simply reused; otherwise, the corresponding browser-specific version is searched for. If you repeat this for other objects of the API, like window.IDBTransaction and window.IDBKeyRange, you have the advantage of being freed from working with browser prefixes in the rest of the program.

12.4.2   Creating a Database

Creating a new database is basically no different from opening a database like we discussed in the previous section. Indeed, the following applies: if you try to open a database that doesn't exist yet, this database will be created implicitly. In other words, the code for opening and creating a database is almost identical. The only difference is that when creating a database, the required object stores should also be created.

Now, of course, the question arises how to distinguish between opening and creating a database. The answer is provided by the onupgradeneeded event handler, which is called whenever either a requested database doesn't yet exist and is therefore created, or when the requested database doesn't yet exist in this particular version. In both cases, the called event handler receives an object of the type IDBVersionChangeEvent as parameter. With this object, you have access to the old and the new version (see Listing 12.30).

```
request.onupgradeneeded = (event) => {
  console.log(event.oldVersion);        // old version of the database
  console.log(event.newVersion);        // new version of the database
  const database = event.target.result; // Access to the database
}
```

Listing 12.30 Event Handler That Is Called when a New Database Is Created or a Database Is Changed

Because onupgradeneeded is called only when a database doesn't yet exist in this form, the corresponding event handler is the appropriate place to create object stores or, more generally, to define the schema of the database (the database schema).

> **Database Schema**
>
> A *database schema* defines the form in which data is stored within the database. In the case of IndexedDB, for example, this includes the object stores contained in the database.

12.4.3 Creating an Object Store

Now that you know how to connect to the database and understand how onupgradeneeded works or in which cases this event is triggered, we'll show you how to create object stores. Usually you'll do this within the onupgradeneeded handler (after all, you only want to create an object store once).

You can create an object store using the createObjectStore() method on the database object. In doing so, you pass the name of the object store and optionally other configuration parameters. In Listing 12.31, for example, an object store is created with the name Books; in addition, the keyPath configuration parameter is used to define that the isbn property (of objects stored in the database) is to serve as the key (more on this in a moment).

```
request.onupgradeneeded = (event) => {
  const database = event.target.result;        // Access to the database object
  const objectStore = database.createObjectStore(  // Create the object store ...
    'Books',                                     // ... where a name...
    { keyPath: 'isbn' }                          // ... and optional parameters ...
  );                                             // ... can be passed.
};
```

Listing 12.31 Creating an Object Store

> **Increasing the Version Number of a Database**
>
> If the version number is incremented when a database is opened, object stores of older versions will persist. You have to consider this because if you try to recreate an already existing object store, an error will be thrown.

12.4.4 Adding Objects to an Object Store

As mentioned, IndexedDB is a database in which objects are stored as a whole, not, as in relational databases, for example, individual properties of an object divided into individual columns of a table. Each object is stored in the object store behind a key that can be used to access the object afterward. What exactly is used as a key is determined by the keyPath and autoIncrement configuration parameters. Table 12.4 shows the different combinations of these two parameters and what they mean for the keys.

keyPath	autoIncrement	Description
Not specified	false	The object store can store all kinds of values, especially for primitive data types like strings or numbers. However, a key must be explicitly specified each time it's added.
Specified	false	Only objects can be stored in the object store (i.e., no primitive data types). However, the prerequisite here is that these objects have a property with the same name as the specified keyPath.
Not specified	true	The object store can store all kinds of values, especially for primitive data types like strings or numbers. Keys are generated automatically but can optionally be specified when adding values.
Specified	true	Only objects can be stored in the object store (i.e., no primitive data types). Keys are automatically created and added to the new object—if it doesn't already have a property with the same name as the specified keyPath. If, on the other hand, the property already exists in the object, then no key is generated, but the value already stored is used as the key.

Table 12.4 Key Generation for IndexedDB

Operations that you perform on a database are encapsulated in transactions (see box) in the case of IndexedDB. How this works is shown in Listing 12.32. The transaction() method is used to access a transaction object (of type IDBTransaction) via the database object. The first parameter of the method is an array of object store names to be accessed in the transaction. If only one object store is to be accessed, a single string can also be passed instead of an array.

> **Transactions**
>
> In general, *transactions* in the database world refers to sequences of operations that are considered closed logical units.

The (optional) second parameter can be used to specify the mode of the transaction: possible values here are readonly (data can only be read), readwrite (data can be read and written), and versionchange (data, object stores, and indexes can be changed; see also Table 12.5). If you don't specify a parameter, readonly is used as the base by default.

However, because the purpose here is to add objects to the object store (i.e., to write data to the database), the value `readwrite` must be used or explicitly specified in the example.

Value	Description
readonly	Data can be read but not changed.
readwrite	Data can be both read and changed.
versionchange	All types of operations on the data are allowed (i.e., read and write). This also includes operations that delete or create object stores and indexes.

Table 12.5 Allowed Values for Transaction Control

In the next step, you access the object stores (which are available within the transaction) via the object of type `IDBTransaction`, which is stored in the `transaction` variable. In the example, this opens the previously created object store named `Books`. The returned object is of type `IDBObjectStore` and has various methods—for example, to be able to add objects, return objects, delete objects, and so on.

In the example, the `add()` method is used to add the objects from the `books` array to the object store one by one. Optionally, the key under which the object is to be stored in the object store can be passed to this method (not shown in the example) as the second parameter. The rules from Table 12.4 apply here.

```
const idbFactory = window.indexedDB;
const request = idbFactory.open(
  'TestDatabase',
  9
);
const books = [
  {
    'isbn': '978-1-4932-2286-5',
    'title': 'JavaScript: The Comprehensive Guide',
    'author': 'Philip Ackermann'
  },
  {
    'isbn': '978-1-4932-2292-6',
    'title': 'Node.js: The Comprehensive Guide',
    'author': 'Sebastian Springer'
  }
]
request.onerror = (event) => {
  const error = event.target.error;
  console.error(error.message);
};
```

```
request.onsuccess = (event) => {
  const database = event.target.result;
  const transaction = database.transaction(          // Open the transaction
    ['Books'],
    'readwrite'                                        // write access
  );
  const objectStore = transaction.objectStore('Books'); // Open object store
  books.forEach(function(book) {
    objectStore.add(book);                            // Adding the objects
  });
};
request.onupgradeneeded = (event) => {
  const database = event.target.result;
  const objectStore = database
    .createObjectStore('Books', { keyPath: 'isbn' });
}
```

Listing 12.32 Adding Objects to an Object Store

Note

In older versions of the IndexedDB API, the READ_ONLY, READ_WRITE, and VERSION_CHANGE constants are available in the IDBTransaction object. However, these constants are no longer included in the current API due to a bug.

Viewing the Contents of Databases

By the way, a very good insight into the structure of databases, object stores, and the objects stored therein can be obtained with the help of various browser tools, just as with cookies and browser stores.

In Chrome DevTools, for example, you can access this feature via **Resources • IndexedDB** (see Figure 12.13).

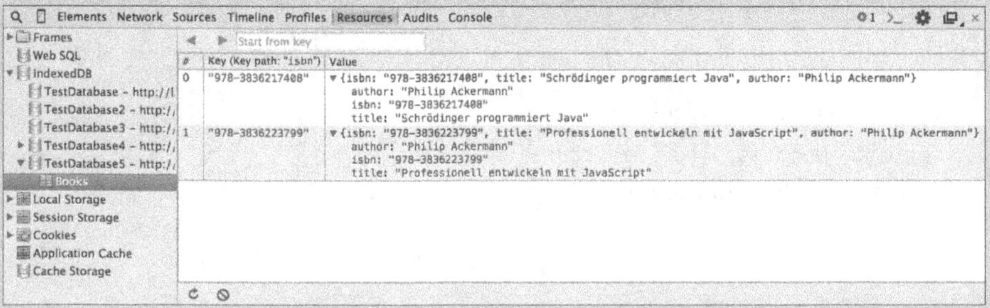

Figure 12.13 Overview of Databases and Object Stores in Chrome DevTools

12.4.5 Reading Objects from an Object Store

Once you understand the principle of how to open an object store, further work with it isn't difficult. For example, to read data from an object store, you basically proceed as you just did: that is, connect to the database, then start a transaction (readonly is sufficient in this case), and access the corresponding object store using the objectStore() method. You already know all of this from the previous sections; it's shown again in Listing 12.33 only for the sake of completeness.

You can then access objects in the object store using the get() method and the key that you pass to this method as a parameter. As a return value, get() returns a request object of type IDBRequest, as you already know from the open() method for opening a database (even though strictly speaking it's an object of type IDBOpenDBRequest there, but the principle is the same). In other words, event handlers can be defined for the normal case (via the onsuccess property) and the error case (via the onerror property). Provided that there is a corresponding object in the object store for the passed key and no error occurs, you then have access to this object within the onsuccess handler.

```
const idbFactory = window.indexedDB;
const request = idbFactory.open('TestDatabase', 9);
request.onerror = (event) => {
  const error = event.target.error;
  console.error(error.message);
};
request.onsuccess = (event) => {
  const database = event.target.result;
  const transaction = database.transaction('Books');    // Open the transaction
  const objectStore = transaction.objectStore('Books'); // Open the object store
  const request = objectStore.get('978-1-4932-2292-6'); // Search for key
  request.onerror = (event) => {                         // Event handler for ...
                                                         // ... Error case
    console.error(event.target.error.message);           // Output of the error message
  };
  request.onsuccess = (event) => {                       // Event handler for ...
                                                         // ... Normal case
    console.log(request.result);                         // Output of the object
  };
};
```

Listing 12.33 Read Access to the Object Store

12.4.6 Deleting Objects from an Object Store

Deleting objects from an object store works according to the same principle with regard to boilerplate code, as shown in Listing 12.34. But because deleting also changes the data in the database, it's necessary to start the corresponding transaction in read-write mode.

To delete an object, you use the delete() method in the object store. This method expects the key of the object to be deleted as its parameter. As before, the return value is a request object of the IDBRequest type.

```javascript
const idbFactory = window.indexedDB;
const request = idbFactory.open('TestDatabase', 9);
request.onerror = (event) => {
  const error = event.target.error;
  console.error(error.message);
};
request.onsuccess = (event) => {
  const database = event.target.result;
  const transaction = database.transaction(         // Open the transaction
    'Books',
    'readwrite'                                      // Write access
  );
  const objectStore = transaction.objectStore('Books'); // Open the object store
  const request = objectStore.delete('978-1-4932-2286-5'); // Delete operation
  request.onerror = (event) => {                    // Event handler for...
                                                    // ... Error case
    console.error(event.target.error.message);      // Output the error message
  };
  request.onsuccess = (event) => {                  // Event handler for...
                                                    // ... Normal case
    console.log('Delete operation successful');
  };
};
```

Listing 12.34 Deleting an Object from the Object Store

If you want to delete not only a specific object from an object store, but all objects, you can achieve this using the clear() method (see Listing 12.35).

```javascript
const idbFactory = window.indexedDB;
const request = idbFactory.open('TestDatabase', 9);
request.onerror = (event) => {
  const error = event.target.error;
  console.error(error.message);
};
request.onsuccess = (event) => {
  const database = event.target.result;
```

```
const transaction = database.transaction(      // Open the transaction
    'Books',
    'readwrite'                                 // Write access
);
const objectStore = transaction.objectStore('Books'); // Open the object store
const request = objectStore.clear();           // Delete operation
request.onerror = (event) => {                 // Event handler for ...
                                               // ... Error case
  console.error(event.target.error.message);   // Output of the ...
                                               // ... error message
};
request.onsuccess = (event) => {               // Event handler for ...
                                               // ... Normal case.
  console.log('Delete operation successful');
};
};
```

Listing 12.35 Deleting All Objects from the Object Store

12.4.7 Updating Objects in an Object Store

Besides adding and deleting objects from the object store, you obviously need a way to update objects in the object store. In principle, everything is familiar again, as shown in Listing 12.36: opening the database, creating a transaction in readwrite mode, opening the object store, and reading the corresponding object using the get() method. You then make the desired changes to the object that is read in this way and then use the put() method on the object store object to update the object in the object store.

```
const idbFactory = window.indexedDB;
const request = idbFactory.open('TestDatabase', 9);
request.onerror = (event) => {
  const error = event.target.error;
  console.error(error.message);
};
request.onsuccess = (event) => {
  const database = event.target.result;
  const transaction = database.transaction(       // Open the transaction
    'Books',
    'readwrite'                                    // Write access
  );
  const objectStore = transaction.objectStore('Books'); // Open the object store
  const request = objectStore.get('978-1-4932-2286-5'); // Read the object
  request.onerror = (event) => {
    console.error(event.target.error.message);
  };
```

```
  request.onsuccess = (event) => {
    const book = request.result;                      // Update the object
    book.title = ' JavaScript: The Comprehensive Guide by Philip Ackermann'
    const requestUpdate = objectStore.put(book);      // Store the object
    requestUpdate.onerror = (event) => {};
    requestUpdate.onsuccess = (event) => {};
  };
};
```

Listing 12.36 Updating an Object in the Object Store

12.4.8   Using a Cursor

If you want to read all objects of an object store, you can use cursors, as shown in Listing 12.37. In the context of databases, cursors are a mechanism to traverse the different records in a database (i.e., the different objects in an object store). The openCursor() method is used to create a request for the creation of a cursor. In the corresponding success event handler, you reach the cursor object itself via the event object. This in turn provides two properties: the key property contains the key of the respective entry, while the value property contains the value itself—that is, the object. The continue() method causes the cursor to move on to the next entry (if there is one), which in turn causes the success event handler to be executed again, and so on.

```
const idbFactory = window.indexedDB;
const request = idbFactory.open(
  'TestDatabaseCursor',
  1
);
const books = [
  {
    'isbn': '978-1-4932-2286-5',
    'title': 'JavaScript: The Comprehensive Guide',
    'author': 'Philip Ackermann'
  },
  {
    'isbn': '978-1-4932-2292-6',
    'title': 'Node.js: The Comprehensive Guide',
    'author': 'Sebastian Springer'
  }
]
request.onerror = (event) => {
  const error = event.target.error;
  console.error(error.message);
};
```

```
request.onsuccess = (event) => {
  const database = event.target.result;
  const transaction = database.transaction('Books');
  const objectStore = transaction.objectStore('Books');
  const request = objectStore.openCursor();
  const books = [];
  request.onsuccess = (event) => {
    const cursor = event.target.result;
    if (cursor) {
      console.log(cursor.key);
      console.log(cursor.value);
      books.push(cursor.value);
      cursor.continue();
    } else {
      console.log(books);
    }
  };
};
request.onupgradeneeded = (event) => {
  const database = event.target.result;
  const objectStore = database.createObjectStore('Books', { keyPath: 'isbn' });
  books.forEach((book) => {
    objectStore.add(book);
  });
}
```

Listing 12.37 Using a Cursor

12.5 Accessing the File System

Via the File API, it's possible to access local files of the user via JavaScript, provided that the user has previously selected the respective files in a corresponding dialog. The specification at *www.w3.org/TR/FileAPI/* defines the following interfaces for working with files:

- The File interface represents a single file and contains information such as the name of the file or the last modification date.
- The FileList interface represents a list of File objects selected by the user.
- The Blob interface represents binary data.
- The FileReader interface provides methods to read objects of type File or Blob.

In principle, there are two options to select files: the file dialog we discussed earlier, and the possibility to drag and drop files into a certain area of a web page to get to the contents of the respective file. Let's take a look at these two options.

12.5.1   Selecting Files via File Dialog

For local files to be accessed via the File API, the user must first select the appropriate file(s). This ensures that arbitrary files cannot be read unnoticed via JavaScript. One option to provide users with a file selection is through the <input> element, whose type attributes you set to the value file (see Listing 12.38).

```
<input type="file" id="files" name="files[]" multiple />
```

Listing 12.38 Definition of a File Selection in HTML

If the user now selects one or more files, the change event for the <input> element is triggered in the background. Therefore, to be able to respond to file selections, you simply need to register an event listener for that event, as shown in Listing 12.39.

```
function handleFileSelected(event) {
  const files = event.target.files;                // all selected files
  let output = '';                                  // variable for result
  for (let i = 0; i < files.length; i++) {         // Iterate via all files ...
    const file = files[i];                          // ... View each file ...
    output += '<li>' +                              // ... and assemble ...
                                                    // result HTML,
                                                    // consisting of:

    '<strong>' + file.name + '</strong>' +          // file name
    ' (' + (file.type || "n/a") + ') - ' +          // file type
    file.size + 'Bytes,' +                          // file size
    ' changed on: ' +                               // modification date
    file.lastModifiedDate.toLocaleDateString() +
    '</li>';
  }
  document.getElementById('list').innerHTML = '<ul>' + output + '</ul>';
}
document.getElementById('files').addEventListener(
  'change',
  handleFileSelected,
  false
);
```

Listing 12.39 Selecting Files via File Dialog

The selected files can then be accessed within the event listener via the files property of the element for which the event was triggered (event.target.files). This list contains all selected files as File objects. These File objects do not yet include the contents of the respective file, but they include general information such as the file name (name property), the file type (type property), the file size (size property), and the last modification date (lastModifiedDate property). In the example, all this information is displayed below the button for file selection (see Figure 12.14).

Choose files   5 files

Screenshot 2022-02-01 at 14.41.45.png (image/png) - 95581 Bytes, last changed: 01/02/2022
Screenshot 2022-02-02 at 14.02.41.png (image/png) - 146150 Bytes, last changed: 02/02/2022
Screenshot 2022-02-02 at 15.20.13.png (image/png) - 777326 Bytes, last changed: 02/02/2022
Screenshot 2022-02-03 at 10.23.07.png (image/png) - 1052483 Bytes, last changed: 03/02/2022
Screenshot 2022-02-03 at 11.25.28.png (image/png) - 277421 Bytes, last changed: 03/02/2022

Figure 12.14 The Selected Files Are Displayed in an HTML List

12.5.2   Selecting Files via Drag and Drop

We'll come back to the Drag and Drop API later in this chapter, but for now we'll show you how to select files using drag-and-drop.

Listing 12.40 shows the corresponding source code. First, you need to define an area within the corresponding web page to be used as the target for the drag-and-drop operation (hereafter referred to as the *drop target* for simplicity). In the example, this is the <div> element with the ID target. Two event listeners are then registered to this element: the event listener for the dragover event (handleDragOver()) is executed when a file is dragged over the element (but not yet dropped). The event listener for the drag event (handleFileSelected()) is executed when the file is then dropped over the element.

For example, within the handleDragOver() event listener, it's possible to deploy an appropriate icon to mark for the user which type of drag-and-drop operation it is (e.g., as shown in Listing 12.39 via event.dataTransfer.dropEffect). The actual selection of the files is done within the handleFileSelected() event listener, where the file information is accessed in the same way as in the selection via the file dialog (see Listing 12.39).

```
function handleFileSelected(event) {
  event.stopPropagation();
  event.preventDefault();

  const files = event.dataTransfer.files;       // all selected files
  let output = '';                              // variable for event
  for (let i = 0; i < files.length; i++) {      // Iterate over all files ...
    const file = files[i];                      // ... view each file ...
    output += '<li>' +                          // ... and assemble ...
                                                // ... result HTML,
                                                // consisting of:
      '<strong>' + file.name + '</strong>' +    // file name
      ' (' + (file.type || "n/a") + ') - ' +    // file type
```

667

```
    file.size + 'Bytes,' +                          // file size
    ' changed on: ' +                               // Modification date
    file.lastModifiedDate.toLocaleDateString() +
    '</li>';
  }
  document.getElementById('list').innerHTML = '<ul>' + output + '</ul>';
}

function handleDragOver(event) {
  event.stopPropagation();
  event.preventDefault();
  event.dataTransfer.dropEffect = 'copy';
}

const dropTarget = document.getElementById('target');
dropTarget.addEventListener('dragover', handleDragOver, false);
dropTarget.addEventListener('drop', handleFileSelected, false);
```

Listing 12.40 Selecting Files via Drag and Drop

Drag files here

Screenshot 2022-02-01 at 14.41.45.png (image/png) - 95581 Bytes, last changed: 01/02/2022
Screenshot 2022-02-02 at 14.02.41.png (image/png) - 146150 Bytes, last changed: 02/02/2022
Screenshot 2022-02-02 at 15.20.13.png (image/png) - 777326 Bytes, last changed: 02/02/2022
Screenshot 2022-02-03 at 10.23.07.png (image/png) - 1052483 Bytes, last changed: 03/02/2022
Screenshot 2022-02-03 at 11.25.28.png (image/png) - 277421 Bytes, last changed: 03/02/2022

Figure 12.15 The Selected Files Are Displayed Again in an HTML List

12.5.3   Reading Files

So far, we've only selected the files, but not yet read their content. In fact, to read the content of files, you must first create an instance of FileReader. This type provides various methods for reading files (see also Table 12.6). These are readAsText() for reading a file as a string, readAsBinaryString() for reading a file as a binary string, readAsDataURL() for reading a file as a data URL (see note box), and readAsArrayBuffer() for reading a file as an array buffer.

If you call one of these methods, you'll be notified about the load event after the file has been successfully read, assuming an appropriately previously defined event handler or registered event listener. If the load event was triggered, the content of the file is also available via the result property (also at the corresponding FileReader instance).

Method	Description
readAsBinaryString()	Reads the data as a binary string.
readAsText()	Reads the data as text.
readAsDataURL()	Reads the data as a data URL (see box).
readAsArrayBuffer()	Reads the data as an array buffer.
abort()	Cancels the read process.

Table 12.6 The Different Methods of FileReader

In addition to the load event or the corresponding onload event handler, there are several other event handlers (or corresponding events) available, which are listed in Table 12.7.

Event Handler	Description
onabort	Handler for the abort event triggered when the read operation is aborted
onerror	Handler for the error event triggered when an error occurs during the read operation
onload	Handler for the load event triggered when the read operation is successfully completed
onloadstart	Handler for the loadstart event triggered when the read operation has been started
onloadend	Handler for the loadend event triggered when the read operation is completed
onprogress	Handler for the progress event triggered during the read operation to give information about the progress

Table 12.7 The Different Event Handlers for FileReader

> **Data URLs**
>
> *Data URLs* are a special scheme for URLs (more precisely, for URIs) to embed data within HTML code. Data URLs start with the string data:, followed by MIME type and encoding information and the corresponding encoded data—for example, data:image/png; base64,jfdsfrRdF for a PNG image with Base64 encoding. So, with the help of data URLs, for example, image data in the form of a string can be used directly within the HTML code, which in turn reduces the number of HTTP requests for a web page because the browser doesn't have to make a second request (for the image).

URL versus URI versus URN

At this point, it's helpful to remember the difference between URL (uniform resource locator) and URI (uniform resource identifier). Often both terms are used (incorrectly) synonymously, but this is not quite correct. According to RFC3986 (*http://tools.ietf.org/ html/rfc3986#section-1.1.3*), URLs, along with URNs (uniform resource names), are a subset of URIs. Or, to put it the other way around, URIs are the superset of URLs and URNs. The following therefore applies: URLs and URNs are always URIs, but the same isn't true in the other direction.

But what are URIs, URLs, and URNs anyway? URIs are used to uniquely identify resources. URLs are URIs that also contain information about how the resource can be located: *http://javascripthandbuch.de*, for example, is a URL because it defines that the resource can be located via the HTTP protocol. On the other hand, *javascripthandbuch.de* is strictly speaking not a URL but a URI because the *http://* specification is missing here (browsers usually know how to deal with this too by automatically inserting a corresponding *http://*, but a valid URL still looks different). URNs, on the other hand, are historically based identifiers that use the *urn* scheme—for example, *urn:isbn:9783836223799*.

An example of reading files is shown in Listing 12.41. For each file selected by the user, the file type is checked to determine whether it's a text file or an image file (other cases are not considered). For a text file, the content is read via readAsText() and added to the DOM tree. For an image file, the content is read via readAsDataURL() as a data URL and an <img> element is created with a thumbnail view of the image.

```
function handleFileSelected(event) {
  const files = event.target.files;
  for (let i = 0; i < files.length; i++) {
    const file = files[i];
    const reader = new FileReader();
    if(file.type.match('text.*')) {
      reader.onload = (event) => {
        const span = document.createElement('span');
        span.innerHTML = reader.result;
        document.getElementById('list').insertBefore(span, null);
      };
      reader.readAsText(file);
    } else if(file.type.match('image.*')) {
      reader.onload = (event) => {
        const span = document.createElement('span');
        span.innerHTML = `<img class="thumbnail" src="${reader.result}"/>`;
        document.getElementById('list').insertBefore(span, null);
      };
```

```
    reader.readAsDataURL(file);
    }
  }
}
document
  .getElementById('files')
  .addEventListener('change', handleFileSelected, false);
```

Listing 12.41 Reading Text and Image Files

12.5.4   Monitoring the Reading Progress

Especially if you want to read large files via the File API, it's helpful to inform users about the progress of the read operation. For this purpose, as you saw in the previous section, the File API or the FileReader type offers the onprogress event handler. The corresponding event object that is sent here is of the ProgressEvent type (see *www.w3.org/ TR/progress-events/*) and contains, among other things, the loaded and total properties, which contain the loaded number of bytes and the complete number of bytes for the respective file.

The current progress can then be easily determined using these two properties, as you can see in Listing 12.42. Figure 12.16 shows a screenshot of the application. As an example, an ISO file of several hundred megabytes in size was used here, mainly so that there was enough time to create the screenshot. Consequently, the code uses the readAsBinaryString() method because the ISO file is a binary file.

Other Event Handlers

In the example, you can also see the use of other event handlers already mentioned: onerror, which is called when an error occurs—for example, if the file could not be found or read; onabort, which is called when the reading of the file is aborted (made possible, by the way, via the abort() method of the FileReader object); and onloadstart, which is called when the reading of the file starts.

```
const progress = document.querySelector('.percent');
const reader = new FileReader();
function updateProgress(event) {
  if (event.lengthComputable) {
    const percentLoaded = Math.round((event.loaded / event.total) * 100);
    if (percentLoaded < 100) {
      progress.style.width = percentLoaded + '%';
      progress.textContent = percentLoaded + '%';
    }
  }
}
```

```javascript
function handleError(event) {
  switch (event.target.error.code) {
    case event.target.error.NOT_FOUND_ERR:
      console.error('File was not found');
      break;
    case event.target.error.NOT_READABLE_ERR:
      console.error('File could not be read');
      break;
    case event.target.error.ABORT_ERR:
      break;
    default:
      console.error('Unknown error');
  }
  ;
}
function handleFileSelected(event) {
  progress.style.width = '0%';
  progress.textContent = '0%';
  reader = new FileReader();
  reader.onprogress = updateProgress;
  reader.onerror = handleError;
  reader.onabort = (event) => {
    console.log('Reading the file aborted');
  };
  reader.onloadstart = (event) => {
    document.getElementById('progress-bar').className = 'loading';
  };
  reader.onload = (event) => {
    progress.style.width = '100%';
    progress.textContent = '100%';
    setTimeout(() => {
      document.getElementById('progress-bar').className = '';
    }, 2000);
  };
  reader.readAsBinaryString(event.target.files[0]);
}

document
  .getElementById('files')
  .addEventListener('change', handleFileSelected, false);

function abortRead() {
  reader.abort();
}
```

```
document
  .getElementById('abort-file-reading')
  .addEventListener('click', abortRead, false);
```

Listing 12.42 Monitoring the Reading Progress

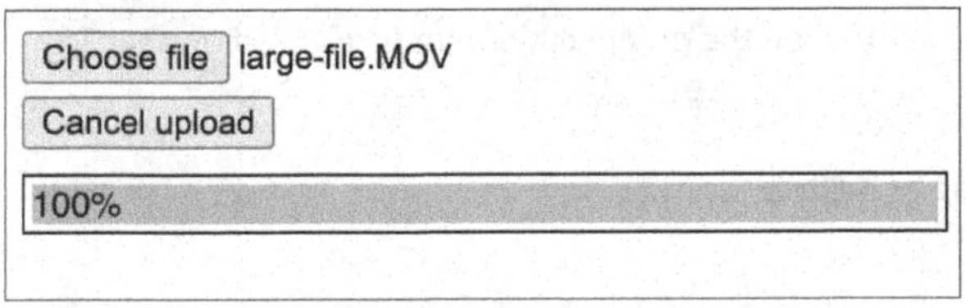

Figure 12.16 The Reading Progress Is Displayed via the Progress Bar

12.6   Moving Components of a Web Page

The term *drag and drop* refers to the "dragging" and "dropping" of screen elements—with regard to web pages, this means the dragging and dropping of elements of a web page. To perform a *drag-and-drop* operation, you click on the element you want to move, hold down the mouse button, drag the element to the desired position, and release the mouse button again to drop the element at the target position.

12.6.1   Events of a Drag-and-Drop Operation

During a drag-and-drop operation, a number of different events are triggered, which are listed in Table 12.8. Their interrelationship is illustrated in Figure 12.17. At the beginning of a drag-and-drop operation, the dragstart event is triggered and shortly thereafter the dragenter event, both on the element that is to be moved (also referred to as the *drag source*). If the element is then dragged over other elements of the web page, the following events are triggered: dragenter when "entering" the other element, dragover while the dragged element is over the other element, and dragleave when "leaving" the other element. When the dragged element is released on the target element (*drop target*), this triggers the drop event on that element and the dragend event on the dragged element.

Event	Description
dragstart	Triggered when an element starts to be dragged
drag	Triggered continuously while an element is dragged
dragend	Triggered when a dragged element is released
dragenter	Triggered for an element when it is "entered" during dragging

Table 12.8 The Various Events of Drag and Drop

Event	Description
dragover	Triggered continuously for an element if you are inside the element while dragging
dragleave	Triggered for an element if the element is "left" during dragging
drop	Triggered for an element when the dragged element is released on that element

Table 12.8 The Various Events of Drag and Drop (Cont.)

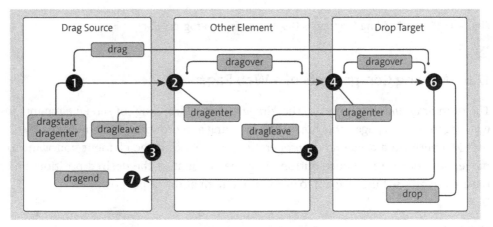

Figure 12.17 Overview of the Different Events in Drag and Drop

12.6.2   Defining Movable Elements

To define an element within a web page that can be moved (the drag source), you simply need to define the draggable attribute of the respective element (either without a value or with the value set to true). In principle, you can mark any elements on a web page as draggable—for example, images, links, or any other DOM elements.

Listing 12.43 and Figure 12.18 show an example of this: the child elements of the <div> element with the ID contacts (in the figure on the left) are all marked as draggable and thus as moveable. Ahead, we'll show you how to move these elements into the <div> element with the ID target (in the figure on the right).

```
<div id="contacts">
  <div class="contact" draggable="true">
    <img class="contact-image" src="img/profile.jpeg" draggable="false">
    <div class="contact-details">
      <div>Name: Philip Ackermann</div>
      <div>Twitter:
        <a href="https://twitter.com/cleancoderocker">@cleancoderocker</a>
      </div>
```

```
      <div>Email:
        <a href="mailto:info@philipackermann.de">info@philipackermann.de</a>
      </div>
    </div>
  </div>
  <div class="contact" draggable="true">
    <img class="contact-image" src="img/profile.jpeg" draggable="false">
    <div class="contact-details">
      <div>Name: Philip Ackermann</div>
      <div>Twitter:
        <a href="https://twitter.com/cleancoderocker">@cleancoderocker</a>
      </div>
      <div>Email:
        <a href="mailto:info@philipackermann.de">info@philipackermann.de</a>
      </div>
    </div>
  </div>
  <div class="contact" draggable="true">
    <img class="contact-image" src="img/profile.jpeg" draggable="false">
    <div class="contact-details">
      <div>Name: Philip Ackermann</div>
      <div>Twitter:
        <a href="https://twitter.com/cleancoderocker">@cleancoderocker</a>
      </div>
      <div>Email:
        <a href="mailto:info@philipackermann.de">info@philipackermann.de</a>
      </div>
    </div>
  </div>
  <div class="contact" draggable="true">
    <img class="contact-image" src="img/profile.jpeg" draggable="false">
    <div class="contact-details">
      <div>Name: Philip Ackermann</div>
      </div>Twitter:
        <a href="https://twitter.com/cleancoderocker">@cleancoderocker</a>
      </div>
      <div>Email:
        <a href="mailto:info@philipackermann.de">info@philipackermann.de</a>
      </div>
    </div>
  </div>
  <div>
  <div class="contact" draggable="true">
    <img class="contact-image" src="img/profile.jpeg" draggable="false">
    <div class="contact-details">
```

```
    <div>Name: Philip Ackermann</div>
    <div>Twitter:
      <a href="https://twitter.com/cleancoderocker">@cleancoderocker</a>
    </div>
    <div>Email:
      <a href="mailto:info@philipackermann.de">info@philipackermann.de</a>
    </div>
  </div>
</div>
<div id="target" class="target">
  Drag contacts here
</div>
```

Listing 12.43 The Basic HTML Structure for Drag-and-Drop Operations

Figure 12.18 Starting Position for the Drag-and-Drop Operations

12.6.3 Moving Elements

After marking the elements to be moved as draggable, the next step is to define what should happen when an element is moved. For this purpose, various event listeners are registered in Listing 12.44.

```
const items = document.getElementsByClassName('contact');
for (let i = 0; i < items.length; i++) {
  const item = items[i];
  item.addEventListener('dragstart', (event) => {
    event.dataTransfer.setData('text/html', event.target.outerHTML);
```

```
  });
}
const target = document.getElementById('target');
target.addEventListener('dragover', (event) => {
  event.preventDefault();
  return false;
});
target.addEventListener('dragenter', (event) => {
  event.target.classList.add('dragover');
});
target.addEventListener('dragleave', (event) => {
  event.target.classList.remove('dragover');
});
target.addEventListener('drop', (event) => {
  event.srcElement.innerHTML += event.dataTransfer.getData('text/html');
  event.target.classList.remove('dragover');
})
```

Listing 12.44 Drag-and-Drop Example for Moving Elements

An event listener for the `dragstart` event is first registered here for all moveable elements. Within this event listener, an object of the `DataTransfer` type is available via the `dataTransfer` property of the event object. This is a container for such data that should be "moved along" with the moved elements during a drag-and-drop operation. This data can be defined via the `setData()` method and then read at the target object later on. In the example, we simply use the HTML content of the drag source (`event.target.outerHTML`).

At the drop target, this data is then accessed within the event listener for the `drop` event via the `getData()` method and added to the custom HTML (via `event.srcElement.innerHTML`). In addition, event listeners are defined for the `dragenter` and `dragleave` events, which add or remove the `dragover` CSS class from the drop target and thus influence the appearance of the drop target. The full result is shown in Figure 12.19.

> **Pass Any Data**
>
> You don't necessarily have to add HTML data to the `DataTransfer` object. You can use any data here; for example, to transfer only the URLs of the thumbnails to the `DataTransfer` object, you would write the contents of Listing 12.45.
>
> ```
> event.dataTransfer.setData(
>   'text',
>   event.target.getElementsByClassName('contact-image')[0].src
> );
> ```
>
> **Listing 12.45** Defining the Content of the DataTransfer Object

Alternatively, you could just take the contact's name, Twitter name, or email address. The DataTransfer object doesn't necessarily have to contain the HTML code of the respective element marked as draggable.

Figure 12.19 After the Drag-and-Drop Operations

12.7 Parallelizing Tasks

JavaScript is a language that is executed as *single-threaded*, meaning that multiple scripts cannot be executed at the same time (see Figure 12.20). Scripts are interpreted and executed one after the other, line by line.

Also, the triggering of events and the associated execution of event listeners do not happen in parallel: the code that triggers an event pauses until the corresponding event listeners have been executed.

The same applies to callback functions. For example, if you make an Ajax request to a server, the script that makes the request continues to execute until the server prepares the response and sends it to the client, but as soon as the callback function that evaluates the response from the server is called, the surrounding code pauses.

Definitions

In software development, a *thread* is an execution string within a program. Programs that are *single-threaded* use only a single thread. This is in contrast to programs that are *multithreaded*, in which not only one thread is used, but several threads, with one taking the role of the *main thread*.

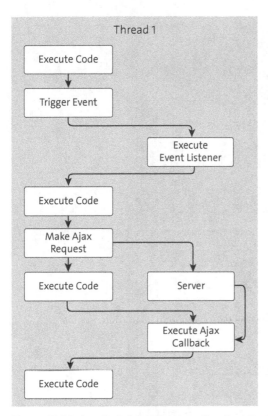

Figure 12.20 JavaScript Applications Run in a Single Thread by Default

12.7.1   The Principle of Web Workers

The Web Worker API (*www.w3.org/TR/workers/*) counteracts this limitation of serial processing of scripts by defining an API for executing background scripts within web applications. With the web workers defined in this API, it's then possible, for example, to execute computing-intensive scripts that would otherwise negatively affect the performance of a web application in the background—that is, in parallel with the main thread.

Web workers are executed in separate threads (see Figure 12.21). Therefore, it's necessary to keep the corresponding code in separate files as well. From the main thread, it's then possible to send messages to or receive messages from individual web workers.

Note

By default, tasks in JavaScript can be executed asynchronously, but not in parallel. Only web workers enable parallel execution.

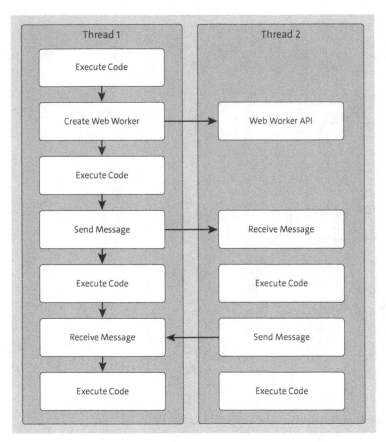

Figure 12.21 Web Workers Are Executed in Separate Threads

12.7.2 Use Web Workers

To create a web worker, use the Worker constructor function, as shown in Listing 12.46. You pass it the name or path to the script to be executed by the web worker as a parameter (see Listing 12.47).

To send messages from the main thread to a web worker, use the postMessage() method, passing any JavaScript object as a message as a parameter. To receive a message on the web worker side, you have to register a corresponding event listener for the message event (see Listing 12.47) or alternatively define the onmessage event handler. To do this, you access the global object of the corresponding web worker via the self variable.

Sending and receiving messages in the other direction works the same way: inside the web worker, you call the postMessage() method to send a message to the main thread. Within the main thread, you can access the message within an event listener for the message event or within the onmessage event handler.

```
// File: main.js
const worker = new Worker("scripts/worker.js");
const message = 'Hello worker';
console.log(`main thread: Send message: ${message}`);
worker.postMessage(message);
worker.addEventListener('message', (event) => {
  console.log(`main thread: Response received from worker: ${event.data}`);
});
worker.addEventListener('error', (event) => {
  console.log('Error occurred');
});
```

Listing 12.46 Content of the Main Thread

```
// File: worker.js
self.addEventListener('message', (event) => {
  console.log(`Worker: Message received: ${event.data}`);
  const workerResult = 'Hello main thread';
  console.log(`Worker: Return response: ${workerResult}`);
  self.postMessage(workerResult);
});
```

Listing 12.47 Worker Content

For the sake of clarity, the communication process in both directions is shown once again in Figure 12.22.

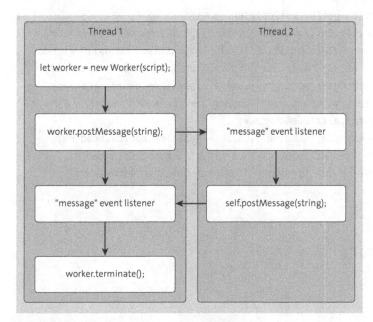

Figure 12.22 Communication with Web Workers

Thus, with the help of web workers, tasks can be executed in parallel to the main thread. However, web workers are subject to restrictions: first, they cannot access the DOM, and second, they cannot access the window object. The reason: web workers are not executed in the browser window, but in the background.

12.8   Determining the Location of Users

Thanks to the Geolocation API (*www.w3.org/TR/geolocation-API*), it's possible to determine the location or position of a user. We'll show you how to do this in the following sections.

12.8.1   Accessing Location Information

The entry point for the Geolocation API is the geolocation property of the navigator object. To get the current position of the user, the geolocation object (of the Geolocation type) provides the getCurrentPosition() method.

Because the position is determined asynchronously, a function is passed to the method as a callback handler, which is called as soon as the position has been determined. Within this function, various information can then be accessed, as shown in Listing 12.48 and Figure 12.23—for example, longitude (coords.longitude), latitude (coords.latitude), and—if provided—speed (speed) and heading (heading).

```
function getPosition() {
  if(navigator.geolocation) {
    navigator.geolocation.getCurrentPosition((position) => {
      document.getElementById('latitude').value = position.coords.latitude;
      document.getElementById('longitude').value = position.coords.longitude;
      document.getElementById('altitude').value = position.coords.altitude;
      document.getElementById('accuracy').value = position.coords.accuracy;
      document.getElementById('altitudeAccuracy').value = ⊃
          position.coords.altitudeAccuracy;
      document.getElementById('heading').value = position.coords.heading;
      document.getElementById('speed').value = position.coords.speed;
      document.getElementById('timestamp').value = position.timestamp;
    });
  }
}
```

Listing 12.48 Determining the Position via the Geolocation API

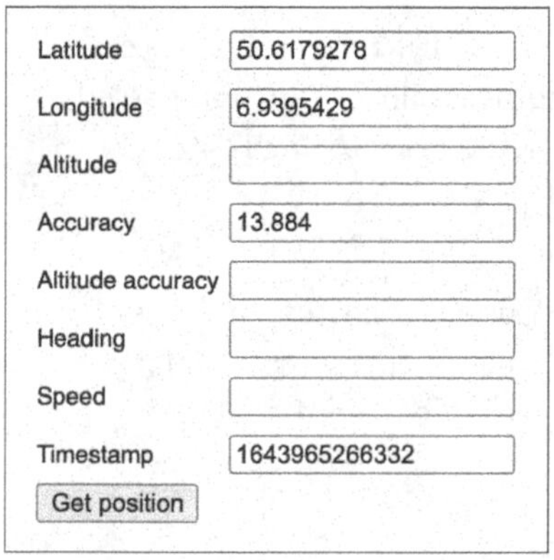

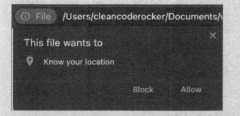

Figure 12.23 Determining the Position in Chrome

Consent of the User

For a user's location to be determined, the user must give their consent. Therefore, as soon as the Geolocation API is used within a web page to determine the location, a corresponding confirmation dialog is displayed (see Figure 12.24, Figure 12.25, and Figure 12.26).

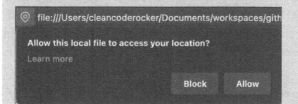

Figure 12.24 Confirmation Dialog in Chrome

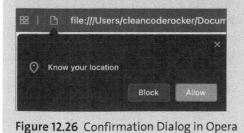

Figure 12.25 Confirmation Dialog in Firefox

Figure 12.26 Confirmation Dialog in Opera

Only if the user gives their consent here can the API be used. If a user refuses access to location information, this can be intercepted via another callback function passed as the second argument to the getCurrentPosition() method (see Listing 12.49).

```
function getPosition() {
  function successHandler(position) {
    document.getElementById('latitude').value = position.coords.latitude;
    document.getElementById('longitude').value = position.coords.longitude;
    document.getElementById('altitude').value = position.coords.altitude;
    document.getElementById('accuracy').value = position.coords.accuracy;
    document.getElementById('altitudeAccuracy').value = ⊃
      position.coords.altitudeAccuracy;
    document.getElementById('heading').value = position.coords.heading;
    document.getElementById('speed').value = position.coords.speed;
    document.getElementById('timestamp').value = position.timestamp;
  }
  function errorHandler(error) {
    // User refuses position determination.
  }
  if(navigator.geolocation) {
    navigator.geolocation.getCurrentPosition(successHandler, errorHandler);
  }
}
```

Listing 12.49 Error Handling if User Refuses Geolocalization

12.8.2   Continuously Accessing Location Information

If you want to determine the location not only once but continuously, the watchPosition() method is a good choice. This method works in principle like getCurrentPosition() but is called continuously or whenever the location information changes. The location information is then accessed again via a corresponding callback function (see Listing 12.50).

As a return value, the method also returns an ID that can be passed to the clearWatch() method at a later time when the determination of location information is to be aborted.

```
const watchID = navigator.geolocation.watchPosition((position) => {
  document.getElementById('latitude').value = position.coords.latitude;
  document.getElementById('longitude').value = position.coords.longitude;
  document.getElementById('altitude').value = position.coords.altitude;
  document.getElementById('accuracy').value = position.coords.accuracy;
  document.getElementById('altitudeAccuracy').value = ⊃
    position.coords.altitudeAccuracy;
```

```
  document.getElementById('heading').value = position.coords.heading;
  document.getElementById('speed').value = position.coords.speed;
  document.getElementById('timestamp').value = position.timestamp;
});
// At a later point in time:
navigator.geolocation.clearWatch(watchID);
```

Listing 12.50 Continuous Determination of Location Information

12.8.3   Showing the Position on a Map

The Geolocation API can be used for various application purposes. It becomes particularly interesting when the determined location information is combined with the *Google Maps API* (*https://developers.google.com/maps/?hl=en*), for example.

You can see a code example for this in Listing 12.51, and the result is shown in Figure 12.27. Here various objects of the Google Maps API are used to show the user's position on a map, provided with a small hint box with the text You are here.

For this purpose, the information on latitude and longitude determined via the Geolocation API is simply passed to the Google Maps API.

```
function getPosition() {
  function successHandler(position) {
    /* here the same code as before for filling the input fields */
    const mapOptions = {
      zoom: 6
    };
    const map = new google.maps.Map(
      document.getElementById('map-canvas'),
      mapOptions
    );
    const googlePosition = new google.maps.LatLng(
      position.coords.latitude,
      position.coords.longitude
    );
    const infowindow = new google.maps.InfoWindow({
      map: map,
      position: googlePosition,
      content: 'You are here.'
    });
    map.setCenter(googlePosition);
  }
  function errorHandler(error) {
    // User refuses position determination
  }
```

```
  if(navigator.geolocation) {
    navigator.geolocation.getCurrentPosition(successHandler, errorHandler);
  }
}
```

Listing 12.51 Using the Geolocation API in Combination with the Google Maps API to Display the User's Position on a Map

Figure 12.27 Displaying the Position with Google Maps

Proprietary APIs

The Google Maps API is not an official API standardized by the W3C or the WHATWG but a proprietary API of Google. Accordingly, the API is not available by default in the various browsers but must be manually integrated with the respective web page using corresponding JavaScript files.

In addition to the Google Maps API, there are numerous other proprietary APIs, not only from Google, but also from other services such as Spotify, LastFM, Twitter, Facebook, Instagram, and many more.

The ProgrammableWeb website at *www.programmableweb.com/apis/directory* provides a good overview of these APIs.

12.8.4   Showing Directions

The Google Maps API is very powerful, and you can do a lot of great things with it that we can't even talk about here due to space limitations. However, we did pick out one interesting use case: displaying directions both textually next to the map and as a connecting line within the map. You can see the code for this in Listing 12.52. Again, based on the determined values for latitude and longitude, the current position is displayed on the map. Based on this position, you get the directions to Alexanderplatz in Berlin.

```
function getPosition() {
  function successHandler(position) {
    /* here the same code as before for filling the input fields */
    const directionsService = new google.maps.DirectionsService();
    const directionsRenderer = new google.maps.DirectionsRenderer();
    const mapOptions = {
      zoom: 6
    };
    const map = new google.maps.Map(
      document.getElementById('map-canvas'),
      mapOptions
    );
    const travel = {
      origin : new google.maps.LatLng(position.coords.latitude,
      position.coords.longitude),
      destination : 'Alexanderplatz, Berlin',
      travelMode : google.maps.DirectionsTravelMode.DRIVING
    };
    const googlePosition = new google.maps.LatLng(
      position.coords.latitude,
      position.coords.longitude
    );
    map.setCenter(googlePosition);
    directionsRenderer.setMap(map);
    directionsRenderer.setPanel(document.getElementById('map-directions'));
    directionsService.route(travel, (result, status) => {
      if (status === google.maps.DirectionsStatus.OK) {
        directionsRenderer.setDirections(result);
      }
    });
  }
  function errorHandler(error) {
    // User refuses position determination
  }
  if(navigator.geolocation) {
    navigator.geolocation.getCurrentPosition(successHandler, errorHandler);
  }
}
```

Listing 12.52 Using the Geolocation API in Combination with the Google Maps API to Display Directions

12.9   Reading the Battery Level of an End Device

Via the Battery Status API (*www.w3.org/TR/battery-status/*), it's possible to access battery information of an end device and thus, for example, adapt a web page accordingly depending on the charging status of the battery. For this purpose, the API defines the BatteryManager interface, which can be used to access various pieces of battery information. Access to an object instance of the BatteryManager type is obtained via the (also new) getBattery() method of the navigator object.

12.9.1   Accessing Battery Information

The BatteryManager interface provides four properties (see Table 12.9). The charging property (of the boolean type) provides information about whether the battery is currently being charged or not. The chargingTime property gives a time (in seconds) that indicates how long it takes for the battery to charge. If the battery is already fully charged, the property has the value 0. On the other hand, if the battery is not currently being charged, the property has the value Infinity. Analogous to chargingTime, the dischargingTime property specifies the time (also in seconds) it takes for the battery to be fully discharged (if the battery is currently being charged, dischargingTime has the value Infinity). Last but not least, the level property indicates the battery level as a floating point number between 0 (not charged) and 1 (fully charged).

Event	Description
charging	Indicates whether the battery is being charged or not
chargingTime	Indicates the time it takes for the battery to be fully charged
dischargingTime	Indicates the time it takes for the battery to be fully discharged
level	Indicates the battery level as a floating point number between 0 (not charged) and 1 (fully charged)

Table 12.9 The Different Properties of BatteryManager

A simple example using the API can be found in Listing 12.53. As you can see, the getBattery() method does not directly return a BatteryManager object, but a Promise object. If you call the then() method on this object, you get to the BatteryManager object in the passed callback function. Figure 12.28 shows the output of the program that shows when the battery is currently being charged. Figure 12.29, on the other hand, shows the output that shows when the battery is currently not being charged.

```
function displayBatteryStatus(battery) {
    document.getElementById('charge').innerHTML = (battery.charging ? 'Yes' : 'No');
    document.getElementById('charging-time').innerHTML = battery.chargingTime;
```

```
  document.getElementById('discharging-time').innerHTML = battery.dischargingTime;
  document.getElementById('battery-level').innerHTML = battery.level;
}
navigator.getBattery().then((battery) =>
{
  displayBatteryStatus(battery);
});
```

Listing 12.53 Reading the Various Properties Relating to the Battery Level

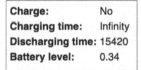

Charge:	Yes
Charging time:	Infinity
Discharging time:	Infinity
Battery level:	0.34

Figure 12.28 The Battery Is Being Charged

Charge:	No
Charging time:	Infinity
Discharging time:	15420
Battery level:	0.34

Figure 12.29 The Battery Is Not Being Charged at the Moment

12.9.2   Responding to Events

In addition to the properties mentioned thus far, event listeners for the following four events can be assigned to the BatteryManager using the addEventListener() method: The chargingchange event is triggered when the charging status changes (that is, from *charging* to *not charging* or from *not charging* to *charging*). The levelchange event is triggered when the charging level changes. And the chargingtimechange and dischargingtimechange events are triggered when the time changes in which the battery is fully charged (chargingtimechange) or discharged (dischargingtimechange; see also Table 12.10). Listing 12.54 shows an example of this.

Event	Description
chargingchange	Triggered when the end device changes its charging status— that is, from charging to not charging or from not charging to charging
levelchange	Triggered when the battery level changes

Table 12.10 The Different Events for the Battery Level

Event	Description
chargingtimechange	Triggered when there is a change in the time it takes for the battery to reach full charge status
dischargingtimechange	Triggered when there is a change in the time it takes for the battery to run down

Table 12.10 The Different Events for the Battery Level (Cont.)

```
if (navigator.getBattery)
{
  function displayBatteryStatus(battery)
  {
    document.getElementById('charge').innerHTML =
      (battery.charging ? 'Yes' : 'No');
    document.getElementById('charging-time').innerHTML = battery.chargingTime;
    document.getElementById('discharging-time').innerHTML =
      battery.dischargingTime;
    document.getElementById('battery-level').innerHTML = battery.level;
  }

  function chargingChangeHandler(event)
  {
    console.log('chargingchange');
    displayBatteryStatus(event.target);
  }

  function chargingTimeChangeHandler(event)
  {
    console.log('chargingtimechange');
    displayBatteryStatus(event.target);
  }

  function dischargingTimeChangeHandler(event)
  {
    console.log('dischargingtimechange');
    displayBatteryStatus(event.target);
  }

  function levelChangeHandler(event)
  {
    console.log('levelchange');
    displayBatteryStatus(event.target);
  }
```

```
navigator.getBattery().then((battery) =>
{
  displayBatteryStatus(battery);
  battery.addEventListener('chargingchange', chargingChangeHandler);
  battery.addEventListener('chargingtimechange', chargingTimeChangeHandler);
  battery.addEventListener('dischargingtimechange', ⊃
                           dischargingTimeChangeHandler);
  battery.addEventListener('levelchange', levelChangeHandler);
});
}
```

Listing 12.54 The Different Events of the Battery Status API

12.10   Outputting Speech and Recognizing Speech

The Web Speech API (*https://dvcs.w3.org/hg/speech-api/raw-file/tip/speechapi.html*) enables web developers to programmatically output speech and recognize speech within a web page. Similarly, the API defines two interfaces: SpeechRecognition for speech recognition (*https://dvcs.w3.org/hg/speech-api/raw-file/tip/speechapi.html# speechreco-section*) and SpeechSynthesis for speech output (*https://dvcs.w3.org/hg/ speech-api/raw-file/tip/speechapi.html#tts-section*). The API has been published by the Speech API Community Group, but it's not yet an official W3C standard.

To find out whether the current browser supports the Web Speech API, you need to test two things: first, whether speech output is supported, and second, whether speech recognition is supported. These two tests are done using feature detection. For speech output, you check whether the window object has the speechSynthesis property (see Listing 12.55). For speech recognition, you check for the presence of the webkitSpeechRecognition property (see Listing 12.56).

```
if(window.speechSynthesis) {
  // Speech output supported
} else {
  // Speech output not supported
}
// Alternative:
if('speechSynthesis' in window) {
  // Speech output supported
} else {
  // Speech output not supported
}
```

Listing 12.55 Checking Browser Support for Speech Output

```
if(window.webkitSpeechRecognition) {
  // Speech recognition supported
} else {
  // Speech recognition not supported
}
// Alternative:
if('webkitSpeechRecognition' in window) {
  // Speech recognition supported
} else {
  // Speech recognition not supported
}
```

Listing 12.56 Checking Browser Support for Speech Recognition

12.10.1   Outputting Speech

Creating speech output is relatively easy using the Web Speech API, as you can see in Listing 12.57. An object of the SpeechSynthesisUtterance type is used to define a kind of configuration object. The text to be output is defined via the text property (alternatively, this text can also be passed directly as a constructor parameter when creating the configuration object).

Then you pass the configuration object to the speak() method provided by the speechSynthesis object. This method ensures that the configuration object is added to a queue, which is processed by the speech output service one by one. This ensures that only a single speech output takes place at a time.

In addition, there are methods to cancel (cancel()), pause (pause()), and resume (resume()) speech output.

```
const utterance = new SpeechSynthesisUtterance();
utterance.text = 'Hello World';
window.speechSynthesis.speak(utterance);
```

Listing 12.57 Creating Speech Output

The getVoices() method is also used to get the voices provided by the browser or the voice objects associated with them. Each voice object has different properties, including a name and an associated country or language abbreviation. Once you've decided on a voice, you can define it using the voices property on a SpeechSynthesisUtterance object instance, as shown in Listing 12.58.

```
const utterance = new SpeechSynthesisUtterance();
utterance.text = 'Hello World';
const voices = window.speechSynthesis.getVoices();
voices.forEach(function(voice) {
  console.log(voice.lang);
```

```
    console.log(voice.name);
});
utterance.voice = voices[1];
window.speechSynthesis.speak(utterance);
```

Listing 12.58 Voice Selection for Voice Output

In addition to the voice, other properties are available to customize the voice output, including the country/language abbreviation, volume, speed, and pitch. The specification of a country/language abbreviation is especially practical, as the appropriate voice for this language is then automatically selected (see Listing 12.59).

```
const utterance = new SpeechSynthesisUtterance();
utterance.text = 'Hello World';   // text in English
utterance.lang = 'en';           // language abbreviation
utterance.volume = 0.5;          // volume
utterance.rate = 0.5;            // speed
utterance.pitch = 0.5;           // pitch
window.speechSynthesis.speak(utterance);
```

Listing 12.59 Further Configuration Options for Voice Output

Last but not least, event handlers can be used to react to various events that are generated as part of the speech output. An example of this is shown in Listing 12.60. You can find a list of all events in Table 12.11.

```
const utterance = new SpeechSynthesisUtterance('Hello World');
utterance.onstart = event => {
  console.log('Start speech output');
};
window.speechSynthesis.speak(utterance);
```

Listing 12.60 Using Event Handlers in Speech Output

Event	Description	Event Handler
boundary	Triggered when a word or phrase limit is reached	onboundary
end	Triggered at the end of the voice output	onend
error	Triggered when an error occurs during voice output	onerror
mark	Triggered when the <mark> tag is found in speech output while processing Speech Synthesis Markup Language (SSML)	onmark
pause	Triggered when the voice output has been paused	onpause

Table 12.11 Events for the Voice Output

Event	Description	Event Handler
resume	Triggered when the voice output has been resumed	onresume
start	Triggered when the voice output is started	onstart

Table 12.11 Events for the Voice Output (Cont.)

12.10.2   Recognizing Speech

Speech recognition is completely separate from speech output and is controlled by the webkitSpeechRecognition object (the browser prefix already hints that the functionality is only available in WebKit-based browsers). The webkitSpeechRecognition object implements the SpeechRecognition interface described in the API.

An example of using speech recognition is shown in Listing 12.61. The continuous property of the webkitSpeechRecognition object (set to false by default) specifies whether speech recognition should be continuous or stop when the user stops speaking. The lang property can also be used to specify the language to which the language targeting should be directed. Finally, the start() method is used to start the speech recognition.

In speech recognition, as in speech output, various events are triggered—for example, as soon as speech is recognized or when an error occurs during speech recognition (an overview of the various events is shown in Table 12.12).

Event	Description	Event Handler
audioend	Triggered at the end of audio recording	onaudioend
audiostart	Triggered when audio recording is started	onaudiostart
end	Triggered when the speech recognition service has been terminated	onend
error	Triggered when an error occurs during speech recognition	onerror
nomatch	Triggered when the speech recognition did not return a result	onnomatch
result	Triggered when the result of the speech recognition is known	onresult
soundstart	Triggered when a sound (e.g., speech) is detected	onsoundstart
soundend	Triggered when sound is no longer detected	onsoundend
speechend	Triggered when speech recognition is finished	onspeechend

Table 12.12 Events for Speech Recognition

Event	Description	Event Handler
speechstart	Triggered when speech is recognized	onspeechstart
start	Triggered when the speech recognition service has been started	onstart

Table 12.12 Events for Speech Recognition (Cont.)

For example, to access the result of speech recognition, you register an event handler for the result event, as shown in Listing 12.61. The corresponding event object then provides a speech recognition list via the results property. Each entry in this list contains one or more speech recognition alternatives in case the speech recognition was ambiguous. Each alternative, in turn, has two properties: the transcript property contains the recognized text, and the confidence property contains a value between 0 and 1 indicating the probability that the text is actually the spoken text. The alternative at the first position (firstResult[0] in the example) represents the result with the highest probability.

```
const recognition = new webkitSpeechRecognition();
recognition.continuous = true;
recognition.lang = 'en';
recognition.onresult = function(event){
  const results = event.results;
  const firstResult = results[0];
  const firstAlternative = firstResult[0];
  const transcript = firstAlternative.transcript;
  const confidence = firstAlternative.confidence;
  console.log(transcript);
  console.log(confidence);
}
recognition.start();
```

Listing 12.61 Using Speech Recognition

12.11   Creating Animations

The Web Animation API (*http://www.w3.org/TR/web-animations/*) enables web developers to define and control animations within a web page via JavaScript. For this purpose, the API defines various new interfaces, which are implemented by Firefox, Chrome, and Opera as of today. Internet Explorer, Microsoft Edge, and Safari do not currently support the API (for more details, check out the Can I Use web page at *http://caniuse.com/#search=web%20animations%20api*). In browsers that do not yet offer support, you can fall back on polyfills such as the one found at *https://github.com/web-animations/web-animations-js*.

12.11.1   Using the API

At the core of the Web Animation API is the `animate()` method, which is newly provided by the API for DOM elements. This method can be used to create individual animations, each of which is represented by an object of the (also new) `Animation` type (see Table 12.13).

Interface	Description
Animation	Represents an animation.
Animatable	Represents an animatable element on a web page. Is implemented by the `Element` interface and the `PseudoElement` interface, giving all DOM elements of a web page the `animate()` method.
AnimationTimeline	Summarizes the animations on a timeline.
AnimationEffectTiming	Represents the effects of an animation (the second parameter that is passed to the `animate()` method).
DocumentTimeline	Summarizes the animations of a web page in a timeline. Derives from `AnimationTimeline`.
KeyframeEffect	Represents the effects of a single keyframe of an animation. Type of objects that are passed as array parameters to the `animate()` function.

Table 12.13 The Main Interfaces of the Web Animation API

Listing 12.62 shows a simple example: The `animate()` method is passed an array of keyframe descriptions as the first parameter and a configuration object as the second parameter, which can be used to define further properties of the animation (see Table 12.14).

The settings you can make with these two parameters are similar to the settings you know from working with CSS animations (see Listing 12.63). The keyframe descriptions can thus be mapped to the `@keyframes` rule, and the configuration object to the (CSS) shorthand property `animation` (or the individual `animation-*` properties).

The `offset` (object) property of each keyframe object can be used to define at which point in time the respective keyframe is to be shown within the animation. If this property is omitted, the individual keyframes are distributed evenly over the defined duration.

In addition, CSS properties such as transform or opacity can be specified for each key-frame (animatable) and their values, which the animated element should assume at the time of the animation. The values between two keyframes are then automatically interpolated.

In a nutshell, if you've already dealt with CSS animations, you'll quickly understand the basics of the Web Animation API. In principle, this all works similarly—only not declaratively, but programmatically.

```
'use strict';
function init() {
  const animation = document.getElementById('circle').animate([
    {
      transform: 'scale(2)',
      opacity: 1,
      offset: 0
    },
    {
      transform: 'scale(3)',
      opacity: 0.8,
      offset: 0.3
    },
    {
      transform: 'scale(4)',
      opacity: 0.6,
      offset: 0.6
    },
    {
      transform: 'scale(5)',
      opacity: 0.7,
      offset: 1
    }
  ], {
    duration: 500,          // Duration in milliseconds
    easing: 'ease-in-out',  // Animation behavior
    delay: 10,              // Delay in milliseconds
    iterations: Infinity,   // Number of repetitions
    direction: 'alternate', // Animation direction
    fill: 'both'            // Fill behavior of animation
  });
}

document.addEventListener('DOMContentLoaded', init);
```

Listing 12.62 Using the Web Animation API

Property	Description
delay	Delay (in milliseconds) after which the animation should be started
endDelay	Delay (in milliseconds) after which the animation should end
fill	Fill behavior of the animation (none, forwards, backwards, both, auto)
iterationStart	Specifies the iteration in which to trigger a particular effect for the animation
iterations	Number of repetitions (infinity or concrete number)
duration	Duration of the animation in milliseconds
direction	Direction of the animation (alternate, normal, reverse, alternate-reverse)
easing	Behavior of the animation (ease, ease-in, ease-out, ease-in-out, cubic-bezier())

Table 12.14 Configuration Options for an Animation

```
@keyframes example {
    0% {
        transform: scale(2);
        opacity: 1;
    }
    30% {
        transform: scale(3);
        opacity: 0.8;
    }
    60% {
        transform: scale(4);
        opacity: 0.6;
    }
    100% {
        transform: scale(5);
        opacity: 0.7;
    }
}
#circle {
    animation: example 500ms ease-in-out 10ms infinite alternate both;
}
```

Listing 12.63 Equivalent CSS Animation

12.11.2   Controlling an Animation

You can control the playback behavior of the animation via the `animation` object obtained from the `animate()` method. The animation can be paused via the `pause()` method and restarted via `play()`. The `cancel()` and `finish()` methods also allow you to cancel or finish an animation.

Listing 12.64 shows a corresponding example for this. Here, various buttons are added to the example of Listing 12.62, which call the corresponding functions on the `animation` object via `click` listeners. You can also see here that you can influence the speed of the animation using the `playbackRate` property.

```
const buttonPause = document.getElementById('button-pause');
buttonPause.addEventListener('click', () => {
  animation.pause();
});
const buttonPlay = document.getElementById('button-play');
buttonPlay.addEventListener('click', () => {
  animation.play();
});
const buttonCancel = document.getElementById('button-cancel');
buttonCancel.addEventListener('click', () => {
  animation.cancel();
});
const buttonFinish = document.getElementById('button-finish');
buttonFinish.addEventListener('click', () => {
  animation.finish();
});

const buttonFaster = document.getElementById('button-faster');
buttonFaster.addEventListener('click', () => {
  animation.playbackRate *= 2;
});
const buttonSlower = document.getElementById('button-slower');
buttonSlower.addEventListener('click', () => {
  animation.playbackRate /= 2;
});
```

Listing 12.64 Controlling an Animation

12.12   Working with the Command Line

Browser tools such as Chrome DevTools, Firebug, or Safari's developer tools are standard tools for any web developer—whether to inspect a web page's DOM tree, generate output on the console, evaluate expressions and function calls, define breakpoints for debugging, go through the individual steps of a web application's JavaScript code, profile the application, or monitor network traffic.

But only some developers know that these tools also provide various functionalities via JavaScript (see Table 12.15). This is a good opportunity to give a brief overview of the relatively unknown Command Line API, which is supported by Chrome (*https://developer.chrome.com/devtools/docs/commandline-api*), Safari (*https://developer.apple.com/library/mac/documentation/AppleApplications/Conceptual/Safari_Developer_Guide/Console/Console.html*), and Firefox (*https://developer.mozilla.org/en-US/docs/Tools/Web_Console*) in their respective developer tools.

Function	Description
`$(selector)`	Alias for `document.querySelector()`.
`$$(selector)`	Alias for `document.querySelectorAll()`.
`$x(xpath)`	Returns the elements that match the passed XPath.
`$0`	Contains the node currently selected in the DOM tree view.
`$1..4`	Contains the nodes last selected in the DOM tree view.
`$_`	Contains the result of the last evaluated expression.
`clear()`	Empties the console.
`copy(object)`	Copies the string representation of an object to the clipboard.
`debug(function)`	Causes the debugger to stop when the passed function is called.
`dir(object)`	Outputs all properties of the passed object (alias for `console.dir()`).
`dirxml(object)`	Outputs the XML representation of the passed object (alias for `console.dirxml()`).
`getEventListeners(object)`	Returns the event listeners registered for an object.
`inspect(object/function)`	Opens the DOM tree view and selects the respective element that was passed or is returned by the passed function.
`keys(object)`	Returns an array containing the names of the properties of an object.
`monitor(function)`	Ensures that when the passed function is called, a corresponding console output is generated, including the respective passed arguments.

Table 12.15 Overview of the Provided Methods

Function	Description
monitorEvents(object[, events])	Starts monitoring events that are triggered by an object.
profile([title])	Starts the JavaScript profiler. Optionally, a title can be passed that is to appear at the corresponding position in the profiling report.
profileEnd()	Stops the JavaScript profiler and creates an appropriate report.
table(data [, columns])	Outputs the passed object in tabular form.
undebug(function)	Stops debugging a function.
unmonitor(function)	Stops the monitoring of a function.
unmonitorEvents(object[, types])	Stops monitoring for the passed events on the passed object.
values(object)	Returns the values of all properties of an object as an array.

Table 12.15 Overview of the Provided Methods (Cont.)

12.12.1 Selecting and Inspecting DOM Elements

From Chapter 10, you'll remember the $ object, which provides jQuery library functionality by default. In the context of the Command Line API, $ represents an alias for the document.querySelector() method.

So the document.querySelector('li') call can be shortened to $('li') even without jQuery included, and it returns the first <li> element on a web page (see Listing 12.65).

```
const firstListItem = $('li');
console.log(firstListItem);
```

Listing 12.65 Selecting the First List Element

> **Note**
>
> In this context, note the following: if a web page embeds jQuery, the alias is understandably not available (unless you've assigned jQuery to another variable).

Analogous to $(), the $$() method represents an alias for the document.querySelector-All() method. For example, the $$('li') call returns all list items on the entire web page, while the $('nav li') call returns only those list items that are inside a <nav> element (see Listing 12.66 and Figure 12.30).

```
const allListItems = $$('li');
console.log(allListItems);
const allNavListItems = $$('nav li');
console.log(allNavListItems);
```

Listing 12.66 Selecting All List Elements within Navigation Elements

Figure 12.30 Selecting Individual or All List Elements

The $x() method, which returns elements for a passed XPath expression, is also particularly handy (see Listing 12.67 and Figure 12.31).

```
const listItems = $x('/HTML/BODY/UL/LI');
console.log(listItems);
```

Listing 12.67 Selecting Elements by Specifying an XPath Expression

Once you've selected an element using one of the $(), $$(), or $x() functions (or using another selection method from the DOM standard), you can display it in the DOM tree view of the respective developer tools using the inspect() function of the Command Line API (see Listing 12.68).

```
const firstListItem = $('li');
inspect(firstListItem);
```

Listing 12.68 Displaying Elements in the Developer Tools

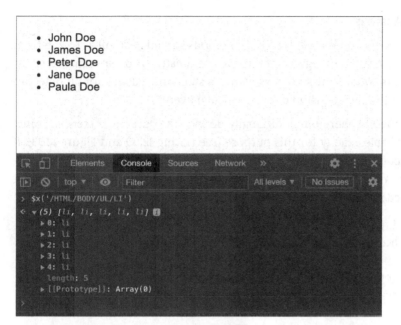

Figure 12.31 Selecting via XPath Expression

Note

By the way, the $0, $1, $2, $3, and $4 shortcuts can be used to access the last five elements selected in the DOM tree (see Figure 12.32).

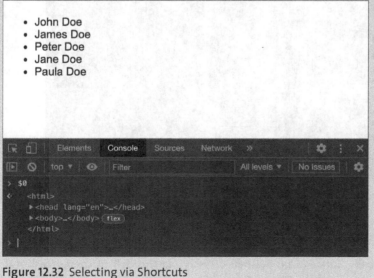

Figure 12.32 Selecting via Shortcuts

12.12.2   Events Analysis

The addEventListener() and removeListener() methods should be familiar to you from Chapter 6. They can be used to register or remove event listeners on specific events for individual elements. What's missing, however, is a standardized way for an object to get to all the event listeners registered for a particular event.

The Command Line API therefore additionally defines the getEventListener() function, which is available exactly for this purpose (see Listing 12.69 and Figure 12.33). If you pass an object to this function, the return value is an object that contains a property with the same name for each event, which in turn contains an array with the event listeners registered for the respective event.

```
window.addEventListener('load', () => {
  console.log('Document loaded');
});
window.addEventListener('resize', () => {
  console.log('Browser window size changed');
});
console.log(getEventListeners(window));
```

Listing 12.69 Output of the Event Listeners Registered for an Object

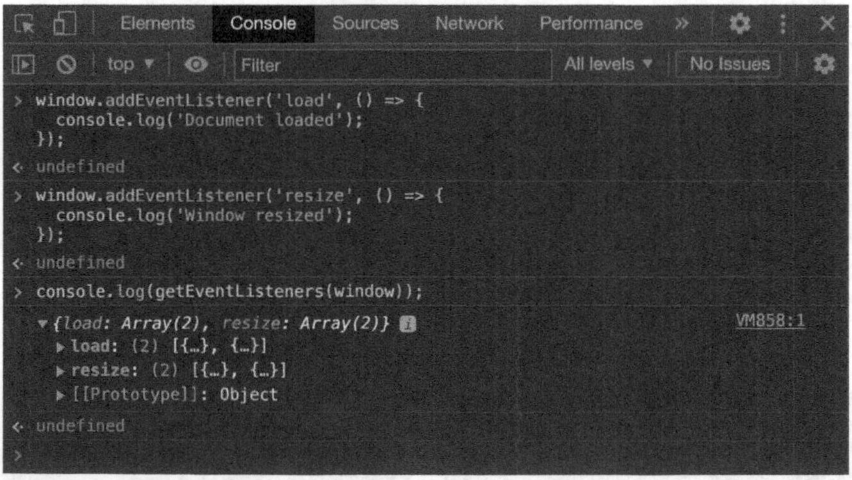

Figure 12.33 Overview of the Event Listeners Registered to an Object

12.12.3   Debugging, Monitoring, and Profiling

As you know, breakpoints can be defined directly via the GUI of the corresponding developer tool or alternatively via the debugger keyword. The Command Line API also provides another option: the debug() method expects a function or object method as a parameter and stops the execution of the respective program each time the passed function or method is called (see Listing 12.70).

```
function createPerson(firstName, lastName, age) {
  return {
    firstName: firstName,
    lastName: lastName,
    age: age
  }
}
debug(createPerson);
const max = createPerson('John', 'Doe', 55);
undebug(createPerson);
```

Listing 12.70 Debugging a Function

If this debugging behavior is to be revoked, calling undebug() is sufficient; the function/method must also be passed as a parameter here.

If you just want to know when and with which arguments a function or method is called, the Command Line API provides the monitor() function. If you pass a function object as an argument to this function, all calls to this function are subsequently documented accordingly.

In Listing 12.71, for example, the call of monitor(createPerson) outputs each call of the createPerson() function, including the arguments passed to it, to the console (see Figure 12.34).

```
function createPerson(firstName, lastName, age) {
  return {
    firstName: firstName,
    lastName: lastName,
    age: age
  }
}
monitor(createPerson);
const max = createPerson('John', 'Doe', 55);
const moritz = createPerson('James', 'Doe', 55);
// later:
unmonitor(createPerson);
```

Listing 12.71 Monitoring a Function

This is particularly practical, for example, to quickly check that a function isn't unintentionally called with incorrect or invalid arguments. To stop the monitoring at a later point in time, you can execute the unmonitor() function in the same way (see Figure 12.35).

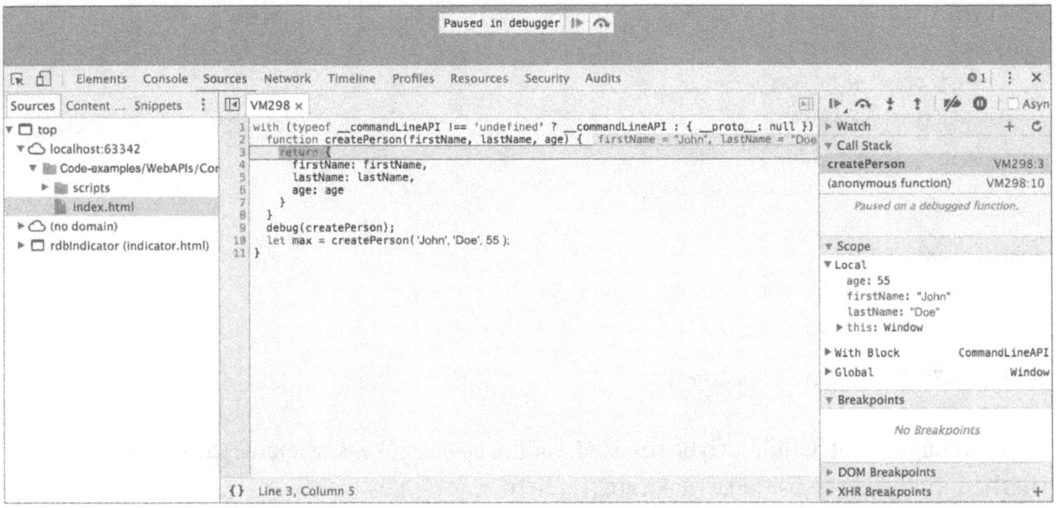

Figure 12.34 Debugging the createPerson() Function

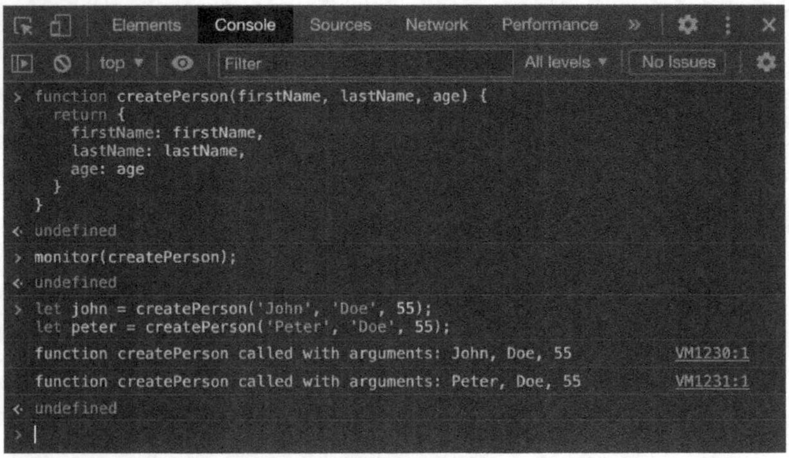

Figure 12.35 Monitoring the createPerson() Function

In addition to monitoring functions and methods, it's also possible to monitor the triggering of events: monitoring can be started with the monitorEvents() function and stopped again with the unmonitorEvents() function (see Listing 12.72 and Figure 12.36). The object that triggers the events and the events for which monitoring is to be performed are passed as arguments. In addition to concrete event names such as mousedown, mouseup, keydown, and keyup, the event types shown in Table 12.16 can also be passed.

```
const button = document.getElementById('button');
button.addEventListener('click', () => {
  console.log('Button pressed');
});
```

```
monitorEvents(button, 'click');
// later:
unmonitorEvents(button, 'click');
```

Listing 12.72 Monitoring Events

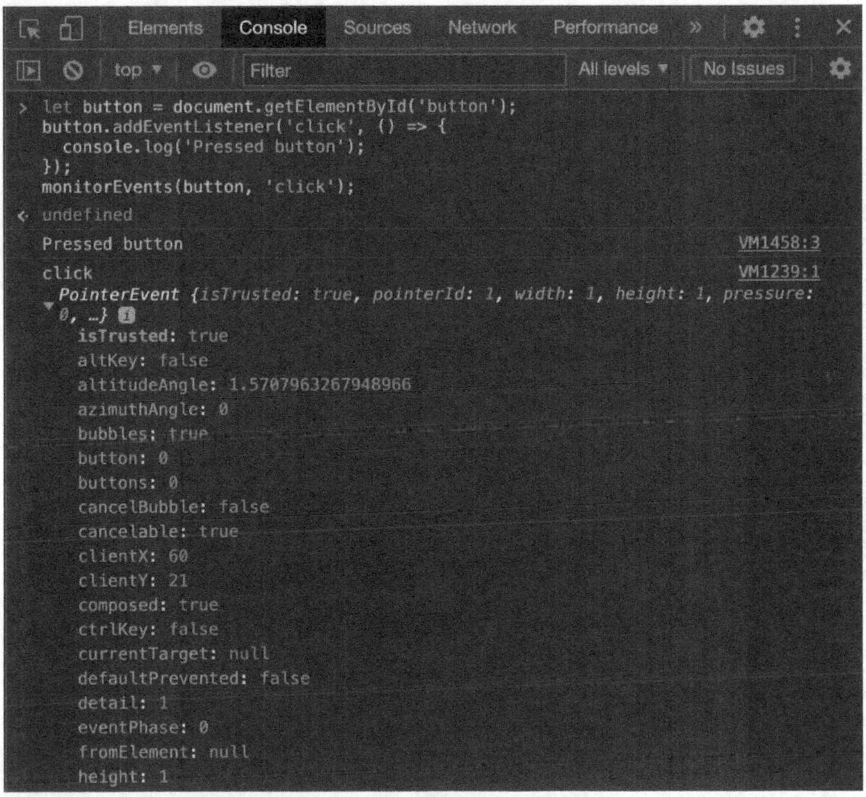

Figure 12.36 Monitoring of the click Event

Event Shortcut	Events
mouse	mousedown, mouseup, click, dblclick, mousemove, mouseover, mouse-out, mousewheel
key	keydown, keyup, keypress, textInput
touch	touchstart, touchmove, touchend, touchcancel
control	resize, scroll, zoom, focus, blur, select, change, submit, reset

Table 12.16 Shortcuts for Monitoring Events

If a website doesn't run smoothly or its performance leaves much to be desired, it's a good idea to take appropriate measurements using browser-internal profiling tools.

This functionality is also provided by the Command Line API: profiling can be started by calling the `profile()` function and stopped again by calling `profileEnd()`, where a name for the profile to be created is to be passed as an argument in each case (see Listing 12.73).

```
// Start profiling/measurement
profile('Sample profiles');
// Execute the code to be measured here
// ...
// Stop profiling/measurement
profileEnd('Sample profiles');
```

Listing 12.73 Profiling a Specific Section of Code

Afterward, the created profile can be found in the **Profiles** tab of the corresponding developer tools (see Figure 12.37).

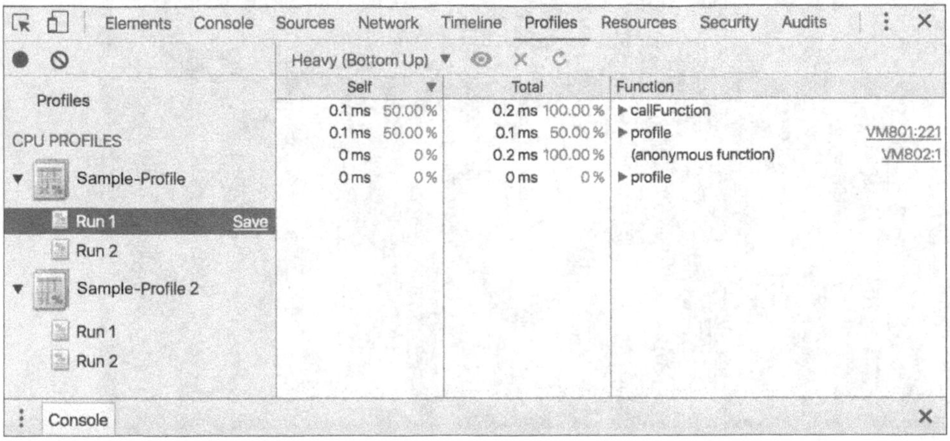

Figure 12.37 Profiling an Application

12.13   Developing Multilingual Applications

As soon as a website or web application is to be multilingual, *internationalization* (*i18n* for short—for the *i* and the last *n* and the 18 letters in between in the word *internationalization*) of the same is inevitable. The idea is to structure an application in such a way that it can be adapted to different languages (or even more generally, to different regions) without much effort.

Usually the text contents of an application are contained in a separate file for each language (or for each *locale*; more about that in a moment) and are then loaded according to the user or language settings. In principle, this is relatively easy to implement within an application if, for example, you use templating engines that obtain the individual text modules from these "dictionary files."

A bit more complex is the handling of different conventions concerning the formatting of numerical values, dates and times, or the comparison of strings. In Germany, the day is listed first, followed by the month and then the year, separated from each other by dots (e.g., for August 12, 2021, 12.08.2021). In the US, on the other hand, the month is in the first position, followed by the day and year, using the slash symbol as a separator (e.g., 08/12/2021). In Great Britain, on the other hand, the arrangement is the same as in Germany, but here, as in the American style, the slash is used as a separator (12/08/2021).

This similarly applies to numerical values or currencies. While in Germany the period is used as the thousands separator and the comma as the separator of the decimal places, and the currency symbol is placed after the numerical value (e.g., € 123.456,79), in the US it's exactly the other way around: here the comma is used as the thousands separator, the period as the decimal separator, and the currency symbol is placed before the numerical value (e.g., $123,456.79). In other parts of the world, the situation is different yet again. Understandably, this could quickly lead to confusion if you had to follow and implement all these rules yourself.

12.13.1   Explanation of Terms

Before we go into detail about the Internationalization API, let's examine some basic information and terminology about internationalization.

A language or a region in which a certain language is spoken is defined, as mentioned, using a *locale*. A locale defines the user's language, region, and any other special preferences—in other words, an identifier (also called a *language tag*) that defines exactly which language is to be used and, consequently, how numeric values, dates, and times are to be formatted and strings compared.

The structure of a language tag is specified in IETF document BCP47 (*https://tools.ietf. org/html/bcp47*). Generally, a language tag consists of letter and number combinations separated by minus signs (these combinations are also called *subtags*).

The first sub tag is the *language subtag*, which may contain either a two-character code from ISO standard 639-1 (*https://en.wikipedia.org/wiki/List_of_ISO_639-1_codes*) or a three-character code from ISO standards 639-2 (*https://en.wikipedia.org/wiki/List_of_ ISO_639-2_codes*), 639-3 (*https://en.wikipedia.org/wiki/List_of_ISO_639-3_codes*), and 639-5 (*https://en.wikipedia.org/wiki/List_of_ISO_639-5_codes*). For example, the locale for German is de, English is en, Italian is it, and so on.

All other subtags are optional and are used to further narrow down the language. For example, the *region subtag* can be used to define the country or region where the language is spoken: the de-DE locale, for example, defines German as it is spoken in Germany, whereas the de-AT locale defines it as it is spoken in Austria. Similarly, the en-US locale defines English as spoken in the US, and the en-UK locale defines English as spoken in the UK.

It's also possible to define the type system to be used via the *script subtag*. For many languages—such as English—this is superfluous because only one writing system can be used. However, there are languages such as Chinese that allow different writing systems. Possible values for the script subtag are defined in ISO 15924 (*https://en.wikipedia.org/wiki/ISO_15924*). For example, the de-Latn locale defines German in Latin script, while the de-Latf locale defines German in Fraktur, the zh-Hans locale defines Chinese in simplified script, and the zh-Hant locale defines Chinese in traditional script.

It's also possible to define certain variants of a language via the *variant subtag*. For example, the de-CH-1996 locale represents the German language in Switzerland after the 1996 spelling reform.

As you can see, there's virtually no language variant that can't be covered by the various subtags. But that's not all: locale definitions can be extended almost arbitrarily using *extension subtags*. For JavaScript, the BCP 47 Extension U defined in RFC 6067 (*https://tools.ietf.org/html/rfc6067*) is relevant in this context. The extension's name is such because of the character u, which is prefixed when defining an extension subtag, followed by a key and a value. The de-DE-u-co-phonebk locale, for example, defines the German language, spoken in Germany, where the sort order (co for *collation*) is the same as in the German telephone book (phonebk is an abbreviation here for *phonebook*).

Other options that arise from the BCP 47 Extension U are the definitions of the calendar to be used (via the ca key for *calendar*—for example, de-DE-u-ca-buddhist), the currency to be used (via the cu key for *currency*), the number system to be used (via the nu key for *numeric system*), and the time zone to be used (via the tz key for *timezone*).

12.13.2   The Internationalization API

The problem of different formatting described earlier is exactly where the ECMAScript 2017 Internationalization API (*https://tc39.github.io/ecma402/*) comes in: it allows language-dependent formatting of numeric values, dates and times, and language-dependent comparison of strings.

The API is based on existing internationalization APIs such as those of the .NET Framework or the Java Internationalization API. The first version of the API was launched by ECMA TC39 back in 2010. In the meantime, the API has been released in its fourth version and is supported by most current browsers (see Listing 12.74). For older browsers, polyfills such as **Intl.js** can be used (*https://github.com/andyearnshaw/Intl.js*).

```
if (window.Intl && typeof window.Intl === 'object'){
  // Internationalization API is supported
} else {
  // Internationalization API is not supported
}
```

Listing 12.74 Checking the Support for the Internationalization API

All objects of the Internationalization API are provided by the central `Intl` object. This object provides three types analogous to the requirements mentioned at the beginning:

- `Intl.Collator`
  Allows you to compare strings, taking into account internationalization information

- `Intl.DateTimeFormat`
  Allows formatting of dates and times, taking into account internationalization information

- `Intl.NumberFormat`
  Allows formatting of numerical values, taking into account internationalization information

Concrete instances of these types can be created using the corresponding constructor functions, passing the respective locale as a string in all cases (see Listing 12.75).

```
const locale = 'de_DE';
const dateTimeFormatGermany = new Intl.DateTimeFormat(locale);
const numberFormatGermany = new Intl.NumberFormat(locale);
const collactorGermany = new Intl.Collator(locale);
```

Listing 12.75 Creating the Format Instances

Alternatively, it's also possible to pass an array of locales instead of a single locale (see Listing 12.76). In this case, the first locale in the array that's supported by the user's system is used. In this case, if a locale isn't supported and consists of multiple subtags, the subtags are successively removed from the locale and rechecked with the locale that was created in each case. If none of the locales contained in the array are supported, the default locale is used.

```
const locales = [
  'zh-Hant', // First "zh-Hant" is checked, then "zh" ...
  'en-US',   // … then "en-US", then "en", ...
  'de-DE'    // … then "de-DE", then "de".
];
const dateTimeFormatGermany = new Intl.DateTimeFormat(locales);
const numberFormatGermany = new Intl.NumberFormat(locales);
const collactorGermany = new Intl.Collator(locales);
```

Listing 12.76 Creating the Format Instances Specifying a Locale Configuration

In addition, all constructor functions can be passed a configuration object as a second parameter, which can be used to control further aspects (more on this in detail later).

> **Note**
>
> You can find out whether a locale is supported by using the `Intl.Collator.supported-LocalesOf()`, `Intl.DateTimeFormat.supportedLocalesOf()`, and `Intl.NumberFormat.supportedLocalesOf()` "static" methods (see Listing 12.77). Each of these methods expects either a single locale or an array of locales as an argument and returns an array of those of the passed locales that are supported.
>
> ```
> const locales = ['zh-Hant', 'en-US', 'de-DE'];
> console.log(Intl.Collator.supportedLocalesOf(locales));
> console.log(Intl.DateTimeFormat.supportedLocalesOf(locales));
> console.log(Intl.NumberFormat.supportedLocalesOf(locales));
> ```
>
> **Listing 12.77** Creating the Format Instances via the Helper Function

In addition to the types defined in the Internationalization API and their methods, the following methods are available for the standard `Array`, `String`, `Number`, and `Date` objects, which are not part of this API, but also take into account the corresponding locale information:

- `Array.prototype.toLocaleString`
- `String.prototype.localeCompare`
- `String.prototype.toLocaleLowerCase`
- `String.prototype.toLocaleUpperCase`
- `Number.prototype.toLocaleString`
- `Date.prototype.toLocaleString`
- `Date.prototype.toLocaleDateString`
- `Date.prototype.toLocaleTimeString`

12.13.3 Comparing Character String Expressions

The `Collator` type is used for comparing strings. For this purpose, it provides the `compare()` method, which expects two strings as parameters and returns one of three numeric values: 1 if the first string is "greater" than the second one—that is, it's placed after the second string in the sorting; -1 if the second string is "greater" than the first one; and 0 if both strings are equal (see Listing 12.78).

```
const nameCollator = new Intl.Collator('de-DE');
console.log(nameCollator.compare('Mustermann', 'Meier'));  // 1
console.log(nameCollator.compare('Meier', 'Mustermann'));  // -1
console.log(nameCollator.compare('Meier', 'Meier'));       // 0
```

Listing 12.78 Comparison of Strings Considering Localization Information

The way in which two strings are compared or which rules are to apply can be further customized via the sensitivity property of the configuration object, which can optionally be passed as the second parameter to the Collator constructor function. The base value, for example, ensures that all characters that have the same base (e.g., the letters á, a, and A) are interpreted as having the same value (see Listing 12.79).

```
const nameCollator = new Intl.Collator('de-DE');
const nameCollatorBase= new Intl.Collator('de-DE',
  {
    sensitivity: 'base'
  }
);
console.log(nameCollator.compare('Mueller', 'mueller'));
// Return value 1, because "M" and "m" are interpreted differently
console.log(nameCollatorBase.compare('Mueller', 'mueller'));
// Return value 0, because "M" and "m" are interpreted as equal
```

Listing 12.79 Comparison of Strings Considering Localization Information

The compare() method can also be conveniently used for sorting arrays, as shown in Listing 12.80. Remember that the sort() array method can optionally be passed a sort or compare function, which then compares the elements in the respective array in pairs and thus creates a sort. If you pass the compare() method of the respective collator, as in the example, it can do the sorting work for you.

```
const names = [
  'Mustermann, Max',
  'Müller, Max',
  'Mustermann, Moritz',
  'Mueller, Moritz',
  'Meier, Petra',
  'Meier, Peter'
  ];
const nameCollator = new Intl.Collator('en', {usage: 'sort'});
console.log(names.sort(nameCollator.compare));
// [
// "Meier, Peter",
// "Meier, Petra,
// "Mueller, Moritz",
// "Müller, Max",
// "Mustermann, Max",
// "Mustermann, Moritz"
//]
```

Listing 12.80 Sorting with Intl.Collator

An overview of all properties that can be set on the configuration object for collator objects is shown in Table 12.17.

Property	Events
localeMatcher	The matching algorithm to be used.
usage	Specifies whether the comparison by the collator is to be used for sorting or for searching strings. Possible values are sort and search, respectively.
sensitivity	Specifies which characters are to be considered unequal. Possible values are base, accent, case, and variant.
ignorePunctuation	Boolean specifying whether punctuation should be ignored.
numeric	Boolean specifying whether strings are to be compared numerically (e.g., "1" < "5" < "10").
caseFirst	Boolean specifying whether lowercase or uppercase letters come first in the sort.

Table 12.17 Overview of Intl.Collator Configuration Options

12.13.4   Formatting Dates and Times

As already mentioned, the DateTimeFormat type allows formatting of dates and times. To do this, it provides the format() method, which expects an object instance of Date as a parameter and returns a string corresponding to the configurations representing the date object (see Listing 12.81 and Listing 12.82). A complete listing of configuration options is shown Table 12.18.

As an alternative to using DateTimeFormat, the toLocaleString(), toLocaleDateString(), and toLocaleTimeString() methods can be used directly on the corresponding Date object instance, also taking into account the locale information passed to the method calls, as mentioned earlier.

```
const date = new Date(Date.UTC(2021, 8, 15, 8, 0, 0));
console.log(new Intl.DateTimeFormat('de').format(date));    // 15.9.2021
console.log(new Intl.DateTimeFormat('en-US').format(date)); // 9/15/2021
console.log(new Intl.DateTimeFormat('en-GB').format(date)); // 15/09/2021
console.log(date.toLocaleString('de'));                     // 15.9.2021, 10:00:00
console.log(date.toLocaleString('en-US'));                  // 9/15/2021, 10:00:00 AM
console.log(date.toLocaleString('en-GB'));                  // 15/09/2021, 10:00:00
console.log(date.toLocaleDateString('de'));                 // 15.9.2021
console.log(date.toLocaleDateString('en-US'));              // 9/15/2021
console.log(date.toLocaleDateString('en-GB'));              // 15/09/2021
```

```
console.log(date.toLocaleTimeString('de'));        // 10:00:00
console.log(date.toLocaleTimeString('en-US'));     // 10:00:00 AM
console.log(date.toLocaleTimeString('en-GB'));     // 10:00:00
```

Listing 12.81 Formatting Dates and Times

```
...
console.log(new Intl.DateTimeFormat('en-US', {
  year: '2-digit',
  month: '2-digit'
}).format(date));
// 09/21

console.log(new Intl.DateTimeFormat('en-US', {
  year: '2-digit',
  month: '2-digit',
  day: '2-digit',
  hour: '2-digit',
  minute: '2 digit',
  second: '2-digit'
}).format(date));
// 09/15/21, 10:00:00 AM

console.log(new Intl.DateTimeFormat('en-US', {
  weekday: 'long',
  era: 'long',
  year: '2-digit',
  month: '2-digit',
  day: '2-digit',
  hour: '2-digit',
  minute: '2-digit',
  second: '2-digit',
  timeZoneName: 'long'
}).format(date));
// Wednesday, 09 15, 21 Anno Domini,
// 10:00:00 AM Central European Summer Time

console.log(new Intl.DateTimeFormat('de', {
  weekday: 'long',
  era: 'long',
  year: '2-digit',
  month: '2-digit',
  day: '2-digit',
```

12

```
  hour: '2-digit',
  minute: '2-digit',
  second: '2-digit',
  timeZoneName: 'long'
}).format(date));
// Mittwoch, 15. 09 21 n. Chr.,
// 10:00:00 Mitteleuropäische Sommerzeit

const formatter = new Intl.DateTimeFormat('de', {
  weekday: 'long',
  era: 'long',
  year: '2-digit',
  month: '2-digit',
  day: '2-digit',
  hour: '2-digit',
  minute: '2-digit',
  second: '2-digit',
  timeZoneName: 'long'
});
console.log(formatter.resolvedOptions());
/*

{
  locale: 'de',
  calendar: 'gregory',
  numberingSystem: 'latn',
  timeZone: 'Europe/Berlin',
  hourCycle: 'h23',
  hour12: false,
  weekday: 'long',
  era: 'long',
  year: '2-digit',
  month: '2-digit',
  day: '2-digit',
  hour: '2-digit',
  minute: '2-digit',
  second: '2-digit',
  timeZoneName: 'long'
}
*/
```

Listing 12.82 Formatting Dates and Times

Property	Events
localeMatcher	The matching algorithm to be used.
timeZone	The time zone to be used.
hour12	Boolean specifying whether 12 hours or 24 hours are to be used as the basis.
formatMatcher	The matching algorithm to be used.
weekday	Specification for formatting the day of the week. Possible values are narrow, short, and long.
era	Specification for formatting the age. Possible values are narrow, short, and long.
year	Specification for formatting the year. Possible values are numeric and 2-digit.
month	Specification for formatting the month. Possible values are numeric, 22digit, narrow, and short.
day	Specification for formatting the day. Possible values are numeric and 2-digit.
hour	Specification for formatting the hours. Possible values are numeric and 2-digit.
minute	Specification for formatting the minutes. Possible values are numeric and 2-digit.
second	Specification for formatting the seconds. Possible values are numeric and 2-digit.
timeZoneName	Specification for formatting the time zone. Possible values are short and long.

Table 12.18 Overview of the Configuration Options of Intl.DateTimeFormat

12.13.5 Formatting Numeric Values

The formatting of numerical values works in principle similarly to the formatting of dates and times: the constructor of NumberFormat expects the locale as the first parameter and optionally a configuration object as the second parameter for further refinement of the formatting. For example, the useGrouping property can be used to define whether separators (e.g., thousands separators) should be used, the currency property can be used to define the currency (if the number should be formatted as a monetary amount), and the minimumFractionDigits and maximumFractionDigits properties can be used to define how many decimal places a number should have as a minimum or maximum. Some more examples of this are shown in Listing 12.83, and a complete overview of the configuration options can be found in Table 12.19.

```javascript
const number = 123456.789;
console.log(
  new Intl.NumberFormat(
    'de-DE',
    {
      style: 'currency',
      currency: 'EUR'
    }
  )
  .format(number)
);
// 123.456,79 €

console.log(
  new Intl.NumberFormat(
    'en-US',
    {
      style: 'currency',
      currency: 'EUR'
    }
  )
  .format(number)
);
// €123,456.79

console.log(
  new Intl.NumberFormat(
    'de-DE',
    {
      style: 'currency',
      currency: 'USD'
    }
  )
  .format(number)
);
// 123.456,79 $

console.log(
  new Intl.NumberFormat(
    'en-US',
    {
```

```
      style: 'currency',
      currency: 'USD'
    }
  )
  .format(number)
);
// $123,456.79

console.log(
  new Intl.NumberFormat(
    'de-DE',
    {
      style: 'currency',
      currency: 'EUR',
      maximumSignificantDigits: 5
    }
  )
  .format(number)
);
// 123.460 €

console.log(
  new Intl.NumberFormat(
    'de-DE',
    {
      style: 'currency',
      currency: 'EUR',
      minimumFractionDigits: 5
    }
  )
  .format(number)
);
// 123.456,78900 €
```

Listing 12.83 Formatting Numeric Values

Property	Events
localeMatcher	The matching algorithm to be used.
style	The formatting style to be used. The following is available: decimal for normal number formatting, currency for currency formatting, and percent for percentages.

Table 12.19 Overview of the Configuration Options of Intl.NumberFormat

Property	Events
currency	The currency to be used in currency formatting—for example, EUR for euros or USD for US dollars.
currencyDisplay	Specification of how the currency is to be displayed in currency formatting. Possible values are symbol for the use of symbols, code for the corresponding ISO currency code, or name for the name of the currency (Euro, Dollar).
useGrouping	Boolean specifying whether separators (e.g., thousands separators) should be used (e.g., 1,000,000).
minimumIntegerDigits	Minimum number of digits a number should have when formatted. If a number doesn't have this minimum number, it's filled with zeros, starting from the beginning.
minimumFractionDigits	Minimum number of decimal places a number should have when formatted. If a number doesn't have this minimum number, it's filled with zeros, starting from the last digit.
maximumFractionDigits	Maximum number of decimal places a number should have when formatted. If a number has more digits, it's rounded accordingly.
minimumSignificantDigits	Minimum number of significant digits a number should have when formatted. If a number doesn't have this minimum number, it's filled with zeros, starting from the last digit.
maximumSignificantDigits	Maximum number of significant digits a number should have when formatted. If a number has more significant digits, it's rounded accordingly.

Table 12.19 Overview of the Configuration Options of Intl.NumberFormat (Cont.)

12.14   Overview of Various Web APIs

Although we haven't described all the web APIs in this chapter, you've already gained a good insight and will be able to learn about other APIs relatively quickly on your own. A slightly larger selection of different APIs is listed in Table 12.20, including a short description and the URL where you can find the corresponding specification.

API	Description	Link
Ambient Light API	Provides a sensor interface to access information about ambient light.	*www.w3.org/TR/ambient-light/*
Battery Status API	Provides access to the battery status of an end device.	*www.w3.org/TR/battery-status/*
Canvas API (HTML Canvas 2D Context)	Enables drawing via JavaScript.	*www.w3.org/TR/2dcontext/*
Command Line API	Provides access to functions of browser developer tools.	Browser-specific: ■ Chrome: *https://developer.chrome.com/devtools/docs/command-line-api* ■ Safari: *https://developer.apple.com/library/mac/documentation/AppleApplications/Conceptual/ Safari_Developer_Guide/Console/Console.html* ■ Firefox: *https://developer.mozilla.org/en-US/docs/Tools/Web_Console*
Device Orientation API	Enables the reading of information with regard to the orientation of end devices.	*www.w3.org/TR/orientation-event/*
Fullscreen API	Enables displaying a web page in full-screen mode.	*https://fullscreen.spec.whatwg.org/*
Geolocation API	Enables access to location information.	*www.w3.org/TR/geolocation-API/*
High Resolution Time API	Enables access to the current time in a higher resolution than, for example, the one used for the system time.	*www.w3.org/TR/hr-time/*
Indexed Database API	Enables access to a client-side browser database.	*www.w3.org/TR/IndexedDB*

Table 12.20 Overview of Various Web APIs

API	Description	Link
Internationalization API	Enables JavaScript applications to be created in multiple languages.	*https://www.ecma-international.org/ecma-402/1.0/*
Media Capture and Streams	Defines an interface for accessing media data such as audio and video.	*www.w3.org/TR/mediacapture-streams/*
Navigation Timing API	Enables access to various temporal information when users interact with a web page.	*www.w3.org/TR/navigation-timing/*
Network Information API	Enables access to connection information of an end device.	*http://w3c.github.io/net-info/*
Notifications API	Enables sending hint messages to a user.	*www.w3.org/TR/notifications/*
Page Visibility API	Allows you to determine whether a web page is currently visible or not (e.g., if it's open in a hidden tab).	*www.w3.org/TR/page-visibility/*
Performance Timeline	Enables access to information to measure performance within a web page.	*www.w3.org/TR/performance-timeline*
Presentation API	Defines an interface for accessing external presentation displays, such as beamers or TVs.	*www.w3.org/TR/presentation-api/*
Pointer Events	Defines a uniform interface for input devices such as a mouse, pen, and touchscreen.	*www.w3.org/TR/pointer-events/*
Progress Events	Defines an interface to access the progress of specific processes. Was used in this chapter, for example, to determine the progress of reading a file (Section 12.5.4).	*www.w3.org/TR/progress-events*
Proximity API	Enables access to information about the location of physical objects such as end devices or users.	*www.w3.org/TR/proximity/*

Table 12.20 Overview of Various Web APIs (Cont.)

API	Description	Link
Resource Timing API	Enables access to temporal information with regard to resources included in a web page—for example, to log how long it takes to load a resource.	*www.w3.org/TR/resource-timing/*
Screen Orientation API	Enables access to orientation information of end devices.	*www.w3.org/TR/screen-orientation/*
Server-Sent Events	Allows sending messages from the server to the client.	*www.w3.org/TR/eventsource*
Touch Events	Defines an interface for accessing touch surfaces.	*www.w3.org/TR/touch-events*
User Timing API	Enables access to various temporal information when users interact with a web page using high-resolution time information.	*www.w3.org/TR/user-timing/*
Vibration API	Enables the use of the vibration function of end devices.	*www.w3.org/TR/vibration/*
Web Animations API	Enables the creation of animations within a web page.	*https://w3c.github.io/web-animations/*
Web Messaging API	Defines an interface for exchanging messages. Is used, for example, with server-sent events or web sockets.	*www.w3.org/TR/webmessaging/*
Web Notification API	Defines an interface for notifications to users.	*www.w3.org/TR/notifications/*
Web Speech API	Enables speech output and speech recognition.	*https://dvcs.w3.org/hg/speech-api/raw-file/tip/speechapi.html*
Web Storage API	Enables access to browser storage.	*www.w3.org/TR/webstorage*
Web Worker API	Enables parallel execution of JavaScript programs.	*www.w3.org/TR/workers*
Web Socket API	Enables bidirectional communication between client and server.	*www.w3.org/TR/websockets*

Table 12.20 Overview of Various Web APIs (Cont.)

12

12.15   Summary

In this chapter, you learned about various Web APIs. We've shown you the following APIs in the process:

- The Web Socket API enables bidirectional communication between client and server.

- Using *server-sent events*, it's possible to actively send messages from the server to the client.

- To store client-side data, you can use cookies, browser storage, or IndexedDB. Browser storage is divided into *local storage* and *session storage*: the former is available to all windows and tabs of a browser, whereas the latter is unique to each window or tab.

- Via the File API, it's possible to access files of the user, provided that the user has selected the files via a selection dialog or a drag-and-drop operation.

- Via *drag and drop*, it's possible to move elements within a web page.

- By default, JavaScript is executed in a single thread. However, using *web workers* and the Web Worker API, the execution of scripts can be distributed across different threads, although web workers do not have access to the DOM or the `window` object.

- The Geolocation API can be used to access the user's location information, provided the user has given their consent. The information obtained can then be combined with the Google Maps API, for example, to display the location or directions on a map.

- The Battery Status API allows you to read information regarding the battery of an end device. This includes the battery status, charging time, and runtime.

- The Web Speech API enables speech output and speech recognition.

- Using the Web Animation API, it's possible to create animations via JavaScript.

- The Command Line API provides some useful features that are helpful during web application development.

- The Internationalization API allows web applications to be multilingual.

Chapter 13
Object-Oriented Programming

Although you've been dealing with objects again and again in the past chapters and the term object-oriented programming has already been briefly mentioned and explained, there's a lot more you should know about this important programming paradigm. If you've already programmed in another object-oriented programming language, you'll notice that JavaScript handles some things fundamentally differently. If you don't have any experience with object-oriented programming, all the better because then these things will probably take less getting used to.

13

In JavaScript, object orientation looks different than in languages like Java. This chapter first explains the core concepts of object-oriented programming (abstraction, data encapsulation, polymorphism, and inheritance) and then shows the different techniques available in JavaScript to implement these concepts.

13.1 The Principles of Object-Oriented Programming

Back in Chapter 3, we briefly mentioned the principle of object-oriented programming, and since then you've already seen in various examples that you're dealing with objects in JavaScript in many places. For example, the various components of web pages are represented as objects in the form of the Document Object Model, the same is true for the various components of the browser window, and even events and errors are nothing but objects.

But the fact that you work with objects alone doesn't necessarily mean that you also work in an *object-oriented* way. Object-oriented programming is based on four essential principles:

- **Abstraction**
  Abstract behavior of objects is summarized in *classes* or *prototypes*.

- **Data encapsulation**
  Properties and methods are encapsulated in the form of classes or prototypes and hidden from external access.

725

- **Inheritance**
  Properties and methods can be inherited from one class to another class or from one object (the prototype) to another object.

- **Polymorphism**
  Objects can take on different types depending on their use.

Other Principles of Object-Oriented Programming

There are several other special principles, such as aggregation, coupling, association, and composition (see, for example, *https://en.wikipedia.org/wiki/Package_principles*), but we won't discuss them here.

Now, of course, the first question is what exactly classes and prototypes are. Therefore, we'll first explain both terms and also discuss their connection with objects before returning to the principles of object orientation.

13.1.1 Classes, Object Instances, and Prototypes

In object orientation, a *class* is a kind of blueprint for objects. A class serves as a template, so to speak, from which individual instances (*object instances*) can be created at the runtime of a program. Within a class, the developer defines the properties and methods that the individual object instances should have. The properties represent the state of the object instances, the methods their behavior. In software development, *class diagrams* in Unified Modeling Language (UML) are often used to model individual classes or to represent the relationship of classes to each other, while the relationship of objects to each other is represented in *object diagrams*.

Figure 13.1 shows a combination of both diagram types, where you can see the Animal class, plus two object instances of this class, bello and bella. In class/object diagrams, both classes and objects are represented by rectangles divided into individual areas.

For classes, the name of the class is at the top, followed by an optional area listing the properties, followed by another optional area listing the methods of the class. Properties are listed with name and data type, methods also with names and data types of the individual parameters. Optionally, other aspects such as return value (for methods) and visibility (for properties and methods) can be specified.

For objects, the name of the respective object is also at the top (lowercase according to convention), followed by a colon and the name of the class of which the respective object is an instance. Properties of objects are specified with names and usually also with concrete values, but a list for methods doesn't exist in object diagrams.

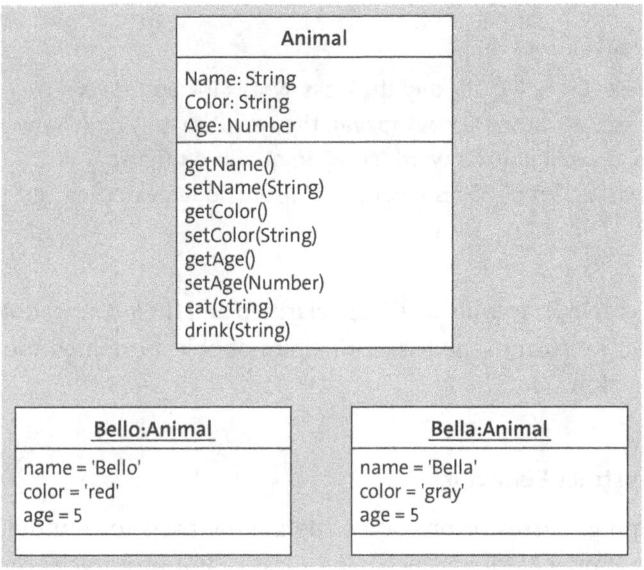

Figure 13.1 A Combination of Class Diagram and Object Diagram to Represent Classes and Objects

An example of a *class-based programming language* is the Java programming language. JavaScript, however, is *not* a class-based programming language, even though there has been a class syntax since ES2015 (more on that in a moment).

JavaScript is instead an *object-based programming language*: object instances are not created here on the basis of classes, but on the basis of other objects. These other objects then represent the *prototype*.

Deviation from UML Standard

Because JavaScript is an object-based programming language and methods are defined directly on objects (and not on classes), we've included some methods in the object diagrams to reflect this fact. Although this deviates somewhat from the UML standard, it simplifies the representation in this case.

Because of this principle of prototypes, the type of programming in JavaScript is also called *prototype-based programming* or *prototypical programming*. An alternative term is *classless programming*, because no classes are used.

Types of Object Orientation

The type of object orientation also has different names depending on the type of programming language: In the class-based programming you speak of *class-based object orientation*, in the object-based and/or prototype-based programming you speak of *prototypical object orientation*.

> **JavaScript Doesn't Know Real Classes**
>
> JavaScript uses the term classes since ES2015, and the class syntax introduced with it, but these aren't genuine classes (like the classes in Java); they're ultimately only "syntactic sugar." Therefore, ahead, we'll put the word "class" in quotation marks if we're referring to these kind of "classes." In all cases where this distinction doesn't matter, we omit the quotation marks.

Now that the concepts of class and prototype have been clarified and their connection to objects has been shown, let's return to the basic principles of object-oriented programming in the following sections.

13.1.2 Principle 1: Define Abstract Behavior

In object-oriented programming, classes or prototypes define the basis for multiple object instances that have a similar state and behavior. Classes and prototypes can therefore also be considered *abstractions* of the (concrete) object instances.

Classes and prototypes define the *abstract behavior* (common to all object instances) or the properties representing the state (also common to all object instances), respectively. In the object instances, the properties are then provided with concrete values, thus defining the *concrete state* (see Figure 13.2).

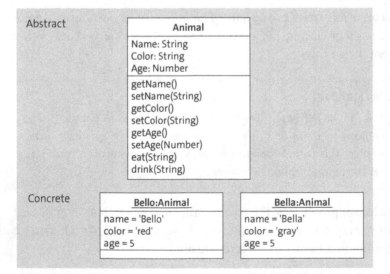

Figure 13.2 Classes Can Be Regarded as Abstractions from the Concrete Object Instances

13.1.3 Principle 2: Encapsulate Condition and Behavior

In object orientation, the term *data encapsulation* (or *information hiding*) refers to the grouping of properties and methods into classes or prototypes, whereas the details of the implementation remain hidden: usually, you provide the properties only through methods to prevent direct access to them and also to prevent an object from being set to an unauthorized state.

In Figure 13.3, this is illustrated in sketch form. The name, color, and age properties are marked as private by the preceding minus sign: direct access to these properties isn't possible from outside, so the call of caller 1 fails.

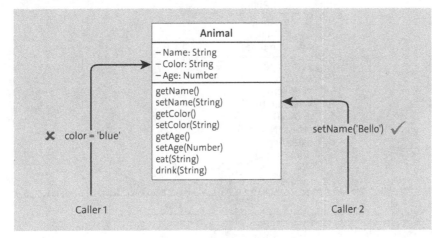

Figure 13.3 Properties Should Only Be Accessed by Methods

Instead, the class provides setter and getter methods to access the properties, so the call to caller 2 succeeds. Such *accessor methods* or simply *accessors* can protect against invalid values being assigned to a property. But if you allow direct access to the properties (and thus do not fulfill the principle of data encapsulation), this isn't guaranteed because values can then also be assigned that are not valid (e.g., the value Doe to the color property).

In programming languages such as Java, special keywords can be used to prevent the values of properties from being changed externally (i.e., from outside an object instance— namely, by marking them as private via the private keyword). JavaScript has long been somewhat cumbersome in this regard, inherently offering only the set and get keywords to mark properties as *access properties*, but not to make properties completely inaccessible from the outside. Only with ES2022 is it now possible to mark private properties as such via a special syntax (Section 13.4.4).

13.1.4   Principle 3: Inherit Condition and Behavior

In class-based object orientation, a class can *inherit* or *derive* properties and methods from another class, which is referred to as *inheritance*.

For example, a Dog class could derive from an Animal class and thus inherit the methods defined there. Figure 13.4 shows the corresponding class diagram for this. You can see that inheritance relationships are indicated by arrows in UML: the Cat and Dog classes derive from the Animal class and inherit its methods, but they also define one further method each.

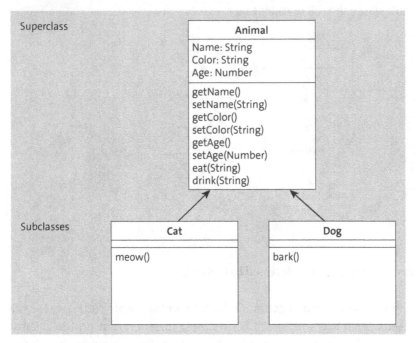

Figure 13.4 Classes Can Inherit Properties and Methods from Other Classes

The class that inherits or *deriving class* is also called the *subclass*; the class that's inherited from is correspondingly called the *superclass*.

Subtypes and Supertypes

In prototypical object orientation, it's possible for objects to inherit from other objects (the prototypes). Because the terms *subobject* and *superobject* are rather uncommon in this context, the terms *subtype* and *supertype* are more commonly used here.

Note

The inheritance of classes or objects represents an as is relationship: An instance of Cat is also an instance of Animal. However, the reverse is not true: an instance of Animal is not necessarily an instance of Cat.

13.1.5   Principle 4: Accept Different Types

Polymorphism is the ability of objects to take on a different type (*shape*) or to present themselves as a different type, depending on the context or their use.

For example, if a function expects an object of the Animal type, then object instances of Animal, but also object instances of subclasses such as Cat or Dog, can be passed as arguments. You can use instances of Cat in all places where you expect instances of Animal or instances of Cat and you can use instances of Dog in all places where you expect instances of Animal or Dog. These instances are *polymorphic*: in one place they can assume the more general type Animal, in another place the more specific type Cat or Dog.

Statically Typed versus Dynamically Typed

In strictly or statically typed programming languages like Java, the language itself emphasizes the topic of polymorphism more than it does in weakly or dynamically typed languages like JavaScript. Because of the weak typing, you can pass any types of objects as arguments for functions, for example, without a compiler grumbling in case of not allowed types.

Note

Object instances of a subclass can be treated like object instances of the respective superclass.

13.1.6   JavaScript and Object Orientation

With regard to object-oriented programming, JavaScript doesn't behave as unambiguously as other languages (like Java, for example, which we often use for comparison). Rather, there are several techniques in JavaScript to program in an object-oriented way. As a good JavaScript developer, you should master all of these techniques.

In principle, distinctions are made among the following:

- **Prototypical object orientation**
  This is the kind of object orientation that is most natural in the JavaScript language because it uses only objects.
- **Pseudoclassical object orientation**
  This is a type of object orientation where you pretend JavaScript is a class-based programming language. Constructor functions are used here.
- **Object orientation with class syntax**
  This type of object orientation represents a syntactic simplification of pseudolassical object orientation.

For didactic reasons, it makes sense to introduce these types of object orientation in exactly the order mentioned, even though in practice—at least for new JavaScript projects—you would probably use the class syntax directly. So let's start with prototypical object orientation first.

13.2 Prototypical Object Orientation

JavaScript is a prototype-based language, so it doesn't know any classes—at least, not real ones. Instead, everything in JavaScript is based on objects. In this section, we'll show you how the classical object orientation based on objects or prototypes (*prototypical object orientation*) works.

13.2.1 The Concept of Prototypes

Every object in JavaScript is based on a *prototype*. At least, almost every object, because some objects—for example, the mother of all objects, Object, or objects whose prototype has been explicitly set to null—have no prototype.

Each object can also serve as a template—that is, as a prototype for another object. In this case, the new object inherits the properties and methods from the prototype. So translated into class-based programming, this is roughly equivalent to creating a subclass: it inherits properties and methods from the derived *superclass* or *parent class*.

> **Note**
> In prototypical inheritance, classes do not inherit from classes, but objects inherit from objects.

> **Access to the Prototype of an Object**
> The prototype of an object is stored in the __proto__ property. First implemented in the Firefox browser as an alias to the internal [[Prototype]] property, this property has since been adopted by almost all browsers or runtime environments. The feature was not permanently adopted in the ECMAScript standard until version 6. Instead of accessing the property directly, it's common and recommended to get the prototype of an object using the Object.getPrototypeOf() method. In addition, it's possible to use Object.isPrototypeOf() to check whether an object is the prototype of another object.

13.2.2   Deriving from Objects

To define an object based on a prototype, use the `Object.create()` method (see also Chapter 4). An example is shown in Listing 13.1. Here, the `animal` object is initially defined, which has the `eat()` and `drink()` methods and the `name`, `color`, and `age` properties (for reasons of space, additional setters and getters for the properties have been omitted here). Subsequently, two further objects are created via `Object.create()` (`cat` and `dog`), where the `animal` object is passed as a prototype.

```
const animal = {
  name: '',
  color: 'Brown',
  age: 0,
  eat: function(food) {
    console.log('Chow chow, ' + food + '!');
  },
  drink: function(drink) {
    console.log('Mmmmmmh, ' + drink + '!');
  }
}
const cat = Object.create(animal);
const dog = Object.create(animal);
```

Listing 13.1 Creating Objects Based on a Prototype

> **Note**
>
> Remember: when creating an object using the object literal notation, no prototype can be specified.

13.2.3   Inheriting Methods and Properties

In prototypical object orientation, objects inherit from objects. In the example of Listing 13.2, for example, the two objects `cat` and `dog` therefore inherit the `eat()` and `drink()` methods, as well as the `name`, `color`, and `age` properties from the `animal` object. Consequently, everything can be accessed via the `cat` and `dog` objects.

```
const animal = {
  name: '',
  color: 'Brown',
  age: 0,
  eat: function(food) {
    console.log('Chow chow, ' + food + '!');
  },
```

```
  drink: function(drink) {
    console.log('Mmmmmmh, ' + drink + '!');
  }
}
const cat = Object.create(animal);   // Objects inherit ...
cat.eat('cat food');                 // ... methods ...
cat.drink('milk');
console.log(cat.color);              // ... and properties from the prototype.
const dog = Object.create(animal);
dog.eat('meat');                     // Output: 'Chow, chow, meat!'
dog.drink('water');                  // Output: 'Mmmmmmh, water!'
console.log(dog.color);              // Output: 'Brown'
```

Listing 13.2 In Prototypical Inheritance, Objects Inherit from Other Objects

13.2.4 Defining Methods and Properties in the Inheriting Object

Of course, it's also possible to define additional properties and methods on objects that inherit from a prototype. In Listing 13.3, for example, the cat object gets the new meow() method and the dog object gets the new bark() method. Of course, these two methods are then only available on the respective objects: the meow() method, for example, cannot be called on the dog object and, conversely, the bark() method cannot be called on the cat object.

```
const animal = {
  name: 'default',
  color: 'Brown',
  age: 0,
  eat: function(food) {
    console.log('Chow chow, ' + food + '!');
  },
  drink: function(drink) {
    console.log('Mmmmmmh, ' + drink + '!');
  }
}
const cat = Object.create(animal);
cat.meow = function() {
  console.log('Meowwwww!');
}
cat.eat('cat food');            // Output: 'Chow, chow, cat food!'
cat.drink('Milk');              // Output: 'Mmmmmmh, milk!'
cat.meow();                     // Output: 'Meowwwww!'
console.log(cat.color);         // Output: 'Brown'
const dog = Object.create(animal);
```

```
dog.bark = function() {
  console.log('Woof woof!');
}
dog.eat('meat');                    // Output: 'Chow, chow, meat!'
dog.drink('water');                 // Output: 'Mmmmmmh, water!'
dog.bark();                         // Output: 'Woof woof!'
console.log(dog.color);             // Output: 'Brown'
```

Listing 13.3 Inheriting Objects Can Define New Methods and Properties

13.2.5   Overwriting Methods

Classes, or in the case of prototypical object orientation, objects that are lower in the inheritance hierarchy, are more special than those that are higher in the inheritance hierarchy. Or put the other way around: classes/objects higher up in the hierarchy are more abstract than those lower down.

Special behavior can arise on the one hand from the fact that—as we have just seen— new methods are added to classes or objects, but on the other hand also from the fact that inherited methods are *overwritten*.

An example of this is shown in Listing 13.4. The previous source code has been extended by a new object, vegetarianDog, which derives from dog. Because vegetarian dogs do not eat meat, the eat() method has been modified and overwritten accordingly: it returns a corresponding error if the string passed to the method contains the value meat.

So if you call the eat() method on the vegetarianDog object now, it's exactly this method that's used and not the method defined in the animal object.

> **Note**
>
> The eat() method on the animal object is of course unaffected by the change to the vegetarianDog object.

```
const animal = {
  name: '',
  color: 'Brown',
  age: 0,
  eat: function(food) {
    console.log('Chow chow, ' + food + '!');
  },
  drink: function(drink) {
    console.log('Mmmmmmh, ' + drink + '!');
  }
}
```

13

```
const cat = Object.create(animal);
cat.meow = function() {
  console.log('Meowwwwww!');
}
const dog = Object.create(animal);
dog.bark = function() {
  console.log('Woof woof!');
}
const vegetarianDog = Object.create(dog);
vegetarianDog.eat = function(food) {
  if(food.indexOf('meat') >= 0 || food.indexOf('meat') >= 0) {
    throw new Error('I don't eat meat!');
  } else {
    console.log('Chow chow, ' + food + '!');
  }
}
vegetarianDog.eat('cheese');
```

Listing 13.4 Overwriting a Method in a Deriving Object

13.2.6   The Prototype Chain

Objects inherit properties and methods from their prototype or all preceding prototypes via the *prototype chain*. The process here is as follows: If you access a property or
method of an object, the JavaScript interpreter first checks whether the corresponding
object has the respective property/method. If so, the property/method is used. If not,
the prototype of the object (which is stored in the __proto__ property, among others) is
accessed. If the property/method isn't present there either, the prototype of the prototype is checked, and so on, until the base Object object is reached at some point (see
Figure 13.5).

Referring to the example, shown in Figure 13.5 in the form of a (slightly modified) object
diagram, this means, for example, that if you call the eat() method on the vegetarian-
Dog object, as in Listing 13.5, it doesn't go up the prototype chain because this method is
defined directly on the object. If, on the other hand, you call the bark() method, it goes
up one level to the dog object via the prototype chain. If you call the drink() method, it
goes up two levels to the animal object. If the toString() method is called, it even goes
up to the Object object because only there is this method defined.

> **Note**
> Thus, the prototype chain is a chain of objects, each of which serves as a prototype for
> the subsequent objects in that chain.

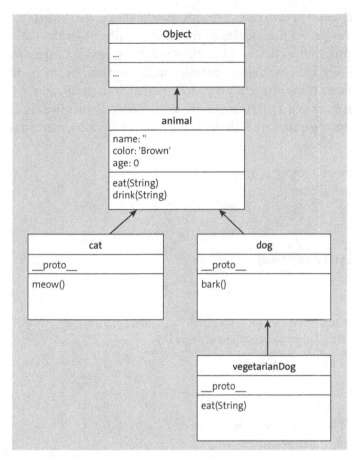

Figure 13.5 Example of a Prototype Chain

```
...
vegetarianDog.eat('cheese');      // Present in vegetarionDog
vegetarianDog.bark();             // Present in dog
vegetarianDog.drink('water');     // Present in animal
vegetarianDog.toString();         // Present in Object
```

Listing 13.5 Calling Methods Defined at Different Places in the Prototype Chain

13.2.7 Calling Methods of the Prototype

To call a method of the prototype of an object, you must first get to the prototype of the object. In principle, you have two options for this: on the one hand, the prototype of an object is stored in its __proto__ property, and on the other hand, you can use the Object.getPrototypeOf() method to determine the prototype of an object. Consequently, the possibilities shown in Listing 13.6 and Listing 13.7 are both valid, although we'd advise you to use the latter for the sake of readability.

What happens here in each case? In both cases, the prototype of the current object (i.e., vegetarianDog) is first accessed via the previously mentioned paths, then the eat() method is called, and on this in turn the call() method is called (see also Chapter 4). Remember: this method, which is available by default for all functions or methods, does nothing other than execute the respective function/method in a specific context. You pass this execution context to it as the first parameter; optionally, you can pass, as shown in the example, further parameters with which the original function/method is to be called.

```
const vegetarianDog = Object.create(dog);
vegetarianDog.eat = function(food) {
  if(food.indexOf('meat') >= 0 || food.indexOf('meat') >= 0) {
    throw new Error('I don't eat meat!');
  } else {
    this.__proto__.eat.call(this, food);
  }
}
vegetarianDog.eat('cheese');
```

Listing 13.6 Calling a Method of the Prototype when Accessed via the __proto__ Property

```
const vegetarianDog = Object.create(dog);
vegetarianDog.eat = function(food) {
  if(food.indexOf('meat') >= 0 || food.indexOf('meat') >= 0) {
    throw new Error('I don't eat meat!');
  } else {
    Object.getPrototypeOf(this).eat.call(this, food);
  }
}
vegetarianDog.eat('cheese');
```

Listing 13.7 Calling a Method of the Prototype when Accessed via the getPrototypeOf() Method

13.2.8   Prototypical Object Orientation and the Principles of Object Orientation

Finally, let's briefly summarize how the four basic principles of object-oriented programming presented at the beginning are implemented in prototypical object orientation.

The first principle, the abstraction of behavior common to different object instances, is given by the fact that this behavior is implemented in prototypes. The behavior is also inherited by deriving objects via the prototype chain (in this respect, the principle of inheritance is also given).

True data encapsulation is possible in JavaScript only via design patterns, which we haven't discussed here. However, it's possible to define access properties using the get and set keywords and thus also to control access to data properties in a certain way or to make further configurations of properties using property attributes (see also Chapter 4).

Polymorphism is a given in JavaScript anyway, because there are no built-in restrictions on the types that are used as arguments to functions, for example.

13.3   Pseudoclassical Object Orientation

In contrast to prototypical object orientation, *pseudoclassical object orientation* is based on the use of constructor functions. The idea is that object-oriented programming with JavaScript feels like doing class-based programming.

13.3.1   Defining Constructor Functions

Remember: *constructor functions* are nothing more than "normal" functions. They only become constructor functions by calling them prefixed with new. Moreover, they're usually written in UpperCamelCase notation (thus following the conventions of good software development). Within a constructor function, the this keyword then refers to the object created by calling the constructor function. An example of a constructor function is shown in Listing 13.8.

```
function Animal(name, color, age) {
  this.name = name;
  this.color = color;
  this.age = age;
};
```

Listing 13.8 Definition of a Function That Can Be Called as a Constructor Function

13.3.2   Creating Object Instances

To create a new object instance using a constructor function, you call the constructor function with the new keyword, as mentioned. In Listing 13.9, for example, a new instance of Animal is created, passing the values Fishy, Green, and 2 as arguments and setting them as values for the corresponding properties on the created instance.

```
const fish = new Animal('Fishy', 'Green', 2);
console.log(fish.name);    // Output: "Fishy"
console.log(fish.color);   // Output: "Green"
console.log(fish.age);     // Output: 2
```

Listing 13.9 Creating an Object Instance Using a Constructor Function

13.3.3   Defining Methods

To create methods that are common to all object instances created using a constructor function, you define them on the object that serves as the prototype for the object instances created by the constructor function. This object is stored in the prototype property of the corresponding constructor function. In Listing 13.10, for example, the eat() and drink() methods are thus defined on the prototype object of the Animal constructor function. Subsequently, the two methods can be called on the fish object instance.

```
Animal.prototype.eat = function(food) {
  console.log('Chow chow, ' + food + '!');
}
Animal.prototype.drink = function(drink) {
  console.log('Mmmmmmh, ' + drink + '!');
}
const fish = new Animal('Fishy', 'Green', 2);
fish.eat('Algae');        // Output: 'Chow Chow, algae!'
fish.drink('water');      // Output: 'Mmmmmmh, water!'
```

Listing 13.10 Definition and Call of Methods

13.3.4   Deriving from Objects

The principle of inheritance in pseudoclassical inheritance is not so easy to understand. So let's explain it using the example shown in Listing 13.11. For a better understanding, you can take a look at Figure 13.6 through Figure 13.11 in parallel; each of these figures graphically represents the state of JavaScript objects after corresponding lines of code in the form of class diagrams (even if they aren't real classes in this case).

```
// Step 1
function Animal(name, color, age) {
  this.name = name;
  this.color = color;
  this.age = age;
};
// Step 2
Animal.prototype.eat = function(food) {
  console.log('Chow chow, ' + food);
}
Animal.prototype.drink = function(drink) {
  console.log('Mmmmmmh, ' + drink);
}
// Step 3
function Dog(name, color, age, type) {
```

```
  Animal.call(this, name, color, age);
  this.type = type;
};
// Step 4
Dog.prototype = new Animal();
// Step 5
Dog.prototype.constructor = Dog;
// Step 6
Dog.prototype.bark = function() {
  console.log('Woof woof');
}
const bello = new Dog('Bello', 'White', 2, 'Maltese');
bello.bark();        // Output: "Woof woof"
```

Listing 13.11 Constructor Functions Are Used in Classical Inheritance

First, you define the `Animal` function that is to serve as a constructor function (step 1). Implicitly, however, much more happens here than just defining a function. The code `function Animal() {...}` also causes an object to be created that is stored in the `prototype` property of the constructor function and in turn links to the constructor function via a `constructor` property (see Figure 13.6).

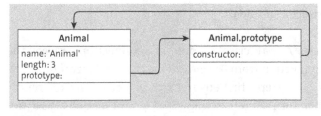

Figure 13.6 Step 1: State after Defining the Animal Constructor Function

The `Animal.prototype` object is, as already stated, the prototype for the objects created by calling the `Animal` constructor function. In the second step, the methods are now defined on this prototype—in this example, the `eat()` and `drink()` methods (see Figure 13.7). We discussed this a moment ago.

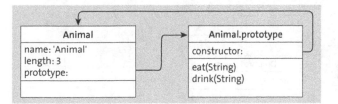

Figure 13.7 Step 2: Defining the eat() and drink() Methods on the Prototype

In the third step, things get interesting with regard to inheritance: in fact, now we are talking about creating a "subclass" of Animal. For this purpose, the Dog constructor function is defined in the example. Figure 13.8 shows the state afterward. As you can see, there is no link between the Dog "class" and the Animal "class" yet. You have to create this link manually as a developer. (By the way: we'll explain what exactly Animal.call(this, name, color, age) does in a few moments.)

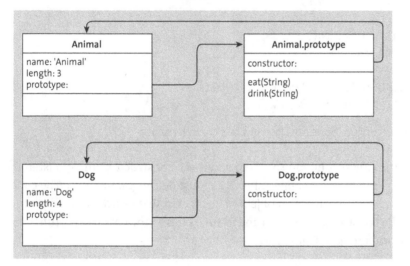

Figure 13.8 Step 3: The Dog Constructor Function

The link from the Dog "class" to the Animal "class" is done via a connection between the prototype objects—that is, a connection from Dog.prototype to Animal.prototype. The line Dog.prototype = new Animal(); in step 4 first ensures that Dog.prototype references a completely new object, which in turn references the Animal.prototype object as a prototype. The current state of the objects is shown in Figure 13.9.

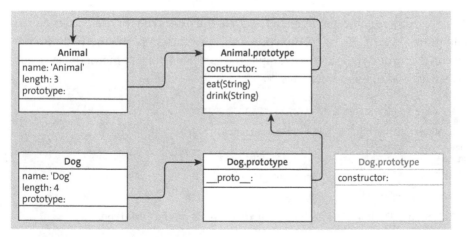

Figure 13.9 Step 4: Redefining the Dog Prototype

Here you can also see that the new `Dog.prototype` object has no `constructor` property compared to the "old" `Dog.prototype` object and thus there is no connection to the `Dog` object. This is corrected in step 5 (see Figure 13.10).

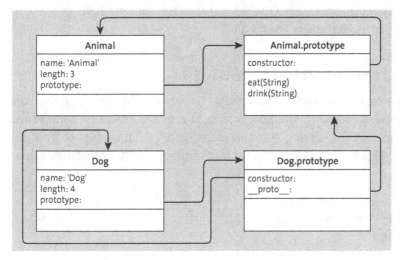

Figure 13.10 Step 5: Linking Prototype to Constructor Function

Finally, you define the methods of the "subclass"—that is, the methods on the `Dog.prototype` object (step 6 and Figure 13.11). Here it's important to add properties and methods only after `Dog.prototype` has been redefined (see step 4); otherwise, they would be defined on the old `Dog.prototype` object and thus lost.

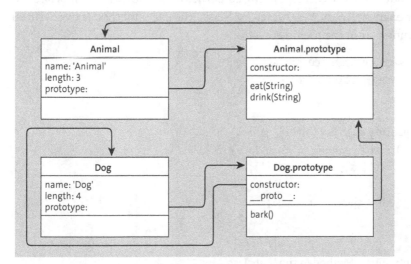

Figure 13.11 Step 6: Defining the bark() Method on the Prototype

Figure 13.11 thus also shows the final state of the objects: Dog and Animal as constructor functions (or "classes") that can be used to create new object instances based on the Dog.prototype and Animal.prototype prototypes.

As you'll see ahead, techniques such as calling constructors and methods of a "superclass" are also easy to understand based on this.

13.3.5   Calling the Constructor of the "Superclass"

To call the constructor of a "superclass," you simply need to call the corresponding constructor function using the call() method, passing this as the execution context and optionally other parameters. Listing 13.12 shows the corresponding snippet from the previous listing, calling the Animal constructor function from the Dog constructor function.

```
function Dog(name, color, age, type) {
  Animal.call(this, name, color, age);
  this.type = type;
};
```

Listing 13.12 Calling the Constructor of the "Superclass"

13.3.6   Overwriting Methods

To overwrite a method in a "subclass," you simply define the corresponding method at the prototype underlying the corresponding constructor function of the "subclass." In Listing 13.13, for example, in the VegetarianDog "class," the eat() method is overwritten with the logic known from the previous sections.

```
function VegetarianDog(name, color, age, type) {
  Dog.call(this, name, color, age);
  this.type = type;
};
VegetarianDog.prototype.eat = function(food) {
  if(food.indexOf('meat') >= 0 || food.indexOf('meat') >= 0) {
    throw new Error('I don't eat meat!');
  } else {
    console.log('Chow chow, ' + food);
  }
}
```

Listing 13.13 Overwriting a Method in the "Subclass"

13.3.7   Calling Methods of the "Superclass"

The call of a method of the "superclass" works like the call of constructors using the call() method. In Listing 13.14, for example, the eat() method of the Animal "class" is called in the eat() method of the VegetarianDog "class".

```
function VegetarianDog(name, color, age, type) {
  Dog.call(this, name, color, age);
  this.type = type;
};
VegetarianDog.prototype.eat = function(food) {
  if(food.indexOf('meat') >= 0 || food.indexOf('meat') >= 0) {
    throw new Error('I don't eat meat!');
  } else {
    Dog.prototype.eat.call(this, food);
  }
}
const vegetarianDog = new VegetarianDog('Bella', 'White', 2, 'Maltese');
vegetarianDog.eat('bread');
```

Listing 13.14 Calling a Method of the "Superclass"

13.3.8   Pseudoclassical Object Orientation and the Principles of Object Orientation

Abstraction of behavior is given by the constructor functions and the prototype underlying them. Inheritance can also be implemented in pseudoclassical object orientation, but it's comparatively complex. Regarding data encapsulation and polymorphism, the same applies as for prototypical object orientation.

13.4   Object Orientation with Class Syntax

Since ES2015, a new class syntax has also found its way into the ECMAScript standard. As mentioned earlier, this class syntax doesn't allow for true class-based programming, but it feels relatively similar due to the keywords and syntax used, among other things. Actually, however, the class syntax only takes away some of the complexity of the pseudoclassical object orientation, because objects and prototypes are still working in the background.

> **Note**
> Developers who come from a language like Java feel especially at home with class syntax. Nevertheless, as a JavaScript developer, it's important for you to have understood and mastered the concepts that actually underlie the JavaScript language, such as prototypical object orientation.

13.4.1   Defining Classes

To define a "class" in JavaScript, you use the class keyword as shown in Listing 13.15 (*class declaration*). After this keyword, you write the name of the class followed by a pair of braces defining the body of the class (the *class body*). Within this class body, the properties and methods of the class can then be defined (but note that properties can only be defined in this way with ES2022).

```
class Animal {

  name = 'John Sample Fish';
  color = 'Gold';
  age = '25';

  constructor(name, color, age) {
    this.name = name ? name : this.name;
    this.color = color ? color : this.color;
    this.age = age ? age : this.age;
  }

  eat(food) {
    console.log(`Chow chow, ${food}`);
  }

  drink(drink) {
    console.log(`Mmmmmmh, ${drink}`);
  }

  toString() {
    return `${this.name}, ${this.color}, ${this.age}`;
  }

}
```

Listing 13.15 Example of a Class

Class Expressions

Besides class declarations, you still have the option to define classes via *class expressions*. The class is assigned to a variable and can later only be referenced via this variable name (see Listing 13.16). The class name after the `class` keyword is optional and applies only within the class itself.

```
const AnimalClass = class Animal {

  name = 'John Sample Fish';
  color = 'Gold';
  age = '25';

  constructor(name, color, age) {
    this.name = name ? name : this.name;
    this.color = color ? color : this.color;
    this.age = age ? age : this.age;
  }

  eat(food) {
    console.log(`Chow chow, ${food}`);
  }

  drink(drink) {
    console.log(`Mmmmmmh, ${drink}`);
  }

  toString() {
    return `${this.name}, ${this.color}, ${this.age}`;
  }

}
```

Listing 13.16 Use of Class Expressions

The `constructor()` method has a special role in classes because this method is always called when a new object instance of the "class" is created (more on this in the next section). In principle, this corresponds roughly to a constructor function: `constructor()` implicitly returns a new object instance. Within the `constructor()` method (and also other methods like in the `toString()` example) you can access this object instance via the `this` keyword. In the example, the `name`, `color`, and `age` properties are overwritten with the passed constructor parameters within the `constructor()` method. The ternary operator ensures that the respective property is only overwritten if the respective parameter also contains a value.

13

13.4.2   Creating Object Instances

To create an object instance of a "class," use the new keyword, as you know from constructor functions and as shown in Listing 13.17. The first call of new Animal() here ensures that a new instance of Animal is created, whose name property has the default value John Sample Fish, color property has the value Gold, and age property has the value 25 (because no parameters were passed to the constructor). The second call of the constructor, on the other hand, creates an object instance in which the properties receive the values passed as constructor parameters.

```
const defaultAnimal = new Animal();
console.log(defaultAnimal.toString()); // "John Sample Fish, gold, 25"


const fish = new Animal('Fishy', 'Green', 2);
fish.eat('Algen');                      // "Chow chow, algae"
console.log(fish.toString());           // "Fishy, Green, 2"
```

Listing 13.17 Creating an Object Instance and Calling an Object Method Using "Classes"

13.4.3   Defining Getters and Setters

In Chapter 4, you learned that you can use the get and set keywords to define getter and setter methods on objects. You can also use the same keywords in combination with "classes" to define getters and setters there. An example of this is shown in Listing 13.18. The two keywords are written as usual in front of the name of the respective method.

It should also be noted that the name of the respective getter or setter method is not the same as the corresponding property, in order to prevent an endless recursion, an associated stack overflow, and thus the crash of the respective program. One option here is to prefix the property name with an underscore (_name, _color, _age) as shown in Listing 13.18.

```
class Animal {

  _name = 'John Sample Fish';
  _color = 'Gold';
  _age = '25';
```

```
constructor(name, color, age) {
  this._name = name ? name : this._name;
  this._color = color ? color : this._color;
  this._age = age ? age : this._age;
}

get name() {
  return this._name;
}

set name(name) {
  this._name = name;
}

get color() {
  return this._color;
}

set color(color) {
  this._color = color;
}

get age() {
  return this._age;
}

set age(age) {
  this._age = age;
}

eat(food) {
  console.log(`Chow chow, ${food}`);
}

drink(drink) {
  console.log(`Mmmmmmh, ${drink}`);
}

toString() {
  return `${this._name}, ${this._color}, ${this._age}`;
}

}
```

```
const snake = new Animal('Hissy', 'Green', 5);
console.log(snake.name);  // "Hissy"
console.log(snake.color); // "Green"
console.log(snake.age);    // 5
```

Listing 13.18 Definition of Getters and Setters

13.4.4   Defining Private Properties and Private Methods

Prefixing a property with an underscore is, of course, just a convention to indicate that the property is private. The underscore in itself doesn't prevent the property from being accessed or overwritten from outside (i.e., from outside the object). Listing 13.19 makes this clear: the code shown is an extension of the previous listing and shows that the three "private" properties (_name, _color, _age) can be easily overwritten with new values.

```
class Animal {

  _name = 'John Sample Fish';
  _color = 'Gold';
  _age = '25';

  constructor(name, color, age) {
    this._name = name ? name : this._name;
    this._color = color ? color : this._color;
    this._age = age ? age : this._age;
  }

  // Setter and getter methods as usual

  eat(food) {
    console.log(`Chow chow, ${food}`);
  }

  drink(drink) {
    console.log(`Mmmmmmh, ${drink}`);
  }

  toString() {
    return `${this._name}, ${this._color}, ${this._age}`;
  }

}
```

```
const snake = new Animal('Hissy', 'Green', 5);
console.log(snake.name);  // "Hissy"
console.log(snake.color); // "Green"
console.log(snake.age);    // 5

snake._name = 4711;
snake._color = 'hello world';
snake._age = 'twenty';

console.log(snake.name);  // 4711
console.log(snake.color); // "hello world"
console.log(snake.age);    // "twenty"
```

Listing 13.19 Overwriting the Object Properties from the Outside Is Not Prevented Here

With ES2022, JavaScript introduces true private properties (and private methods). However, the syntax for this takes some getting used to. Instead of an intuitive keyword such as private (as is available in Java), in JavaScript private properties are marked by a # sign prefixed to the name of the respective property. Private properties can be accessed only in the initialization part of the object properties, in the constructor, and in object methods, as shown in Listing 13.20. Accessing private properties from outside, on the other hand, results in a SyntaxError.

```
class Animal {

  #name = 'John Sample Fish';
  #color = 'Gold';
  #age = '25';

  constructor(name, color, age) {
    this.#name = name ? name : this.#name;
    this.#color = color ? color : this.#color;
    this.#age = age ? age : this.#age;
  }

  get name() {
    return this.#name;
  }

  set name(name) {
    this.#name = name;
  }

  get color() {
    return this.#color;
```

```
    }

    set color(color) {
      this.#color = color;
    }

    get age() {
      return this.#age;
    }

    set age(age) {
      this.#age = age;
    }

    eat(food) {
      console.log(`Chow chow, ${food}`);
    }

    drink(drink) {
      console.log(`Mmmmmmh, ${drink}`);
    }

    toString() {
      return `${this.#name}, ${this.#color}, ${this.#age}`;
    }

}

const snake = new Animal('Hissy', 'Green', 5);
console.log(snake.name);  // "Hissy"
console.log(snake.color); // "Green"
console.log(snake.age);   // 5

// snake.#name = 4711;            // SyntaxError
// snake.#color = 'hello world';  // SyntaxError
// snake.#age = 'twenty';         // SyntaxError
```

Listing 13.20 Private Properties Cannot Be Accessed or Overwritten from the Outside

In the same way that you can define private properties, you can mark private methods as such. That is, you simply prefix the name of the method with a # character (see Listing 13.21). With regard to access, the same applies as for private properties: only constructors and other object methods can access private methods.

```
class Animal {

  #name = 'John Sample Fish';
  #color = 'Gold';
  #age = '25';

  constructor(name, color, age) {
    this.#name = name ? name : this._name;
    this.#color = color ? color : this._color;
    this.#age = age ? age : this._age;
  }

  // Setter and getter methods as usual

  #eat(food) {
    console.log(`Chow chow, ${food}`);
  }

  #drink(drink) {
    console.log(`Mmmmmmh, ${drink}`);
  }

  toString() {
    return `${this.#name}, ${this.#color}, ${this.#age}`;
  }

}

const snake = new Animal('Hissy', 'Green', 5);
// snake.#eat('bird'); // SyntaxError
// snake.#drink('water'); // SyntaxError
```

Listing 13.21 Private Methods Cannot Be Called (or Overwritten) from Outside

13.4.5   Deriving from "Classes"

Using the extends keyword, it's possible for one "class" to inherit or derive from another "class." As shown in Listing 13.22, the keyword is simply written after the (new) "class" to inherit; the keyword is then followed by the name of the "class" to inherit from. If you create an instance of the "subclass" as in Listing 13.22, it has all the methods defined in the "superclass" and the methods defined in the "subclass."

```
...
class Dog extends Animal {
```

```
  _type;

  constructor(name, color, age, type) {
    super(name, color, age);
    this._type = type ? type : this._type;
  }

  get type() {
    return this._type;
  }

  set type(type) {
    this._type = type;
  }

  bark() {
    console.log('Woof woof');
  }
}

const dog = new Dog('Bello', 'White', 2, 'Maltese');
dog.eat('cheese');      // "Chow chow, cheese"
dog.bark();             // "Woof woof"
console.log(dog.type); // "Maltese"
```

Listing 13.22 Example of a Deriving Class

Inside the constructor of the deriving "class," the constructor of the "superclass" (the *parent constructor*) can be called via super(). By the way, it's very important to do this before you access this inside the constructor. Otherwise, an error will occur (more precisely, a ReferenceError), as shown in Listing 13.23.

```
...
class Dog extends Animal {

  _type;

  constructor(name, color, age, type) {
    this._type = type ? type : this._type;    // Error: this is not defined!
    super(name, color, age);
  }

  get type() {
    return this._type;
  }
```

```
  set type(type) {
    this._type = type;
  }

  bark() {
    console.log('Woof woof');
  }
}

const dog = new Dog('Bello', 'White', 2, 'Maltese'); // Error!
dog.eat('cheese');
dog.bark();
console.log(dog.type);
```

Listing 13.23 The Constructor of the "Superclass" Must Be Called before Accessing This

The same is true if you omit the call to the parent constructor altogether within a constructor. Accordingly, Listing 13.24 would also result in an error.

```
...
class Dog extends Animal {

  _type;

  constructor(name, color, age, type) {
    // error, because no call of parent constructor
  }

  get type() {
    return this._type;
  }

  set type(type) {
    this._type = type;
  }

  bark() {
    console.log('Woof woof');
  }
}

const dog = new Dog('Bello', 'White', 2, 'Maltese'); // Error!
```

```
dog.eat('cheese');
dog.bark();
console.log(dog.type);
```

Listing 13.24 The Call of the Parent Constructor Must Not Be Omitted

However, it's possible to omit the constructor of a "class"—that is, the constructor()
method—altogether. In this case, a constructor is implicitly used internally, which
passes all parameters to the parent constructor (see Listing 13.25). In the example, however, this ensures that the _type property is not initialized (because this had previously
happened in the constructor of the Dog class) and therefore retains the value undefined.

```
...
class Dog extends Animal {

  _type;

  // The following constructor is used implicitly:
  // constructor(...args) {
  //   super(...args);
  // }

  get type() {
    return this._type;
  }

  set type(type) {
    this._type = type;
  }

  bark() {
    console.log('Woof woof');
  }
}

const dog = new Dog('Bello', 'White', 2, 'Maltese');
dog.eat('cheese');      // "Chow chow, cheese"
dog.bark();             // "Woof woof"
console.log(dog.type); // undefined
```

Listing 13.25 The Constructor Can Optionally Be Omitted Altogether

Class Syntax Creates Same Structure as Pseudoclassical Object Orientation

The structure generated internally by the Animal (see Listing 13.18) and Dog (see Listing 13.22) "classes" corresponds exactly to the structure generated by the comparable pseudoclassical object orientation (see Figure 13.11).

Deriving from Standard Classes

Since ES2015, it's also possible to derive from standard objects like Error and Array. In Listing 13.26, for example, the InvalidValueError "class" is created as a "subclass" of Error: it calls the parent constructor with a specific error message and also remembers the invalid value in the value property.

```
class InvalidValueError extends Error {
  constructor(value) {
    super(`Invalid value: ${value}`);
    this.value = value;
  }

  get value() {
    return this._value;
  }

  set value(value) {
    this._value = value;
  }
}

throw new InvalidValueError(5);
```

Listing 13.26 Standard Objects Like Error Also Can Be Derived

13.4.6 Overwriting Methods

To overwrite a method in a "subclass," you simply define a corresponding method with the same name as the method to be overwritten. An example of this can be found in Listing 13.27, Listing 13.28, and Listing 13.29 . As in the examples for the other types of object orientation, the goal is to create a new VegetarianDog class that derives from Dog and overrides the eat() method.

To make the example a bit more object-oriented and to change the eat() method to expect an object instance instead of a string as the parameter, you first create a simple class hierarchy for food (see Listing 13.27). This consists of the Food "base class" and the two Meat and Bread "subclasses." As a parameter, the constructor expects a description of the respective food in the form of a string. The toString() method, which returns only this description, also ensures that the console output of the eat() method of the Animal "class" doesn't need to be adjusted and continues to produce decent output.

```
class Food {

  _description

  constructor(description) {
    this._description = description ? description : this._description;
  }

  get description() {
    return this._description;
  }

  set description(description) {
    this._description = description;
  }

  toString() {
    return this.description;
  }

}
class Meat extends Food {}

class Bread extends Food {}

const bread = new Bread('wheat bread');
console.log(bread.description);        // "wheat bread"
const meat = new Meat('steak');
console.log(meat.description);         // "steak"
```

Listing 13.27 A Simple Object Model for Food

Listing 13.28 then shows the VegetarianDog "class." Now, within the eat() method (as in the examples with the other types of object orientation), whether the value Meat or meat is contained in a string isn't checked; only whether the passed argument is an instance of the Meat "class" is checked. If this is the case, an error is thrown; otherwise, appropriate output is generated.

```
class VegetarianDog extends Dog {

  eat(food) {
```

```
    if (food instanceof Meat) {
      throw new Error('I don't eat meat!');
    } else {
      console.log(`Chow chow, ${food.description}!`);
    }
  }
}
```

Listing 13.28 Overwriting a Method

Subsequently, the method can be called as shown in Listing 13.29, passing instances of Food (or its "subclasses") in each case.

```
const dog = new VegetarianDog('Bello', 'White', 2, 'Maltese');
dog.eat(new Bread('wheat bread')); // "Chow, chow, wheat bread!"
dog.eat(new Meat('steak'));        // Error: "I don't eat meat!"
```

Listing 13.29 Calling the Overwritten Method

> **Note**
> The structure shown here, which uses a separate "class" to represent food, corresponds to the object-oriented idea more than the use of a string and the search for specific values within that string.

13.4.7 Calling Methods of the "Superclass"

If you want to call another method of the same "class" within a method, you can do this by using the this keyword. If, on the other hand, you want to specifically call a method of the "superclass" within a method, you use the super keyword, which is a reference to the "superclass," so to speak. Referring to the previous example, you could, for example, reuse the eat() method of the Animal "superclass" in the VegetarianDog "class" precisely for the case in which the food passed to the method is not meat. Listing 13.30 shows how this works.

```
class VegetarianDog extends Dog {

  eat(food) {
    if (food instanceof Meat) {
      throw new Error('I don't eat meat!');
    } else {
      super.eat(food);
    }
```

```
    }

}

const dog = new VegetarianDog('Bello', 'White', 2, 'Maltese');
dog.eat(new Bread('wheat bread')); // "Chow, Chow, wheat bread!"
dog.eat(new Meat('steak'));        // Error: "I don't eat meat!"
```

Listing 13.30 Calling the Method of the "Superclass"

Avoiding Duplicate Code

The advantage of this type of reuse is that duplicate code is avoided. For example, if the output is to be changed within the eat() method, this only has to be done in one place—namely, in the Animal "class." But if you leave the code as it is in Listing 13.28, the output would also have to be adapted in the eat() method of the VegetarianDog "class."

Access to Methods of the "Superclass"

You can also access methods of the "superclass" via this, but only if the respective method doesn't exist in the "subclass". If the respective method does exist in the "subclass," it's used when accessing via this.

13.4.8   Defining Static Methods

In object-oriented programming, *static methods* are methods that are called directly on the class and not on an object instance. Static methods are always suitable if you want to use them to provide functionality that belongs thematically to the respective class but doesn't necessarily require an object instance. In the JavaScript class syntax, you define a method as static by prefixing it with the static keyword. Subsequently, the method can be called directly via the "class." In Listing 13.31, for example, the static get-AnimalColors() method is defined, which returns an object with predefined color values. The method can only be called on the Animal "class," not on its object instances.

```
class Animal {

  _name = 'John Sample Fish';
  _color = 'Gold';
  _age = '25';

  constructor(name, color, age) {
    this._name = name ? name : this._name;
```

```
    this._color = color ? color : this._color;
    this._age = age ? age : this._age;
  }

  static getAnimalColors() {
    return {
      WHITE: 'White',
      BLACK: 'Black',
      BROWN: 'Brown',
      GREEN: 'Green',
      YELLOW: 'Yellow',
      ORANGE: 'Orange'
    }
  }

  ...

}

console.log(Animal.getAnimalColors());
// {
//    WHITE: 'White',
//    BLACK: 'Black',
//    BROWN: 'Brown',
//    GREEN: 'Green',
//    YELLOW: 'Yellow',
//    ORANGE: 'Orange'
// }
const bird = new Animal('Birdie', Animal.getAnimalColors().BLACK, 5);
console.log(bird.name);  // "Birdie"
console.log(bird.color); // "Black"
console.log(bird.age);    // 5
// console.log(bird.getAnimalColors()); // error because method is static
```

Listing 13.31 Definition and Call of a Static Method

Static Methods Are Methods on the Function Object
Because the class syntax including the static keyword is ultimately only a syntactic refinement of the pseudoclassical object orientation, static methods are actually methods that are defined on the respective function object of the constructor function, and static properties are actually properties of the function object.

13.4.9   Defining Static Properties

In addition to static methods, object orientation also includes the concept of *static properties*. Analogous to static methods, static properties are defined directly on a class, and you don't need an object instance to access those properties. In Listing 13.32, a static ANIMAL_COLORS property is added to the Animal class.

```
class Animal {

  _name = 'John Sample Fish';
  _color = 'Gold';
  _age = '25';

  static ANIMAL_COLORS = {
    WHITE: 'White',
    BLACK: 'Black',
    BROWN: 'Brown',
    GREEN: 'Green',
    YELLOW: 'Yellow',
    ORANGE: 'Orange'
  }

  constructor(name, color, age) {
    this._name = name ? name : this._name;
    this._color = color ? color : this._color;
    this._age = age ? age : this._age;
  }

  ...

}

console.log(Animal.ANIMAL_COLORS);
// {
//    WHITE: 'White',
//    BLACK: 'Black',
//    BROWN: 'Brown',
//    GREEN: 'Green',
//    YELLOW: 'Yellow',
//    ORANGE: 'Orange'
// }
const bird = new Animal('Birdie', Animal.ANIMAL_COLORS.BLACK, 5);
console.log(bird.name);  // "Birdie"
console.log(bird.color); // "Black"
```

```
console.log(bird.age);    // 5
// console.log(bird.ANIMAL_COLORS); // undefined
```

Listing 13.32 Definition of a Static Property with Keyword

Note

The option to explicitly define static properties within the class body is still relatively new (ES2022) and isn't yet supported by all browsers or runtime environments as of the time of writing (June 2021; a good place to find out if a feature is supported or not is the website at *https://kangax.github.io/compat-table/es2016plus*). As an alternative to using the static keyword, however, you can also "emulate" static properties by defining them as properties of the "class" outside of the class syntax, as shown in Listing 13.33.

```
Animal.ANIMAL_COLORS = {
  WHITE: 'White',
  BLACK: 'Black',
  BROWN: 'Brown',
  GREEN: 'Green',
  YELLOW: 'Yellow',
  ORANGE: 'Orange'
}
console.log(Animal.ANIMAL_COLORS);
// {
//    WHITE: 'White',
//    BLACK: 'Black',
//    BROWN: 'Brown',
//    GREEN: 'Green',
//    YELLOW: 'Yellow',
//    ORANGE: 'Orange'
// }
const bird = new Animal('Birdie', Animal.ANIMAL_COLORS.BLACK, 5);
console.log(bird.name);  // "Birdie"
console.log(bird.color); // "Black"
console.log(bird.age);    // 5
// console.log(bird.ANIMAL_COLORS); // undefined
```

Listing 13.33 Definition and Call of a Static Property without Keyword

---

13.4.10   Class Syntax and the Principles of Object Orientation

Because the class syntax is a simplification of the pseudoclassical object orientation, similar things apply here as there, but the implementation is easier for developers:

instead of constructor functions, abstract behavior is grouped into "classes" here, so that object instances of the respective "class" inherit the behavior.

Defining inheritance relationships via the extends keyword is also easier than with pseudoclassical object orientation. For the encapsulation of data, however, there are no special native ways of restricting the visibility of properties and methods, for example, apart from the options mentioned thus far for prototypical and pseudoclassical object orientation. For polymorphism, the same applies as for the other types of object orientation.

13.5   Summary

This chapter introduced object orientation in general and object-oriented programming in JavaScript in particular. You should take away the following points from this chapter:

- Object-oriented programming is based on the following four principles (among others):
  - **Abstraction**
    Abstract behavior of objects is summarized in classes or prototypes.
  - **Data encapsulation**
    Properties and methods are encapsulated in the form of classes or prototypes and hidden from external access.
  - **Inheritance**
    Properties and methods can be inherited from one class to another class or from one object to another object.
  - **Polymorphism**
    Objects can take on different types depending on their use.
- In JavaScript, there are several types of object-oriented programming:
  - **Prototypical object orientation**
    This is the type of object orientation that is most natural in the JavaScript language. In this process, objects are created based on other objects. These other objects are then also referred to as *prototypes*.
  - **Pseudoclassical object orientation**
    This is a type of object orientation in which you pretend that JavaScript is a class-based programming language. *Constructor functions* are used here. Overall, it's quite elaborate for developers to program according to this approach.
  - **Object orientation with class syntax**
    This type of object orientation represents a syntactic simplification of the pseudoclassical object orientation. "Classes" can be defined using the class keyword and inheritance relationships using the extends keyword. In addition, static methods are defined using the static keyword.

Chapter 14
Functional Programming

Besides object-oriented programming, introduced in the previous chapter, functional programming is another important programming paradigm that plays a central role in JavaScript. In this chapter, we briefly present various functional concepts. More complex topics are beyond the scope of this book.

JavaScript is a programming language that contains concepts from object-oriented programming (as you saw in the previous chapter) and concepts from functional programming. But what does functional programming mean, anyway? What's the difference between it and object-oriented programming? We'll answer these and other questions in this chapter and also show you how to program functionally with JavaScript.

14

14.1 Principles of Functional Programming

Functional programming, like other programming paradigms, follows different principles or has special characteristics. These are essentially as follows:

- **Principle 1: Functions are first-class objects**
  Functions are *first-class objects* (also referred to as *first-class citizens*). You saw what this means in Chapter 4: functions can be assigned to variables like other objects and primitive values, and they can be used as arguments of other functions or as their return value. In nonfunctional programming languages, however, functions are not represented as objects and consequently can't be treated as such.

- **Principle 2: Functions work with immutable data structures**
  Data structures in functional programming are usually unchangeable or are not changed. Rather, operations performed on data structures create new data structures if necessary and return them as results. In *purely functional programming languages*, for example, once lists or other data structures have been created, they cannot be changed later (or only in a roundabout way). By the way, JavaScript is not a *purely* functional programming language, which is why arrays can be changed here at any time.

- **Principle 3: Functions have no side effects**

  Taking the previous point a bit further, there is also the fact that in functional programming the functions usually have *no side effects* at all and behave more like mathematical functions. This means that functions in functional programming always return the same result for the same input but do not trigger any side effects. In purely functional languages, side effects are already prevented by the language itself. JavaScript, as a programming language that isn't purely functional, does allow functions to return different results for the same input.

- **Principle 4: Functional programs are declarative**

  Imperative programming is a programming paradigm in which you give the computer very precise individual instructions on *how* to solve a problem. Imperative programs use explicit loop statements (`while` loops, `for` loops, etc.), conditional statements (`if-else`), and sequences of these (so far in this book, we've always programmed imperatively within functions).

  Functional programs, on the other hand, are *declarative*, meaning that you, as the developer, formulate your program more to say *what* should be done. As a result, functional programs are usually more readable, more meaningful, and more compact than the equivalent imperative code. In Section 14.2, we'll demonstrate this with some examples.

Figure 14.1 shows how to classify the functional programming paradigm.

Unlike *object-oriented programming*, functional programming focuses on functions, not objects. JavaScript combines the two programming paradigms. For example, you can structure your program in an object-oriented manner—that is, work with objects—and then program functionally in turn within object methods.

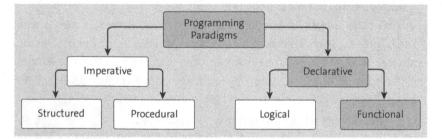

Figure 14.1 Principles of Functional Programming

Note

Functional programs are usually leaner than the equivalent variant in object-oriented or imperative programming.

> **Functional Programming Languages**
>
> Examples of (almost) purely functional programming languages include Haskell, Lisp, and Miranda. JavaScript is, as already mentioned, not a purely functional programming language. For example, data structures such as arrays can be modified even after they have been defined, whereas in Haskell, for example, this is not allowed.

14.2   Imperative Programming and Functional Programming

In this section, we'll show you the advantages of functional programming compared to imperative programming. To do this, we'll introduce four methods available to arrays in JavaScript:

- The `forEach()` method for iterating over arrays (which we discussed in Chapter 4)
- The `map()` method for mapping elements of one array to new elements in another array
- The `filter()` method for filtering elements in an array
- The `reduce()` method for reducing the elements of an array to a single value

14.2.1   Iterating with the forEach() Method

If you want to iterate via an array or a list, you have several (imperative) options, which you've already learned about in this book (for example, in Chapter 3):

- Via a `for` loop
- Via a `while` loop
- Via a `do-while` loop
- Via a `for-in` loop
- Via a `for-of` loop

Listing 14.1 shows again for repetition how the elements of an array can be output using a `for` loop. The array that's iterated over here contains various objects, which in turn contain information about various artists (the artist's name and their published albums).

The source code in Listing 14.1 is only supposed to output each value of the array. This is *what* is supposed to happen. However, the code is actually far too concerned with *how* the whole thing is supposed to work: initialize counter variable, check termination condition, index-based access to the array, and then increment the counter variable.

As you can see, imperative programs contain a lot of extra code (*boilerplate code*), which doesn't make the program very readable, but rather unnecessarily bloats it.

Surely, as a developer, you'll eventually have an eye for such imperative control structures, and in simple cases you'll know right away what a for loop does in a specific case.
In practice, however, it isn't always as simple as in the example shown: often loops are
nested, and within the loops you can find conditional statements, branches, and so on,
so you can quickly lose the overview.

```
const artists = [
  {
    name: 'Kyuss',
    albums: [
      {
        title: 'Wretch',
        year: 1991
      },
      {
        title: 'Blues for the Red Sun',
        year: 1992
      },
      {
        title: 'Welcome to Sky Valley',
        year: 1994
      },
      {
        title: '...And the Circus Leaves Town',
        year: 1995
      }
    ]
  },
  {
    name: 'Ben Harper',
    albums: [
      {
        title: 'The Will to Live',
        year: 1997
      },
      {
        title: 'Burn to Shine',
        year: 1999
      },
      {
        title: 'Live from Mars',
        year: 2001
      },
      {
```

```
      title: 'Diamonds on the Inside',
      year: 2003
    }
  ]
  }
];
for(let i=0; i<artists.length; i++) {
  console.log(artists[i].name);
}
```

Listing 14.1 Imperative Iteration with a Normal for Loop

Using functional programming, problems can often be formulated in a much more readable way. For the given problem, for example, the forEach() method is much more suitable, as you can see in Listing 14.2. As an argument, you pass a function (*callback function*) to it, which is then called in turn for each element in the array with three arguments: the element, the index of the element, and the array itself.

```
artists.forEach(
  (                       // function called for each element
    artist,               // (1) current element
    index,                // (2) Index of the current element
    artists               // (3) the entire array
  ) => {
    console.log(artist.name);
  }
);
```

Listing 14.2 Functional Iteration Using the forEach() Method

And even though the code isn't necessarily shorter in terms of the number of lines (on the contrary, it's longer, but that's just because of the formatting), it's already a lot more readable. In contrast to the imperative variant, the focus is now on the logic of the program (the what), not on the loop itself (the how). If you leave out all the comments in Listing 14.2 and adjust the formatting a bit, it becomes even clearer, as shown in Listing 14.3.

```
artists.forEach((artist, index, artists) => {
  console.log(artist.name);
});
```

Listing 14.3 Without the Comments and with Adjusted Formatting, the Example Is Even More Readable

If you pass a named function instead of an anonymous function, as in Listing 14.4, the program can be read almost like natural language ("artists for each print name").

```
function printName(artist, index, artists) {
  console.log(artist.name);
}
artists.forEach(printName);
```

Listing 14.4 Named Functions Instead of Anonymous Functions Increase Readability Even More

> **Note**
>
> Using the forEach() method, you can iterate over the elements of an array with relative ease. Compared to imperative code variants such as the for loop, the code is thus easier to read.

14.2.2   Mapping Values with the map() Method

It's often the case that you not only want to iterate over the elements of an array, but also simultaneously determine a value for each element and store this in another array—for example, to calculate the square for each number for an array of natural numbers or (less boring) to read a property from each object for an array of objects and copy the corresponding value into a new array.

Let's take the object model from Listing 14.1 as an example. Suppose that from the array of artist objects shown there, the names of the artists should be copied into a new array. In imperative fashion, you would probably solve this problem as shown in Listing 14.5.

```
const artistNames = [];
for(let i=0; i<artists.length; i++) {
  artistNames.push(artists[i].name);
}
console.log(artistNames);  // ['Kyuss', 'Ben Harper']
```

Listing 14.5 Imperative Mapping with a Normal for Loop

As in the example from the previous section, the for loop takes up a large part of the code here, even though it's only a means to an end. With the map() method, on the other hand, the code becomes much more meaningful (see Listing 14.6). As an argument, this method expects a function, which is then called for each element in the array. The return value of this function determines the value to be written to the target array for the respective element.

```
const artistNames = artists.map(
  (                      // function called for each element
    artist,              // (1) current element
    index,               // (2) Index of the current element
```

```
  artists               // (3) the entire array
) => {
  return artist.name;   // Return value determines the
                        // new value in the result array.
}
);
console.log(artistNames);  // ['Kyuss', 'Ben Harper']
```

Listing 14.6 Functional Mapping Using the map() Method

> **Note**
>
> Using the map() method, you can create a new array relatively based on an array, call-
> ing the specified mapping function for each element in the source array and taking its
> return value to the destination array.

14.2.3   Filtering Values with the filter() Method

In Chapter 4, you learned how to search for elements in an array using the indexOf()
and lastIndexOf() methods. Remember: these methods determine the index of an element passed to them if it occurs in the array, or return the value -1 if the element
passed doesn't occur in the array.

But you can be much more flexible with the filter() method. As an example, let's take
an array that contains various objects, each representing a music album. Starting from
this array, all albums released before the turn of the millennium are to be filtered out.

> **Note**
>
> For didactic reasons, the object model in Listing 14.7 is structured in a slightly different
> way than in the preceding examples.

```
const albums = [
  {
    title: 'Push the Sky Away',
    artist: 'Nick Cave',
    year: 2013
  },
  {
    title: 'No more shall we part',
    artist: 'Nick Cave',
    year: 2001
  },
  {
```

```
    title: 'Live from Mars',
    artist: 'Ben Harper',
    year: 2003
  },
  {
    title: 'The Will to Live',
    artist: 'Ben Harper',
    year: 1997
  }
];
```

Listing 14.7 A Simple Object Model That Is to Be Used as a Basis for Filtering

Imperatively, you would probably implement this task as shown in Listing 14.8 using a for loop. For each album object in the array, it's checked here within the loop whether the value for the year of publication (year property) is smaller than 2000. If so, the element is added to the albumsBefore2000 result array.

```
const albumsBefore2000 = [];
for(let i=0, i<albums.length; i++) {          // For all albums:
  if(albums[i].year < 2000) {                 // Check if published before 2000.
    albumsBefore2000.push(albums[i]);         // If yes, include in result.
  }
}
console.log(albumsBefore2000.length);         // 1
```

Listing 14.8 Filtering Specific Elements of an Array with Imperative Programming

With the mentioned filter() method, this is much easier. As with forEach() and map(), the argument is a function that is called for each element in the array. Its return value determines in this case whether an element is transferred to the new array. If the function returns true, the corresponding element is included in the new array; otherwise, it is not. Inside the callback function, you again have access to the current element and its index, as well as to the whole array.

```
const albumsBefore2000 = albums.filter(  // The filter() method expects ...
  (                                      // ... a callback function.
    album,                               // (1) the respective element
    index,                               // (2) the index of the element in the array
    albums                               // (3) the entire array
  ) =>
  {                                      // The method returns only the albums ...
    return album.year < 2000;            // ... that were released before 2000.
```

```
  }
);
console.log(albumsBefore2000.length);    // 1
```

Listing 14.9 Functional Filtering Using the filter() Method

Note

You can use the `filter()` method to filter out elements from an array based on a filter function. The method returns an array containing all elements for which the filter function returns `true`.

14.2.4   Reducing Multiple Values to One Value with the reduce() Method

Another one of the "functional methods" for arrays is the `reduce()` method. This method is used to determine a single representative value based on the elements of an array—that is, to *reduce* the elements of an array to a single value.

To illustrate this method, let's assume that based on the object model in Listing 14.10, the number of all albums (not per artist, but in total) is to be determined.

```
const artists = [
  {
    name: 'Kyuss',
    albums: [
      {
        title: 'Wretch',
        year: 1991
      },
      {
        title: 'Blues for the Red Sun',
        year: 1992
      },
      {
        title: 'Welcome to Sky Valley',
        year: 1994
      },
      {
        title: '...And the Circus Leaves Town',
        year: 1995
      }
    ]
  },
  {
    name: 'Ben Harper',
```

14

```
  albums: [
    {
      title: 'The Will to Live',
      year: 1997
    },
    {
      title: 'Burn to Shine',
      year: 1999
    },
    {
      title: 'Live from Mars',
      year: 2001
    },
    {
      title: 'Diamonds on the Inside',
      year: 2003
    }
  ]
  }
];
```

Listing 14.10 A Simple Object Model to Be Used as a Basis for Reduction

In an imperative way, this problem would probably be solved as shown in Listing 14.11 via a *for* loop (which, by the way, should hopefully be getting on your nerves by now).

```
let totalAlbumCount = 0;                        // Number of all albums
for(let i=0, i<artists.length; i++) {           // For all artists:
  const albumCount = artists[i].albums.length;  // Get the number of ...
                                                // ... of albums ...
  totalAlbumCount += albumCount;                // ... and increase the ...
                                                // ... total number.
}
console.log(totalAlbumCount);                   // 8
```

Listing 14.11 Imperative Variant for Determining the Total Number of Music Albums

Via the reduce() method, this is easier again. As an argument, you pass a function (you know the principle by now), which is called as usual for each element in the array. As with the other methods discussed, you have access to the element, the index, and the entire array within this passed function.

In addition, the function gets the current accumulated value of the previous iteration as an argument. You can optionally specify the start value as the second argument of the reduce() method. In the example, the initial value of the accumulation is 0 (see Listing 14.12).

For each element in the `artists` array, the passed function is now called, and the number of albums of the respective artist is added to the total number of all albums (`result`).

```
const totalAlbumCount = artists.reduce(          // The reduce()-method ...
  function(                              // ... expects a callback function.
    result,                              // (1) current intermediate result
    artist,                              // (2) the respective element
    index,                               // (3) the index of the element in the array
    artists                              // (4) the array
  ) {
    const albumCount = artist.albums.length;  // number of albums of the artist
    return result + albumCount;               // Increase total count
  },
  0                                      // Number of all albums
);
console.log(totalAlbumCount);         // 8
```

Listing 14.12 Functional Variant for Determining the Total Number of Music Albums

Note

The `reduce()` method can be used to reduce the elements or values within an array to a representative element or value.

Other Functional Methods of Arrays

There are several other methods of arrays that are worth mentioning in this context but that won't be discussed in detail here:

- The `every()` method can be used to check whether each element in the array satisfies the criterion defined by the passed callback function.
- The `find()` method can be used to search for the first element that satisfies the criterion defined by the passed callback function.
- The `some()` method can be used to check whether at least one element in an array satisfies the criterion defined by the passed callback function.
- The `reduceRight()` method works in principle like the `reduce()` method, but it goes through the elements from right to left rather than from left to right.

14.2.5 Combination of the Different Methods

You can see that the methods shown for arrays that are available by default already make the source code a lot more readable and make the solution of the problems much more elegant.

However, the true advantage becomes apparent when the methods are combined and the calls are linked—for example, to first filter out the artists from the artist array that have at least one album that was released after 2000, then to "map out" the names of these artists and then to iterate over them. The code that achieves this is extremely readable in the functional variant, especially if you define the individual callback functions with names rather than anonymously (see Listing 14.13). As a result, the program outputs the string Ben Harper because Kyuss (unfortunately) didn't release a new album after 2000.

```
function after2000(album) {
  return album.year > 2000;
}
function hasAlbumAfter2000(artist) {
  return artist.albums.filter(after2000).length > 0;
};
function getArtistName(artist) {
  return artist.name;
};
function printName(name) {
  console.log(name);
}
artists
  .filter(hasAlbumAfter2000)
  .map(getArtistName)
  .forEach(printName);
```

Listing 14.13 The Combination of the Presented Methods Provides Very Readable Code

The imperative equivalent would be more extensive and include various if queries and nested for loops. We'll spare you the code for that at this point. Hopefully, you've acquired enough of a taste to get more involved with functional techniques.

14.3   Summary

In this chapter, we offered a first introduction to functional programming with Java-Script. Of course, the subject of functional programming is far more complex than presented here.

If you want to learn more about this topic, and especially about its application in Java-Script, please refer to the book *Composing Software: An Exploration of Functional Programming and Object Composition in JavaScript* by Eric Elliott (2018), which introduces some advanced functional techniques that are commonly used in professional development with JavaScript.

From this chapter, you should take away the following:

- In JavaScript, functions are *first-class objects*, which means they can be assigned to variables, used as arguments or return values of functions, and stored as values in an array, for example.

- Unlike object-oriented programming, *functional programming* focuses on functions, not objects. However, both programming paradigms can certainly be combined with each other.

- In contrast to *imperative programming*, where you use control structures or statements to tell in a relatively elaborate way how to solve a problem, programs in functional programming tend to be formulated to tell you what is being done, making them very readable and self-explanatory.

- Important array methods that reflect the functional concept (i.e., working on data) include the following:
  - `forEach()` for convenient iteration over the elements of an array
  - `map()` to map elements of an array to new values
  - `filter()` for filtering elements out of an array
  - `reduce()` and `reduceRight()` to reduce the elements to a single value
  - `every()` to check whether each element in an array satisfies a given criterion
  - `some()` to check if at least one element in an array satisfies a given criterion

14

Chapter 15

Correctly Structuring the Source Code

The larger a software project becomes, the more important it is to structure the source code correctly, both to have an overview of the code and to encapsulate data and methods appropriately, and to avoid naming conflicts among variables, objects, and functions, both within your own source code and when using third-party libraries.

By default, JavaScript offers the option to combine source code via modules since ES2015. But even in the past, various design patterns and approaches had emerged that can be used to implement this requirement. In this chapter, we'll first discuss these design patterns for historical reasons and for didactic reasons, and then we'll take a closer look at the native modules introduced with ES2015.

15.1   Avoiding Name Conflicts

As soon as you develop a slightly more extensive application in which the logic is distributed across several JavaScript files, or if you include third-party libraries over whose variable and function names you have no control, you should think about how you group source code components (variables, functions, objects, etc.). After all, it can quickly happen that name conflicts arise when everything is defined on a global level.

Figure 15.1 shows an example: The two JavaScript files **script1.js** and **script2.js** each define a variable with the same name (MAX) and a function with the same name (add()). So long as both scripts are used separately (**script1.js** from **index1.html** and **script2.js** from **index2.html**), there are no conflicts. But as soon as both scripts are used at the same time (**index3.html**), the order of loading then determines which value the variable MAX gets and which of the two functions is available under add().

In languages such as C# and Java, a grouping of components is possible using features such as *packages* and *namespaces*, so that within different packages/namespaces, components with the same name may occur without influencing each other. However, neither packages nor namespaces exist in JavaScript—but the option to emulate namespaces does. This technique is called *namespace design pattern*.

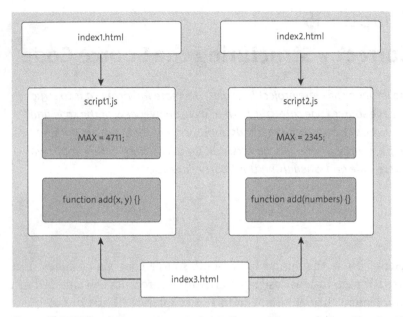

Figure 15.1 Without Namespaces or Some Form of Encapsulation, Naming Conflicts between Different Scripts Can Quickly Occur

The idea is to combine related variables and the like in a separate object that exists only once within an application and serves as a simple container (see Figure 15.2). This way, you've at least brought some structure into your source code and avoid defining variables in the global scope. So long as such container objects have a globally unique name (MathUtilities and MoreMathUtilities in the example), this approach doesn't lead to any naming conflicts.

Listing 15.1 shows the source code for the components shown in Figure 15.2. The MathUtilities object forms the container or namespace for the MAX variable and the add() function; the MoreMathUtilities object in turn forms the namespace for the components of the same name, MAX and add(). The variables and functions are accessed then via the container object.

```javascript
var MathUtilities = MathUtilities || {};
MathUtilities.MAX = 4711;
MathUtilities.add = function(x, y) {
  return x + y;
};
var result = MathUtilities.add(2, 2);
console.log(result);            // 4
console.log(MathUtilities.MAX); // 4711
MathUtilities.MAX = 2345;
console.log(MathUtilities.MAX); // 2345
```

Listing 15.1 Namespace Design Pattern

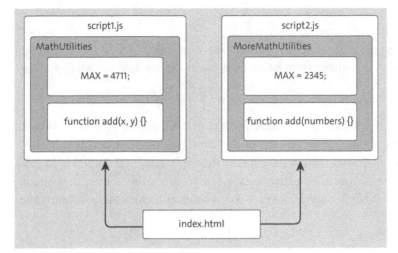

Figure 15.2 Namespaces Prevent Naming Conflicts

> **Note**
>
> To keep the following listings as realistic as possible, we use the var keyword to create variables, rather than the let and const keywords. JavaScript runtime environments that support the newer keywords usually also have support for the native modules mentioned previously, so using let, for example, in combination with the following design patterns would be rather unusual—or in some cases wouldn't work at all (see next note box).

The call according to the var MathUtilities = MathUtilities || {}; pattern prevents a possibly already existing MathUtilities object from being overwritten.

In the more compact object-literal notation, the whole thing then looks as shown in Listing 15.2.

```javascript
var MathUtilities = MathUtilities || {
  MAX: 4711,
  add: function(x, y) {
    return x + y;
  }
};
```

Listing 15.2 Namespace Design Pattern in Object Literal Notation

> **Note**
>
> The notation with the let keyword (i.e., let = MathUtilities || {}) doesn't work in this case; it produces a ReferenceError.

> **Note**
> The namespace design pattern doesn't prevent variables, functions, and so on of the corresponding container object from being reset (overwritten) from outside (see also Listing 15.1).

Now, of course, when assigning the name for a container object, you may choose a name for which there is already a variable of the same name (e.g., in an included Java-Script library). To get around this, in practice, as shown in Listing 15.3 and Listing 15.4, namespaces can also be nested (*nested namespacing*), using the convention already known from Java or C# of deploying reverse-written domain names depending on the respective project.

```
var de = de || {};
de.philipackermann = de.philipackermann || {};
de.philipackermann.javascript = de.philipackermann.javascript || {};
```

Listing 15.3 Nested Namespace Design Pattern

```
var de = de || {
  philipackermann : {
    javascript : { }
  }
};
```

Listing 15.4 Nested Namespace Design Pattern in Object Literal Notation

> **Advantage of Domain Names with Namespaces**
> The advantage of using reverse-spelled domain names as the basis for a namespace structure is that domains are unique worldwide. This ensures that no other developer in the world uses the same namespace (assuming everyone adheres to this convention).

With the namespace design pattern, the problems of name conflicts are solved, but not, as you've seen, those of the visibility of variables and functions. However, true to the concept of *information hiding* (also known as *data encapsulation*), when modeling objects it makes sense to make only as much information available to the outside world as is absolutely necessary. In the next section, we'll introduce the *module design pattern*, which can be used to group individual components as with namespaces, but which also allows data encapsulation.

15.2   Defining and Using Modules

Some languages like Python already support modules natively. JavaScript, by contrast, lacked such support until recently. Only with version ES2015 are modules a part of the standard and thus of the JavaScript language. But because this hasn't been the case for a relatively long time, various design patterns and techniques have emerged over time to build source code in a modular fashion and group it into reusable modules.

In the course of this, two quasi standards have also developed, which have the modularization of the source code as their goal: on the one hand, CommonJS, which primarily addresses the use of modules on the server side—for example, for use under Node.js; and on the other hand, asynchronous module definition (AMD), which is used to deploy modules on the client side—that is, those modules that are used in the browser.

In this section, we'll introduce these different concepts and techniques, as well as the still relatively new native module support.

15.2.1   The Module Design Pattern

For a long time, JavaScript developers had to help themselves if they wanted to structure and modularize their source code in any way. The design pattern that has evolved as a result of this is commonly referred to as the *module design pattern*.

Definition

In software development, a *design pattern* (or *pattern*) refers to certain code modules that can be used as a proven solution to frequently occurring problems. Each programming paradigm and language has its own design patterns.

The module design pattern is based on the use of the namespace design pattern just introduced, as well as the encapsulation of data via closures and Immediately Invoked Function Expressions (IIFEs), which are both rather advanced concepts that we'll only briefly introduce here (in the next two note boxes).

Using Closures

A *closure* (also called a *function closure*) is a function that is returned by another function and that "encloses" the values of variables and parameters of this function and virtually remembers them.

Listing 15.5 shows a code example in which the principle of a closure is used. The counter() function expects a parameter (name) and defines a variable (i) in the first line. The function returns another function as a return value. This returned function accesses both the name parameter and the i variable.

Each call to the `counter()` function now creates a function that "includes" the current variable and parameter assignment in each case. The function stored in the `counter1` variable thus includes the value `counter 1`, and the function in the `counter2` variable includes the value `counter 2`. It's important to understand that the functions returned by the `counter()` function do not influence each other. A call to `counter1()` increments the "included" variable `i` available to this function, but not the variable `i` "included" by `counter2()`.

```
function counter(name) {
  let i=0;
  return function() {
    i++;
    console.log(name + ': ' + i);
  }
}
const counter1 = counter('Counter 1'); // Create a counter
counter1();                            // Counter 1: 1
counter1();                            // Counter 1: 2
const counter2 = counter('Counter 2'); // Create a counter
counter2();                            // Counter 2: 1
counter2();                            // Counter 2: 2
```

Listing 15.5 In a Closure, the Variables and Parameters of the Outer Function Are "Enclosed" in the Inner Function

Using IIFEs

An IIFE is a function that is called directly when defined. As you can see in Listing 15.6, the function is surrounded by two parentheses before it's called.

This way, the interpreter doesn't evaluate the function as a declaration (which would cause a syntax error in this case), but as an expression.

```
(function() {
  console.log('This function is declared and called immediately.')
})();
```

Listing 15.6 The Process of Defining and Directly Calling a Function Is Called IIFE

In principle, this code from Listing 15.6 does the same as the code in Listing 15.7. Here, a function is also created and then called directly, but it differs in two ways from the IIFE. The first difference is that it uses two separate statements. The second difference is that the IIFE is anonymous and can therefore only be called once, whereas the function in Listing 15.7 can be called several times because it has a name.

```
const namedFunction = (function() {
    console.log('This function is declared and called immediately.')
});
namedFunction();
```

Listing 15.7 An IIFE Is Somewhat Equivalent to This Code

IIFEs are usually used to define a separate scope for code that is to be executed directly.

The idea of the module design pattern is as follows: with the help of an IIFE, a separate scope is created, which ensures that none of the properties and functions of the module are accessible from the outside.

The IIFE also returns an object containing the methods and properties provided by the module (*export object*—the public API, so to speak). Methods of this export object have access to all properties and functions defined within the module (i.e., a *Closure* is defined here).

Listing 15.8 shows a simple example of this technique. Here you can see the Module module, which contains two variables, x and y, which are only visible within the module. The IIFE returns an export object, which in turn contains the getX() and getY() methods, two simple *getter methods* for the two previously mentioned (private) variables (see Figure 15.3).

```
var Module = Module || (function () {
  // private variable
  const x = 5;
  // private variable
  const y = 4711;
  // public API
  return {
    // public function
    getX: function() {
      return x;
    },
    // public function
    getY: function() {
      return y;
    }
  }
})();
console.log(Module.getX());  // 5
console.log(Module.getY());  // 4711
Module.x = 888;
```

15

```
Module.y = 888;
console.log(Module.getX());  // 5
console.log(Module.getY());  // 4711
```

Listing 15.8 The Module Design Pattern as a Combination of Closure and IIFE

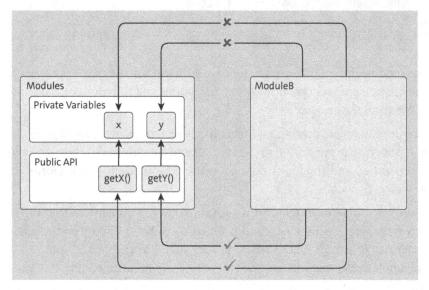

Figure 15.3 The Module Design Pattern Encapsulates the Code, Allowing Certain Variables to Be Kept Private

Only the methods of the export object can now be accessed from outside the module—in this case, the getX() and getY() methods. If you try to overwrite the private properties (i.e., the x and y variables), as shown in the listing, this has no effect on the variables.

OR Operation on Namespace Design Pattern

A small detail to note here, which you already know from the namespace design pattern: the OR operation at the beginning of the module prevents a module from being initialized more than once. If the Module variable already exists, it's also used, but if not, the IIFE is called and the module is initialized once.

15.2.2   The Revealing Module Design Pattern

Something else that isn't so nice about the implementation in Listing 15.8 is that if you want to call other methods of the same module within a method of a module, then you always have to prefix the name of the module to these method calls.

In Listing 15.9, for example, the module was extended by a print() method, which in turn calls the getX() and getY() methods. Both calls work only if they are called on the Module object—that is, via Module.getX() and Module.getY().

```
var Module = Module || (function () {
  const x = 5;
  const y = 4711;
  return {
    getX: function() {
      return x;
    },
    getY: function() {
      return y;
    },
    // Access to own methods
    print: function() {
      console.log(
        'x: ' +
        Module.getX() +
        ', y: ' +
        Module.getY()
      )
    }
  }
})();
```

Listing 15.9 Function Call in the Classic Module Design Pattern

To get around this inconvenience, you can use a technique commonly known as the *revealing module* or *revealing module pattern*. The idea is that a method to be exported is not defined inside the export object itself, but outside of it. Within the export object, you only reference this method.

Listing 15.10 shows how you can use this technique to call the getX() and getY() methods directly inside the print() method, without prefixing the module name.

```
var Module = Module || (function () {
  const x = 5;
  const y = 4711;
  function getX() {
    return x;
  }
  function getY() {
    return y;
  }
  function print() {
    console.log(
      'x: ' +
      getX() +
```

```
    ', y: ' +
    getY()
  )
}
// Return object contains only references.
return {
  getX: getX,
  getY: getY,
  print: print
}
})();
Module.print();
```

Listing 15.10 Function Call in Revealing Module Design Pattern

Importing Modules

To import a module within another module, you simply pass the module to be imported to the other as an argument of the IIFE. In Listing 15.11, for example, you can see two modules: the already known Module module (now named ModuleA) and the new ModuleB module. By passing the latter as an argument to the other module, the printHelloWorld() method of ModuleB can be accessed within the print() method. If you want to import several modules, you can of course continue the process by simply passing multiple arguments.

```
var ModuleB = ModuleB || (function () {
  function printHelloWorld() {
    console.log('Hello World');
  }
  return {
    printHelloWorld: printHelloWorld
  }
})();

var ModuleA = ModuleA || (function (moduleB) {
  // Within the module, dependencies ...
  // ... are available via the ...
  // ... corresponding argument.
  const x = 5;
  const y = 4711;
  function getX() {
    return x;
  }
  function getY() {
```

```
    return y;
  }
  function print() {
    moduleB.printHelloWorld();
    console.log(
      'x: ' +
      getX() +
      ', y: ' +
      getY()
    )
  }
  return {
    getX: getX,
    getY: getY,
    print: print
  }
  // Dependency is passed as an argument.
})(ModuleB);
ModuleA.print();
```

Listing 15.11 Importing a Module

Module Augmentation

If you want to distribute the source code for a module to several source code files, you can use a little trick, a technique called *module augmentation*. To do this, you simply pass the module itself to the IIFE as an argument, add properties and functions, and finally use the module itself as a return value (see Listing 15.12).

```
// File 1
var ModuleA = ModuleA || (function (moduleA) {
  // Add properties and functions
  const x = 5;
  const y = 4711;
  moduleA.getX = function() {
    return x;
  }
  moduleA.getY = function() {
    return y;
  }
  // Module itself as return value
  return moduleA;
  // Loose augmentation
})(ModuleA || {});
```

```
// File 2
var ModuleA = (function (moduleA) {
  // Add properties and functions
  moduleA.print = function() {
    console.log(
      'x: ' +
      moduleA.getX() +
      ', y: ' +
      moduleA.getY()
    )
  }
  // Module itself as return value
  return moduleA;
  // Tight augmentation
})(ModuleA);

// File 3
ModuleA.print();
```

Listing 15.12 Module Augmentation

Module augmentation is available in two variants: loose augmentation and tight augmentation. With *loose augmentation*, if the module hasn't yet been created an empty object is passed as argument (ModuleA || {} in Listing 15.12, for example). *Tight augmentation*, on the other hand, assumes that the module already exists (i.e., at least one other source code file has already been loaded). This can be seen in Listing 15.12 in the section below the File 2 comment: here only ModuleA is passed as an argument. In the example, this makes sense in that the print() method (which is defined in File 2) depends on the getX() and getY() methods (which in turn are defined in File 1).

The advantage of loose augmentation is that scripts contributing to the module can be loaded asynchronously. It doesn't matter which script is loaded first, because in case of doubt the module will be recreated. This isn't the case with tight augmentation. Here the application assumes a certain sequence when loading the scripts. The advantage of this is that within a file you can rely on the fact that other files have already been loaded and that properties and methods added to the module exist there accordingly (such as the getX() and getY() methods used within the print() method).

Regardless of which type of module augmentation you use, there is one common drawback: functions defined in one source code file for a module do not have access to private variables defined in another source code file for the same module. For example, within the print() method (which was defined in File 2), the x and y variables (which were defined in File 1) could not be accessed directly.

15.2.3   AMD

AMD is a module definition technique that enables asynchronous loading to address applications that run in the browser. AMD is implemented by **require.js** (*http://requirejs.org*), for example.

Listing 15.13 shows the definition of a module in AMD. If you look closely, you can recognize the module design pattern. For registering a module, the define() method is available, which expects at least one module function as the (third) argument, in which you define the corresponding module.

Optionally, the name of the module can be defined as the first argument, and a list of the modules on which the current module depends can be defined as the second argument (in the example, the module named ModuleB). These are then available as arguments within the module (in the example, via moduleB).

The function that defines the module (the third argument) returns an object that represents the public API, similar to the module design pattern.

```
// Definition of ModuleA
define(
  'ModuleA',          // Name of the module
  ['ModuleB'],        // Modules to be imported
  function (moduleB) { // Function that defines the module
    const x = 5;
    const y = 4711;
    const module = {
      getX: function() {
        return x;
      },
      getY: function() {
        return y;
      },
      print: function() {
        moduleB.printHelloWorld();
        console.log(
          'x: ' +
          this.getX() +
          ', y: ' +
          this.getY()
        )
      }
    }
    return module;
  }
);
```

15

```
// Definition of 'ModuleB'
define(
  'ModuleB',            // Name of the module
  [],                   // Modules to be imported
  function () {         // Function that defines the module
    const module = {
      printHelloWorld: function() {
        console.log('Hello World');
      }
    }
    return module;
  }
);
```

Listing 15.13 Module Definition with AMD

To include modules, AMD defines the `require()` function, the use of which you can see in Listing 15.14. As with `define()`, the names of the modules to be included are passed in the form of an array. The corresponding modules are then available within the code.

```
require(['ModuleA'], function(moduleA){
    moduleA.print();
});
```

Listing 15.14 Using a Module with AMD

15.2.4   CommonJS

Unlike AMD, CommonJS (or more precisely, its module specification; see *http:// wiki.commonjs.org/wiki/Modules/1.1*) addresses the use of modules on the server side and is used, for example, in Node.js.

In Listing 15.15, you can see the somewhat more compact definition of a module in CommonJS compared to AMD. It's immediately clear that the source code is not encapsulated in its own IIFE like in AMD. CommonJS is based on the principle of treating each source code file as a separate module per se with its own scope. Within such a scope, there are essentially three different components available—the `require()` method, the `exports` object, and the `module` object:

- It's possible to load a module via the `require()` method. The name of the respective module or its path is passed to the method. In Listing 15.15, for example, the call `const moduleA = require('ModuleA')` loads the **ModuleA.js** file or the module defined there into the `moduleA` variable.

- The `exports` object represents the export object—that is, the public API. To this object, you add the components that the module should provide to the outside. Listing 15.15, for example, exports the `print()` method in `ModuleA` and the `print-HelloWorld()` method in `ModuleB`.

- The `module` object (not used in the listing) provides additional meta information for the current module, such as the module ID or the URL where a module can be found.

```
// File "ModuleA.js"
// Loading a module
const moduleB = require('ModuleB');
const x = 5;
const y = 4711;
function getX() {
  return x;
}
function getY() {
  return y;
}
function print() {
  moduleB.printHelloWorld();
  console.log(
    'x: ' +
    getX() +
    ', y: ' +
    getY()
  );
}
// public API
exports.print = print;

// File "ModuleB.js"
function printHelloWorld() {
  console.log('Hello World');
}
// public API
exports.printHelloWorld = printHelloWorld;

// File "main.js"
// Loading a module
const moduleA = require('ModuleA');
moduleA.print();
```

Listing 15.15 Module Definition with CommonJS

15

15.2.5   Native Modules

Since ES2015, the standard provides a native module system for JavaScript. This involves a compromise between AMD and CommonJS in the specification of the corresponding module component of the standard. So on the one hand, the notation is similarly compact as that of CommonJS (if not even more compact); on the other hand, there's the possibility to load modules both synchronously (as in CommonJS) and asynchronously (as in AMD). Consequently, native ES2015 modules can be used both on the server side and on the client side.

Defining Modules

The principle of native modules is similar to that of CommonJS: a module is nothing more than an ordinary script file into which you "export" objects and functions that the module is to provide to the outside world. This export of structures can be done in several ways: Either you specify the structures to be exported explicitly (this is referred to as a *named export*; see Listing 15.16), or you specify a single *default export*, which quasi represents the main part of the module (see Listing 15.17). In both cases, you use the export keyword.

```
// File: logger.js
export function info(message) {
  console.log(message);
}
export function debug(message) {
  console.debug(message);
}
export function warn(message) {
  console.warn(message);
}
export function error(message) {
  console.error(message);
}
```

Listing 15.16 Definition of Designated Exports

```
// File: Album.js
export default class Album {
  constructor(artist, title, year) {
    this.interpret = interpret;
    this.titel = titel;
    this.year = year;
  }
}
```

Listing 15.17 Definition of a Default Export

The advantage of default exports is that when you import the corresponding module into another module (more on that in a moment), you don't need to know what the exported structure is called within the module.

> **Note**
> If you want to use the native module syntax under Node.js, you need to set the `type` entry to the `module` value in the respective **package.json** file.

Importing Modules

Several options are available for importing modules. Assume that the module defined previously in Listing 15.16 is stored in the **logger.js** file. Then you could import individual named exports of this module directly, as shown in Listing 15.18, specifying the `import` keyword and the respective named export. In the example, the imported functions are assigned to variables with the same name in the current module.

```
import {
  info,
  debug,
  warn,
  Error
} from './logger.js'

info(4711);    // Call the 'info' function of the 'logger' module
debug(4711);   // Call the 'debug' function of the 'logger' module
warn(4711);    // Call the 'warn' function of the 'logger' module
error(4711);   // Call the 'error' function of the 'logger' module
```

Listing 15.18 Import Individual Functions from a Module

You also have the option to import exports under a different name (an *alias*). This can help, for example, to avoid naming conflicts when the "imported exports" have the same name in their respective modules. To define an alias, use the as keyword followed by the alias name after the respective imported export, as shown in Listing 15.19.

```
import {                  // Import ...
  info as i,              // ... of the 'info' function under alias 'i'
  debug as d,             // ... of the 'debug' function under alias 'd'
  warn as w,              // ... of the 'warn' function under alias 'w'
  error as e              // ... of the 'error' function under alias 'e'
} from './logger.js'

e(4711); // Call the error function of the 'logger' module
```

Listing 15.19 Importing Different Exports under a Different Name

If you import a module that defines a default export (discussed earlier), you can import it as shown in Listing 15.20 (the name of the import can be selected freely).

```
import Album from './Album.js';
const album = new Album('Monster Magnet', 'Dopes to Infinity', 1994);
```

Listing 15.20 Importing the Default Component of a Module

Importing Modules Dynamically

The import keyword can be used only at the top level. So, for example, you can't use it inside an if block or any other code block. This also makes it impossible, for example, to dynamically import modules using the import keyword. Since ES2020, this is remedied by the function-like import() statement (which is not a real function!).

The import() statement can be used to load modules dynamically, passing the path to the corresponding module as a parameter. Because the import of modules is asynchronous, the return value is a promise object, which can be used as usual in combination with then()/catch() or async/await (see Listing 15.21).

```
'use strict';
const loadModule = true;

if (loadModule) {
  const moduleSpecifier = './logger.js';
  import(moduleSpecifier)
    .then(module => {
      // Calling the info function of the 'logger' module
      module.info('Module loaded dynamically!');
      // Calling the debug function of the 'logger' module
      module.debug('Module loaded dynamically!');
      // Calling the warn function of the 'logger' module
      module.warn('Module loaded dynamically!');
      // Calling the error function of the 'logger' module
      module.error('Module loaded dynamically!');
    }).catch(error => {
        console.error('Error loading the module')
    });
}
```

Listing 15.21 Importing Different Components under a Different Name

---

Note

Another advantage of importing modules dynamically is that the path to the modules to be imported can also be determined dynamically.

15.3   Summary

In JavaScript, there are several solutions with regard to the modularization of source code:

- You can use the *namespace design pattern* to prevent naming conflicts among variables, objects, functions, classes, and other components.
- The principle of the namespace design pattern can basically be nested as deeply as required, in which case this is referred to as the *nested namespace design pattern*.
- The namespace design pattern solves the problem of name conflicts, but not that of data encapsulation. The *module design pattern*, on the other hand, solves both.
- The module design pattern exists in different variants: the *classic module design pattern* and the *revealing module design pattern*.
- Besides the module design pattern, you have the option to use AMD or CommonJS for structuring modules. The former loads modules asynchronously and is therefore suitable for browser use; the latter loads modules synchronously and is therefore more suitable for browser-independent applications.
- *Native modules*, however, have only been included in the JavaScript language set since ES2015.
- Since ES2020, it's also possible to import native modules dynamically.

15

Table 15.1 provides a comparison of the different techniques for modularizing JavaScript source code.

	Syntax	Synchronous	Asynchronous	Client	Server
Module Design Pattern	Rather complex	Tight augmentation	Loose augmentation	Yes	Yes
CommonJS	Compact	Yes	No	Partly (but only with tools such as Browserify)	Yes
AMD	Complex	No	Yes	Yes	No
Native Module (ES2015)	Compact	Yes	Yes	Yes	Yes

Table 15.1 Comparison of the Different Techniques for Modularization

Chapter 16

Using Asynchronous Programming and Other Advanced Features

In this chapter, we'll discuss asynchronous programming. We'll also discuss other advanced topics that can be helpful for development with JavaScript.

Let's start with asynchronous programming. We'll take a look at what exactly this is and what the different options are. We'll then discuss three features that fall into the advanced programming category: iterators, generators, and proxies.

16.1   Understanding and Using Asynchronous Programming

One of the fundamental principles of developing in JavaScript is *asynchronous programming*, whether it's formulating an Ajax request or—later in this book in Chapter 17—reading files under Node.js. In many cases, you call functions and also pass functions as parameters, which are called exactly when the result of the called function is determined—for example, when the requested data has been downloaded from the server or the contents of a file have been read. Then the flow of the program is not synchronous, but *asynchronous*.

In this section, we'll introduce three different methods of asynchronous programming in JavaScript:

- **The callback design pattern**
  The classic variant, which can quickly become syntactically confusing for more complex use cases

- **Promises**
  The modern variant introduced as of ES2015, which remains relatively clear syntactically even for more complex use cases

- **Async functions**
  Essentially, two new keywords introduced with ES2016 (async/await) that further simplify working with promises and that are the clearest in terms of syntax

16.1.1   Using the Callback Design Pattern

Passing a function as a parameter to another function, where the latter calls the passed function at a later time, is called following a *callback design pattern*, and the passed function is called a *callback function, callback handler,* or just *callback* for short.

The general structure of the callback design pattern is shown in Listing 16.1: the (asynchronous) asyncFunction() function expects a function (callbackFunction) as a parameter and calls it somewhere within the function body.

```
function asyncFunction(callbackFunction) {
  // More code here
  console.log('Prior to callback');
  callbackFunction();
  console.log('After callback');
  // More code here
}
function callbackFunction() {
  console.log('Calling callback');
}
asyncFunction(callbackFunction);
// Output:
// "Prior to callback"
// "Calling callback"
// "After callback"
```

Listing 16.1 General Structure of the Callback Pattern

Passing Functions, Instead of Calling Them

When working with callbacks, avoid the careless error shown in Listing 16.2, one that's often made and that results in the function that is intended as a callback function not being passed, but instead being called, and its result being mistakenly passed as the supposed callback function. If the result is not a function, this leads to the object is not a function error, as shown in Listing 16.2, and the program terminates.

```
asyncFunction(callbackFunction());
```

Listing 16.2 Caution: Here the Function Is Not Passed, but Called!

Pitfall 1: Return Values of Asynchronous Functions

Asynchronous functions do not return the result of the asynchronous calculation via the return keyword but pass it as a parameter to the callback function. Let's illustrate this with an example. For this purpose, we take a simple asynchronous function that waits two seconds via the setTimeout() call and then sets the result value (see Listing 16.3).

```
function asyncFunction(callbackFunction) {
  let result;
  setTimeout(
    () => {
      // This only happens after two seconds.
      result = Math.floor(Math.random() * 100) + 1;   // Random number
    },
    2000
  );
  return result;
}
```

Listing 16.3 An Asynchronous Function in Which return Is Used

If this asynchronous function is called as if it were a synchronous function, this quickly leads to unwanted program behavior, as shown in Listing 16.4. The program continues to run without waiting for the result of the asynchronous function, so the supposed result in the result variable is therefore undefined.

```
const result = asyncFunction();
console.log(result); // undefined
```

Listing 16.4 The Result of the Asynchronous Function Is undefined

We'll show you in a moment what this example should look like when set up correctly—both in terms of calling the callback function or returning the result, and calling the asynchronous function. But before we do that, let's show you a second thing to keep in mind about asynchronous functions.

Pitfall 2: Throwing Errors in Asynchronous Functions

Inside an asynchronous function, you can't "throw" errors in the usual way that's attempted in Listing 16.5. The reason: by the time the error is thrown, the calling code has already moved on and there is no one left to catch the error.

```
function asyncFunction(callbackFunction) {
  let result;
  setTimeout(
    () => {
      result = Math.floor(Math.random() * 100) + 1;
      if(result < 50) {
        throw new Error(`Random number ${result} less than 50.`);
      }
    },
    2000
  );
```

16

```
    return result;
}

try {
  const result = asyncFunction();
} catch(error) {
  console.error(`Fehler: ${error}`); // This line is not called!
}
```

Listing 16.5 Errors Thrown by Asynchronous Functions Cannot Be Caught

Passing Results and Errors to Callback

Asynchronous functions that use callbacks can therefore neither return a return value to the calling code nor inform about errors in the "normal" way (i.e., in the synchronous way).

This is exactly where the callback functions just introduced come into play: they represent the link, so to speak, between the asynchronous function and the calling (synchronous) code. The calling code passes the callback function, and the asynchronous function calls this callback function with the result value (the *return value*) or, in case of an error, with the error object as a parameter. The calling code can then respond to both within the callback function (see Listing 16.6).

```
function asyncFunction(callbackFunction) {
  let result;
  setTimeout(
    () => {
      // This only happens after two seconds.
      result = Math.floor(Math.random() * 100) + 1;
      if(result >= 50) {
        callbackFunction(
            null,        // null --> no error
            result       // result value
        );
      } else {
        callbackFunction(
          new Error(`random number ${result} less than 50.`), // Error
          undefined                                  // no result value
        );
      }
    },
    2000
  );
}
```

```
asyncFunction(
  (error, result) => {
    if(error) {
      console.error(error);  // Error handling in the callback
    } else {
      console.log(result);   // Result handling in the callback
    }
  }
);
```

Listing 16.6 Error and Result Handling via Callbacks

> **Parameters of a Callback Function**
>
> Usually, the callback function is passed a possible error object as the first parameter (or the value `null` if no error occurred) and the result of the asynchronous calculation as the second parameter. This convention has become an established best practice in the JavaScript community.

The Problem of Asynchronous Programming with Callbacks

The use of callback functions is an essential feature of JavaScript programming. However, the overuse of callback functions can lead to a code structure known among JavaScript developers as the *pyramid of doom* or *callback hell.*

This code structure occurs when asynchronous function calls are nested excessively often; that is, if another asynchronous function is called in the callback of an asynchronous function, and then another asynchronous function is called in that asynchronous function's callback, and so on.

Listing 16.7 shows an exaggerated example of this, and it also illustrates the reason for the name *pyramid of doom*: the more callback functions are nested, the more these functions move to the right, resulting in a pyramid-like structure overall.

```
asyncFunction(
  (error, result) => {
    // more code
    asyncFunction2(
      // more code
      (error2, result2) => {
        // more code
        asyncFunction3(
          (error3, result3) => {
            // more code
            asyncFunction4(
```

```
        (error4, result4) => {
          // more code
          asyncFunction5(
            (error5, result5) => {
              // more code
            }
          );
        }
      );
    }
  );
    }
  );
  }
);
```

Listing 16.7 The Pyramid of Doom, Feared among JavaScript Developers

16.1.2   Using Promises

Due to the many indentations needed, the nesting of callbacks leads to the pyramid of doom, as shown in the previous section. The *promises* introduced with ES2015 prevent such code structures but still allow asynchronous programming or asynchronous programs to be formulated so that they look like synchronous programs. So with promises, it's generally easier to control an asynchronous program flow.

Promises themselves are nothing more than objects (of the Promise type) that serve as placeholders, so to speak, for the result of an asynchronous function (see Listing 16.8). Instead of the asynchronous function itself being passed the callback handlers, it returns a Promise object that has access to two encapsulated callback functions: one to inform about the result value and one to inform about errors (usually the names of these callback functions are resolve() and reject() to clarify their intent). This simple but effective trick allows the synchronous code to continue working with the Promise object.

```
function asyncFunction() {
  const promise = new promise(
    function(resolve, reject) {
      setTimeout(
        () => {
          const result = Math.floor(Math.random() * 100) + 1;  // Random number
          if(result >= 50) {
            resolve(result);  // Result
          } else {
```

```
            reject(`random number ${result} less than 50.`);  // Error
        }
    }, 2000);
  }
);
return promise;
}
```

Listing 16.8 Asynchronous Function That Returns a Promise Object

Processing a Promise

So from the point of view of the calling code, you no longer pass a callback parameter to the asynchronous function. Instead, you now pass this parameter to the Promise object that you get from the asynchronous function as a return value. The Promise object provides the then() method for this purpose. It can be passed a callback handler for handling the result and a callback handler for handling errors, as shown in Listing 16.9.

```
asyncFunction().then(
   (result) => {
     console.log(result);
   },
   (error) => {
     console.error(error);
   },
);
```

Listing 16.9 Calling an Asynchronous Function Using Promises

The relationship between the asynchronous function and the calling code is illustrated in Figure 16.1.

As an alternative to specifying a callback function as the second parameter of then(), you can also pass it to the catch() method as in Listing 16.10. This variant is now also used more often because catch() makes it clear at first glance where the error handling happens.

```
asyncFunction()
  .then(
   (result) => {
     console.log(result);
   })
```

```
    .catch(
      (error) => {
        console.error(error);
      }
    )
);
```

Listing 16.10 Using catch() for Error Handling

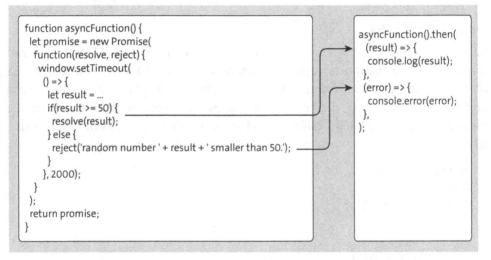

Figure 16.1 Connection of Promise Object and Callbacks

Since ES2018, the `finally()` method is also available, which can be used to specify callback functions that are *always* executed, regardless of whether an error occurs or not (see Listing 16.11).

```
asyncFunction()
  .then(
   (result) => {
    console.log(result);
  })
  .catch(
   (error) => {
      console.error(error);
    }
  )
  .finally(() => {
    console.log('Always executed.');
  });
);
```

Listing 16.11 Using finally() for Error Handling

Concatenating Promise Calls

Thanks to the Promise API's Fluent API, calls to then() can be lined up relatively conveniently one after the other because then() always returns a Promise object itself as well. In the example in Listing 16.12, the first callback handler returns the result of asyncFunction() multiplied by two, implicitly creating a Promise object. The return value of the callback handler is then used as input for the second callback handler.

```
asyncFunction()
  .then((result) => {
    return result * 2;
  })
  .then((result) => {
    // Here result contains the result from above multiplied by two.
    console.log(result);
  });
```

Listing 16.12 A Chain of Promises

> **Note**
>
> The then() method always implicitly returns a Promise object.

Thanks to this ability to concatenate promises, the pyramid of doom of Listing 16.7 can also be avoided, as Listing 16.13 shows. By concatenating the then() method and passing appropriate callback functions, the code remains on one level.

```
asyncFunction()
  .then((result) => {
    // Contents of asyncFunction2
  })
  .then((result) => {
    // Contents of asyncFunction3
  })
  .then((result) => {
    // Contents of asyncFunction4
  })
  .then((result) => {
    // Contents of asyncFunction5
  });
```

Listing 16.13 Much Clearer than the Pyramid of Doom: Concatenation of Promises

The States of Promises

Internally, a Promise object assumes one of three states (see also Figure 16.2):

- *Pending* means that the asynchronous function is not yet completed.
- *Fulfilled* means that the asynchronous function completed successfully (and the Promise object contains a result value). This state is reached when the callback function resolve() has been called.
- *Rejected* means that the asynchronous function did not complete successfully or resulted in an error (and that the Promise object contains the reason for the error). This state is reached when the reject() callback function has been called.

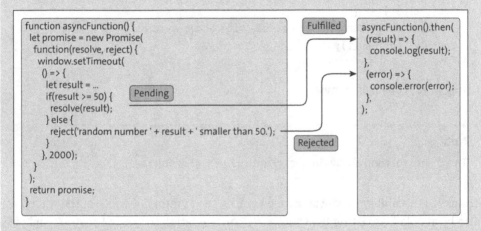

Figure 16.2 The Different States of Promises

In connection with states of promises, the term *settled* is also relevant: if a promise is settled, it means that it has either been fulfilled or rejected. In other words, it is no longer in the pending state.

Using Promises Helper Methods

In addition to the methods discussed, the Promise class also provides various static helper methods that are useful when working with promises, especially when calling various asynchronous functions in parallel that work with promises. For example, the Promise.all() method expects an array of promises (more precisely, an iterable of promises) and itself also returns a promise that is fulfilled if all submitted promises have been fulfilled and is rejected if any of the submitted promises have been rejected. If all promises have been fulfilled, the promise returned by Promise.all() returns the respective result values as an array. If one of the promises results in an error (i.e., it is rejected), this error is passed to Promise.all().

Listing 16.14 shows how to use the method: First, three promises are created here, with the first and third promises being fulfilled and the second promise being rejected.

Therefore, the first call of the `Promise.all()` method (where promise number 2 is not passed) returns the result values of promise 1 and promise 3. The second call, however (promise number 2 is now also passed), results in an error.

```
// Promise 1 is "resolved"
const promise1 = new Promise((resolve, reject) => resolve('1'));
// Promise 2 is "rejected"
const promise2 = new Promise((resolve, reject) => reject('2'));
// Promise 3 is "resolved"
const promise3 = new Promise((resolve, reject) => resolve('3'));

Promise
  .all([promise1, promise3])
  .then((result) => {
    console.log(result);
  })
  .catch((error) => {
    console.error(`Error: ${error}`);
  });

// Output: [ '1', '3' ]

Promise
  .all([promise1, promise2, promise3])
  .then((result) => {
    console.log(result);
  })
  .catch((error) => {
    console.error(`Error: ${error}`);
  });

// Output: "Error: 2"
```

Listing 16.14 Using the Promise.all() Method

The `Promise.race()` method works similarly to `Promise.all()`, but it ends directly at the first promise that is fulfilled or rejected. Figuratively speaking, the individual promises passed thus run a race (hence the name of the method): the asynchronous function that is *settled* first—that is, either resolved or rejected—wins the race.

Listing 16.15 shows a simple example. The three promises defined at the beginning of the listing have been slightly modified compared to the previous listing to better illustrate the use of `Promise.race()`: promise 1 and promise 3 use the `setTimeout()` method to simulate two asynchronous functions that resolve after five seconds, while promise

2 rejects after two seconds. In other words, promise 2 wins the race, and `Promise.race()` returns the error thrown by promise 2.

```
const promise1 = new Promise((resolve, reject) => {
    setTimeout(() => resolve('1'), 5000);
});
const promise2 = new Promise((resolve, reject) => {
    setTimeout(() => reject('2'), 2000);
});
const promise3 = new Promise((resolve, reject) => {
    setTimeout(() => resolve('1'), 5000);
});

Promise
  .race([promise1, promise2, promise3])
  .then((result) => {
    console.log(result);
  })
  .catch((error) => {
    console.error(`Error: ${error}`);
  });

// Output: 1
```

Listing 16.15 Using the Promise.race() Method

The `Promise.allSettled()` method works slightly different from `Promise.all()`: it also expects an array or iterable of promises and also returns a promise, but unlike `Promise.all()`, the returned promise is not rejected once one of the given promises has been rejected. Instead, the promise is fulfilled when all passed promises have completed (i.e., when they settle), regardless of whether they have been fulfilled or rejected. As a result, the promise returns an array of objects, each of which contains the result of each promise. Listing 16.16 shows an example.

```
const promise1 = new Promise((resolve, reject) => resolve('1'));
const promise2 = new Promise((resolve, reject) => reject('2'));
const promise3 = new Promise((resolve, reject) => resolve('3'));

Promise
  .allSettled([promise1, promise3])
  .then((result) => {
    console.log(result);
  })
```

```
    .catch((error) => {
      console.error(`Error: ${error}`);
    });

// Output:
// [
//   { status: 'fulfilled', value: '1' },
//   { status: 'fulfilled', value: '3' }
// ]

Promise
  .allSettled([promise1, promise2, promise3])
  .then((result) => {
    console.log(result);
  })
  .catch((error) => {
    console.error(`Error: ${error}`);
  });

// Output:
// [
//   { status: 'fulfilled', value: '1' },
//   { status: 'rejected', reason: '2' },
//   { status: 'fulfilled', value: '3' }
// ]
```

Listing 16.16 Using the Promise.allSettled() Method

In addition to the three methods presented thus far, ES2021 introduced the `Promise.any()` method. As the name of the method suggests, it returns a promise that is fulfilled as soon as *one* of the passed promises has been fulfilled and rejected only if *all* given promises have been rejected (see Listing 16.17).

```
const promise1 = new Promise((resolve, reject) => resolve('1'));
const promise2 = new Promise((resolve, reject) => reject('2'));
const promise3 = new Promise((resolve, reject) => resolve('3'));

Promise
  .any([promise1, promise2, promise3])
  .then((result) => {
    console.log(result);
  })
  .catch((error) => {
```

```
    console.error(`Error: ${error}`);
  });
```

// Output: 1

```
Promise
  .any([promise2])
  .then((result) => {
    console.log(result);
  })
  .catch((error) => {
    console.error(`Error: ${error}`);
  });
```

// Output: "Error: AggregateError: All promises were rejected"

Listing 16.17 Using the Promise.any() Method

In addition to all these helper methods, Promise.resolve() and Promise.reject() provide two more methods to generate a promise that is fulfilled (Promise.resolve()) or rejected (Promise.reject()). For example, the previous code example can be rewritten using these two helper methods as shown in Listing 16.18.

```
const promise1 = Promise.resolve('1');
const promise2 = Promise.reject('2');
const promise3 = Promise.resolve('3');

Promise
  .any([promise1, promise2, promise3])
  .then((result) => {
    console.log(result);
  })
  .catch((error) => {
    console.error(`Error: ${error}`);
  });
```

// Output: 1

```
Promise
  .any([promise2])
  .then((result) => {
    console.log(result);
  })
```

```
.catch((error) => {
  console.error(`Error: ${error}`);
});
```

```
// Output: "Error: AggregateError: All promises were rejected"
```

Listing 16.18 Using the Promise.resolve() and Promise.reject() Methods

16.1.3   Using Async Functions

Compared to callback functions, promises thus greatly simplify writing asynchronous code. But it gets even better: in version ES2016, an additional option was introduced with the *async functions*, which further simplify the formulation of asynchronous code.

The async keyword can be used to mark asynchronous functions as such, where the keyword is written before the declaration of the corresponding function (see Listing 16.19).

```
async function someAsyncFunction() {
  // asynchronous calculation here
  const result = ...;
  return result;
}
```

Listing 16.19 Using the async Keyword

> **Note**
>
> Internally, a Promise object is implicitly created and returned for a function marked async. So the result can be accessed as before via the direct use of promises (see Listing 16.20).
>
> ```
> someAsyncFunction()
> .then(result => console.log(result));
> ```
>
> **Listing 16.20** Access to the Result of an Asynchronous Function via Direct Use of Promises

Within an asynchronous function marked with async, the await keyword can now be used. If you prepend this keyword to a function call, the calling function waits until the result of the asynchronous function call is determined.

Listing 16.21 shows a simple example. The randomNumber() function returns a random number between 1 and 100 with a time delay (to simulate the asynchrony aspect). Within the addTwoRandomNumbers() calling function, the specification of await is now sufficient to cause the execution of the function to be continued only when the execution of randomNumber() has been completed in each case. So first the value for a is determined, then the value for b, and after that the expression a + b is calculated—exactly as you would expect for the corresponding synchronous code.

Note that the call of addTwoRandomNumbers() using await cannot be used at the top level. Instead, an anonymous function is created in the listing, marked with the async keyword and called directly (an exception to this is the *top-level await*, which allows the use of await at the top level at least in combination with the EMCAScript module syntax; see *https://github.com/tc39/proposal-top-level-await*).

```
function randomNumber() {
  return new Promise(resolve => {
    setTimeout(() => {
      const x = Math.floor(Math.random() * 100) + 1;
      resolve(x);
    }, 2000);
  });
}


async function addTwoRandomNumbers() {
  console.log('Calculation of first random number');
  const a = await randomNumber();
  console.log(`Result: ${a}`);
  console.log('Calculation of second random number');
  const b = await randomNumber();
  console.log(`Result: ${b}`);
  return a + b;
}


(async () => {
  const result = await addTwoRandomNumbers();
  console.log(`Summe: ${result}`);
})();


// Sample output:
// Calculation of first random number
// Result: 38
// Calculation of second random number
// Result: 58
// Total: 96
```

Listing 16.21 Using the await Keyword

In contrast to the use of callback functions, this source code is much easier to read and understand. This becomes especially clear when several asynchronous function calls are lined up one after the other, as in Listing 16.22. What would grow into a confusing jumble of nested and indented function calls with callback functions remains much clearer with async functions. Even the code listed in the listing for comparison for the use of promises is not quite as clear anymore compared to the marking via await. By the way, you can also see in the listing that normal try/catch statements can also be used when await is used—just as you're used to from synchronous function calls.

```
class UserRepository {

  constructor() {
    this._users = new Map();
  }

  async save(user) {
    this._users.set(user.id, user);
    return Promise.resolve(user);
  }

  async find(id) {
    const user = this._users.get(id);
    return Promise.resolve(user);
  }
}

const repository = new UserRepository();

// Using await
async function saveAndFindJames() {
  const james= {
    id: 4712
    firstName: 'James',
    lastName: 'Doe'
  };
  try {
    const result = await repository.save(james);
    const user = await repository.find(result.id);
    console.log(user);
  } catch (error) {
    console.error(error);
  }
}
saveAndFindJames();
```

```
// Using promises
function saveAndFindJohn() {
  const john = {
    id: 4711
    firstName: JOHN
    lastName: 'Doe'
  };
  repository.save(john)
    .then(result => repository.find(result.id))
    .then(user => console.log(user))
    .catch(error => console.error(error));
}

saveAndFindJohn();
```

Listing 16.22 Clear Asynchronous Code Thanks to async and await

16.2   Encapsulating Iteration over Data Structures

In this book, you've already learned about different ways to iterate over data structures such as arrays, maps, or sets. You've also already seen that the Map and Set data types (and Array, for that matter) return iterators via the keys(), values(), and entries() methods, which can then be used directly as input in for-of loops.

16.2.1   The Principle of Iterators

In general terms, *iterators* abstract iteration over data structures. In simple terms, these are objects that contain a kind of pointer to an underlying data structure that can be moved on the iterator via calls of the next() method. The respective element to which the pointer then points is returned by next() (see Figure 16.3).

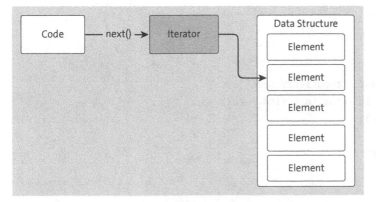

Figure 16.3 Iterators Are a Kind of Pointer to the Elements of a Data Structure

16.2.2 Using Iterators

Listing 16.23 shows an example of this using an iterator that is returned by the values() method of an array. On the iterator, the next() method is called several times in succession until the end of the iterator is reached and all values are output. The next() method returns an object with the done and value properties and advances the internal pointer of the iterator. The value property contains the value of the current iteration, while the done property contains a specification of whether the end of the iterator has been reached.

```
const artists = [
  'Deep Purple',
  'Jimi Hendrix',
  'The Doors',
  'King Crimson'
];
const iterator = artists.values();  // Creating the iterator
const artist = iterator.next();     // First value in the iterator
console.log(artist);                // Output: {value: 'Deep Purple', done: false}
artist = iterator.next();           // Continue in the iterator
console.log(artist);                // Output: {value: 'Jimi Hendrix', done: false}
artist = iterator.next();           // Continue in the iterator
console.log(artist);                // Output: {value: 'The Doors', done: false}
artist = iterator.next();           // Continue in the iterator
console.log(artist);                // Output: {value: 'King Crimson', done: false}
artist = iterator.next();           // Continue in the iterator
console.log(artist);                // Output: {value: undefined, done: true}
```

Listing 16.23 The next() Method Can Be Used to Control the Iterator

16.2.3 Creating Your Own Iterator

As you've seen, you can access predefined iterators of the Array, Set, and Map data structures. However, you also have the option to create your own iterators.

Now we'll show this with an example and create an iterator that outputs the elements of an array in *reverse order*—that is, first the last element, then the second last, and so on, then finally the first element last.

The code for this is shown in Listing 16.24. You can see the implementation of the iterator inside the createIterator() function. Here first the counter counter variable is initialized, which here represents the internal pointer of the iterator, which points to the respective current element in the array. Initially, the variable has the value determined from the array.length-1 expression and thus points to the last element in the array.

Then the function returns the iterator object. Its next() method implements the iteration behavior: if the counter counter variable (or pointer variable) is greater than or

16

equal to 0, next() returns an object whose done property has the value false (because the iterator has not yet reached the end, or in this case the beginning, of the array) and whose value property contains the corresponding element from the array pointed to by the counter variable.

The decrement operator (--) is used to count down the counter variable directly by one after determining the respective element. When the counter variable has reached 0 (i.e., the iterator has reached the end), next() returns an object whose done property has the value true and whose value property has the value undefined.

```
const artists = [
  'Deep Purple',
  'Jimi Hendrix',
  'The Doors',
  'King Crimson'
];
function createIterator(array) {
  let counter = array.length-1;
  // Return of the iterator object
  return {
    next: function(){
      if (counter < 0) {
        return {
          value: undefined,
          done: true
        };
      } else {
        return {
          value: array[counter--],
          done: false
        };
      }
    }
  }
};
const iterator = createIterator(artists);
const artist = iterator.next();   // First value in the iterator
console.log(artist);              // Output: {value: 'King Crimson', done: false}
artist = iterator.next();         // Continue in the iterator
console.log(artist);              // Output: {value: 'The Doors', done: false}
artist = iterator.next();         // Continue in the iterator
console.log(artist);              // Output: {value: 'Jimi Hendrix', done: false}
artist = iterator.next();         // Continue in the iterator
console.log(artist);              // Output: {value: 'Deep Purple', done: false}
```

```
artist = iterator.next();         // Continue in the iterator
console.log(artist);              // Output: {value: undefined, done: true}
```

Listing 16.24 Creating and Using Your Own Iterator

16.2.4   Creating an Iterable Object

Now that you know how to create your own iterator, it is not difficult to create an *iterable object*. To do this, as shown in Listing 16.25, you first define an object that serves as a container for the array and is the object that is about to be made iterable.

```
const artists = [
  'Deep Purple',
  'Jimi Hendrix',
  'The Doors',
  'King Crimson'
];
const arrayWrapper = {
  array: artists
}
```

Listing 16.25 The Object That Is About to Be Made Iterable

The only thing you need to do after that is to define the Symbol.iterator property on the container object and to specify as its value a function that returns an iterator.

As shown in Listing 16.26, this is similar to the implementation just illustrated in Listing 16.24. The only difference is that a parameter is not passed to the Symbol.iterator function (or method), but the array stored in the container object is accessed within the function.

```
arrayWrapper[Symbol.iterator] = function() {
  const array = this.array;
  let counter = this.array.length-1;
  // Return of the iterator object
  return {
    next: function(){
      if (counter < 0) {
        return {
          done: true
        };
      } else {
        return {
          value: array[counter--],
          done: false
        };
```

16

```
    }
   }
  }
};
```

Listing 16.26 Implementation of the Iterator and the Method That Returns the Iterator

---

Note

In JavaScript, an object is *iterable* if it has an internal Symbol.iterator method that returns an iterator (Figure 16.4).

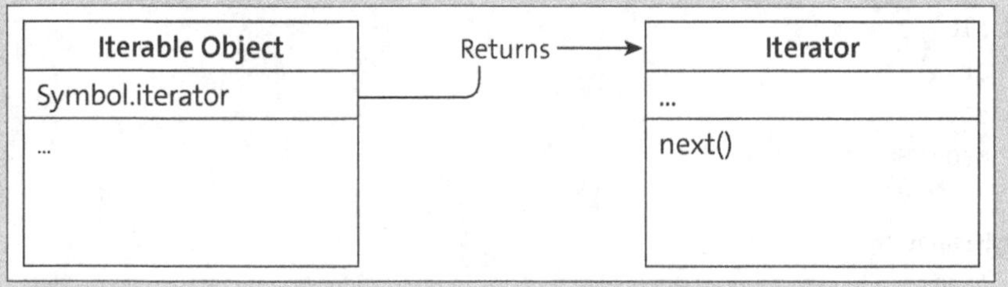

Figure 16.4 Relationship between Iterable Objects and Iterators

---

16.2.5   Iterating over Iterable Objects

Now that you've made the object iterable, you can easily use it as input for a for-of loop, just like maps, sets, and arrays (see Listing 16.27).

```
for(let artist of arrayWrapper) {  // Iteration over the iterator
  console.log(artist);
  // Output one after the other:
  // "King Crimson"
  // "The Doors"
  // "Jimi Hendrix"
  // "Deep Purple"
}
```

Listing 16.27 Using the Iterable Object in a for-of Loop

16.3   Pausing and Resuming Functions

With ES2015, a feature has been added to the ECMAScript standard that allows functions to be paused or interrupted at certain points and resumed at a later time. The constructs that are used here are called *generators*. They are generated via *generator functions*.

16.3.1 Creating a Generator Function

Generator functions are defined using the function keyword, immediately followed by an asterisk (function*). When a generator function is called, it returns a generator that can be used to control the execution of the code defined in the generator function.

A generator is interrupted using the newly introduced yield operator. The yield operator, like return, returns a value and causes a step out from the generator. The highlight here is that when the generator is called the next time, the execution of the function continues after the yield. The generator function in Listing 16.28 thus returns a generator that returns 1 on the first call and 2 on the second call.

```javascript
function* returnOneThenReturnTwo() {
  console.log('A');
  yield 1;                 // Generator stops here and returns the value 1.
  console.log('B');        // On the next call, the generator continues ...
                           // ... to execute from here ...
  yield 2;                 // ... up to this line, at which the generator stops...
                           // ... again and returns the value 2 this time.
  console.log('C');
}
```

Listing 16.28 A Simple Generator Function

16.3.2 Creating a Generator

Let's show the generator's behavior just theoretically described in practice with an example. In Listing 16.29, a generator is initially created by calling the returnOneThenReturnTwo() generator function. Here, it's important that this call doesn't yet invoke the generator itself. You achieve this by using the next() method on the generator object.

This method is not only similar in name to iterators, but also returns an object that has two properties: The done property contains information about whether the end of the generator has been reached, and the value property contains the actual value returned by yield in each case.

Repeated calls of the next() method on the generator cause the control flow to step out of the generator function at yield and back in again behind it.

```javascript
const generator = returnOneThenReturnTwo();
// Calling the generator function creates a generator.

let result = generator.next();    // Output: "A"
console.log(result);              // Output: {done: false, value: 1}
result = generator.next();        // Output: "B"
console.log(result);              // Output: {done: false, value: 2}
result = generator.next();        // Output: "C"
```

821

```
console.log(result);                    // Output: {done: true, value: undefined}

const generator2 = returnOneThenReturnTwo();    // a second generator
let result2 = generator2.next();   // Output: "A"
console.log(result2);                   // Output: {done: false, value: 1}
result2 = generator2.next();       // Output: "B"
console.log(result2);                   // Output: {done: false, value: 2}
result2 = generator2.next();       // Output: "C"
console.log(result2);                   // Output: {done: true, value: undefined}
```

Listing 16.29 Creating and Using a Generator

> **Note**
>
> Generators are therefore nothing but a special kind of iterator. As with iterators, calls of next() on a generator always return an object with the done and value properties. The done property provides information about whether the end of the generator has been reached, and the value property contains the value returned by the current yield.

16.3.3   Iterating over Generators

Because generators are a special form of iterators, they can also be used directly as input for a for-of loop. Listing 16.30 shows a corresponding example.

```
const generator = returnOneThenReturnTwo();
for(let value of generator) {
  if(value) {
    console.log(value);
  } else {
    break;
  }
}
// Output:
// A
// 1
// B
// 2
// C
```

Listing 16.30 Generators within a for-of Loop

16.3.4   Creating Infinite Generators

It's also possible to create generators that can generate infinite sequences. As an example, let's take a generator function that works like a counter and always returns the next highest number, starting at 0. Because the yield operator can in principle appear at any place within a function, such a counter functionality can be implemented relatively quickly by simply placing yield within an infinite loop, as shown in Listing 16.31.

```
function* counter() {
  let counter = 0;
  while(true) {
    counter++;
    yield counter;
  }
}
```

```
const counter1 = counter();
console.log(counter1.next());        // {done: false, value: 1}
console.log(counter1.next());        // {done: false, value: 2}
console.log(counter1.next());        // {done: false, value: 3}
console.log(counter1.next());        // {done: false, value: 4}
console.log(counter1.next());        // {done: false, value: 5}
// and so on
```

Listing 16.31 A Generator Function for Counting Up

16.3.5 Controlling Generators with Parameters

Sometimes it can be helpful to be able to influence a generator from the outside—for example, to control when it should be terminated. To achieve this, a parameter can be passed to the next() method, which is then used within the generator as the input value of the yield statement.

Listing 16.32 shows the previous counter() generator function, which has been adapted accordingly and evaluates the return value of yield (or the parameter passed in each case).

```
function* counter() {
    let counter = 0;
    while(true) {
        counter++;
        const restart = yield counter;
        if(restart === true) {
            counter = 0;
        }
    }
}
```

Listing 16.32 A Generator Function with yield Return Value

The restart variable receives the value that was passed as a parameter to the call of next(). Depending on this value, the counter variable is reset or not. So if next() is called with true as in Listing 16.33, then the corresponding generator starts counting from the beginning again.

```
const counter1 = counter();
console.log(counter1.next());        // {done: false, value: 1}
console.log(counter1.next());        // {done: false, value: 2}
console.log(counter1.next());        // {done: false, value: 3}
console.log(counter1.next());        // {done: false, value: 4}
console.log(counter1.next());        // {done: false, value: 5}
console.log(counter1.next(true));    // {done: false, value: 1}
console.log(counter1.next());        // {done: false, value: 2}
console.log(counter1.next());        // {done: false, value: 3}
console.log(counter1.next());        // {done: false, value: 4}
console.log(counter1.next());        // {done: false, value: 5}
```

Listing 16.33 Using next() with Parameters

16.4   Intercepting Access to Objects

Another concept, known as a *design pattern* in many programming languages, was introduced natively to the JavaScript language in ES2015. We're talking about proxies.

16.4.1   The Principle of Proxies

In software development, a *proxy* is an object that's upstream of another object and is called as a substitute for the object. The proxy object allows you to intercept, process, and forward accesses to the source object and also to intercept and influence the return values of intercepted methods (see Figure 16.5).

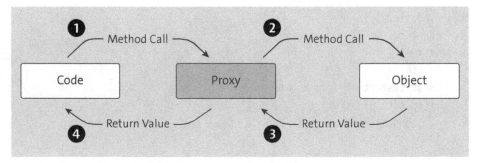

Figure 16.5 Method Calls to Objects Can Be Intercepted via Proxies

16.4.2   Creating Proxies

A proxy object is created via the call `Proxy(targetObject, handler);` (see Listing 16.34). The `Proxy()` function expects two arguments: `targetObject` represents the source object whose accesses are to be intercepted, and `handler` designates the object that is to react to the accesses to the source object. In the subsequent code, you then address the proxy object instead of the source object.

```
const targetObject = {
  firstName: null,
  lastName: null
};
const handler = {/* is about to be implemented*/};
const proxy = new Proxy(targetObject, handler);
proxy.firstName = 'John';
proxy.lastName = 'Doe';
console.log(proxy.firstName);
console.log(proxy.lastName);
```

Listing 16.34 Creating a Proxy

16.4.3   Defining Handlers for Proxies

Proxies thus provide the framework for intercepting method calls. The method calls to be intercepted and how to react to them are defined in handler objects: there are a number of predefined methods (referred to as *traps*) that can be implemented on a handler object and then called depending on the operation being performed on the proxy object. The relationship between the proxy operation and the method called on the handler is shown in Table 16.1.

Method in Handler	Operation	Remark

apply(
  target,
  thisArgument,
  argumentsList
)
	proxy.apply(
	  thisArgument,
	  argumentsList
	)
	
	or
	
	proxy.call(
	  thisArgument,
	  ...argumentsList
	)
	
	or
	
	proxy(...argumentsList)
		Only if the proxy object is a function

Table 16.1 Correlation between Proxy Operations and Handler Methods

825

Method in Handler	Operation	Remark

construct(
  target,
  argumentsList,
  newTarget
)
	new proxy(
	  ..argumentsList
	)
		Only if the proxy object is a function

defineProperty(
  target,
  property,
  propertyDescriptor
)
	Object.defineProperty(
	  proxy,
	  property,
	  propertyDescriptor
	)
		For all objects

deleteProperty(
  target,
  property
)
	delete proxy[property]
	or
	delete proxy.property
		For all objects

enumerate(target)	for(var i in proxy)	Removed from the current working version of the ECMAScript standard—that is, the successor of ES2015

get(
  targetObject,
  property,
  proxy
)
	proxy[property]
	or
	proxy.property
		For all objects

getOwnPropertyDescriptor(
  target,
  property
)
	Object.getOwnPropertyDescriptor(
	  proxy,
	  property
	)
		For all objects

getPrototypeOf(
  target
)
	Object.getPrototypeOf(
	  Proxy
	)
		For all objects

has(property)	property in proxy	For all objects
isExtensible(target)	Object.isExtensible(proxy)	For all objects

Table 16.1 Correlation between Proxy Operations and Handler Methods (Cont.)

Method in Handler	Operation	Remark
ownKeys(target)	Object.getOwnPropertyProper-tyNames (proxy) or Object.getOwnPropertyProperty-Symbols (proxy) or Object.keys(proxy)	For all objects
preventExtensions(target)	Object.preventExtensions(proxy)	For all objects

set(
  targetObject,
  property,
  value
)
	proxy[property] = value
	or
	proxy.property = value
		For all objects

setPrototypeOf(
  target,
  proto
)
	Object.setPrototypeOf(proxy,
	proto)
		For all objects

Table 16.1 Correlation between Proxy Operations and Handler Methods (Cont.)

An example of using a handler is shown in Listing 16.35. Here, the set and get methods were defined on the handler object. Consequently, all accesses are intercepted where a property of the underlying object is read or set.

```
const person = {
  firstName: 'John',
  lastName: 'Doe',
  email: 'johndoe@javascripthandbuch.de',
  age: 42
}

const handler = {
  get(target, property) {
      console.log(`Read "${target[property]}" from property "${property}"`);
      return target[property];
  },

  set(target, property, value) {
    console.log(`Write "${target[property]}" to property "${property}"`);
    target[property] = value;
  }
```

16

```
}

const proxy = new Proxy(person, handler);
proxy.firstName = 'John';          // Call set() of handler
// Output:
// Write value "John" to property "firstName"

proxy.lastName = 'Doe';            // Call set() of handler
// Output:
// Write value "Doe" to property "lastName"

console.log(proxy.firstName);      // Call get() of handler
// Output:
// Read value "John" from property "firstName"
// John

console.log(proxy.lastName);       // call get() of handler
// Output:
// Read value "Doe" from property "lastName"
// Doe

console.log(proxy.age);            // call get() of handler
// Output:
// Read value "42" from property "age"
// 42
```

Listing 16.35 Using a Proxy

We can extend the example a bit by, for example, including a validation for the age within the trap for writing properties. You can see the code for this in Listing 16.36. Whenever an attempt is made to assign a value to the age property, a check is made to ensure that the value is actually a number and that the number is not less than 0. If either of these is not the case, a corresponding error is thrown.

```
const person = {
  firstName: 'John',
  lastName: 'Doe',
  email: 'johndoe@javascripthandbuch.de',
  age: 42
}

const handler = {
  get(target, property) {
      console.log(`Read "${target[property]}" from property "${property}"`);
```

```
      return target[property];
  },

  set(target, property, value) {
    if (property === 'age') {
      if (typeof value !== 'number') {
          throw new Error('Age must be a number');
      }
      if (value < 0) {
          throw new Error('Age must not be less than 0')
      }
    }
    console.log(`Write "${target[property]}" to property "${property}"`);
    target[property] = value;
  }
}

const proxy = new Proxy(person, handler);
proxy.age = -42; // Error: Age must not be less than 0.
```

Listing 16.36 Proxy with Validation of Age

16.5 Summary

In this chapter, we introduced asynchronous programming, an important concept in JavaScript. You also learned about various advanced features. Here's what you should take away from this chapter:

- In asynchronous programming, the call of a function and the return of the result are not directly coupled to each other as in synchronous programming. Instead, the return value (or the result of the function) and also errors are transferred to the calling code in a different way. The following variants are available in JavaScript for this purpose:

  - *Callbacks* simplify the writing of asynchronous code by encapsulating the callback functions of the asynchronous function. The new async and await keywords introduced in ES2017 make asynchronous code even more readable.

  - *Promises* make writing asynchronous code easier by encapsulating the callback functions of the asynchronous function in their own objects, on which the then(), catch(), and finally() methods are available.

  - *Async functions* internally work with promises but lead to even clearer code thanks to the async and await keywords.

- *Iterators* encapsulate the behavior for the iteration on data structures.
- *Generators* allow functions to be stopped or interrupted at certain points and resumed at a later time.
- *Proxies* make it possible to intercept accesses to objects.

Chapter 17

Creating Server-Based Applications with Node.js

For a long time, JavaScript was limited to use within browsers. In recent years, however, the language has opened up a number of new areas of application, which we'll introduce in this and the following two chapters. We'll start here with the development of server-based applications with JavaScript based on the Node.js runtime environment.

Node.js allows JavaScript to be executed outside the browser. It's based on the V8 runtime environment, which is also used in Chrome, and has contributed significantly to the renewed success of JavaScript in recent years.

17.1 Introduction to Node.js

Strictly speaking, Node.js is more than "just" a runtime environment: it also provides various software components (*modules* or *packages*) for JavaScript—for example, to read files, create web servers, access databases, and much more. To make this possible, Node.js contains native components partly written in C or C++.

17.1.1 The Architecture of Node.js

The popularity of Node.js is not least due to the fact that it's relatively fast and scalable, using certain concepts that will be explained ahead. To better understand this functionality or the architecture of Node.js, let's first take a look at how traditional servers such as IIS or Apache Tomcat work for comparison (see Figure 17.1).

With these servers, each request from a user to the server results in a new thread being created or the server selecting a thread from the thread pool and assigning it to the request. This also happens if a user reloads a web page (thus generating a new request to the server). For these reasons, these types of servers are also called *multithreaded servers*.

Usually, the requests also involve some form of *blocking input and output* (*blocking I/O*): for example, a search query to a database, loading a very specific file, and so on. The thread now waits until the result of the corresponding operation is available, but of course it still occupies memory.

If many requests are executed, this leads to higher memory usage for the server. The longer the input and output operations take, the more it becomes apparent: as long as threads are blocked, the server must also create new threads for new requests.

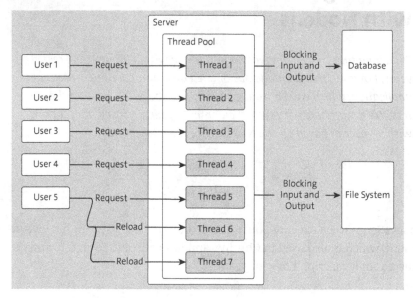

Figure 17.1 The Architecture of Traditional Servers

This is exactly where the Node.js architecture comes into play (see Figure 17.2). Instead of one thread per request, Node.js uses a single (main) thread that receives all requests and manages them in a *request queue* (Node.js is thus a *single-threaded server*).

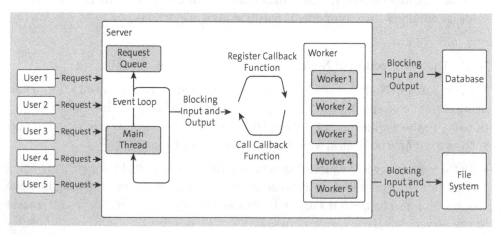

Figure 17.2 The Architecture of Node.js

Within this thread, a so-called event loop is executed, which is a loop that continuously checks requests from the event queue and processes events from input and output operations (more on this in a moment). If a user makes a request to a Node.js server, a check is made within the event loop to see whether the next request requires a blocking input or output operation. If not—that is, if it's *nonblocking input/output* (*nonblocking I/O*), the request is processed directly and a corresponding response is sent to the user.

If, on the other hand, a request requires a blocking input or output operation, one of several Node.js-internal workers (in principle threads, just Node.js-internal) is triggered to perform this operation. Here, a callback function is passed, which in turn is called as soon as the input or output operation has been performed (these are the events processed by the event loop, so to speak).

But the crucial thing is that the main thread doesn't stop during the blocking input and output operations: the event loop makes its rounds constantly, checks new requests, and so on. Through this architecture, Node.js prevents more and more threads from being created and occupying computing power, even though they're only waiting for the results of input or output operations.

17.1.2 Installing Node.js

The installation of Node.js is relatively simple: For Windows and Mac, installation or executable files are available for download at *http://nodejs.org/download/*. For other operating systems, Node.js can be installed via appropriate package managers. Corresponding installation scripts can be found at *https://nodejs.org/en/download/package-manager/*.

After successful installation, the node command is available on the command line, which you can use to execute JavaScript code. You can also use node --version or node -v to display the version of the Node.js installation to ensure that the installation was successful.

To execute a JavaScript file, you pass the name of the file (including the path to the file, if applicable) to the node command as an argument—for example, node main.js.

> **Read-Eval-Print Loop**
>
> In addition to executing JavaScript files, you can also use the node command to start a *read-eval-print* loop (*REPL*), which basically is a command line through which you can enter JavaScript instructions and have them executed directly.

17.1.3 A Simple Application

The simplest application for Node.js is certainly just to write the console.log('Hello world'); statement to the appropriate script file and call it using node main.js: Node.js interprets the script, executes it, outputs the message Hello World on the console, and that's it.

In contrast, a somewhat more interesting *Hello World* example is shown in Listing 17.1. Here you can see how to use the http package to set up a simple web server that runs under `localhost` on port 8000 and responds to every request with the message `Hello World`. If you call this script with the `node` command, the web server runs until you cancel the script (e.g., by pressing `Ctrl` + `C`).

As you can see in the listing, Node.js follows the CommonJS specification regarding the use of packages: therefore, to import a package, use the `require()` function. We'll discuss the remaining methods in more detail later in this chapter when we discuss the http package. But you can already see that under Node.js, it's possible to create a simple web server with relatively few lines of code.

```
'use strict';
const http = require('http');
http.createServer((request, response) => {
  response.writeHead(200, {
    'Content-Type': 'text/plain'
  });
  response.write('Hello World');
  response.end();
}).listen(8000);
```

Listing 17.1 A Simple Node.js Application

17.2   Managing Node.js Packages

There are many different modules available for Node.js. Some, like the http package already briefly shown, are included in the installation of Node.js; others can be installed later via the Node.js Package Manager (NPM).

17.2.1   Installing the Node.js Package Manager

You have several options to install the NPM tool: MSI and **.pkg** installation files are available for Windows and Mac, and a corresponding installation script is available for Unix systems. Further installation options are described in detail at *https://github.com/npm/npm*.

However, much more common than a separate installation of NPM is indirect installation via Node.js. Since version 0.6.3, NPM is already included in the installation of Node.js. As already described, the latter can be downloaded from *http://nodejs.org/download/* as an installation or executable file for the various operating systems. After installing Node.js, NPM is also directly available to you as the `npm` command line command. You can verify the installation by running the `npm --version` command, which outputs the version number of the installed NPM.

Version Numbers of NPM and Node.js

The version number of NPM is not identical to the version number of Node.js. Currently, for example, the node --version command on my computer outputs version 16.2.0, while the npm --version command outputs version 7.13.0.

17.2.2   Installing Packages

With NPM, you can install packages either locally or globally. The former is useful if you want to install a particular Node.js package as a dependency of one of your applications, while the latter makes sense in cases where you want a Node.js package to be globally available to all of your applications, or if it's a tool like mocha or Grunt that you want to be globally available (see also Chapter 21).

Installing Packages Locally

The command for installing a package is npm install <package> (or in short form: npm i <package>), where <package> stands for the package to be installed. For example, to install the lodash package (*https://lodash.com/*), you call the following command: npm install lodash (or npm i lodash).

Then NPM creates a new directory named **node_modules** in the current directory if there is no such directory already and installs the lodash package into this directory.

NPM not only ensures that the package specified is installed, but also, as mentioned, that all dependencies of the package are installed. This is done recursively for each package to be installed until all dependencies have been resolved and installed as well.

Strictly speaking, you can use not only the name of a package for <package>, but also, for example, URLs, such as those pointing to a GitHub repository. You can find an overview of the various package installation options at *https://docs.npmjs.com/cli/install*.

Installing a Package with a Specific Version

By default, NPM installs the last current version of a package. But if you want to install a specific version of a package, simply specify it after the name of the package—for example, npm install lodash@4.3.5.

Installing Packages Globally

To install a package globally, the -g (or --global) flag must be passed as an argument to the install command. Because, depending on the configuration, the global packages are located in a directory for which you only have write access with administrator permissions, in such cases the command should be executed under the appropriate

17

identifier. In Unix-based environments, for example, you would execute `sudo npm install -g <package>`.

Updating NPM

Because NPM usually is updated more frequently than Node.js, you can also update NPM separately. Conveniently, this can be done via NPM itself by running the `sudo npm install -g npm` command, because NPM itself is also an NPM package.

Overview of Various Web APIs

If you enter the name of a package for `<package>`, it must be registered in the *NPM registry*, a directory for available packages. NPM obtains all packages from the registry at *http://registry.npmjs.org* by default. In principle, however, a customized registry can also be hosted on its own server. For an overview of the packages available in the default registry, see *www.npmjs.org*. Currently, over a million packages are listed there (as of May 2021). For comparison: There were about 475,000 packages in October 2017, 250,000 in May 2016, and 95,000 in September 2014.

A small selection of known packages is shown in Table 17.1.

Package Name	Description	Installation Command	Link
async	Library with many useful helper functions for asynchronous programming	`npm install async`	*https://github.com/caolan/async*
bower	Package manager for web applications	`npm install -g bower`	*http://bower.io*
browserify	Tool for using Node.js packages in the browser	`npm install -g browserify`	*http://browserify.org*
commander	Helper tools for creating command line applications	`npm install commander`	*https://github.com/tj/commander.js*
cordova	Command line tools for creating Cordova-based applications	`npm install -g cordova`	*https://cordova.apache.org*
express	Web framework for Node.js	`npm install express`	*https://github.com/strongloop/express*

Table 17.1 Using Packages

Package Name	Description	Installation Command	Link
grunt/ grunt-cli	Tool for automating tasks or building applications	`npm install -g grunt-cli`, `npm install grunt`	*http://gruntjs.com*
gulp/ gulp-cli	Tool for automating tasks or building applications	`npm install -g gulp-cli`, `npm install gulp`	*http://gulpjs.com*
lodash	Library with many useful helper functions for functional programming	`npm install lodash`	*https://lodash.com*
mocha	Test framework for JavaScript applications	`npm install -g mocha`	*https://mochajs.org*
mongodb	Driver for connecting to the MongoDB database	`npm install mongodb`	*https://github.com/ mongodb/node- mongodb-native*
pm2	Process management for Node.js	`npm install -g pm2`	*http://pm2. keymet- rics.io*
request	A simple HTTP client	`npm install request`	*https://github.com/ request/request*
socket.io	Server for socket connections	`npm install socket.io`	*http://socket.io*
underscore	Library with many useful helper functions for functional programming	`npm install underscore`	*http://under- scorejs.org*
validator	Library for validating strings	`npm install validator`	*https://github.com/ chriso/validator.js*

Table 17.1 Using Packages (Cont.)

As mentioned, Node.js and thus NPM follow the CommonJS module format. This means that to use a package, you must include or import it via `require()`.

An example is shown in Listing 17.2. The lodash package you just installed is integrated via `require('lodash')` and assigned to the _ variable. This variable subsequently contains references to all functions and objects exported by the lodash package (see also Chapter 15). One of these functions is the `includes()` function, which checks an array to see if it contains a particular value, and is applied to the names array in the example.

```
const _ = require('lodash');
const names = ['John', 'James'];
console.log(_.includes(names, 'James')); // Output: true
```

Listing 17.2 Using the lodash Package in Node.js

17.2.3   Creating Your Own Packages

Of course, it's also possible to create your own packages for Node.js. To do this, you can use the npm init command, which guides you through the steps using a command line wizard. The information highlighted in Listing 17.3 is queried consecutively. The result of the wizard is a file named **package.json** (the *package configuration file*), the contents of which can be seen at the end of the listing.

```
This utility will walk you through creating a package.json file.
It only covers the most common items, and tries to guess sane defaults.

See `npm help json` for definitive documentation on these fields
and exactly what they do.

Use `npm install <pkg> --save` afterwards to install a package and
save it as a dependency in the package.json file.

Press ^C at any time to quit.
name: (package) sample package
version: (0.0.0) 1.0.0
description: Sample package JavaScript manual
entry point: (main.js)
test command: mocha
git repository:
keywords: javascript
author: Philip Ackermann
license: (ISC) MIT
About to write to /Users/philipackermann/Documents/Arbeit/Rheinwerk/
JavaScriptHandbuch/Quelltext/Kapitel17/package/package.json:

{
  "name": "sample package",
  "version": "1.0.0",
  "description": "Sample package JavaScript Manual,
  "main": "main.js",
  "scripts": {
    "test": "mocha"
  },
```

```
  "keywords": [
    "javascript"
  ],
  "author": "Philip Ackermann",
  "license": "MIT"
}
```

Is this ok? (yes)

Listing 17.3 Command Line Wizard for Creating an NPM Package

This configuration file is a JSON file that contains various pieces of information about a package. The file must be present in each package and must contain at least the name and version number of the respective package; otherwise, it can't be installed. The combination of name and version number uniquely identifies a package. Both are required by NPM to resolve and download dependencies.

Dependencies of a Package

In addition to general data about the package, the dependencies to other packages are also defined in the configuration file. If you install a package via NPM, the dependencies are installed directly from this file in the correct version if necessary.

The JSON format used is loosely based on the package descriptor file format defined under CommonJS (*http://wiki.commonjs.org/wiki/Packages/1.0#Package_Descriptor_ File*). Table 17.2 provides an overview of the most important properties that can be used in this context. For a complete list, visit *https://docs.npmjs.com/files/package.json*.

Property	Description
name	The name of the package.
version	The version of the package. The name of a package plus the version of the package serves as a unique ID for the entire package. Semantic versioning is supported here (see also *http://semver.org*).
description	A description of the package.
main	The main file/entry file into the package.
keywords	An array of keywords to classify the package thematically. For example, these keywords are searched when you perform a search query via npm search.
homepage	The URL of the project homepage.

Table 17.2 The Various Properties of the package.json Configuration File

Property	Description
license	The license of the package.
author	The (main) author of the package. Only one person can be specified here. Additional authors can be listed using the contributors property. A Person object consists of the name, email (optional), and url (optional) properties.
contributors	An array of Person objects.
repository	This can be used to specify the repository under which the source code of the package is managed.
dependencies	Here you can define dependencies of the package to other packages. Dependencies are defined by name and version of the corresponding package. Among other things, you can define whether the version number of the referenced package must match exactly or whether the version must be greater than (or equal to) or less than (or equal to) the specified version number. Various additional placeholders can be used to flexibly determine when a dependency is fulfilled. Dependencies are installed directly when a package is installed.
devDependencies	This is where all the packages are managed that are only required during development, but not when the respective package is used productively. Packages for unit testing, checking code quality, the build process, and so on can usually be found here.
os	This property allows you to define the operating systems under which the respective package is executable.

Table 17.2 The Various Properties of the package.json Configuration File (Cont.)

Get Information about Packages

You can use the npm info <package> command to output the **package.json** file of the corresponding package without the package having to be installed on your computer. NPM retrieves the information from the NPM registry and outputs the file on the console. This can be handy if you want to check certain prerequisites before installing a package—for example, dependencies used, support of a certain operating system, and so on.

Adding Dependencies to the package.json File

By specifying the additional --save parameter in the npm install command, the dependency is not only downloaded, but also directly marked as a dependency in the **package.json** file:

```
npm install lodash --save
```

The `--save-dev` parameter analogously writes the dependency to the development dependencies (`devDependencies`) of the configuration file:

```
npm install mocha --save-dev
```

After executing the preceding commands, the **package.json** file from just now would look as shown in Listing 17.4.

```
{
  "name": "sample package",
  "version": "1.0.0",
  "description": "Sample package JavaScript Manual",
  "main": "index.js",
  "scripts": {
    "test": "mocha"
  },
  "keywords": [
    "javascript"
  ],
  "author": "Philip Ackermann",
  "license": "MIT",
  "dependencies": {
    "lodash": "~4.17.21",
  },
  "devDependencies": {
    "mocha": "~8.4.0"
  }
}
```

Listing 17.4 The package.json Configuration File Extended by Dependencies

17.3   Processing and Triggering Events

Much of Node.js is event-driven. The events are triggered by *event emitters*—that is, objects of the `EventEmitter` type. In this section, we'll briefly show you how to use this basic programming paradigm (which you already know in principle from Chapter 6) in Node.js.

17.3.1   Triggering and Intercepting an Event

The `EventEmitter` type has two main methods (you can see a detailed listing in Table 17.3). The `on()` method can be used to define callback functions to be executed when a specific event occurs—in other words, event listeners can be registered this way. You can use the second method of EventEmitter, the emit() method, to trigger events.

The first parameter to be passed to the on() method is the name of the event for which the event listener is to be registered; the second parameter is the event listener in the form of a function. The emit() method is passed the name of the event and the arguments used to call the event listeners registered for the event.

An example of this is shown in Listing 17.5. After importing the events package (which is included in the Node.js installation by default, like the http package), an instance of EventEmitter is created here, then an event listener is registered for the (self-defined) personAdded event, and then the event with the two values John and Doe is triggered via the emit() call.

```
'use strict';
const events = require('events');          // Include events package
const emitter = new events.EventEmitter(); // Create emitter
emitter.on(                                // Intercept event
  'personAdded',                           // Event name
  (firstName, lastName) => {               // Callback function
    console.log(firstName + ' ' + lastName);
  }
);
emitter.emit(                              // Trigger event
  'personAdded',                           // Event name
  'John',                                  // Parameter firstName
  'Doe'                                    // Parameter lastName
);                                         // Output: "John Doe"
```

Listing 17.5 Triggering and Intercepting an Event

Property/Method	Description
EventEmitter.defaultMaxListeners	Default maximum number of event listeners that can be registered for an event. This value can be overwritten. Alternatively, a maximum number can be defined individually for each event emitter using the setMaxListeners() method.

addListener(
  eventName,
  listener
)
	Alias for the on() method. Registers a new event listener for an event.

Table 17.3 Methods for Working with Events

Property/Method	Description

emit(
  eventName
  [, arg1]
  [, arg2]
  [, ...]
)
	Triggers an event.

eventNames()	Returns an array containing the names of the events for which an event emitter has registered event listeners.
getMaxListeners()	Specifies the maximum number of event listeners for the given event emitter.
listenerCount(eventName)	Returns the number of event listeners registered for an event.
listeners(eventName)	Returns an array with the event listeners registered for an event.
on(eventName, listener)	Registers a new event listener for an event.

once(
  eventName,
  listener
)
	Registers a new event listener for an event, but executes it once at most.

prependListener(
  eventName,
  listener
)
	Registers a new event listener for an event and places it at the beginning of the array of event listeners registered for that event.

prependOnceListener(
  eventName,
  listener
)
	Like prependListener(), except that the corresponding event listener is called once at most.

removeAllListeners([eventName])	Removes all event listeners registered for an event.

removeListener(
  eventName,
  listener
)
	Removes the passed event listener for the passed event.

setMaxListeners(n)	Sets the maximum number of event listeners that can be registered for each event in an event emitter.

Table 17.3 Methods for Working with Events (Cont.)

17

17.3.2   Triggering an Event Multiple Times

Of course, it's also possible to call the `emit()` method for an event multiple times and thus trigger the event multiple times. In Listing 17.6, for example, the `personAdded` event is triggered twice and the corresponding event listener is executed twice as a result.

```
'use strict';
const events = require('events');              // Include events package
const emitter = new events.EventEmitter();     // Create emitter
emitter.on(                                    // Intercept event
  'personAdded',                               // Event name
  (firstName, lastName) => {                   // Callback function
    console.log(firstName + ' ' + lastName);
  }
);
emitter.emit(                                  // Trigger event
  'personAdded',                               // Event name
  'John',                                      // Parameter firstName
  'Doe'                                        // Parameter lastName
);                                             // Output: "John Doe"
emitter.emit(                                  // Trigger event
  'personAdded',                               // Event name
  'James',                                     // Parameter firstName
  'Doe'                                        // Parameter lastName
);                                             // Output: "James Doe"
```

Listing 17.6 Triggering and Intercepting Multiple Events

17.3.3   Intercepting an Event Exactly Once

If you want a registered event listener to be called only once—regardless of how often an event is triggered—use the `once()` method instead of the `on()` method to register the corresponding event listener. Listing 17.7 shows an example for this: here again, the `personAdded` event is triggered twice, but the event listener is executed only once.

```
'use strict';
const events = require('events');              // Include events package
const emitter = new events.EventEmitter();     // Create emitter
emitter.once(                                  // Intercept event
  'personAdded',                               // Event name
  (firstName, lastName) => {                   // Callback function
    console.log(firstName + ' ' + lastName);
  }
);
```

```
emitter.emit('personAdded', 'John', 'Doe');        // Output: "John Doe"
emitter.emit('personAdded', 'James', 'Doe');       // Event listener is not...
                                                   // ... triggered.
```

Listing 17.7 Intercepting a Single Event

> **Note**
>
> Event listeners registered via once() are triggered the first time an event occurs and removed from the event emitter.

17.3.4   Intercepting an Event Multiple Times

There's nothing against calling the on() method multiple times for an event and registering multiple event listeners for a single event this way. Listing 17.8 shows an example of this, where one event listener was registered to output the first name when the personAdded event occurs and another event listener registered to output the last name.

```
'use strict';
const events = require('events');              // Include events package
const emitter = new events.EventEmitter();     // Create emitter
emitter.on(                                    // Intercept event
  'personAdded',                               // Event name
  (firstName, lastName) => {                   // Callback function
    console.log('First name: ' + firstName);
  }
);
emitter.on(                                    // Intercept event
  'personAdded',                               // Event name
  (firstName, lastName) => {                   // Callback function
    console.log('Last name: ' + lastName);
  }
);
emitter.emit(                                  // Trigger event
  'personAdded',                               // Event name
  'John',                                      // Parameter firstName
  'Doe'                                        // Parameter lastName
);
```

Listing 17.8 Intercepting a Single Event Multiple Times

17.4   Accessing the File System

Node.js offers a myriad of functions for working with the file system. You can read files, write files, create directories, rename files and directories, change permissions on both, and much, much more. We'll only look at an excerpt of these functions here.

17.4.1   Reading Files

The internal and default package available with every Node.js installation that provides the helper functions is the fs package (*fs* is for *file system*; see *https://nodejs.org/api/ fs.html*).

For example, to read files, you have the option to do this asynchronously or synchronously (as is the case with many of the other file operations). Asynchronous reading is done with the readFile() function, which, as shown in Listing 17.9, expects two parameters: the path to the file to be read and a callback function to get the file contents or, in case of an error, the corresponding error information.

```
'use strict';
const fs = require('fs');
fs.readFile('input.txt', (error, data) => {
  if (error) {
    return console.error(error);
  }
  console.log(data.toString());
});
```

Listing 17.9 Asynchronous Reading of a File

Note
The readFile() method can also be called with three parameters: in the first place, the path to the file; in the second place, a configuration object, via which you can set, for example, the encoding to be used; and in the third place, the callback function.

As an alternative to the asynchronous readFile() function, you can use the read-FileSync() method to read a file synchronously. Instead of using a callback function, you can access the contents of the corresponding file directly via the return value of the function. Therefore, as you can see in Listing 17.10, you only pass the path to the file as a parameter and optionally a configuration object as a second parameter.

```
'use strict';
const fs = require('fs');
```

```
const data = fs.readFileSync('input.txt');
console.log(data.toString());
```

Listing 17.10 Synchronous Reading of a File

Reading Files from the Browser and under Node.js

You know from Chapter 12 that it isn't possible to access users' files from JavaScript code that's executed in the browser without their consent. In Node.js, things are a bit different: here, it depends on the user ID under which the respective Node.js application or JavaScript is executed and whether the respective user has sufficient rights to access a file.

17.4.2 Writing Files

For writing files, you also have both an asynchronous function and a synchronous function at your disposal. You can see the use of the former, the writeFile() method, in Listing 17.11. As parameters, you pass the path to the file to be written, the content to be written, and a callback function that's called when the file has been written or an error has occurred. In Listing 17.12, by contrast, you can see the use of the writeFileSync() function. As expected, the callback function is omitted here, but the rest of the call is the same.

```
'use strict';
const fs = require('fs');
fs.writeFile('output.txt', 'Hello World', (error) => {
  if (error) {
    return console.error(error);
  }
  fs.readFile('output.txt', (error, data) => {
    if (error) {
      return console.error(error);
    }
    console.log('Content: ' + data.toString());
  });
});
```

Listing 17.11 Asynchronous Writing of a File

```
'use strict';
const fs = require('fs');
fs.writeFileSync('output.txt', 'Hello World');
```

```
const data = fs.readFileSync('output.txt');
console.log(data.toString());
```

Listing 17.12 Synchronous Writing of a File

Note

The writeFile() and writeFileSync() functions can also optionally pass a configuration object as an additional parameter (in the case of writeFile(), inserted before the callback function), which can be used to specify the encoding of the data to be written, among other things.

17.4.3   Reading File Information

To read file information, you can use the stat() function. It provides, as shown in Listing 17.13 and Listing 17.14, a number of different pieces of information about a file, such as creation date, file size, and much more (see also *http://man7.org/linux/man-pages/man2/stat.2.html*).

```
'use strict';
const fs = require('fs');
fs.stat('input.txt', (error, stats) => {
  if (error) {
    return console.error(error);
  }
  console.log(stats.isFile());        // true
  console.log(stats.isDirectory());   // false
  console.log(stats);                 // See next listing
});
```

Listing 17.13 Reading File Information

```
{ dev: 16777218,
  mode: 33188,
  nlink: 1,
  uid: 501,
  gid: 20,
  rdev: 0,
  blksize: 4096,
  ino: 57181993,
  size: 10,
  blocks: 8,
  atime: Mon May 24 2021 20:03:35 GMT+0200 (CEST),
  mtime: Mon May 24 2021 20:02:32 GMT+0200 (CEST),
```

```
ctime: Mon May 24 2021 20:03:35 GMT+0200 (CEST),
birthtime: Mon May 24 2021 20:02:32 GMT+0200 (CEST) }
```

Listing 17.14 Sample Output of File Information

> **Note**
>
> Also, for stat() there is again the synchronous counterpart, in the form of the stat-Sync() function. But as we can assume that you understand the difference between asynchronous and synchronous operation by now, we'll refrain from giving a corresponding example at this point.

17.4.4   Deleting Files

To delete a file, you use the unlink() (or unlinkSync()) function. It expects the path to the file to be deleted as the parameter, as well as a callback function that's called after deleting the file or in case of an error. An example of this is shown in Listing 17.15: here, a file is first created via writeFile() and then deleted again in the callback function of this function via unlink().

```
'use strict';
const fs = require('fs');
fs.writeFile('output.txt', 'Hello World', (error) => {
  if (error) {
    return console.error(error);
  }
  console.log('File created');
  fs.unlink('output.txt', (error) => {
    if (error) {
      return console.error(error);
    }
    console.log('File deleted again');
  });
});
```

Listing 17.15 Deleting a File

17.4.5   Working with Directories

The fs package also provides a number of functions for working with directories: for example, you can use the mkdir() and mkdirSync() functions to create directories (see Listing 17.16), the readdir() and readdirSync() functions to list all files within a directory (see Listing 17.17), and rmdir() and rmdirSync() to delete a directory (see Listing 17.18).

849

```
'use strict';
const fs = require('fs');
fs.mkdir('test', (error) => {
  if (error) {
    return console.error(error);
  }
  console.log('Directory created');
});
```

Listing 17.16 Asynchronous Creation of a Directory

```
'use strict';
const fs = require('fs');
fs.readdir('test', (error, files) => {
  if(error) {
    return console.error(error);
  }
  files.forEach((file) => {
    console.log(file);
  });
});
```

Listing 17.17 Asynchronous Reading of a Directory

```
'use strict';
const fs = require('fs');
fs.rmdir('test', (error) => {
  if(error) {
    return console.error(error);
  }
});
```

Listing 17.18 Asynchronous Deletion of a Directory

> **Note**
>
> All the packages we've introduced so far in this chapter are already included in Node.js by default. There are, of course, a few more that Node.js also comes with, but we'll introduce two packages in the next two sections that are not included in Node.js: first, the Express.js web framework, and second, the mongodb package, which makes it possible to access the MongoDB database.

17.5 Creating a Web Server

Before we introduce Express.js, let's briefly review the http package that we used for the *Hello World* example earlier in the chapter.

17.5.1 Starting a Web Server

Listing 17.19 shows how to create a web server using the http package (*https://nodejs.org/api/http.html*): after importing the http package, you create a server object using the createServer() method, passing this function a callback function that receives requests to the server and prepares the server's responses to the client. Within this callback function, you have access to an object representing the request to the server (request parameter) and an object representing the response from the server (response parameter).

To generate a response, as shown in the example, it's sufficient to set an appropriate Content-Type header on the response object via the writeHead() method and the data to be included in the response via the end() method.

To then start the server, you call the listen() method on the server object. The script can then be started using the node main.js command. If you now call the URL *http://localhost:8080* in a browser, you get the output Hello World.

```
'use strict';
const http = require('http');
const PORT = 8080;
function handleRequest(request, response){
  response.writeHead(200, {'Content-Type': 'text/plain'});
  response.end('Hello World');
}
const server = http.createServer(handleRequest);
server.listen(PORT, () => {
  console.log("Server is running at: http://localhost:%s", PORT);
});
```

Listing 17.19 A Simple Server with the http Package (Contents of the server.js File)

Alternatively, you can write it all down a bit more compactly, as shown in Listing 17.20.

```
'use strict';
const http = require('http');
http
  .createServer((request, response) => {
    response.writeHead(200, {'Content-Type': 'text/plain'});
    response.end('Hello World');
```

851

```
})
.listen(8080);
```

Listing 17.20 More Compact Starting of a Web Server

> **Server-Sent Events**
>
> Remember Chapter 12? There we had also started a web server via the http package to trigger server-sent events. So if you skipped the example back then, now is a good time to take another quick look at it.

17.5.2   Making Files Available via Web Server

To read an HTML file from the file system and return its contents to the client, simply use the fs package shown earlier in this chapter, as shown in Listing 17.21, and pass the contents of the file to the write() method.

```
'use strict';
const http = require('http');
const url = require('url');
const fs = require('fs');
// 1.) Create server
http.createServer((request, response) => {
   // 2.) Find path
   const pathname = url.parse(request.url).pathname;
   // 3.) Read file for path
   fs.readFile(pathname.substr(1), (error, data) => {
      if (error) {
         return console.error(error);
         // 3.1.) File not found
         // HTTP status: 404 : NOT FOUND
         // Content-Type: text/plain
         response.writeHead(404, {'Content-Type': 'text/plain'});
      } else {
         // 3.2.) File found
         // HTTP status: 200 : OK
         // Content-Type: text/plain
         response.writeHead(200, {'Content-Type': 'text/html'});
         response.write(data.toString());
      }
      // 4.) Send response
      response.end();
```

```
  });
}).listen(8080);
```

Listing 17.21 Reading an HTML File and Sending It to the Client

17.5.3   Creating a Client for a Web Server

You can use the http package not only to create a web server, but also to make requests to a web server yourself. To do this, use the `request()` function as shown in Listing 17.22, using a configuration object to configure the web server to be requested or its host, port, and possibly a path specification, and passing a callback function that processes the response from the server.

```
'use strict';
const http = require('http');
const options = {
   host: 'localhost',
   port: '8080',
   path: '/index.html'
};
function handleResponse(response){
  let body = '';
  response.on('data', (data) => {
    body += data;
  });
  response.on('end', () => {
    console.log(body);
  });
}
const request = http.request(options, handleResponse);
request.end();
```

Listing 17.22 Creating a Client and a Request to a Web Server

> **Note**
>
> In the example, you can see from the on() method of the response object that it derives from EventEmitter.

17.5.4   Defining Routes

When the client makes a request to a web server, the server must decide what response to send back to the client. This process is commonly referred to as *routing*: the server selects a certain route based on the client's request and delivers a corresponding response. Criteria for selecting a route can include, for example, the requested URL, the transmitted parameters, or the HTTP method used. Listing 17.23 shows an example of this. Depending on the requested URL (stored in the url property of the request object), the server generates a different response: the / URL responds with the text Hello World, the /about URL with the text About Us, and the /contact URL with the text Contact Information. In all other cases, the server generates an appropriate error message and returns it to the client along with the 404 status code.

```
'use strict';
const http = require('http');
http.createServer((request, response) => {
  if(request.url === '/') {
    response.writeHead(200, {'Content-Type': 'text/html;charset=UTF-8'});
    response.end('Hello World');
  } else if(request.url === '/about') {
    response.writeHead(200, {'Content-Type': 'text/html;charset=UTF-8'});
    response.end('Über Uns');
  } else if(request.url === '/contact') {
    response.writeHead(200, {'Content-Type': 'text/html;charset=UTF-8'});
    response.end('Contact information');
  } else {
    response.writeHead(404, {'Content-Type': 'text/plain'});
    response.end('Requested URL not found');
  }

}).listen(8080);
```

Listing 17.23 Depending on the Requested URL, a Different Response Is Sent to the Client

What's still quite manageable in the example can quickly become quite confusing in more complex web applications. This is exactly one of the points that is simplified by the Express.js web framework presented next.

17.5.5 Using the Express.js Web Framework

Express.js (*http://expressjs.com*) is a web framework for Node.js that takes a lot of work out of developing web applications. To use Express.js, it must be installed as a local dependency for the corresponding project via the npm install express -save command.

The use of the package is shown in Listing 17.24. After including the package via require(), the express() call creates an object that represents the respective web application. Using its get() method, you define a route for GET requests, passing as parameters a URL pattern and a callback function that generates the response to the client. This callback function is also called a *middleware function* in the context of Express.js.

```
'use strict';
const express = require('express');
const app = express();
app.get('/', (request, response) => {
  response.send('Hello World');
});
const server = app.listen(8080, () => {
  const port = server.address().port;
  console.log("Server is running at: http://localhost:%s", port);
});
```

Listing 17.24 A Simple Server with the express Package (Contents of the server.js File)

Having an Express.js Application Generated

If you want to create a web application based on Express.js, you can also use the express-generator package (*https://github.com/expressjs/generator*). This package provides a command line tool that can be used to generate a basic framework for Express.js applications.

In addition to the get() method, other methods are available, each with the same name as the corresponding HTTP method: among others, these include post() for POST requests (see Listing 17.25), put() for PUT requests (see Listing 17.26), and delete() for DELETE requests (see Listing 17.27).

```
app.post('/something', (request, response) => {
  response.send('POST request processed');
});
```

Listing 17.25 Handling a POST Request

```
app.put('/something', (request, response) => {
  response.send('PUT request processed');
});
```

Listing 17.26 Handling a PUT Request

```
app.delete('/something', (request, response) => {
  response.send('DELETE request processed');
});
```

Listing 17.27 Handling a DELETE Request

You can find a complete listing of HTTP methods for which Express.js provides eponymous methods in Table 17.4.

HTTP Method	Method Call in Express.js
CHECKOUT	app.checkout()
COPY	app.copy()
DELETE	app.delete()
GET	app.get()
HEAD	app.head()
LOCK	app.lock()
MERGE	app.merge()
MKACTIVITY	app.mkactivity()
MKCOL	app.mkcol()
MOVE	app.move()
M-SEARCH	app['m-search']()
NOTIFY	app.notify()
OPTIONS	app.options()
PATCH	app.patch()
POST	app.post()
PURGE	app.purge()
PUT	app.put()
REPORT	app.report()
SEARCH	app.search()
SUBSCRIBE	app.subscribe()
TRACE	app.trace()
UNLOCK	app.unlock()
UNSUBSCRIBE	app.unsubscribe()

Table 17.4 HTTP Methods and Corresponding Method Calls in Express.js

Using Middleware

An essential part of Express.js is the middleware functions we just briefly mentioned. These are functions that can be connected in series to process requests, implementing different functionalities such as cookie parsing or more complex issues such as security and access control. Each middleware function has access to the request object, the response object, and the next middleware function.

You can see an example of the use of such middleware in Listing 17.28. Here the body-parser middleware package is used, through which the content of an HTTP request can be parsed, for example, into JSON format, as shown in the listing. The parsed content is then accessible within the callback function via the body property of the request object. You can also see that to use a middleware function, you pass the appropriate call to the use() method on the application object.

```
'use strict';
const express = require('express');
const bodyParser = require('body-parser');
const app = express();
app.use(bodyParser.json())
app.get('/', (request, response) => {
  const json = request.body;
  // here normal processing of the request
});
app.listen(8080);
```

Listing 17.28 Providing the Request Content as JSON

You can see another example in Listing 17.29. Here the cookie-parser middleware package is used to parse the cookies sent in the corresponding header into an array. This array is then available within the callback function in the cookies property of the request object.

```
'use strict';
const express = require('express');
const cookieParser = require('cookie-parser');
const app = express();
app.use(cookieParser());
app.get('/', (request, response) => {
  const cookies = request.cookies;
  // here normal processing of the request
});
app.listen(8080);
```

Listing 17.29 Providing the Cookies of a Request

The morgan middleware package shown in Listing 17.30 can be used to log requests automatically—for example, as shown here, to a specific file.

```
'use strict';
const express = require('express');
const fs = require('fs');
const morgan = require('morgan');
const app = express();
const accessLogStream = fs.createWriteStream(
  __dirname + '/access.log',
  {
    Flags: 'a'}
  )
app.use(morgan('combined', {stream: accessLogStream}))
app.get('/', (request, response) => {
  // here normal processing of the request
});
```

Listing 17.30 Logging All Requests to a File

Installing Middleware Packages

Because most middleware functions are in separate packages and not included in Express.js, you must first install packages you want to use via npm install. To install all the middleware packages shown in the examples, you can use the following command: npm install body-parser cookie-parser morgan.

Other Middleware Packages

A list of additional middleware packages can be found online at *http://expressjs.com/ en/resources/middleware.html.*

Configuring Static Files

To provide static files—for example, images, CSS files, or JavaScript files—through the server, routing as described earlier makes little sense: the routes would be too extensive if you had to specify every single image there.

Therefore, there is also special middleware for providing static files, which is an integral part of Express.js. The corresponding express.static() function expects the directory whose contents are to be made available as a static resource as the first parameter, and optionally a configuration object as the second parameter, which can be used to define, for example, which file types are not to be taken into account.

In Listing 17.31, for example, the middleware function is used several times in succession to mark the styles, scripts, and images directories as static or to make the files contained therein available. The files are then available at the following URLs: *http://localhost:8000/images, http://localhost:8000/styles*, and *http://localhost:8000/scripts*.

```
'use strict';
const express = require('express');
const app = express();
app.use(express.static('styles'));
app.use(express.static('scripts'));
app.use(express.static('images'));
```

Listing 17.31 Providing Static Files

Alternatively, it's possible to specify a prefix path under which the static files are to be provided. In Listing 17.32, we slightly change the previous example and pass the static prefix to the use() method. The files are then available at *http://localhost:8000/static/images, http://localhost:8000/static/styles*, and *http://localhost:8000/static/scripts*.

```
'use strict';
const express = require('express');
const app = express();
app.use('static', express.static('styles'));
app.use('static', express.static('scripts'));
app.use('static', express.static('images'));
```

Listing 17.32 Providing Static Files with Prefix Path

17.6 Accessing Databases

With the help of Node.js or JavaScript, it's also possible to access databases. One of the better-known databases in this context is the MongoDB database (*https://www.mongodb.com*). This is a NoSQL database—more precisely, a *document-oriented database*—where data is stored in the form of JSON. To access this database via JavaScript, you can use the mongodb package (*https://github.com/mongodb/node-mongodb-native*).

17.6.1 MongoDB Installation

To be able to use the mongodb package, you first need to install MongoDB on some server or— an option that is easier for when you're starting out —locally on your development computer. Corresponding installation instructions for the various operating systems can be found at *https://docs.mongodb.com/manual/installation/*. For Windows, for example, there is an MSI installation file, for Linux there are—depending on the distribution—.rpm or **.deb** packages, and under macOS MongoDB can be installed most easily via the brew installation tool.

MongoDB stores records in a directory (e.g., on macOS, it stores records in **/data/db** by default). Therefore, before you start MongoDB, you need to make sure of the following:

1. This directory exists.
2. The user who starts MongoDB has write access to the directory—for example, via the following commands:
   - sudo mkdir /data/db
   - sudo chmod 777 /data/db

Configuring the MongoDB Directory

If you want to use a directory other than the default directory, you can define it using the --dbpath parameter when starting MongoDB: mongod --dbpath <path_to_directory>.

You can then start the MongoDB server using the sudo mongod command (without a *b* on the end).

17.6.2   Installing a MongoDB Driver for Node.js

To be able to access MongoDB from JavaScript under Node.js, you need a corresponding driver, which comes in the form of the mongodb package and can be installed via the npm install mongodb command.

17.6.3   Establishing a Connection to the Database

Communication to a MongoDB database takes place through the MongoClient object, as shown in Listing 17.33. To connect to a database, use its connect() method, passing the URL to the database and a callback function that will be called once the connection is established or an error has occurred while establishing the connection. If the connection was established successfully, inside the callback function you then have access to an object representing the database.

```
'use strict';
const mongoDB = require('mongodb');                        // Include mongodb package
const client = mongoDB.MongoClient;                        // Create client
const url = 'mongodb://localhost:27017/exampleDB';         // URL to the database
client.connect(url, (error, db) => {                       // Establish connection
  if (!error) {                                            // If there is no ...
                                                           // ... error, ...
    console.log('Connection established');                 // ... the connection ...
                                                           // ... was established
                                                           // ... successfully.
```

```
    db.close();                                  // Close connection
  }
});
```

Listing 17.33 Establishing a Connection to MongoDB

17.6.4   Creating a Collection

MongoDB stores records in *collections*, the equivalent of tables in relational databases. To create a new collection, you execute the `createCollection()` method on the database object, as shown in Listing 17.34. You pass the name of the collection to be created and a callback function that will be called if the collection was created or an error occurred. In the former case, you get an object that represents the collection (the `collection` object in the example).

```
'use strict';
const mongoDB = require('mongodb');                // Include mongodb package
const client = mongoDB.MongoClient;                // Create client
const url = 'mongodb://localhost:27017/exampleDB'; // URL to the database
client.connect(url, (error, db) => {               // Establish connection
  if (!error) {                                    //
    db.createCollection(                           // Create collection
      'persons',                                   // Name of collection
      (error, collection) => {                     // Callback handler
        if(!error) {
          console.log('Collection created');
        }
        db.close();
      }
    );
  }
});
```

Listing 17.34 Creating a Collection in a MongoDB Database

> **Alternative Method for Creating a Collection**
>
> As an alternative to the `createCollection()` method, you can also use `collection()`. The difference is that the latter doesn't create the named collection until a first entry is stored in the collection.

Working with MongoDB (as with other databases) is based on four basic data operations: create, read, update, and delete (CRUD). In the following four sections, we'll show you how to perform each of these operations in a MongoDB database.

17.6.5   Saving Objects

For saving objects, the insert() method is available on the object that represents a collection. An example of this is shown in Listing 17.35: here, after connecting to the database and creating a collection, a person object is created and added to the collection via insert().

```javascript
'use strict';
const mongoDB = require('mongodb');                      // Include mongodb package
const client = mongoDB.MongoClient;                      // Create client
const url = 'mongodb://localhost:27017/exampleDB';       // URL to the database
client.connect(url, (error, db) => {                     // Establish connection
  if (!error) {
    db.collection(                                       // Create collection
      'persons',                                         // Name of collection
      (error, collection) => {                           // Callback handler
        if(!error) {
          const person = {                               // Object to be...
            firstName:'John',                            // ... saved
            lastName: 'Doe'
          };
          collection.insert(                             // Saving the ...
            person,                                      // ... object
            (error, result) => {                         // Callback handler
              if(!error) {
                console.log(result);
              }
              db.close();
            }
          );
        }
      }
    );
  }
});
```

Listing 17.35 Saving Objects in a Collection

17.6.6   Reading Objects

To read an object from a collection, use the find() method. Without parameters, it returns all objects contained in the respective collection (see Listing 17.36).

```javascript
'use strict';
const mongoDB = require('mongodb');                      // Include mongodb package
const client = mongoDB.MongoClient;                      // Create client
```

```
const url = 'mongodb://localhost:27017/exampleDB';    // URL to the database
client.connect(url, (error, db) => {                  // Establish connection
  if (!error) {
    const collection = db.collection('persons');      // Find collection
    const cursor = collection.find();                 // Create cursor
    cursor.each( (error, document) => {               // Iterate cursor
      if(document) {
        console.log(
          document._id,                               // internal ID
          document.firstName,                         // here: "John"
          document.lastName                           // here: "Doe"
        );
      } else {
        db.close();
      }
    });
  }
});
```

Listing 17.36 Reading All Objects from a Collection

If you want to select only those objects that match a certain criterion, you have the option to pass a corresponding configuration object to the find() method. In Listing 17.37, for example, a search is performed that contains as a result only objects whose lastName property has the value Doe.

```
'use strict';
const mongoDB = require('mongodb');                   // Include mongodb package
const client = mongoDB.MongoClient;                   // Create client
const url = 'mongodb://localhost:27017/exampleDB';    // URL to the database
client.connect(url, (error, db) => {                  // Establish connection
  if (!error) {
    const collection = db.collection('persons');      // Find collection
    const cursor = collection.find(                   // Create cursor
      {                                               // only persons...
        lastName:                                     // ... whose last name is...
        'Doe'                                         // ... Doe
      }
    );
    cursor.each( (error, document) => {
      if(document) {
        console.log(
          document._id,
          document.firstName,
          document.lastName
```

17

```
    );
  } else {
    db.close();
  }
 });
 }
});
```

Listing 17.37 Searching Objects by Property

Furthermore, you can use comparisons and logical AND as well as OR links within the configuration object (see Table 17.5).

Property	Description

Greater than	```find(
	  {
	  'age': {
	  $gt: 30
	  }
	  }
	)```

Less than	```find(
	  {
	  'age': {
	  $lt: 30
	  }
	  }
	)```

Logical AND	```find(
	  {
	  'lastName': 'Doe',
	  'age': 30
	  }
	)```

Logical OR	```find(
	  $or: [
	  {
	  'lastName': 'Doe'
	  },
	  {
	  'age': 30
	  }
	  ]
	)```

Table 17.5 Overview of Various Search Criteria

17.6.7   Updating Objects

Collections provide three different methods to update objects: with updateOne() you can update a single object, with updateMany() multiple objects, and with replaceOne() objects can be replaced. All three methods expect three parameters: a configuration object that describes the objects to be updated, a configuration object that describes the changes to be made, and a callback function that is called after updating the objects or in case of an error. An example of the use of updateOne() is shown in Listing 17.38.

```javascript
'use strict';
const mongoDB = require('mongodb');                 // Include mongodb package
const client = mongoDB.MongoClient;                 // Create client
const url = 'mongodb://localhost:27017/exampleDB';  // URL to the database
client.connect(url, (error, db) => {                // Establish connection
  if (!error) {
    const collection = db.collection('persons');    // Find collection
    collection.updateOne(                           // Update object ...
      {                                             // ... which applies ...
        firstName: 'John',                          // ... to these ...
        lastName: 'Doe'                             // ... properties
      },
      {                                             // Update the ...
        $set: {                                     // ... object with ...
          firstName: 'James'                        // ... these ...
        }                                           // ... properties
      },
      (error, results) => {
        if(!error) {
          console.log(results);
        }
        db.close();
      }
    )
  }
});
```

Listing 17.38 Updating an Object in a Collection

17.6.8   Deleting Objects

To delete objects from a collection, you can use two methods: the deleteOne() method deletes a single object, while the deleteMany() method deletes multiple objects. Both methods expect a configuration object as a parameter, which describes which object(s) are to be deleted. In Listing 17.39, for example, calling deleteMany() will delete all entries of the persons collection whose lastName property has the value Doe.

```
'use strict';
const mongoDB = require('mongodb');                       // Include mongodb package
const client = mongoDB.MongoClient;                       // Create client
const url = 'mongodb://localhost:27017/exampleDB';        // URL to the database
client.connect(url, (error, db) => {                      // Establish connection
  if (!error) {
    const collection = db.collection('persons');          // Find collection
    collection.deleteMany(                                // Delete persons ...
      {
        lastName:                                         // ... whose last name is ...
        'Doe'                                             // ... Doe
      },
      (error, results) => {
        if(!error) {
          console.log(results);
        }
        db.close();
      }
    );
  }
});
```

Listing 17.39 Deleting an Object from a Collection

The MEAN Stack

You may come across the term *MEAN* (or *MEAN stack*) in the context of web application development under Node.js. This is an abbreviation for four basic technologies that are used in the process: MongoDB as the database (M), Express.js as the server-based web framework (E), Angular as the client-based web framework (A), and finally Node.js (N).

17.7   Working with Streams

One concept that plays an important role in Node.js is that of *streams*. This refers to data streams that either read or write data. Advantages of streams compared to other types of input and output include their performance and the option to combine streams very easily.

17.7.1   Introduction and Types of Streams

Overall, Node.js provides four different types of streams:

- *Readable streams* are used to read data from data streams.
- With *writable streams*, on the other hand, it's possible to write data to data streams.

- *Duplex streams* are those that can be used to both read and write data.
- *Transform streams* in turn build on duplex streams, but they provide a simplified API (see Figure 17.3).

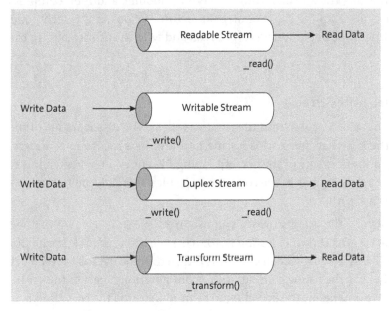

Figure 17.3 Different Types of Streams

17.7.2 Stream Use Cases

The use of streams always makes sense in those cases where you have continuous streams of data or where there might be performance or memory problems when reading or writing data. For example, if you want to process a large amount of data (such as large image, video, or log files) or download large files from a web server, you should use streams. For comparison: if you were to read large files without streams (e.g., under Node.js as shown previously using the readFile() method from the fs package), the entire file must be loaded into memory! Depending on the size of this file and the available memory, this can quickly lead to performance or memory problems. With streams, however, data can be read in piece by piece and processed in chunks.

In addition to processing large files, the use of streams is useful in many other cases where data is being processed. Thus, streams are also suitable for processing (large) HTTP requests from the client that are processed on the server. For example, if you want to implement an application where clients should be able to upload files to the server, you should definitely implement the corresponding upload process based on streams. Of course, the reverse is also true if a web application requires large files to be downloaded from the server. Further application areas of streams are the transfer of data via sockets and the processing of standard output and standard error output of child processes in the respective parent process.

In addition, many Node.js packages provide their APIs in the form of stream APIs, making them very easy to combine and/or integrate into an existing stream architecture. For example, you can read files via streams (using the streams from the fs module), then encrypt them (using the streams from the crypto module), and then compress them (using the streams from the zlib module). But before we look at this technique, called *piping*, let's briefly look at how data can be read and written with streams in the first place.

17.7.3 Reading Data with Streams

In Section 17.4.1, you learned how to read files under Node.js. The disadvantage of the approach shown there is that the readFile() method and its synchronous variant, readFileSync(), read the contents of the corresponding file completely into memory before you can access the contents in the code. For large files, this can lead to memory problems as mentioned earlier.

To read the contents of a file using streams, you use the createReadStream() method (also from the fs package) as shown in Listing 17.40 to first create a *readable stream* for the corresponding file. By default, readable streams return the read data as a raw *binary buffer*. Alternatively, as in the listing, you can pass a configuration object to the createReadStream() method and define the encoding to be used there via the encoding property.

Because all stream classes work on an event basis, they derive from the EventEmitter class (the default class from the Node.js API for supporting events; Section 17.3), and various event listeners can be registered via the on() method. The readable event, for example, signals that new data is available in the stream, which can then be read by calling the read() method. The end event, on the other hand, is called when there is no more data in the stream and the end of the data has been reached.

```
'use strict';
const fs = require('fs');
const path = require('path');

const INPUT = path.join(__dirname, '..', 'large.file');

const readableStream = fs.createReadStream(INPUT, {
  encoding: 'utf-8'
});

readableStream.on('readable', () => {
  const data = readableStream.read();
  console.log(data);
});
```

```
readableStream.on('end', () => {
  console.log('File reading completed');
});
```

Listing 17.40 Reading Files via Streams

Basically, the Stream API distinguishes between two different modes: in *paused mode* (shown in Listing 17.41), as mentioned earlier, you are informed via the readable event that data in the stream is ready to be read. Reading this data must then be actively triggered by calling the read() method. The consumer of the data therefore sets the speed.

In the second mode, on the other hand, the *flowing mode*, the data from the data source is written to the stream as fast as possible; that is, the producer of the data specifies the speed. Data may therefore get lost if the producer sends the data faster than the consumer can process it. This mode is not enabled by default and must first be explicitly enabled—for example, by registering an event listener for the data event, as shown in Listing 17.41.

```
'use strict';
const fs = require('fs');
const path = require('path');

const INPUT = path.join(__dirname, '..', 'large.file');

const readableStream = fs.createReadStream(INPUT);

readableStream.on('data', (data) => {
  console.log(data.toString('utf-8'));
});

readableStream.on('end', () => {
  console.log('File reading completed');
});
```

Listing 17.41 Reading Files in Flowing Mode

17.7.4 Writing Data with Streams

How to write a (large) file using a *writable stream* is shown in Listing 17.42. Similar to the createReadStream() method used before for creating a readable stream, here you first use the createWriteStream() method to create a writable stream. You can then use the write() method to write data to the stream. As the first parameter, you pass the data to be written, either in the form of a string or in the form of a buffer. Optionally, you can use the second parameter to define the encoding of the data and the third parameter to define a callback function that is called after the respective data is written.

To signal that you're done writing the data, you use the end() method. The signature of the method is the same as that of the write() method, although unlike the latter, all three parameters are optional in end(): as the first parameter, you can pass additional data to be written to the stream before closing it; as the second parameter, you can define the encoding to be used; and as the third parameter, you can pass a callback function that will be called when the writing and closing of the stream have been performed.

```
'use strict';
const fs = require('fs');
const path = require('path');

const INPUT = path.join(__dirname, '..', 'large.file');

const writableStream = fs.createWriteStream(INPUT);

for (let i = 0; i <= 100000; i++) {
  writableStream.write(
    'Lorem ipsum dolor sit amet, consectetur adipisicing elit, sed do eiusmod
tempor incididunt ut labore et dolore magna aliqua...\n',
    'utf-8',
    () => {
      // Callback when data is written
    }
  );
}

writableStream.end(
    'Last line',
    'utf-8',
    () => {
      // Callback when writing of data is finished
    }
);
```

Listing 17.42 Writing Files via Writable Streams

17.7.5   Combining Streams Using Piping

One strength of streams is the piping option mentioned earlier. This makes it possible to combine several streams with each other or to connect them one after the other. This allows data from a readable stream (or a transform stream) to be passed directly into a writable stream (or a transform stream). Piping is comparable to the eponymous concept of Unix-based shells, in which command line commands can be combined with each other in many different ways using the | symbol (the pipe symbol).

In principle, the piping of streams works under Node.js, as outlined in Listing 17.43, using the pipe() method.

```
readableStream
  .pipe(transformStream1).
  .pipe(transformStream2).
  .pipe(writableStream);
```

Listing 17.43 Piping Principle

To make the whole thing a bit more tangible and practical, we have an example ahead that can be solved very easily under Node.js using piping: compressing (zipping) and decompressing (unzipping) files.

Real-Life Example: Compressing Files

For compressing and decompressing, the Node.js API provides the zlib module (*https://nodejs.org/api/zlib.html*), which directly provides corresponding streams for these operations.

In Listing 17.44, you can see how to compress files using this API and using streams. For this purpose, a total of three streams are created: As you know, the fs.createRead-Stream() method is used to create a readable stream that reads the data to be compressed from a file. The zlib.createGzip() method in turn creates a transform stream that performs the actual compression. Subsequently, a writable stream is created via the call of fs.createWriteStream(), which in turn ensures that the compressed data is written to a (new) file.

After initializing the three streams, they are connected in series using the pipe() method. This method is first called on the readable stream (inputStream), passing as a parameter the stream to which the read data should be forwarded (i.e., the stream named gzipStream). Because the return value of pipe() is again a stream, the individual calls can be sequenced very clearly. Thus, in the second step, the compressed data from the gzipStream is passed to the writable stream (outputStream) via another call of pipe(), which finally writes the data to the destination file.

```
'use strict';
const fs = require('fs');
const path = require('path');
const zlib = require('zlib');

const INPUT = path.join(
  __dirname,
  '..',
  'data',
  'input',
```

```
  'someFile.txt'
);
const OUTPUT = path.join(
  __dirname,
  '..',
  'data',
  'someFile.txt.gz'
);

// 1. Stream for reading the file to be compressed
const inputStream = fs.createReadStream(INPUT);

// 2. Stream for compressing the read data
const gzipStream = zlib.createGzip();

// 3. Stream for writing the archive file
const outputStream = fs.createWriteStream(OUTPUT);

inputStream              // Read the file
  .pipe(gzipStream)      // Compress the read file
  .pipe(outputStream);   // Write the archive file
```

Listing 17.44 Zipping Files with Streams

Real-Life Example: Decompress Files

Conversely, the data previously compressed can be decompressed just as easily via piping. You can see the source code for this in Listing 17.45. The procedure is analogous to the previous one, only in the other direction: First, the zipped file is read via a readable stream. Its output, in turn, is used as input to the stream that performs the decompression (gunzipStream) via a call of the pipe() method. Its output, in turn, serves as input for the writable stream, which finally writes the unpacked data to the destination file (outputStream).

```
'use strict';
const fs = require('fs');
const path = require('path');
const zlib = require('zlib');

const INPUT = path.join(__dirname, '..', 'data', 'someFile.txt.gz');
const OUTPUT = path.join(__dirname, '..', 'data', 'output');
const OUTPUT_FILE = path.join(OUTPUT, 'someFile.txt');

fs.emptyDirSync(OUTPUT);
```

```
// 1. Stream for reading the file to be decompressed
const inputStream = fs.createReadStream(INPUT);

// 2. Stream for decompressing the read data
const gunzipStream = zlib.createGunzip();

// 3. Stream for writing the archive file
const outputStream = fs.createWriteStream(OUTPUT_FILE);

inputStream                 // Read the file
  .pipe(gunzipStream)       // Decompress the read data
  .pipe(outputStream);      // Write the archive file
```

Listing 17.45 Unzipping Files with Streams

17.7.6 Error Handling during Piping

As simple as using the pipe() method is, it also has a disadvantage: it doesn't provide for direct error handling. What does this mean? The answer is simple: if an error occurs at any point within a stream pipeline, this error is not communicated to the other streams. This in turn leads to these streams not being closed automatically, and this can then quickly lead to memory problems.

Node.js version 10 therefore introduced the pipeline() function, which solves exactly this problem. Listing 17.46 shows how to adjust the compression example accordingly. As a parameter, you pass the individual streams to be connected in series as a pipeline to the pipeline() function. Optionally, a callback function can be passed as the last parameter, which is called if an error occurs within the pipeline. Exactly at this point, you now have the option to react to errors and perform any cleanup work, such as closing streams or the like.

```
'use strict';
const fs = require('fs');
const path = require('path');
const zlib = require('zlib');
const { pipeline } = require('stream');

const INPUT = path.join(__dirname, '..', 'data', 'input', 'someFile.txt');
const OUTPUT = path.join(__dirname, '..', 'data', 'someFile.txt.gz');

const inputStream = fs.createReadStream(INPUT);
const outputStream = fs.createWriteStream(OUTPUT);
const gzipStream = zlib.createGzip();

pipeline(
```

```
    inputStream,
    gzipStream,
    outputStream,
    (error) => {
      if (error) {
        console.error('Compression failed.');
      } else {
        console.log('Compression successful.');
      }
      // Perform cleanup ...
      // ... for example, close streams, etc.
    }
  );
```

Listing 17.46 Error Handling for Streams since Node.js 10

17.8 Summary

In this chapter, we gave you a brief introduction to Node.js, a runtime environment and platform for JavaScript that has significantly contributed to the renewed success of JavaScript in recent years. If you want to delve deeper into Node.js, we can point you to one more book on the subject, also published by Rheinwerk Publishing: *Node.js: The Comprehensive Guide* by Sebastian Springer gives a comprehensive introduction to Node.js. I had the pleasure of providing my technical expert opinion to that book.

For now, remember the following points from this chapter:

- Node.js is a *single-threaded server* consisting of the following major components:
  - An *event loop* that regularly processes new requests to a Node.js server and reacts to events
  - Several internal *workers* that execute *blocking input and output operations* (*nonblocking input and output operations*, on the other hand, are processed directly by the event loop)
  - The V8 runtime environment, which is also used in Google Chrome
  - Native modules, written in C or C++, that act as wrappers around functionalities that would not be possible with JavaScript directly
- Node.js modules (also referred to as *packages*) are also managed via the Node.js Package Manager.
- Node.js already comes with a lot of default packages, but there is a true wealth of other packages on the internet for almost any use case.
- You can work with the file system via the standard fs package: you can create or delete files and directories, read file information, and much more.

- The standard events package supports event-driven programming. The `EventEmit-`
  `ter` type contained in it can be used to register event listeners and trigger events.
  Many other objects within Node.js derive from `EventEmitter` and therefore also have
  the corresponding `on()` and `emit()` methods.

- Using the standard http package, you can create your own web server in just a few
  minutes.

- Express.js is a web framework that can save you a lot of work when building web
  applications. It can be extended modularly through middleware packages with additional functionalities, such as parsing the request text into JSON, parsing the cookie
  header into a corresponding array, or logging requests.

- The mongodb package can be used to access the MongoDB database, a document-
  based NoSQL database that stores documents in JSON format.

- Using the Stream API, data can be read or written piece by piece. This always makes
  sense when you're dealing with a lot of large data—for example, when reading very
  large files or uploading large image files to a server.

17

Chapter 18

Creating Mobile Applications with JavaScript

It should be no news to you that the use of mobile devices such as smartphones and tablets has increased enormously in recent years. Mobile applications, or apps, are therefore a correspondingly large market—one in which JavaScript has been involved for several years.

In this chapter, we'll show you how to create mobile applications using JavaScript. As a representative of the many libraries that now exist for this purpose, we'll introduce React Native as an example. But first, we'll give you an overview of the different types of mobile applications.

18.1 The Different Types of Mobile Applications

Basically, mobile applications are divided into native applications, mobile web applications, and hybrid applications.

18.1.1 Native Applications

Native applications (also called *native apps*) are applications that have been developed specifically for a particular (mobile) operating system, such as Android or iOS, and can thus make optimal use of its functionalities and features.

Technologies

For smartphones and tablets that use Android as their operating system, native applications are developed in Java or Kotlin (using the Android SDK), for example. For Apple devices such as the iPhone and iPad, on the other hand, native applications are developed in Objective-C or Swift. For Windows Mobile, Visual C# is used, for example.

Advantages

The advantage of native applications is that you can optimally access the functionalities and features of the respective end device here, as already mentioned. In addition, native applications are still faster than the other types of applications presented in the later sections in terms of performance, because here the entire application is compiled for the respective operating system before execution (see Figure 18.1). Another advantage is the existing documentation and other resources, which are usually provided directly by the manufacturer. In addition, the respective communities are quite respectable.

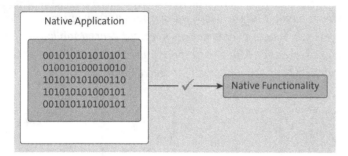

Figure 18.1 Native Applications Can Access Native Functionality

Disadvantages

For a long time, the big disadvantage of native applications was that a separate version of the application had to be implemented for each operating system to be supported. The development costs, the required developer know-how, and the maintenance effort were correspondingly high: in case of doubt, the team then needed at least one Android or Java developer, one Objective-C or Swift developer, and someone to implement the version for Windows Mobile.

18.1.2   Mobile Web Applications

Mobile web applications (*mobile web apps*) are, as the name suggests, quite ordinary web applications, that are optimized for use on mobile devices.

Technologies

Mobile web applications are developed in HTML5, CSS3, and JavaScript using responsive design principles (this is why they're sometimes also referred to as *HTML5 apps* or *responsive apps*) and then run on the respective end device within a browser installed there. As with ordinary websites, the source code of the application resides on a server, then is downloaded to the end device and executed there.

Responsive Design and CSS3 Media Queries

Responsive design or *responsive web design* refers to a paradigm in website development in which the layout of the website adapts to the resolution of the end device on which the particular website is viewed. CSS3 media queries are primarily used here to define CSS rules for specific resolutions.

Advantages

The advantage of mobile web applications is that updates can be imported relatively easily, which then—because they are imported on the server—has a direct impact on all distributed applications. Another advantage is also the fact that you only have to create one version of the application, which can then run on all common mobile operating systems (although this advantage is put into perspective again by solutions such as React Native). This reduces both the initial development effort and the associated development costs, as well as the maintenance effort and the corresponding maintenance costs. "Only" HTML, JavaScript, and CSS knowledge is required from the developer to be able to implement these types of applications.

Disadvantages

A disadvantage of mobile web applications is the restricted access to native hardware functions such as GPS, camera, microphone, and the like for security reasons (see Figure 18.2). Plus, this type of application can't be installed on the respective end device like a native application, but must always be executed in the browser.

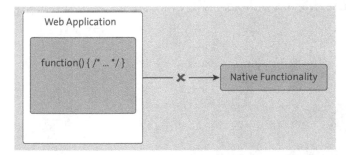

Figure 18.2 Mobile Web Applications Usually Cannot Access Native Functionalities

---

W3C Standards

Although the W3C has now published or is working on many different specifications that standardize access to hardware features of mobile devices (e.g., the Geolocation API, *www.w3.org/TR/geolocation-API/*, or the Battery Status API, *www.w3.org/TR/battery-status*), it will still take some time before all conceivable features are both standardized by an API and implemented accordingly by the various mobile browsers.

18.1.3 Hybrid Applications

Hybrid applications (*hybrid apps*) take a hybrid approach, attempting to combine the advantages of native applications with the benefits of mobile web applications.

In principle, a mobile web application is displayed within a native application. For this purpose, the corresponding platforms such as Android or iOS offer *web views*, which are special GUI components that contain a rendering engine and can display the content of web applications. The web application can then be loaded from a server as well as kept offline in the respective hybrid application.

Technologies

Just like for mobile web applications, the technologies used for hybrid applications are HTML5, CSS3, and JavaScript. In addition, a native part is required that forms the (native) framework of the application and provides, among other things, the web view component. You can then use the native part of the application to install the hybrid application on the respective end device like a native application (and, incidentally, also to make it available for download in app stores) and to access various hardware features and features of the mobile platforms (see Figure 18.3).

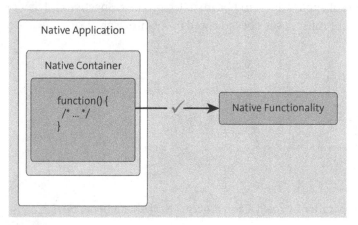

Figure 18.3 The Native Container Allows the Native Functionality to be Accessed from the JavaScript Code in Hybrid Applications

Advantages

Hybrid apps thus combine the advantages of native apps and mobile web apps: they can be installed natively, are mostly platform-independent, and actually require "only" knowledge of HTML5, CSS3, and JavaScript.

Disadvantages

But there is also a disadvantage, although it's relatively small compared to the benefits: frameworks like Cordova (*https://cordova.apache.org*) try to implement APIs for different hardware features and features of the mobile platforms that are kept as general as possible—that is, that represent the lowest common denominator of different mobile platforms, so to speak. In individual cases, however, one platform may provide different hardware features than the other, which are then not taken into account by these general APIs. In a nutshell: native applications still offer more opportunities here than hybrid applications.

18.1.4   Comparison of the Different Approaches

Which of the described types you choose for developing an application depends on various factors: Do you want to make the application available in an app store? Then mobile web applications are omitted and you have to develop either a native or a hybrid app. Does the application have to be as fast as possible—that is, as performant as possible? Then you would probably choose a native application because compiled code is used, which can be executed faster than JavaScript.

An overview and possibly also decision support for choosing the application type that is suitable for your respective project is available in Table 18.1, in which the three types are compared in regard to the different relevant aspects.

Aspect	Native	Web	Hybrid
Development	One application must be created per platform.	Only one application needs to be developed, which can then be run on all platforms.	Only one application needs to be developed, which can then be installed like a native application thanks to appropriate native components.
Programming Languages and Other Languages	Objective-C, Swift, Java with Android SDK, Visual C#	HTML5, CSS3, JavaScript	HTML5, CSS3, JavaScript plus native component for each platform
Platform Independence	No	Yes	Yes
Development Effort and Costs	High	Low	Medium
Maintenance Effort and Costs	High	Low	Medium
Reusability between Platforms	Low	High	High

Table 18.1 Comparison of the Different Types of Mobile Applications

Aspect	Native	Web	Hybrid
Offline Use	Usually, no connection to the internet is required to switch back and forth between individual views of a native application. A connection to the internet is only required if an application uses explicit online functions (e.g., to access web services or similar).	Here, there tends to be more of a need to have a connection to the internet in order to use a mobile web application. However, this can be counteracted with the help of HTML5 features such as the application cache and offline databases.	Hybrid applications also generally do not require a connection to the internet, unless the application itself needs to access the internet.
Performance	Native applications have a high performance compared to the other types of mobile applications because they use compiled code.	Mobile web applications are usually the slowest of the three types of mobile applications. One reason for this is that the code of a mobile web application that is written in JavaScript is interpreted. (For comparison: in case of native applications, the code is compiled in the appropriate languages.)	Hybrid applications are typically slower than native applications, but faster than mobile web applications.
Deployment	Native apps are usually downloaded and installed from the respective app store.	Mobile web applications are hosted on a server and not installed on the respective end device.	Hybrid apps are downloaded and installed like native applications from the respective app stores.

Table 18.1 Comparison of the Different Types of Mobile Applications (Cont.)

Note

The jQuery Mobile (*https://jquerymobile.com*) and Apache Cordova (*https://cordova. apache.org*) libraries have become increasingly less important in recent years. Instead, people today use more modern solutions such as NativeScript (*https://nativescript. org*), Ionic (*https://ionicframework.com*), or React Native (*https://reactnative.dev*), the latter of which is presented in the following section.

18.2   Creating Mobile Applications with React Native

React Native (*https://reactnative.dev/*) is based on the React web framework, which is one of the most widely used frameworks along with Angular and Vue.js. In principle, of course, it's an advantage if you've already gained experience with the React framework before you start working with React Native. However, because both are based on JavaScript, you should be able to follow along with the following examples without any knowledge of React. Where things get a bit more React-specific, we'll provide background information at the relevant point.

React Native aims to facilitate the development of mobile web applications by providing, among other things, UI components that have the typical *look and feel* of mobile applications' native UI components (also called *widgets*), as well as the ability to define transitions between individual "pages" of an application.

18.2.1   The Principle of React Native

Using React Native, it's possible—as the name suggests—to create hybrid applications with a native UI for mobile devices (*native apps*). The convenient thing about this is that you can use JavaScript to implement the application, and React Native then takes care of getting that code into "the right shape" for the respective mobile operating system. This is a huge advantage for you as a developer: you don't need to learn a new programming language to create native apps—no Swift to build native iOS apps and no Java to build native Android apps. This shows once again how important and versatile JavaScript has become.

18.2.2   Installation and Project Initialization

In principle, there are several ways to install React Native and create a React Native–based application. The standard way is through the Expo tool (*https://expo.io*), which makes the application build and deployment process much easier. To use the tool, you must first install it as a global Node.js package—for example, via NPM. The command to do this is `npm install --global expo-cli`. Then you can use the `expo` command, which in turn has several subcommands.

To create a new project based on React Native, simply use the `expo init` command followed by the name of the application you want to create:

```
expo init hello-world
```

A command line wizard will then open to guide you through the configuration of the application. You can choose between different templates, based on which the programming language used is then selected (JavaScript and TypeScript are available for selection). Select the default template *blank* here so that you use JavaScript as the programming language.

This command creates a set of files and directories. Take a quick look at Table 18.2 to see what this is all about and get an overview of a typical project structure in a React Native application.

File/Directory	Description
.expo	Contains configuration files for Expo
.expo-shared	Contains optimized files for Expo
assets	Contains additional files such as images, videos, and audio files
node_modules	External dependencies (libraries and packages) required by the application
.gitignore	Configuration file that can be used to define which files should be ignored by the Git version management system (see Chapter 21)
App.js	The entry point into the application
app.json	Configuration file that contains build information for the application
babel.config.js	Configuration file for the JavaScript compiler Babel.js (*https://babeljs.io*) used by React Native
package.json	Configuration file in which, among other things, the dependencies used by the application or scripts can be configured
yarn.lock	File used to (automatically) record exactly which versions of which dependency are used for the application

Table 18.2 The Files and Directories Generated by Expo for the React Native Application

18.2.3   Starting the Application

The `expo` command has other subcommands in addition to the `init` subcommand. These include, for example, `start` for starting a React Native application. Conveniently, as part of the project generation in the previous section, some preconfigured commands have already been written to the `scripts` section in the **package.json** configuration file (see Listing 18.1) so that you can start the application for different operating systems or in different emulators.

```
{
  "main": "node_modules/expo/AppEntry.js",
  "scripts": {
```

```
    "start": "expo start",
    "android": "expo start --android",
    "ios": "expo start --ios",
    "web": "expo start --web",
    "eject": "expo eject"
  },
  "dependencies": {
    "expo": "~42.0.1",
    "expo-status-bar": "~1.0.4",
    "react": "16.13.1",
    "react-dom": "16.13.1",
    "react-native": "https://github.com/expo/react-native/archive/ ↄ
sdk-42.0.0.tar.gz",
    "react-native-web": "~0.13.12"
  },
  "devDependencies": {
    "@babel/core": "^7.9.0"
  },
  "private": true
}
```

Listing 18.1 The package.json Configuration File

The following commands are available:

- npm start or expo start opens the Expo Dev Tools web interface in the browser (see Figure 18.4). Starting from this interface, you have several options: for example, you can open the application from here in different *emulators*, special software that emulates a mobile device on your development computer so that you as a developer can see directly during development how the application looks and behaves on the respective mobile operating system (iOS or Android). Alternatively, you can start the application directly in an emulator using the following commands:

- npm run android or expo start --android opens Expo Dev Tools in the browser and also starts the application within the Android emulator. Note that a corresponding emulator has to be installed separately—for example, within Android Studio (*https:// developer.android.com/studio*).

- npm run ios or expo start --ios opens Expo Dev Tools in the browser and also starts the application within the iOS emulator (see Figure 18.5). Note that a corresponding emulator must also be installed separately for this—for example, as part of Xcode (*https://developer.apple.com/xcode*).

- npm run web or expo start --web opens Expo Dev Tools in the browser and also starts the application in another browser window (see Figure 18.6). This variant is useful if you don't have an emulator installed for one of the two platforms mentioned (iOS or Android).

18

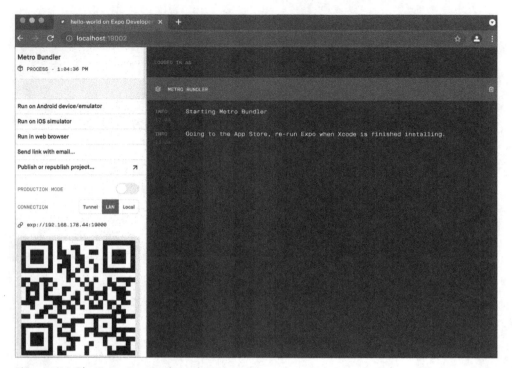

Figure 18.4 The Expo Dev Tools in the Browser

Figure 18.5 The Sample Application in the iOS Emulator

Figure 18.6 The Sample Application in the Browser

18.2.4 The Basic Structure of a React Native Application

Let's take a closer look at the generated code, especially the JavaScript code in the **App.js** file. This file is the entry point to the application, which can be recognized by the subtle note displayed when starting the application in the emulator or in the browser window: "Open up App.js to start working on your app!" That's exactly what we're going to do now. The good thing is that if the application has been started with one of the commands described earlier in the emulator or alternatively in the browser, the Expo Dev Tools ensure in the background that the application is reloaded directly when changes are made to the source code. Try it: open the **App.js** file in an editor or development environment and change the welcome text to "Hello World!" as shown in Listing 18.2. The application should immediately update itself in the emulator/browser.

```
import { StatusBar } from 'expo-status-bar';
import React from 'react';
import { StyleSheet, Text, View } from 'react-native';
```

```
export default function App() {
  return (
    <View style={styles.container}>
      <Text>Hello World!</Text>
      <StatusBar style="auto" />
    </View>
  );
}

const styles = StyleSheet.create({
  container: {
    flex: 1,
    backgroundColor: '#fff',
    alignItems: 'center',
    justifyContent: 'center',
  },
});
```

Listing 18.2 The App.js File Is the Entry Point to the Application (Here with Customized Welcome Text)

While we're at it, let's briefly explain the rest of the code. As you can already see in the first lines, React Native uses the native module syntax for importing JavaScript modules. This way, various components from different external libraries are loaded: a StatusBar component from Expo, the full React library, and some components from the React Native library used in the example.

The export keyword, in turn, exports the App() function, which is called internally by React Native and which defines the application as such as a return value. What strikes the trained JavaScript eye here is the strange syntax behind return—that is, what the return value reflects. React and thus React Native support their own special syntax in the form of the JSX format, in which it's possible to "mix" JavaScript code and HTML code (for details, see *https://reactjs.org/docs/introducing-jsx.html*).

The example also uses three concrete components from the React Native library: The View class provides a container, so to speak, in which further UI components can be defined. The Text class represents—as the name suggests—simple text. In addition, the StyleSheet class is used to define the appearance of individual UI components. Here you can define aspects such as the background color of components, the color or alignment of texts, and much more via conventional CSS rules.

Note
JSX allows "mixing" of HTML code, CSS code, and JavaScript code in React and in React Native. However, there is a small difference between React and React Native in this

regard: while with React you can use elements that are translated one-to-one into HTML elements (which are later interpreted—that is, "understood" and rendered by the browser), with React Native you can't use normal HTML elements because later on the code is converted not into HTML, but into the corresponding native code. Therefore, we won't speak of HTML code ahead, but of *markup code*.

This similarly applies to the CSS code: though the CSS properties available for React Native are, by name, largely the same as the CSS properties from the CSS standard, no real CSS is used internally by React Native.

18.2.5   Using UI Components

React Native provides a whole set of UI components that you can use directly in your application. For an overview of these components, refer to the official React Native documentation at *https://reactnative.dev/docs/components-and-apis*. In the earlier example, you saw that the View and Text components are included in the **App.js** file. Basically, React Native provides a great many UI components, supplemented by other libraries that are based on React Native and provide additional UI components. Ahead, we'll introduce the use of buttons and text input fields as examples.

Using Buttons

To use buttons, simply import the Button component. You define the component itself within the markup code, just like you defined the Text component before. You can use the title property to specify which text should be displayed on the button and the onPress property to specify which function is to be called when the button is clicked. In Listing 18.3, an anonymous arrow function is specified in which an alert dialog is called using Alert.alert(). Alert is another UI component provided by React Native.

```
import { StatusBar } from 'expo-status-bar';
import React from 'react';
import { Alert, Button, StyleSheet, Text, View } from 'react-native';

export default function App() {
  return (
    <View style={styles.container}>
      <Text>Hello World!</Text>
      <Button
        title="Click here"
        onPress={() => Alert.alert('Button clicked')}
      />
      <StatusBar style="auto" />
    </View>
  );
```

```
}

const styles = StyleSheet.create({
  container: {
    flex: 1,
    backgroundColor: '#fff',
    alignItems: 'center',
    justifyContent: 'center',
  },
});
```

Listing 18.3 Using Buttons and Displaying Hint Messages

If you haven't stopped the application yet, it should refresh itself within the emulator or browser window and display the button (see Figure 18.7).

Figure 18.7 A Simple Button

If you now click on the button, the previously defined anonymous function is called and the hint dialog is displayed (see Figure 18.8).

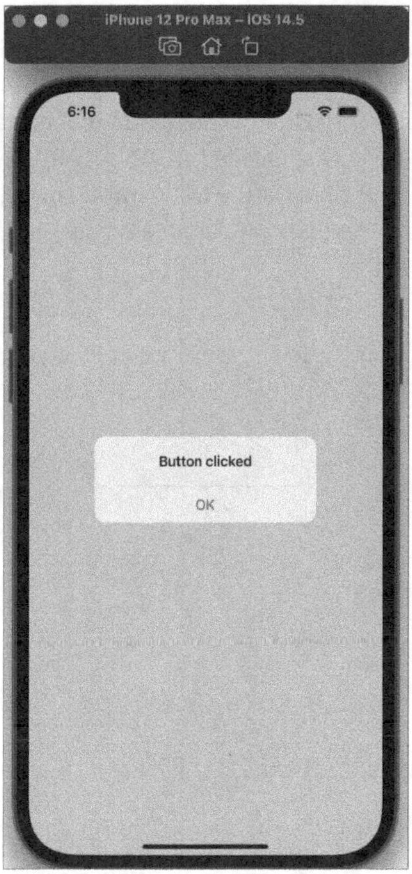

Figure 18.8 The Hint Dialog That Appears when the Button Has Been Clicked

Using Input Fields

In React Native, text input fields are represented by the TextInput class. The import works, as shown in Listing 18.4, just like the import of the other classes like Text and Button before. In addition, however, two other things can be seen in the example: on the one hand, the appearance of the text input fields is configured via additional CSS rules; on the other hand, the use of the useState() function from the React library stands out. With this function, it's possible to manage the *state* of a component.

A call of the useState() function returns an array with two elements, each of which is written directly to two variables in the example using array destructuring (described in Chapter 4). The first value in this array (firstName or lastName in the example) contains the property in the state; the second value (setFirstName or setLastName in the example) contains a function that can be used to update the respective property in the state. Optionally, a default value can be passed to the useState() function as a parameter, which is initially assigned to the respective property.

In the example, two text input fields are defined (one for the first name, one for the last name), where the onChangeText property can be used to specify a function that is called when the text in the input field changes. Here, the corresponding function is passed in each case, which was previously created via useState(). That is, if the text in the input field for the first name changes, the setFirstName() function is called and the firstName variable in the state is updated. If the text in the input field for the last name changes, the setLastName() function is called accordingly and the lastName variable is updated.

```javascript
import { StatusBar } from 'expo-status-bar';
import React, { useState } from 'react';
import { Alert, Button, StyleSheet, Text, TextInput, View } from 'react-native';

export default function App() {

  const [firstName, setFirstName] = useState('');
  const [lastName, setLastName] = useState('');

  return (
    <View style={styles.container}>
      <Text>Hello World!</Text>
      <TextInput
        style={styles.input}
        onChangeText={(firstName) => setFirstName(firstName)}
        value={firstName}
        placeholder='First name'
      />
      <TextInput
        style={styles.input}
        onChangeText={(lastName) => setLastName(lastName)}
        value={lastName}
        placeholder='Last name'
      />
      <Button
        title="Click here"
        onPress={() => Alert.alert(`Hello ${firstName} ${lastName}`)}
      />
      <StatusBar style="auto" />
    </View>
  );
}

const styles = StyleSheet.create({
  container: {
    flex: 1,
    backgroundColor: '#fff',
```

```
    alignItems: 'center',
    justifyContent: 'center',
  },
  input: {
    height: 40,
    width: '80%',
    padding: 12,
    margin: 12,
    borderWidth: 1,
    borderRadius: 5,
    borderColor: 'grey'
  },
});
```

Listing 18.4 Use of Input Fields

In the Listing 18.4, the message that is output in the hint dialog has also been adjusted. Instead of the previous **Button Clicked** message, a personalized welcome message is now displayed that accesses the values of the first name and last name (see Figure 18.9).

Figure 18.9 The Customized Hint Dialog with Personalized Welcome Message

18.2.6   Communication with the Server

Mobile applications usually communicate with a server—for example, to retrieve data from it or send data to it. Conveniently, React Native supports the Fetch API in this regard, which you already know about from Chapter 9. The communication with the server is therefore comparatively simple. Listing 18.5 is an extension of the familiar code from Listing 18.4, where default values for the first name and the last name are now loaded from the server and written into the state of the component (and thus into the text fields). As you can see, another feature from React is used here: by using use-Effect() it's possible to define *page effects* (*https://reactjs.org/docs/hooks-effect.html*), such as the initial loading of server data. In the callback function, which is to be passed to the useEffect() function as a parameter, another function is defined in the example (loadData()), which loads the data from the server via the Fetch API, converts the HTTP response into a JSON structure, and from this structure writes the data for firstName and lastName to the state.

```
import { StatusBar } from 'expo-status-bar';
import React, { useState, useEffect } from 'react';
import { Alert, Button, StyleSheet, Text, TextInput, View } from 'react-native';

export default function App() {

  const [firstName, setFirstName] = useState('');
  const [lastName, setLastName] = useState('');

  useEffect(() => {
    async function loadData() {
      const response = await fetch('http://localhost:3000/settings');
      const data = await response.json();
      setFirstName(data.firstName);
      setLastName(data.lastName);
    }
    loadData();
  });

  return (
    <View style={styles.container}>
      ...
    </View>
  );
}


...
```

Listing 18.5 Loading the Default Data from the Server for First Name and Last Name

18.2.7 Building and Publishing Applications

In addition to developing, debugging, and running in emulators, Expo also provides you with functionality to build and publish an application—that is, upload it to Apple's App Store or the Google Play store. Only then can your application be installed and used by other users! The information relevant to building and publishing an application is configured via the **app.json** file (which is automatically generated when an application is created via Expo). To build the application, you use the `expo build:android` or `expo build:ios` command, depending on the target platform. But for the build to work correctly, you will need an account at *https://expo.io/*, which is free and can be created either from the website or from the command line as part of the build process. For details on publishing React Native apps using Expo, visit *https://docs.expo.io/distribution/building-standalone-apps*.

18.3 Summary

In this chapter, you've seen the role JavaScript plays in creating mobile applications. You've learned about different types of mobile applications and the React Native library. The following list summarizes the most important points from this chapter:

- Mobile applications are divided into three different types:
  - *Native applications* are applications that have been developed specifically for a (mobile) operating system and can thus make optimal use of its functionalities and features. Programming languages used include Java (with the Android SDK), Objective-C, and Swift, or alternative solutions such as React Native.
  - *Mobile web applications* are ordinary web applications that are optimized for use on mobile devices. The technologies used are HTML5, CSS3, and JavaScript.
  - *Hybrid applications* are applications that attempt to combine the advantages of native applications with the benefits of mobile web applications. Hybrid applications are largely developed with HTML5, CSS3, and JavaScript, but must have a small native portion that allows access to hardware features, among other things.
- One library that can help with native web application development is React Native. The logic is programmed in JavaScript and the graphical interface via JSX (or TSX, if you use TypeScript), which is then converted accordingly for iOS or Android, depending on the target platform.
- The easiest way to develop a React Native application is to use the Expo tool. Through Expo, a React Native application can be started, debugged, and published in various emulators for iOS and Android.

18

Chapter 19
Desktop Applications with JavaScript

Desktop applications can now also be implemented with JavaScript. In recent years, two main frameworks have emerged for this purpose, which will be presented in this chapter.

Thanks to modern web technologies, web applications have become increasingly popular in recent years and in many cases have replaced classic desktop applications or offer equivalent solutions; these are called rich internet applications. However, desktop applications still make more sense in many cases, depending on the use case or requirements.

The advantages of desktop applications over web applications include the following:

- **Access to native features**
  In contrast to web applications, which cannot access native features and hardware resources of the computer at all or only to a very limited extent (e.g., via corresponding web APIs or browser plug-ins), this restriction doesn't apply to desktop applications. A classic example of this is access to the file system: while within a web application (via the file API; see Chapter 12, Section 12.5) you can only access files that have been explicitly selected by the user, within a desktop application you can basically access the entire file system (provided you have the appropriate rights).

- **No need to worry about browser versions**
  When developing web applications, a considerable amount of development time usually has to be dedicated to the topic of browser compatibility. This includes questions such as: What features are supported by what browsers? As of what browser version? What are the special features or bugs in a browser? How can these be remedied? Of course, *polyfills* can help in this context—that is, libraries that emulate a certain feature if a browser doesn't support it. Cross-browser testing tools, which automatically test a web application in different constellations of browser, version, and operating system, are also a tremendous help during development. With desktop applications, however, this issue is completely eliminated as you don't have to deal with different browsers or browser engines in the first place (although it must be honestly noted that with desktop applications, you have roughly comparable stress with the different operating systems, operating system versions, architectures, etc.).

19

- **No internet access required**
  Web applications require a connection to the internet. Although this can be minimized as much as possible using offline-first technologies such as the Service Worker API, the IndexedDB API, and the Web Storage API, it's usually much easier to design desktop applications to run smoothly without internet access.

- **No download time**
  The complexity of web applications and the number of integrated third-party libraries and frameworks have a corresponding effect on the time it takes to initially launch the application. If it takes a long time, this negatively affects the usability of an application. Although caching mechanisms of the various browsers counteract this, this problem doesn't even arise for desktop applications. Nevertheless, desktop applications must, of course, be downloaded initially so that you can install them on your own computer.

- **Performance with high user traffic**
  For web applications, high access rates can have a negative impact on performance. For desktop applications, the number of concurrent active users is irrelevant (at least for the UI code). Only if a desktop application integrates external (web) services can these become the bottleneck of the application.

On the other hand, of course, web applications offer a lot of advantages over desktop applications, including one very significant one: *cross-platform capability*—that is, the ability of an application to run on all operating systems, including mobile operating systems (Windows, Linux, macOS, Android, iOS), assuming a corresponding runtime environment that comes in the form of a browser. The effort to create corresponding cross-platform-capable desktop applications natively and the necessary programming skills are correspondingly high in comparison.

This is exactly where the NW.js and Electron frameworks, which we'll present in the following sections, come in: they combine modern web technologies with the ability to use them to create desktop applications. The approaches of both frameworks are similar, but on closer inspection, they do show differences.

19.1   NW.js

NW.js (*https://nwjs.io/*) is an open-source framework for creating desktop applications in HTML, CSS, and JavaScript and was developed by Intel in 2011. The idea of NW.js is to combine the Node.js JavaScript runtime environment with the WebKit browser engine (the framework's original name was node-webkit) and make it available in a platform-independent way.

By combining WebKit and Node.js, NW.js is able, on the one hand, to display applications implemented in HTML, CSS, and JavaScript within a desktop window (which is possible through WebKit) and, on the other hand, to interact with the underlying operating system—that is, to use native functionalities (which in turn is possible through Node.js).

Simply put, NW.js allows web developers who "only" know HTML, CSS, and JavaScript to also implement desktop applications. And the whole thing even works cross-platform because NW.js takes care of generating the appropriate application files for the various operating systems—Windows, Linux, and macOS—based on a single code base in the languages mentioned (more on that later).

19.1.1 Installing and Creating an Application

The installation of NW.js is quite simple: on the project's website, you'll find corresponding installation files for all operating systems. For developing NW.js-based applications, you need to download the software development kit (SDK) version.

A minimal NW.js application consists of two to three files: a configuration file, an HTML file that is the entry point of the application, and usually at least one JavaScript file that contains the logic of the application. Let's take a quick look at what these three files look like for the sample application.

The **package.json** configuration file (also known as the manifest file) is used to manage general metadata about the application, such as the name, the version number, the specification of the file that is the entry point for the application, and external dependencies, just like for Node.js packages.

The name, version, and entry point are also the minimum requirements for a **package.json** file for NW.js applications. The combination of the name and version properties serves as an identifier for the application; the main property specifies which HTML file is loaded initially.

So a minimal configuration file for an application named *helloworld* in version 1.0.0, where the **index.html** file marks the entry point, looks like the content of Listing 19.1.

```
{
  "name": "helloworld",
  "version": "1.0.0",
  "main": "index.html"
}
```

Listing 19.1 Example Structure of the package.json File

Listing 19.2 shows the content of the corresponding HTML file. As you can see, this is normal HTML. The logic, in turn, is sensibly outsourced to a separate JavaScript file (more on that in a moment).

```
<!DOCTYPE html>
<html>
```

19

```
<head>
  <title>Hello World!</title>
</head>
<body>
  <h1>Hello World!</h1>
  <div>
    Your operating system is: <span id="platform"></span>
  </div>
  <script type="text/javascript" src="./scripts/main.js"></script>
</body>
</html>
```

Listing 19.2 The Entry Point Is an HTML File

NW.js provides its API via a global object, nw, which can be used to create UI components such as context menus or the like. The DOM API and the various Node.js APIs, on the other hand, can be accessed directly. Listing 19.3 shows a combination of the latter two. Here, on the document object (DOM API), an event listener for the DOMContentLoaded event is registered, in which the information about the platform used is then read via the os Node.js module (Node.js API) and this information is then written to the element with the platform ID (again using the DOM API).

```
const os = require('os');
// Register event listener (DOM API)
document.addEventListener('DOMContentLoaded', () => {
  // Read information about the operating system (or platform) (Node.js API)
  const platform = os.platform();
  // Write information to the DOM tree (DOM API)
  document.getElementById('platform').textContent = platform;
});
```

Listing 19.3 Access to the Node.js API

Note

Within an NW.js application, you can use the entire DOM API and the entire Node.js API (plus additional libraries and packages, of course). Furthermore, NW.js extends the DOM API and the Node.js API with some added features—for example, additional properties for text input fields or additional properties for the process object.

19.1.2   Starting the Application

To run the application shown above in the previous listings, you need the SDK for NW.js, which was installed at the beginning of this chapter. Then, on the command line, go to the root directory of the project and run the command <NWJS_TOOLS> ., where the

`<NWJS_TOOLS>` placeholder varies from operating system to operating system as shown in Listing 19.4.

```
# For Windows
/path/to/nwjs/nw.exe .

# For Linux
/path/to/nwjs/nw .

# For macOS
/path/to/nwjs/nwjs.app/Contents/MacOS/nwjs .
```

Listing 19.4 Launching an NW.js Application

After launching, the application should look like Figure 19.1. Because we started the application in macOS, the screenshot shows the value darwin. If you use a different operating system, you will of course see a different value here.

Figure 19.1 The NW.js Application after Starting

19.1.3 Packaging of the Application

For packaging NW.js applications—that is, the "packaging" of source code files into an executable file—the nwjs-builder-phoenix package (*https://github.com/evshiron/nwjs-builder-phoenix*) is a good choice. It can be installed as a development dependency via the npm install nwjs-builder-phoenix --save-dev command, after which it will show up accordingly in the **package.json** file under the devDependencies section (see Listing 19.5).

```
{
  "name": "helloworld",
  "version": "1.0.0",
  "main": "index.html",
  "devDependencies": {
    "nwjs-builder-phoenix": "^1.15.0"
  }
}
```

Listing 19.5 Exemplary Structure of the package.json File

In order to "package" the project for the different operating systems, you also need two more entries in this configuration file (see Listing 19.6): First, you need to configure which version of NW.js to use via the `build` section. Then, it's helpful to add a corresponding entry under `scripts` for the rather long `build` command for packaging the application. This way, you can call the build process using the much shorter `npm run dist` command. You specify which platforms you want to package the application for using the `-tasks` parameter. In the example, a total of three packages are generated in this way: one for Windows, one for Linux, and one for macOS (each in the 64-bit variant).

```
{
  "name": "helloworld",
  "version": "1.0.0",
  "main": "index.html",
  "scripts": {
    "dist": "build --tasks win-x64,linux-x64,mac-x64 --mirror ⊃
https://dl.nwjs.io/ .",
  },
  "devDependencies": {
    "nwjs-builder-phoenix": "^1.15.0"
  },
  "build": {
    "nwVersion": "0.14.7"
  }
}
```

Listing 19.6 The package.json File Extended with Build Information and a Build Script

19.1.4 More Sample Applications

The sample application shown in the previous sections is obviously very simple. In principle, of course, you can give free rein to your knowledge of HTML, CSS, JavaScript, and Node.js to implement amazing desktop applications. A few inspirations to show what's possible with NW.js are listed in Table 19.1.

Name	Type of Application	URL
Facebook Messenger Desktop	Messenger	*https://github.com/Aluxian/Facebook-Messenger-Desktop*
Gitter Desktop	Gitter client	*https://github.com/gitterHQ/desktop*
Mango	Markdown editor	*https://github.com/egrcc/Mango*
WhatsApp Desktop	Messenger (not official)	*https://github.com/bcalik/Whatsapp-Desktop*

Table 19.1 Applications Based on NW.js

19.2   Electron

The second popular framework for creating desktop applications in JavaScript is Electron (*https://electron.atom.io/*). Electron was originally used by GitHub as part of the development of the Atom code editor, but it was made available to the public as a separate framework in 2013.

In principle, Electron is similar to NW.js. No wonder—one of the original developers of NW.js, who previously worked at Intel, now continues to develop Electron for GitHub. Still, there is a key difference between NW.js and Electron that is important for developers to understand: while Node.js and WebKit share a single JavaScript context in NW.js, there are multiple contexts in Electron—one for the background process that controls the application, and one for each application window. Another difference is the definition of the starting point of an application: in NW.js, as already described, this is an HTML file, whereas in Electron it's a JavaScript file.

Other Differences

Unlike Electron, NW.js also allows the JavaScript code to be compiled into *native* code to prevent the source code from being shipped with the application in a readable form—but then the compiled code runs about 30% slower. In addition, NW.js has an integrated PDF viewer and print preview. Under Electron, on the other hand, you have to resort to external libraries such as pdf.js (*https://mozilla.github.io/pdf.js/*).

As stated earlier, Electron distinguishes between two different types of processes: the main process and the renderer processes. The main process (usually contained in a **main.js** file) provides the entry point for an Electron application and controls the lifecycle of an application. For example, native components such as the file system can also be accessed from the main process.

This is contrasted by the renderer processes, which essentially represent a (browser) window within an Electron application and contain a combination of HTML, CSS, and JavaScript. Consequently, within a renderer process (or the corresponding JavaScript code), you have access to the DOM of the corresponding window. In addition, however, you also have access to the full Node.js API within a renderer process.

Note

Within an application, there can therefore be several renderer processes, but understandably only one main process.

19

19.2.1 Installing and Creating an Application

The easiest way to have an Electron project generated is via the electron-quick-start Git repository, which can be cloned via the `git clone https://github.com/electron/electron-quick-start` command and contains a minimal sample application consisting of the **package.json** file, a **.gitignore** file, a license and readme file, and the following files:

- A JavaScript file containing the code for the main process, which in turn creates the main window of the application (**main.js**)
- An HTML file that is loaded into the main window (**index.html**) and provides the code for the renderer process of this window
- A JavaScript file that is included by this HTML file (**renderer.js**) and contains the code that is processed by the renderer process (initially, this file is still empty except for some comments)

A somewhat customized version of the generated main process code (**main.js**) is shown in Listing 19.7. As usual with Node.js applications, the electron package is included via the `require()` function. The `app` variable imported here represents the application; `BrowserWindow` represents a single application window. The code in the listing ensures that once the application is loaded, a new application window with a width of 800 pixels and a height of 600 pixels is created via the `createWindow()` function.

```
const { app, BrowserWindow } = require('electron');
const path = require('path');

function createWindow() {
  const mainWindow = new BrowserWindow({
    width: 800,
    height: 600,
    webPreferences: {
      preload: path.join(__dirname, 'preload.js')
    }
  })
  mainWindow.loadFile('index.html');
}

app.whenReady().then(() => {
  createWindow();

  app.on('activate', () => {
    if (BrowserWindow.getAllWindows().length === 0) {
      createWindow();
    }
  })
})
```

```
});

app.on('window-all-closed', () => {
  if (process.platform !== 'darwin') {
    app.quit();
  }
});
```

Listing 19.7 Code for the Main Process

Calling loadFile() in turn loads the specified HTML file, **index.html**, into the created application window. You can see the code of this file in Listing 19.8.

```
<!DOCTYPE html>
<html>
  <head>
    <meta charset="UTF-8">
    <meta http-equiv="Content-Security-Policy" content="default-src 'self'; ⊃
script-src 'self'">
    <title>Hello World!</title>
  </head>
  <body>
    <h1>Hello World!</h1>
    <div>Node.js Version: <span id="node-version"></span></div>
    <div>Chromium Version: <span id="chrome-version"></span></div>
    <div>Electron Version: <span id="electron-version"></span></div>
    <script src="./renderer.js"></script>
  </body>
</html>
```

Listing 19.8 Code for the Main Window

In addition, when the BrowserWindow constructor is called, another JavaScript file is loaded (**preload.js**), which in turn ensures that the information about the versions of Chrome, Node.js, and Electron used is written into the HTML placeholder elements provided for this purpose (see Listing 19.9).

```
window.addEventListener('DOMContentLoaded', () => {
  const replaceText = (selector, text) => {
    const element = document.getElementById(selector);
    if (element) {
      element.innerText = text;
    }
  }
```

19

```
  for (const type of ['chrome', 'node', 'electron']) {
    replaceText(`${type}-version`, process.versions[type]);
  }
})
```

Listing 19.9 Contents of the preload.js File

Next, let's look at how to launch the sample application shown. Before this is possible, however, you must first install the required dependencies via the npm install command.

19.2.2   Starting the Application

Starting the application isn't particularly difficult: you just need to run the npm start command, and Electron will do the rest in the background. Then the application window we created earlier using the createWindow() function opens, which looks like the screenshot in Figure 19.2 for our example.

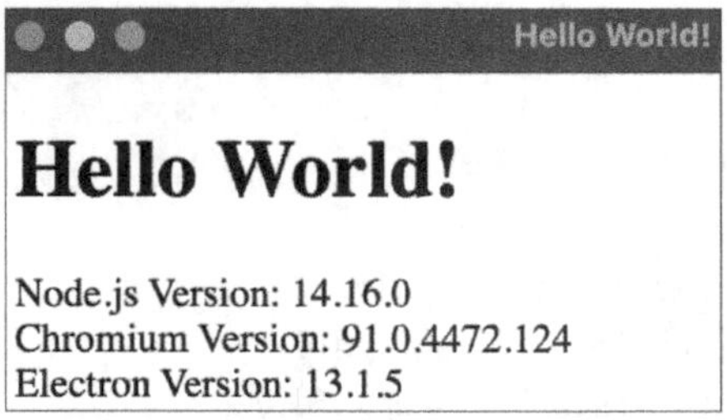

Figure 19.2 The Electron Application after Starting

19.2.3   Packaging

Just as with NW.js, applications can be packaged for different operating systems with Electron. One option is to use the electron-packager package (*https://github.com/electron-userland/electron-packager*). This package can be called both programmatically and from the command line. For the former, it's sufficient to install it locally via the npm install electron-packager --save-dev command; for the latter, the module must be installed globally via the npm install -g electron-packager command.

On the command line, start the packaging with the electron-packager command. Here, you must specify the source directory, the name of the application, the target platforms (darwin, linux, mas, win32) and their architecture (ia32, x64, armv71) as parameters. For example, the electron-packager . hello-world --platform=win32,linux,darwin --arch=x64 command packages the application for Windows, Linux, and macOS as 64-bit binaries.

Because the command for packaging the application can become relatively long under certain circumstances, it's a good idea—as was previously the case with NW.js—to include an appropriate script in the **package.json** file (see Listing 19.10). After that, you can call the build process via a simple npm run dist.

```
{
  "name": "electron-helloworld",
  "version": "1.0.0",
  "main": "main.js",
  "scripts": {
    "start": "electron .",
    "dist": "electron-packager . hello-world --platform=win32,linux,darwint ⊃
--arch=x64"
  },
  "devDependencies": {
    "electron": "^13.1.5"
  }
}
```

Listing 19.10 Configuration File package.json for the Electron Sample Application

19.2.4 More Sample Applications

The selection of sample applications created using Electron is significantly more extensive than those created using NW.js, so it seems that Electron is the more popular framework (also, Electron has a higher number of "Stargazers" on GitHub, which is another indicator of its popularity).

A small selection of Electron-based applications is shown in Table 19.2. As you can see, among them are some that you as a web developer may already be using on a daily basis (e.g., Atom, Postman, Slack, or Visual Studio Code), but you may not have been aware of the underlying technology.

Name	Type of Application	URL
Abricotine	Markdown editor	*https://github.com/brrd/Abricotine*
Atom	Code editor	*https://github.com/atom/atom*
Caret	Markdown editor	*http://caret.io/*
Flow	Risk management	*https://www.getflow.com/*
GitKraken	Git client	*https://www.gitkraken.com/*
Kitematic	Docker container management	*https://kitematic.com/*
Min	Web browser	*https://github.com/minbrowser/min*

Table 19.2 Applications Based on Electron

Name	Type of Application	URL
Mongotron	MongoDB management tool	*https://github.com/officert/ mongotron*
Nocturn	Twitter client	*https://github.com/k0kubun/ Nocturn*
Nylas N1	Email client	*https://www.nylas.com/*
Playback	Video player	*https://github.com/mafintosh/ playback*
Postman	REST or HTTP client	*https://www.getpostman.com/*
Slack	Desktop application for Slack	*https://slack.com/downloads*
Space Radar	Hard disk visualization	*https://github.com/zz85/space- radar*
Visual Studio Code	Code editor	*https://github.com/Microsoft/ vscode*
Wagon	SQL analysis tool	*http://www.wagonhq.com/*
WebTorrent	Torrent client	*https://github.com/feross/ webtorrent-desktop*
WhatsApp	Messenger	*https://www.whatsapp.com/ download/*
WordPress Desktop	CMS	*https://desktop.wordpress.com/*

Table 19.2 Applications Based on Electron (Cont.)

19.3 Summary

With NW.js and Electron, it's relatively easy to create platform-independent desktop applications based on HTML, CSS, and JavaScript.

You should remember the following points from this chapter:

- NW.js and Electron work similarly in principle, combining WebKit and Node.js.
- Both frameworks allow you to use the DOM API and the various APIs of Node.js.
- An HTML file is the entry point for NW.js; for Electron it's a JavaScript file.
- While in NW.js, Node.js and WebKit share a single JavaScript context, in Electron there are multiple contexts because there a distinction is made between the main process and renderer processes.
- Both NW.js and Electron allow applications to be packaged for different operating systems and architectures.

Chapter 20

Controlling Microcontrollers with JavaScript

In addition to server-based, mobile, and desktop applications, another application area for JavaScript programming has emerged in recent years: its use in microcontrollers or embedded systems, which form the basis for the Internet of Things. In this chapter, we'll introduce some technologies and libraries that are relevant in this context and, as an example, show you how you can read temperature sensors or control LED lamps via JavaScript.

You've probably heard the term Internet of Things (IoT) before. In the broadest sense, this refers to the networking of *things*—that is, everyday objects—via the internet. Classic examples of such networked everyday objects are the intelligent refrigerator that knows when to order new milk online, the coffee machine that independently prepares fresh coffee in the morning when the alarm clock rings, or the smart home, in which lamps, heating, and shutters are controlled automatically.

Among other things, microcontrollers work in the background, reading sensors (temperature sensors, motion sensors, etc.) or controlling actuators, such as LEDs in the simplest case, or switching motors on and off, for example.

There are now so many different proprietary IoT solutions and various protocols via which the individual objects, microcontrollers, and the like communicate with each other (Wi-Fi, Bluetooth Low Energy, radio, etc.) that entire books could be filled on this topic as well. However, my intention here is to show you how you can run JavaScript on a selection of microcontrollers (and microcomputers) to, for example, read sensors or control actuators.

Specifically, we'll look at the following:

- The Espruino microcontroller
- The Tessel microcontroller
- The BeagleBone Black microcomputer
- The Arduino microcontroller

> **Note**
>
> So that the code from this chapter can also be executed on older versions of the micro-controllers mentioned, no "newer" features such as the `let` and `const` keywords are used in this chapter.

20.1   Espruino

The Espruino (see Figure 20.1) is a microcontroller that does not execute C or even assembler code (as you are used to from other microcontrollers), but JavaScript code.

Figure 20.1 The Espruino Board Is Just Half the Size of a Credit Card

20.1.1   Technical Information

The Espruino has its own lightweight JavaScript interpreter on board, which can in principle also be installed and used on other devices and which is based on 128 KB of flash memory and 8 KB of RAM. Much more would not be possible on an Espruino as it has just 48 KB of RAM and a 256 KB flash memory. Not much for industrial use, but quite sufficient for prototypical development. It's also equipped with a 72 MHz Arm Cortex-M3 processor.

Moreover, the Espruino provides a microSD card slot, a micro USB port, two push buttons, three LED lights (red, green, and blue), and 44 general-purpose input/output (GPIO) pins that can be used to connect external components such as sensors and actuators (for more details, see the product description on the manufacturer's website at *www.espruino.com*).

At 2.2 x 1.6 inches, the Espruino is only about half the size of a credit card, which is why it is ideally suited for prototypical development in IoT projects—for example, to test and evaluate the interaction of different sensors.

20.1.2 Connection and Installation

To develop with an Espruino, you must first connect the microcontroller to a PC or Mac using a micro USB cable. Under Windows, you must then install a few special drivers. Under Linux, you need to assign some permissions, whereas macOS provides the board directly via plug-and-play.

In principle, after a successful connection, the Espruino can be accessed with any terminal program. Especially during development, however, Espruino Web IDE comes in handy. This is a browser plug-in that the manufacturer provides on its website (see Figure 20.2). This development environment makes it relatively easy to load JavaScript code onto the Espruino board and execute it there on a test basis.

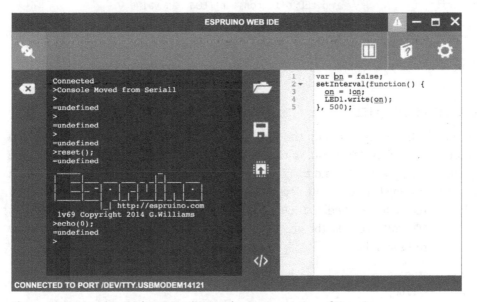

Figure 20.2 Espruino Web IDE Facilitates the Programming of Espruino

After connecting to the Espruino board via a terminal program or web IDE, you find yourself on the board's command line, which can in principle be used to directly execute any JavaScript instructions. More complex programs can be loaded to the board manually or via the IDE.

20.1.3 First Example

In addition to objects and functions that you already know from the standard for JavaScript, Espruino provides its own objects and functions that can be used to control the board. For example, for addressing the individual pins (e.g., GPIO pins, LEDs, and push buttons), corresponding global objects are available in each case (such as the objects LED1, LED2, and LED3), which are all instances of the Pin class. The latter has different methods: With read(), for example, the value or level of the corresponding pin can be read; with write() the value of the pin can be written; with set() you can set directly to the value 1; and with reset() you can set directly to the value 0 (see Listing 20.1).

```
LED1.set();             // Red LED on
LED1.read();            // Output: true
LED1.reset();           // Red LED off
LED1.read();            // Output: false
LED1.write(1);          // Red LED on
LED1.write(0);          // Red LED off
LED1.write(true);       // Red LED on
LED1.write(false);      // Red LED off
LED1.write(HIGH);       // red LED on, constant HIGH has value 1
LED1.write(LOW);        // red LED off, constant LOW has value 0
LED2.write(1);          // Green LED on
LED3.write(1);          // Blue LED on
```

Listing 20.1 Different Objects—LED1, LED2, and LED3—Abstract Working with Pins

20.1.4 Controlling LEDs

A simple example that lights up the three built-in LEDs at short intervals—the *Hello World* example of the IoT world, so to speak—is shown in Listing 20.2. First the three toggleRed(), toggleGreen(), and toggleBlue() functions are defined here, which switch the corresponding LEDs on or off. Second, setInterval() defines in which time interval the functions are to be called. In the example, the red LED is switched on or off in this way every 400 milliseconds, the green LED every 420 milliseconds, and the blue LED every 440 milliseconds.

```
var red = true;
var green = true;
var blue = true;

function toggleRed() {
  red = !red;
  LED1.write(red);
}
function toggleGreen() {
  green = !green;
  LED2.write(green);
}
```

```
function toggleBlue() {
  blue = !blue;
  LED3.write(blue);
}
setInterval(toggleRed, 400);
setInterval(toggleGreen, 420);
setInterval(toggleBlue, 440);
```

Listing 20.2 Interval-Controlled Switching on and off of the LED Lights

As an alternative to the read() and write() methods of Pin, the digitalWrite() and digitalRead() global functions are available for writing and reading the pins, respectively. The digitalWrite() function is passed the pin number and the value to be written to the respective pin. The previous example could therefore be adapted using digitalWrite() as shown in Listing 20.3.

```
var red = true;
var green = true;
var blue = true;

function toggle1() {
  red = !red;
  digitalWrite(LED1, red);
}
function toggle2() {
  green = !green;
  digitalWrite(LED2, green);
}
function toggle3() {
  blue = !blue;
  digitalWrite(LED3, blue);
}
setInterval(toggle1, 400);
setInterval(toggle2, 420);
setInterval(toggle3, 440);
```

Listing 20.3 Interval-Controlled Wwitching on and off of the LED Lights Using digitalWrite()

Analogous to writing values via digitalWrite(), the digitalRead() function is used to read the values of individual pins. If you pass it the number of the pin, you'll get the level currently measured there. An example in which an LED is switched on or off via a push button is shown in Listing 20.4.

To read the status of the push button (*pressed* or *not pressed*), the digitalRead() method is used in the listing. The setWatch() function is used to continuously monitor the status of a pin. If it changes, the program executes the passed callback function. In the example, the status of the push button is monitored in this way (BTN1), and as soon as it's pressed (which can be seen from the return value 1), the red LED is switched on or off, which is controlled by the code inside the callback function.

```
var red = true;
setWatch(function() {
 if (digitalRead(BTN1) === 1) {
    digitalWrite(LED1, red);
    red = !red;
  }
}, BTN1, true);
```

Listing 20.4 Reading the Status of the Push Button via digitalRead()

20.1.5   More Modules

You can find an overview of the available functions and objects (including old acquaintances for JavaScript developers like the JSON or the console object) in the Espruino documentation. In addition, a number of JavaScript modules are available out of the box. For example, an Espruino board can also be used as an HTTP client or as an HTTP server via the http module, as shown in Listing 20.5 and Listing 20.6.

```
var http = require('http');
http.get("http://www.espruino.com", function(res) {
 res.on('data', function(data) {
    console.log(data);
  });
});
```

Listing 20.5 The Espruino Board as HTTP Client

```
var http = require('http');
http.createServer(function (req, res) {
  res.writeHead(200);
  res.end('Hello World');
}).listen(8080);
```

Listing 20.6 The Espruino Board as HTTP Server

The fs module also allows developers to access the file system of the microSD card. Listing 20.7 shows, for example, how you can write to a file using the writeFileSync() method and read the contents using the readFileSync() method.

```
var fs = require('fs');
fs.writeFileSync('file.txt', 'Hello World');
console.log(fs.readFileSync('file.txt'));
```

Listing 20.7 Access to the File System

More Modules

For a complete reference of the modules provided by default, visit *www.espruino.com/ Reference.*

20.1.6 Reading Sensors

Additional external modules can also be integrated—for example, to access sensors, actuators, or other connected components. They are all installed via the Node.js package manager (npm). If you use Espruino Web IDE, it automatically loads the modules on your Espruino when you upload code. Alternatively, the modules can be copied to the SD card in the **node_modules** folder or—if Espruino has a Wi-Fi connection—downloaded directly from the internet.

A complete overview of the available modules can also be found on the project page. Among other things, there is one for reading a temperature sensor, as shown in Listing 20.8.

```
var ow = new OneWire(A1);
var sensor = require("DS18B20").connect(ow);
setInterval(function() {
  // Output of the measured temperature value
  console.log(sensor.getTemp());
}, 1000);
```

Listing 20.8 Reading a Temperature Sensor

From the name of the module (here DS18B20, you can see that the individual modules are usually very hardware-specific. This means, for example, that there is no generic module that can be used with any temperature sensors.

Although the example only shows how the value of the temperature sensor can be read, it can be extended relatively easily—assuming appropriate knowledge of electrical engineering—to switch a connected heater on or off depending on this value, for example.

20

> **Even Smaller: Espruino Pico**
>
> If the Espruino is already a pipsqueak, the Espruino Pico goes one step further: with dimensions of 1.3 x 0.6 inches, it's just a quarter of the size of its older brother. However, this comes at the expense of the hardware: instead of three LEDs, the Espruino Pico only has two (red and green); instead of two push buttons, it has a single one; and instead of 44 GPIO pins, it only has 22. The memory, on the other hand, has been upgraded: an 84 MHz Arm Cortex-M4 processor, 384 KB flash memory, and 96 KB RAM is used. In terms of price, the Espruino Pico at around $30 is even cheaper, slightly, than the Espruino at around $35.

20.2   Tessel

Like the Espruino, the Tessel board (see) interprets JavaScript natively and is primarily characterized by its modular extensibility.

20.2.1   Technical Information

The Tessel board (in version 1) has an Arm Cortex-M3 processor with 180 MHz, 32 MB flash memory, 32 MB RAM, a built-in Wi-Fi module, a GPIO strip, four LEDs, two push buttons, one micro USB port, and four slots for adding external Tessel hardware modules.

Figure 20.3 The Tessel Board Is Characterized by Its Modular Expandability. Image source: *https://tessel.io/press*

The Tessel 2 (see), on the other hand, is equipped with a 580 MHz MediaTek MT7620N processor, 32 MB of flash memory and 64 MB of DDR2 RAM, one micro USB port and two USB ports, a Wi-Fi module, and an Ethernet port. Instead of four slots for connecting Tessel modules, however, there are only two on the Tessel 2.

Figure 20.4 The Tessel Board in Version 2. Image source: *https://tessel.io/press*

20.2.2 Connection and Installation

For development, the Tessel board is connected to the PC or Mac via micro USB. Before development can begin, the tessel Node.js module must be installed globally via NPM on the respective host computer:

```
npm install -g tessel
```

Afterward, the `tessel` command is available on the command line, which can be used to execute JavaScript programs on the connected board or upload them to it. The `run` parameter is used to start the program:

```
tessel run index.js
```

With this parameter, the Tessel loads the corresponding program into RAM and executes it there. However, the program isn't loaded into the flash memory; that is, if you disconnect the Tessel board from the host computer again, the program is lost. To load the program into the flash memory—that is, to *deploy* a program on the Tessel board—you must use the `push` parameter:

```
tessel push index.js
```

20.2.3 Controlling LEDs

To be able to control the Tessel board within a JavaScript program, the corresponding Node.js module must be included via `require('tessel')` (see Listing 20.9).

```
var tessel = require('tessel');
```

Listing 20.9 Integrating the tessel Module

This module can be used to access the LEDs of the board (via the tessel.led array), the programmable push button (via the tessel.button variable), and the individual ports—that is, the module connections and the GPIO connector strip (via the tessel.port map; a complete description of the API can be found in the Tessel documentation).

The code example in Listing 20.10 shows—analogous to the code for the Espruino board—a program for the alternating switching the LEDs on and off. The state of the LEDs is buffered via the red, green, blue, and amber Boolean variables, and the toggleGreen(), toggleBlue(), toggleRed(), and toggleAmber() functions via setInterval() are executed in certain time intervals.

> **Note**
> The following code examples all refer to the first version of the Tessel board.

```
var tessel = require('tessel');
var red = true;
var green = true;
var blue = true;
var amber = true;
function toggleGreen() {
  green = !green;
  tessel.led[0].write(green);
}
function toggleBlue() {
  blue = !blue;
  tessel.led[1].write(blue);
}
function toggleRed() {
  red = !red;
  tessel.led[2].write(red);
}
function toggleAmber() {
  amber = !amber;
  tessel.led[3].write(amber);
}
setInterval(toggleRed, 400);
setInterval(toggleGreen, 420);
setInterval(toggleBlue, 440);
setInterval(toggleAmber, 460);
```

Listing 20.10 Interval-Controlled Switching On and Off of the LED Lights for Tessel

Alternatively, you can use the toggle() method, which relieves you of the cumbersome task of remembering the state (see Listing 20.11).

```
var tessel = require('tessel');
var greenLED = tessel.led[0].write(0);
var blueLED = tessel.led[1].write(0);
var redLED = tessel.led[2].write(0);
var amberLED = tessel.led[3].write(0);
function toggleGreen() {
  greenLED.toggle();
}
function toggleBlue() {
  blueLED.toggle();
}
function toggleRed() {
  redLED.toggle();
}
function toggleAmber() {
  amberLED.toggle();
}
setInterval(toggleRed, 400);
sctIntcrval(toggleGreen, 420);
setInterval(toggleBlue, 440);
setInterval(toggleAmber, 460);
```

Listing 20.11 Interval-Controlled Switching On and Off of the LED Lights for Tessel with the toggle() Helper Function

20.2.4 Programming the Push Buttons

As already mentioned, the Tessel board has two push buttons. One is used to restart the Tessel board. The other doesn't (yet) provide any special function and can therefore be programmed according to your own needs. The button object provides the on() method for this purpose, which can be used to define event handlers for the press and release events. A corresponding example can be found in Listing 20.12: when the button is pressed, the LED is switched on; when it's released, it's switched off again.

```
var tessel = require('tessel');
tessel.button.on('press', function(time, type) {
  tessel.led[0].write(1);
});
tessel.button.on('release', function(time, type) {
  ctessel.led[0].write(0);
});
```

Listing 20.12 Controlling LEDs of the Tessel Board

20.2.5   Extending the Tessel with Modules

The special feature of the Tessel is the modular extensibility via two or four module connections. Many modules are available for different applications, including, for example, a Bluetooth adapter, an accelerometer (an acceleration sensor), or a servo control.

All of these modules are designed for use with a Tessel board and are accordingly optimized for programming with JavaScript (although this is also noticeable in the price of the modules, which—compared to nonproprietary components—are considerably more expensive).

Each Tessel module can be controlled via a corresponding Node.js module. Listing 20.13 shows an example of using a module for camera control.

```javascript
var tessel = require('tessel');
var camera = require('camera-vc0706').use(tessel.port['A']);
var notificationLED = tessel.led[3];
camera.on('ready', function() {
  notificationLED.high();
  camera.takePicture(function(err, image) {
    if (err) {
      console.error(err);
    } else {
      notificationLED.low();
      var name = 'picture-' +
        Math.floor(Date.now()*1000) +
        '.jpg';
      process.sendfile(name, image);
      camera.disable();
    }
  });
});
camera.on('error', function(err) {
  console.error(err);
});
```

Listing 20.13 Controlling the Camera Module of the Tessel Board

While the example is again deliberately kept simple, it's already easy to imagine what is possible with a camera module: in combination with a motion sensor, for example, a prototype for a motion-dependent monitoring system would be relatively easy to implement. Recorded photos could also be stored on a central server or sent directly by email. Thanks to the built-in Wi-Fi module, the Tessel board doesn't even have to be connected via Ethernet.

20.3 BeagleBone Black

The BeagleBone Black (*http://beagleboard.org/BLACK*; see Figure 20.5) is a single-board microcomputer similar to the Raspberry Pi and thus plays in a different league than the Espruino or Tessel microcontrollers because it offers more performance and computing power in comparison.

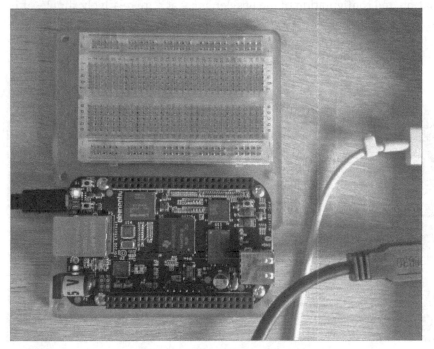

Figure 20.5 BeagleBone Black Is a Full-Fledged Microcomputer

20.3.1 Technical Information

The BeagleBone Black features an 1 GHz ARM Cortex A8 processor from the AM335x series; USB, HDMI, and Ethernet ports; and four LEDs. It comes with 2 GB of flash memory and 512 MB of RAM. The BeagleBone Black can be extended with additional functions and components via various extension boards (referred to as *capes*; see *http://beagleboard.org/cape*). These include liquid crystal displays (LCDs), a motor controller, breadboards for experimenting with circuits, and much more.

An overview of the available capes can be found on the Embedded Linux website at *http://elinux.org/Beagleboard:BeagleBone_Capes*.

In principle, the BeagleBone Black can also be programmed with other languages, such as C, Python, Java, and so on, because the operating system installed by default is full-fledged Linux (Debian). In addition, other operating systems (including Android) can be installed.

JavaScript can be executed directly on the board thanks to the Node.js runtime environment. To do this, you can either use the node command on the command line or the Cloud9 IDE that the BeagleBone Black provides by default.

20.3.2   Connection and Installation

The installation and configuration of the BeagleBone Black are relatively simple: after connecting the microcomputer to the PC or Mac via USB and installing the driver subsequently, you can access the web interface of the BeagleBone in the browser via *http://192.168.7.2/* and an installation of Cloud9 IDE at *http://192.168.7.2:3000/* (see Figure 20.6).

Figure 20.6 Cloud9 IDE is Recommended for Development with the BeagleBone Black

The preinstalled BoneScript library (*http://beagleboard.org/support/bonescript*) is available for programming the board, which can be integrated into the respective program via the require('bonescript') command as is usual for Node.js modules. It simplifies access to the hardware components of the BeagleBone Black. Listing 20.14 shows, for example, how you can access the individual LEDs via this module.

The digitalWrite() method is used to write a value to the pin that is passed respectively as in the corresponding code example for the Espruino. In the listing, all four LEDs are simply set to the value 1; that is, they are switched on.

```
var b = require('bonescript');
b.pinMode('USR0', b.OUTPUT);      // LED 0 on output mode
b.pinMode('USR1', b.OUTPUT);      // LED 1 on output mode
b.pinMode('USR2', b.OUTPUT);      // LED 2 on output mode
b.pinMode('USR3', b.OUTPUT);      // LED 3on output mode
b.digitalWrite('USR0', b.HIGH);   // Switch on LED 0
```

```
b.digitalWrite('USR1', b.HIGH);   // Switch on LED 1
b.digitalWrite('USR2', b.HIGH);   // Switch on LED 2
b.digitalWrite('USR3', b.HIGH);   // Switch on LED 3
```

Listing 20.14 Switching LEDs on and off on BeagleBone Black

> **Note**
>
> Calling pinMode() is advisable at this point to explicitly define the corresponding LED pins (USR0, USR1, USR2, and USR3) as outputs (by default, all pins are defined as inputs after switching on BeagleBone Black).

20.3.3   Controlling LEDs

Listing 20.15 shows the code for switching an LED on and off via a connected push button (details on the wiring for the example can be found at *http://beagleboard.org/Support/BoneScript/pushbutton*). The pin with the number P8_19 (to which the push button is connected) is defined as input and pin P8_13 (to which the LED is connected) as output.

Using setInterval(), you define that the check() function is to be called every 100 milliseconds. It reads the value of the pin with connected pushbutton via digitalRead() or passes the value to the checkButton() callback function. Within this function, the LED is then switched on or off via digitalWrite() based on the measured value (1 for *push button pressed* and 0 for *push button not pressed*).

```
var b = require('bonescript');
b.pinMode('P8_19', b.INPUT);
b.pinMode('P8_13', b.OUTPUT);
setInterval(check, 100);
function check(){
  b.digitalRead('P8_19', checkButton);
}
function checkButton(x) {
  if(x.value == 1){
    b.digitalWrite('P8_13', b.HIGH);
  }
  else{
    b.digitalWrite('P8_13', b.LOW);
  }
}
```

Listing 20.15 Switching LEDs on and off via Push Button on BeagleBone Black

20.4   Arduino

The Arduino single-board computer (*www.arduino.cc*; see Figure 20.7) remains the most mature platform for IoT development. However, developing in C might not be everyone's cup of tea, so it's now also possible to remotely control an Arduino via JavaScript.

Figure 20.7 The Arduino Uno Can Be Addressed via the Firmata Protocol Using JavaScript

Arduino Yún

For the sake of completeness, however, it should be noted that unlike other Arduinos such as Uno, which is used in the examples that follow, the Arduino Yún even includes an installation of Node.js to run JavaScript directly.

20.4.1   The Firmata Protocol

The Firmata protocol is based on the MIDI message format (*www.midi.org/techspecs/midimessages.php*) and allows you to communicate from a remote computer with an Arduino (or microcontrollers and microcomputers in general). In principle, any microcontroller can implement the protocol, but the implementation for Arduino boards (*https://github.com/firmata/arduino*) is currently the most common.

20.4.2 Connection and Installation

By default, there is no Firmata server on the Arduino, which means that you must first install it manually. The easiest way to do this is to use the Arduino IDE, which can be downloaded from the Arduino website (*www.arduino.cc/en/main/software*) for Windows, macOS, or Linux. After successful installation and start of the IDE, the Arduino must be connected to the PC or Mac via USB. In the **Tools** menu, you then select the appropriate board and port so that the upload process from your PC/Mac to the Arduino board and thus the installation of the Firmata server work smoothly (see Figure 20.8).

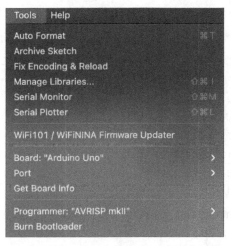

Figure 20.8 Selecting the Board and Port

Next, select **StandardFirmata** from the **File** · **Examples** · **Firmata** menu to open the **StandardFirmata** sketch. This is a source code file that contains the code for the Firmata server. Afterward, click the **Upload** button in the editor window that appears to get the code onto the Arduino board accordingly. The installation is now finished: you can close the Arduino IDE again, and the Firmata server is ready on Arduino.

20.4.3 The Johnny Five Node.js Module

On the client side, there are several libraries that implement the Firmata protocol—for example, for languages such as Python, Perl, Ruby, Clojure, Java, .NET, PHP, and JavaScript. For the latter, the Johnny Five library (*https://github.com/rwaldron/johnny-five*) is probably the best-known implementation.

Johnny Five is installed using the `npm install johnny-five` command (on client side, not on Arduino). You can then use `require('johnny-five');` to integrate the module into the respective JavaScript program. Listing 20.16 shows a simple example for controlling an LED on the Arduino (this requires a setup like the one shown in Figure 20.7).

```
var five = require('johnny-five');
var board = new five.Board({
  port: '/dev/cu.usbmodem14131'
});

var LEDPIN = 13;
var OUTPUT = 1;

board.on('ready', function() {
  var value = 0;
  this.pinMode(LEDPIN, OUTPUT);
  this.loop(2000, function() {
      value = value ? 0 : 1;
    this.digitalWrite(LEDPIN, value);
  });
});
```

Listing 20.16 Switching an LED on and off with Johnny Five

You communicate with the Arduino via an instance of Board. The program uses the on() method to define an event handler for the ready event, which is executed when you establish the connection to the Arduino board.

The loop() function then ensures that the event handler passed to it is executed several times (here every two seconds). The handler contains the functions that make sure that the LED behind the specified pin is switched on and off alternately using digitalWrite().

What was done manually in the code just now can be simplified via the Led class, as shown in Listing 20.17. It abstracts the communication with LED lamps and uses, for example, the blink() method for alternately switching an LED on and off.

```
var five = require('johnny-five');
var board = new five.Board({
  port: '/dev/cu.usbmodem14131'
});
board.on('ready', function() {
  var led = new five.Led(13);
  led.blink(2000);
});
```

Listing 20.17 Switching an LED on and off with Johnny Five via the LED Class

In addition, classes are available for working with push buttons, keyboards, joysticks, sensors (distance sensor, motion sensor, temperature sensor, etc.), and much more. For example, the program can be extended relatively easily to switch the LED on and off using the push button, as shown in Listing 20.18.

```
var five = require('johnny-five'), button, led;
var board = five.Board({
  port: '/dev/cu.usbmodem14131'
}).on('ready', function() {
  button = new five.Button(7);
  led = new five.Led(13);
  button.on('hit', function() {
    led.on();
  }).on('release', function() {
    led.off();
  });
});
```

Listing 20.18 Switching LEDs on and off via Push Button on Arduino

20.5 Cylon.js

If you look at the code examples of the previous listings, you'll notice that they are all very similar in principle and differ only in the details. This is exactly where the Cylon.js framework (*http://cylonjs.com*) comes in by creating a unified interface for various IoT platforms, including Tessel, BeagleBone Black, and Arduino. (Espruino is currently not supported.)

You install Cylon.js as a Node.js module using the npm install cylon command. Afterward, the module is integrated via require('cylon'); as usual.

20.5.1 Controlling the BeagleBone Black with Cylon.js

Listing 20.19 shows how Cylon.js can be used to control the BeagleBone Black. You can see directly that Cylon.js provides a relatively understandable API. The connection() method is used to establish the connection to the respective microcontroller—in this case, the BeagleBone Black—whereas the corresponding configuration is made via the adaptor property of the passed configuration object. Subsequently, you can use the device() method to configure various components such as LEDs and buttons.

The first argument to be passed to the device() method is the name of the respective component, which can then be accessed within the JavaScript code. The respective type of the component is specified via the driver property of the configuration object passed as the second argument; the pin property determines to which pin the respective component is connected. After the configuration is complete, you start the whole thing using the start() method.

20

```
var Cylon = require('cylon');
Cylon
  .robot()
  .connection('beaglebone', { adaptor: 'beaglebone' })
  .device('led', { driver: 'led', pin: 'P9_12' })
  .device('button', { driver: 'button', pin: 'P9_14' })
  .on('ready', function(robot) {
    robot.button.on('push', function() {
      robot.led.toggle();
    });
  });
Cylon.start();
```

Listing 20.19 Controlling BeagleBone Black with Cylon.js

20.5.2   Controlling the Tessel Board with Cylon.js

The JavaScript code necessary to control a Tessel board with Cylon.js is basically no different from the code for controlling a BeagleBone Black, as you can see in Listing 20.20. The only difference is the connection information used and the configuration of the components or their pins.

```
var Cylon = require('cylon');
Cylon
  .robot()
  .connection('tessel', { adaptor: 'tessel' })
  .device('led', { driver: 'led', pin: 1 })
  .device('button', { driver: 'button', pin: 'config' })
  .on('ready', function(robot) {
    robot.button.on('push', function() {
      robot.led.toggle();
    });
  });
Cylon.start();
```

Listing 20.20 Controlling a Tessel Board with Cylon.js

20.5.3   Controlling an Arduino with Cylon.js

When controlling an Arduino via Cylon.js, the corresponding JavaScript code is essentially the same again (see Listing 20.21). Only the connection information and the configuration of the LED and the button differ.

```
var Cylon = require('cylon');
Cylon
  .robot()
```

```
  .connection('arduino', { adaptor: 'firmata', port: '/dev/cu.usbmodem14131' })
  .device('led', { driver: 'led', pin: 13 })
  .device('button', { driver: 'button', pin: 2 })
  .on('ready', function(robot) {
    robot.button.on('push', function() {
      robot.led.toggle();
    });
  });
Cylon.start();
```

Listing 20.21 Controlling an Arduino with Cylon.js

20.6 Summary

There is now a whole range of microcontrollers and microcomputers that can run Java-Script applications. In this chapter, we've introduced you to some of the best known of these and shown you an (admittedly simple) example of controlling LEDs. In summary, remember:

- The Espruino microcontroller can run JavaScript natively.
- The Tessel microcontroller can also run JavaScript out of the box and is relatively easy to extend with special hardware modules.
- The BeagleBone Black microcomputer is a full-fledged minicomputer similar to the Raspberry Pi.
- Most variants of the Arduino microcomputer cannot run JavaScript, but can still be controlled remotely using the Firmata protocol.
- The Johnny Five Node.js module is a client for the Firmata protocol.
- The Cylon.js JavaScript library creates a unified API for working with various micro-controllers.

20

Chapter 21

Establishing a Professional Development Process

Professional software development also includes a professional develop-
ment process. How can repetitive tasks be automated? How can the
source code be checked automatically? And what is the best way to
manage the source code? In this chapter, we'll give you answers to these
questions and show you the first steps toward setting up a professional
development process for JavaScript application development.

In this chapter we'll describe the following aspects of software development with Java-Script in greater detail:

- Automating repetitive tasks (Section 21.1)

- Automatic testing of source code (Section 21.2)

- Source code management using a version control system (Section 21.3)

21.1 Automating Tasks

As a developer, you'll eventually find that certain tasks need to be performed over and over again when developing software or web applications. So it's only logical that rather than always performing these tasks yourself, you instead use appropriate tools that can relieve you of a lot of work. In the following sections, we'll introduce two such tools commonly used in the JavaScript environment: Grunt and Gulp.

21.1.1 Automating Tasks with Grunt

Grunt (*http://gruntjs.com*) is a JavaScript-based *build tool* that takes over tasks from the developer and executes them automatically. Grunt can be installed via NPM as a Node.js package, although you should install Grunt locally for each project rather than globally. Because you usually use Grunt only during the development of an application, it's sufficient here to add the dependency only as a development dependency. The corresponding command is then as follows:

```
npm install grunt --save-dev
```

In addition, you need the grunt-cli package, which provides the command line command `grunt` globally (more on this later in this chapter) and needs to be installed globally via the following command:

```
npm install -g grunt-cli
```

You define the tasks to be automated by Grunt (referred to simply as *tasks*) per project in a configuration file called **Gruntfile.js**, which is usually located in the root directory of the respective project. You can already tell from the suffix that the file is a JavaScript file. Its general structure is shown in Listing 21.1.

```
'use strict';
module.exports = function (grunt) {
  // 1.) configuration
  grunt.initConfig({
    // ...
  });
  // 2.) Load plug-ins and tasks
  grunt.loadNpmTasks('...');
  // 3.) Define tasks
  grunt.registerTask('default', [ '...' ]);
};
```

Listing 21.1 General Structure of the Gruntfile.js File

Inside the anonymous function, which is exported in familiar CommonJS fashion, the actual configuration happens in three steps:

1. You specify the project and task configurations via `initConfig()`.
2. The existing plug-ins and tasks—that is, automated tasks—can be loaded using `loadNpmTasks()`.
3. Your own tasks can be defined via `registerTask()`.

Listing 21.2 shows the definition of a simple task that simply outputs the message `Hello World` on the console. The first parameter of the `registerTask()` method is the name of the task, the second parameter is a short description, and the third parameter is a callback function containing the actual logic of the task. The task can then be called using the `grunt example` command.

```
'use strict';
module.exports = function (grunt) {
  grunt.registerTask('example', 'A sample task.', () => {
    console.log('Hello World')
  });
};
```

Listing 21.2 A Sample Task for Grunt

Within the callback function, you can automate tasks of any complexity. For example, you can use the fs package to copy files from A to B, restart a web server, and much more. For many such tasks, plug-ins already exist, each of which you can later install as Node.js packages. In the following sections, we'll therefore focus on the use of such plug-ins and not on defining custom tasks (in this context, you have all the freedom JavaScript grants under Node.js).

Using Plug-ins

Grunt offers a veritable wealth of existing plug-ins, which can be viewed at *http:// gruntjs.com/plugins*. Table 21.1 shows a small selection of well-known plug-ins. As you can see, there are plug-ins for checking code quality, minifying JavaScript or CSS files, generating documentation, running automated tests, and, as already mentioned, a great deal of other tasks.

Plug-in	Description
grunt-contrib-jshint	Validation of JavaScript code using JSHint (*http://jshint.com*)
grunt-contrib-uglify	Minification of JavaScript code using UglifyJS (*https://github.com/ mishoo/UglifyJS* or *https://github.com/mishoo/UglifyJS2*)
grunt-contrib-concat	Merging multiple JavaScript files into a single JavaScript file
grunt-contrib-cssmin	Minification of CSS files
grunt-contrib-watch	Execution of certain Grunt tasks as soon as observed files change
grunt-contrib-qunit	Execution of unit tests based on QUnit (*https://qunitjs.com/*; see also Section 21.2.3)
grunt-contrib-yuidoc	Creation of documentation using YUIDoc (*http://yui.github.io/ yuidoc/*)
grunt-mocha-test	Execution of server-side unit tests based on mocha (*https://mochajs.org/*; see also Section 21.2.4)

Table 21.1 Overview of Some Plug-ins for Grunt

Installing Plug-ins

The use of a plug-in for Grunt is described ahead using the grunt-contrib-uglify plug-in, which can minify the source code using UglifyJS, among other things. To be able to use a plug-in, it must first be installed for the respective project; for the plug-in mentioned, for example, you can do that via the following command:

```
npm install grunt-contrib-uglify --save-dev
```

Listing 21.3 shows the use of the plug-in within the **Gruntfile.js** file. The UglifyJS plug-in is first configured within initConfig(), specifying, among other things, the source directory and target directory of the JavaScript files to be processed (src and dest) in addition to the name of the task (uglify) and whether the directory structure in the target directory should be retained or the target code should be combined into one file (expand).

The plug-in is then loaded via the loadNpmTasks() call. The subsequent registerTask() call is optional at this point and only ensures that the task is defined as the default task. This allows you to call the task not only via the grunt uglify command, but also via the grunt command.

```
'use strict';
const path = require("path");
module.exports = function (grunt) {
  const binDir = path.join(__dirname, "dist", "bin");
  grunt.initConfig({
    uglify: {
      module : {
        files: [
          {
            expand : true,
            src : [
              '**/*.js',
              '!dist/**/*.js',
              '!node_modules/**/*.js',
              '!Gruntfile.js'
            ],
            dest : binDir
          }
        ]
      }
    }
  });
  grunt.loadNpmTasks('grunt-contrib-uglify');
  grunt.registerTask('default', [ 'uglify' ]);
};
```

Listing 21.3 Using the UglifyJS Plug-in for Grunt

Default Task

If you have defined several tasks in a basic configuration file, it makes sense to define one of these tasks or a composition of different tasks as the default task.

The bigger a project gets, the bigger the configuration file for Grunt gets; critical voices therefore consider Grunt too configuration-heavy (mainly you define the behavior of the tasks via JavaScript objects, which you pass to the `initConfig()` method).

As a competitor to Grunt, another tool has therefore become increasingly popular in recent years, one that is significantly less configuration-heavy and takes an overall programmatic approach.

21.1.2 Automating Tasks with Gulp

The somewhat younger alternative to Grunt is called Gulp (*http://gulpjs.com*) and can also be installed globally via NPM:

```
npm install -g gulp-cli
```

After the global installation, Gulp and some plug-ins should ideally directly be added as dependencies to the **package.json** file via the following commands:

```
npm install --save-dev gulp
npm install gulp-jshint gulp-sass gulp-concat gulp-uglify gulp-rename --save-
dev
```

Like Grunt, Gulp is configured via a JavaScript configuration file, but with the name **gulpfile.js**. For example, such a configuration file for Gulp looks like the one shown in Listing 21.4.

```
const gulp = require('gulp');
const concat = require('gulp-concat');
const uglify = require('gulp-uglify');
const rename = require('gulp-rename');
gulp.task('example', () => {
  return gulp.src('scripts/*.js')      // all JavaScript files ...
    .pipe(concat('all.js'))            // ... concatenate ...
    .pipe(gulp.dest('dist'))           // ... copy to a destination folder ...
    .pipe(rename('all.min.js'))        // ... rename file ...
    .pipe(uglify())                    // ... minify ...
    .pipe(gulp.dest('dist'));          // ... and copy the minified file
});

gulp.task('default', ['example']);
```

Listing 21.4 General Structure of the gulpfile.js File

In Gulp, individual tasks can be defined using the `task()` method, where you pass the name of the task and a function that contains the logic of the task. The `pipe()` method can be used to connect individual steps of a task sequentially. The result is then much more readable than a comparable configuration in Grunt.

The task defined in the example can be called via the `gulp example` command or—because the task was also defined as a default task—via the `gulp` command.

21.2   Automated Testing of Source Code

The more source code you create, or the more complex the source code is and the more difficult and costly it is to verify that the source code does what it's supposed to do. Automated tests, especially so-called unit tests, can help you execute source code automatically and formulate certain criteria that the tested source code should fulfill.

21.2.1   The Principle of Automated Tests

The principle of automated testing is outlined in Figure 21.1. The idea is essentially that you write specific programs (*test programs* or *unit tests*) that call the code to be tested and check the results of the code.

The *code under test* can be a single function, as shown in the figure, but also a combination of various functions or different classes and objects. In general, we also speak of a *class under test* or, even more generally, of a *system under test*. The checks within a unit test are also referred to as *assertions*. A unit test usually also consists of several *test cases*.

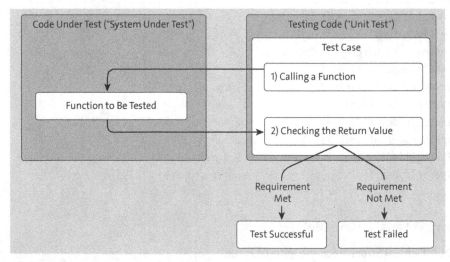

Figure 21.1 The Principle of a Unit Test

Let's suppose you implemented an `add()` function that's supposed to add two numbers and return the result. A unit test would then call this function as shown in Figure 21.2

(e.g., with arguments 5 and 6) and check whether the *actual result* matches the *expected result*. If it does, the test is successful; otherwise, it fails.

Now why would you write unit tests at all? Why would you bother writing additional source code that checks your other (the "correct") source code? There are several reasons. First, you use tests to ensure that subsequent changes to the code don't have any unwanted side effects because if those side effects occur, the corresponding tests will fail. Second, writing unit tests also makes you think more about the structure of your code in general because you automatically pay more attention to writing simple and easily testable code. This in turn usually has the positive side effect of making the code easier for others to use and understand.

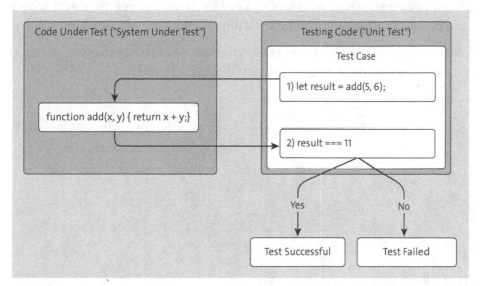

Figure 21.2 Testing an Addition Function

21.2.2 The Principle of Test-Driven Development

When you integrate the principle of automated testing into your development workflow, this is referred to as *test-driven development* (*TDD*). The basic concept here is an iterative approach: before starting to implement a new component (e.g., a function), you first define unit tests and determine what requirements the new component must meet. You therefore pursue the following steps in TDD (see also Figure 21.3):

1. **Write test**
   Before you start implementing the new component, you use assertions in the unit test to define the requirements for the component to be implemented.

2. **Run test**
   Next you run the test that will fail at the beginning (because you haven't implemented the required functionality yet).

3. **Implement component**

   In this step, you implement the component, with the goal of meeting the require-ments of the test so that it passes after a new run.

4. **Run test again**

   Now you verify that you have implemented the requirements correctly by rerun-ning the test. Only when the test is successful do you move on to the next step. If, on the other hand, the test fails, you must adjust the component accordingly and then start a new test run.

5. **Optimize component**

   In the next step of the iteration, you can now optimize the component (this is also referred to as *refactoring*). By rerunning the test, you can always make sure that opti-mizations don't affect the actual functionality.

This sequence of steps is also called *red-green-refactor* because in many tools, failed tests are marked red, whereas successful tests are marked green.

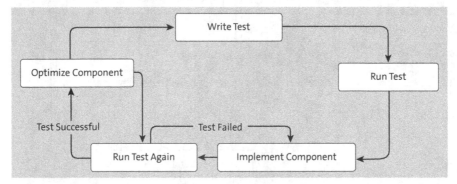

Figure 21.3 Workflow of Test-Driven Development

Module, Unit, Component

By the way, the terms *module, unit*, and *component* are often used synonymously in the context of testing. For this reason, we also speak of *module tests, unit tests*, or *component tests*.

In the following sections, we'll introduce two representative tools: QUnit, which is best suited for testing JavaScript with dependencies on the DOM (i.e., testing client-side code), and mocha, which we recommend for testing Node.js modules (i.e., server-side code). Basically, however, it's possible to test both client-side and server-side code with both tools. JavaScript code that's independent of a runtime environment can be tested equally well with both frameworks anyway.

21.2.3   Automated Testing of Source Code with QUnit

QUnit (*http://qunitjs.com*) was originally developed by John Resig as part of the jQuery library with the main goal of testing the internal code of jQuery. Then in 2008 it became a standalone project—still tightly coupled to jQuery, but at least from then on it was possible to test custom code based on the jQuery library. A year later, in 2009, the dependencies on jQuery were completely resolved, so today QUnit can be used for testing any JavaScript code.

Installing QUnit

Among other things, QUnit can be installed via NPM (`npm install qunit`), which ensures that the required JavaScript and CSS files are downloaded by QUnit and added as a dependency to the corresponding project. Alternatively, you can download these files manually from the website. Basically, you need two files: the JavaScript file that contains the source code of QUnit and a CSS file that's used to format the test results.

Writing a Test

Let's demonstrate QUnit with a concrete example: The function `MathFunctions.compare()` is to be implemented. It's supposed to compare two numbers with each other and return one of three return values: the value 1 if the first number is greater than the second number, the value -1 in case the first number is less than the second number, and the value 0 if both numbers are equal.

First, you need a container for running QUnit tests: an HTML file (referred to as a testrunner file ahead), as shown in Listing 21.5. The tests themselves are usually written in individual JavaScript test files, which are then included separately in this testrunner file. The testrunner file should contain two `<div>` elements: the element with the `qunit` ID represents the container for the test report, the element with the `qunit-fixture` ID the container for the so-called test fixture. The latter is used in tests in which the DOM of a web page is tested to provide the DOM code to be tested.

```html
<!DOCTYPE html>
<html>
<head>
  <meta charset="utf-8">
  <title>QUnit example</title>
  <link rel="stylesheet" href="https://code.jquery.com/qunit/qunit-2.16.0.css">
</head>
<body>
  <div id="qunit"></div>
  <div id="qunit-fixture"></div>
  <script src="https://code.jquery.com/qunit/qunit-2.16.0.js"></script>
  <script src="src/MathFunctions.js"></script>
```

21

```
    <script src="test/MathFunctionsTest.js"></script>
</body>
</html>
```

Listing 21.5 The testrunner.html file

Following the TDD methodology, the next thing you do is write the test—that is, the contents of the **MathFunctionsTest.js** file (see Listing 21.6). Each test case in QUnit is defined by a call of the test() method. The first parameter describes the intention of the test in the form of a character string. The text you enter here should be as meaningful and unambiguous as possible, as it will be used later in the presentation of the results.

As the second parameter of test(), you specify the actual contents of the test, the *test procedure*, as a callback function. Within this function, you formulate the individual assertions.

In the example, three different requirements are now placed on the MathFunctions.compare() function in three test cases:

- If the first of the two numbers is greater, the function should return the value 1.
- If the first of the two numbers is smaller, the function should return the value -1.
- If both numbers are equal, the function should return the value 0.

To ensure this, the assertion method equal() is used in each test case, which is available within the callback through the assert object. The first parameter represents the actual result, while the second parameter is the expected result. The third parameter can also be used to further influence the result display by means of a character string.

```
'use strict';
// 1. Test case
QUnit.test('MathFunctions.compare() should return 1 if the first number is ⊃
greater.', (assert) => {
  const number1 = 7;
  const number2 = 5;
  const result = MathFunctions.compare(number1, number2);
  assert.equal(
    result,                 // actual result
    1,                      // expected result
    '7 is greater than 5'   // additional message
  );
});
// 2. Test case
QUnit.test('MathFunctions.compare() should return -1 if the first number ⊃
is smaller.', (assert) => {
  const number1 = 5;
  const number2 = 7;
```

```
  const result = MathFunctions.compare(number1, number2);
  assert.equal(
    result,                 // actual result
    -1,                     // expected result
    '5 is smaller than 7'   // additional message
  );
});
// 3. Test case
QUnit.test('MathFunctions.compare() should return 0 if both numbers are equal.',
 (assert) => {
  const number1 = 5;
  const number2 = 5;
  const result = MathFunctions.compare(number1, number2);
  assert.equal(
    result,                 // actual result
    0,                      // expected result
    '5 is equal to 5'       // additional message
  );
});
```

Listing 21.6 A Simple Unit Test with QUnit

In addition to equal(), QUnit provides other assertions, an overview of which is shown in Table 21.2.

Assertion	Meaning
ok()	Checks if the passed value is true
equal()	Checks if the two passed values are equal (==)
notEqual()	Checks whether the two values passed are not equal (!=)
strictEqual()	Checks if the two passed values are strictly equal (===)
notStrictEqual()	Checks whether the two values passed are strictly unequal (!==)
deepEqual()	Recursive check for equality
notDeepEqual()	Recursive check for inequality
propEqual()	Strict type and value comparison of the (direct) properties of an object for equality
notPropEqual()	Strict type and value comparison of the (direct) properties of an object for inequality
throws()	Checks if a function throws an error

Table 21.2 Overview of Assertions in QUnit

21

Runing a Test

If you open the testrunner file in the browser at this point, you'll notice that the test will fail (see Figure 21.4). That's logical because there is no MathFunctions object yet, let alone a compare() method. But both can be implemented quickly, as you'll see in the next step.

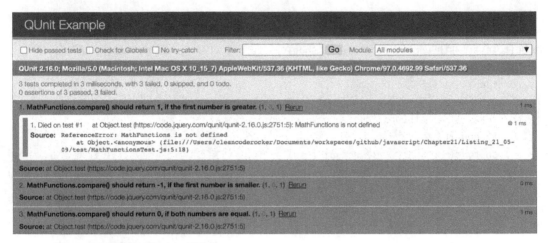

Figure 21.4 Failed Test in QUnit

Implementing the Component and Running the Test Again

The functionality of the MathFunctions.compare() function is relatively simple to implement, as shown in Listing 21.7. Inside the function, the two passed values are compared and a corresponding result is returned.

```
const MathFunctions = {
  compare(number1, number2) {
    if(number1 > number2) {
      return 1;
    } else if(number2 > number1) {
      return -1;
    } else {
      return 0;
    }
  }
}
```

Listing 21.7 A Simple Function for Comparing Two Numbers

When you now load the testrunner file again, the test should be successful and the result should match the screenshot shown in Figure 21.5.

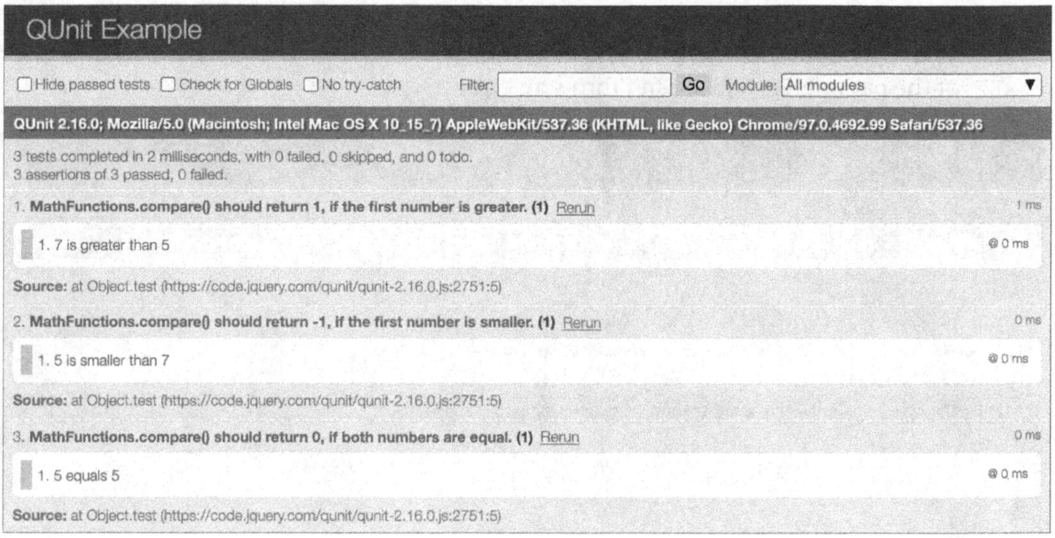

Figure 21.5 Passed Test in QUnit

Writing Another Test

We could now consider adding another test, defining the requirement that only numerical values can be passed to the compare() method; otherwise, the method should throw a TypeError.

To check whether an error gets thrown, QUnit provides the throws() method, which can also be called on the assert object, as shown in Listing 21.8. This method is passed a function to be executed as the first parameter, the expected error as the second parameter, and optionally a string to be used in the result display as the third parameter.

```
QUnit.test(
  'MathFunctions.compare() is supposed to throw an error if no numbers ⊃
were passed.',
  (assert) => {
    const number1 = "5";
    const number2 = "5";
    assert.throws(
      () => MathFunctions.compare(number1, number2),
      new TypeError('Only numbers allowed.'),
      'Strings are not accepted.'
    );
  }
);
```

Listing 21.8 This Test Expects an Error

If you now run this test (together with the tests you already know), it will fail (see Figure 21.6) because the implementation of the compare() method doesn't yet check the types of the parameters and doesn't throw an error.

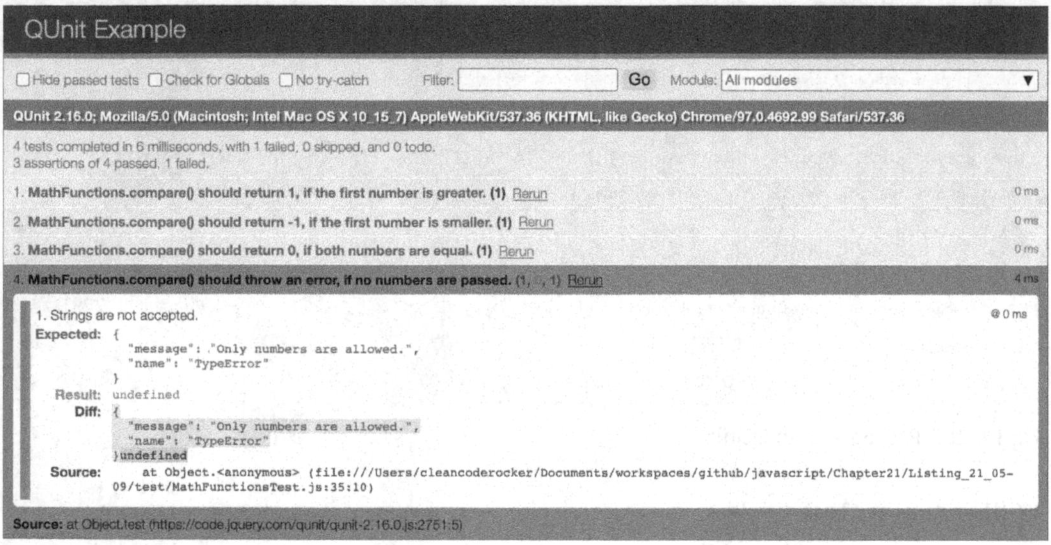

Figure 21.6 The New Test Fails

So the next step would be to adapt the implementation accordingly and accept only numerical values as parameters.

Listing 21.9 contains the code for this: as soon as one of the two parameters is not of the number type, the function throws a TypeError. If you now run the test again, it won't fail anymore (see Figure 21.7).

```
const MathFunctions = {
  compare(number1, number2) {
    if(
      typeof number1 !== 'number' ||
      typeof number2 !== 'number'
    ) {
      throw new TypeError('Only numbers allowed.');
    } else {
      if(number1 > number2) {
        return 1;
      } else if(number2 > number1) {
        return -1;
      } else {
        return 0;
      }
    }
```

```
    }
}
```

Listing 21.9 The Adjusted Implementation Now Throws an Error

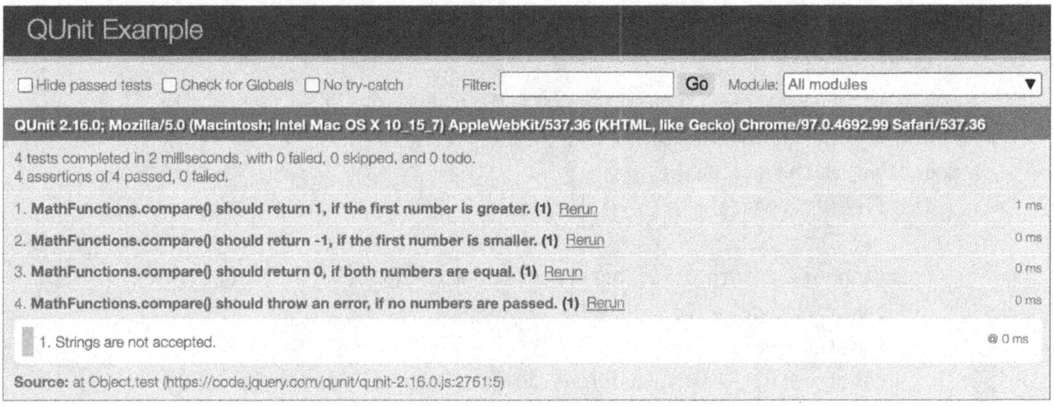

Figure 21.7 With the Adjustment the Test Is Now Successful

So as you can see, unit tests allow you to gradually refine the implementation and add specific requirements. For the preceding example, it would be conceivable to add appropriate tests to make sure that exactly two parameters are passed. By always running all the tests for a component, you ensure that when you implement the new requirement, you won't cause any side effects (reintroduce bugs into the code, as it were) that would prevent you from meeting other requirements.

21.2.4   Automated Testing of Source Code with mocha

Another testing framework that can be used independently of the runtime environment used is mocha (*http://mochajs.org*). If you want to use mocha in the browser, you can proceed similarly to how you used QUnit: you create an HTML testrunner file and include a JavaScript and a CSS file from the mocha library, as well as the appropriate unit tests (see *http://mochajs.org/#browser-support* for more details).

But in the following sections, we'll show you how you can use mocha on the command line. To do this, you need to install the mocha package globally via the `sudo npm install -g mocha` command (on Windows, without `sudo`), which will make the `mocha` command available to you.

Writing a Test

The basis of a unit test in mocha is the `describe()` function, which can be used to initiate a group of tests, as shown in Listing 21.10. The first parameter represents the name of the group; the second parameter defines a function that contains the actual test or additional `describe()` calls—that is, subsets of tests.

You define a single test case using the it() function. The first parameter is a description of the test, while the second parameter is a callback function that contains the actual test procedure.

By default, the assertion library is the assert package, which is already part of Node.js and therefore doesn't need to be installed separately.

```
'use strict';
const MathFunctions = require('../src/MathFunctions')
const assert = require('assert');
describe('MathFunctions', () => {
  describe('#compare()', () => {
    // 1. Test case
    it('should return 0, if both numbers are equal.', () => {
      const number1 = 7;
      const number2 = 5;
      const result = MathFunctions.compare(number1, number2);
      assert.equal(
        result,                    // actual result
        1,                         // expected result
        '7 is greater than 5'      // additional message
      );
    });
    // 2. Test case
    it('should return -1, if the first number is smaller.', () => {
      const number1 = 5;
      const number2 = 7;
      const result = MathFunctions.compare(number1, number2);
      assert.equal(
        result,                    // actual result
        -1,                        // expected result
        '5 is smaller than 7'      // additional message
      );
    });
    // 3. Test case
    it('should return 0, if both numbers are equal.', () =>{
      const number1 = 5;
      const number2 = 5;
      const result = MathFunctions.compare(number1, number2);
      assert.equal(
        result,                    // actual result
        0,                         // expected result
        '5 is equal to 5'          // additional message
      );
    });
```

```
      // 4. Test case
    it('should throw an error if no numbers were passed.', () => {
      const number1 = '5';
      const number2 = '5';
      assert.throws(
        () => {
          MathFunctions.compare(number1, number2)
        },
        TypeError                // the expected error type
      );
    });
  });
});
```

Listing 21.10 A Unit Test in mocha for the MathFunctions Object

For the `MathFunctions` object to be included via `require()`, it must be converted to a CommonJS module, as shown in Listing 21.11.

```
const MathFunctions = {
  compare(number1, number2) {
    if(
      typeof number1 !== 'number' ||
      typeof number2 !== 'number'
    ) {
      throw new TypeError('Only numbers allowed.');
    } else {
      if(number1 > number2) {
        return 1;
      } else if(number2 > number1) {
        return -1;
      } else {
        return 0;
      }
    }
  }
}
module.exports = MathFunctions;
```

Listing 21.11 The MathFunctions Object Adapted to CommonJS

Running a Test

The execution of the unit tests can be started via the mocha command. If you don't use any special parameters, mocha will search for them by default in a directory named **test** and execute all tests contained there. Alternatively, you can specify a concrete path or pattern, such as `mocha test/MathFunctionsTest.js` or `mocha test/**/*Test.js` to specifically run individual tests or a group of tests.

Several types of so-called reporters are supported when mocha is used on the command line; these affect the format of the test results. You can see an overview of different reporters in Table 21.3. A reporter can be defined via the `-R` parameter as follows:

```
mocha -R spec
```

The `spec` reporter specified here outputs the results of the test clearly on the command line in Listing 21.12.

```
MathFunctions
    #compare()
        should return 0, if both numbers are equal.
        should return -1, if the first number is smaller.
        should return 0, if both numbers are equal.
        should throw an error, if no numbers were passed.
  4 passing (14ms)
```

Listing 21.12 Output of the spec Reporter

Reporter	Description
dot	Minimalist output, where individual tests are output as dots on the console.
spec	Output that reads like a specification.
TAP	Output in Test Anything Protocol (TAP) format (see *http://en.wikipedia.org/wiki/Test_Anything_Protocol*), which enables integration into CI systems, for example.
list	Similar to spec, except that the individual tests are not output hierarchically but as a list.
json	Output in JSON format.
json-cov	Output in JSON format, which contains additional information about the test coverage, provided that an appropriate code coverage library has been included.
html-cov	Output in HTML format, which contains additional information about the test coverage, provided that an appropriate code coverage library has been included.
min	Minimal output, where only the total result of all tests is contained.
doc	Output similar to HTML documentation that nests test groups and tests in `<section>` elements.

Table 21.3 Selection of Available Reporters

Reporter	Description
html	Reporter that's automatically used when the test execution of mocha is performed in the browser. When run on the console, this reporter causes an error because certain browser-specific JavaScript objects such as document are not available there by default.

Table 21.3 Selection of Available Reporters (Cont.)

21.3   Source Code Version Management

To conclude this chapter and also this book, we'll provide a brief and compact introduction to the topic of version management. While entire books can be written about this topic (and have been), the goal here is to give you the most important facts about this topic as concisely as possible.

21.3.1   Introduction to Version Management

Sooner or later, you'll have to think about how to store your source code in a way that ensures you have a backup and, if you're working with multiple developers on a project, how to keep the source code up-to-date between developers and make changes made by one developer visible and accessible to the others. In short, you need to worry about *version management*. However, that doesn't mean you'll have to reinvent the wheel: there are various so-called version management systems (or version control systems [VCSs]) available that fulfill exactly the requirements just mentioned.

Version control systems are used within software projects to log changes to the source code over time. The advantage of this is: that if you want to access an old source code state, you can do this conveniently via the VCS. In addition, changes to files can be easily tracked and reverted to old states if necessary. And version control systems are virtually indispensable in professional teamwork.

In the context of version control systems, a basic distinction is made between two different approaches: centralized VCSs and decentralized VCSs. Central VCSs were the standard in professional software development for a long time. Examples of this include CVS and Subversion. The idea behind such central VCSs is that all versioned files of a software project are managed within a so-called repository on a central server, which can then be accessed by every developer of a development team. As a developer, you retrieve (via appropriate CVS or Subversion commands) the files of a project you want to work with on your own computer, edit them or add new files, and then synchronize again (also via appropriate commands) with the central server. Figure 21.8 illustrates this procedure.

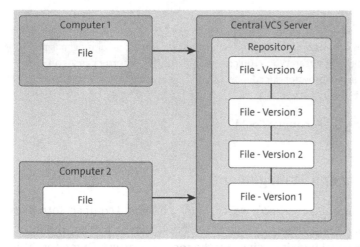

Figure 21.8 The Principle of Centralized Version Control Systems

The disadvantage of a central VCS is that the corresponding server on which the repository is located must always be available in order to upload your own changes or download updates from other developers from the system to your own computer. If the server isn't available, the developer has a problem. It gets even worse if the server or its hard disk, on which all the data is stored, crashes. Then the history of the data is irretrievably lost—unless you have made a backup upfront, which is usually not the case. The only thing that remains in such a case is the current state of the data the developers have on their computers.

It is precisely these two problems that are addressed by decentralized or distributed version control systems such as Mercurial (*www.mercurial-scm.org*) or Git (*https://git-scm.com*), which are widely used and described in the following sections. The difference between decentralized VCSs and centralized VCSs is that individual developers no longer have only the latest version of the data on their machines; each has a complete copy of the entire repository (see Figure 21.9) in a so-called local repository.

The first advantage: in such local repositories, developers can "upload" changes to the data without being connected to the server, and later—when connected again—synchronize the local repository with the *remote repository*.

The second advantage: if the server is damaged in any way such that the data in the (central) remote repository is lost, it can be restored completely—including the entire history—from any developer computer (provided it's up to date). In addition, developers can synchronize their repositories with each other even without a server, which opens up a range of completely different possibilities with regard to workflows compared to central VCSs.

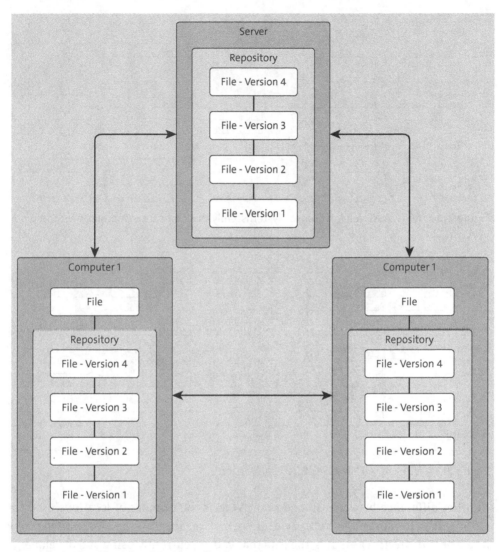

Figure 21.9 The Principle of Decentralized Version Control Systems

The way Git stores information about the data in the repository is fundamentally different from most other version control systems (whether centralized or decentralized). While in most other VCSs all information is stored as a list of changes from the first version of a file to the previous version (as so-called deltas; see Figure 21.10), Git stores the complete state of all files of the respective repository with each commit (this is also what "saving" is called in Git).

So Git takes an image (a *snapshot*) of the entire repository for each commit (see Figure 21.11). What looks like a waste of memory at first glance actually saves a relatively large amount of memory in practice. For example, no new copies are created for unchanged files as only shortcuts are created.

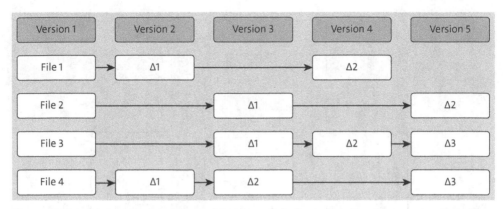

Figure 21.10 With Most Version Control Systems, Only the Respective Changes Are Stored per Version

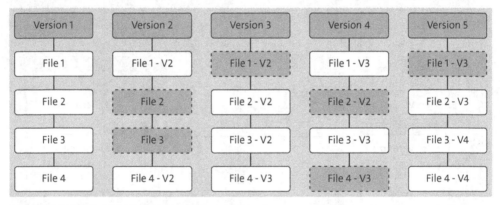

Figure 21.11 With Git, All Files Are Stored per Version

Another difference between Git and other VCSs is the number of locations used for storing data. In most other VCSs, there are two places for this: the *local working copy* (the *working directory*)—that is, the data that you are currently using as a developer— and the repository—that is, the data that has already been *committed*.

But in Git, there is another area besides these two, called the *staging area* (also referred to as the *index*; see Figure 21.12).

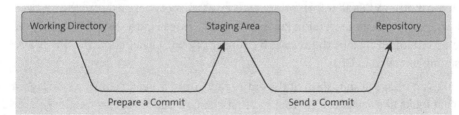

Figure 21.12 The Different Areas in Version Control with Git

This is where you specifically compile the changes you have made to your working copy and which you want to transfer, or *commit*, to the repository. The advantage of this third section and the associated decoupling between the working directory and the repository is that you are much more flexible when compiling a commit.

> **Git versus GitHub**
>
> By the way, Git is not the same as GitHub (*https://github.com*). The latter is "merely" an online service that uses Git and on which Git repositories can be managed. Many open-source projects are now available on GitHub (as you've no doubt noticed throughout the book itself).

21.3.2   Installing and Configuring the Git Version Control System

The installation of Git is relatively simple, regardless of the operating system used. On Linux, depending on the distribution, you use yum or apt-get—that is, either the following command for yum:

```
$ sudo yum install git
```

Or the following command for apt-get:

```
$ sudo apt-get install git
```

For Windows and macOS, on the other hand, corresponding installation files can be downloaded from the Git website. The installation programs started should then be self-explanatory.

After installing Git, the VCS is available to you via the git command. First, you should use the git config command to configure the username and email address that will be associated by default with each commit you make (if needed, both can also be set later on a project-by-project or repository-by-repository basis):

```
$ git config --global user.name "John Doe"
$ git config --global user.email "john.doe@javascripthandbuch.de"
```

The first step after installation and configuration is to create a new Git repository. You do this not only once, but for every project you want to version using Git. There are basically two ways to create a new local Git repository. On the one hand, you can initialize a directory on your own computer as a Git repository; on the other hand, you can download or clone an existing repository from another computer (or from a server) to your own computer (see Figure 21.13).

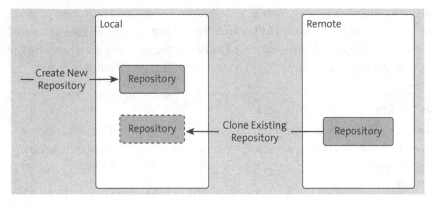

Figure 21.13 The Different Ways to Create a New Local Repository

You choose the former if you want to create a completely new project in Git that doesn't yet exist on any server. The latter comes into play if, for example, you're a new developer joining a team that already manages a project via a remote repository.

21.3.3   Creating a New Local Repository

To initialize a local directory as a Git repository, you must run the git init command:

```
$ mkdir example-project
$ cd example-project
$ git init
Initialized empty Git repository in /example-project/.git/
```

This creates the **.git** directory in the respective project folders (here, **example-project**) in the background. Git subsequently stores all information about the repository in that directory (e.g., the history of the files and directories in the respective repository; see Figure 21.14).

Figure 21.14 The .git Folder Contains All Information about a Repository

21.3.4   Cloning an Existing Repository

To create a copy of an existing repository from a server on your machine, you should use the git clone command. This command will transfer the entire data of the remote repository, including all versions (i.e., the entire history of the data), to your computer. For example, to clone the source code of the jQuery library from GitHub (*https://github.com/jquery/jquery*), you must use the following command:

```
git clone git://github.com/jquery/jquery.git
```

The output then looks something like this:

```
Cloning into 'jquery'...
remote: Counting objects: 41130, done.
remote: Total 41130 (delta 0), reused 0 (delta 0), pack-reused 41130
Receiving objects: 100% (41130/41130), 24.45 MiB | 1.50 MiB/s, done.
Resolving deltas: 100% (29238/29238), done.
Checking connectivity... done
```

21.3.5 Transferring Changes to the Staging Area

The git init command is only used to initialize the corresponding directory as a Git repository. Any files and subdirectories that may exist there aren't automatically added to the repository by this command, but are first located in the workspace mentioned earlier. So to add them to the repository, you have to transfer them to the staging area first and then to the repository.

The former action, adding files to the staging area (see Figure 21.15), is achieved via the git add command:

```
$ git add *.js
$ git add **/*.js
$ git add package.json
```

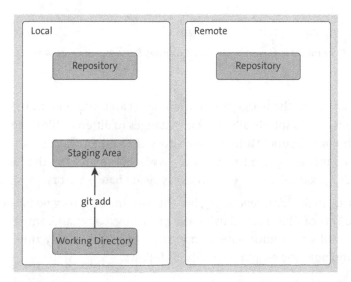

Figure 21.15 The git add Command Is Used to Add Changes to the Staging Area

21.3.6   Transferring Changes to the Local Repository

Once you've added all the files to be included in a commit to the staging area, you can commit them to the local repository using the git commit command (see also Figure 21.16):

```
$ git commit -m "Initial commit"
```

The output then looks like the following example:

```
[master (root-commit) 671cbc4] Initial commit
4 files changed, 14 insertions(+)
create mode 100644 index.js
create mode 100644 lib/examples.js
create mode 100644 package.json
create mode 100644 tests/examples-tests.js
```

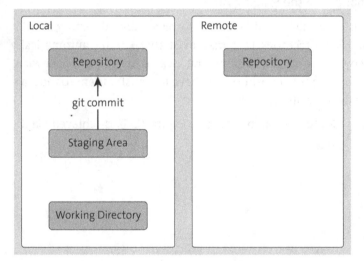

Figure 21.16 The git commit Command Is Used to Commit Changes from the Staging Area to the Local Repository

This two-step transfer of data from the workspace to the staging area and then to the local repository makes it possible to specifically combine changes to different files into one commit and transfer them as a bundle into the repository. If you then select meaningful *commit messages* (which are passed to the git commit command via the -m parameter as in the preceding example), this leads to a very clear change history.

Once committed, the files are in the local repository, but the working directory no longer contains any changes. This can be checked using the git status command, which can be used to retrieve useful status information about the repository at any time. When you call the command now, the output should be as follows:

```
$ git status
# On branch master
nothing to commit, working directory clean
```

In other words, the workspace now doesn't contain any changes that could be committed.

21.3.7   The Different States in Git

Files can assume one of several states in Git: *untracked* (or *unversioned*) means that a file isn't yet even considered by version control; *modified* (or *edited*) means that the file has been modified since the last commit; *unmodified* (or *unedited*) means that it hasn't been modified since the last commit; and *staged* means that a modified file is scheduled for the next commit (see Figure 21.17).

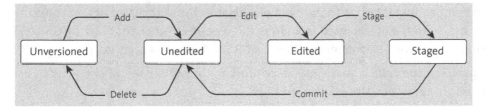

Figure 21.17 The Different States of Files in Version Control with Git

If you now change files in the working copy or add new files, you can use git status to find out which files are affected and what their status is:

```
$ git status
# On branch master
# Changes not staged for commit:
#   (use "git add <file>..." to update what will be committed)
#   (use "git checkout -- <file>..." to discard changes in working directory)
#
#       modified:   lib/examples.js
#
# Untracked files:
#   (use "git add <file>..." to include in what will be committed)
#
#       lib/examples2.js
#       tests/examples2-tests.js
no changes added to commit (use "git add" and/or "git commit -a")
```

For example, the preceding output says that one file has been modified (**lib/examples.js**) and two files have been detected as untracked—that is, not versioned yet (**lib/examples2.js** and **tests/examples2-tests.js**). We can also see that the changes to the modified file are only in the workspace, not in the staging area (recognizable by the Changes not staged for commit output). You could now commit the changes back to the repository via git add and git commit.

21.3.8 Transfering Changes to the Remote Repository

All commits so far are only in the local repository. The next step is therefore to set up a remote repository. If, on the other hand, you have cloned an already existing remote repository onto your own computer using the git clone command, this step is of course not necessary because then the remote repository is already available.

A new remote repository can be added using the git remote add command:

```
$ git remote add origin ssh://cleancoderocker@workspace/volume1/repository/
example-project.git/
```

The first parameter (origin in the example) denotes the short name of the repository that can subsequently be used to address the repository when formulating Git commands. The second parameter specifies the URL of the remote repository.

To push the commits from the local repository to the remote repository, you can use the git push command (see also Figure 21.18).

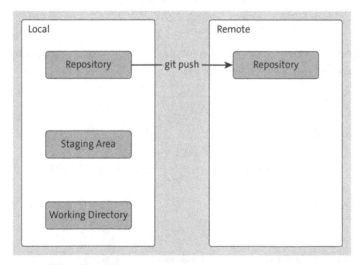

Figure 21.18 The git push Command Is Used to Push Changes from the Local Repository to the Remote Repository

The first parameter is the name of the remote repository (basically, several remote repositories can be linked to a local repository), and the second parameter is the branch from which the commits are to be transferred (more on branches later). By default, this is the so-called master branch:

```
$ git push origin master
Counting objects: 12, done.
Delta compression using up to 4 threads.
Compressing objects: 100% (9/9), done.
Writing objects: 100% (12/12), 1.05 KiB | 0 bytes/s, done.
Total 12 (delta 1), reused 0 (delta 0)
To ssh://cleancoderocker@workspace/volume1/repository/example-project.git/
 * [new branch]      master -> master
```

21.3.9   Transferring Changes from the Remote Repository

If you work on a team, it's usually the case that before you *push* your own changes (or commits) to the remote repository, you transfer the changes of other developers from the remote repository to your own computer or to the local repository. This is done using the git fetch command, which is assigned the name of the remote repository as a parameter (see also Figure 21.19):

```
$ git fetch origin
```

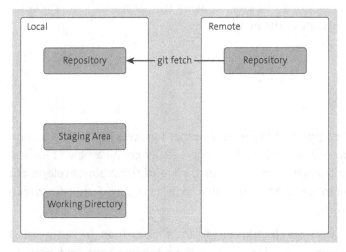

Figure 21.19 The git fetch Command Is Used to Commit Changes from a Remote Repository to the Local Repository

This means that all commits from the remote repository that aren't yet in the local repository are transferred there, to so-called remote branches, which are development branches that exist in parallel to the main development branch (usually the master branch). In this way, you have the opportunity to review appropriate changes before you subsequently incorporate them into your own master branch. The latter in turn is done via the git merge command, which is passed the name of the remote branch as a parameter:

```
$ git merge origin/master
```

Here it can happen that changes of other developers cause conflicts with your own changes. These conflicts can then be solved manually via the command line or the editor or development environment used in each case. As an alternative to the combination of git fetch followed by git merge, you can also use the git pull command, which implicitly executes both steps one after the other.

21.3.10 Working in a New Branch

An essential part of working with Git is the branches feature mentioned previously. These are development branches that allow you to develop new features or perform bug fixing independently of the main development branch. By default, you work on the master branch (which is created by the git init command by default).

The git branch command can be used to list all branches of a repository—for our example, only one branch is listed, the master branch:

```
$ git branch
* master
```

New branches, on the other hand, can be created using the git branch <branch> command, where <branch> is the name of the new branch:

```
$ git branch feature-xyz
$ git branch
feature-xyz
* master
```

Branches are an important component of the development process in Git. If, for example, you want to add a new feature or fix a bug, you usually create a new branch to encapsulate the associated changes from the source code of the main development branch. In this way, you can make sure that unstable code is not transferred directly to the main development branch.

Figure 21.20 illustrates this strategy. In addition to the master branch, two isolated development lines can be seen here: a feature branch on the one hand and a bugfix branch on the other.

To switch branches, you can use the git checkout <branch> command, where <branch> again represents the name of the branch you want to switch to. For example, to switch to the feature-xyz branch you just created, you should write the following:

```
$ git checkout feature-xyz
```

After that you'll receive the message Switched to branch 'feature-xyz'. You can also check whether you're in the new branch at any time by using the git branch command: The active branch is marked with a * symbol in the subsequent output:

```
$ git branch
* feature-xyz
master
```

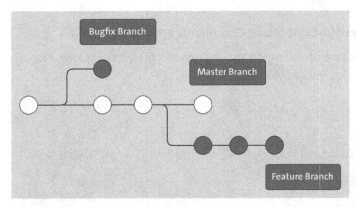

Figure 21.20 Different Branches Enable You to Develop Individual Features or Bug Fixes in Isolation from the Main Development Branch

21.3.11   Adopting Changes from a Branch

Once you're done with a new feature or fixing a bug in the corresponding branch and want to merge the associated changes into the main development branch, you must first switch to the branch you want to merge the changes into and then use the `git merge` command (see Figure 21.21):

```
$ git checkout master
$ git merge feature-xyz
Merge made by the 'recursive' strategy.
 lib/examples.js | 2 ++
 1 file changed, 2 insertions(+)
```

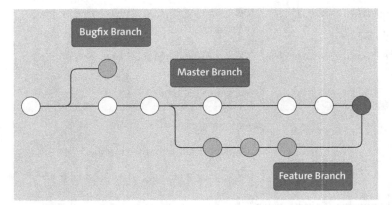

Figure 21.21 The git merge Command Can Be Used to Transfer the Changes from One Branch to Another

In the command line dialog that appears, you can customize the commit message (by default, this message reads Merge branch <branch>, where <branch> again stands for the branch name).

21.3.12 Overview of the Most Important Commands and Terms

Figure 21.22 summarizes the most important commands for working with Git and shows their connection with the individual Git areas.

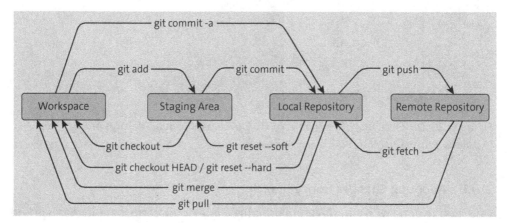

Figure 21.22 The Areas of Git and the Different Commands

Table 21.4 contains a detailed overview of a selection of commands commonly used in practice, and the most important terms for working with Git are listed in Table 21.5.

Command	Description
Creating a Repository	
git init	Initializes a new Git repository
git clone ssh://<username> @<domain>/ <repositoryname>.git	Clones an existing repository based on the passed URL
git clone git@github.com: <username>/ <repositoryname>	Clones an existing repository based on the passed GitHub URL
Local Changes	
git status	Outputs status information
git diff	Displays changes to the versioned files
git add .	Adds all local changes to the next commit

Table 21.4 The Most Important Commands in Git

Command	Description
git add -p FILE	Adds the changes to a file to the next commit
git commit -a	Commits all tracked changes
git commit -m "Update"	Commits the changes from the staging area
git commit --amend	Modifies the last commit (note: do not modify commits that have already been uploaded to a remote repository)
Commit History	
git log	Outputs all commits, starting with the last commit
git log -p <file>	Outputs all commits for a file, starting with the last commit
git blame <file>	Outputs who has made what changes to a file and when
git stash	Transfers the local changes from the workspace to the clipboard
git stash pop	Transfers the local changes from the clipboard to the workspace
Branches and Tags	
git branch -av	Lists all branches
git checkout <branch>	Switches to the existing branch
git branch <branch>	Creates a new local branch
git checkout --track <remote>/<branch>	Creates a new local branch based on a remote branch
git branch -d <branch>	Deletes a local branch
git tag <tagname>	Adds a tag to the current commit
Updating and Publishing	
git remote -v	Lists all remote repositories
git remote show <remote>	Displays information about a specific remote repository
git remote add <shortname> <url>	Adds a new remote repository

Table 21.4 The Most Important Commands in Git (Cont.)

21

Command	Description
git fetch <remote>	Downloads all changes from the remote repository, but no integration in HEAD (i.e., the current branch).
git pull <remote> <branch>	Downloads all changes from the remote repository and integrates or merges them directly into HEAD
git push <remote> <branch>	Uploads the local changes to the remote repository
git branch -dr <remote>/<branch>	Deletes a branch in the remote repository
git push --tags	Uploads the tags to the remote repository
Merging and Rebasing	
git merge <branch>	Merges the changes from a branch into the current HEAD
git rebase <branch>	Rebases the current HEAD to the specified branch
Undo	
git reset --hard HEAD	Discards all local changes in the workspace
git checkout HEAD <file>	Discards local changes to a single file in the workspace
git revert <commit>	Reverts a commit
git reset --hard <commit>	Resets the HEAD to a previous commit and discards any local changes that have occurred since then
git reset <commit>	Resets the HEAD to a previous commit and keeps all local changes that have taken place since then
git reset --keep <commit>	Resets the HEAD to a previous commit and keeps any local changes that have occurred since then and have not yet been committed

Table 21.4 The Most Important Commands in Git (Cont.)

Concept	Meaning
Repository	Contains all files of a (software) project including previous versions
Remote repository	Remote repository
Working directory	Workspace
Index/staging area	Area where changes are prepared for committing to the local repository
Commit	Transfer of changes from the staging area to the local repository
Push	Transfer of changes transferred to the local repository to the remote repository
Pull	Transfer of changes from the remote repository to the local repository
Checkout	Retrieval of a working copy from a branch or a commit
Clone	Copying of a remote repository
Branch	A separate development branch
Merge	The combining of changes from one branch to another branch
Fork	Offshoot of a repository
HEAD	Current branch

Table 21.5 The Most Important Terms in Git

21.4   Summary

This chapter has provided a brief introduction to the key aspects of a professional development process. In this context, three main aspects were discussed in greater detail (there are more). The most important points are as follows:

- For automated execution of certain repetitive tasks, you can use the Grunt and Gulp tools. Grunt can require a great deal of configuration work depending on the number of automated tasks, whereas Gulp is much more readable due to its Fluent API.

- In *test-driven development*, before implementing a new component, you first formulate what the new component must do in a *unit test* using *assertions*.

- An iteration in test-driven development consists of five steps: writing the test, running the test, implementing a component, running the test again, and refactoring the component.

- In JavaScript, there are many different unit testing frameworks, two of which we introduced in this chapter: QUnit, which is particularly well suited for testing client-side JavaScript, and mocha, which is particularly well suited for testing server-side JavaScript. However, both frameworks can also be used in both contexts.

- You should manage your source code using a *version control system*. On the one hand, this facilitates the work with the team, and on the other hand, it also provides a history (and thus an implicit backup) of the entire source code.

- Probably the most popular VCS at the moment is Git—a so-called decentralized VCS, in which every developer has a complete image of all source code versions on their computer.

The Author

 **Philip Ackermann** is CTO of Cedalo GmbH and author of several reference books and technical articles on Java, JavaScript and web development. His focus is on the design and development of Node.js projects in the areas of Industry 4.0 and Internet of Things.

Index

S

- Your complete guide to backend programming with JavaScript

- Install the Node.js environment and learn to use core frameworks

- Debug, scale, test, and optimize your applications

Sebastian Springer

Node.js

The Comprehensive Guide

If you're developing server-side JavaScript applications, you need Node.js! Start with the basics of the Node.js environment: installation, application structure, and modules. Then follow detailed code examples to learn about web development using frameworks like Express and Nest. Learn about different approaches to asynchronous programming, including RxJS and data streams. Details on peripheral topics such as testing, security, performance, and more, make this your all-in-one daily reference for Node.js!

approx. 834 pp., avail. 09/2022
E-Book: $49.99 | **Print:** $49.95 | **Bundle:** $59.99

www.rheinwerk-computing.com/5556

- Your all-in-one overview of full stack web development, from design and interactivity to security and operations

- Learn about frontend tools, including HTML, CSS, JavaScript, APIs, and more

- Work with backend technologies, including Node.js, PHP, web services, and databases

Philip Ackermann

Full Stack Web Development

The Comprehensive Guide

Full stack web developers are always in demand—do you have the skillset? Between these pages you'll learn to design websites with CSS, structure them with HTML, and add interactivity with JavaScript. You'll master the different web protocols, formats, and architectures and see how and when to use APIs, PHP, web services, and other tools and languages. With information on testing, deploying, securing, and optimizing web applications, you'll get the full frontend and backend instructions you need!

740 pages, 1st edition, pub. 08/2023
E-Book: $54.99 | **Print:** $59.95 | **Bundle:** $69.99

www.rheinwerk-computing.com/5704